THE TURN TO TRANSCENDENCE

Glenn W. Olsen

THE
TURN
TO
TRANSCENDENCE

The Role of
Religion in the
Twenty-First
Century

THE CATHOLIC UNIVERSITY OF AMERICA PRESS

Washington, D.C.

Library of Congress Cataloging-in-Publication Data

Olsen, Glenn W. (Glenn Warren), 1938–

The turn to transcendence : the role of religion in the

twenty-first century / Glenn W. Olsen.

p. cm.

Includes bibliographical references and index.

ISBN 978-0-8132-1740-6 (cloth : alk. paper)

1. Christianity and culture—History—21st century.

2. Christianity—21st century.

I. Title.

BR115.C8O49 2010

261'.109045—dc22   2009042034

UXORI CARISSIMAE

CONTENTS

Ancient and medieval Western writers used various metaphors, especial-ly of cosmic harmony or the music of the spheres, to express the idea that humans are of their nature aligned with or "fit" to the universe. They are a part of nature and take their bearings from the structures they find around them in nature, but, as Plato so clearly saw, are also oriented to something "above" themselves. This "something above" has had many names, but the philosophers tended to think of it under the terminology of transcendence, using especially the terms the one, the good, the true, and the beautiful to describe that which transcends human life, but which humans are at least in part capable of knowing and experiencing. For the theologians, the transcendent was more explicitly to be identified with God and with what eventually were called supernatural realities.

In recent centuries, the sense that humans, while living in nature and history, are oriented to transcendence has seemingly diminished. Some have claimed that this is as it should be: for them the race, while beginning in a theological or mythical state of life, close to God or the gods, eventually in modernity properly passed to a desacralized or secular life from which the gods have disappeared, or in which they are very feeble. This book is about those who have not accepted this development and who propose various alternatives to it in favor of underlining the centrality of an orientation to transcendence for human life. The number of those who refuse to accept the story of permanent desacralization is growing, and the idea that the future of the world involves the disappearance of God has become increas-ingly improbable. Much evidence suggests the opposite, for in many parts of the world religion in various forms is growing by leaps and bounds. My own view is that all along, in all periods, desacralization and resacralization have taken place simultaneously. Things formerly thought "holy" and cen-tral to life, perhaps honored through sacrifice or liturgy, have become rela-tively marginalized, and things formerly marginal or hardly thought about have moved more and more to the center of life.

Usually the sacred is thought of as "the permanent things," those things that stand at the center of life and give it its meaning. In specifically theo-logical or philosophical formulation, these permanent things have been as-sociated with the idea that at the heart of our present temporal life can be found that which in some sense is also of another order and gives life its meaning, or measures it. This can be expressed in two ways, both as the trans-worldly, and as the transparency of the cosmos to the trans-worldly, hence as the liturgical-sacramental. In the one, transcendence is found in things, is "in but not of the world." In the other, which we might associate especially with Plato and his descendants, our cosmos is transparent to a reality caught best in liturgy and sacramental action, in which the transcendent "shines into" or "shines through" our world. There is an important sense in which liturgy, understood as something visible bearing something invisible, is our best expression of transcendence.

The place of liturgy in life tracks the story of desacralization and resacralization. Clearly in the modern period many have lost their sense of God and of the sacredness of the creation. Others, living in a culture in which desacralization is taking place, have in one way or another fought against this. They have "turned to transcendence," commonly becoming cultural critics or dissenters, perhaps experimenters with forms of transcendence with which moderns might identify. As one of its central tasks this book traces both the loss of transcendence and attempts to recover it, before, in the final chapter, making its own proposals. A key chapter (chapter 3) treats modernism in the arts, not just in an attempt to sort out the many ways in which this term has been used, but to show that, though much that has been called modern has been part of a drive to create a cultural space free from the past and from religion, much has also been part of a rebellion against the loss of transcendence in modernity. Some modern art—perhaps Piet Mondrian (1872–1944) could be taken as a case—may be viewed as a contemporary form of search for the transcendent.

The approach this book takes is intended to be neither reactionary nor modernist, that is, neither disapproving of all break with tradition nor desiring systematic abandonment of the past. The question rather is how, under the conditions of modern life, some form of the sacred and some form of the secular might both flourish at the same time. If, as Christopher Dawson (1889–1970) argued, religion is at the center of culture, that is, cultures even in the modern period are in some way embodied religions, the place of transcendence in life is not a problem that will go away. Its presence or absence will both be an expression of and impact our politics and social life. This especially chapters 1, 2, 5, and 6 try to show.

Chapter 1 is an overview of the relation of religion and mass culture in the modern period, especially of those discontent with the forms culture has taken. The argument is that certain characteristics of the present, such as the forms democracy and individualism have taken, compound the problem of finding a proper place for transcendence in contemporary life. Chapter 2 considers three premises which the author believes must be affirmed if there is to be any desirable resolution of the problem of the relation of transcendence and religion to culture as it now is: 1) humans are made for a "communitarian," non-individualistic, social life which supports their deepest beliefs and makes it possible to pass these beliefs on to their children, 2) the still very widespread belief in general progress which continues to form many people's ideas of what can and should be expected of the political and economic orders is wrong and must be abandoned, and 3) related to this latter, also to be abandoned are the various forms of utopianism which have in fact become the common coin of our culture, and make difficult the anti-utopianism or anti-perfectionism on which all decent politics depends because they articulate the limits of what politics reasonably can achieve.

Chapter 4 travels from the ancient world to the High Middle Ages, showing the forms transcendence took before the modern period. Chapter 5 treats the origins, development, and nature of the forms of liberalism, personal autonomy, and democracy so central to culture today, and to the concomitant secularization of life and attack on authority and tradition. Finally, chapter 6, which asks the reader to think of Christianity as a culture in its own right, considers a range of alternatives to life as it now is, specifically alternatives involving a reconception of religion and transcendence. The author's hope is to stimulate reconsideration of the most basic premises of our life in society today, and this chapter argues that a religion unwilling to maintain itself with its own overt architecture, language, and calendars, "face-to-face" against an enveloping secular culture, is destined for oblivion.

This book is the outcome of a long period of reflection, in which I have become indebted to many people. I want most to thank my wife, Suzanne, a living dictionary of the languages of Europe, who has throughout shown her customary generosity and patience. This book is dedicated to her. Most of the research and travel grants I have received over the years have been in support of projects in medieval history, but from the first, with the receipt of a Fulbright grant for study in Rome, these awards have placed me in situations in which I could become increasingly aware of the questions treated in the present book. I am especially grateful for recent grants from my department and college at the University of Utah, which have allowed for the presentation of papers on the subject of this book in Europe. My thought has been nourished in innumerable ways by contact with the *communio* theologians associated with the journal of that name. A special thanks is owed to Adrian Walker, who capped a visit to Austria, where I was teaching, with a typically searching reading of my entire manuscript. I also give many thanks to an anonymous reviewer for the Catholic University of America Press, and to James Hitchcock, who was quite willing to have the press identify him as the second reviewer. David McGonagle, the press's director, encouraged me throughout.

ABBREVIATIONS

AB   *Adoremus Bulletin*

AHR   *American Historical Review*

An   *Anales de la Fundación Francisco Elías de Tejada*

CH   *Church History*

CHR   *Catholic Historical Review*

Co   *Communio: International Catholic Review*

CSSR   *Catholic Social Science Review*

DMN   *Deseret Morning News*

DN   *Deseret News*

DUC   *Daily Utah Chronicle*

EC   *Ethics and Culture: The Newsletter of the Notre Dame Center for Ethics and Culture*

EME   *Early Medieval Europe*

FQI   *Fides Quaerens Intellectum*

FR   *Faith and Reason*

FCSQ   *Fellowship of Catholic Scholars Quarterly*

FT   *First Things*

HCW   *Houston Catholic Worker*

HPS   *Hebraic Political Studies*

HR   *Historical Review*

HS   *Historically Speaking*

IC   *Intermountain Catholic*

In   *Interpretation: A Journal of Political Philosophy*

IR   *Intercollegiate Review*

IHT   *International Herald Tribune*

JECS   *Journal of Early Christian Studies*

JHI   *Journal of the History of Ideas*

THE TURN TO TRANSCENDENCE

Chapter One

INTRODUCTION

I curse love's sweet transcendent call,
My curse on faith! My curse on hope!
My curse on patience above all!

 —Johann Wolfgang Goethe, *Faust,* Part I[1]

The impulse of our century has been to substitute earth for
god as an object of reverence. This seems an implicit rejection
of the eternal. But the religious mind, with its hunger for
meaning and disposition to awe, its craving for the path, the
continuum, the unbroken line, for what is final, immutable,
cannot sustain itself on matter and natural process.

 —Louise Glück, *Averno*[2]

In January 1944 the English Catholic historian Christopher Dawson
posed what he called "the basic sociological problem of our time," the relation of religion and mass culture.[3] Writing in the midst of World War II,
Dawson saw the choice facing the West as between spiritual renewal, on
the one hand, and technocracy and totalitarianism, on the other: "Unless
we find a way to restore the contact between the life of society and the life
of the spirit our civilization will be destroyed by the forces which it has
had the knowledge to create but not wisdom to control."[4] Dawson was
right. In the long half-century since he wrote, liberal democracy has shown
itself incapable of, indeed largely uninterested in, providing the renewal of
which Dawson wrote. Indeed, we now have analyses even more sobering
than Dawson's.

 1. Lines 1604–6, tr. David Luke (Oxford: Oxford University Press, 1987), 49.
 2. Quoted by Charles Simic, "The Power of Ruins," *NYRB* 53, 11 (June 22, 2006): 16–19 at 19.
 3. "Religion and Mass Civilization—The Problem of the Future," *The Dublin Review* 214
(January 1944): 1–8 at 8.
 4. Ibid.

John Lukacs, in a kind of updating of Dawson's views, argues that we are living at the end of an age in which some of the most valued achievements of the last five hundred years, including print culture and liberal education themselves, have been diminished beyond recovery.[5] Democracy, so dependent if it is to be intelligent on these things, is in terminal arrest, if not dead, replaced by democratic populism. Constitutional democracy, to function well, depends on families, churches, and communities, but these are disappearing under the onslaught of mass culture and consumerism, the desire for the ephemeral. Standards of civility are far gone. If history is any guide, thinks Lukacs, on the other side of this lies tyranny.[6] Further, "print culture" was itself "just" the form that a book culture going back to late antiquity took when the printing press was invented. This is the world in which Christianity came to center stage, and we can reasonably ask what the passing of the book, that is, of a culture built on reading, means for Christianity, a *"Buchreligion."*[7]

In the world that is upon us, nature is increasingly apprehended as indeterminate in the sense of having no inviolable structure, as being a mere object.[8] Whereas in the pre-modern world it tended to be presumed that the cosmos had an underlying structure to which man was to conform, the modern project of mastering nature has increasingly encouraged thinking of individual things as "heaps," aggregations which one can reorder at will. Objects can be broken down without reference to the whole of which they were once part, and reassembled in some other way. Technology aims at erasing the distinction between human nature and artifice, and the sense of intrinsic limits fades as man increasingly becomes his own redesigner.[9] Life is less and less viewed as a gift; more and more it is viewed as infinitely malleable by autonomous individuals responsible only to themselves.[10] The spirit of the Enlightenment, the belief that humans can and should ever more dominate nature, seems largely to have prevailed, though a good deal

---

5. *At the End of an Age* (New Haven, Conn.: Yale University Press, 2002). The situation in the Middle Ages, when the so-called oral and written cultures co-existed and interacted, was more complicated than Lukacs imagines: see Patrick J. Geary, *Phantoms of Remembrance: Memory and Oblivion at the End of the First Millennium* (Princeton, N.J.: Princeton University Press, 1994), 11–16, and "Land, Language, and Memory in Europe, 700–1000," *Transactions of the Royal Historical Society,* 6th ser., 9 (1999): 169–84.

6. John Lukacs, *Democracy and Populism: Fear and Hatred* (New Haven, Conn.: Yale University Press, 2005).

7. *Normieren, Tradieren, Inszenieren: Das Christentum als Buchreligion,* ed. Andreas Holzem (Darmstadt: Wissenschaftliche Buchgesellschaft, 2004).

8. Hans Jonas, *Philosophical Essays: From Ancient Creed to Technological Man* (Englewood Cliffs, N.J.: Prentice-Hall, 1974). Cf. William H. Vanderburg, *Living in the Labyrinth of Technology* (Toronto: University of Toronto Press, 2005).

9. Adrian Walker, "Not Neutral: Technology and the 'Theology of the Body,'" *SS* 7 (2006): 26–32 at 28–29, and see my "The Return of Purpose," *Co* 33 (2006): 666–81.

10. Marc Ouellet, "Theological Perspectives on Marriage," *Co* 31 (2004): 419–34 at 419–20.

of science fiction is written in dread of what is coming, and with profound ambivalence about the benefits of technology.

Many have noted the ways in which a culture of science, consumerism, and capitalism seizes the young to teach rebelliousness against tradition and commitment to the new, and one of the most pessimistic of the critics has written: "No, technology cannot be controlled by any kind of 'humanistic' recoding; yes, bio-genetic manipulation has opened wide and irreversibly the gates of the brave new world: neither Left nor Right is likely to deal with what is science today."[11] This critic goes on to wonder whether, because of its inability to control technology, democracy itself is not to be impugned:

Democratic governance may not be an ideal worth pursuing. . . . The industrial-technological end-station looms like an ever-swelling tumor. We have reached the point where we must assume, in a complete reversal of the assumptions crowding behind us, that enlightened modern man is no better and no wiser than history's so-called irrational and barbaric forces.[12]

One comes to wonder whether Augustine was not really right about how corrupt human beings are, how incapable they are of controlling *curiositas*. There seems to be something demonic here, for we are all swept into the flood occasioned by the least reflective and morally most uninhibited amongst us:

A good many people, presumably, would have chosen to "stay out of the nuclei." But that was a choice they did not have. When a few scientists decided to go in, they decided for everybody. This "freedom of scientific inquiry" was immediately translated into the freedom of corporate and/or governmental exploitation. And so the freedom of the originators and exploiters has become, in effect, the abduction and imprisonment of all the rest of us. Adam was the first, but not the last, to choose for the whole human race.[13]

The "fallacy of technology," that "because a thing can be done, it must be done," rules, and "the means absorb completely, and man becomes blind to the very concept of ends."[14]

The apparent increase in human dominion over nature—secure until the viruses wreak their revenge in some awful pandemic—has "dazzled all but the most thoughtful."[15] Though in some quarters the very idea of prog-

11. Thomas Molnar, "Tradition, Science and the Centuries," *An* 9 (2003): 171–77 at 174–75.
12. Ibid., 175. Molnar's disenchantment with democracy itself, to be pursued below, may be viewed through the lens of Loren J. Samons II, *What's Wrong with Democracy? From Athenian Practice to American Worship* (Berkeley: University of California Press, 2004).
13. Wendell Berry, *Life Is a Miracle: An Essay against Modern Superstition* (Washington, D.C.: Counterpoint, 2001), 76–77.
14. Richard M. Weaver, *Ideas Have Consequences* (Chicago: University of Chicago Press, 1948), 60.
15. Ibid., 8.

ress has been called into question, among most scientists it continues in the form of "progress through science" to undergird the scientific project itself. The scientists are often schizophrenic here, urging that we must follow the logic of progress, while acknowledging that brakes must be put on development if the environment is not to perish.[16] There seems no light at the end of the tunnel unless—a goal of the present book—we can change our evaluation of ourselves and of what we want from this world, and as a result change our treatment of that world.[17] We need what some have called a second Enlightenment, a reconsideration of the premises of the first Enlightenment and of the world which has been built on them. That Augustine did not quite have it right when he portrayed the power of curiosity seems witnessed to by the lives of certain heroic men such as Enrico Fermi or I. I. Rabi, refusing to participate in the development of the H-bomb.[18]

The gravest physical dangers which face humans—atomic and biological weapons, the destruction of natural resources and of the atmosphere—are largely man-made, one result of the intrusion of applied science into ever more areas of life.[19] One hardly knows where to look for deliverance: in the last decades the universities, for instance, have been transformed by commercial forces and seriously compromised especially by the pharmaceutical and biomedical industries.[20] At one level this is completely understandable, for the pharmaceutical industry has also brought immense benefits in regard to health, and probably the perception of most people is that only with modernity have they escaped a burdensome and sickly past.[21]

This is one of the reasons it is so difficult to classify religion today: a case can be made that fundamentalism, whether Protestant or Islamic, is not so much a throwback to some more religious age, as a new form of technology-based life bent on dominating the world.[22] In similar fashion, though we might more commonly associate the indiscriminate development of technology with a classical liberal politics advocating commercial and capital expansion, the twentieth century presented notable cases of a

16. Tom Wessels, *The Myth of Progress: Toward a Sustainable Future* (Hanover: University of Vermont Press, 2006).

17. Philip Sherrard, *Human Image, World Image: The Death and Resurrection of Sacred Cosmology* (Ipswich, England: Golgonooza Press, 1992).

18. Thomas Powers, "An American Tragedy," *NYRB* 52, 14 (September 22, 2005): 73–79 at 75.

19. Lukacs, *End of an Age,* 37–43, on this and the following.

20. Marcia Angell, "The Truth About the Drug Companies," *NYRB* 51, 12 (July 15, 2004): 52–58; Jennifer Washburn, *University Inc.: The Corporate Corruption of American Higher Education* (New York: Basic Books, 2004).

21. Eric Cohen, "Rival Immortalities," *FT* 149 (January 2005): 38–41 at 40, who notes that "in Europe and Canada, there is a secular idea of human dignity and a deeper skepticism about the unequivocal goodness of technological progress. . . . American scientists, who are probably no more secular than their European and Canadian counterparts, are much less willing to accept any limits at all on their research (41)."

22. Pankaj Mishra, "A Cautionary Tale for Americans," *NYRB* 52, 9 (May 26, 2005): 8–11 at 10.

"push for modernization" in the hands of authoritarian governments ranging from Franco to Hitler.[23] Some years ago Andrei Tarkovsky's last film,
The Sacrifice (1986), brilliantly critiqued the exploitation of nature, which
he saw as connected to the setting aside by democratic technological culture
of Christianity, in the name of progress and the pursuit of the power that is
at the heart of technology.[24] Similarly the artist David Jones converted to
Catholicism when he came to view (even) the human-made world as sacramental. He came to see his own Protestantism as incapable of resisting the
world that technology was forming, and to see that Catholicism provided a
sacramental alternative to technology which, if anything, could resist it.[25]
We will pursue this in a later chapter.

Such warnings are not new, only largely ineffective. One hardly knows
where to take up the story. At the origins of American history was a sharp
dispute between a Jeffersonian and Hamiltonian view of what the future
should be. In the words of one historian:

Jefferson's vision . . . was "a fantasy of America as an agrarian paradise with limited household manufacturing" and minimal government. . . . Hamilton's vision
of America was an urban one, in which a strong central government would foster
the accumulation of capital in private hands as a means of creating the growth of
commerce, manufacturing, and national power.[26]

Thus a supporter of Hamilton's view puts the matter. The choice as thus
passed down the generations is agonizing, between "fantasy" and—under
the presumption that Hamilton's view inevitably sanctions the Industrial
Revolution—"pollution." The decision that an industrial vision of society
is to prevail is not one the "Jeffersonians" have ever accepted, so at the least
they have served the useful function of questioning whether, granted that
the Industrial Revolution cannot be undone, it can be limited, its "pollution" controlled. The more communitarian vision of the Jeffersonians has
to the present queried "unbridled capitalism."

The division of opinion about the track we should follow has remained
to the present, and the literature of protest against the track actually taken
is vast.[27] In a book still well worth reading, Jackson Lears chronicled the

23. Eduardo Gonzalez Calleja, *La España de Primo de Rivera. La modernización autoritaria:
1923–1930* (Madrid: Alianza Editorial, 2005).

24. I am indebted to Gabriel F. Giralt's excellent analysis of this film, "Andrei Tarkovsky's
Adaptation of Motifs Embedded in Leonardo Da Vinci's *The Adoration of the Magi,*" *Canadian
Journal of Film Studies* 14, 2 (Autumn 2005): 71–83. Professor Giralt also sent me a longer un-
published form of this study.

25. Adam Schwartz, *The Third Spring: G. K. Chesterton, Graham Greene, Christopher Dawson, and David Jones* (Washington, D.C.: The Catholic University of America Press, 2005).

26. Edmund S. Morgan, "The Whirlwind," *NYRB* 51, 14 (September 23, 2004), 34–39 at 34,
quoting Ron Chernow, *Alexander Hamilton* (New York: Penguin Press, 2004).

27. John Brewer, "Selling the American Way," *NYRB* 53, 19 (November 30, 2006): 58–61, is
an instructive musing on a vast literature on commercial culture and commodity consumption
and political attempts to manage these.

anti-modernist tradition, with its alliance with the arts and crafts movement, its love for things medieval, and its opposition to what was coming to be called a consumer society.[28] Though Catholics had tended to be
somewhat foreign in the American body politic, and their views often not
very influential, from before 1900 there was a specifically American form
of a worldwide Catholic critique of modernity; and some Protestants saw
Catholicism not just as an antidote to the individualism and lack of concern about the common good so common in Protestant culture, but as "the
religion of beauty," always an alternative in its worship and art to the aesthetics of Puritanism, but more radically an alternative way of being in the
world.[29]

G. K. Chesterton played a transatlantic role here, for while contribut-
ing to the English Catholic critique of modernity, he also arguably wrote
the best book ever written about American democracy, better than Alexis
de Tocqueville's *Democracy in America,* in the process doubting that Americans would be able to resist the corrupting influences of science and capitalism.[30] The "distributist" Chesterton lived too early to know the word
"globalization," but in his lament over what the increasing place of "communications" in human life was doing to local liberty and experience, he
already criticized what a later generation was to call globalization, but under the name of a capitalist spirit "that is proud of having sold a hundred
hats to Spanish peasants without thinking of what it is doing or what it is
displacing."[31]

One of the most worrisome aspects of contemporary life elucidated in
the film *The Fog of War,* Errol Morris's documentary of the life of Robert S.
McNamara, is McNamara's almost wholly technocratic formation.[32] Hold-

28. *No Place of Grace: Antimodernism and the Transformation of American Culture 1880–1920*
(New York: Pantheon Books, 1981).

29. Thomas E. Woods Jr., *The Church Confronts Modernity: Catholic Intellectuals and the
Progressive Era* (New York: Columbia University Press, 2004). Lears, *No Place of Grace,* 183–215,
241–60, treats the place of Catholic aesthetic sensibility in America.

30. Eugene McCarraher, "Remarks on John McGreevy's Catholicism and American Freedom," *HS* (September/October 2004): 28–31 at 29, in a brilliant article, describes Chesterton's
What I Saw in America as "the finest Catholic, or even foreign, reflection on American democracy ever written, far superior to Tocqueville's *Democracy in America* in points of literary style,
intellectual prowess, and critical acuity." We will return to McCarraher in a later chapter.

31. Quoted in Stratford Caldecott, "Chesterton for Today: A Tribute to *The Chesterton Review,*" *SS* 7 (2006): 69–72 at 70, noting that Chesterton's distributism "is in many ways the
ancestor of today's radical movements in defense of life, ecology, the family, agriculture, small
shops and small communities. . . . And it stood against Imperialism." Cf. on the "culture death"
that often follows the imposition of capitalism, Charles Taylor, "A Different Kind of Courage,"
NYRB 54, 7 (April 26, 2007): 4–8.

32. See also the book, *The Fog of War: Lessons from the Life of Robert S. McNamara,* ed. James
G. Blight and Janet M. Lang (Lanham, Md.: Rowman and Littlefield, 2005). Arthur M. Schle-
singer Jr., "The Turning Point," *NYRB* 54, 15 (October 11, 2007): 10–12, publishes excerpts from
McNamara's journal which suggest more insight.

ing the most awesome powers of life and death over others, of pursuing war or peace, McNamara is revealed as almost completely innocent of history and the history of moral reflection, not a bad man but a kind that Americans and technocratic education keep thrusting on the stage of world history.

McNamara was virtually an inevitable product of education as it has become, of the disintegration of the liberal arts tradition into technologies, as well as a prime exhibit of the fact that "Americans are simply not competent imperialists."[33]

To stick with the former point, a good deal of sociological study of the academic world leads to the conclusion that students in business and technocratic fields "learn to take the prevailing social order as a given, while they focus on the creation and utilization of material resources."[34] We note in passing that such disciplines, which typically do not study religion, produce graduates who "are least knowledgeable about religious issues, but are the most likely to believe in God, attend church, and have religious experiences."[35] The larger point is that a technocratic training such as McNamara's predisposes the student not to question prevailing technocratic assumptions about the use of the earth's material resources, and therefore to be very unclear about when and why one might resist the advance of technology.

It would appear that in some cases the only solution to specific problems is simply the prohibition of some applications of science, but who, what government, what international authority, will issue and enforce such prohibitions? How many have the historical sense and inbred caution and piety to know that we virtually never know the long-term effects of attempts to refashion nature? In a grudging acknowledgment that John Paul II might have known what he was talking about when he warned of the burgeoning commercial exploitation of science, Richard Horton warns us that the universities and especially the pharmaceutical firms are now in such close collusion that it is difficult to apply any effective brake.[36]

The growth of fields such as bioethics, which might have provided some

33. Arthur Schlesinger Jr., "The Making of a Mess," *NYRB* 51, 14 (September 23, 2004): 40–43 at 41. Although I have much sympathy with the "realist" views of Robert D. Kaplan, who saw in the end of the cold war not the triumph of the West but the coming anarchy in which we now find ourselves, and I accept his argument that if anyone has the power forcefully to intervene in world affairs it is the United States, I do not accept his conclusion that America now has an imperial historical task. I agree rather with John Gray, "The Mirage of Empire," *NYRB* 53, 1 (January 12, 2006): 4–8, who observes that "America lacks most of the attributes that make an imperial power."

34. James D. Davidson, "Field of Study Affects the Way People Think about Religion and Society," *IC*, September 16, 2005, summarizing the research of Barbara Hargrove and Alan Mock.

35. Ibid., summarizing the research of Edward C. Lehman Jr. and Donald W. Shriver Jr.

36. "The Dawn of McScience," *NYRB* 51, 4 (March 11, 2004): 7–9 at 7.

braking, seems almost counterproductive, since much of what comes out of the philosophy departments seems in connivance with each new technological discovery, ethics making straight the advance of bourgeois culture, philosophy as cheerleading.[37] Clearly, one of those shifts of public opinion that sometimes occurs in democracies, and now seems found in growing receptivity to some forms of environmentalism, would be necessary for Sheila and David Rothman to be shown in any way wrong: as one of their reviewers remarks, refusing to accept their counsel of despair, "It is just possible—now for the first time in the history of modern science—that the moment has finally come when society might reconsider whether the curiosity and enthusiasm of scientists alone should determine the direction of research into certain technologies."[38]

The ironies multiply. In the United States, at least, many conservatives are in favor of capitalism and technological progress, and hardly "conserve" at all: "Conservatives . . . are not on the side of the angels, and many of them seem to worry more about an efficient free-market than about a balanced cosmology."[39] They seem hardly aware of the conversation that has been going on at least since de Tocqueville's day about the relationship between material desire and democracy.[40] The conservative failure to conserve is part of a larger reorientation and confusion in which neither of the major American political parties stands for what it once stood for, and the labels "liberal" and "conservative" have become quite dated. The Republicans, once isolationist, now largely support a kind of nationalist interventionism, and both "conservatives" and "liberals" have strong nationalist and populist tendencies.[41]

In explaining why he would not support the Kyoto protocols on global warming, President George W. Bush declared: "We will not do anything that harms our economy. . . . That's my priority."[42] Such a view is very far from that of an old-fashioned organic conservative like George Kennan, who despaired of our democratic self-gratification, the leveling effects of mass democracy, and our waste of energy.[43] Many liberals, on the other hand, still in sway to the Enlightenment, refuse to consider any questions

37. Anthony Fisher, "Bioethics and the Culture of the Family," *SS* 4 (2003): 12–17 at 13. *Re-Ordering Nature: Theology, Society and the New Genetics*, ed. C. Deane-Drummond, B. Szerszynski, and R. Grove-White (New York: T & T Clark, 2003), has articles which do propose placing limits on what is to be tolerated.

38. Sherwin B. Nuland, "Getting in Nature's Way," *NYRB* 51, 2 (February 12, 2004): 32–35 at 35.

39. Molnar, "Tradition, Science and the Centuries," at 175, and see 177.

40. Kathleen G. Donohue, *Freedom from Want: American Liberalism and the Idea of the Consumer* (Baltimore: Johns Hopkins University Press, 2003).

41. Lukacs, *Democracy and Populism*.

42. Quoted in Bill McKibben, "The Coming Meltdown," *NYRB* 53, 1 (January 12, 2006): 16–18 at 18.

43. Ronald Steel, "George Kennan at 100," *NYRB* 51, 7 (April 29, 2004): 8–9.

about the validity and claims of science. Too many "greens," while able to avoid the mistakes of the conservatives and the liberals, that is, while preferring "the conservation of Nature to the inroads of Finance and Science," propose a view of nature from which humans are excluded.[44] The modern age was not wrong about everything, and especially in countries like Germany learned how to evolve a high urban culture within a natural context, that is, without destroying the environment, but this seems lost on, or unknown to, many environmentalists, who have little appreciation for a perspective in which one measure of human achievement is intelligent modification of the natural environment.[45] The German case suggests that Norbert Wiener, the inventor of cybernetics, though right in his belief that technology has the potential for great good as well as evil, lived a life that witnessed the difficulty of achieving meaningful control over the dangers technology presents.[46]

Increasingly a gap widens "between people who are still unthinking believers in technology and in economic determinism and people who are not."[47] Bill McKibben's *Enough: Staying Human in an Engineered Age* is written on behalf of those who are frightened to death of what is coming.[48] For

44. Lukacs, *End of an Age,* 38–39 at 38. Cf. Murray Jardine, *The Making and Unmaking of Technological Society: How Christianity Can Save Modernity from Itself* (Grand Rapids, Mich.: Brazos Press, 2004).

45. Thomas M. Lekan, *Imagining the Nation in Nature: Landscape Preservation and German Identity, 1885–1945* (Cambridge, Mass.: Harvard University Press, 2003). For the measurement of civilizational achievement by successful modification of the natural environment, see Felipe Fernández-Armesto, *Civilizations: Culture, Ambition, and the Transformation of Nature* (New York: Free Press, 2001), and Thomas P. Hughes, *Human-Built World: How to Think about Technology and Culture* (Chicago: University of Chicago Press, 2004). While teaching in a forested area of Austria, I, coming from the western United States where dead animals on the highways are an everyday event, asked why I had seen no road kill and was told that every landowner is assigned by the government a maximum number of wild animals that may inhabit his property. Whatever number is above what the government determines the land can sustain must be killed, or the landowner will be fined.

46. Freeman Dyson, "The Tragic Tale of a Genius," *NYRB* 52, 12 (July 14, 2005): 10–13.

47. John Lukacs, "It's the End of the Modern Age," *Chronicle of Higher Education,* April 26, 2002, B7. Edward J. O'Boyle, "Getting the Hard-Core Concepts of Economics Right," *Lo* 7, 1 (Winter 2004): 147–73, is a sometimes brilliant criticism of widespread assumptions within economics that center this discipline on the concept of the individual rather than on communitarian categories of the person. O'Boyle wants economics reimbedded in culture.

48. (New York 2003); also see Margaret Atwood, "Arguing Against Ice Cream," *NYRB* 50, 10 (June 12, 2003): 6–10 at 6. See also McKibben's "Crossing the Red Line," *NYRB* 51, 10 (June 10, 2004): 32–38, on global warming, which virtually no one in the scientific community denies is an immediate problem. McKibben closes with the following quotation from the Stockholm Environmental Institute, which imagines "a planet where preferred lifestyles combine material sufficiency with qualitative fulfillment. Conspicuous consumption and glitter are viewed as vulgar throwbacks to an earlier era. The pursuit of the well-lived life turns to the quality of existence—creativity, ideas, culture, human relationships and a harmonious relationship with nature. . . . The economy is understood as the means to these ends, rather than an end in itself." This is a vision with which many could agree. On the other hand, as McKibben seems to recognize, it is also the wildest utopianism, and he has nothing to say about how democracy itself stands in the way of such dreams.

these it is silly to speak about globalization "working" without taking such things as the impending energy crisis into the calculation.[49] Thus some of the weightiest thinkers of the century agree with Dawson's animadversions on technocracy. Even an associate editor of such a mainline magazine as the *Atlantic Monthly* sees technology to have doomed any "fight for decency in American popular culture."[50] Hans-Georg Gadamer (1900–2002) observed that in becoming masters of the world, we have become deaf and cannot hear things as they are in themselves. We have become homeless. According to Gadamer, continuing a tradition to be explored below, we must awaken to "the voice of Being."[51] For this we must recover a Socratic sense of our own finitude and limitations. When the Delphic oracle announced "Know that you are a man and no god," we were told that we will never be masters of the world.[52]

As elemental to humans as curiosity is greed. Thus in so many ways laissez-faire capitalism, belief in progress, belief in historical inevitability, and other scourges of the age are given free reign. Behind such sunny beliefs, articulated once more in Deirdre McCloskey's vision of "the bourgeois virtues" as lying behind most that is good in society, lie "the black and merciless things that are behind the great possessions," portrayed by Henry James in *The Ivory Tower*.[53] The result of such greed is a kind of glut, warned of by G. K. Chesterton in a 1930 speech given in Toronto:[54]

The coming peril is the intellectual, educational, psychological and artistic overproduction, which, equally with economic overproduction, threatens the well-being of contemporary civilisation. People are inundated, blinded, deafened, and

49. Martin Wolf, *Why Globalization Works* (New Haven, Conn.: Yale University Press, 2004). Nicolas Kristof, "Wretched of the Earth," *NYRB* 54, 9 (May 31, 2007): 34–36, lists some of the real economic successes of globalization, but without discussion of the accompanying cultural changes. Patricia Cohen, "In Economic Departments, A Growing Will to Debate Fundamental Assumptions," *NYT,* July 11, 2007, A17, is an instructive description of growing doubts about free-market economics, the benefits of free trade and globalization, and the role of mathematics in economics.

50. Ross Douthat, "Lost and Saved on Television," *FT* 173 (May 2007): 22–26 at 22: "Every successive technological innovation weakened the power of regulators . . . while expanding the venues where human weakness could be exploited for fun and profit." But Douthat also argues that the very pop culture he laments takes religion more seriously than did the "family values" culture of the 1950s.

51. Edward Tingley, "Gadamer & the Light of the Word," *FT* 139 (January 2004): 38–45 at 38–39.

52. Ibid., 42–43.

53. Deirdre McCloskey, *The Bourgeois Virtues: Ethics for an Age of Commerce* (Chicago: University of Chicago Press, 2006); and for James see *The Ivory Tower,* introduction by Alan Hollinghurst, with an essay by Ezra Pound (New York: New York Review Books, 2004). See the essay on James's dislike of the modernization of New York—on what had been done in the name of material progress—and loss of the past by Colm Tóibín, "Henry James's New York," *NYRB* 53, 2 (February 9, 2006): 33–37.

54. One of several relevant documents quoted in "Last Things," *SS* 4 (2003): 79–80 at 80.

mentally paralyzed by a flood of vulgar and tasteless externals, leaving them no time for leisure, thought, or creation from within themselves.

Comfort has come to be worshipped, with its attendant logic of a life lived wholly in the world, from which transcendence has been evacuated.[55]
As Gabriel Marcel put it at mid-century:

In our contemporary world it may be said that the more a man becomes dependent on the gadgets whose smooth functioning assures him of a tolerable life at the material level, the more estranged he becomes from an awareness of his inner reality. . . .
It would be no exaggeration to say that the more progress "humanity" as an abstraction makes towards the mastery of nature, the more actual individual men tend to become slaves of this very conquest.[56]

It becomes almost impossible to say "enough, I have enough." The spirit that animated the medieval attempt to limit usury, the Amish attempt to examine and then accept or reject each new technology on the basis of spiritual criteria and the common good, is now if anything more marginal than formerly.[57]
Very few are able to admit that they have consented to a logic of perpetual disappointment, in which no amount of income is ever adequate to their "needs," and it is almost impossible to entertain the idea that they might be happier if they could only be satisfied with a stable list of necessities.[58] Without much sense of history and self-knowledge, Americans and others can accept the ideas of those who with a straight face tell them that their prosperity is the result of a benevolent union of personal initiative and free choice of an upright life under the kindly hand of some impersonal destiny: even the most elementary knowledge of history shows that the farthest things from, say, the mind of the sixteenth- or seventeenth-century English entrepreneur was free trade or obedience to the doctrine of the just price. What was wanted was a nation that preferred merchants' interests to all else. All was fair, so far as foreigners were concerned, that gave advantage. Every trick could be used. Though one should be a gentleman with one's fellows, what was wanted was a pragmatic, unprincipled, life of commerce.[59] Usu-

55. Weaver, *Ideas Have Consequences,* 117.
56. *Men against Humanity* (London: Harvill Press, 1952), quoted in ibid., 80.
57. Atwood, "Arguing Against Ice Cream," 10; Glenn W. Olsen, *Beginning at Jerusalem: Five Reflections on the History of the Church* (San Francisco: Ignatius Press, 2004), esp. ch. 3.
58. Weaver, *Ideas Have Consequences,* 14–15.
59. Liah Greenfeld, "Speaking Historically about Globalization and Related Fantasies," *HS* 5, 3 (January 2004): 23–28 at 25–26, noting how misunderstood Adam Smith, who approved the Acts of Navigation and state intervention in the economy so long as it fostered national power, has been. Smith made fun of the *Économistes,* the French inventers of laissez faire, and Greenfeld makes clear how different the histories and economic ideas of the two countries, at least until the second half of the eighteenth century, were, provocatively arguing that the French were rational, i.e., worked to live, while the English were irrational, i.e., lived to work.

ally hardly appearing in this story is a nod to the central role slavery played in the prosperity of early America.[60]

⌒

Classical late-eighteenth- and nineteenth-century laissez-faire liberalism was well fashioned to allow what the merchants wanted, and from it evolved more modern forms of liberalism.[61] Understood as Alasdair MacIntyre understands it, liberalism as a philosophy came to allow *liberté* (from *libertas* = unbounded or unrestricted) to trump all other values.[62] There are no greater symbols of this than the Statue of Liberty, greeting the visitor coming from Europe, or the statue of Freedom on the dome of the Capitol in Washington, D.C.[63] In both England and the United States the outcome of *liberté* trumping all other values has been a modernizing empire too intellectually lazy and morally debilitated to engage in serious reflection on whether there is any exit from the path it has fallen upon. Liberalism has revealed itself as not so much a position with an internal coherence as the end product, or latest stage, of a series of responses to various historical contingencies.[64]

When we speak of a liberalism derived from *liberté* trumping all other values, an important distinction must be made between what we may call the liberalism of elites and the liberalism of the average person. Later chapters will develop the idea that in the way they conceive of such things as the will, most Americans are liberals. This does not mean that they do not at the same time think of themselves as religious, only that it is likely that their religion has been shaped by liberal premises. The elites actually pushing for ever-greater secularization and the elimination of religion from life may be relatively small in number. In either case, whether we are speaking

60. Gordon S. Wood, "What Slavery Was Really Like," *NYRB* 51, 18 (November 18, 2004): 43–47 at 43.

61. Richard Bellamy, *Liberalism and Modern Society: A Historical Argument* (University Park: Pennsylvania State University Press, 1992), traces the evolution of liberal thought, showing the contingency of its assumptions.

62. See especially *After Virtue: A Study in Moral Theory*, 3rd ed. (Notre Dame, Ind.: University of Notre Dame Press, 2007), as at 195; *Three Rival Versions of Moral Enquiry: Encyclopaedia, Genealogy, and Tradition* (Notre Dame, Ind.: University of Notre Dame Press, 1990); and *Dependent Rational Animals: Why Human Beings Need the Virtues* (Chicago: Open Court, 1999); see also my "America as an Enlightenment Culture," *Actas del IV Congreso "Cultura Europea,"* ed. Enrique Banús and Beatriz Elío (Pamplona: Aranzadi, 1998), 121–28. Christopher Wolfe, "American Liberalism: Past, Present, Future," *Razón práctica y multiculturalismo,* ed. Enrique Banús and Alejandro Llano, Studia Europea Navarrensis 1 (Pamplona: Centro de Estudios Europeos, Universidad de Navarra, 1999), 207–14, at 208, 210–11, makes shrewd comments about why American liberalism has worked as well as it has.

63. David Hackett Fischer, *Liberty and Freedom* (Oxford: Oxford University Press, 2005), while making clear the great profusion of ideas about liberty in American history, gives a celebratory history of these ideas hardly touched by their treatment by philosophers such as MacIntyre.

64. Richard Bellamy, *Liberalism and Modern Society: A Historical Argument* (University Park: Pennsylvania State University Press, 1992).

of elites or the average person, to the degree that liberty is allowed to trump all other values, contemporary liberalism fosters an attitude intrinsically solvent of any public philosophy or shared worldview and destabilizing of any long-term effort to control technology in the name of agreed-on non-commercial human values.[65]

As MacIntyre has described the career of liberalism in the United States, it has become committed to the prohibition of the dominance of any single idea of the good in public life.[66] In this sense, multiculturalism, the deep pluralism in which a society cannot agree about the good, is simply an end-point of liberalism.[67] Liberalism's goal is process rather than substance.[68] It results in the growing social and cultural separation of people. Further, if MacIntyre is right that the self itself is a product of community and social context, that is, if its nature is ordered by that which is outside it, the liberal self, replicating as it does a social order from which the idea of a common good and any hierarchy of public goods has been largely evacuated, is intrinsically disordered and dysfunctional, the copy of a public order filled with "procedure" rather than quest for the good, true, and beautiful.[69] It represents "the fracture of good order."[70]

It is not an accident that pragmatism is the most common philosophy in America. First Emerson lost his belief in God, while retaining confidence in nature, the heart, and himself, thus becoming a kind of founding father of "the theology of experience." Then Melville lost confidence in nature, and concluded that there are no objective norms by which human life can

65. This is an extension of my argument in "The Quest for a Public Philosophy in Twentieth-Century American Political Thought," *Co* 27 (2000): 340–62. J. Budziszewski, *The Revenge of Conscience: Politics and the Fall of Man* (Dallas: Spence, 1999), similarly argues that shared life is not possible on the myth of neutrality, the notion that we need not commit ourselves to some view of reality.

66. *Whose Justice? Which Rationality?* (Notre Dame, Ind.: University of Notre Dame Press, 1988).

67. Christopher Shannon, "Catholicism as the Other," *FT* 139 (January, 2004): 46–52 at 47.

68. Ibid., 48.

69. *After Virtue*, as at 172–73. Jeffrey Stout, *Democracy and Tradition* (Princeton, N.J.: Princeton University Press, 2004), gives sustained criticism of MacIntyre's views. Robert D. Putnam, *Bowling Alone: The Collapse and Revival of American Community* (New York: Simon & Schuster, 2000), describes the growing disconnection and loss of social capital in American life. It is interesting to observe that criticisms similar to MacIntyre's are coming from very different directions. Ruiping Fan, a philosopher at the City University of Hong Kong, argues in Confucian fashion for the autonomy of the family, observing: "The most important moral values are not individual liberty as self-determination or equality of opportunity, but rather the virtues for preserving and promoting bonds for human flourishing, especially in the family." Quoted in "The 19th Annual Clarke Family Medical Ethics Conference," *EC,* June 2004: 2–3 at 2. It is a shame that the American press uncomprehendingly reduces the important criticisms of liberalism coming from Asia to some mindless and irrational "Asian values."

70. Jason C. Bivins, *The Fracture of Good Order: Christian Antiliberalism and the Challenge to American Politics* (Chapel Hill: University of North Carolina Press, 2003), on a number of thinkers often thought of as "to the left" rather than as anti-liberal.

be lived. In the words of one of his most astute students: "Our fate as human beings is to live by norms that have no basis in divine truth, but that have functional truth for the conduct of life."[71] Thus pragmatism drifts into liberalism, a worldview for those not honest enough to admit that the logic of saying there are no norms is that "anything goes."

Such liberalism is good at driving religion out of the world, especially through the idea that modern states may control the education of the young so as to form "good citizens" by an education from which religion has been excised (individualism and the notion that one can affirm one's private good typically give way before the claims of the state). Commonly liberalism is blind to its own sectarianism in labeling religious views "sectarian," while presenting its own secularism as "neutral," when in fact a definite formation is being forced on the citizenry.[72] A good argument can be made in this regard that "liberalism . . . should be seen as a vehicle that constructs people for the benefit of the state, not the state for the benefit of people."[73] In any case in the United States the growing secular left is united in—almost defined by—hostility to fundamentalism and to pro-lifers, viewed as illegitimately intruding religion into the public sphere.

A deep hypocrisy of many on the left is the claim that liberalism stands for toleration: liberalism, like most political positions, tolerates those things of which it approves, but is intolerant of the rest. Thus Gloria Feldt, the president of Planned Parenthood Federation of America, responding to the attempt of health workers to secure "conscience clauses" that would allow them to refuse to perform abortions, stated: "It's part of the anti-choice arrogance in which they believe they have the right to impose their ideology on everyone else."[74] Feldt seems completely oblivious to her own intolerance and arrogance in demanding that those who think abortions to be murder be forced to participate in them. She shows no sense of the tragedy of pluralism, that someone's conscience is going to be violated in a serious

<hr />

71. Andrew Delbanco, *Melville: His World and Work* (New York: Knopf, 2005), 311, cited by Roger Lundin, "'As If God Were Dead': American Literature and the Question of Scripture," in *The Bible and the University*, ed. David Lyle Jeffrey and C. Stephen Evans, Scripture and Hermeneutics Series 8 (Grand Rapids, Mich.: Zondervan, 2007), 253–83, useful on both Emerson and Melville.

72. Robert Royal, "Dawson's History: Resurrecting the Work of Christopher Dawson," *The Weekly Standard*, March 17, 2003, 33–35 at 35. Cf. *The Secular Revolution: Power, Interests, and Conflict in the Secularization of American Public Life*, ed. Christian Smith (Berkeley: University of California Press, 2003), and Talal Asad, *Formations of the Secular: Christianity, Islam, Modernity* (Stanford, Calif.: Stanford University Press, 2003). More generally see Winnifred Fallers Sullivan, *The Impossibility of Religious Freedom* (Princeton, N.J.: Princeton University Press, 2005).

73. These are the words of a letter by Harry G. Hutchison in *FT* 139 (January 2004): 8–9 at 9. Michael Lerner, *Spirit Matters* (Charlottesville, Va.: Hampton Roads, 2000), is a challenge to anti-spiritual liberalism by a leading American Jewish intellectual.

74. Quoted by David Crary in an Associated Press article, "Abortion Foes Expand Efforts," *DMN*, September 17, 2004.

way on such issues, that there is no neutral ground. Only a few in public life dare stand up to the liberal demand that consciences be violated.

Even the generous-spirited Kwame Anthony Appiah does not seem fully aware of the premises of his position. Appiah accepts the common narrative of the history of toleration, examined in the next chapter, that beginning in the early modern period embracing toleration was the most realistic way of forestalling war. Over time this de facto toleration has turned more and more into de jure toleration, that is, a toleration mandated by law. An example of this is American anti-hate legislation. Appiah does not think that a full relativism should result from the acceptance of "multiculturalism," and wishes to construct a global ethic on the basis of certain standards of morality. But he seems not fully to realize that formally his views are not different from those of a religious person who wishes all to embrace his religion. Appiah may be "nicer" than some of these religious persons, but he still finally wants everyone to accept his notions of rationality and morality, his "universalist missionary creed."[75]

David Brooks is much more perceptive here. He began an op-ed piece of April 21, 2005, in the *New York Times,*

Justice Harry Blackmun did more inadvertent damage to our democracy than any other 20th century American. When he and his Supreme Court colleagues issued the Roe v. Wade decision, they set off a cycle of political viciousness and counter-viciousness that has poisoned public life ever since. . . . Religious conservatives became alienated from their own government, feeling that their democratic rights had been usurped by robed elitists. . . . The fact is the entire country is trapped. Harry Blackmun and his colleagues suppressed that democratic abortion debate the nation needs to have. . . . Unless Roe v. Wade is overturned, politics will never get better.

Here Brooks recognizes the peremptory intolerance of the left, expressed in Blackmun's case in a judicial form that Feldt merely continues.

Continuing blindness about one's own intolerance seems largely the situation of the left in at least the first world. In the United States the Democratic Party itself has eliminated the "conscience clause" from the abortion clause in its platform, making assent to the culture of death (or dissimulation) almost a prerequisite for membership (a few brave souls identify themselves as pro-life Democrats).[76] In Spain the Socialist prime minister, José Rodriguez Zapatero, distinguished between a civil sphere (of which he was in control) and a sphere of private convictions, to which he relegated religion, apparently without any sense of his own intolerance.[77]

75. Edward Feser, "We Are The World," *NR* 58, 4 (March 13, 2006): 42–43 at 43, reviewing Appiah's *Cosmopolitanism: Ethics in a World of Strangers* (New York: W. W. Norton, 2006).

76. William McGurn, "Bob Casey's Revenge," *FT* 149 (January 2005): 6–8 at 7.

77. "Catholic Politician Confident Spanish Church, State Can Solve Dispute," *IC,* Decem-

◦

In spite of a growing environmental consciousness in some quarters and some successes for systems labeled democratic, many have concluded that the situation vis-à-vis both technology and totalitarianism has worsened in the half-century since Dawson wrote.[78] Early-twentieth-century American progressivism, which unlike populism did not in principle oppose business and thought that economic growth could improve life, already had wondered whether an emphasis on individual freedom had not resulted in an undesirable concentration of wealth in the hands of the few, and whether the only way available to redress this was a strong central government.[79] At mid-century, Joseph Schumpeter was unsure capitalism itself could survive.[80] Writers such as the Swiss economist Wilhelm Röpke tried to give the market its due while warning of its intrinsic limits and of capitalism's self-destructive elements, recognizing that the market must be subordinated to higher, communal goods.[81] In many ways this remains a central issue, for the "globalization" advocated by many Americans centers on free markets and pro-business policies, while many Europeans in particular view such advocacy as denial of the state's obligations to provide public services and safety nets for the ill and the poor.[82]

Truly scarifying are the views of the Nobel economist Robert Fogel, who observes the worldwide breakdown of village life.[83] This is often missed by those living in the first world, but for most of world history most human beings have lived in villages. These have been the main means of inculturation and cultural stability, in spite of the fact that survival in village life was commonly precarious. Now threatened or in decay as capitalism advanc-

---

ber 10, 2004, 2, describing the attempt of a Catholic group within the Socialist Party to have Zapatero adopt a position more tolerant of religion.

78. Sigurd Bergmann, *Geist, der Natur befreit: Die trinitarische Kosmologie Gregors von Nazianz im Horizont einer ökologischen Theologie der Befreiung* (Mainz: Matthias-Grünewald-Verlag, 1995), is among other things an apology for the role of theology in confronting the ecological problems of our day.

79. Ronald Steel, "Where It Began," *NYRB* 51, 14 (September 23, 2004): 58–61 at 58; and Jeff Madrick, "The Way to a Fair Deal," *NYRB* 53, 1 (January 12, 2006): 37–40 at 38.

80. Jerry Z. Muller, *The Mind and the Market: Capitalism in Modern European Thought* (New York: Knopf, 2002), is a very astute study of thinkers from Voltaire to Schumpeter.

81. John Zmirak, *Wilhelm Röpke: Swiss Localist, Global Economist* (Wilmington, Del.: ISI Books, 2001).

82. Stanley Hoffmann, "The Foreign Policy the US Needs," *NYRB* 53, 13 (August 10, 2006): 60–64 at 60. Pankaj Mishra, "Impasse in India," *NYRB* 54, 11 (June 28, 2007): 48–51, gives an idea for one country of the pros and cons of globalization. See also the analysis of globalization in Pierre Manent, *A World Beyond Politics? A Defense of the Nation-State* (Princeton, N.J.: Princeton University Press, 2006), who among other things argues that one result of present advocacy of universal human rights is a "universal man," who is only incidentally anything specific, a citizen, a spouse, or a father.

83. For this and what follows, see William H. McNeill, "Bigger and Better?" *NYRB* 51, 16 (2004): 61–63.

es, around the world cities have only very imperfectly either absorbed the social networks of village life, or have replaced these with something less stable. People are more and more removed from familial and religious connections, and left in their professions without the guide of either tradition or religion. Fogel sees cultural continuity as never as much at risk as in the twenty-first century. His views are not exactly new, and thinkers as different as Emile Durkheim (1858–1917) and Simone Weil (1909–43) lamented the *anomie,* the rootlessness which had resulted from the loss of community that accompanied the abandonment of village life as people left the land for the big city. The move of a French peasant to Paris was commonly accompanied by what might be called his secularization, his loss of faith, and, among other things, a growth in the suicide rate.[84]

Important dimensions of these developments are missed by almost all. It is common to view computer technology as something neutral, something like a knowledge of arithmetic (also viewed as neutral), which every child should be taught. But of course every tool of reason carries its own cultural assumptions:

Computers reinforce or marginalize culturally specific patterns of thought and communication in how the technology encodes the cultural assumptions of those who design them. Unfortunately users who share with creators the same cultural assumptions do not see this inherent bias. However, members of other cultures are aware that when they use computers they must adapt themselves to radically different patterns of thought and deep, culturally bound ways of knowing. If they accept computers uncritically as a culturally neutral technology and as the latest expression of progress, they may not recognize how their interactions with computers are changing them.[85]

It is as much the first as the third world that is threatened in such matters, and Victoria de Grazia, distinguishing between the traditional bourgeois culture of recent European centuries and the consumer society that has developed in America, argues that the latter has conquered the former.[86]

In many of the foregoing analyses, "capitalism" is at most a convenient

---

84. Emmet Kennedy, "Simone Weil: Secularism and Syncretism," *JHS* 5 (2005): 203–25 at 212–13. I cannot stress too much how complicated the question of secularization is. We may think of the upper classes as often the first to secularize, forgetting how common in the nineteenth century some form of integralism was, and how many leaders of Church and state regularly presented themselves as experts in both. Gladstone and Bismarck thought of themselves as theological experts, and untold numbers of clergy delivered themselves of opinions on political thought and economics: Michael Burleigh, *Earthly Powers: The Clash of Religion and Politics in Europe from the French Revolution to the Great War* (New York: HarperCollins, 2005); see also Russell Hittinger, "The Churches of Earthly Power," *FT* 164 (June/July 2006): 27–32 at 27.

85. C. A. Bowers. *Let Them Eat Data: How Computers Affect Education, Cultural Diversity, and the Prospects of Ecological Sustainability* (Athens: University of Georgia Press, 2000).

86. *Irresistible Empire: America's Advance through Twentieth-Century Europe* (Cambridge, Mass.: Harvard University Press, 2005).

shorthand for a whole range of shifts, at the center of which for those now living is a communications revolution which took place after World War II. Already Paul Valéry described the situation at the end of World War I: "The system of causes controlling the fate of every one of us, and now extending over the whole globe, makes it reverberate throughout at every shock; there are no more questions that can be settled by being settled at one point."[87] How much more the communications revolution after World War II rendered this pronouncement true! Satellites made the rapid growth of multinational corporations and nongovernmental organizations possible. When analysts now cast about for a label that better catches the new web of reality than does "capitalism," they sometimes light on "globalization" to designate a certain weakening of boundaries.[88]

John Gray has pointed out that this process now called globalization has long been perceived, and that Marx and Engels wrote in 1848 in the *Communist Manifesto*:

The need of a constantly expanding market for its products chases the bourgeoisie over the whole surface of the globe. It must nestle everywhere, settle everywhere, establish connections everywhere. The bourgeoisie has through its exploitation of the world market given a cosmopolitan character to production and consumption in every country. . . . It compels all nations, on pain of extinction, to adopt the bourgeois mode of production; it compels them to introduce what it calls civilization into their midst, i.e. to become bourgeois themselves. In one word, it creates a world after its own image.[89]

Gray goes on to note the similarities between Marxism and neo-liberalism, and their shared disabling limitations. Above all, for them "politics and culture are secondary phenomena [to economic forces], sometimes capable of retarding human progress; but in the last analysis they cannot prevail against advancing technology and growing productivity." For Gray there is a measure of truth in such technological determinism, but also an oversimplified unidirectional view of history which ignores the persistent strength of religion and nationalism. Sharing Marx's blind spots, neo-liberalism glosses over some of Marx's most important insights, above all into the self-destructive and disruptive nature of capitalism. In Gray's words:

As capitalism spreads, it turns society upside down, destroying entire industries, ways of life, and regimes. . . . The expansion of European capitalism . . . involved . . . many . . . forms of imperial conquest and rivalry. . . . Over the past two hun-

87. Quoted in Pankaj Mishra, "Massacre in Arcadia," *NYRB* 52, 15 (October 6, 2005): 8–11 at 8.

88. Ulrich Teusch, *Was ist Globalisierung? Ein Überblick* (Darmstadt: Wissenschaftliche Buchgesellschaft, 2004).

89. Quoted in John Gray, "The World Is Round," *NYRB* 52, 13 (August 11, 2005): 13–15 at 13, for this and the two following quotations.

dred years, the spread of capitalism and industrialization has gone hand in hand with war and revolution.

In such a perspective globalization is the latest chapter of the centuries-long economic developments that comprised "capitalism," but centers on the weakening or disappearance of cultural, economic, and linguistic boundaries, and leads one to wonder about what, if anything, is to replace them.[90] Gray's view is not only that globalization is reversible, but that "its disruptive effects tend to result in deglobalization."[91] Others note that capitalism is not one thing, and that distinction should be made between a capitalist model, common after World War II, in which corporations were seen to have a responsibility for their employees' well-being and to the community, and the more recent "Washington consensus model" in which corporation managers are only responsible for creating short-term "value."[92] This is an uncontrolled capitalism which can wreak damage at any level of society. Amy Chua believes that the exportation of this free market democracy has bred global instability.[93] But there is disagreement and Robert Ashford and Rodney Shakespeare show ways in which free markets can be made compatible with access of the poor to capital.[94] It seems fairly clear that in certain places, as India, the multitude of developments that parade under the label globalization have in fact reduced poverty.[95] Particularly level-headed is Kevin Phillips's analysis, which with the United States in mind and against many laissez-faire thinkers stresses how much government has contributed to economic growth, indeed that government has arguably been an even greater source of prosperity than technology.[96] Joseph Stiglitz suggests that the economic conditions of various parts of the world are so different that what should be attempted rather than universal deregulation is free-trade blocs composed of countries of roughly the same level of economic development.[97] There is so much to sort out! Clearly there is false representation on all sides, anti-globalism, for instance, often being a cloak for the protection of local economic interests which are not viable against open

90. Tony Judt, "Europe vs. the US," *NYRB* 52, 2 (February 10, 2005): 37–41 at 41.

91. John Gray, "The Global Delusion," *NYRB* 53, 7 (April 27, 2006): 20–23 at 22.

92. William Pfaff, "France: The Children's Hour," *NYRB* 53, 8 (May 11, 2006): 40–43 at 42–43.

93. *World on Fire: How Exporting Free Market Democracy Breeds Ethnic Hatred and Global Instability* (New York: Doubleday, 2003).

94. *Binary Economics: the New Paradigm* (Lanham, Md.: University Press of America, 1999).

95. Thomas Friedman, "India's Lesson for the Antiglobalizers," *IHT,* June 8, 2004; Pankaj Mishra, "The Neglected Majority Wins!" *NYRB* 51, 13 (August 12, 2004): 30–37.

96. *Wealth and Democracy: A Political History of the American Rich* (New York: Broadway Books, 2002); see also Jeff Madrick, "The Power of the Super-Rich," *NYRB* 49, 12 (July 18, 2002): 25–27 at 26, noting that for Phillips "globalization is the equivalent of the Social Darwinism of the late 1800s."

97. Pfaff, "Children's Hour," 43.

competition. What is often presented as simply the exploitation of workers in third world countries, though involving wages which are absurdly low by Western standards, nevertheless may represent an improvement of the local third world economy involved, and jobs where none existed before.

Gray believes that the globalization of the neo-liberals, like Marxism before it, elides two propositions, the first, that we are living in a time of rapid technological innovation, obviously true, and the second, that this is leading to a single world economy, which is simply groundless ideology. There is no good reason to think that globalization leads to either peace or liberal democracy. It more likely leads to new great powers such as India and China. It seemed the United States most benefited from the free flow of capital, goods, and ideas that globalization and the Internet revolution in the 1990s signified; but a good argument can be made that in the twenty-first century the United States has become the victim of these same developments.[98] In any case, the existence of "globalization" understood as the breakdown of barriers and the prying open of the most closed social systems by the Internet and the communications revolution can hardly be denied. One result is the paradox of the use of the most modern technologies in jihad, a struggle against modernity.

Fifty years ago Herbert Simon expressed doubt about the tenet of classical economics which holds that people choose on the basis of all available information. As a product of the Enlightenment, classical economics had always tended to a rationalist and mathematical view of human life not justified, he thought, by the historical record. Simon thought humans not that "rational," and the universe of available information too large for classical theory to be true. He suggested the more sober and modest view that people commonly choose the first option they meet that satisfies their needs. Such modesty still is uncommon among economists, and Robert H. Nelson has suggested that indeed market economics is itself a religion.[99] It may be a deep delusion to think that unfettered research, market freedom, and technological development expand human choice:

It is not enough to contend that research should be pursued in the name of scientific freedom and that, in the name of market freedom, people should be able to take it or leave it as they see fit. We should know by now that almost every major technology introduced in the name of expanded personal choice sooner or later is overtaken by cultural patterns and practices that finally shape everyone's behavior, whittling away almost to nothing the range of the choice.[100]

98. Patrick Radden Keefe, "Quartermasters of Terror," *NYRB* 52, 2 (February 10, 2005): 33–36 at 33, arguing that terrorists were among the first to understand and take advantage of rapid deregulation carried by globalization.

99. *Economics as Religion: From Samuelson to Chicago and Beyond* (University Park: Pennsylvania State University Press, 2001).

100. Daniel Callahan, "Visions of Eternity," *FT* 133 (May 2003): 28–35 at 34.

George Soros, while a believer in global civil society, has noted how globalization has distorted the allocation of material goods at the expense of various public goods.[101] To him laissez-faire economics is as unscientific as Marxism, and he notes the tendency of markets to overshoot their marks, resulting in cycles of boom and bust.[102] A similar argument informs the writings of George P. Brockway, who shows how the wrenching of economics away from philosophy and its wedding to mathematics has resulted in conceiving economic life as impersonal, as free from the restraints which should inform any human activity.[103] Liah Greenfeld goes further and claims that the very nature of modern nationalism is inherently competitive and tied to a notion of prestige which can never be satisfied. That is, modern economies are tied to an unending race in which growth itself is the always receding prize in view. Because by definition one can never be satisfied, it is impossible to calculate efficiency, and thus the modern economy is deeply irrational. Greenfeld likens the "preoccupation with growth for its own sake" to an addiction.[104]

Of course both traditional culture/religion and, where it exists, the nation state, fight back against globalization at every step, and should not be expected to disappear at any early date, for in the nature of things, nations have divergent interests and will compete until history's last day. Indeed, one author argues that it is precisely the high level of nationalism remaining in America which will undo all attempts to achieve American global dominance.[105] The basis of international politics remains the calculation of national interests and quest for a stable balance of power, and this neither a United Nations, a European Union, nor globalization can replace.[106] The analysis of Anne-Marie Slaughter is particularly helpful. Slaughter argues that the United States is already inextricably tied to and integrated with a

101. George Soros, *George Soros on Globalization* (New York: Public Affairs, 2002); see also Joseph E. Stiglitz, "A Fair Deal for the World," *NYRB* 49, 9 (May 23, 2002): 24–28. As we have already noted, "globalization" is a devilishly difficult term to define. Among the articles in "Free Trade and Modern History: A Forum" in *HS* 5, 3 (January 2004): 17–30, a wise, if occasionally overly clever, piece by Liah Greenfeld, "Speaking Historically about Globalization," 23–28, argues that there is no such thing as globalization. Tony Judt, "Its Own Worst Enemy," *NYRB* 49, 13 (August 15, 2002): 12–17, points out many reasons why globalization will be only one trend of the future, including the contradictory policies practiced by its advocates. See also the articles in "The British Empire and Globalization: A Forum," *HS* 4, 4 (April 2003): 21–39.

102. John Gray, "The Moving Target," *NYRB* 53, 15 (October 5, 2006): 22–24, explaining the fallibility of all economic models based on the assumption of perfect knowledge, and the limitations of all social science.

103. *The End of Economic Man: An Introduction to Humanistic Economics,* 4th ed. (New York: W. W. Norton, 2001). Already some in the Austrian school (F. A. Hayek, etc.) argued that economics was as much a branch of moral philosophy as a science.

104. "Speaking Historically about Globalization," 25.

105. Neil Smith, *The Endgame of Globalization* (New York: Routledge, 2005).

106. James Chace, "Empire, Anyone?" *NYRB* 51, 15 (October 7, 2004): 15–18 at 17.

host of international organizations, from the World Trade Organization to international securities commissioners.[107] The decisions of these organizations shape much of life in America, as elsewhere. This is the truth of "globalization." But this does not mean either that the world is moving toward world government or that the nation-state is at an end. It simply means that the nation-state cannot be as autonomous as it was in the nineteenth century, and that therefore all forms of imperialism are ever more difficult to practice.

Without a response to Dawson's problem, the relation of religion and mass culture, it seems that the future will be divided between jihad and "McWorld."[108] Terrorism and neo-liberalism are revealed as sharing a common tendency toward, if not reveling in, global anarchy, to be so preoccupied with one idea (the victory of one's cause in the case of terrorism, the freedom of markets in the case of neo-liberalism) as to refuse to address all those questions of subsidiarity and the common good which build up the texture of actual societies.[109] On the one side will be the forces of tribal and religious fundamentalism, unable to assimilate the legitimate advances of the Enlightenment,[110] and on the other hand those of consumerist capitalism and globalization, mindlessly and nihilistically pursuing technology wherever it leads, with little regard to the fact that man is first of all a spiritual being.[111]

A good case can be made that those countries that have followed the French-German social model, while obtaining the satisfaction of the retention of familiar and socially responsible patterns of life, have paid the price

107. *A New World Order* (Princeton, N.J.: Princeton University Press, 2004), discussed in Tony Judt, "Dreams of Empire," *NYRB* 51, 17 (November 4, 2004): 38–41 at 41.

108. Benjamin R. Barber, *Jihad vs. McWorld* (New York: Ballantine Books, 1995), has many fine insights, but does not seem to me finally to come to terms with the legitimacy of the distaste for democracy found in religious and tribal fundamentalism, and liberal democracy's role in generating such distaste. Although Barber's views are often very realistic, his hopes for "global democracy" seem to me unreasonably optimistic.

109. Christian Caryl, "Tyrants on the Take," *NYRB* 49, 6 (April 11, 2002): 27–30 at 27, notes that "terrorism seems to be establishing itself as the dark twin of globalization."

110. Charles Taylor, *A Catholic Modernity? Charles Taylor's Marianist Award Lecture*, ed. James L. Heft (New York: Oxford University Press, 1999), gives an idea of what a post-secularist understanding of religion might look like, and this is the subject of the last chapter of the present book.

111. John Gray, *False Dawn: The Delusions of Global Capitalism* (New York: New Press, 1998); Zygmunt Bauman, *Globalization: The Human Consequences* (New York: Columbia University Press, 1998); and Joseph E. Stiglitz, *Globalization and Its Discontents* (New York: W. W. Norton, 2002), are on the limitations of global capitalism. For a critique of Gray's views, see Alan Ryan, "Live and Let Live," *NYRB* 48, 8 (May 17, 2001): 54–56, and M. A. Casey, "How to Think about Globalization," in *FT* 126 (October 2002): 47–56 at 47–48. See also the articles gathered in the Autumn issue of *Co* 27, 3 (2000), and Tony Judt, "The French Difference," *NYRB* 48, 6 (April 12, 2001): 15–22. David Reynolds, *One World Divisible: A Global History since 1945* (New York: W. W. Norton, 2000), argues that a dialectical process is at work in which unifying developments such as better communication and globalization fuel new regionalisms.

in high unemployment and slow growth, while those countries like Ireland, generally on the periphery of the European Union, which have embraced globalization, have prospered astoundingly. Ireland has in one generation moved from being an alleged "sick man" of Europe to being the second richest, after Luxembourg.[112] But at what cost? Ireland's traditional religious culture has disintegrated in the same generation, and one remembers the biblical query "What does it profit a man if he gain the whole world but lose his soul?"

The deep cleavage between the United States and what the second Bush administration called "Old Europe" in the events leading up to the second Gulf War, in 2003, has been characterized by Robert Kagan as a struggle between a Kantian Europe and an imperial America. There is some truth in this. On the side of the former we find the belief or hope "that the world (or at least Western Europe) has entered a Kantian era of perpetual peace in which virtually all disputes can be contained using international organizations."[113] Europe, in the view of Romano Prodi as European Commission president, has a new *mission civilisatrice,* the bringing of universal peace to the world.[114] On the side of the latter ("American") view, we perhaps have not so much one single position as a widespread suspicion that a universal order built on rights, law, and perpetual peace is beyond human attainment (the uneasy juxtaposition of the notion that American power can be used to "build nations" with the practice of *realpolitik* indicates that we do not really have one American position, or that the "official" position is deeply contradictory). In any case the Kantians—and Americans who agree with them—are almost certainly wrong, and it is unlikely that perpetual peace is in anyone's future. Though the boundaries he draws between civilizations may be too simplistic, Samuel Huntington warns us that what is coming— what we have entered—is not a universal order of peace and prosperity, but a time of prolonged clash between civilizations.[115] In a partly parallel vein, Emmanuel Todd warns of an impending breakdown of the American order, which has never been as powerful as some think.[116]

In sum, "the problem with globalization as it currently operates is its tendency to foster secularization among peoples and cultures that are not

112. Thomas L. Friedman, "Ireland Has Found Gold at Rainbow's End," *DMN,* June 30, 2005, A13.

113. Paul Carrese, "The Ironies of American Power," *FT* 135 (September 2003): 39–42 at 40, a review of Robert Kagan, *Of Paradise and Power: America and Europe in the New World Order* (New York: Knopf, 2003). See also in *FT* 140 (February 24, 2004): 18–25 at 18–19, George Weigel, "Europe's Problem—and Ours."

114. Weigel, "Europe's Problem," 19.

115. *The Clash of Civilizations and the Remaking of World Order* (New York: Simon & Schuster, 1996).

116. *After the Empire: The Breakdown of the American Order* (New York: Columbia University Press, 2003).

secular and do not want to be secular."[117] In the Islamic world especially, secularism can be perceived as a failed Christian ideal; and the liberal insistence that political advance can only come through the renunciation of religion is often viewed as temptation to a hollow life associated with the West.[118] With a growing number of sociologists, thinkers with ties to the Muslim world wonder whether secularism has the presumed inevitability and universality many liberals have granted it.[119] Important Christian thinkers agree: Alister McGrath, in *The Twilight of Atheism: The Rise and Fall of Disbelief in the Modern World,* and David L. Schindler, taking a quite different position, believe that secularization is reversible if we come once again to see the implications of Christianity for each area of human life and thought.[120]

Raising the question of the relation of globalization and secularization brings us to the central concerns of the present book, what place religion might have in the twenty-first century, and what alternatives the twenty-first century might find to a human life totally absorbed in and exhausted by its worldly context, without transcendence. Here only a few words can be said in anticipation. William T. Cavanaugh has mounted a theological critique of globalization which agrees with its more severe critics. For Cavanaugh globalization represents a "false catholicity" to which must be opposed new models of space, time, and tradition rooted in the liturgy.[121] Ultimately this is the goal of the present book, but it must be admitted that such a view is almost "off the radar screen" not just of secular thinkers, but also of most religious people, and we must proceed slowly. Our goal includes a different model of community, one which conceives of the center neither in liberal fashion, as seeking "to maintain the independence of individuals from each other," nor in fascist fashion, as seeking "to bind individuals to each other through the center."

We get in the struggle between fundamentalism and globalization a re-

---

117. Casey, "How to Think about Globalization," 55. Pippa Norris and Ronald Inglehart, *Sacred and Secular: Religion and Politics Worldwide* (Cambridge: Cambridge University Press, 2004), is one of a new breed of secularization studies which tries to correct the old belief that religion is dying in the face of secularization.

118. *Islam and Secularism in the Middle East,* ed. John L. Esposito and Azzam Tamimi (New York: New York University Press, 2000). Olivier Boulnois, "The Modernity of the Middle Ages," *Co* 30 (2003): 234–59 at 249–50, develops an approach to secularization from Western history that is useful here, viewing secularization not as a one-way movement, but as, in Western terms, a dialectic between modernity and the Middle Ages.

119. Asad, *Formations of the Secular.*

120. (New York: Doubleday, 2004). On Schindler see Adrian Walker, "'Constitutive Relations': Towards a Spiritual Reading of *Physis,*" an article to be published in a festschrift for David L. Schindler.

121. These and the words quoted below are the description in an anonymous review in *SS* 4 (2003): 70–71, of William T. Cavanaugh, *Theopolitical Imagination* (New York: T & T Clark, 2002). See also Cavanaugh's *Being Consumed: Economics and Christian Desire* (Grand Rapid, Mich.: Eerdmans, 2008).

play at the social level of the problem of the One (globalization) and the Many (attachment to the particular).[122] The poet Czeslaw Milosz (1911–2004) thought the Russian Lev Shestov was right in thinking that finally the struggle is between the philosopher's quest for the universal and the poet's—or the historian's—attachment to the contingent and particular:[123]

> The true enemy of man is generalization.
> The true enemy of man, so-called History.
> Attracts and terrifies with its plural number.
> Don't believe it.

The "History" under attack by Milosz is that of the Hegelians and Marxists, a generalization claiming to reveal historical necessities before which we must bow, or with which we must join. Milosz, a defender of the religious dimension of life, "our right to infinity," believed such ways of thinking are always belied by attention to detail, and was instinctively on the side of the Schumachers or Berrys, the defenders of the particular and local.[124] However, we may—and in what follows will—fairly wonder if preference for the particular is any more adequate than preference for the general. Discernment lies in what once was called "subsidiarity," judging the place of the particular within the general.[125]

⌒

The struggle between the "Enlightenment" and its enemies, the struggle over modernity, continues, and is revisited in the "culture wars" of the present.[126] The *New York Times* described Prime Minister Necmettin Erbaken of Turkey as "dangerously religious" for his attempt to roll back the preju-

122. William T. Cavanaugh, "Balthasar, Globalization, and the Problem of the One and the Many," *Co* 28 (2001): 324–47, is a brilliant theological exposition of the issues.

123. Quoted in Charles Simic, "A World Gone Up in Smoke," *NYRB* 48, 20 (December 20, 2001): 14–18 at 18. Simic puts the poets on the side of the historians rather than, with Aristotle, on the side of the philosophers. I propose a new way of dealing with the relation of the universal and the particular in culture in "Why We Need Christopher Dawson," *Co* 35 (2008): 115–44.

124. The phrase is from the obituary by Adam Zagajewski, "On Czeslaw Milosz (1911–2004)," *NYRB* 51, 14 (September 23, 2004): 65, who goes on to write, "The telegram Nietzsche sent to inform Europeans of God's death reached him [Milosz], of course, but he refused to sign the receipt and sent the messenger packing. . . . Following in the great Simone Weil's footsteps, he set forth a model of thought linking metaphysical passion with responsiveness to the plight of the simple man. And this in a century that scrupulously and mean-spiritedly insisted that religious thinkers and writers be perceived as right-wingers."

125. Glenn W. Olsen, "Unity, Plurality, and Subsidiarity in Twentieth Century Context," in *Actas del III Congreso "Cultura Europea,"* ed. Enrique Banús (Pamplona: Aranzadi, 1996), 311–17; and *Subsidiariedad: historia y aplicación,* ed. Enrique Banús (Pamplona: Universidad de Navarra, 2000).

126. Isaiah Berlin, *The Roots of Romanticism,* ed. Henry Hardy (Princeton, N.J.: Princeton University Press, 1999); *Three Critics of the Enlightenment: Vico, Hamann, Herder,* ed. Henry Hardy (Princeton, N.J.: Princeton University Press, 2000); and *Political Ideas in the Romantic Age: Their Rise and Influence on Modern Thought,* ed. Henry Hardy, introduction by Joshua L. Cherniss (Princeton, N.J.: Princeton University Press, 2006), are useful for entrance into this subject, though Berlin like Virgil is at a certain point unable to guide further.

dice against religion, expressed in the exclusion of religious Muslims from the civil service and army that had been Kemel Atatürk's legacy there.[127] Such newspapers seem to have a difficult time understanding that many of the problems of the modern world, starting with Islamic terrorism, are rooted at least as much in militant secularism—that of Reza Shah or the various secularisms of Egypt, Syria, and Algeria—as in militant religion.[128] The irony is that the latter is commonly a predictable result of the former. More desirable is the stance of Joseph Ratzinger, now Benedict XVI, who has written, "To this extent we must be grateful to secular society and the Enlightenment. It must remain a thorn in our side, as secular society must accept the (Christian) thorn in its side."[129]

In Turkey, as generally in Europe, the secular party bans head scarves in public schools and buildings.[130] With the French leading, the European Union, ever more an anti-democratic bureaucratic organization, successfully resisted any explicit mention in its draft constitution of Christianity as the spiritual and cultural foundation of European identity.[131] This refusal even to mention the Christian roots of Europe was for Pope Benedict XVI, who before becoming pope had long worked for the re-evangelization of Europe, one more piece of evidence that the Church's "euphoric post-conciliar solidarity" with contemporary culture after Vatican Council II had been naively optimistic: Ratzinger himself had advocated a nonconformism in which the Church would confront, rather than collude with, this culture.[132] Of course one could plausibly argue that all the European Union did in refusing to mention Christianity was to ratify the relativism and skepticism which have followed on the disintegration of the various European empires in the wake of World War II.[133] According to this view, it is European identity itself, as it was once understood, which has disappeared, and the secular party is unwilling to found whatever European confederation is emerging on anything but the Enlightenment.

What the politicians have learned from the historians is that all iden-

127. February 13, 1997, described by Richard John Neuhaus, "Who Will Rid Us of This Turbulent Democracy," *FT* 73 (May 1997): 65.

128. Ian Buruma and Avishai Margalit, "Seeds of Revolution," *NYRB* 51, 4 (March 11, 2004): 10–13 at 12.

129. Quoted in John O'Sullivan, "Benedict's Task," *New York Post* online edition, April 20, 2005. Cf. the exchange between Jurgen Habermas and Joseph Ratzinger, now Pope Benedict XVI, in their *The Dialectics of Secularization: On Reason and Religion* (San Francisco: Ignatius Press, 2007).

130. "Turkish Bash Brings Ire on Secular Elite," *SLT,* October 30, 2003, A18.

131. Weigel, "Europe's Problem," 20.

132. Eamon Duffy, "On the Other Side," *Times Literary Supplement,* December 16, 2005, 8–9 at 9. Benedict's last book before becoming pope, *Christianity and the Crisis of Cultures,* with Marcello Pera (San Francisco: Ignatius Press, 2006), takes as its starting point the refusal of mention of the Christian roots of Europe in the preamble to the European Union constitution.

133. Barry Strauss, "The Rebirth of Narrative," *HS* 6, 6 (July/August 2005): 2–5 at 2.

tity is built on a combination of remembering and forgetting: if one wants to strengthen the thin identity of a secular "Enlightenment" Europe, first the competition—Europe's former Christian history—must be obliterated. Thus Rocco Buttiglione, the representative of Italy to the European Union and a practicing Catholic, was rejected by the European Union as commissioner for justice for holding Catholic views on human sexuality.[134] It has been observed that the very myth of the social contract on which much Anglo-American political thought since Thomas Hobbes (1588–1679) and much French political thought since Jean-Jacques Rousseau (1712–78) rests is "a clever piece of imaginative rhetoric to detach nation states and the civilizations that inhabit them from their religious foundations and reestablish them on rationalistic, immanent grounds."[135] Here even the "methodological atheist" Jürgen Habermas has been roused to protest that Christianity is the historical ground for liberty, conscience, human rights, and democracy. "To this day we have no other options. We continue to nourish ourselves from this source. Everything else is postmodern chatter."[136]

Anything incompatible with secularism is to be erased. In the United States there is a campaign to remove the phrase "under God" from the Pledge of Allegiance, a campaign which splits conservatives because some (rightly) see this as one more attempt to secularize society, and others (rightly) see the Pledge of Allegiance as itself a problem, arguing that it is one more expression of civic religion, "a slavish ritual of devotion to the state."[137] Tony Judt declares "'Christian Europe' . . . is a dead letter," and tells Israel that a Jewish state, that is, a state "in which one community—Jews—is set above others . . . has no place" today.[138] His respondents point out that a Jewish Israel is no more an anachronism than Poland, Serbia, or indeed Germany, France, or the European Union itself, each of which in its own way privileges some common culture.[139] One would think that, especially

134. Richard John Neuhaus, "While We're At It," *FT* 152 (April 2005): 60–72 at 69. Buttiglione got caught up in a struggle between "the two Europes," which I have described in an article of that name published in *The European Legacy: Toward New Paradigms* 14, 1 (2009): 133–48.

135. William A. Frank, "Western Irreligion and Resources for Culture in Catholic Religion," *Lo* 7, 1 (Winter 2004): 17–44 at 22. Cf. on Rousseau, Mark S. Cladis, *Public Vision, Private Lives: Rousseau, Religion, and 21st-Century Democracy* (New York: Oxford University Press, 2003).

136. Jurgen Habermas, "A Time of Transition," quoted in Neuhaus, "While We're At It," *FT* 152 (April 2005): 69. The question of the place of Christianity in European definition is very complicated. At one pole we have the views of Christopher Dawson, at another Lester K. Little, "Cypress Beams, Kufic Script, and Cut Stone: Rebuilding the Master Narrative of European History," *Sp* 79 (2004): 909–928, esp. 919–20.

137. Gene Healy, "What's so conservative about the Pledge of Allegiance?" *SLT,* October 23, 2003.

138. "Israel: The Alternative," *NYRB* 50, 16 (October 23, 2003): 8–10 at 10. Particularly interesting has been the exchange between Judt and Michael Burleigh, whom Judt in a review, *NYT,* March 11, 2007, describes as seeking "to write Christianity back into European political history"; Richard John Neuhaus, "While We're At It," *FT* 174 (June/July 2007): 70.

139. See "An Alternative Future: An Exchange," *NYRB* 50, 19 (December 4, 2003): 57–61.

in democracies, what should be defended is the right of each to try to persuade others of the merit of his or her views, religious or not. In the so-called real world honest argument rarely prevails, but for religious people, that is, people unwilling to obtain their point by deceit or violence, there is no alternative.

In Europe resistance against militant secularism takes many forms, sometimes, as in France or Austria, in tandem with defense by conservative minority political parties of "family values," a rural way of life, and anti-immigration sentiment.[140] For the most part such protest falls on deaf ears. The intellectuals and journalists erase Christianity every day, one of the more egregious examples being the failure of many of them to acknowledge the centrality of Pope John Paul II in the fall of communism, certainly one of the best contemporary examples of the fact that an individual can redirect the course of history.[141] But even the treatment of John Paul II pales besides the stunning silence—with a few honorable exceptions—of the journalists about "the largest pattern of persecution in the world" today, contemporary persecution of Christians.[142]

Christoph Cardinal Schönborn observed Christians "are increasingly regarded as foreign bodies, disturbing the peace in a neo-pagan society."[143] So unremitting has become the antagonism in some quarters to the Catholic Church—in its defense of its understanding of homosexual acts, say, or of the sexes as complementary—that some now portray the Church as subject to the hate campaign of a secular inquisition.[144] In the United States, the Supreme Court casts religion as a danger from which children must be protected.[145] This should not be surprising: as Justice Douglas conceded in *Engel v. Vitale* (1962) in regard to the intrinsic logic of the Jeffersonian "separation of church and state" then so popular, even if without constitutional

140. "Dans l'Ouest, Villiers défend les racines chrétiennes de l'Europe," *Le Figaro,* June 8, 2004, 8. On the same page see further "Un 'non' commun à la Turquie," on related sentiment that Turkey, because not part of the Judeo-Christian tradition, should not be admitted to the European Union. See also in the same issue, p. 11, "Le message aux nouveaux arrivants: tradition chrétienne et liberté de religion," a description of a film shown to legally arriving immigrants, *Vivre en France,* which describes France as "un pays de tradition chrétienne où chacun peut pratiquer la religion de son choix."

141. George Weigel, *The Final Revolution: The Resistance Church and the Collapse of Communism* (New York: Oxford University Press, 1992). See also "L'identité française n'est pas une donnée immanente!" *Le Figaro,* June 8, 2004, 13, an intelligent article insisting, partly against those who associate France solely with an identity forged in the French Revolution, that France has been many things.

142. A. J. Bacevich, "The Seed of the Church," *FT* 74 (June/July 1997): 53–55 at 53.

143. Richard John Neuhaus, "While We're At It," *FT* 132 (April 2003): 88–89.

144. "Vatikan beschwert sich über neue Inquisition," *Spiegel Online,* October 18, 2004: www.spiegel.de/politik/ausland/0,1518,323758,00.html.

145. Russell Hittinger, *The First Grace: Rediscovering the Natural Law in a Post-Christian World* (Wilmington, Del.: ISI Books, 2003). In general see James Hitchcock, *The Supreme Court and Religion in American Life,* 2 vols. (Princeton, N.J.: Princeton University Press, 2004).

foundation, "there can be no logical stopping point until the last vestige of religious expression or aid to religion is erased from the public realm."[146]

In a very striking book, Philip Hamburger completely undid the historical claims of the Jeffersonian myth of a wall of separation between Church and state used by Justice Douglas, showing that for the United States the idea became widespread only in the middle of the nineteenth century as an aspect of American anti-Catholicism.[147] It remains today a tenet central to the "theology" of the secular state, a principal way of keeping religious people "in their place."[148] Others besides Hamburger have shown that for years there has been a confusion about the meaning of the First Amendment, in which the two clauses of the amendment have been turned against each other, the establishment clause being employed to limit public expression of religious belief. This clause, rather, was intended to protect religion from governmental interference.[149] An element of the Democratic Party thinks that not just support of abortion should be a litmus test for nomination to the federal bench, but, as the *Wall Street Journal* described a Senate vote of July 6, 2004, on a Catholic nominee, religious belief itself. That Douglas's desire to erase religion from public life has not already occurred is but the result of the justices' second and third thoughts since then.

Muslims in America are only the latest to see if they can have their cake and eat it too, to see whether their faith and identity can be preserved as they enter the headwaters of the stream of globalization.[150] The Jewish experience here is not exactly hopeful.[151] One might argue that Orthodoxy

146. The phrase quoted is from Cory L. Andrews's summary, "The Metaphor as Wrecking Ball," *IR* 39, 1–2 (Fall 2003/Spring 2004): 66–69 at 66–67. Hitchcock, *Supreme Court and Religion,* studies the personal religious histories of the justices, and notes a shared belief among the high separationists (Black, Douglas, Frankfurter, etc.) that religion is irrational, and should be restricted to the private realm. I have studied the separationist assumptions about religion in "Separating Church and State," *FR* 20 (1994): 403–25.

147. Philip Hamburger, *Separation of Church and State* (Cambridge, Mass.: Harvard University Press, 2002). Hamburger distinguishes between the religious liberty demanded by most dissenters early in American history and an anticlerical understanding of Church-state relations, and argues that the latter was fueled in nineteenth-century America by a bigotry similar to that of European, especially French, laicism.

148. As Judge Diarmuid F. O'Scannlain has written of *Newdow II,* the decision that the expression "under God" in the Pledge of Allegiance is unconstitutional, "*Newdow II* . . . confers a favored status on atheism in our public life. . . . The absolute prohibition on any mention of God in our schools creates a bias *against* religion. . . . One wonders, does atheism become the default religion protected by the Establishment Clause?": quoted in Richard John Neuhaus, "While We're At It," *FT* 133 (May 2003): 88.

149. Patrick M. Garry, *Wrestling with God: The Courts' Tortuous Treatment of Religion* (Washington, D.C.: The Catholic University of America Press, 2006).

150. *Muslims on the Americanization Path?* ed. Yvonne Yazbeck Haddad and John L. Esposito (New York: Oxford University Press, 2000).

151. Jonathan D. Sarna, "American Judaism in Historical Perspective," *HS* 5, 5 (May/June 2004): 11–15, describes the issues, but seems to me unreasonably optimistic. A. Alvarez, "A Double Bind," *NYRB* 51, 20 (December 16, 2004): 76–77, describing Judaism in Britain during the last four centuries as a liberal secular Jew, has a similarly optimistic, Whiggish view, basically

has not given up the battle, witness the relative decline of those forms of Judaism which have wanted to be both Orthodox and modern, and the surge in more traditionalist Orthodoxy.[152] But this of course has meant that this traditionalism has in significant degree given up on assimilation itself, and inclines to some form of relative isolationism.

To judge by the ongoing history of Latino immigration, the answer to the general question of whether faith can be preserved in the process of assimilation to contemporary American culture must be a qualified no. A recent survey by the Pew Hispanic Research Center establishes that, though Latinos born outside the United States have as a group a conservatism and family orientation distinctly different from the general American population, those born in the United States hardly differ at all.[153] It has been suggested that the only thing that stops the United States from looking like Europe religiously is the continuing flow of Hispanic immigrants into the former.[154] That is, (Western) Europe is secular because it has no continuing flow of Christian immigrants, and for the most part it mightily does what it can to marginalize Islamic immigrants. Aside from the continuing strength of Protestant evangelicalism, America is kept relatively more religious by Hispanic immigration, this argument goes, but, in spite of Latinos' family values when they enter the country, one can wonder about the quality of Hispanic belief in coming generations. The question is much complicated by the continuing vitality of evangelical Christianity in the United States, and a good case can be made that in America "as many aspects of public culture become more secular . . . , exclusivist religion flourishes as a more or less private option. . . . American culture is both remarkably religious and remarkably secular."[155] But certainly both in America and in Europe the story has been that in their hearts many ostensibly religious people, including many priests and bishops, have long accommodated to liberal culture. In the middle of the twentieth century, Romano Guardini noted, many German theology professors hesitatingly kept their liberalism in check "by a reluctant obedience to dogma. . . . The faith was experienced as a fetter, an imposed burden, a set of rules."[156] No wonder they interpreted the "opening to the world" of Vatican II as sanctioning what they had long wanted, to be free.

---

seeing the assimilation that has produced himself as largely benign. Alvarez understands that "in England the price of tolerance was Englishness," without wondering why this should be called tolerance. Cf. Eric Michael Mazur, *The Americanization of Religious Minorities: Confronting the Constitutional Order* (Baltimore: Johns Hopkins University Press, 1999).

152. David Singer, "For Torah and Culture," *FT* 153 (May 2005): 27–32.

153. Diane Urbani, "Latino Values Fit Right with Utah's," *DMN*, October 20, 2003, B1–2.

154. Michael Enright, "The Second Most Important Question," *SA* 8 (2003): 25–27 at 25.

155. George Marsden, "Can Jonathan Edwards (and His Heirs) Be Integrated into the American History Narrative?" *HS* 5, 6 (July/August 2004): 13–15 at 13.

156. George Sim Johnston, "After the Council: Living Vatican II," *IC,* December 17, 2004.

Not everyone would accept the way in which Dawson framed the question of the relation of religion to mass culture, though it has been observed that "every European social and political theorist since the first French Revolution" has been anxious about Alexis de Tocqueville's problem, the implications of democracy for shared life in society.[157] Dawson bluntly saw democracy as one of the great problems/evils of the modern age, and thought that it developed in alliance with bureaucracy in such a way that the political intruded into every area of life more thoroughly than in any totalitarian state.[158]

Space does not allow response to the wide range of possible objections to Dawson's position. In some ways not much can be said to those who view religion and man's spiritual aspirations as delusions, or as a stage of human development to be left behind, or as at most something to be tolerated privately but not allowed into the public sphere.[159] Yet, because I take such positions to be deeply dehumanizing, they must be addressed in a generic way, if only with the hope of evincing a certain embarrassment by raising the question of the forms of intolerance and hypocrisy specific to liberal democracy.[160] As James Hitchcock summarized the blind spots and contradictions of American liberalism in the conclusion to his two-volume study *The Supreme Court and Religion in American Life*:

Liberal thought cannot conceive of persons belonging to communities bound by moral ties that are antecedent to choice, an attitude that inevitably sees strong religious groups as dangerous. Contemporary liberalism seems bifurcated, in that it is obsessed with "rights talk" even as it treats certain rights, especially those having to do with religion, as though they were conferred by the state. The ultimate

157. Alan Ryan, "My Way," *NYRB* 47, 13 (August 10, 2000): 47–50 at 47. See J. Judd Owen, *Religion and the Demise of Liberal Rationalism: The Foundational Crisis of the Separation of Church and State* (Chicago: University of Chicago Press, 2001).

158. Christopher Dawson, *Religion and the Modern State* (New York: Sheed & Ward, 1936), 38–45.

159. The distinction between public and private introduces constructs of modern liberalism problematic in any historical situation: Raymond Geuss, *Public Goods, Private Goods* (Princeton, N.J.: Princeton University Press, 2001), 12–74, uses examples from ancient history to illustrate the many ways in which this distinction can be drawn, and how difficult it is to make it clearly.

160. Michael J. Sandel, *Liberalism and the Limits of Justice,* 2nd ed. (New York: Cambridge University Press, 1998), is a gentle survey of the question. Two books by Stephen L. Carter explore the situation in the United States: *The Culture of Disbelief: How American Law and Politics Trivialize Religious Devotion* (New York: Basic Books, 1993), and *God's Name in Vain: The Wrongs and Rights of Religion in Politics* (New York: Basic Books, 2000). Jeff Spinner-Halev, *Surviving Diversity: Religion and Democratic Citizenship* (Baltimore: Johns Hopkins University Press, 2000), in arguing for the reconciliation of religious identity with citizenship, explores the forms of intolerance commonly practiced by liberal multicultural societies. *Toleration: An Elusive Virtue,* ed. David Heyd (Princeton, N.J.: Princeton University Press, 1996), is a well-named book which deals with the paradoxes of toleration. Paul J. Griffiths, "Proselytizing for Tolerance, Part I," *FT* 127 (November 2002): 30–34, is a brilliant exploration of the origins and rhetoric of toleration as itself a species of proselytism.

issue is whether citizens possess natural rights, which the Constitution merely promises to respect, or whether rights are conditionally bestowed by the state.[161]

One can only hope that those who with Amartya Sen would praise the creation of the secular state and the privatization of religion might be brought to the admission that their position involves forever attenuating the lives of religious people so that secular people like themselves can flourish.[162] Positions such as Sen's are according to the present analysis part of the spiritual crisis of the age rather than of any possible solution.[163] As Leo Strauss once observed of liberal tolerance's tendency to become "a seminary of intolerance," any claim which might impede "the uninhibited cultivation of individuality" is perceived as something not to be tolerated.[164] In the United States "the last acceptable prejudice" remains anti-Catholicism, and a supposedly tolerant culture continues to be filled with prejudice against its largest religious group.[165]

So far as I can see, and here Judaism is a particularly poignant example, every religion which has fulsomely embraced the Enlightenment and has declared some equivalent of "be a Jew in your tent and a 'mensch' [man] when you go out," that is, has privatized religion in favor of an allegedly neutral public sphere, has ended with only the tag-ends of a religion. As Elliott Abrams commented on those words of J. L. Gordon from the mid-1880s, "Gordon did not foresee that those who stopped being Jews in the street and on the job almost inevitably would stop being Jews in their tents as well."[166] In part this is because it is not possible to draw the line between sacred and secular as starkly as the Sens of this world would have it.[167] The "fretful orthodoxy" of modern Orthodox Judaism is but one of the more poignant examples of trying simultaneously to live the fullness of a religion

161. II, 162. I have explored the history of toleration in "Setting the Boundaries: Early Medieval Reflections on Religious Toleration and their Jewish Roots," *HPS* 2 (2007): 164–92, and "The Middle Ages in the History of Toleration: A Prolegomena," *MS* 16 (2008): 1–20.

162. "East and West: The Reach of Reason," *NYRB* 47, 12 (July 20, 2000): 33–38, an article depressing in its lack of awareness of its own premises, in its naïve belief that there can be such a thing as the religious neutrality of the state, and in imprecisions of every kind. Some of these latter are criticized by Paul Seabright, "The Road Upward," *NYRB* 48, 5 (March 26, 2001): 41–43.

163. The same might be said of the puzzling review of Sen by Alan Ryan, "The Way to Reason," *NYRB* 50, 19 (December 4, 2003): 43–45. Ryan's analysis lays bare the contradictions at the heart of a liberalism of Sen's form and the superficiality, what I would call ahistoricity, of so much thought in economic and political theory, but Ryan draws back from severe judgment.

164. *Natural Right and History* (Chicago: University of Chicago Press, 1965), 5–6. James Hitchcock, "The Enemies of Religious Liberty," *FT* 140 (February 2004): 26–28, considers some representatives of liberal intolerance.

165. Mark S. Massa, *Anti-Catholicism in America: The Last Acceptable Prejudice* (New York: Crossroad, 2003).

166. "Judaism or Jewishness," *FT* 74 (June/July 1997): 18–25 at 21.

167. Keith J. Pavlischek, "At the Border of Church and State," *FT* 72 (April 1997): 47–50. Cf. Alan Mittleman, *Religion as a Public Good: Jews and Other Americans on Religion in the Public Square* (Lanham, Md.: Rowman and Littlefield, 2003).

while submitting to the "way of the land," issuing in more "a style than a coherent intellectual vision."[168]

If Dawson is right that every historic culture is the embodiment of a religion, and that for any civilization to survive it must inculcate the texts of its religion in the young, then a position such as Sen's, which tends to "privatize" such texts, is tantamount to a cultural death sentence.[169] Of course in the secularizing West, where one project has long been the separation of the historic cultures from the religions that formed them, the execution of this death sentence is far advanced. This has been suggested by some examples above, and may be further illustrated in a slightly roundabout way. Christianity has affirmed tolerance of being misunderstood as one of the more difficult virtues. It is a form of humility, especially prominent in the Franciscan tradition, not to defend oneself at every point, but simply to obey God's law whether one is praised or reviled, whether one's worth is recognized or not, whether one is understood or not. But what is one to do in a world which has so lost its Christianity by excluding that faith from the public order that it is not even understood that tolerance of misunderstanding is a virtue? Not only will such a world be unable to understand the Christian virtues as portrayed by Jane Austen, say in the person of Anne Elliot in *Persuasion,* it will be a world in which refusal to defend oneself is tantamount to admission that one is wrong.[170] This world, returned to a pre-Christian Greek inability even to see that humility is a virtue, will be a place in which it will be not just very difficult for Christians to pass on their faith, but, unless Nietzsche was right, it will be impossible for humans to flourish except as proud supermen (of course the present emphasis on self-fulfillment places us well down that road).

⌒

There is on first view not much to be said to those who, simply in reading the historical record, cannot see that, as the Latin word *religio* (a connection between the human and the greater-than-human) suggests, humans are by nature religious animals. As such they are beings ordered, among other things, to transcendence.[171] Plato's *Euthyphro* contains a long discussion of piety, which Plato sees as involving some form of fear or awe, and suggests is a part of justice, something native to man. Piety, cooperation

168. Alan Mittleman, "Fretful Orthodoxy," *FT* 136 (October 2003): 23–35 at 24.

169. The idea that cultures are founded on religions is basic to all Dawson's writings: see my "The Maturity of Christian Culture: Some Reflections on the Views of Christopher Dawson," in *The Dynamic Character of Christian Culture: Essays on Dawsonian Themes,* ed. Peter J. Cataldo (Lanham, Md.: University Press of America, 1984), 97–125, and "Why We Need Christopher Dawson."

170. These thoughts are occasioned by a reading of Daniel Callam, "Jane Austen's Catholic Sensibility," *SS* 5 (2004): 22–29, at 26.

171. Stephen M. Barr, "The Devil's Chaplain Confounded," *FT* 145 (August/September 2004): 25–30 at 26.

with the gods in acceptance of the order they have instituted, almost defines the human.[172] Catherine Pickstock emphasizes that before Christianity taught that the sacred completes the rational, this was Plato's view in the *Phaedrus*.[173] After him Virgil embraced a similar, if Roman, view of piety, drawing the figure of pious Aeneas, the man obedient to providence. The Christian form of this is found in St. Irenaeus of Lyons's declaration around A.D. 180 in *Against Heresies*: "God is man's glory. Man is the vessel which receives God's action and all his wisdom and power." But a similar claim can be made in the categories of the history of religion:

We experience transcendence as the inclination for a life not limited to finite realities . . . the encounter with the sacred is the answering response to this impulse. . . . The sacred is not God himself but his presence in the world. Even though we might say that God is always the substance or the form of the sacred, his Divinity is still concealed in its mode of presentation. The sacred always has something of the sign or symbol about it.[174]

Almost from its beginning as a field of study, witness Albert Réville's (1826–1906) *Prolégomènes de l'Histore des Religions,* the history of religion has provided a reading of the historical record that reveals man the religious animal to any fair-minded person.[175] This does not at all mean that traditional or primitive man is deeply pious, or uniformly religious: in all periods, such things vary. Of course the turn to the subjective in modernity has affected the history of religion, and there has long been a standing temptation to turn from the mystery of the divine life to merely man-centered or anthropological categories, to see religion as simply human.[176]

Much has been written about secularization and modernization that suggests that religion is no more than a stage of human development eventually left behind. Such a perspective seems to me not much more than scholarly wish fulfillment, "premature secularization."[177] What Benedetto Croce (1866–1952) remarked, that "the problem of modernity is above all a religious problem," seems much closer to the truth:

Religion is born of the need for orientation as regards life and reality. . . . Without religion, or rather without this orientation, either one cannot live, or one

172. Weaver, *Ideas Have Consequences,* 170–71.

173. *After Writing: On the Liturgical Consummation of Philosophy* (Oxford: Blackwell, 1998), part 1.

174. Frank, "Western Irreligion," 30, and on religion as a natural architectonic moral virtue. I have attempted to argue man's religious nature in such articles as "'You Can't Legislate Morality': Reflections on a Bromide," *Co* 2 (1975): 148–62, and "Separating Church and State."

175. (Paris 1881), translated as *Prolegomena of the History of Religions,* tr. A. S. Squire (London: Williams and Norgate, 1884).

176. Paul O'Callaghan, "Is Christianity a Religion? The Role of Violence, Myth and Witness in Religion," *FCSQ* 29, 4 (Winter 2006): 13–28 at 16.

177. Donald Winch, *Riches and Poverty: An Intellectual History of Political Economy in Britain, 1750–1834* (Cambridge: Cambridge University Press, 1996), 23.

lives unhappily with a divided and troubled soul. Certainly it is better to have a religion that coincides with philosophical truth, than a mythological religion; but it is better to have a mythological religion than none at all.[178]

Today the eminent psychologist Robert Coles fights against those who would diminish the place of mystery and the sacred in life.[179] Michael Walzer writes of a bankruptcy of the left which includes an inability to acknowledge the continuing power of religion.[180] Scholars who had tended "to equate modernity with the 'disenchantment of the world,'" now re-evaluate religion's persistent force in modern societies.[181] It has long been observed that the neo-pagan church of Julian the Apostate, who reigned 361–63, or the ten-day secular week introduced in France in the wake of the French Revolution look suspiciously like Christian antecedents they were intended to replace, but more recent is the observation, made in relation to various European rituals of labor and the left, that the ritual form of strikes, the singing of revolutionary songs, and the totemic identification of various places along the routes of marches are new or inverted forms of religious rituals and processions.[182]

Talal Asad insists that religious practice not be reduced to something other than itself, to therapeutic need, outdated science, sublimated sex, or social resentment, but be seen as "a distinctive space of human practice and belief which cannot be reduced to any other."[183] Some scholars (including Peter Berger himself) now argue that secularization theory got things precisely backward: the dislocations and uncertainties generated by modernity seem to have stimulated not a decline, but a global resurgence of religiosity. Thomas Howard has pointed out the insidious effects of many historians' simply dropping religion from the narrative of European history with the coming of the French Revolution, and of the absence from the European narrative of a host of figures from Félicité de Lammenais to John Paul II. But everything has its day, and Howard now notes a "religious turn" among

178. Quoted in Emilio Gentile, "The Sacralisation of Politics," *Totalitarian Movements and Political Religions* (electronic resource) 1, 1 (Summer 2000): 31.

179. Daniel Berrigan and Robert Coles, *The Geography of Faith: Underground Conversations on Religious, Political, and Social Change* (Woodstock, Vt.: Skylight Paths, 2001).

180. "Can There Be a Decent Left," *Dissent* (Spring 2002): 19–23.

181. Thomas Albert Howard, "A 'Religious Turn' in Modern European Historiography?" *HS* 5, 4 (June 2003): 24–26 at 24, and see *Säkularsierung, Dechristianisierung, Rechristianisierung im neuzeitlichen Europa,* ed. Hartmut Lehmann (Göttingen: Vandenhoeck & Ruprecht, 1997), and John Van Engen, "Introduction: Formative Religious Practices in Premodern European Life," in *Educating People of Faith: Exploring the History of Jewish and Christian Communities,* ed. John Van Engen (Grand Rapids, Mich.: Eerdmans, 2004), 1–26 at 1–3, on religion as a constant in human life.

182. Rod Kedward, *France and the French: A Modern History* (Woodstock, N.Y.: Penguin, 2006).

183. *Genealogies of Religion: Discipline and Reasons of Power in Christianity and Islam* (Baltimore: Johns Hopkins University Press, 1993), 27, quoted in Van Engen, "Formative Religious Practices," 2–3 at 3.

the historians themselves.[184] Many have noted, as Pico Iyer does regarding India, that vast numbers of people "carry on their lives as if religion had not been unsettled by science, and Nietzsche had not arrived to tell them about the death of God."[185]

The confines of a single essay do not allow tracing all the ways in which the religious nature of human beings reasserts itself in the most secular and oppressive of civilizations.[186] My colleague Vincent Pecora has shown how the sacred is remade in the modern world and how demystification passes into remystification.[187] More mundanely, although there is an ever-growing literature debating the question of how monolithic Soviet society of the Communist period was, few would deny that religion survived and today has a kind of revival, if often still in service to nationalism.[188] Neither do the limitations of an essay allow the development of the argument that in all cultures secularization and sacralization simultaneously occur.[189] Indeed, there is some irony in the fact that, taking Europe as a whole, its apparent secularization was accompanied by a Hegelian history centered on "man's gradual self-divinization in history."[190] Many have puzzled over a certain continuing religiosity in American society, which seems in stark contrast to Europe. One is tempted to attribute this above all to the fact that religion has been more centrally under attack by the lay party for longer in Europe than in America, and that the kind of anti-religious bigotry displayed by such politicians as Prime Minister Zapatero of Spain has cowed most believing politicians into simply not speaking of God in public. But in an interview with a representative of the Italian religious movement Communione e Liberazione, the American Methodist theologian Stanley Hauerwas upset this conventional view. According to Hauerwas:

184. "A 'Religious Turn,'" 25–26.

185. Pico Iyer, "Passage to Bombay," *NYRB* 49, 16 (October 24, 2002): 30–31 at 31.

186. *The Desecularization of the World: Resurgent Religion and World Politics,* ed. Peter L. Berger (Grand Rapids, Mich.: Eerdmans, 1999).

187. *Households of the Soul* (Baltimore: Johns Hopkins University Press, 1997).

188. Aileen Kelly, "The Secret Sharer," *NYRB* 47, 4 (March 9, 2000): 33–37, reviews the historiography, and see also her "In the Promised Land," *NYRB* 48, 19 (November 15, 2001): 45–48.

189. Glenn W. Olsen, "Cultural Dynamics: Secularization and Sacralization," in *Christianity and Western Civilization,* ed. Wethersfield Institute (San Francisco: Ignatius Press, 1995), 97–122, and Coles, *Secular Mind,* esp. ch. 1. Marjule Anne Drury, "Anti-Catholicism in Germany, Britain, and the United States: A Review and Critique of Recent Scholarship," *CH* 70 (2001): 98–131, both introduces recent scholarship and gives a good idea of the complexity of the question. Alan Mittelman, "From Jewish Street to Public Square," *FT* 125 (September 2002): 29–37, brilliantly displays the misguesses of secularization theory in not anticipating the recent growth of Orthodox Judaism in the United States, or the effect of this growth on reconceiving church-state issues in favor of positions more favorable to a religious presence in public life.

190. Mark Lilla, "The Big E," *NYRB* 50, 10 (June 12, 2003): 46–47 at 46. "God and the Enlightenment," *AHR* 108 (2003): 1057–1104, gives review essays considering the current state of secularization and modernization studies. These essays attempt to reverse the view that religion and modernity are antithetical categories.

America, though oftentimes identified as one of the more religious cultures still in existence, is much more determined by the secular than is Italian culture. I know that sounds extremely odd, but in Italy, Christianity is in the stones, and in America, we have no stones. The Christianity in America is not thick in practices that actually form bodies to understand better what it means to be Christian. And that has everything to do with the kind of Protestantism that shaped American society, which both produced and has then been reproduced by a certain understanding of the relationship with God that is gnostic in character.[191]

As if to buttress Hauerwas's use of the example of Italy, a ferocious row broke out there in 2003 about a judge's decision to order the removal of a crucifix from an Italian classroom (Italian law permits crucifixes in school). In this case the plaintiff in the suit was a Muslim activist. One can doubt the accuracy of the judge's declaration that the presence of the crucifix shows "the state's unequivocal will to place Catholicism at the center of the universe . . . in public schools, without the slightest regard for the role of other religions in human development," and in fact in 2002 the country's minister of education had sent instructions to all public schools to authorize a room for prayers for non-Catholic students, if such a space was requested.[192] In such conflicts a secular "naked classroom" almost certainly will win out if there is not present some theory of the rights of both majorities and minorities.[193] But the struggle continues, and in August 2005 Pope Benedict XVI upped the ante, encouraging the placement of crucifixes in public buildings. No believer in the "naked public square," he said that God should be present in community life.[194]

Hauerwas goes on to explain that by gnostic he means a Christianity of God and the soul, unmediated by Church. In America

the mediated character of Christianity is simply unknown and that means your educational task is not surrounded by the kind of thick practices that are necessary to sustain it (as any serious business). . . . The deepest hindrance is capitalism. We are a consumer culture and therefore Christianity is seen as just one more possible consumer item you might buy that gives you a lot of meaning.

One might wish, especially in regard to his last comment, that Hauerwas knew more about contemporary Italy, but such a point of view should bring us up short in thinking secularism is easily located, described, or judged.

Leszek Kolakowski wrote a famous essay, "The Revenge of the Sacred

191. Interview, *Traces* 5, 5 (May 2003): 22.

192. "Italian Judge Sets Off Debate after Removal of Crucifix," *IC,* October 31, 2003. This controversy is not new. The liberal movements which preceded Mussolini removed crucifixes from public school classrooms, and as premier, he put them back, while refusing to let a mosque be built in Rome: Robert E. Herzstein, "Judgment and Restitution: Goldhagen, the Catholic Church, and Anti-Semitism," *JHS* 3, 3–4 (Summer/Fall 2003): 471–92 at 476.

193. "Judge's Order to Remove Crucifix from School Sparks Outrage," *SLT,* October 27, 2003.

194. "Italy," *DMN,* August 16, 2005.

in Secular Culture."[195] Some now argue that Western Europe is the anomaly in a world which is desecularizing.[196] Philip Jenkins writes in *The Next Christendom* of the explosive growth of Christianity going on at present in many parts of the world.[197] He suggests that in his own country, the United States, many are unaware of this because they have been taught a "myth of American religious diversity" in which the numbers and influence of minority (non-Christian) religions are consistently overstated by a media with a "vested interest in exaggerating the strength and significance of minority faiths."[198] The vested interest is in denying that America is a Christian nation, in discounting such things as Protestant fundamentalism, interpreted as declining in the face of the new pluralism. But a book full of subtle observations argues that contemporary conversion to Christianity is commonly conversion to a specifically modern form of Christianity, and also to a religious form of modernity.[199] This is not an isolated observation, and one of the editors of an excellent collection of essays on the holy in the Americas from 1500 to 1800 observes that the European "'spiritual conquest' of the Americas" was at the same time "the American 'conquest' of Christianity."[200]

In conclusion, after centuries in which the forces of secularization seem to have had the upper hand, especially in European history, it now can be seen that the story is more complicated than being simply a tale of the loss of God and transcendence: alongside the undoubtedly strong forces of secularization, a quest for that which transcends history and orients life remains. Since man is by nature a religious animal, and religion of some form is at the heart of every culture, after a period in which much was done to marginalize the transcendent dimensions of life, a life wholly of this world has become the subject of growing criticism and discontent. This book is about this discontent, but more importantly about alternative ways of viewing life which

195. In *Modernity on Endless Trial* (Chicago: University of Chicago Press, 1990), 63–74.

196. Richard John Neuhaus, "Secularization in Theory and Fact," *FT* 104 (June/July 2000): 86–89.

197. Subtitle: *The Coming of Global Christianity* (New York: Oxford University Press, 2002).

198. "A New Religious America," *FT* 125 (September 2002): 25–28 at 27, trying to explain the "rapturous reception" accorded Diana L. Eck, *A New Religious America: How a "Christian Country" Has Now Become the World's Most Religiously Diverse Nation* (San Francisco: HarperSanFrancisco, 2002), whose thesis Jenkins believes is "flat wrong." He notes that the present immigration policies of the United States are making the country inexorably more Christian (in a head-counting sense), while those of Europe are increasing the Muslim presence.

199. Peter Van der Veer, *Conversion to Modernities: The Globalization of Christianity* (New York: Routledge, 1995). David Martin, "Living in Interesting Times," *FT* 124 (June/July 2002): 61–64 at 63, reviewing Jenkins's *Next Christendom,* believes that Jenkins speaks too easily of the new Christendom as being homogenizing: especially in Africa, it is fissiparous.

200. Jodi Bilinkoff, "Introduction," in *Colonial Saints: Discovering the Holy in the Americas, 1500–1800,* ed. Alan Greer and Jodi Bilinkoff (New York: Routledge, 2003), xiv–xv.

allow the transcendent a fuller place. The recognition of the unsatisfactori-
ness of life as it is currently lived leads to a reconsideration of all aspects of
our lives, political, social, economic, religious, artistic, and this reconsideration is part of our story. Particularly pressing is the question of the capacity
of mass culture, typically of a democratic form, to respond to the challenges
of the age ranging from the technological to the spiritual. At the center of
our concern is the question of how a life both of and not of this world can
be sustained today.

Chapter Two

THREE PREMISES

Under socialism, man will be ten-foot tall.

—Leon Trotsky

Whenever I hear people speak of the brotherhood of man,
I think of Cain and Abel.

—Evelyn Waugh[1]

Three premises of this book's analysis need explicit articulation and defense: 1) the claim that there is a natural fit between a religious and a communal existence, that is, the claim for the superiority of a "communitarian"
over an "individualistic" form of life for nurturing the religious individual;
2) the claim that, despite increasing attacks on ideas of progress during the
past century and the demonstration of the inadequacy of such ideas for understanding history and politics, they largely continue, to our detriment, to
shape our lives; and 3) the claim that politics must be founded on a non- or
anti-utopian view of the world. This chapter is devoted to exploration of
these premises.

To turn to the first, one scholar has generalized about Islam:

Islam substantially merges the personal with the communal. Religion is not simply a matter of private, individual practice. The Islamic ethos rather secures a
congenial fusion of personal and public happiness, giving believers a sense of
belonging to a vaster entity, regulating their way of life and their modes of interaction, and generating in them a harmonious sense of completeness in a world
that they . . . [feel] to be whole and integrated.[2]

1. For the first quotation, see Peter Schrag and Stephan Thernstrom, "'Must Schools Fail?'
An Exchange," *NYRB* 52, 3 (February 24, 2004). For the second, see "The Disturbing Light of
Reality: Sin and Redemption in the Writing of Graham Greene and Evelyn Waugh," *EC* (Spring
2005), 3–5 at 3 (anon.).
2. Salma Khadra Jayyusi, "Andalusi Poetry: The Golden Period," in *The Legacy of Muslim
Spain,* 2 vols., ed. Salma Khadra Jayyusi (Leiden: E.J. Brill, 1994), I, 317–66 at 352.

Allowing for the idealization that colors this passage and does not mention the envy, conformity, and lack of privacy that can suffocate, especially in small-scale communities,[3] the passage would not need much adjustment to describe most religious people's sense of the kind of world in which they— and their children—could flourish. It is not a world in which the communal suffocates the individual, but in which the community is the condition which allows the individual to flourish.

A common caricature of traditional societies is that they value only the communal. This is at the core of Jacob Burckhardt's famous contrast between a Middle Ages which lacked individualism and creativity, and a Renaissance which allowed these to flourish. A fascinating reply to Burckhardt is found in Meyer Schapiro's study of Romanesque sculpture, the sculpture of a highly religious society. Here, according to Schapiro, we have not the unrelenting submission of the individual to some overarching architectural or social order, a limitation of the human imagination, but "a model for a particular perfection" in which "every individual found his place and acquired a form from his place in the whole."[4] The individual is not perfected in isolation, but in a community, from which he derives his individuality.

One scholar writing of Judaism states that we are not meant to live as isolated individuals, each with our "rights," but contextually in a "nation" with its own particularity.[5] This "nation" need not literally be a nation, but must be something particular. "As in our own time the permafrost of modernity has at last begun to melt . . . the world we are seeing is not a strange new world, revealed as the glaciers draw back, but a strange old world: kinship, locality, embodiment, domesticity, affect."[6] Thus the desire after the individualistic age of "sprawl" for "neighborhoods," for living in a traditional manner in which daily activities are proximate to one's home, and at least most of them within walking distance.[7] Few will be able to return to the particularity of "the king living among us," for most of the monarchies are gone, replaced by a less embodied, more impersonal, state, but still people will want some symbol of unity and a common life.

Whatever their religion, people long for some shared conception of life which effectively "privileges" one view of the world over others. This they

3. Alexandre Nasri, "Gaudin renonce au projet de grande mosquée à Marseille," *Le Figaro,* June 4, 2004, 10, brings one down to earth, where the "communauté muslmane," as in Iraq, is often a fiction. In Marseilles, now 25 percent Muslim, a project to build a great mosque, three years in the planning, had to be abandoned because the various Muslim groups could not agree.

4. *Romanesque Architectural Sculpture,* ed. Linda Seidel (Chicago: University of Chicago Press, 2006), 34–36, 61–64 at 62, and see lectures 2, 3, and 5, an extended response to Burckhardt's views.

5. Steven Grosby, "The Biblical 'Nation' as a Problem for Philosophy," *HPS* 1, 1 (Fall 2005): 7–23 at 16. Grosby argues that the primordial category is "kinship" (23).

6. Alan Bray, *The Friend* (Chicago: University of Chicago Press, 2003), 306.

7. See the summary of a lecture by Philip Bess, "After Urbanism: The Strange Bedfellows of Neo-Traditional Architecture and Town Planning," in *EC* (Fall 2006): 4.

perhaps once had in an "established" religion, but once disestablishment took place, they understood that many things which had helped maintain a privileged worldview weakened.[8] Sometimes this results in something Alexis de Tocqueville (1805–59) found in mid-nineteenth-century Americans, internalized standards and controls; sometimes it does not. In any event—and for a host of reasons—what occurred in the American case was a developing language of individual choice.

The United States originated in a seventeenth-century attempt to create a godly commonwealth in which the whole social order was "organized for fellowship with God and with God's people."[9] Still in the eighteenth century a reformed Protestant communalism often prevailed.[10] Though the godly commonwealth as such did not survive the eighteenth century, a weak form of this idea is at the core of American history. Thus Samuel Huntington has observed that historically one became an American by "adopting America's Anglo-Protestant culture and political values."[11] Today mainline Protestantism has lost its grip on America, and there seem not one but several quite different, in some ways incompatible, Americas.[12]

The inclination of like to seek like is broader than religion, for arguably most people assume any society should have a center and some agreement about ends: this is what is missed today. A deeply pluralist society does not seem capable of resolution of such debates as that over abortion, and the question is whether "public reason" is a meaningful idea in such a society.[13] One fears, rather, such things as the *Goodridge* decision of the Massachusetts Supreme Court in 2003, which, without explaining why it is irrational to hold a natural law position or to affirm that the sexes are complementary rather than equal, simply declared that there was "no rational reason" to oppose same-sex marriage, and that such opposition had to be the result of "persistent prejudices."[14] To a practicing Orthodox Jew or many Chris-

8. John D'Emilio and Estelle B. Freedman, *Intimate Matters: A History of Sexuality in America* (New York: Harper & Row, 1988), as at 49, treat the link between the disestablishment of churches after the American Revolution and changes in sexual morality.

9. Mark Noll, "Founding Fathers?" *FT* 140 (February 2004): 38–41.

10. Barry Alan Shain, *The Myth of American Individualism: The Protestant Origins of American Political Thought* (Princeton, N.J.: Princeton University Press, 1994).

11. These words from Huntington's *Who Are We? The Challenges to America's National Identity* (New York: Simon & Schuster, 2004) are discussed by Andrew Hacker, "Patriot Games," *NYRB* 51, 11 (June 24, 2004): 28–31 at 28. Hacker does not like Huntington's belief that the Protestant origins of America play a major role in its identity today. He writes that "imposing a specific religious component onto our American political culture strikes me not only as redundant, but divisive as well," and follows this with the truly bizarre non sequitur, "After all, a Catholic signed the Declaration of Independence."

12. Charles Simic, "Difference in Similarity," *NYRB* 51, 4 (March 11, 2004): 21–23 at 21.

13. Fred M. Frobock, *Public Reason: Mediated Authority in the Liberal State* (Ithaca, N.Y.: Cornell University Press, 1999).

14. The phrases quoted are part of the discussion by M. A. Casey, "Democracy and the Thin Veneer of Civilisation," *FSCQ* 29, 4 (Winter 2006): 4–9 at 7.

tians, this means that their religion—but also their sense of what it is to live the life of reason—is so beneath contempt that it may simply be dismissed without argument.

⌒

One Parisian wrote in the wake of the riots of young Muslims in October and November 2005 in France: "My country is in the middle of a deep national identity crisis. The population doesn't know what it wants, and the politicians don't know what to offer voters."[15] It is unclear whether the Parisian writer of 2005 saw any link between the French identity crisis and the refusal of the French left even to tolerate mention of Christianity in the European Union's constitution, but one can argue that the French crisis has been long in preparation.[16] De Tocqueville famously argued that nothing resembled France before the French Revolution so much as France after the French Revolution. That is, the emphasis on centralized rule, statist and protectionist, characterized the post-revolutionary Republic as much as or more than the *ancien regime,* and has persisted to the present. In line with this insight, we might say that the dominant French approach to identity since the Revolution has been to replace the *ancien regime* notion of an identity simultaneously religious, national, and cultural at the center of life with an Enlightenment sense of identity, thinner and more secular but still highly nationalist and insisting on agreement among citizens. "France is a 'universal nation' of people who are unmistakably French."[17] Today Germany might allow a limited *de facto* practice of Sharia law in its Muslim communities (i.e., tolerate wife-beating), but in France thus far the *desideratum* has been complete integration, an integration into the Enlightenment so thorough that the alternative cultures implicitly present in Catholicism or Islam can only be allowed if tailored to "liberté, egalité, fraternité."[18] Talal Asad has observed that Islam is so preoccupied with state power today not because of some commitment to nationalism intrinsic to Islam, but because Islam is confronted by the claim of the modern nation-state to be

15. John-Edouard Silva, "Streets of Fire," *Time,* December 5, 2005, 16. A good case can be made that these riots were "a feature of being poor and marginal, not of being Muslim": Richard John Neuhaus, "The Much Exaggerated Death of Europe," *FT* 173 (May 2007): 32–38 at 35.

16. By comparison, Aleksander Kwasniewski, the atheist president of Poland, stated, "There is no excuse for making references to ancient Greece and Rome, and to the Enlightenment, without making reference to the Christian values which are so important to the development of Europe." Quoted in Michael Burleigh, *Earthly Powers: The Clash of Religion and Politics in Europe from the French Revolution to the Great War* (New York: HarperCollins, 2005), 15. Burleigh has continued his analysis of the clash between religion and secularist states in *Sacred Causes: the Clash of Religion and Politics, from the Great War to the War on Terror* (New York: HarperCollins 2007).

17. Neuhaus, "Much Exaggerated Death," 37.

18. Leslie S. Lebi, "Create Space for 'Rule of Law' Muslims," *DMN,* April 8, 2007, G6. On the voluminous literature on European Islam, see Malise Ruthven, "The Islamic Optimist," *NYRB* 54, 13 (August 16, 2007): 61–65.

the source of social identity.[19] This is a claim that most Frenchmen have accepted, but, as Christopher Dawson observed in many writings, nationalism itself commonly is a kind of tribalism, an idealization of the particular.[20] Always one must distinguish between a proper universalism, which tries to continue the Roman quest for the way of life best suited to human nature, and a proper particularism, without which a notion of "home" is not possible. The universal must temper the particular, but life has no flavor without the particular.

Islam tends to lack two differentiations found in the history of Christianity, especially Catholic Christianity, and this makes Islam's way in the modern world especially difficult.[21] The second is the distinction between Church and state, but before that there was a first, more primordial distinction, between grace and nature, which, properly made, allows nature to stand forth with an integrity of its own, embodying laws which can be codified into science. Though undoubtedly the distinction of Church from state was a development in Christianity of the distinction between grace and nature, the two distinctions are not the same. When the early Christians declared that they belonged to "another City," to a City transcending space and time, they relativized loyalty to all earthly cities in a way almost unimaginable (Plato's *Apology* shows Socrates imagining but rejecting this possibility) to the citizens of Periclean Athens or Augustus's Rome or Saladin's Baghdad. For most, as in the quotation with which this chapter began, one's city or community was one's religion.

In France especially have two contradictory notions of tolerance born of the Wars of Religion and the Enlightenment uneasily stood next to one another, commonly with neither aware of its premises: on the one hand, there has been the Enlightenment ideal of a universal civilization, which implies the (hoped for) victory of one best way of life and set of values; on the other, there has been an understanding of toleration as aiming at peaceful coexistence of different ways of life, and therefore not at some ultimate victory of one view.[22] The first view politically expressed in fact tends to remain nationalistic in presuming that the common universal culture to be achieved will look very much like French Enlightenment culture; while the second view is more open to the retention of a religious center—or religious centers—in life. Things could have been different, for historically the uni-

---

19. *Formations of the Secular: Christianity, Islam, Modernity* (Stanford, Calif.: Stanford University Press, 2003).

20. See for example C. J. McNaspy, "A Chat with Christopher Dawson," *America* (October 28, 1961): 122.

21. This and the following develop William A. Frank, "Western Irreligion and Resources for Culture in Catholic Religion," *Lo* 7, 1 (Winter 2004): 17–44 at 39–40.

22. John Gray, *Two Faces of Liberalism* (New York: New Press, 2000). Arnold Angenendt, *Toleranz und Gewalt: Das Christentum zwischen Bibel und Schwert* (Münster 2007), is masterful.

versalism of the first position was attached to the Church rather than the nation. What has happened in the modern period since the Treaty of Westphalia (1648) and the acceptance of the permanent division of Christendom into nation-states, is that nations have acted imperially.[23] Those who today wish to intervene, for instance, in the case of mass murder, across national borders, or use international law to intervene in nations with serious problems of justice, implicitly hold that the national absolutism created by Westphalia has had its day.

Of course the immigrant rioters of 2005 would not likely have been placated by a thicker French identity in which the religious (i.e., Christian) component was more tolerated or prominent, but they even less wished to identify with a regime as hostile to religion as the French left or lay or Jacobin party has been to its own inherited Christianity. And it will not help, as commentators such as Timothy Garton Ash seem to think it will, if the attempt is made to assimilate Muslim immigrants to some European civic identity, if that identity in turn is aggressively secular.[24] Few, especially liberals, can see that the disappearance of a center is the inevitable result of a certain understanding of "democracy," of wanting a society with no distinctions or hierarchy or commonly accepted truths.[25] If the hope during the period of the European immigrations to America was that one could keep the culture one had brought with one while accepting also the culture of one's new country, it is not so clear in France how many Muslims want to prosper as Frenchmen, if that means as highly assimilated. At least so far many of them do wish to prosper, but as Muslims.[26] As elsewhere, many of them are the "in-between people," at home neither in Europe nor in the country of their parents' origins.[27]

In America one of the tragedies of the civil-rights era was the way in which urban Catholic enclaves were caught between the desire, generally coming from outside their communities, to extend equal rights to all and their own desire to maintain the ethnic neighborhoods which had allowed them a kind of shared public Catholic life in the midst of a generally hostile, larger, Protestant culture.[28] This came to a head in the matter of busing.

23. Christopher Dawson, *The Dividing of Christendom* (New York: Sheed & Ward, 1965), stressing that Christendom was not a political but a cultural entity based on religion.

24. "Islam in Europe," *NYRB* 53, 15 (October 5, 2006): 32–35.

25. Richard M. Weaver, *Ideas Have Consequences* (Chicago: University of Chicago Press, 1948; reprinted 1984), 35.

26. Jonathan Laurence and Justin Vaisse, *Integrating Islam: Political and Religious Challenges in Contemporary France* (Washington, D.C.: Brookings Institution Press, 2006), argues that most French Muslims are fairly well integrated.

27. Garton Ash, "Islam in Europe," 33.

28. John T. McGreevy, *Parish Boundaries: The Catholic Encounter with Race in the Twentieth-century Urban North* (Chicago: University of Chicago Press, 1996), discussed by Eugene McCarraher, "Remarks on John McGreevy's Catholicism and American Freedom," *HS* (September/

Inevitably, working- and middle-class Catholics seemed (and were) bigots, defending their communities through exclusion and hostility toward outsiders. Liberals generally refused to see this as a tragic situation, and simply preferred the legitimate aspirations of blacks by ignoring the legitimate aspirations of Catholics.

Pretty much by definition religious people incline to a communitarian vision of a life of shared public affirmations. Islam is often merely a particularly clear case of not wishing compartmentalization in life, of not wanting the kind of schizoid stance going under the idea of "the separation of Church and state" in the United States, in which one separates one's faith from a sphere which allegedly secular principles govern.[29] From such an Islamic point of view, it is almost inevitable that by comparison democracy seems a human system that does not center on God.[30] John Gray goes further and points out in the case of Iraq that "democratization" cannot be the answer. Democratization will not bring stability, but only (more) misery. In a country in which the populations have long been divided, liberal democracy will promote continuing fragmentation: "In these conditions liberal democracy is a utopian project. A kind of democracy may be established, but it will be democracy Iranian-style—an Islamist version of Rousseau's illiberal dream."[31]

The question is broader than religion. No one is able to form a sense of individual identity except against some larger communitarian background, whether the local football team or one's nation. If one was in the majority, a shared common life was always one advantage of the confessional state, which probably outlawed certain forms of behavior as unsuitable to the shared life of some religious majority.[32] It is precisely a high level of reli-

---

October 2004): 28–31 at 29. McCarraher notes that the subsequent predominant Catholic narration of the "march to the suburbs" has been triumphalist and Whiggish, a success story of assimilation into the larger culture in which the "old neighborhoods" have come to be viewed as restricting "ghettoes."

29. Francisco Canals Vidal, "Por Qué Descristianiza el Liberalismo?" *Verbo* 439–40 (November–December 2005): 817–28, excellently distinguishes the forms of liberalism.

30. Carrie Moore, "Can Mideast Ever Embrace Western Democracy?" *DMN,* November 5, 2005, E2.

31. John Gray, "The Mirage of Empire," *NYRB* 53, 1 (January 12, 2006): 4–8 at 6. There are Muslims who disagree. Reza Aslan, arguing against "Muslims" such as Salman Rushdie, who think that their religion ought be depoliticized and confined to some personal sphere in the manner that Christianity has been secularized, contends, something in the manner of an Islamic Richard John Neuhaus, that the public square need not be naked, and that a modern democratic Islamic state should not be built on a privatized Islam, but on some form of public Islam both respectful of tradition and protective of individual rights, on some form of compromise that resists the absolutists of right and left: Pankaj Mishra, "The Misunderstood Muslims," *NYRB* 52, 18 (November 17, 2005): 15–20.

32. Adam Schatz, "In Search of Hezbollah," *NYRB* 51, 7 (April 29, 2004): 41–44 at 44, quotes the remarks of one of the leaders of Hezbollah about an Islamic Lebanese state: "We believe the requirement for an Islamic state is to have an overwhelming popular desire, and

gious diversity that so frightens parts of the Islamic world and sets them off against the West. Many Moslems see in Europe and America cultures in which parents have lost control of their children to a popular culture saturated with infantilism and commerce, corrupting the souls of all.[33] They see in "globalization" the spread of an individualistic ethos quite ready to trample traditional cultures, often with a certain hectoring in which these cultures are told they are "backward" and should change.

Most of this has very ancient roots. The *convivencia* or "living together" of the three religions of the Book found in medieval Spain always was precarious and guarded, each community largely living its own life with only limited contact with the others. We sometimes forget that the forced ghettoization of late medieval and early modern history was preceded by centuries when especially Jews formed their own neighborhoods, that is, chose to live together, as they already were doing in ancient Alexandria.[34] When this was replaced with *apartamiento,* a forced "living apart" in the late Middle Ages, especially in large "multicultural" towns, we are not surprised to find that religious cleansing was not far behind.[35] One might argue that though it is difficult to keep nations with radically different worldviews at peace with one another, it is even more difficult to keep seriously different subcultures at peace within one state.

Many argue that one of the most important unresolved issues of the Balkan wars of the 1990s is the insistence that people who hate one another must live together in multiethnic states. States such as Slovenia or Croatia, which chose to build their identity around a relatively homogenous ethnicity and religion, and in the case of Croatia fought to drive out what they considered "foreign bodies," have flourished; those that were forced to be multiethnic, above all Bosnia, seem lost in time, consumed with hatred against internal Others. Some now acknowledge that democracy and a national state which forces people who do not like or trust each other to live together is not a universal panacea for the woes of the world and can be counterproductive, as has been the case for so long in the Tyrol.[36] Further,

we're not talking about fifty percent plus one, but a large majority. And this is not available in Lebanon and probably never will be." This must express the views of many religious people who would prefer a confessional state, but not at any cost.

33. David Solomon, "From the Director," *EC* (June 2004): 1–3 at 1.

34. I treat both the desire of all three religions to draw boundaries between themselves and others, and the nature of *convivencia,* in "Setting Boundaries: Early Medieval Reflections on Religious Toleration and Their Jewish Roots," *HPS* 2 (2007): 164–92, and "The Middle Ages in the History of Toleration: A Prolegomena," *MS* 16 (2008): 1–20.

35. James F. Powers, Review, *CHR* 91 (2005): 516–17.

36. Tim Parks, "Tyrol: Retreat to Reality," *NYRB* 51, 9 (May 27, 2004): 50–52 at 51, speaking of "the pathos and drama of two peoples absolutely locked up in the past and prisoner to the overwhelming desire that they not be obliged to live together." The crowning irony is that the South Tyrol, like Croatia, has become an international tourist designation precisely because it has retained its "quaint," Catholic, agricultural culture, full of wood carvers and such like. As Parks

one of the grim facts of life seems to be that many countries seem to need some "glue" to hold themselves together, some shared hatred. If this cannot be found in religion, it may be found in some virulent form of nationalism, perhaps in anti-Semitism or anti-Catholicism. Israel's continuing harassment of Christians may partly be viewed in this light.[37]

We noted in the last chapter that Amy Chua has shown in considerable detail that the spread of a market economy and democracy do not necessarily make the world a safer place.[38] Easily enough they lead to resentment and terrorism. Commenting on her analysis, a pair of reviewers agree that "there is a lot of evidence that democracy works best in ethnically and religiously homogeneous societies."[39] But this is true of all forms of government. This is the hard truth the French, more generally the European Union, had to face during the riots of 2005. In the case of Iraq, a united Iraq may be in no one's interest. Better to "go back" before the nation-state was imposed on peoples who had not lived together, and allow Iraq to break down, perhaps in a federal form of government, into its "natural" (i.e., pre-national) components, Kurdish, Shia, and Sunni.[40]

The natural desire to live among similarly minded people does not make everyone a cultural conservative, but does mean that if one does not have a preferred language, religion, or set of customs, one probably gravitates to cosmopolitan centers, where—the crowning irony—one can find people like oneself. The large majority prefer a fair degree of homogeneity, a minority a fair degree of variety.[41] This is quintessentially expressed in the French idea, already alluded to, that to be French is not a matter of race or origins but of accepting French culture.[42] It is the opposite of what the North Americans call multiculturalism, which most experience as cultures

---

remarks, "What does the globalized world of free travelers feel nostalgic for, if not the closed, traditional community? The more the tourists come, particularly Italian tourists, the more the locals cling to their traditions. And the more they cling to their traditions the more the tourists come." Beginning in 2003 travelers in Europe have been inundated with advertisements to visit Croatia to see "the Mediterranean as it used to be."

37. "Vatican Delegation Astonished by Cancellation of Meeting with Israel," *IC,* December 24, 2004, 2, on "what appears to be a pattern of last-minute, unilateral cancellations by Israel of crucially important meetings," in this case to attempt to resolve tax issues concerning church property which have been ongoing for a dozen years. The Israelis arguably are trying to change the tax laws so as to close Catholic institutions.

38. *World on Fire: How Exporting Free Market Democracy Breeds Ethnic Hatred and Global Instability* (New York: Doubleday, 2003).

39. Vijay Joshi and Robert Skidelsky, "One World?" *NYRB* 51, 5 (March 25, 2004): 19–21 at 21.

40. Georgie Anne Geyer, "Insistence on United Iraq May Defeat Us All," *DMN,* December 3, 2003, A15.

41. Christopher Jencks, "Who Should Get In?" *NYRB* 48, 19 (November 29, 2001): 57–63 at 57–58.

42. Though the question seems more complicated to me than this, some in Europe contrast the French model of integration, in which as articulated by Jacques Chirac immigrants accept "secularism, France's cherished separation of religion and state, [which] remains a cornerstone of

living next to one another in uneasy juxtaposition in the manner of New York City or Los Angeles. These latter are witnesses to the phenomenon of the "global city," each with sub-populations tied to many corners of the globe, but with people from the same ethnic communities seeking one another out, as if to find some respite from unending diversity, as well as non-acceptance.[43]

A million things, starting with the raising of children, are easier if one lives with those with whom one agrees. In many historical situations multiculturalism is inevitable, but in certain obvious ways multicultural societies fail humans.[44] Multiculturalism may have a certain short-term attractiveness, but it is doubtful that a civilization or nation can last long without a fair degree of shared vision of reality.[45] By definition anything more than façade-multiculturalism—I like cappuccino, you like tacos—involves disagreement about reality.[46] If that disagreement is sufficiently pluriform, if a culture does not at the least contain sufficiently cohesive subcultures, even the individual will be incapable of forming a firm identity as a member of some shared narrative story and there will be no clear criteria for the definition of any shared good.[47] Not only will there be no censorship or public norms, there will be no principled sense of cooperation in any common project.[48] Thus today observers of European society note "deep conflict

French values, providing neutral ground for different religions to coexist in harmony," and "the Anglo-Saxon model of integration—admired by some French Muslims—where ethnic communities guard their customs and separateness": John Leicester, "Chirac Aims to Secularize France," *DMN,* December 18, 2003.

43. Jencks, "Who Should Get In?" 62.

44. Enrique Banús, "¿Desde o Hacia el Multiculturalism? Un Concepto y su Plasmación en la Unión Europea y el Consejo de Europa," in *Razón Práctica y multiculturalismo,* ed. Enrique Banús and Alejandro Llano (Pamplona: Centro de Estudios Europeos, Universidad de Navarra, 1999), 258–77, is a very useful overview of various European statements about and definitions of multiculturalism.

45. Neil Bissoondath, *Selling Illusions: The Cult of Multiculturalism in Canada* (Toronto: Penguin Books, 1994), abridged in "I Am Canadian," *Saturday Night* (October 1994): 11–22, is a very intelligent exploration of the limits of diversity, which views both the (older, U.S.) ideal of the melting pot and the (current, Canadian) ideal of multiculturalism as untrue to what selves in history are.

46. I have discussed the difference between a deep pluralism, which involves affirmation of incompatible goods, and cultural pluralism, which involves different styles of life, in such essays as "The Catholic Moment?" *Co* 15 (1988): 474–87.

47. Alasdair MacIntyre, *After Virtue: A Study in Moral Theory,* 3rd ed. (Notre Dame, Ind.: University of Notre Dame Press, 2007), 226–27, 236, within the larger argument of esp. chs. 15–16. At 232–36 MacIntyre observes what happens to societies which lose a shared conception of the good.

48. Roger Shattuck, *Forbidden Knowledge: From Prometheus to Pornography* (New York: St. Martin's Press, 1996). Leszek Kolakowski, "Where Are Children in Liberal Philosophy?" in *My Correct Views on Everything* (South Bend, Ind.: St. Augustine's Press, 2005), argues that the neutrality required by liberal ideology makes it impossible to generate the public virtues needed for sustenance of a common good. Paradoxically, liberalism's weakening of any common culture causes the state to legislate obsessively on the minutiae of everyday life.

among people who want to believe in a multiethnic national culture but now fear its effects."[49]

An American therapist who had worked in Europe for thirty years, speaking of the growth of anti-immigrant sentiment well before the French riots of 2005, stated: "The anxiety is incredible. . . . People who are strong liberals wake up in the morning and want their country back."[50] Of course the very refusal of these strong liberals to have children, at least at the rate of population replacement, is the engine behind this "problem," for the immigrants are little more than the inevitable nature abhorring a vacuum caused by declining population in still-rich countries. Against such a background, some now argue that a liberal view of immigration is mistaken in not allowing regulation according to national identity and economic reality, and the concerns of native-born working-class people who might be displaced by cheap labor, or otherwise affected by immigration, for instance, by changed schools in which knowledge of the host language varies significantly.[51] It is in the interest of few, the argument goes, to allow immigration decade after decade if the economy has been unable to produce anything close to full employment, even taking into consideration the less attractive jobs that usually are the entrance into society for immigrants. Further, economics more or less aside, the argument may also be that states may legitimately craft immigration policies which express some particular vision of political community.[52] Thus in campaigning for the French presidency in 2007, Nicolas Sarkozy took the so-called conservative position that immigrants must, in the words of the *New York Times,* be made "to embrace the secular values of the republican state."[53]

An opposition to John Paul II's embrace of virtually unrestricted immigration formed in the Curia itself, and within the Italian episcopate. How, it was asked, can a country like Italy preserve its Christian identity in the face of unlimited Islamic immigration and of the intolerance of other religions Islam commonly brings with it?[54] Some form of this question is being

49. "Europe Grapples with New Kind of World," *DN,* September 4, 2002. Multiethnicity in itself seems to me no problem at all, so the anonymous author must assume in using that word that ethnicity is a carrier of culture.

50. Barry Goodfield as quoted in ibid.

51. What Peter C. Meilaender writes about the American context is transferable worldwide: "Immigration: Citizens & Strangers," *FT* 173 (May 2007): 10–12, and see his *Toward a Theory of Immigration* (New York: Palgrave, 2001).

52. Unsigned review of Meilaender, *Theory of Immigration,* in *FT* 126 (October 2002): 8–10.

53. Elaine Sciolino, "Tensions Over French Identity Shape Candidates' Voter Drives," *NYT,* March 30, 2007, A1–A6 at A1. The Socialist candidate, Ségolène Royal, who was apparently on vacation during the various French riots beginning in 2005, responded, "Foreign workers have never threatened French identity."

54. Renzo Guolo, *Xenophobes and Xenophiles: Italians and Islam;* and see Richard John Neuhaus, "While We're At It," *FT* 138 (December 2003): 76. I have been unable to see or get complete information on this book.

asked across Europe: hence the explosion of so-called far right parties, wishing to restrict especially Islamic immigration. Filip Dewinter, the leader of Vlaams Belang (Flemish Interest), a party which has had the allegiance of about 25 percent of the population of Dutch-speaking Flanders, describes Belgium's liberal immigration policies as very naïve, and calls "tolerance Europe's Achilles' heel and immigration Islam's Trojan horse."[55] The feeling is growing that one rarely plays on a level field with Islam, which denies to others the freedom of religious practice it wishes for itself.

The failure of multicultural societies generally to satisfy man is nowhere more obvious than in the matter of religion, which only restricts itself to a private sphere if made to do so. Left to itself, religion fills all life, like any great passion. This is especially true of the historically dominant European religion, Christianity, which is incarnational. Some of the Oriental religions so insist on the transcendence of the Divine Nature and so widen the gulf between man and the divine that they impugn the good of the material order. But Christianity—more so in its Catholic forms, less so in its Calvinist forms—views matter and history as things to be perfected. It tries to satisfy the mind, and is interested in education. It tries to fill the soul, and expresses itself in music and dance. It is concerned with justice, and tries to form good human beings. To come to the point, it tries to shape and fill the public order, and in the words of Vatican Council II is interested "to impress the divine law on the affairs of the earthly city (*Gaudium et Spes*, 43)."[56] This is why liberalism so fears it.

None of this means that the religious man is not also interested in those who differ in worldview, just that his first instinct is to live in a public order which makes it easy, rather than difficult, to practice his religion and pass it on to his children.[57] The religious person would rather not have public monies spent to support exhibitions in which art is used as a weapon to attack his religion.[58] As I have already suggested, the same can be said of

55. Craig S. Smith, "Fear of Islam Drives Growth of Belgian Far Right," *DMN*, February 13, 2005, A5.

56. Cf. John Paul II's message to the 2000 U.S. National Prayer Breakfast, printed in "The Pope at the National Prayer Breakfast," *FT* 104 (June–July 2000): 85–86 at 85: "Such a responsibility [the building of a world more worthy of the human person], by its very nature, cannot be reduced to a purely private matter. The light of Christ should illumine every thought, word, and action of believers; there is no area of personal or social life which it is not meant to penetrate, enliven, and make fruitful."

57. *Beyond the Persecuting Society: Religious Toleration Before the Enlightenment*, ed. John Christian Laursen and Cary J. Nederman (Philadelphia: University of Pennsylvania Press, 1997), and Cary J. Nederman, *Worlds of Difference: European Discourses of Toleration, c. 1100–c. 1550* (University Park: Pennsylvania State University Press, 2000), dismantle the generalization that before the rise of secularism intolerance held sway in Europe, but even better, reframe the question to show that medieval and early modern people saw toleration not as an end in itself, but as something flowing from our fallen nature.

58. Lynne Munson, *Exhibitionism: Art in an Era of Intolerance* (Chicago: Ivan R. Dee, 2000).

secular man, for whom, whatever else it is, the secular state is a device to make the lives of those without religion easy. Unfortunately, secular man tends to be largely unaware of what we might call the theological premises of the secular state, and especially of the ways in which secularism itself commonly takes the form of religion and strives for dominance of the public order.[59]

There is perhaps no more astonishing example of this than the prohibition of home schooling in the Netherlands: so concerned is the state to dominate the public order that parents who attempt to teach their own children are labeled child abusers.[60] The French have been the masters here, and have perfected the use of the public school system to foster and allow only a secular point of view or identity. Indeed to the French, with their two-hundred-year history of the state's driving religion from the public arena via control of education, it is the Americans, with their toleration of home schooling by parents who wish to limit or reject such "progressive" universal schooling, who look odd. In his announcement in 2003 that France must outlaw any obvious religious signs in schools, Jacques Chirac declared that France would not tolerate a religious challenge to its core values, carved above school and town hall doors: liberty, equality, fraternity.[61] In reply, three thousand women, most of them Muslim, veiled and singing the Marseillaise, took to the streets of Paris, marching to the Place de la Bastille (!) and shouting "the veil, my choice."[62] This was to no avail, and on February 10, 2004, the National Assembly by an overwhelming vote banned the scarves.[63] One must wish the Averroes Lycée in Lille, the first

59. Karl Löwith, *Meaning in History: The Theological Implications of the Philosophy of History* (Chicago: University of Chicago Press, 1949), is a classic analysis of the lack of self-awareness of the implicit theological premises of their thought of many of the most influential modern philosophers of history. We see this lack of awareness in many areas of modern thought: see the running criticism of Edward O. Wilson's *Consilience: The Unity of Knowledge* (New York: Knopf, 1998), by Wendell Berry, *Life Is a Miracle: An Essay Against Modern Superstition* (Washington, D.C.: Counterpoint, 2000). Berry views Wilson's attempt to unify the disciplines as actually the imposition of materialism on the arts and religion, and the turning of science into religion.

60. "Institute Continues International Outreach with Amsterdam Conference," *Acton Notes: The Newsletter of the Acton Institute* 12, 10 (October 2002): 3. State concern about the quality of home schooling is of course legitimate, and I note that in, for instance, Austria, home-schooled children must take national exams annually.

61. Leicester, "Chirac Aims to Secularize France."

62. John Leicester, "'The Veil, My Choice' Say French Muslims," *DMN*, December 22, 2003, A10. The article also describes the position of Gerhard Schroeder, who was then German chancellor, on the issue, which allows girls to cover their heads in public classrooms. For the division in Germany on the question of Muslim teachers wearing head scarves in public schools, see the Associated Press article "German Officials at Odds over Religious Symbols," *DMN*, January 3, 2004. In response to Chirac's declaration that his goal was to protect secularism, the minister of the British Foreign Office declared: "In Britain, we are comfortable with the expression of religion, seen in the wearing of the hijab, crucifixes, or the kippa." He added, "Integration does not require assimilation": "Muslims around Globe Protest French Scarf Ban," *DMN*, January 18, 2004.

63. Elaine Ganley, "French Parliament Passes Scarf Ban," *DMN*, March 4, 2004. Joan Wal-

Muslim high school in France, well, with its commitment, exceptionally, to allowing the head scarf.[64] But the fact is that by October 2004 resisting Muslim girls who insisted on wearing head scarves in school were being expelled, one observing: "What they want is to see us in tight pants like all the girls."[65] In Germany about the same time a court ruled that a ban on veils should be extended to the habits of nuns, many of whom teach in the public schools. Opinion was divided as to whether this covered all nuns, or only those teaching so-called secular subjects. Some wished the ban on habits extended to Catholic schools.[66]

⌒

James F. McMillan has revealed for nineteenth-century France a pattern with many analogues elsewhere: the quarrel about the place of religion in politics was precipitated by republicans who first legislated anti-clerical laws circumscribing the place of religion in public life, and then labeled Catholic opposition "clericalism," "illicit interference on the part of the clergy in the sphere of politics and public life."[67] Any historian who has worked the archives of Europe has probably used materials now gathered in national holdings which were once the property of some ecclesiastical institution and then were seized by the state.[68] Some such pattern of "republican persecution" has continued to the present and has found a home in the bureaucracy and committees of the European Union, and among those who say American Catholic bishops have no right to discipline politicians who claim to be Catholic but dissent from Catholic teaching.[69]

---

lach Scott, *The Politics of the Veil* (Princeton, N.J.: Princeton University Press, 2007), concentrates on France.

64. Elaine Ganley, "French Muslim School Opens," *DMN,* September 4, 2003, detailing the warning by Prime Minister Jean-Pierre Raffarin that a law could be passed "'if necessary' to impose secularism."

65. Elaine Ganley, "France Expels Students with Head Scarves," *DMN,* October 21, 2004.

66. "German Court Ruling on Veils Could Affect Nuns in Public Schools," *IC,* October 22, 2004. The German Constitutional Court declared in September 2003 that the separate German states could each decide whether to ban the veil. Baden-Württemberg, Lower Saxony, Saarland, and Hesse then banned the head scarf.

67. The phrases quoted are from a review by Loretta Sharon Wyatt in *CHR* 87 (2001): 713–14 at 713, of *The Politics of Religion in an Age of Revival: Studies in Nineteenth-Century Europe and Latin America,* ed. Austen Ivereigh (London: Institute of Latin American Studies, 2000), in which McMillan's essay is found. In this volume the editor has an article on Argentina, which again has wide application: in the summary of Wyatt's review, 714, "While the Church asserted that the state should reflect society and its values, including the religious, liberals contended that the state was an entity above its society with the responsibility to unify and to mold its citizens through such methods as a public education that was rational and wholly secular in nature."

68. *I manoscritti datati del Fondo Conventi Soppressi della Biblioteca Nazionale Centrale di Firenze,* ed. S. Bianchi et al. (Florence: SISMEL: Edizioni del Galluzzo, 2002), listing the manuscripts now in Florence confiscated from ecclesiastical institutions either by the French in 1808 or by the Italian government in 1866. More generally, see Derek Beales, *Prosperity and Plunder: European Catholic Monasteries in the Age of Revolution, 1650–1815* (New York: Cambridge University Press, 2003).

69. James Hitchcock, "Bureaucracy—a Force for Change," *Voices* 17, 2 (2002): 29.

A shrewd analysis of how Indian history has been written reveals some-thing similar. Partha Chatterjee has shown that nineteenth-century Indian historiography copied Western periodization, dividing history into ancient, medieval, and renaissance periods.[70] As in the West, the ancient, Hindu, period became the model for a desirable Indian modernity, while the sub-sequent Muslim period became the Indian equivalent of the Western Dark Ages. Hence many historians nurtured what is now called Hindu funda-mentalism, the identification of Hinduism with India, and once again, what is now called fundamentalism, both Hindu and Muslim, was one as-pect of the birth of nationalism. To write Islam back into the story, other historians had to construct a different medieval period, this time viewed as a time of toleration and freedom, in which both religions lived a shared commercial life.

Secular man, especially in the United States, typically views the secu-lar state as merely a pragmatic response to cultural and religious diversity, without seeing that every response carries its own ideological freighting.[71] He retains for the political order an idea widely discredited elsewhere, that there is a public domain governed solely by canons of critical reason in which, for instance, to draw an analogy with my own field of study, a histo-rian can write a simply objective history with no reference to his or her own beliefs or disbeliefs.[72] This "myth of neutrality," this idea that we can some-how live together without committing to some view of reality, represents philosophical naiveté of a high order, but a naiveté absolutely essential to most forms of contemporary liberalism.[73] In states which have sizable pop-ulations of both religious and ostensibly irreligious people, it is difficult to see how problems of the place of religion in society can even be addressed

70. I am following the analysis of Chatterjee and others by Kathleen Biddick, "Translating the Foreskin," in *Queering the Middle Ages,* ed. Glenn Burger and Steven F. Kruger (Minneapo-lis: University of Minnesota Press, 2001), 193–212 at 204–6.

71. Ronald F. Thiemann, *Religion in Public Life: A Dilemma for Democracy* (Washington, D.C.: Georgetown University Press, 1996), while on the United States, has good discussions, as in ch. 4, of liberalism and the "myth of neutrality." Thiemann tries both to save liberalism and to move it beyond neutrality. See Frederick Christian Bauerschmidt, *Julian of Norwich and the Mystical Body Politic of Christ* (Notre Dame, Ind.: University of Notre Dame Press, 1999), for the more general position "that all politics is 'theological' and that all theology is 'political'" (3).

72. Peter Novick, *That Noble Dream: The "Objectivity Question" and the American His-torical Profession* (Cambridge: Cambridge University Press, 1988). James D. Tracy, "Believers, Non-Believers, and the Historian's Unspoken Assumptions," *CHR* 86 (2000): 403–19, defends a more modest view of "a public realm of intellect," as does Thomas L. Haskell, *Objectivity Is Not Neutrality: Explanatory Schemes in History* (Baltimore: Johns Hopkins University Press, 1998), 145–73. Maureen C. Miller, "Religion Makes a Difference: Clerical and Lay Cultures in the Courts of Northern Italy, 1100–1300," *AHR* 105 (2000): 1095–1130, is a splendid exploration for my own field of historical specialization of the use of "willfully secular" (1097) models of culture in contemporary scholarship which leave out the central historical role of religion in forming identity.

73. J. Budziszewski, *The Revenge of Conscience: Politics and the Fall of Man* (Dallas: Spence, 1999).

until the so-called lay or liberal or secular party becomes much more aware of and honest about its various historical bigotries in this regard.

⟨—

My second premise is that most people who have passed through the Enlightenment still accept as true what I will call the Whig Grand Narrative of history, though, as Yeats remarked, "saints and drunkards are never Whigs."[74] Here by "Whig" I mean principally the view that history is progressive and the story of increasing liberty, but also the view that Anglo-Saxon history is a particular carrier of this story of progress.[75] I cannot attend to all the things labeled "Whig" at this or that point of history, and do not mean to deny that people called Whigs sometimes stood for desirable policies, such as a national bank in Abraham Lincoln's day. Early on, the idea that history is progressive and the story of liberty often was closely tied to a notion of providence particularly approving of the Anglo-Saxons (but every European people had something similar), and had a specifically religious flavor. Thus John Foxe's (1516–87) *Book of Martyrs* saw England as the "elect nation," an idea carried by the English colonists to the "New World" (new to them).[76]

Though originating in a close alliance of nationalism and religion, over time the Whig Grand Narrative increasingly expressed the "metaphysics of clarity" advanced by the Enlightenment. This was particularly attractive to those who could not take much mystery or enigma in their lives, or admit that the Greeks—or later Nietzsche—were on to something important when they insisted on the tragic dimension of life, all the ways in which things do not cohere, let alone turn out well.[77] Presumably few people in any civilization "check their facts" and most people show great deference to

74. A narrative already attacked by Weaver, *Ideas Have Consequences*, 1, and see 110, for Yeats. Cf. my "Why and How to Study the Middle Ages," *Lo* 3, 3 (Summer 2000): 50–75 at 53–54, 63–64, and "Middle Ages in the History of Toleration"; and J. G. A. Pocock, *Barbarism and Religion*, 4 vols. (New York: Cambridge University Press, 1999–2005). G. K. Chesterton, *Orthodoxy* (Garden City, N.Y.: Image Books, 1959), 30–45, without using the word "Whig," had already given over a chapter to the explanation of the problems with general theories of progress. I will for the purposes of the present article speak of the Enlightenment in the singular, but the direction of recent scholarship, including that of Pocock, vol. 1, esp. 5–9, is to speak of it in the plural and to stress the variety of Enlightenment thought.

75. In a review of an unconvincing defense of the Whig view, David Spadafora, *AHR* 109 (2004): 860–61, discusses the slippery problem of definition. Reinhold Niebuhr, *The Nature and Destiny of Man; a Christian Interpretation* (New York: Scribner, 1949), gave a probing examination of how the idea of progress derived from or is a secularized version of the biblical view of history, lacking much understanding of the tragic dimension of history. See the discussion in Richard John Neuhaus, "The Idea of Moral Progress," *FT* 95 (August/September 1999): 21–27 at 24.

76. Paul Johnson, "The Almost-Chosen People," *FT* 164 (June/July 2006): 17–22 at 17.

77. See the line of thought running through Dennis Schmidt, *On Germans and Other Greeks: Tragedy and Ethical Life* (Bloomington: Indiana University Press, 2001). The phrase "metaphysics of clarity" is used by Charles Bambach, "German Philosophy and the Ethical Life," *MA* 48, 1 (Winter 2006): 85–89 at 88.

power: what better than a Whig view that allows one to accept the historical narrative of government and the nation the powerful give?[78] The United States has always preferred the upbeat history the Whig tells, and thus
Hannah Arendt wrote of the Vietnam War that "'the greatest power on
earth' lacked the inner strength to live with defeat."[79] This strength could
have come from Yeats's saints, that is, from those who knew that life is not
primarily about categories such as success and progress, but about things
such as fidelity, come what may. Before the "metaphysics of clarity" beloved
of the Whig existed, the saint's life, especially its masculine form, witness
St. Francis of Assisi, had been centered on the idea of the conversion of
the soul, of abrupt and radical change, of at one moment being one thing,
at the next another.[80] In this pre-Enlightenment view history was subject
to supernatural intervention, and conversion was often not gradual, but
precipitous. Hence perhaps one sense of Yeats's declaration that saints are
never Whigs: the Whig was to make the world impervious to the adventure
that is Christianity. Thus the eighteenth-century novel lost interest in tales
of conversion, preferring tales of character improvement.

Other European peoples have had variations on the idea of progress,
and we might see the Hegelian view of history, centered on Germany rather
than England in the modern period, as a more dialectical version of Whig
claims, and like it a kind of secularized theodicy.[81] Fichte (1762–1814) wrote
of Germany needing a new religion, "a Fatherland religion," and even the
great sociologist of religion Ernst Troeltsch (1865–1923) stated at the time of
World War I: "The German faith is a faith in the inner moral and spiritual
content of Germanness, the faith of the Germans in themselves, in their
future, in their world mission."[82] I intend no more precision in defining
"Whig" as a view of history than as designating the progressive story of

78. Russell Baker, "Goodbye to Newspapers?" *NYRB* 54, 13 (August 16, 2007): 8–12 at 12.

79. Quoted in Jeremy Waldron, "What Would Hannah Say," *NYRB* 54, 4 (March 15, 2007):
8–12 at 8.

80. In such books as *Holy Feast and Holy Fast: The Religious Significance of Food to Medieval
Women* (Berkeley: University of California Press, 1987), Caroline Bynum argued that men's and
women's spirituality, at least in the Middle Ages, differed, women's being gradual or developmental. One can think of enough exceptions to this idea to wonder how general this pattern
has been. Were it true, it would make the Enlightenment a period in which women's ways of
viewing the world had some measure of triumph. J. M. Coetzee, "Sleeping Beauty," *NYRB* 53, 3
(February 23, 2006): 4–8 at 5, comes close to suggesting that what the Whig world calls "magic
realism" in Latin American literature is not much more than its Catholicism, the ways in which
Latin American life refuses to be Whig and remains "medieval" or Quixotic.

81. Mark Lilla, "Slouching Toward Athens," *NYRB* 52, 11 (June 23, 2005): 46–48 at 47. Lilla
treats the story of secularism at greater length in *The Stillborn God: Religion, Politics, and the
Modern West* (New York: Knopf, 2007).

82. Both quotations are from Russell Hittinger, "The Churches of Earthly Power," *FT* 164
(June/July 2006): 27–32 at 28–29, who also comments on the "new" nineteenth-century na-
tionalist ideas of providence, which in some ways were quite old, as the medieval *Gesta Dei per
Francos* should remind us.

increasing liberty, and acknowledge that, as with all the big words, "liberalism," "Enlightenment," etc., the best one can do under a single heading is to nod in the direction of some generalization. Gertrude Himmelfarb has made a good case that at the least we should differentiate between the French and English Enlightenments, the former preoccupied with reason, rights, liberty, equality, tolerance, science, and progress, but not with virtue, the preeminent preoccupation of the English, whose Enlightenment by comparison was only mildly progressive and rather socially conservative.[83]

To say that most English-speaking peoples and many Europeans are still in thrall to the Whig view of history means that though our leading thinkers may have become postmodern, and many of our historians may doubt the possibility of writing a master narrative "generated by the European experience," most of us still live in the midst of modernity.[84] In spite of what writers such as Gustave Flaubert (1821–80) long ago concluded to—the lack of probity in humankind, the lack of intelligence in governments, the failure of science to progress—we accept almost without question a humanist narrative in which the discovery of the printing press, for instance, advances enlightenment, without any remark on the use of this new technology, say, to broadcast anti-Jewish ideology.[85] Similarly we unquestioningly accept a narrative of progress in which "bastard feudalism," that is, the recovery of regional strength which delayed the march of central administrations in the late Middle Ages, must be disapproved as unprogressive.[86] In general we accept a narrative silent about the undesirable effects of each claimed progressive step, as if "advance" does not always involve some form of loss or tragedy. We accept the notion that progress consists in perpetual adaptation to the new.[87]

In America, in spite of much sobering counterevidence typified by the Vietnam and Iraq Wars, the dominant notes are still of progress, and the attitude to be expected of the citizenry is one of optimism. The writings of people such as William Pfaff seem to have had little impact. Like a darker

83. *The Roads to Modernity: The British, French, and American Enlightenments* (New York: Knopf, 2004), with Alan Ryan, "Faith-Based History," *NYRB* 51, 19 (December 2, 2004): 22–24. As Ryan notes, Himmelfarb emphasizes the benign role that religion played, and plays, in a well-ordered society, and shows that her eighteenth-century Enlightened Englishmen agreed.

84. The phrase is from a review by David Martin, "Living in Interesting Times," *FT* 124 (June/July 2002): 61–64 at 61. *The Decline of Christendom in Western Europe, 1750–2000*, ed. Hugh McLeod and Werner Ustorf (Cambridge: Cambridge University Press, 2003), considers the master narrative of religious decline. David W. Noble, *Death of a Nation: American Culture and the End of Exceptionalism* (Minneapolis: University of Minnesota Press, 2002), is indicative of how far many historians have abandoned progressive views of history, especially as centered on the idea of American exceptionalism.

85. Julian Barnes, "Flaubert, C'est Moi," *NYRB* 53, 9 (May 25, 2006): 12–15 at 13.

86. Bray, *Friend*, 308, and see 311–12.

87. Joel Best, *Flavor of the Month: Why Smart People Fall for Fads* (Berkeley: University of California Press, 2006).

Christopher Dawson, Pfaff, having observed that no African nor Asian traditions have viewed history as a tale of progress, and that the view that man may rationally manipulate his environment to the better is specifically Western, for forty years has been calling into question the West's self-presentation as the vanguard of the march to the future. For Pfaff this "march to the future" in fact has made the West the source and carrier of some of the worst features of the twentieth century, utopianism, communism, and a mission of bringing liberty to the world which in fact visits appalling violence on the world.[88]

Of course there have always been countercurrents and disbelievers. Without these the "culture wars" of the present would not be possible. Long before Herbert Butterfield (1900–79) expressed doubts about the Whig view of history, Moses Mendelssohn (1729–86) had against Kant denied any overall progressive movement to history and suggested that Enlightenment was not the latest stage of a progressive history, but something shared in by various peoples and religions scattered over time. No more than his progressive descendants could Kant (see especially his *An Old Question Raised Again: Whether the Human Race is Constantly Progressing*, 1798) bear history's "pointlessness" as Mendelssohn understood it.

Again, from the American Civil War on, some Americans became more aware of tradition as a social force, and came to view tradition more positively than had the Revolutionary generation, with a concomitant suspicion of the general faith in progress.[89] But this was not the dominant stance. The various immigrant communities that have formed the country have been made, even by historians writing from within these communities, to fit in to a Whiggish tale in which, for instance, Catholicism in America becomes the story of "the triumph of Americanist Catholics over retrograde conservatives."[90] Only quite recently have historians such as John T. McGreevy begun to treat this specific story as a kind of Hegelian tragedy, in which all along incompatible views of the world clashed, and no resolution was possible of the incompatibilities between the understanding of freedom Catholic immigrants brought with them, usually suspicious of "perverse individualism" and in any case presuming that the individual is embedded in "an ensemble of social relations," and the understanding of freedom present

---

88. Pankaj Mishra, "A Cautionary Tale for Americans," *NYRB* 52, 9 (May 26, 2005): 8–11 at 8. Dawson tended to rejoice in the creative energy of the West, while Pfaff sees the merit of quietism and compromise. *The Bullet's Song: Romantic Violence and Utopia* (New York: Simon & Schuster, 2004), is Pfaff's latest attack on the idea of total transformation of society through politics, whether of the right (free trade), left (communism), or both (science).

89. Michael D. Clark, *The American Discovery of Tradition, 1865–1942* (Baton Rouge: Louisiana State University Press, 2005).

90. George Marsden, "Can Jonathan Edwards (and His Heirs) Be Integrated into the American History Narrative?" *HS* 5, 6 (July/August 2004): 13–15 at 13.

in the low-church Protestant culture they entered, centered on freedom as individual autonomy, and, with classical Protestantism, understanding will as at the center of the human person.[91]

In my own field of medieval studies, though for a century various ways in which Whig and Romantic nationalist ideas have distorted the telling of English history have often been noted and criticized, these ideas are still very common in the general population and are still being rooted out even among scholars.[92] Anthony Giddens argues that, rather than postmodernity, our own period is one of "high modernity": characteristic of the age is the radicalization and universalization of the consequences of modernity.[93] When all is said and done, amid growing doubts, most Europeans still accept a narrative in which history is about the progressive emancipation of mankind through the motor of European history, specifically through the European national state and, on the Continent, the ideals of the French Enlightenment and Revolution.[94] Even if they do not accept all the bloodier and more heroic nineteenth-century definitions of the nation, Europeans generally view it as a legitimate successor to what went before, Christendom or a shared European culture founded in a shared religion, though not in a common political system.

Though no side might wish to defend the policies of the generally ineffectual Louis XV (1710–74), his brutalization of the Protestant minority in France by forbidding Protestant church services and marriages and declaring that all newborn children must be baptized Catholic, he was not only an easy target for Voltaire's *Treatise on Tolerance,* but an example of the intolerance of the *ancien régime* which the French revolutionaries could see

91. *Catholicism and American Freedom: A History* (New York: W. W. Norton, 2003), as at 36–37, 265. The first phrase quoted is from Fr. John Ryan, the "Right Reverend New Dealer," as quoted in an article by Leo P. Ribuffo, "The American Catholic Church and Ordered Liberty," *HS* (September/October 2004): 26–28 at 28, and the second phrase quoted is from another article discussing McGreevy's book in the same issue by McCarraher, "Remarks on John McGreevy's Catholicism," 28–31 at 30. Ribuffo observes that, if their behavior is examined, American Catholics and Protestants seem not to differ as much as when only their ideas are examined.

92. William Calin, *The French Tradition and the Literature of Medieval England* (Toronto: University of Toronto Press, 1994); Bray, *Friend,* 35–41, 98, showing how the debate about the nature of medieval male friendship has been impeded by the conventional narration of the growth of English government.

93. *Consequences of Modernity* (Stanford, Calif.: Stanford University Press, 1990).

94. I say this despite all the "postcolonial" attacks on Europe detailed in my "The Changing Understanding of the Making of Europe from Christopher Dawson to Robert Bartlett," in *Actas del V Congreso "Cultura Europea,"* ed. Enrique Banús and Beatriz Elío (Pamplona 2000), 203–10, and in another version in *Quidditas* 20 (1999): 193–201. Patrick J. Geary, *The Myth of Nations: The Medieval Origins of Europe* (Princeton, N.J.: Princeton University Press, 2002), details the still-present nationalist myths about the origins of the European nations. Hans Peter Duerr, *Nudité et pudeur: Le mythe du processus de civilisation,* preface by André Burguíeere, translated from the original German by Véronique Bodin (Paris: Maison des sciences de l'homme, 1998), shows how the idea of the process of civilization is an analogue to the ideology used to justify colonialism.

themselves as definitively destroying.[95] By contrast to this *ancien régime,* eighteenth-century ameliorists such as Benjamin Franklin could present themselves as the bearers of practical progress. Their projects, such as the University of Pennsylvania, could promise an unending growth in useful knowledge. Though the notion that each generation sees farther because it stands on the shoulders of all who have gone before goes back to the Middle Ages, it took special force in the thought of Charles W. Eliot, the president of Harvard from 1869 to 1909, who declared "each successive generation of youth shall start with all the advantages which their predecessors have won."[96] George Santayana thought Eliot an ominous first-fruit of the destruction of liberal education in the name of preparation for successful careers.

Only recently have some historians begun to see how much the very story of the origins of nationhood has been conceived from an Enlightenment perspective. Anthony D. Smith offers a very different view in which the argument is that, worldwide, the only ground for the rise of any nation is the presence of the idea that a given people is chosen and lives in a "holy land."[97] Over time, as apparently more secular national identities develop, these continue to be based in earlier sacred foundations. In this sense, religion continues to provide the binding commitments of the community. Though we may doubt the universal applicability of this idea, it is illuminating, revealing the shared ground between, say, Americans' view of themselves as "a light to the nations," the French view of themselves as the carriers of all that is highest in human life, and secular Israelis' insistence that Jerusalem is theirs. In trying to locate a common denominator in suicide terrorism, Robert Pape takes a somewhat different tack, suggesting that the common denominator is not to be found in religion but in response to occupation of a national homeland.[98] That is, religion is an aggravating factor, but central to such terrorism is offended nationalism, the attempt to drive out an occupier. In any case religion is bent in the national interest. Others argue that over the last two centuries politics has often taken on the character of religion.[99]

With adjustments, the idea of a "holy land" has been carried to other parts of the world such as China. If America is the last bastion of the worst

95. Algis Valiunas, "Fleeting Light," *FT* 149 (January 2005): 49–53 at 53.

96. Andrew Delbanco, "Colleges: An Endangered Species," *NYRB* 52, 4 (March 10, 2005): 18–20 at 20.

97. *Chosen Peoples: Sacred Sources of National Identity* (New York: Oxford University Press, 2003), with the helpful review by Donald Harman Akenson, *AHR* 110 (2005): 105.

98. Christian Caryl, "Why They Do It," *NYRB* 52, 14 (September 22, 2005): 28–32, 30–32 on Pape.

99. Emilio Gentile, *Politics as Religion,* tr. George Staunton (Princeton, N.J.: Princeton University Press, 2006).

European ideas of the eighteenth century, China is the last bastion of the worst European ideas of the nineteenth century, above all patriotism expressed in the form of a "holy mother China." Of course China has its own indigenous patriotism, but in important respects she still lives in the nineteenth century of the European lay party, continuing the persecution of religion and the insistence that religion serve the purposes of the nation. When one underground community of Catholics in China wrote to Pope Benedict XVI on his accession, asking not to be forgotten, they informed the pope of a set of religious-affairs regulations which had taken effect on March 1, 2005. According to these, Catholic priests must make a weekly report to religious-affairs officials about their activities, and may not leave their parishes without permission from the security officials.[100]

In particular, a presumed progress made possible through the development of science in recent centuries—I say "presumed" because this question is unendingly complicated by all the undesirable environmental and technological results of this presumed progress—has conditioned people to the unending benefits of "newness." "Progress" as the "metaphysical handmaiden" to science has encouraged a kind of insanity in which becoming has been exalted over being, and most people have become "presentists," resulting in the provincialism modernism can be, a refusal to look beyond the present horizon.[101] Already when in the eighteenth century the new scientific societies were tending in Europe to replace the universities as the principal locus of scientific discovery, the American Philosophical Society, founded in 1744 by Benjamin Franklin, defined itself as existing

for the promotion of useful knowledge. . . . All new Arts, Trades, Manufactures, etc., that may be proposed or thought of . . . And all philosophical Experiments that let Light into the Nature of Things, tend to increase the Power of Man over Matter, and multiply the Conveniences or Pleasures of Life.[102]

The emphasis on the new was by Franklin's day in firm alliance with a promise of increased power over nature and a growth in human comfort.

Though the reputation of the university as a place of science and reason was to rebound in the nineteenth century, in the eighteenth century "newness" made its way, as is often the case, by attacking the old, and part of the campaign for science involved attack on the universities as clerically dominated and therefore unprogressive. In 1753 *The Independent Reflector* marked the founding of King's College, now Columbia University, by urging:

100. "Chinese Underground Catholics Tell Pope, 'Do Not Forget Us,'" *IC,* May 6, 2005, 2.
101. Weaver, *Ideas Have Consequences,* 67.
102. *Year Book 2000–2001. The American Philosophical Society* (Philadelphia; American Philosophical Society, 2001), 306–7; and see John O'Malley, *Four Cultures of the West* (Cambridge, Mass.: Belknap Press, 2004), 119–22.

Let not the seat of literature, the abode of the Muses, and the nurse of science, be transformed into a cloister of bigots, a habitation of superstition, a nursery of ghostly tyranny, a school of rabbinical jargon. The legislator alone should have direction of so important an establishment.[103]

The state, not the Church, was to be the patron of the new learning, and the school was to be less a place of contemplation than a center of world transformation.

There have been many local variations on the theme of unending progress, such as the Scottish Enlightenment of the eighteenth century, in which the vision was of human progress through stages, culminating in a modern commercial life. This has been much more than a Scottish vision, and from Europe has gone forth the notion of the state as a vast bureaucracy in the service of appetite, aimed above all at the promotion of economic life and comfort.[104] Most commonly, whether we are speaking of Marx, Spencer, or Comte, the idea has been that modern life is moving toward a shared global system.[105] Often it has been less "Europe" that carries the story of progress, than France, Britain, or, for the early modern period, Spain.[106] Thus the British experience in India, where the East India Company presented itself as bringing civilization, science, rationality, and progress to less developed peoples.[107] Other European countries and trends tended to fall out of the story until, "belatedly," as in the case of Germany or Italy from the second half of the nineteenth century, they consciously tried to catch up with the trendsetters. The conservative tendencies of early-nineteenth-century Europe, or places which challenge the teleological assumptions of the master story, such as Venice or the Tyrol, were passed over.[108]

It is beyond liberal belief that the life of such areas might actually be better than that of the world of liberalism, nationalism, and commerce. Thus liberal incomprehension of Christopher Dawson's observation about the parts of Europe in which the presence of an earlier Baroque culture is still felt: "Where its traditions survived into the nineteenth century, as in

103. Quoted in O'Malley, *Four Cultures,* 120.

104. Weaver, *Ideas Have Consequences,* 38, and see 40 on de Tocqueville's perception of the link between the decline of hierarchy and the growth of comfort. However, I find Weaver's excoriation of the middle class somewhat ahistorical, especially in its comparison of bourgeois and peasant.

105. John Gray, "The Global Delusion," *NYRB* 53, 7 (April 27, 2006): 20–23 at 20. On Marxism as the most radical form of belief in progress, see Benedict XVI, *Deus Caritas Est,* 31, b (Vatican City 2005).

106. David A. Bell, *The Cult of the Nation in France: Inventing Nationalism, 1680–1800* (Cambridge, Mass.: Harvard University Press, 2001).

107. Pankaj Mishra, "The Empire Under Siege," *NYRB* 51, 12 (July 15, 2004): 33–35 at 33–34.

108. David Laven, *Venice and Venetia under the Habsburgs, 1815–1835* (Oxford: Oxford University Press, 2002), kills two birds with one stone, showing the strength of conservatism after the French Revolution, and how Venice ill fits the Whig narrative. See also Parks, "Tyrol," 50–52.

Austria and Spain and parts of Italy and South Germany, one still feels that life has a richer savour and a more vital rhythm than in the lands where the bourgeois spirit is triumphant."[109] Those Catholic movements, commonly peasant or rural, which over the centuries but especially in and since the French Revolution have challenged the development of the world as it has become, are similarly seen as simply quixotic. The nineteenth-century Tyrolers or Basques must move aside in the name of the modern "isms," especially nationalism.[110] Only belatedly are some now ready to admire, say, the native peoples of a country like the United States, who arguably were not as competitive and acquisitive as the American colonists.[111]

In the development of political life it is often assumed that the past is past and has nothing to teach us.[112] Even countries which have seemed to be at the center of the narrative of progress, such as France, have things about them which only with difficulty can be fit into the master narrative. Typically these inconvenient facts are neglected: if we look at French rural areas, we hardly find the nation-state until late in the nineteenth century. Arguably it was only then that peasants were turned into Frenchmen, only then that a country of many languages and ways of living was turned through such things as the railroads and public schools into a national culture.[113] But Venice and rural France can be made into merely laggard participants in a tale of general progress. Most still find it impossible to acknowledge that it is the very idea of general progress that is wrong, and most are unable to see that Pope Pius IX and the *Syllabus of Errors* of 1864 was more right than wrong in condemning reconciliation to "progress."

This is too radical a message for liberal, bourgeois society, which, if aware of it, almost always has misconstrued the thought of people such as Leo Strauss, who rejected especially the idea that democracy is the inevitable goal at which progress aims.[114] A more recent thinker such as John Gray has had much difficulty in convincing others that the rates of "progress" (economic development) vary greatly from place to place, and that the hybrid regimes of the world are in fact developing in many directions,

109. *The Dynamics of World History*, ed. John J. Mulloy (New York: Sheed & Ward, 1956), 207–8.

110. Of course by the twenty-first century the story, especially in the Basque country, with one of the most prosperous urban economies in Spain, becomes extremely complicated.

111. Gordon S. Wood, "Apologies to the Iroquois," *NYRB* 53, 7 (April 6, 2006): 50–52 at 52.

112. But then see Oliver O'Donovan and Joan Lockwood O'Donovan, *Bonds of Imperfection: Christian Politics, Past and Present* (Grand Rapids, Mich.: Eerdmans, 2004).

113. Eugen Weber, *Peasants into Frenchmen: The Modernization of Rural France, 1870–1914* (Stanford, Calif.: Stanford University Press, 1976), and see now Graham Robb, *The Discovery of France: A Historical Geography from the Revolution to the First World War* (New York: W. W. Norton, 2007).

114. Mark Lilla, "The Closing of the Straussian Mind," *NYRB* 51, 17 (November 4, 2004): 55–59, at 56. Strauss's *Natural Right and History* (Chicago: University of Chicago Press, 2000) was especially directed against Whiggish perspectives.

not one.[115] In the same vein, those who believe in general progress cannot take seriously those who, if not rejecting modernity root and branch, believe we have gone seriously astray. It is simply impossible to believe that other ways of life and thought, especially earlier ways, might have been better than what we now know. What Pat Moynihan called the "liberal expectancy," "the belief that nationalism, religion and ethnicity would be of steadily diminishing importance because of the inexorable advance of modernity—education, science, secularism, prosperity," must be true.[116] Of course many are of two minds. A New Yorker may in many ways be a true believer in progress, but find New York attractive precisely because it still is a city of neighborhoods; a European may accept the technological imperative, but also value the pedestrian areas at the center of his cities, which in some ways return life to an earlier age. One question of the present book is whether such double-mindedness does not suggest a way into the future.

From the sixteenth century the very notion of "civilization" increasingly carried with it the idea of a continuing, expanding progress, impersonal or secular rather than providential.[117] This has taken many forms and has penetrated into every corner, often unobserved. It is only recently, for instance, that historians have noticed that even such things as human emotional life have been portrayed as progressive: people in the Middle Ages, it had been said, were childish, violent, and unrestrained, whereas they now are disciplined and under control.[118] The nineteenth-century liberal promised peace through cosmopolitanism and free trade, which would render archaic the former world of kingly and aristocratic war.[119] Today, as we have noted, it is "globalization" which is made into an impersonal secular trend (though, besides factors no human can control, this "trend" is in fact the accumulation of thousands of separate decisions made over five hundred years by individual actors trying to judge their own circumstances).[120] Largely forgotten is the older Christian sense of Providence, in which the future, though in God's hands, is unfathomable. In this older view God has his own purposes, which humans cannot read. The proper attitude toward the future is hope, a theological virtue that trusts in God, rather than op-

---

115. "Global Delusion," 20.

116. George F. Will, "Kerry Caught Between Good and Bad News," *DMN* (September 12, 2004), AA2.

117. Liah Greenfeld, "Speaking Historically about Globalization and Related Fantasies," *HS* 5, 3 (January 2004): 23–28 at 24, who comments on the implicit teleology of much language about impersonal secular trends. See Greenfeld's *The Spirit of Capitalism: Nationalism and Economic Growth* (Cambridge, Mass.: Harvard University Press, 2001).

118. Barbara H. Rosenwein, "Worrying about Emotions in History," *AHR* 107 (2002): 821–45.

119. Brink Lindsey, "The Origins and Progress of the Industrial Counterrevolution," *HS* 5, 3 (January 2004), 17–21 at 18, 20.

120. Greenfeld, "Speaking Historically about Globalization," 28.

timism, a banal confidence that things by a secular measure will turn out well and are getting better.

Some prominent historians who have made the transition from writing national history to writing world history continue to present a Whig view of human progress, now on a global stage. Thus J. R. and William H. McNeill write that "the general direction of history has been toward greater and greater social cooperation—both voluntary and compelled—driven by the realities of social competition."[121] Leaving aside such questions as what can possibly be meant by a "compelled social cooperation," this is an extraordinarily benign view of the horrors of the twentieth century. In spite of what influential writers such as Michel Foucault have said about the formation of "the rationality of modern state power" along the two axes of "reason of state" and the "doctrine of police," the sinister aspects of this development are discounted even in the face of totalitarianism.[122]

Even those who understand globalization to limit older forms of capitalism as well as the nation-state itself sometimes observe that the nation continues to be the central focus of life for the majority of the world's population.[123] Nation-states are not just a European nor a nineteenth-century development, and have not always served an expansionist foreign policy. Their limiting borders may actually enhance the possibilities for peace, and when we remember the frightful nation-based wars of the twentieth century, we should not forget that those areas of the world today which are the home of poverty, drug production, and mass murder are often places where nation-states do not exist. The nation-state has long fostered real communities, and those who have only negative things to say about it should wonder what a world without the nation-state at all might look like.[124] We imperil our future if, in thinking a new world order of transnational and cooperative impulses is dawning, we neglect the old realities of competition between nation-states.[125]

Most Europeans do not listen to those who assert the need for radical reconsideration of the idea of progress; and most Americans have a view

121. Quoted in Jonathan Spence, "The Whole World in Their Hands," *NYRB* 50, 15 (October 9, 2003): 35. William H. McNeill, "Man Slaughters Man," *NYRB* 55, 6 (April 12, 2008): 43–48 at 48, acknowledged his writings have too much emphasized human cooperation.

122. Ed Cohen, "Legislating the Norm: From Sodomy to Gross Indecency," *South Atlantic Quarterly* 88, 1 (Winter 1989), 181–217 at 194, for the phrases cited, with Michel Foucault, "Omnes et Singulatim: Towards a Critique of Political Reason," in *Tanner Lectures on Human Values,* ed. Sterling McMurrin (Salt Lake City: University of Utah Press, 1981), 224–54 at 245–50.

123. Alexander Stille, "Apocalypse Soon," *NYRB* 49, 17 (November 7, 2002): 47.

124. Diana Muir, "The Value of the Nation-State," *HS* 7, 1 (September/October 2005): 37–40.

125. Jonathan Haslam, *No Virtue Like Necessity: Realist Thought in International Relations Since Machiavelli* (New Haven, Conn.: Yale University Press, 2002); see also Paul Kennedy, "The Modern Machiavelli," *NYRB* 49, 17 (November 7, 2002): 52–55 at 53, also reviewing other books on the current status of nation-states.

similar to that of the Europeans, simply replacing Europe with America and the ideals of the American Revolution as the motor of history.[126] Commonly this is tied to American exceptionalism, to the notion that America has a divinely given mission and is really different from other nations, more virtuous, a new beginning, "the last, best hope of mankind."[127] This can express itself in an American form of the idea of the white man's burden: many Americans see themselves, as in Iraq for instance, engaged in democratic nation building, in spreading democracy in the Middle East.

In its Jeffersonian or less overtly religious form, the idea has been that "America is nature's nation, a place free of the encumbrances and tyrannies of older civilizations, where the New Man of a democratic future would be forged."[128] Mark Noll, centering on the career of Evangelical Christianity and the Calvinist tradition in America, has told the story by which, in the nineteenth century, Christianity increasingly allied itself with the American experiment, placing itself in service to a market and bourgeois culture, and to nation building.[129] As in Europe, one result was that the state increasingly arrogated spiritual prerogatives to itself. The common faith became a generic civil religion, faith in America and the American way of life. It was not that Americans became less religious, at least according to some definitions, but that their religion was increasingly an Americanized form of republican deism in which God was left in heaven so men could profitably make their way on earth. Growing democratic sentiment undermined traditional forms of hierarchy; Protestantism increasingly defined itself by devotion to liberty; and a chief goal of religion was promotion of civic virtue. This might be called "secularization under the cover of religion," because while religion became increasingly irrelevant to large areas of life and was less valued for itself than for its patriotism, most Americans continued to think of themselves as "under God." Indeed, from time to time they can catch us up, as when in his 2003 State of the Union address George W. Bush delivered a very orthodox rendition of Providence: "We do not know—we do not claim to know all the ways of Providence, yet we can

126. *History and the Idea of Progress,* ed. Arthur M. Melzer et al. (Ithaca, N.Y.: Cornell University Press, 1995).

127. Wilfred M. McClay, "The Continuing Irony of American History," *FT* 120 (February 2002): 20–25 at 23. The phrase, from Abraham Lincoln, shows the ease with which even realists lose their bearing in America. "Exceptionalism" can bear various meanings, two of which especially should be distinguished. A theological use implies divine approval of a country's history. A historical use claims that empirically something exceptional about a country can be shown. My primary concern is with the first usage. By definition every national experience has something unique to it.

128. Ibid., 23.

129. *America's God: From Jonathan Edwards to Abraham Lincoln* (New York: Oxford University Press, 2002). See also Noll's *The Civil War as a Theological Crisis* (Chapel Hill: University of North Carolina Press, 2006).

trust in them, placing our confidence in the loving God behind all of life, and all of history."[130]

According to the progressive view of history common to both Europe and America, the Renaissance freed us from the Middle Ages, the Reformation from Catholicism, the birth of modern science from superstition, and the secular state from intolerance.[131] The Marquis de Sade (1740–1814) gave classic expression to the idea that the world would never be safe as long as religion held sway:

And once again wars of religions are ready to devastate Europe. Boheman, leader and agent of a new sect of "purified" Christianity, has just been arrested in Sweden, and the most disastrous plans were found among his papers. The sect to which he belonged is said to want nothing less than to render itself master of all the potentates of Europe and their subjects. In Arabia new sectarians are emerging and want to purify the religion of Mahomet. In China, even worse troubles, still and always motivated by religion, are tearing apart the inside of that vast empire. As always it is gods that are the cause of all ills.[132]

If only religion would disappear, so would rancor and division, thought de Sade as he forced himself on some unsuspecting woman. Of course it is true that religion has been the main rival to and limit on the claims of state sovereignty, but one might wish to regard this as a good, rather than bad, thing.[133]

In any case the question is broader than that of religion. Henry Adams's observation that "politics, as a practice, whatever its professions, has always been the systematic organization of hatreds" is so true that one pauses before seeing any one area of human life as uniquely responsible for the social ills that plague us.[134] Indeed, to trace the world's hatreds uniquely to religion does little more than reveal one's own irrational hatred.

⌒

130. Quoted in Richard John Neuhaus, "While We're At It," *FT* 141 (March 2004): 61–72 at 65.

131. In addition to my "Humanism: The Struggle to Possess a Word," *Lo* 7 (2004): 97–116, see Peter Wallace, "The Long European Reformation: A Proposal for a New Interpretive Model," *HS* 6, 2 (November/December 2004): 2–4. Henry Kamen, *The Spanish Inquisition: A Historical Revision* (New Haven, Conn.: Yale University Press, 1998), esp. 305–20, and Maurice A. Finocchiaro, *Retrying Galileo, 1633–1992* (Berkeley: University of California Press, 2005), are indicative of how far scholarship has come in "deconstructing" and complicating the Whig narrative.

132. Diary of the Marquis de Sade, quoted by Abdelwahab Meddeb, *The Malady of Islam,* tr. Pierre Joris and Ann Reid (New York: Basic Books, 2003), and then by Max Rodenbeck, "Islam Confronts Its Demons," *NYRB* 51, 7 (April 29, 2004): 14–18 at 14, in an article which tends to embody the views I am attacking. For a response to these see Keith Ward, *Is Religion Dangerous?* (Grand Rapids, Mich.: Eerdmans, 2007).

133. See the multilayered analysis of James J. Sheehan, "The Problem of Sovereignty in European History," *AHR* 111 (2006): 1–15 at 4–5.

134. Quoted in Anthony Hecht, "Knowing the Score," *NYRB* 49, 19 (December 5, 2002): 54–57 at 54.

The progressive treatment of the so-called Wars of Religion is exemplary of acquiescence in the claims of the nation-state vis-à-vis religion.[135] There is a historical scholarship here, of which most people are unaware, that bears directly on the question of the relation between the life of society and the life of the spirit. It should go without saying that many terrible things have been done in the name of religion, and that in important ways specifically Christianity helped bring on itself its marginalization in European life.[136] If the nation-state's drive to centralize often displaced and marginalized religion, this infrequently had as one cause the fact that religion *had* been divisive. Nationalism, on the other hand, shrewdly directed, can be unifying and bring social classes together. Of course it also may well become a replacement for traditional religion (religion often can live comfortably with patriotism, but when patriotism becomes aggressive nationalism, religion suffers).[137] The very kind of cultural criticism the present study attempts frequently in the hands of the religious has not been much more than a jeremiad against the present, lamenting all that has been lost without acknowledging the many ways in which some form of traditionalism has again and again sanctioned very gross injustice, ignored present defect, or opposed new life a-budding and better ways of understanding and confronting the world. No doubt the emphasis on "interests," that is, on a rational or commercial calculation of life, in writers such as Montesquieu (1689–1755) and Adam Smith (1723–90) was an attempt to find a replacement for the martial passions which had divided seventeenth-century Europe.[138] By mocking religion and advocating toleration and directing philosophy to practical goals, Enlightenment thinkers "imagined a world of satisfied citizens and shopkeepers, and nearly succeeded in creating it."[139]

Clearly from 1560 to 1660 religion was a source of division in Europe.

135. Cf. A. J. Conyers, *The Long Truce: How Toleration Made the World Safe for Power and Profit* (Dallas: Spence 2001), attempts to show the ways in which toleration has undermined the peace it was intended to establish, and to show that our choices include more than that between political conflict and the suppression of transcendent concerns. Conyers advances as a model the Christian understanding of humility, in opposition to the notion of indifference.

136. Peter Partner, *God of Battles: Holy Wars of Christianity and Islam* (Princeton, N.J.: Princeton University Press, 1998), is a history of religious violence which is made more precise by the fine review by Jonathan Riley-Smith, *Sp* 75 (2000): 719–21, who makes the critical point that the architects of the sixteenth-century "beginning of the decline of the idea of divinely ordained violence," Vitoria, Suarez, and Ayala, sought the authority for force in the idea of the common good, rather than in a divine plan, thus moving such arguments from theology to law. James Turner, *Without God, Without Creed: The Origins of Unbelief in America* (Baltimore: Johns Hopkins University Press, 1985), in arguing that "religion caused unbelief" makes points that illuminate European experience also. Cf. Douglas Farrow, "Three Meanings of Secular," *FT* 133 (May 2003): 20–23.

137. For the distinction between patriotism and nationalism see John Lukacs, *Democracy and Populism: Fear and Hatred* (New Haven, Conn.: Yale University Press, 2005).

138. Daniel J. Mahoney, "A Noble Failure," *FT* 139 (January 2004): 57–61 at 59.

139. Mark Lilla, "Leo Strauss: The European," *NYRB* 51, 16 (October 21, 2004): 58–60 at 59.

Neither Catholicism nor Protestantism was guiltless.[140] But one can easily be tricked here. Enlightenment historians, for instance, loved to portray the Crusades as emblematic of all that is bad about religion, even to offer a sanitized version of Saladin as a humane contrast to Christian barbarism. The general public may still accept such moralizing caricatures, but many historians have become very uneasy about such views, one suggesting that John Paul II's apology for the Crusades was anachronistic.

Most great religions have elements of both tolerance and intolerance built into them: intolerance because they believe they carry the truth, perhaps the sole truth, and tolerance because they also speak of humanity, the common origins of mankind, concepts of divine justice, and a humane order for all. Violence does not flow from religion alone—even bigoted religion. After all, the greatest horrors and killing machines in history stemmed from the Western, secular ideologies of fascism and communism.[141]

Many people are insufficiently aware of how much Christianity and other religions have been manipulated by forces stronger than themselves. David Abulafia, the editor of volume 5 of *The New Cambridge Medieval History,* in correcting such views goes so far as to argue that the thirteenth-century struggle between pope and emperor was already somewhat anachronistic, seen in the light of the constantly tightening bonds between subjects and monarchs which resulted by 1300 in the triumph of kings.[142] In an earlier situation, Europe had been rather like Africa, and politics, even before chivalry, had been "chivalric," centered on face-to-face contact, without such abstractions as "the state."[143] A ruler like Otto III of Germany (who reigned 983–1002) did not rule a state, but practiced a kind of "political theater," exercising power through ritual and various "rules of the game" rather than ideologies or even policies.[144] Without such abstractions as "the state," it was almost impossible to develop a single narrative story of

---

140. "*AHR* Conversation: Religious Identities and Violence," *AHR* 112 (2007): 1433–79, is a useful discussion.

141. Christopher Tyerman, *God's War: A New History of the Crusades* (Cambridge, Mass.: Belknap Press, 2006); see also Eamon Duffy, "The Holy Terror," *NYRB* 53, 16 (October 19, 2006): 41–45 at 45. Cf. Tomaz Mastnak, *Crusading Peace: Christendom, the Muslim World, and Western Political Order* (Berkeley: University of California Press, 2002), 229–347. John Paul II's apology for the Church's behavior in the Galileo case similarly seemed unaware of recent scholarship on the complexity of this case: see my "The Return of Purpose," *Co* 33 (2006): 666–81, and Maurice A. Finocchiaro, "The Church and Galileo," *CHR* 94 (2008): 260–83.

142. Subtitle: *C. 1198–c. 1300* (Cambridge: Cambridge University Press, 1999), esp. the preface and introduction.

143. Alan Harding, *Medieval Law and the Foundations of the State* (New York: Oxford University Press, 2002), gives an up-to-date narrative of the development of the state from the time of the Carolingians. *Das Frühmittelalterliche Königtum. Ideelle und religiöse Grundlagen,* ed. Franz-Reiner Erkens (Berlin: De Gruyter, 2005), considers sacral kingship and African parallels.

144. Gerd Althoff, *Otto III,* tr. Phyllis G. Jestice (University Park: Pennsylvania State University Press, 2003), challenges modern "statist" assumptions.

political progress. "Politics was a dynamic process of personal interaction rather than relationships stabilized by 'hegemony' or 'legitimacy' or any of the other modern fictions necessary to explain 'structures' that work by abstraction rather than through continuous, real-time confrontation and collaboration."[145] But by the middle of the thirteenth century we find a "religion of the state," in which even some theologians justified increasing state sovereignty.[146] The state and sovereignty thus worshipped was not a natural form of association, but a voluntarist construct or power of ruling, only now seen as such in postmodernity.[147]

Theocratic monarchy, government in which the ruler claims either to be God or to rule for him, was probably the most common form of government in the ancient world and into the Middle Ages, and persisted long after the Middle Ages in the claims of such absolute monarchs as Elizabeth I of England (1533–1603). From the first, medieval theocratic monarchies had tried to "cap" transcendence, sometimes with and sometimes against the clergy.[148] In the early Middle Ages many churchmen accepted such control of the Church by the monarch, or intervention in the Church's life by him: the canonist Burchard of Worms, born around 965 and holding that ecclesiastical law was superior to secular law, was quite unusual in his day in holding that secular law had no authority in Church law.[149] More usual, in spite of the subsequent Investiture Controversy of the eleventh century, with its attempt on the side of the Church to create a Christian society purified of a wide range of abuses, was acquiescence in, if not actual advocacy of, some degree of royal control over the Church.[150] Still in the fourteenth century John Wyclif urged kings to seize Church property, but of course they had been doing this for centuries, and Wyclif's proposals were not that different from Dante's vision, earlier in the century, of a poor Church, a Church unable to thwart the political ambitions of cities such as his beloved Florence.[151]

145. Joseph C. Miller, "Beyond Blacks, Bondage, and Blame: Why a Multi-centric World History Needs Africa," *HS* 6, 2 (November/December 2004): 9, describing Africa.

146. Alain Boureau, *La Religion de l'État: La construction de la république étatique dans le discours théologique de l'occident médiéval (1250–1350)* (Paris: Belles Lettres, 2006).

147. Robert Sokolowski, "Theology and Deconstruction," *Telos* 110 (Winter 1998): 155–66 at 166.

148. Elisabeth Magnou-Nortier, "*L'Admonitio generalis*: Etude critique," in *Jornades internacionals d'estudi sobre el bishe Feliu d'Urgell* (Barcelona 2000), 95–142, in brilliantly showing that the document most associated with Charlemagne's ecclesiastical policy is a forgery, establishes the means by which bishops tried to gain control over the empire.

149. Greta Austin, "Jurisprudence in the Service of Pastoral Care: The *Decretum* of Burchard of Worms," *Sp* 79 (2004): 929–59 at 946–47.

150. *Vom Umbruch zur Erneuerung? Das 11. Und beginnende 12. Jahrhundert—Positionen der Forschung*, ed. Jörg Jarnut and Matthias Wemhoff (Munich: Fink, 2006).

151. Stephen E. Lahey, *Philosophy and Politics in the Thought of John Wyclif* (Cambridge: Cambridge University Press, 2003). Though Dante of course does not advocate royal control of the Church, his scapegoating of the papacy and papal states as the cause of Italian disunity

William Chester Jordan has written a splendid narrative of royal triumph in France from 1290 to 1321, laying bare the tensions between the Church and the French crown, the attempt of kings to force churchmen to accept policies they knew to be incompatible with the freedom of the Church.[152] This was part of a larger process—illuminated by Foucault, if with various imprecisions—in which the accumulation of capital in the High Middle Ages made possible the replacement of relatively chaotic "feudal" forms of power with the "technology of subjection."[153] Though in the days of the Plantagenet Empire (1154–1224), the nobility still possessed considerable resources by which to resist the king and the king's relatively weak infrastructure, a modern writer describes the Plantagenet king at this period as already a "master of propaganda," aiming at aristocratic complaisance.[154] Already an "analytics of power" was developing whereby increasingly power was defined juridically and resided with a legislator.[155]

With variations, Jordan's story could be written for much of Europe. The general reader is familiar with some of the great conflicts between the rising national states and the Church, the so-called Investiture Contest of the eleventh century, the Beckett controversy in the twelfth century, or the confrontation between Henry VIII and the papacy in the sixteenth, but all through the later Middle Ages clashes occurred. Henry of Nördlingen was only one of those priests who chose exile and obedience to the pope rather than obey Louis the Bavarian and the Imperial Diet when, in 1358, they declared invalid the interdict Pope John XXII laid on Germany after Louis crowned himself Holy Roman Emperor.[156] The papal schism of the fourteenth and fifteenth centuries only increased the leverage of temporal rulers over the Church, allowing after the Council of Constance (1414–17) a series of concordats ratifying increased royal control over what was becoming, at the expense of Christendom, effectively regional churches subject to their sovereigns. The "long war of the nation-state" against all opposition to itself, religious or aristocratic, had begun.[157]

With the weakening of the medieval (transnational) idea of Christendom, the early modern nation-state much more vigorously tried to "control

---

effectively left much more culpable parties, such as his own Florence, largely free to pursue their aggressive ambitions.

152. *Unceasing Strife, Unending Fear: Jacques de Thérines and the Freedom of the Church in the Age of the Last Capetians* (Princeton, N.J.: Princeton University Press, 2005).

153. *Discipline and Punish,* tr. Alan Sheridan (New York: Vintage Books, 1979), 220–21.

154. Martin Aurell, *The Plantagenet Empire 1154–1224,* tr. David Crouch (New York: Pearson Education, 2007), 84–94 at 84. See also 110–19, "The Limits of the Sacred."

155. Michel Foucault, *The History of Sexuality: An Introduction,* vol. 1, tr. Robert Hurley (New York: Vintage Books, 1978), 82–90, sketches this process over the modern period.

156. John W. Coakley, *Women, Men, and Spiritual Power: Female Saints and Their Male Collaborators* (New York: Columbia University Press, 2006), 149–69.

157. This is the title of a section in Philip Bobbitt, *The Shield of Achilles: War, Peace and the Course of History* (New York: Knopf, 2002).

God."[158] In the degree of their submission to the laws of God and to the pope in spiritual matters, Louis IX of France and Alfonso X of Castile-Leon in the thirteenth century were unusual, for the kings of the High Middle Ages frequently ignored or fought against the teachings of the Church, just as had the kings of the early Middle Ages.[159] But in the early modern period famous examples such as that of Henry VIII made clear in an especially public way that a single king could pretty much do what he wanted, that kings such as Henry were individually capable of facing down the pope.[160] In 1534 when by the Act of Supremacy Henry became Head of the Church of England, there were 825 religious houses in England; a half dozen years later, as a result of the Dissolution of the Monasteries, there were none.[161] Those who did not flee were persecuted mercilessly. Thus began the time of the priest-hides or priest holes, underground hole and tunnel systems for hiding priests, still visible today at places such as Ufton Court, thirty miles from London.[162] The fact of being a Catholic priest meant the death penalty and the death was horrible: throttling followed by being butchered alive. Priest hunters roamed the land.

Increasingly the discipline given society by religious institutions or military groups passed over to national governments, engaged in producing "useful individuals."[163] The Church often either lost or ceded authority to the state, resulting in absolutism and unceasing war, often described as religious, but commonly the result of a quest by the state for material and political advantage. The visitor to Germany today has perhaps heard someone referred to as a "country Catholic," as someone whose traditional, say Bavarian, rural religion has been little touched by the modern world. The division on which this remark is founded was appearing in the early mod-

---

158. Pierpaolo Donati, "El desafío universalismo en una sociedad multicultural postmoderna: un planteamiento relacional," *Razón práctica y multiculturalismo,* ed. Enrique Banús and Alejandro Llano, Studia Europea Navarrensis 1 (Pamplona: Centro de Estudios Europeos, Universidad de Navarra, 1999), 1–34 at 10–17.

159. One reservation I have about the views of some of the practitioners of radical orthodoxy discussed in the last chapter below is a tendency on their part to view the nation-state as a unique evil, and in so doing insufficiently to note continuities in the age-old practice of "theocratic monarchy." Catherine Pickstock, "Medieval Liturgy and Modern Reform," *Antiphon* 6, 1 (2001): 19–25 at 23, in conveying medieval normative ideas about kingship, and placing kings "within the liturgical congregation," does not seem to me to give sufficient attention to theocratic patterns.

160. William Chester Jordan, *The French Monarchy and the Jews: From Philip Augustus to the Last Capetians* (Philadelphia: University of Pennsylvania Press, 1989) not only brilliantly portrays the character of the thirteenth-century kings, but, as at 252–53, makes very astute comparisons between medieval and early modern monarchy.

161. John Vidmar, *The Catholic Church Through the Ages: A History* (New York: Paulist Press, 2005), 210.

162. Joanna Bogle, "Ufton Court: A Reminder of Catholic Heritage," *Voices* 22, 1 (2007): 21–22 at 21, on this and the following.

163. Foucault, *Discipline,* 211.

ern period, in which increasingly urban elites associated themselves with a kind of practical rationalism which justified and advanced their increasing material prosperity ("progress"), and in contrast to which the world of the rural dweller was described as superstitious.[164]

We must be careful here and not take the everlasting struggle for influence in society to be unproblematically a secularizing process. A brilliant book on the religion of the Italian communes from 1125 to 1325 has made this very clear. A long-accepted view saw in this period continuous secularization in which the Italian communes became essentially secular regimes. How then are we to explain why "communal . . . Italy produced the single largest concentration of lay saints in Christian history, the modern age included"?[165] Augustine Thompson, the author of these words, argues that the truth is closer to the opposite of secularization, that lay government did not become secularized, but rather ever more expressed itself in rhetoric and rituals it had learned from the Church.[166] This was not just in Italy, but throughout the early modern world, and is a very complicated matter to judge: as in other historical periods we seem to have sacralization and secularization going on simultaneously; indeed, processes which seem to have been both at the same time. The communes learned their rhetoric and ritual from the Church, thus giving society a more religious form, while not infrequently using this rhetoric and ritual to increase their power at the expense of the Church. In Russia later, which as much as the Hapsburg Empire learned how coexistence with Islam was possible and toleration could be an instrument of imperial government, religion typically was controlled by the state, but was also the ground of state authority.[167] A new scholarship tells us that under Peter the Great (1672–1725) there existed a kind of political or court theater with a kind of liturgification or sacralization of life rather than secularization (something like the Italian communes earlier)—of course on the monarch's terms, that is, attempting to control religion. A "political theology" drawn from the liturgy and religious texts was used, here as elsewhere, to exalt the imperial office.[168]

The early modern dynastic territory and national state, descendants of the theocratic monarchies of the ancient and medieval worlds, commonly continued the claim that the state possesses an authority higher than that of

164. Wallace, "Long European Reformation," 4.

165. Augustine Thompson, *Cities of God: The Religion of the Italian Communes, 1125–1325* (University Park: Pennsylvania State University Press, 2005), 4. Thompson goes on to show, as at 258, that the notion of a passive laity, not for instance understanding the Latin mass, is far from the truth.

166. Thompson, "Cities of God," as at 3.

167. Orlando Figes, "Islam: the Russian Solution," *NYRB* 53, 20 (December 21, 2006): 74–77.

168. Ernest A. Zitser, "Review Essay. Post-Soviet Peter: New Histories of the Late Muscovite and Early Imperial Russian Court," *HS* 7, 2 (November/December 2005): 37–39.

any church.[169] For these early modern "theocrats," it could not be accepted that Christians (or Jews) intrinsically belonged to something higher than the national culture, call it Church, Chosen People, or City of God, founded not by human authority but by God.[170] Loyalty to kingdom or state could not be provisional as under the judgment of final loyalty to God or Church. Previously even relatively simple Christians had understood otherwise, witness the teaching of the anonymous fourteenth-century *Prickynge of Love* that though the Christian must show respect to worldly powers, these powers must be subordinate to God's will.[171] This association of Christianity with a duty to resist evil government was a traditional part of Christian teaching.

As we enter an early modern Europe divided between Catholic and Protestant, on the one side, generally Catholic, stood natural law thinking, with its insistence that the ruler is under the law of God.[172] The canon law of the medieval Church, as well as its theology, had long formed such a view, and the first recension of the *Decretum* of Gratian, the great collection of Church law composed no earlier than 1139, began with a Distinction on the law of nature, also stating that ignorance of natural law is a more serious offence than ignorance of civil law.[173] Distinction 8 then twice quoted (cc.5–6) a tag favored by the eleventh-century Gregorian Reformers in their struggle to free the Church from German lay theocratic control: "For the Lord said in the Gospel 'I am the Truth.' He did not say 'I am the custom.'" That is, Catholics are to obey God/Church, not man/Emperor. Sometime before 1158, canons were added in the second recension of the *Decretum* (C. 11, q. 3, canons 97–98), which transmitted the idea that in cases of conflict, one must obey God (= Church) rather than secular rulers. Thomas More offered a classical exposition of this when he insisted that he was "the

169. Isnard Wilhelm Frank, *A Concise History of the Medieval Church,* tr. John Bowden (New York: Continuum, 1995), 48, does a particularly good job of evoking the early medieval situation, in which a "church of the realm" or "King's church" expressed an archaic sense of religion, in which "all religion is public and all that is public is religious." Here we have a kind of undifferentiated sacred, in which nothing in society is able to find its proper autonomy and, paradoxically, the sacred itself is controlled by a sacral "lay" ruler. Insufficient differentiation has taken place.

170. How different is the Carolingian Empire as church from Elizabeth I's national church? Obviously there are differences, but the similarities are also striking: Mayke de Jong, "The Empire as *Ecclesia:* Hrabanus Maurus and Biblical *Historia* for Rulers," in *The Uses of the Past in the Early Middle Ages,* ed. Yitzhak Hen and Matthew Innes (Cambridge: Cambridge University Press, 2000), 191–226.

171. Ed. Harold Kane (Salzburg 1983), 75.

172. Stephen J. Grabill, *Rediscovering the Natural Law in Reformed Theological Ethics* (Grand Rapids, Mich.: Eerdmans, 2006), describes the forms of natural law thinking that remained in Protestantism and why they disappeared. Cf. my "The Natural Law: The First Grace," *Co* 35 (2008): 354–73.

173. Anders Winroth, *The Making of Gratian's "Decretum"* (Cambridge: Cambridge University Press, 2000), 113, 160. There is an invaluable collection, *From Irenaeus to Grotius: A Sourcebook in Christian Political Thought, 100–1625,* ed. Oliver O'Donovan and Joan Lockwood O'Donovan (Grand Rapids, Mich.: Eerdmans, 1999).

king's good servant, but God's first": the king was as much under God's law as was More.

One could not overestimate the effect in Protestant lands of the ceasing of the study of this Catholic tradition of limited loyalty to the state. Of course this does not mean that, Calvinism, for example, especially when in a minority position, was particularly obeisant and did not provoke rebellion. But often there was in Protestantism, especially Lutheranism, the idea that the ruler's will defines the law and that there may be no appeal from it to some higher law.[174] It took centuries for the struggle between the opposed positions to work itself out, but, at least to the Enlightenment, the Catholic side, as represented say by the Jesuits, insisted on "irreducible beliefs about the irreplaceable centrality of order, hierarchy, monarchy, and obedience in any collectivity."[175] One of the great questions of modern political thought, considered in the last chapter of the present work, is whether the Jesuits were in any respect mistaken.

In many ways the great watershed was the Peace of Westphalia of 1648. Here the ancient and medieval Christian idea of sovereignty, that rulers were morally responsible under God and the natural law and had to justify things like war by universal criteria applicable to all, was replaced with a new idea of national sovereignty. Effectively each ruler had to represent only the demands of his own nation in regard to questions such as territorial integrity. The nation, not Christendom, set the boundaries of justified action, and over time sovereignty became more and more a matter of procedure concerning such things as the defense of the principle of noninterference in domestic matters. Always there had been tyrants, but such ideas were conducive to a kind of "tyranny within the nation" in which rulers could oppress, rob, and murder their own citizens.[176] In a best case scenario in which the ruler genuinely put the interests (as defined by the Enlightenment) of his people first, as with Charles III of Spain (1716–88), strong regalism remained, constantly trying to diminish the power of the Church.[177]

It has often been difficult for those brought up on the propaganda of especially the Protestant nation-state, for instance on the idea that the Ref-

---

174. Martin Versfeld, *The Perennial Order* (London: Society of St. Paul, 1954), 140–41, is a classic exposition. Philip S. Gorski, *The Disciplinary Revolution: Calvinism and the Rise of the State in Early Modern Europe* (Chicago: University of Chicago Press, 2003), explores the relation between Protestant discipline and the enhancement of the power of the state.

175. Harro Höpfl, *Jesuit Political Thought: The Society of Jesus and the State, c. 1540–1630* (New York: Cambridge University Press, 2004), 51. Höpfl's brilliant exposition demolishes many commonplaces. He shows how the tendency of Protestantism to see the Church as invisible was to leave everything "visible," including Church administration, in the hands of the secular magistrate, thus encouraging state interference in the life of the Church.

176. James Turner Johnson, "Just War, As It Was and Is," *FT* 149 (January 2005): 14–24 at 16.

177. J. H. Elliott, "Barbarians at the Gates," *NYRB* 53, 3 (February 23, 2006): 36–38 at 38.

ormation advanced religious toleration, to see all this, to see that from Luther to the Peace of Westphalia, all invocation of toleration "had no other result than to consolidate the principle of State religion *(cuius regio illius et religio),* and the religious, civil, and political inferiority of the dissenting minority."[178] But, as Christopher Dawson saw, all modern states, following generally their ancient and medieval predecessors, have sought to limit the power of the churches within them.[179] Some Catholic monarchies were more Gallican or nationalistic than others, but in some degree all became "Protestant," attempting to limit the pope's authority within their national boundaries.[180] One of the great contemporary questions is whether, as the relative power of the nation-state recedes in the face of such entities as the European Union and the multinationals, religion itself will not have a resurgence as a vehicle for imparting identity.

Although many Enlightenment thinkers and rulers continued to be highly nationalistic, against this background, one can read the quest for "universal rights" and "perpetual peace" from the Enlightenment to the present as an attempt to find some secular replacement for the old idea of Christendom, some United Nations system to replace the Church.[181] Although this has long been presented as a kind of Kantian advance of the law, Foucault was probably closer to the truth when he insisted that the language of constitutions and codes since roughly the time of the French Revolution marks a recession rather than advance of the law: as the state has increasingly lost its age-old function of the sword, of possessing the power of life and death in defense of the sovereign, and following the logic of popular sovereignty has taken on the modern function of fostering the length and quality of life, the law has been increasingly incorporated into the medical and administrative spheres, becoming in the process less juridical and more regulative or normative.[182]

Protestantism could more easily give up the idea of Christendom, that all rulers ruled under the same law, but on both sides of Westphalia the religious divide was far from clean, both between and within countries.[183]

---

178. Luigi Sturzo, *Church and State,* 2 vols., tr. A. Robert Caponigri (Notre Dame, Ind.: University of Notre Dame Press, 1962), II, 273. James Simpson, *Burning to Read: English Fundamentalism and Its Reformation Opposition* (Cambridge, Mass.: Belknap Press, 2007), though eccentric in some of its views, is fundamentally right in its argument that the Protestant Reformers were not the ancestors of liberalism.

179. *Religion and the Modern State* (London 1935).

180. Höpfl, *Jesuit Political Thought,* shows this in detail.

181. James Turner Johnson, "Just War," 21. Johnson does not intend his argument to be against the nation-state per se, which has behaved as well as badly, but against the narrowing of the obligations of the sovereign ruler flowing from Westphalia.

182. *History of Sexuality,* vol. 1, 144. Foucault notes that much of the redefinition of law as regulative has gone under the banner of "rights" (145).

183. See for instance Keith P. Luria, *Sacred Boundaries: Religious Coexistence and Conflict in Early-Modern France* (Washington, D.C.: The Catholic University of America Press, 2005).

Henry II of France (reigned 1547–59), for instance, refused to recognize the Council of Trent (1545–63), fearing the elevation of the pope's authority over the Church in France above his own.[184] An allegorical fresco entitled *The Unity of the State* in the François I Gallery at Fontainebleau (1528) shows Henry's predecessor François I holding a pomegranate, the many seeds in one fruit symbolizing the power gathered in one hand by François. In all kinds of ways, the kings of early modern Europe employed such symbol and ritual to show forth their sacred status.[185] Religion and politics stood in a symbiotic relationship, Luther providing sanction to the Protestant Princes of Germany.[186] Edward Gibbon's (1737–94) *Decline and Fall of the Roman Empire,* perhaps the greatest literary expression of the idea that the Church should serve the state, shows how influential views originating in theocracy were still in the eighteenth century.[187] On the other hand, early Protestant America, as in the person of John Adams, insisted that all people have rights antecedent to government derived from the Creator, and that no government or earthly law could restrain such rights. Government exists not to grant rights, but to protect them. These were ideas Catholics could approve.

The insidious role of the early modern state is presented nowhere more clearly than in Eamon Duffy's portrayal of the manner in which the English monarchy, against the wishes of most Englishmen, undermined late medieval Catholicism, in the process creating a body of anti-Catholic propaganda still widely believed today.[188] Duffy has since shown in great detail how one Catholic village rebelled, was punished, and had Anglicanism imposed on it by Elizabeth.[189] A spate of revisionist histories have followed

184. In general see Paul Kléber Monod, *The Power of Kings: Monarchy and Religion in Europe, 1589–1715* (New Haven, Conn.: Yale University Press, 1999).

185. Sergio Bertelli, *The King's Body: Sacred Rituals of Power in Medieval and Early Modern Europe,* tr. R. Burr Litchfield (University Park: Pennsylvania State University Press, 2001).

186. David M. Whitford, "*Cura Religionis* or Two Kingdoms: The Late Luther on Religion and the State in the Lectures on Genesis," *CH* 73 (2004): 41–62, surveys the wide range of readings of Luther to the present, arguing that the arrangements after the Peace of Augsburg of 1555 would not have been welcomed by Luther, who saw the earlier involvement of princes in religion as necessitated by emergency and not intrinsically desirable. Whitford argues that Luther "repeatedly resisted efforts to coerce religious uniformity and belief by force" (62). The question seems more complicated to me than this. Cf. *Luther and Calvin on Secular Authority,* ed. Harro Höpfl (Cambridge: Cambridge University Press, 1993).

187. Peter Brown, "Gibbon's Views on Culture and Society in the Fifth and Sixth Centuries," *Daedalus* (Spring 1976): 73–86. Harding, *Medieval Law,* is fundamental.

188. *The Stripping of the Altars: Traditional Religion in England, 1400–1580,* 2nd ed. (New Haven, Conn.: Yale University Press, 2005). Richard Rex is another of the Cambridge historians sympathetic to late medieval Catholicism: see his *The Theology of John Fisher* (New York: Cambridge University Press, 1991). Ethan H. Shagan, *Popular Politics and the English Reformation* (New York: Cambridge University Press, 2003), basically approves the type of revisionism represented by Duffy. Helen L. Parish, *Monks, Miracles and Magic: Reformation Representations of the Medieval Church* (New York: Routledge, 2005), tells the story by which Protantism rewrote the medieval past.

189. *The Voices of Morebath: Reformation and Rebellion in an English Village* (New Haven, Conn.: Yale University Press, 2001).

Duffy's breakthrough, for instance, telling us that in the years immediately preceding the Dissolution of the Monasteries (1536–41) the religious orders, especially the Benedictines, rather than being in decay, experienced various forms of institutional reform and intellectual revival.[190]

Such research has been pushed back into the late Middle Ages, and again, instead of the decadence and corruption customarily attributed to late medieval English Catholicism, has found much evidence of health.[191] Studies of such things as the reading of Scripture by laymen in the late Middle Ages have revealed that stereotypes long dear to Protestant polemic need serious rethinking.[192] The decree of the Fourth Lateran Council of 1215 that bishops or their designates must preach regularly is now seen to lie behind a golden age of preaching from the mid-fourteenth to the mid-fifteenth century.[193] In the early sixteenth century the clerical vocation remained popular in England, and recent study suggests a high level of conscientious function among parish priests, who were well integrated into their local communities: it is difficult to sustain the idea that the Reformation in England was a result of popular anti-clericalism.[194] The life of someone like the Jesuit martyr Edmund Campion (1540–81) was played out against a background of Catholic networks and loyalties composed of people clinging to and fighting for their faith.[195] Though there is debate about how widespread or deep were the Catholic practices Duffy details, clearly the changes beginning with Henry VIII had a cumulative force that was revolutionary.[196]

What counted most in early modern state formation was *"Le primat de la guerre,"* the use of force by monarchs to impose their will; as always,

190. *The Religious Orders in Pre-Reformation England,* ed. James G. Clark (Rochester, N.Y." Boydell & Brewer, 2002). For an example of flourishing monasticism, see James G. Clark, *A Monastic Renaissance at St. Albans: Thomas Walsingham and His Circle c. 1350–1440* (New York: Clarendon Press, 2005). For the religious policy of Henry VIII himself, see G. W. Bernard, *The King's Reformation: Henry VIII and the Remaking of the English Church* (New Haven, Conn.: Yale University Press, 2005).

191. *The Church and Learning in Late Medieval Society: Studies in Honour of Professor R. B. Dobson,* ed. Caroline Barron and Jenny Stratford (Donington, England: Shaun Tyas/Paul Watkins, 2002).

192. A. Gow, "Challenging the Protestant Paradigm: Bible Reading in Lay and Urban Contexts of the Later Middle Ages," in *Scripture and Pluralism. Reading the Bible in the Religiously Plural Worlds of the Middle Ages and Renaissance,* ed. T. J. Heffernan and T. E. Burman (Boston: Brill, 2005).

193. *A Macaronic Sermon Collection from Late Medieval England,* ed. and tr. Patrick J. Horner (Toronto: Pontifical Institute of Mediaeval Studies, 2006).

194. Tim Cooper, *The Last Generation of English Catholic Clergy: Parish Priests in the Diocese of Coventry and Lichfield in the Early Sixteenth Century* (Rochester, N.Y.: Boydell & Brewer 1999).

195. Gerard Kilroy, *Edmund Campion: Memory and Transcription* (Burlington, Vt.: Ashgate, 2005). On the clandestine community at Cambridge University, see Stephen Greenblatt, "Who Killed Christopher Marlowe?" *NYRB* 53, 7 (2006): 42–46 at 44.

196. James Simpson, *The Oxford English Literary History,* vol. 2, *1350–1547: Reform and Cultural Revolution* (New York: Oxford University Press, 2002).

those intellectuals were particularly valued who provided a rationale for the emerging order.[197] In England only when he had written two-thirds of *The Laws of Ecclesiastical Polity* did the great Elizabethan theologian Richard Hooker (1553/54–1600) come to realize how far the Elizabethan Settlement had departed from the ideals of his hero, Thomas Aquinas. The Settlement was a monarchy dominating a church, not the two functioning in harmony. The honest Hooker's work remains unfinished, for Hooker came to see that Thomism could not be used to justify what was really a lay theocracy.[198]

That Elizabeth, who persecuted Catholics viciously over a long reign, should be called "Good Queen Bess," while Mary, who persecuted Protestants viciously over a short reign, should be called "Bloody," suggests, in addition to the fact that history is written by the victors, the persistence of this anti-Catholic, Whiggish propaganda to the present.[199] Only recently has the notion that, a century later, Oliver Cromwell (1599–1658) treated Catholics benignly, been dismantled: he was little different from the monarchs who preceded him.[200] In the civil war of the mid-century the murderous zeal of the parliamentary forces looted libraries and defaced monuments in a manner recollecting Huguenot barbarism in France earlier, only in turn to be countered by the Restoration of Charles II (1630–85).[201]

State manipulation of religion characterized the French Revolution, with its eventual sale, closure, or destruction of 95 percent of the 2,500 Benedictine monasteries and convents that had existed in France on the eve of the Revolution.[202] "We have no king but Caesar—Caesar—Caesar!"[203]

197. The phrase quoted is the title of the first chapter of Jean-Philippe Genet, *La genèse de l'état moderne. Culture et société politique en Angleterre* (Paris: Presses univeritaires de France, 2003).

198. Peter Munz, "Past and Present Cross-Fertilized," *HS* 5, 5 (May/June 2004): 26–28 at 26.

199. Rafael E. Tarragó, "Bloody Bess: The Persecution of Catholics in Elizabethan England," *Lo* 7, 1 (Winter 2004): 117–33. See also on the newer scholarship, more favorable to Mary, the review essay by Colin Armstrong, "English Catholicism Under Mary Tudor," *CHR* 93 (July 2007): 588–93. Cf. Anne McLaren, "Gender, Religion, and Early Modern Nationalism: Elizabeth I, Mary Queen of Scots, and the Genesis of English Anti-Catholicism," *AHR* 107 (2002): 739–67, and Stephen Greenblatt, "Shakespeare and the Uses of Power," *NYRB* 54, 6 (April 12, 2007): 75–82 at 81 n. 8, on Elizabeth's as the English reign when torture was most used, predominantly against Catholics. Neil Hanson, *The Confident Hope of a Miracle: The True History of the Spanish Armada* (New York: Knopf, 2003), writes a story of the Spanish Armada in which Elizabeth I and Sir Francis Drake are the villains.

200. Albert J. Loomie, "Oliver Cromwell's Policy Toward the English Catholics: The Appraisal by Diplomats, 1654–1658," *CHR* 90 (2004): 29–44.

201. Bray, *Friend*, 256–57, treats Hereford.

202. H. Tristram Engelhardt Jr., "Life & Death After Christendom: The Moralization of Religion & the Culture of Death," *Touchstone* 14, 5 (June 2001): 18–26 at 23. On the following, see Nigel Aston, *Religion and Revolution in France, 1780–1804* (Washington, D.C.: The Catholic University of America Press, 2000).

203. These are the words used by John Tavener in *The Myrrh-Bearer* (1993) as "the ultimate denial of God": John Tavener, *The Music of Silence: A Composer's Testament*, ed. Brian Keeble (London: Faber and Faber, 1999), 75.

All church lands were designated national property in 1789, and the religious orders were suppressed the next year. The Civil Constitution of the Clergy of 1790 was perhaps the most ruthless exercise in "lay theocracy" yet, though it followed in general outline the pattern of control of the Church established by Henry VIII. A national church was established in which all clergy had to swear loyalty to the Revolution. Initially many if not most refused, and Counter-Revolution was found in many places, but, from 1793, especially in the west of France. On March 11 of that year about a thousand Counter-Revolutionaries, largely peasant farmers attempting to defend the Church against attacks coming from the Revolutionary government, converged on the town of Machecoul. Over the following weeks they killed many of the Revolutionary officials, and began the War of the Vendée, which though apparently involving the deaths of more than 100,000 people, was largely ignored by nineteenth- and twentieth-century historians.[204] The response was the Terror. We need not detail the Terror and the subsequent history of the Jacobin Republic, but the course of the Jacobinism which subsequently runs through French history had been set.[205] All French universities, ecclesiastical institutions from their foundations, were dissolved, to be refounded by Napoleon after the Revolution under state control.[206]

All through the nineteenth century, in spite of—or in alliance with—the recovery of religion, political religion was enthroned, with the deification of nation and state, arguably to issue in the bitter fruit of twentieth-century totalitarianism.[207] Both left and right participated. Pius IX penned his *Syllabus of Errors,* warning about nationalism, but the left vilified him, as it continues to do. It must be said that Pius like many churchmen missed many opportunities.[208] Yet as Bishop Dupanloup of Orléans wrote in defense of his intransigence in the matter of nationalism, "Where do we find it written 'Outside the *Code Napoléon* there is no salvation'?"[209] In France, the attack on the Church continued. University status was taken away from Catholic

204. Edward J. Woell, *Small Town Martyrs and Murderers: Religious Revolution and Counterrevolution in Western France, 1774–1914* (Milwaukee, Wis.: Marquette University Press, 2006), and François Furet, "Vendée," in *A Critical Dictionary of the French Revolution,* ed. Francoise Furet and Mona Ozouf (Cambridge, Mass.: Harvard University Press, 1989), 169. Cf. Alan Forrest, *Paris, the Provinces and the French Revolution* (New York 2004).

205. The foregoing is taken from John Merriman, *The Stones of Balazuc: A French Village in Time* (New York: W. W. Norton, 2002), 62–66, where one can find the history of Jacobinism as it has affected one village to the present.

206. Christopher Dawson, *The Gods of Revolution* (London: Sidgwick & Jackson, 1972), 55.

207. On the revival of French Catholicism in the 1830s, see Philip Mansel, *Paris Between Empires: Monarchy and Revolution, 1814–1852* (New York: St. Martin's Press, 2003), as at 305.

208. Burleigh, *Earthly Powers.*

209. Quoted in Hittinger, "Churches of Earthly Power," 30. Hittinger's interesting analysis views the political thought of Leo XIII as motivated by the judgment "that Catholicism had not responded adequately to the Enlightenment" (31).

higher educational institutions, and religious education in state schools was prohibited in 1852. Nuns and priests were prohibited from teaching in state schools in 1886, and in the opening years of the twentieth century members of religious orders were prohibited from teaching in any school, causing the closing of thousands of schools.[210] All through the nineteenth century the necessity for government approval of the building of churches meant that the expanding working-class sections of many cities were left almost church-less.[211] After the abrogation of the 1801 Concordat in 1905, most religious orders were banned altogether.

The story varies from country to country, but conflict between liber-alism *(liberté)* and Catholicism is a central theme of nineteenth-century European history. In 1866, for instance, the Italian government decreed the seizure of the houses of all religious congregations.[212] The story of the sei-zure of Church lands by "new men" in the wake of Giuseppe Garibaldi's (1807–82) ventures is a theme of Giuseppe di Lampedusa's *The Leopard.* In Germany the nineteenth-century is filled with a "war against Catholi-cism."[213] As in the United States, where the *New York Times,* already the paper of record for anti-Catholic bigotry, could in 1861 announce that "'in-telligent minds in every country' thought Catholic belief a 'fast-vanishing quality,'" one of the results of such anti-Catholicism could be Catholic re-vival. Many countries experienced such revival at some point in the cen-tury, mass attendance, for instance, becoming more regular, and the aver-age Catholic more willing to seek or accept direction from outside his own national culture, that is, from the pope.[214]

Not all art lovers today, as they tramp from museum to museum, realize that one reason they have to travel so far to see, say, the great altarpieces of the Gothic and Renaissance eras is that the secularizing Napoleonic laws scattered them all over Europe.[215] Many, especially the bourgeois classes, the chief beneficiaries of the half-millennia-long Bourgeois Age which is

210. Hugh McLeod, *Secularisation in Western Europe, 1848–1914* (New York: St. Martin's Press, 2000), 66.

211. Thomas Kselman, *European Religion in the Age of the Great Cities, 1830–1930* (London: Routledge, 1995), 179.

212. Raymond Grew, "Liberty and the Catholic Church in 19th Century Europe," in *Free-dom and Religion in the Nineteenth Century,* ed. Richard Helmstadter (Stanford, Calif.: Stanford University Press, 1997).

213. Michael B. Gross, *The War against Catholicism: Liberalism and the Anti-Catholic Imagi-nation in Nineteenth-Century Germany* (Ann Arbor: University of Michigan Press, 2004).

214. John T. McGreevy, "Catholicism and American Freedom," *HS* (September/October 2004): 25–26, at 26, citing the *Times,* and see Margaret Lavinia Anderson, "The Limits of Secu-larization: On the Problem of the Catholic Revival in 19th-Century Germany," *HR* 38 (1995): 647–70. For Bismarck's culture war against Catholic religion and cosmopolitanism, see R. J. W. Evans, "Mighty Prussia: Rise and Fall," *NYRB* 54, 14 (September 27, 2007): 64–67 at 64.

215. Caterina Virdis Limentani and Mari Pietrogiovanna, *Great Altarpieces Gothic and Re-naissance* (New York: Vendome Press, 2002).

just closing, had much reason to be on the side of the nation-state, and to favor strong monarchs.[216] But there can be no doubt that the culture wars of the present are deeply rooted in especially the secular-Catholic conflict of the nineteenth century, that is, in either advocacy of or resistance to the manipulation of religion.[217]

The consummation of this manipulation of religion was achieved in movements such as Nazism or in "the universal nationalization of everything, and thus the nationalization of human beings" found in the twentieth-century totalitarianism flowing from Marxism, with its vicious persecution of religion and elimination of God as the most dangerous possible points of resistance to the final subjection of everything to the state.[218] Here the goal was the final destruction of religious institutions, which had been still imperfectly attained in spite of the best efforts for more than a century of the European left; perhaps, as in the case of Nazism, the replacement of traditional with a new religion. A contemporary liberal form of this subjection of all to the state is Cass Sunstein's proposal that, because strong religious beliefs threaten civic peace, the liberal state must as "a divine instrument" force the intolerant to be tolerant.[219] The more Orwellian among contemporary liberal thinkers, such as Amy Gutmann and Dennis Thompson, allow systems of state education to violate the rights of believers.[220]

Few really understand that the practice of Marxism or the proposals of a Sunstein both ratify habits of state found round the world. The argument of the present analysis has been that the ancient hope of the Church to form society has in the modern age given way to a very similar hope, now practiced by most states, whatever they call themselves. This is particularly advanced in a country such as France, where from the Revolution there has been in the name of *liberté*—this is the supreme irony—an attempt to control ever more aspects of life, many more than ever any medieval government, especially the Church, attempted. As de Tocqueville recognized, this pattern of state control traces back to the increasingly efficient bureaucracy of the *ancien régime,* which through an expanding use of experts by stages fostered modern technocracy.[221] As the Marquis de Condorcet expressed

216. John Lukacs, *At the End of an Age* (New Haven, Conn.: Yale University Press 2002), 15–17.

217. *Culture Wars: Secular-Catholic Conflict in Nineteenth-Century Europe,* ed. Christopher Clark and Wolfram Kaiser (New York: Cambridge University Press, 2003).

218. Leszek Kolakowski, "What Is Left of Socialism?" published first in *FT* 136 (October 2002): 42–46 at 44, and then in *My Correct Views.*

219. Cass Sunstein, *The Partial Constitution* (Cambridge, Mass.: Harvard University Press, 1993), quoted in James Hitchcock, "The Enemies of Religious Liberty," *FT* 140 (February 2004): 26–28 at 27. The use of the phrase "a divine instrument" continues the cynicism and inability of the lay tradition, already obvious in Hobbes, to found its views on anything more than arbitrary will and power, some fairy tale such as the myth of the social contract.

220. *Democracy and Disagreement* (Cambridge, Mass.: Belknap Press, 1996).

221. P. N. Furbank, "The Scientific Takeover," *NYRB* 52, 9 (May 26, 2005): 39–40 at 39.

it in the Plan of Public Instruction at the end of the eighteenth century, French education should henceforth be scientific, a bulwark against medieval superstition.[222]

The forms of public control ever advance, especially in the most intimate aspects of life. In France the state intervened in abortion in 1975, in contraception in 1976, in the donation of sperm in 1978, in the donation of embryos in 1984, and so it goes.[223] More and more the consciences of people are compelled by the state, and no place is found for conscientious objection to state policy. No matter that Catholics may regard a given practice as immoral, the state increasingly forces them to act against their consciences if they wish to continue participating in public life. A given individual may come down in favor of or against a given state intervention, but the massive fact behind the pattern of intervention is the presence of a "lay confession" which effectively or commonly constitutes a new lay church. In a provocative book centering on France, Marc Fumaroli has called the outcome the "culture state," the replacement of religion by culture, or culture as religion, to the end of the continual propagandization of the populace.[224]

⌒

What commonly happened in the so-called Wars of Religion of the seventeenth century was that secular rulers and the nobility took advantage of religious division to unify their states and territories.[225] One part of this was the substantial achievement of the old dream of subordinating religion to politics.[226] This was to remain a pattern, reappearing in the manipulation of confessional antagonism in the nineteenth century by Prussia to achieve German unification.[227] That is, these wars were more caused by national and royal ambition than by religion. Religious controversy often was a pre-

222. Ibid., 39.

223. Dominique Memmi, "Verso una confessione laica? Nuove forme de controllo pubblico dei corpi nella Francia contemporanea," in *Corpi e storia: Donne e uomini dal mondo antico all'età contemporanea,* ed. Nadia Maria Filippini, Tiziana Plebani, and Anna Scattigno (Rome: Viella, 2002), 229–49 at 229.

224. *L'État culturel: Une religion moderne* (Paris: Editions de Fallois, Libraire générale française, 1991).

225. William T. Cavanaugh, "'A Fire Strong Enough to Consume the House': The Wars of Religion and the Rise of the State," *MT* 11 (1995): 397–420; "The City: Beyond Secular Parodies," in *Radical Orthodoxy,* ed. John Milbank, Catherine Pickstock, and Graham Ward (New York 1999), 182–200; and *The Theopolitical Imagination: Christian Practices of Space and Time* (Edinburgh: T & T Clark, 2003), esp. 9–52.

226. Always there are degrees, and of course no early modern state achieved the control of religion found in the totalitarian states of the twentieth and twenty-first centuries. On the range of subgroups found in pre-modern European society, see John Van Engen, "Introduction: Formative Religious Practices in Premodern European Life," in *Educating People of Faith: Exploring the History of Jewish and Christian Communities,* ed. John Van Engen (Grand Rapids, Mich.: Eerdmans, 2004), at 18, 20–21.

227. Marjule Anne Drury, "Anti-Catholicism in Germany, Britain, and the United States: A Review and Critique of Recent Scholarship," *CH* 70 (2001): 98–131, at 111–13. Cf. David Martin, *Does Christianity Cause War?* (New York: Oxford University Press, 1997).

text that made possible the "Wars for the Unification of the Nation-State." Arguably one of the benefits of the reduction of the Empire to Austria after the Thirty Years War was Austria's relative lack of a historical identity, and therefore of nationalism. In Austria was possible a Baroque Catholic culture with a universalist spirit more akin to medieval Christendom than to the modern state.[228] In the British Isles, by comparison, we have had the attempt of more than half a millennium by England to make Ireland a Protestant state, in which religion has been the locus of resistance.[229] By today, it is the papacy itself which virtually stands alone as the advocate of a universal humanity tied to a universal faith. None of this means that religion was not a troublesome matter and a cause of trouble in the sixteenth and seventeenth centuries, but that to see it as the singular cause of the wars during this period is to accept the narrative of these events first written by the apologists of the monarchy and since approved by a liberalism anxious to reduce religion to a private sphere so as itself to dominate the public sphere, and anxious to redefine the state as the protector of property, rather than the protector of the spiritual order.

A reading of early modern history which gives insufficient attention to the drive of the state to control religion is as inadequate as thinking that the events some years ago in Kosovo were more about religion than about nationalism or the ambitions of individual leaders.[230] The common wisdom has been that problems in the Balkans are caused by "ancient ethnic hatreds."[231] But according to scholars such as Misha Glenny, John B. Allcock, and Mark Mazower, "violence among ethnic or religious communities is . . . more the consequence than the cause of Balkan instability."[232] Glenny

228. Thus Dawson, *Dividing of Christendom,* 22, 156–62, 168–70. Robert Darnton, "A Euro State of Mind," *NYRB* 49, 3 (February 28, 2002): 30–32, in giving a very laicist view of what constitutes Europe (the Enlightenment), and in almost completely neglecting Christendom, nevertheless stresses the destructiveness of nationalism, attributing to Enlightenment universalism and cosmopolitanism the broadening of horizons Dawson attributed to Christendom.

229. Marcus Tanner, *Ireland's Holy Wars: The Struggle for a Nation's Soul, 1500–2000* (New Haven, Conn.: Yale University Press, 2001).

230. Timothy Garton Ash, "Kosovo: Was It Worth It?" *NYRB* 47, 14 (September 21, 2000): 50–60, is a perceptive survey which remarks: "The deepest cause of the Kosovo war was that, since the emergence of modern Serbian and Albanian nationalisms from amid the crumbling Ottoman Empire, political and intellectual leaders of both nations had repeatedly told their peoples that they could only be fully themselves if they had this territory as part of their own national state" (52). See the new introduction, "The Resumption of History in the New Century," to Daniel Bell, *The End of Ideology: On the Exhaustion of Political Ideas in the Fifties* (Cambridge, Mass.: Harvard University Press, 2000), xi–xxviii, which argues that the fall of communism signaled the return of traditional conflicts, ethnic and religious.

231. See the review of scholarship by Richard Crampton, "Myths of the Balkans," *NYRB* 48, 1 (January 11, 2001): 14–18.

232. Ibid., 14, describing the argument of Misha Glenny, *The Balkans: Nationalism, War and the Great Powers* (New York: Viking, 2000). All three authors mentioned tend to see an imported modern nationalism as central to the problems of the Balkans. Cf. Neal Ascherson, "In the Black Garden," *NYRB* 50, 18 (November 20, 2003): 37–40, with the darker view that many

further argues that in the eastern Balkans the weakness of civil society partly is the result of the supineness of the Orthodox Church in the face of the
state: the persistence of theocratic or caesaro-papist structures, the weakness of the church before the nation-state, has harmed civil society.[233] In
such matters it is always difficult to determine what is cart, and what horse.
The twelfth-century historian 'Abd al-Wahid al-Marrakushi described "the
natural lightness with which . . . [the feared Almohads of North Africa]
shed blood," but does this mean that Islam fostered bloodiness, or that a
people habituated to bloodiness, having become Muslim, shocked fellow
Muslims with their barbarity?[234]

I do not want to be misunderstood. I am not trying to lay the groundwork for a return to some integralist past, though I do think it a misreading
of the Second Vatican Council—a misreading almost universal in the United States—to say confessional states are now out of bounds for Catholics.[235]
Such states merely, in my opinion, are not in the European or American
cards. And in important ways, aspects of the so-called secularization of the
past two centuries have been good for religion and good for man. Often
loss and gain have gone hand in hand. The secularization of time designated by the expression "the time of the merchants," in which time becomes
money, or the national unification of time which allowed Count Helmuth
von Moltke (1800–91) to choreograph the muster of German troops for the
Franco-German war of 1870–71, advanced various worldly purposes; but
one can regret the destructiveness such efficiency made possible, as well
as the loss of a time centered on the liturgical calendar.[236] Much that was
taken as sacred well beyond the *ancien régime* was ultimately properly secularized, that is, given an autonomy appropriate to it. As regards the Church
itself, two generations after the French Revolution five of every six bishops

---

ethnically mixed communities have been held together by the shared fear of some strong outside
authority: when this authority is removed, the communities' tolerance for each other dissolves.

233. Crampton, "Myths of the Balkans," 16.

234. "The Admirable in Abridgment of the News of the West," tr. John A. Williams, in *Medieval Iberia: Readings from Christian, Muslim, and Jewish Sources,* ed. Olivia Remie Constable
(Philadelphia: University of Pennsylvania Press, 1997), 185–89 at 188.

235. I give my argument against the common misreading in "The Meaning of Christian
Culture: A Historical View," in *Catholicism and Secularization in America,* ed. David L. Schindler (Notre Dame, Ind.: Communio Books, 1990), 98–130 at 114–15, and will return to this
question in the final chapter. See also Thomas Storck, *Foundations of a Catholic Political Order*
(Beltsville, Md.: Four Faces Press, 1998), esp. ch. 2 and appendix 2. There seems to have been
some slippage in the meaning of "integralist" in the recent past. I understand the traditional
modern European reference to be to a regime in which Church and state are closely allied. During a visit to France in the summer of 2004, I noticed the usage of much of the press seemed
to have become more militantly laicist: any presence of religion in public life now received the
label "integralist."

236. Peter Galison, *Einstein's Clocks and Poincaré's Maps: Empires of Time* (New York: W. W.
Norton, 2003); see also Donald A Yerxa, "Einstein's Clocks, Poincaré's Maps: An Interview with
Peter Galison, Part I," *HS* 5, 2 (November 2003): 5–9 at 6.

in France were still appointed by the state. The Austrian Emperor vetoed a papal conclave as recently as 1903.[237] Certainly it has been to the advantage of the freedom of the Church to be released from subjection to such lay theocracy.

Another way of putting this is to say that, alongside the continuing presence of a lay theocratic tendency in European political life seeking to keep religion in the control of the state, there has been a second tendency, sometimes called secular, to find in the political order a relative autonomy protecting citizens from all unlimited government, whether of state or Church, giving a constitutional practice more under law than individual will. This "secular" tendency, rooted ultimately in the fact that Christianity was born in an imperial setting in which Roman law provided practices not specifically derived from any revealed religion, is what we do not generally find in regions which have not known significant Christian influence. Thus Roger Scruton argues in addressing globalization that there is a fundamental gulf between those nations stemming from the Roman and Christian tradition which have formed states with the rule of law, and those nations which are not really states at all, but pre-national personal fiefdoms.[238] Traditional Islam, because it does not recognize a "secular" law or government, tends to the latter condition of life.

This lack of compatibility between the Arab world and the Western democracies would be present even if the West became more religious than it currently is. It is not so much democracy as a form of political life as it is constitutionalism and a state with bounded authority which keep personal, national, and religious excess in bounds. Thus the argument of Richard A. Posner that democracy today should not be understood as a system of direct participation in government by each citizen.[239] This would be undesirable, since effective government demands time and expertise beyond what the actual citizen has and can give. Democracy in its political sense rather is a way of competing for power through regular elections. It does not aim at rule by the wise or good, but at the stability orderly succession provides. Finally, it provides a means for the generality of humans to limit the tendency of those in power to use government to enrich themselves.[240]

⌒

237. This data is taken from Russell Hittinger, "Christ and the Sanctification of the *Saeculum*," *Magnificat* 22 (September 2000): 5–7 at 5.

238. *The West and the Rest: Globalization and Terrorist Threat* (Wilmington, Del.: ISI Books, 2002), on this and the following. Scruton's tendency to view the nation-state as the greatest of Western achievements—a view the present writer does not share—is something of an antidote to the political naiveté of the radical orthodox, which tends to under-appreciate the goods that have come from the nation-state.

239. *Law, Pragmatism, and Democracy* (Cambridge, Mass.: Harvard University Press, 2003).

240. Anne Barton, "The Romantic Survivor," *NYRB* 52, 20 (December 15, 2005): 24–26 at 25.

A third premise of my analysis is anti-utopian or anti-perfectionist. In the words of Pope John Paul II's 1991 encyclical *Centesimus Annus* (25), the great danger is that "politics becomes a 'secular religion' which operates under the illusion of creating paradise in this world."[241] This, including the idea that (perfect) social harmony is possible, which as Isaiah Berlin pointed out has no basis in lived experience, is one of the most debilitating of the Enlightenment inheritances: "an ideal for which more human beings have, in our time, sacrificed themselves and others than, perhaps, for any other cause in human history."[242] Mao Zedong (1893–1976), apparently believing that human nature itself could be changed and that he was the instrument of cosmic transformation, exempted himself from the normal rules of morality, killing millions in the process.[243] It is not that harmony is not desirable, but that conflict and disagreement are permanent characteristics of social life. The repression practiced by the Communist regimes was not the result of backwardness or the misapplication of theory, but of the "resolute attempt to realize an Enlightenment utopia."[244]

The philosophical and literary idea of utopia is much older than the Enlightenment, witness Plato, and various expressions of it run through Jewish and Christian history. The Dead Sea Scrolls, for instance, reveal a sect trying to create in the present the purity of the end times.[245] More than a thousand years later, after many Jewish and Christian messianic and millenarian movements, we find an attempt to give utopia visual form in "The Ideal City," a painting attributed to Luciano Laurana (ca. 1430–79), and now in the Palazzo Ducale in Urbino. Not surprisingly this picture of an urban landscape, or rather of a number of buildings, is all measured (mathematical) perspective and lacks human beings altogether, in impact as cold and unappetizing as the social arrangements found in Thomas More's *Utopia*. We find the opposite of this detachment in the passions of the nineteenth century, perhaps nowhere more than in Auguste Comte's (1789–1857) bizarre proposal that the earth's path be changed from circular to elliptical to favor a more moderate climate. Here all the absurdities of

241. Quoted with discussion in Richard John Neuhaus, "The Liberalism of John Paul II," *FT* 73 (May 1997): 16–21 at 20.

242. Although Berlin does not seem to me to have been a thinker of the first rank, he made many shrewd judgments on prudential matters: John Gray, "The Case for Decency," *NYRB* 53, 12 (July 13, 2006): 20–22 at 21 for the quotation. Gaabril Motzkin, *Time and Transcendence: Secular History, the Catholic Reaction, and the Rediscovery of the Future* (Dordrecht: Kluwer Academic Publishers, 1992), as at 145, is a powerful statement of the need to think of society as necessarily imperfect.

243. Jung Chang and Jon Halliday, *Mao: The Unknown Story* (New York: Knopf, 2005).

244. Gray, "Case for Decency," 21. The novels of Vladimir Sorokin are unrelenting examinations of Soviet utopianism and its transmutations to the present: Christian Caryl, "Ice Capades," *NYRB* 54, 14 (September 27, 2007): 60–63.

245. Shemaryahu Talmon, *The World of Qumran from Within: Collected Studies* (Jerusalem: Magnes Press, 1989), 273–300.

nationalism, belief in technology and progress, and utopianism united.[246]

The valuing of prudence and the Christian tradition's accompanying sense of the intrinsic limits of the temporal realm—exemplified by Thomas Aquinas's explanation of why, though human or positive law is to lead one to virtue, one should not aim at a perfectly virtuous world (*ST* I-II, Q. 96, A. 2)—has tended in the Kantian liberalism considered especially in chapter 5 of the present book to be replaced with the idea of progress toward perpetual peace.[247] Indeed in large perspective the body politic of Kant and Hegel is utopian, "one in which heaven takes the place of a contingent and imperfect earth."[248] There is a profound ambiguity about the question of whether perfection is ever achieved, or whether always we are "on the way," blocked from final attainment by something the existence of which liberalism can but deny or ignore. The teaching of Kant's *Theory and Practice* (1792) is not only the duty of constant progress, but the duty to hope for a world state. Three years later the very title *Toward Perpetual Peace* expresses the idea that utopia is not yet: we are only "on the way." In liberal as well as Marxist thought this "on the wayness" puts off forever any precise accounting, while implicitly recognizing that human perfection is unattainable.[249]

Again and again "the delusion that man is by nature good" and therefore must progress works itself out.[250] Machiavelli suffered from no such delusion, and is a touchstone for the more "realistic" idea that political changes are dangerous: people get used to one form of government or another, and if a government works tolerably, it is best to leave well enough alone. The temptation always is to think that one's own historical moment presents a unique opportunity for "a comprehensive elimination of evil."[251] There never will be some one best regime gathering all under its umbrella. History will always have to be given its due, and as Montesquieu saw, laws will always have to be adapted to local conditions.

In his first encyclical, *Deus Caritas Est,* having stated that the political task cannot be the Church's immediate responsibility, Benedict XVI warned of the Church itself becoming utopian: "The Church cannot and must not take upon herself the political battle to bring about the most just

---

246. Hittinger, "Churches of Earthly Power," 27, commenting on Burleigh, *Earthly Powers.*

247. Robert Kraynak, "The Illusion of Christian Democracy," *CSSR* 9 (2004): 87–95 at 87.

248. Michael Mack, *German Idealism and the Jew: the Inner Anti-Semitism of Philosophy and German Jewish Responses* (Chicago: University of Chicago Press, 2003), 4–5.

249. Kolakowski, *My Correct Views,* explains with reference to Marxism why the work of the dictatorship of the proletariat, the transformation of society, is never done, and thus the end in view, the withering away of the state, never achieved. Kolakowski lays bare the central (soteriological) myth of Marxism, that a communal way of life can be grounded in individualism.

250. Weaver, *Ideas Have Consequences,* 9. For Christianity humans of course are ontologically good, but in history seriously flawed.

251. Frederick Christian Bauerschmidt, "Confessions of an Evangelical Catholic: Five Theses Related to Theological Anthropology," *Co* 31 (2004): 67–84 at 83.

society possible" (no. 28).[252] Here lies the false but seductive idea that the state can become so just as to eliminate the need for charity. Mother Teresa was sometimes criticized for spending her time ministering to the individually poor and sick, rather than fighting for a society that would eliminate poverty and sickness. The pope warns that though such a fight is admirable, it is not sufficient: "In the end, the claim that just social structures would make works of charity superfluous masks a materialist conception of man: the mistaken notion that man can live 'by bread alone.'" Love "will always prove necessary even in the most just society. There is no ordering of the state so just that it can eliminate the need for a service of love. . . . There will always be suffering which cries out for consolation and help. There will always be loneliness. There will always be situations of material need where help in the form of concrete love of neighbor is indispensable" (no. 28).

One may forget the most elementary facts of existence, say the fact that impermanence is of the very essence of living in history. "Here we have no abiding place." My attitude is close to that of *The Rebellion of Beasts*, possibly by Leigh Hunt, a little monarchist exercise in pessimism of 1825 leading to the conclusion that, however justified they are in the beginning, revolutions—and republics themselves—generally come to a bad conclusion. We note that many of the great modern converts to Catholicism, G. K. Chesterton and Christopher Dawson among them, not only were rebels against modernity, but shared a vivid sense of original sin.[253] One does not have to be a convert to Catholicism to appreciate the horrors of modernity, and in a wonderfully dystopian book, *House of Meetings*, which in depicting the unending bloodiness of Stalin's Russia suggests the folly of Enlightenment hope and confidence in human reason, and therefore of most of the assumptions of the modern world, Martin Amis has joined hands with Joseph de Maistre before him to depict the world as an altar on which unending immolation takes place.[254]

In the twentieth century, utopianism mightily affected religion itself, and the social gospeler Walter Rauschenbusch went so far as to write:

We have the possibility of so directing religious energy by scientific knowledge that a comprehensive and continuous reconstruction of social life in the name of God is within the bounds of human possibility.[255]

True religion and the life of the mind is greatly disadvantaged by such views, though we might wish to describe Rauschenbusch as liberal rather

252. This and the following quotations are taken from the Vatican translation, Libreria Editrice Vaticana 2005.

253. Adam Schwartz, *The Third Spring: G. K. Chesterton, Graham Greene, Christopher Dawson, and David Jones* (Washington, D.C.: The Catholic University of America Press, 2005).

254. John Banville, "Executioner Songs," *NYRB* 54, 3 (March 1, 2007): 14–17.

255. Quoted in McClay, "Continuing Irony of American History," 22.

than utopian. In some ways this is a fine distinction, for liberalism generally shares with a more full-blown utopianism a neglect to take seriously the burden of evil carried by the race, and consequently plans for imaginary futures impossible to attain. Thus the marked tendency in mainline Protestantism of recent generations, a tendency now increasingly found among Catholics, to view war itself as something humanity might eliminate "because of the increasing perfection of human social institutions."[256] Oddly, this "Kantian" view of the possibility of universal peace often persists among those who have grown skeptical of the universal anthropology and rights theory on which it was historically grounded.

The first truths on which any decent political life must be founded are acknowledgment that people are seriously flawed, that therefore by definition all government will be imperfect and should pursue modest goals, and that until the end of history the wheat and tares will grow together.[257] It was not just Augustine (354–430) who saw all this: a recent book has observed that, precisely because most bishops of his day had to serve as judges, if only informally, their common conclusion was that justice cannot be guaranteed in this world and is more a quality of the next life.[258] Although certain of the American Founding Fathers were not convinced that humans are seriously flawed, for the most part all these first truths of a decent political life were acknowledged at the beginning of American history. This in part is why generally Americans of the late eighteenth century described themselves as republicans, not as democrats. It was not seen as desirable to replace one form of tyranny, the monarchy of George III, with another, democracy, and the Declaration of Independence and Constitution never use the word "democracy," but speak of "a Republican Form of Government" (Constitution, IV, Section 4).[259]

From roughly the 1840s, however, in spite of such obvious limitations as restricting the vote to white men, a democratic ethos prevailed, and the idea of equality reshaped important areas of (especially Protestant) life, among other things, making the hierarchical character of Catholicism a sticking point just at the time waves of Catholic immigrants were entering the country. John T. McGreevy has observed that as Americans in general became more enthusiastic about democracy, the papacy and elements of the

256. James Turner Johnson, "Just War," 15.

257. John F. Quinn, "Why *Is* He a Catholic? Garry Wills' Spiritual Odyssey," *FCSQ* 27:2 (Summer 2004): 12–23 at 16. John Kekes, *The Illusions of Egalitarianism* (Ithaca, N.Y.: Cornell University Press, 2003), explains the illusionary character of unwarranted faith in basic human goodness.

258. Kevin Uhalde, *Expectations of Justice in the Age of Augustine* (Philadelphia: University of Pennsylvania Press, 2007).

259. According to John Adams, "Democracy never lasts long. It soon wastes, exhausts, and murders itself. There was never a democracy yet that did not commit suicide." Quoted by Walter E. Williams. "True 'Democracy' Was Never What Our Founders Intended," *DMN,* January 5. 2005, A15.

Roman Catholic Church in America were becoming less so.[260] Again, different ideas of freedom were involved, and the hierarchical Church could not easily be content with the expansion of personal freedom as increasing numbers of Americans understood this. This was one of the reasons favoring an affiliation of Catholicism and the Democratic Party: both thought of capitalism—and democracy itself—as merely means to social goods, not things to be pursued for themselves. The primary category was not individual will or freedom, but the common good.[261]

The present analysis separates itself from those who think democracy the form of government most suited to human beings as they are, and regards the spread of the ideology of democracy with a kind of Tocquevillian awe and horror.[262] This needs some elaboration, and here I follow not de Tocqueville, who because he had a somewhat superficial understanding of philosophy and theology is not finally an adequate guide, but Chesterton, the writer of the most profound book on America ever written, *What I Saw in America,* one that few Americans—indeed few American historians—are familiar with. Chesterton has done about as good a job as can be done at getting at the nature of the irrationalism and voluntarism that undergird democracy in its modern, liberal, American form. The first thing to be said is that American democracy is unintelligible without its dual ancestry in the Enlightenment and in Protestant Christianity. It is the latter which is of interest here, for the idea of democracy as we find it in America springs from the Christian idea that humans are made in the image of God and thus are each of infinite worth. This does not mean that they are equal in their talents or in any observable way, but equal in their dignity. In agreement with this insight, when Pope John Paul II spoke of democracy, what he primarily intended was not a form of governance at all, but the notion that all humans have God-given rights, including the right to a constitutional order that protects their rights.

At the beginning, most Americans believed that their equal dignity was a gift from God, and this idea is enshrined in the Declaration of Independence. Then in the First Amendment we have, not the later liberal idea that the amendment creates a right, but the idea that government cannot impinge on the religious liberty that comes from natural right.[263] The histori-

260. *Catholicism;* and see the amusing commentary by Ribuffo, "American Catholic Church," 26–27. Steven D. Smith, *Getting over Equality: A Critical Diagnosis of Religious Freedom in America* (New York: New York University Press, 2001), explores the incoherence of doctrines of equality.

261. Ribuffo, "American Catholic Church," 27.

262. For an introduction to some of the central questions, see Paul Woodruff, *First Democracy: The Challenge of an Ancient Idea* (New York: Oxford University Press, 2005).

263. Thomas J. Curry, *Farewell to Christendom: The Future of Church and State in America* (New York: Oxford University Press, 2001).

cal career of liberalism since roughly the mid-nineteenth century has been to downplay man's divine origin while trying to retain an idea of equality, now either undefended or placed on some secular premise.[264] But there is no such premise, and an honest thinker acknowledges that if we follow reason and observation, what is striking about humans is their natural inequalities, their unsuitability for democracy.[265] Their natural form of governance is by elites. Only by, so to speak, going against the facts can we affirm that humans are made for democracy. Absent the revelation that man is made in God's image, that is, absent dogma, it is only brute willfulness or sentimentality that can assert that men are in any sense equal: "Any secular groundwork was 'a sentimental confusion, full of merely verbal echoes of the older creeds.'"[266] A new generation of French historians, some of whom regard the French Revolution as a disaster, has been saying similar things about French history, Pierre Chanau going so far as to suggest that, removed from its Christian background, the French trinity *(liberté, egalité, fraternité)* is dangerous, and that if one has the Lord's Prayer and the Ten Commandments, the Declaration of 1789 is unneeded.[267]

The historical role of liberalism and pragmatism in American history has been precisely to ground democracy in willfulness or sentimentality, and refuse to discuss the question further. If we are Christians, we may be democrats (though confusion would remain, for we would not have answered the "natural" or philosophical objections to democracy), but if we deny the existence of the God of the three Abrahamic religions, we have no right at all to democracy. Rule by the *demos,* the people, is always possible as one of the disordered forms of government feared by virtually every pre-modern political thinker, but there can be no grounding in any-

264. It would take a big book to trace the evolution from Plato's or Aristotle's idea that humans are by nature unequal to modern notions that they are by nature equal. Probably pivotal here would be "slippage" from Christian ideas of the essential equality or equal dignity of all humans to more political ideas of equality. The ninth-century Carolingian reform bishop, Jonas of Orléans, probably presuming the Augustinian definition of "natural" as "prelapsarian," for instance, held both for the essential natural equality of all humans and for an inequality of capacity in humans as we actually find them after the Fall: see *De institutione laicali* 2.22 and 3.14, *Patrologiae cursus completus. Series Latina,* ed. J.-P. Migne (Paris 1800–75) vol. 106.213A–215B, 259B, and *De institutione regia ad Pippinum regem,* 5, in the same volume, 294BC, echoing the Council of Paris of 829, *Concilium Parisiense 829* 2.3, *Monumenta Germaniae Historica, Concilia,* 2: *Concilia aevi Karolini,* 2 vols., 2nd ed. Albert Werminghoff (Munich 2003), p. 654.11, and the article of David Appleby, "Sign and Church Reform in the Thought of Jonas of Orléans," *Viator* 27 (1996): 11–33. Alain Finkielkraut, *In the Name of Humanity: Reflections on the Twentieth Century,* tr. Judith Friedlander (New York: Columbia University Press, 2000), begins with a history of the ideal of universal humanity which explains the difference between ancient and medieval universal and modern egalitarian ideals.

265. I have worked this out in "John Rawls and the Flight from Authority: The Quest for Equality as an Exercise in Primitivism," *In* 21 (1994): 419–36, and see the last chapter below. The present analysis depends on McCarraher, "Remarks on John McGreevy's Catholicism," 28.

266. Ibid., 29, quoting Chesterton.

267. See Steven Kaplan, *Farewell Revolution: The Historians' Feud: France, 1789/1989* (Ithaca, N.Y.: Cornell University Press, 1995), 40.

thing other than religion for such ideas as that people are equal or—a more complicated question—deserve equal rights. This—that the American idea of democracy presumes biblical religion—is what de Tocqueville did not clearly see, and what is at the heart of Chesterton's book. To the extent that democracy makes sense, it makes sense rooted in Christian, not secular, ground. Secularism is the insidious enemy of democracy because it encourages, or is incapable of giving any but pragmatic reasons for limiting, all the awful developments the cataloguing of which began the present book, laissez-faire capitalism, unlimited science and technology, and an instrumentalist or pragmatic understanding of reason.

A decent political life is based on acknowledgment that good and evil are, on the one hand, objective categories, and, on the other hand, found in each person. Insofar as this is possible, government is obliged to encourage good and curb evil. Neutrality toward all claimed conceptions of the good of the form advocated by John Rawls's liberalism is not something desirable, but the destruction of shared human life. The liberal model of politics presumes good and reasonable persons, but this precisely may not be presumed; and it aims at things not of this world, equal freedom and resources.[268] The utopians will always have their proposals, forcing the religious or sane man to be negative, to say "this will not work," but of course this religious or sane man, because not himself a utopian, will have no alternative grand schemas of his own. It is frustrating, like being surrounded by laughing people at a Michael Moore movie.

Tzvetan Todorov, who considered the totalitarian impulse to be the one truly original twentieth-century contribution to political development, sees this impulse as virtually always promoted by those with a vision of a better world: Nazism in particular has been portrayed as in its earliest stages a variety of utopian remedies to socio-political crisis.[269] Though many on the left, such as Eric Hobsbawm and George Bernard Shaw, were "slow learners" in regard to the Soviet experiment, fortunately elements of the left, as well as the right, have come to see the dangers of such totalitarianism.[270] Hobsbawm now acknowledges that his dream of international harmony and good will has crumbled.[271]

268. Again explained by Kekes, *Illusions.* What I say is not intended as an apology for deep disparity in property, but as an attack on egalitarianism and wishful thinking.

269. *Hope and Memory: Lessons from the Twentieth Century,* tr. David Bellos (Princeton, N.J.: Princeton University Press, 2003). Roger Griffin, Review, *AHR* 109 (2004): 1530–31 at 1531, discusses Nazism as utopianism.

270. François Furet, *The Passing of an Illusion: The Idea of Communism in the Twentieth Century,* tr. Deborah Furet (Chicago: University of Chicago Press, 1999), and Michael Scott Christofferson, *French Intellectuals against the Left: The Antitotalitarian Moment of the 1970's* (New York: Berghahn Books, 2004).

271. *The Age of Extremes: A History of the World, 1914–91* (New York: Vintage Books, 1994). Emmet Kennedy, "Simone Weil: Secularism and Syncretism," *JHS* 5 (2005): 203–25 at 216–17, considers Weil's opinions of Shaw and others who praised Stalin.

The same growth in the capacities of government which characterized the early modern period and resulted in the increasing ability of the state to control the Church also increased the temptation to try to realize the most ancient utopian dreams of the race. Humans could be manipulated in ways hardly contemplated earlier, and the road to totalitarianism was opened. Two styles of politics, in Michael Oakeshott's formulation, appeared.[272] One, typified by Francis Bacon, believed that the chief goal of politics was the perfection and improvement of the material conditions of life, and for this the chief instrument is government. It seeks power and wishes always to expand the range of things governed. It expresses a kind of faith, but in the ability of government to bring about human perfection. The other style of politics could not bring itself to believe any of these things, and indeed views them as dangerous, and in this sense is characterized by skepticism. It sees the government's primary responsibility as the preservation of order. Though I think the contrasts should not be so starkly drawn as Oakeshott does, I also think the politics of skepticism is much closer to the truth.

I take human beings to be seriously flawed, as well as capable of greatness. They have powerfully irrational and antisocial inclinations which must be moderated by many things, above all law and the learned habits we call civility. Freedom understood as the ability to choose between alternatives is a sine qua non of a properly human existence, not its end, and therefore freedom must not trump things higher than itself such as the transcendentals, whether expressed philosophically as the good, true, and beautiful, or in a religious form. History and customary ways of doing things must play a large role in human calculations, if they are not to end in disaster. This means that we should be reluctant to undermine, in the name of something more perfect, modes of life which have served well enough. Although military intervention by a country or countries in the life of another is sometimes necessary, this should be for the cause of providing the security on which all human development depends, and not to spread democracy. It is fine with Roman jurisprudence or the Enlightenment to seek for some best law system, some law most suited to human nature which should be applied to the entire race, for this opens the range of human possibility before us, but we should not apply this jurisprudence without attention to the ways that history is unlikely to be overridden. Above all, we should not insist that all political regimes should look alike. We must abandon "the illusion that there is only one way of being modern, one way of being democratic, and one way of building and managing a free economy."[273]

272. For this and the following, see Michael Oakeshott, *The Politics of Faith and the Politics of Scepticism,* ed. Timothy Fuller (New Haven, Conn.: Yale University Press, 1996); see also Peter Berkowitz, "The Styles of Modern Politics," *FT* 72 (April 1997): 38–42 at 39.

273. M. A. Casey, "How to Think About Globalization," *FT* 126 (October 2002): 47–56, at 55.

Robert P. Kraynak, whom we will consider at some length in the last chapter, is right to insist that there is no necessary connection between Christianity and liberal democracy, and that liberal democracy is not the only form of government which secures human dignity, if indeed it does that.[274] Though our strong preference should be for political systems with an explicit constitutional and legal order, we must abandon the idea that all must be democratic (it is in this sense that we should be open to the possibility of a confessional state, open to the possibility that in some historical tradition such a state works, not "best," but well enough). A particularly lethal combination since the late eighteenth century has been the tying of the idea of "reconstruction," the remaking of an entire society, to the idea of war as mission, "the use of coercive force to impose betterment on those who are deemed ignorant or evil."[275] One writer has argued that World War II never ended, but changed into the cold war when America realized it had not achieved its aim of imposing democracy and free enterprise on Europe.[276] Writing on the place of America in the twenty-first century, Robert Skidelsky says: "The most important need today is not to create a universal democracy—a parliament of the world—but to restore collegiality among those countries which, however unevenly, have power to shape the future."[277]

Large and abstract schemas of social renewal such as the French Revolution, Communism, and Wilsonian democracy, while always having something good that can be said about them, have tended toward the disastrous.[278] Two hundred years of Russian utopianism, infecting almost all shades of political opinion and only modestly tempered by the thought of an Ivan Turgenev (1818–83) or Boris Slutsky (1919–), have exacted a terrible price.[279] Overridden was Turgenev's sense that freedom could as much be threatened by revolutionary radicalism and a doctrine of historical necessity

274. *Christian Faith and Modern Democracy: God and Politics in the Fallen World* (Notre Dame, Ind.: University of Notre Dame Press, 2001). This book makes searching critique of all personalist positions, including that of Pope John Paul II, arguing that it has not been wise to incorporate so much of Kant into current Catholic thinking.

275. Donald A. Yerxa, "Cultures of Defeat: An Interview with Wolfgang Schivelbusch," *HS* 5, 2 (November 2003): 16–17 at 17.

276. Gregor Dallas, *1945: The War That Never Ended* (New Haven, Conn.: Yale University Press, 2005).

277. "The American Contract," *Prospect Magazine,* July 2003, quoted in Brian Urquhart, "'A Great Day in History,'" *NYRB* 51, 1 (January 15, 2004): 8–10 at 10.

278. Ronald Steel, "Mr. Fix-It," *NYRB* 47, 15 (October 5, 2000): 19–21, and "The Missionary," *NYRB* 50, 18 (November 20, 2003): 26–35, are excellent discussions of Wilson's heritage. See also the comparison between Wilson and Theodore Roosevelt in James Chace, "TR and the Road Not Taken," *NYRB* 50, 12 (July 17, 2003): 35–38 at 36–37, and Andrew J. Bacevich, "Does Empire Pay?" *HS* 4, 4 (April 2003): 32–33. Michael M. Uhlmann, "The Supreme Court Rules," *FT* 136 (October 2003): 26–35 at 28, makes shrewd comments on how progressivism prepared the way for Wilson's views.

279. Aileen Kelly, "The Secret Sharer," *NYRB* 47, 4 (March 9, 2000): 33–37 at 35, and

à la Hegel as by authoritarianism.[280] Sometimes, as in the case of Stalin himself, it is difficult to distinguish between utopianism and madness.[281] Following a line of thought already laid out by Dostoevsky in *The Possessed*, Richard Pipes, arguing against the common view that terrorism is born in poverty or oppression, sees it rather as a kind of self-destructive urge in which the utopian instinct is a pretext for violence.[282]

In a brilliant essay, Aileen Kelly has shown how the Russian socialist obsession with eradicating the pre-socialist past, which we might understand as a form of modernism defined as assault on the past and attempt to sever the future from the past, resulted in having virtually no present at all.[283] Evermore defining themselves by machine culture, and not a little influenced by the ideas of Frederick Winslow Taylor, the American "father of time-and-motion study," Russians came to live in a future defined by accelerating production processes.[284] The present was constantly devalued in the name of a bright future, resulting in Homo Sovieticus:

> Passive in the face of authority, infinitely pliable in his behavior and values, with no horizons beyond the needs of the moment . . . this unappetizing creature was the end product of the first attempt in the modern age to realize a Western utopia.[285]

John Gray sees a common descent from the Enlightenment through the Soviet experiment, which of course viewed as a kind of modernization had many American supporters, to both Al Quaeda and the neo-liberal dream of a worldwide free market.[286] He knows that one does not have to be a wide-eyed fanatic to be taken in by such dreams, and sees that the belief that globally life is converging can take a "business-utopian" form.[287] It is doubtful whether in Russia even all the disarray caused by rapid transition to a market economy, with its attendant corruption and crime, permanent-

---

Anthony Grafton, "Stoppard's Romance," *NYRB* 54, 9 (May 31, 2007): 30–33 at 32. Anthony Grafton, "Over the Rainbow," *NYRB* 47, 19 (November 30, 2000): 4–6, reviews recent books on utopianism more generally, including that promoted by futurism, Nazism, and communism.

280. Gray, "Case for Decency," 22.

281. Ian Buruma, "Master of Fear," *NYRB* 51, 7 (May 13, 2004): 4–6.

282. Orlando Figes, "Murder, Russian Style," *NYRB* 51, 6 (April 8, 2004): 52–55 at 53–54.

283. "In the Promised Land," *NYRB* 48, 19 (November 15, 2001): 45–48, on this and the following.

284. Mauro Guillén, *The Taylorized Beauty of the Mechanical: Scientific Management and the Rise of Modernist Architecture* (Princeton, N.J.: Princeton University Press, 2006), tells Taylor's story, and connects him to the modernist architecture discussed in the next chapter below.

285. "In the Promised Land," 48.

286. *Al Qaeda and What It Means to be Modern* (New York: New Press, 2003). David C. Engerman, *Modernization from the Other Shore: American Intellectuals and the Romance of Russian Development* (Cambridge, Mass.: Harvard University Press, 2003), is a searing indictment of those who allowed universalistic visions to justify great suffering.

287. "Global Delusion," 20–21, especially approving Daniel Cohen, *Globalization and Its Enemies* (Cambridge, Mass.: MIT Press, 2006).

ly dampened the utopian tendency, but some Russians now, in advocating "managed democracy," speak with an unaccustomed modesty about what politics can achieve.[288]

❧

Though Americans have always been tempted by the tradition of Benjamin Franklin, the "can-do" attitude which sees no limits to what is possible, speaking modestly used to be a respectable mode of discourse in the United States. Famously, Abraham Lincoln warned his countrymen against the change of character that would follow from a shift from republic to empire. In the 1840s he was one Whig opposed to the doctrine of Manifest Destiny, to the notion of a continuing expansion of the United States. Americans should be proud of what they had achieved, but not attempt to export it. Further, he thought "self-interest," often viewed as part of the Whig program, as sapping the strength of democracy, and held that if there was a conflict between the man and the dollar, the man should prevail.[289] Such views incarnate a modesty and prudence about the political order far removed from utopianism. These sensibilities presumably have been especially found among those labeled conservative, but have not been the sole possession of any political party. Franklin Delano Roosevelt, for instance, is usually considered among the more progressive American presidents, but what president would now dare repeat his words, spoken in a fireside chat during the Great Depression, "It is common sense to take a method and try it: if it fails, admit it frankly and try another."[290] Roosevelt, too, thought that Americans should not imitate European colonialism, should not be a colonial power.

Again, how realistic the words of another Democrat, John F. Kennedy, now sound: "We must face the fact that the United States is neither omnipotent or omniscient . . . that we cannot impose our will upon the other 94 percent of mankind—that we cannot right every wrong or reverse each adversity."[291] How far such statements are from the rampant utopianism of J. F. K.'s Democratic successor, Lyndon Baines Johnson, who in 1965 said of his proposal for the Great Society, "I want to be the President who helped to end hatred among his fellow men and who promoted love among the people of all races, all regions, and all parties. I want to be the President who helped to end war among the brothers of this earth."[292] This is but

288. Christian Caryl, "Window on Russia," *NYRB* 50, 9 (May 29, 2003): 26–29 at 29. Vladimir Putin gives "managed democracy" a sinister meaning.

289. David Bromwich, "How Lincoln Won," *NYRB* 53, 16 (October 19, 2006): 46–49.

290. Quoted in James Chace, "The Winning Hand," *NYRB* 51, 4 (March 11, 2004): 17–20 at 17.

291. Quoted in Arthur Schlesinger Jr., "History and National Stupidity," *NYRB* 53, 7 (April 27, 2006): 14–16 at 16.

292. Quoted in Richard John Neuhaus, "Explaining the Strange Death of American Lib-

a secular—and compared to the rhetoric of "defeat of terrorism" or "victory over evil," relatively peaceful—rendition of the sense of mission which has defined America from the beginning.[293] Wilson had made the national myth of exceptionalism into a doctrine of international action, and Johnson was pleased to express this in the most utopian terms.[294]

During the early cold war the language was often of bringing freedom and democracy to Eastern Europe, but when the crunch came in November 1956, President Eisenhower, who never had any intention of militarily helping the Hungarian insurgents, pulled American troops away from Hungary. An argument can be made that this was the prudent thing to do, but such actions reveal the immense gap between the language of the spread of freedom and democracy, and the realities of power.[295] Americans, typically modern in their resentment of the past because it confuses them—no need to discuss American education here—and because it inhibits them, are almost always characterized by the shallow optimism that comes from ignorance of history, and hence are particularly prey to schemes of perfectibility.[296]

Ronald Reagan was a particularly interesting case. Usually classified a conservative and very important in the demise of Communism, in important ways he was closer to Thomas Paine than Edmund Burke. Reagan liked to quote Paine's "we have it in our power to begin the world over again," and it has been argued that he made the 1980s into an "Emersonian moment," in which Romanticism and Transcendentalism were united.[297] Another tag Reagan liked to quote was Emerson's "no law can be sacred to me but that of my nature." Some took Reagan's preternatural calm for stupidity and sloth, but arguably he had an Emersonian confidence in his own

eralism," *FT* 120 (February 2002): 83–86 at 85: he writes, "There is an unforgettable scene in Lincoln Steffens' *Autobiography* which tells of a proposal made by Clemenceau at the Versailles Peace Conference. The astute Frenchman, having listened to much talk that this was a war to end war forever, asked Wilson, Lloyd George, and Orlando whether they were taking the idea seriously. After obtaining assent from each of the somewhat nonplussed heads of state, Clemenceau proceeded to add up before them the cost. The British would have to give up their colonial system, the Americans would have to get out of the Philippines, to keep their hands off Mexico; and on and on it went. Clemenceau's colleagues soon made it plain that this was not at all what they had in mind, whereupon the French realist bluntly told them that they wanted not peace but war."

293. William Pfaff, "The American Mission?" *NYRB* 51, 6 (April 8, 2004): 24–28 at 28.

294. William Pfaff, "Manifest Destiny: A New Direction for America," *NYRB* 54, 2 (February 15, 2007): 54–59 at 55.

295. Tony Judt, "A Story Still to Be Told," *NYRB* 53, 5 (March 23, 2006): 11–15 at 14.

296. Weaver, *Ideas Have Consequences*, 176–77. Weaver goes on to discuss the idea that the sexes are equal as one of the results of utopian rather than historical thinking. That is, the members of classes as large as a sex could only be thought of as equal if viewed as a mathematician might view them, devoid of all their historical characteristics. His larger idea is that equality destroys fraternity, and that the relation between the sexes can take the form of one or the other, but not both (178).

297. Quoted by George Will, "Conservatives Must Temper Worship of Reaganism," in *DMN*, February 11, 2007, G4, used in what follows.

internal light that trumped all else, and an Emersonian God: not a God of judgment, but a God of approval. In a very shrewd book, John Patrick Diggins suggests that this was a religion that enabled the forgetting of religion, and further that Reagan was so popular because he rarely blamed individuals for malfeasance, and never suggested that much that didn't work was a direct result of the limitations of democracy.[298] It was not the individual or democracy that was the source of social evil, but, largely, government. Hence Reagan's idea, expressed in his first Inaugural Address but even more popular after his death, that "we [Americans] are all heroes." Granted, this idea was first expressed at a time when very serious problems such as the Iranian hostage debacle were faced by the country and Americans needed "bucking up." A case can be made that Reagan's lofty rhetoric was "just what the doctor ordered." Still, the sobriety and pessimism of any serious conservatism has completely disappeared in flattery of the *demos* and populist utopianism.

Having both Reformation Protestantism and Enlightenment Republicanism as its forebears, the American sense of mission has sometimes taken the form of changing the rest of the world by example, sometimes the form of changing it by force. Perhaps no nation has much to be proud of here, but the brutality and arrogance of Protestant American culture, expressed in so much from genocide directed against Indians, through harassment of Mormons, to the anti-Catholicism which runs through American culture to the present, complicates any claim to be God's special agent.[299] There seems to have been deep (self?) deception here, expansionism and quest for wealth, sometimes using violence, made into a providential and progressive story. In such a story Abraham Lincoln with a certain distaste for the Protestant millennialism that identified the Union cause with God's kingdom come on earth, comes as something of a relief with his language of Americans as God's "almost chosen people."[300]

Part of the schizoid quality of the form of Protestantism in which the United States originated was the simultaneous Calvinist insistence on human depravity and on our duty to create, if not heaven on earth, "Genevas."[301] Again and again the resultant sense of mission has led to war, "to

---

298. *Ronald Reagan: Fate, Freedom, and the Making of History* (New York: W. W. Norton, 2007).

299. McCarraher, "Remarks on John McGreevy's Catholicism," 30, commending Mark Massa's study of anti-Catholicism [*Anti-Catholicism in America: The Last Acceptable Prejudice* (New York: Crossroad, 2003)] for its insistence on how dominant this tradition remains. In the same issue of *HS* (September/October 2004), see Thomas Schoonover, "Uncle Sam's War of 1898 and Globalization," 36–37, on the War of 1898. The point is not that the United States was worse than other nations in its behavior, but that it was not markedly better.

300. James Nuechterlein, "Lincoln Both Great and Good," *FT* 165 (August/September 2006): 36–41 at 41.

301. Neither Huntington, *Who Are We?* nor his reviewer, Richard John Neuhaus, "To Be

the conquest of Indian lands, the expulsion of first the French and then the British Empires, western expansion, . . . and America's accession to global power status after 1914."[302] Of course, America's entrance into World War I was more something thrust on it than desired, and the United States has continued to waver between isolationism and expansionism. Still, World War I was a "war for righteousness" waged by a messianic America.[303]

To foster democracy worldwide is very far from traditional conservatism, with its distrust of grand theories and utopian projects.[304] The European country that matches the United States in hubris is France, also forged in revolution, and, not surprisingly, we often find the projects of these two countries at loggerheads.[305] The "cost of empire" has always been a matter of debate, and at a deeper level, one can doubt that rational imperialism, if it ever was possible, works in the contemporary world, especially for democracies, which tend to be unwilling over the long run to pay empire's costs.[306]

In regard to America's tremendous expansion since 1940, the wise George Kennan wrote: "To see ourselves as the center of political enlightenment and as teachers to a great part of the rest of the world [is] unthought-through, vainglorious, and undesirable. . . . This planet is never going to be ruled from any single political center, whatever its military power."[307] Even Arthur Schlesinger Jr. acknowledged that constitutional democracy is not the wave of the future: "The world got along without democracy until two centuries ago, and there is little evidence that constitutional democracy is likely to triumph in the century ahead."[308] A fact always underestimated in advocacy of democracy is the mind-deadening level of education to which democracies have tended. It is not just that "American voters are jaw-droppingly ignorant about politics," it is that they are jaw-droppingly ignorant of almost everything. One must stand in astonishment before such proposals as that

American," *FT* 145 (August/September 2004): 89–97 at 94, though both producing worthy studies, seem to me adequately to take the measure of the deep contradictions of the Protestantism on which America was built, which have persisted to the present.

302. Linda Colley, "Tough Guys," *NYRB* 51, 8 (May 13, 2004): 40–41. See also Robert Kagan, *Dangerous Nation* (New York: Knopf, 2006).

303. Richard M. Gamble, *The War for Righteousness: Progressive Christianity, the Great War, and the Rise of the Messianic Nation* (Wilmington, Del.: ISI Books, 2003).

304. Arthur Schlesinger Jr., "The Making of a Mess," *NYRB* 51, 14 (2004): 40–43 at 40, using the thought of Anne Norton to explain the departure of neoconservative thought from conservatism.

305. Thus Ian Buruma, "The Indiscreet Charm of Tyranny," *NYRB* 52, 8 (May 12, 2005): 35–37 at 37.

306. Tony Judt, "Dreams of Empire," *NYRB* 51, 17 (November 4, 2004): 34–38, at 38.

307. Richard Ullman, quoted in Pfaff, "American Mission?" 24. See also Paul Kennedy, "Mission Impossible?" *NYRB* 51, 10 (June 10, 2004): 16–19, discussing the various reasons why Americans cannot "hack it" on a world stage, and why a looming American fiscal crisis is virtually inevitable.

308. Arthur M. Schlesinger Jr., *War and the American Presidency* (New York: W. W. Norton, 2004), quoted in James Chace, "Empire, Anyone?" *NYRB* 51, 15 (October 7, 2004): 15–18 at 16.

we institute a "deliberation day" before elections, as if a day of focus groups could remedy the systemic failures of an educational system in which there is "no child left behind."[309] There has to be something diabolical about an educational system and culture in which people are encouraged to express opinions about things of which they know nothing, as if "one man's opinion is as good as another's." There is something astonishing about studies which show how willingly people will express themselves even when questioned about nonexistent policies and legislation.[310]

Again, I do not want to be misunderstood. The very fact of having a shared experience suggests that every nation or culture must have some form of exceptionalism, some way in which it thinks of itself as different from all the others. This is not in itself bad. Most modern nations, whether in significant degree secularized or not, also have a sense of mission. There is probably a good and bad form of most senses of mission. The American mission is seen most plausibly when it is formulated as Margaret Thatcher did in her eulogy at the funeral of President Reagan on June 11, 2004, saying that what America stands for is "freedom and opportunity for ordinary people." One would have to qualify even such aspirations, but at least they seem on the surface more desirable than seeing the mission of America as imposing democracy on the world.

Surveying history since 1945, David Reynolds sagely concludes that the world is not moving toward an "American" norm. In the words of his reviewer: "Even the developed capitalist societies exhibit a protean range of social forms with varying proportions of public and private ownership and very different attitudes toward both the market and the state."[311] Francis Fukuyama was wrong to suggest that the human search for a civilizational model was over with the discovery of democracy/capitalism.[312] Part of the wave of utopian credulity incident on the fall of Communism from 1989, Fukuyama was only one of those who thought a more peaceful and prosperous world was a-borning, when all the end of the cold war marked was an unfreezing of history that allowed an earlier clash of states and religions to resume.[313] William Pfaff has a better grip on the facts when, observing the insistence of India and China that they sit at the same consumerist table as the West, he foresees a world of unceasing struggle and perpetual war.[314] There is indeed something to be said for the view of historians such

---

309. Alan Ryan, "Time Out?" *NYRB* 51, 16 (October 21, 2004): 51–53, does not come close to taking the measure of the foolishness contained in Bruce Ackerman and James S. Fishkin, *Deliberation Day* (New Haven, Conn., Yale University Press, 2004).

310. Ryan, "Time Out?" 51.

311. Judt, "Story of Everything," 67.

312. *The End of History and the Last Man* (New York: Free Press, 1992).

313. Joshi and Skidelsy, "One World?" 19.

314. Mishra, "Cautionary Tale," 11, also noting Pfaff's belief that even today others can recognize spiritual distinction in a nation.

as John Elliott and James Muldoon, who observe that we are now in a position to appreciate the early modern dynastic state as it existed before the centralized nation-state.[315] In some ways, such states, with their welter of ways of dealing with problems of sovereignty, language, and ethnicity look less unsatisfactory than they once did.

Because man is a sinner with a marked tendency toward the mediocre, irrational, and particular, we should not expect that human beings will ever come to some common form of life, liberal, totalitarian, or otherwise. Indiscriminate use of the word "democracy" hides how very different the political orders of the world remain. Since liberalism is a taste, ideology, or pragmatic conclusion rather than something philosophically compelling, it should not be the only model for our life in society.[316] Democracy itself, with its persistent tendency to base policy on counterfactual assumptions such as belief in human equality, tends also to the ideological rather than to the philosophical. The Italian philosopher Emanuele Severino goes so far as to argue that contemporary thought has in accepting such ideology and in demanding that the world conform to our projects returned to the age of myth from which Greek philosophy—briefly, as it turns out—delivered us.[317]

⌒

A rather catty reviewer has described the project of the philosopher Hilary Putnam in recent years as being an attempt "to make the world safe for religion."[318] That is a goal of the present book. The hostility of the secular left to religion for more than two centuries now has had many successes, and religion is itself a dead issue for large numbers of people, especially in Europe. But there are others for whom religion remains the center of reality, and others again who are open to some transcendental orientation. If freedom of conscience is to be respected, but balanced against the interests of society, all these points of view must somehow get along, none getting a public order with which he or she is completely comfortable. Some degree of "accommodationism" is in order.[319]

---

315. See Muldoon, *Empire and Order;* and see the review by Peter Hulme, *AHR* 105 (2000): 1270–71.

316. Olsen, "John Rawls." G. A. Cohen, *If You're an Egalitarian, How Come You're so Rich?* (Cambridge, Mass.: Harvard University Press, 2000), seeing justice to be a matter of attitudes as well as rules, attempts to correct Rawls, in the process developing a treatment of equality close to one strand of the Judeo-Christian ethical tradition.

317. *La filosofia antica* (Milan 1984), 33.

318. Simon Blackburn, review of Hilary Putnam, *The Threefold Cord: Mind, Body, and World* (New York: Columbia University Press, 1999) [see esp. "Lecture Two"], in *NeR* April 17 and 24, 2000, in turn reviewed by Richard John Neuhaus, "While We're At It," *FT* 106 (October 2000): 100–101.

319. This is the position I argue for in "Separating Church and State," *FR* 20 (1994): 403–25. Cf. Andrew Kohut, John C. Green, Scott Keeter, and Robert C. Toth, *The Diminishing Divide: Religion's Changing Role in American Politics* (Washington, D.C.: Brookings Institution Press, 2000).

This does not try to reduce religious differences to some lowest common denominator, but, while realizing that this is a compromise rather than some best order, lets the religions and the cultures they form coexist. It takes the lead of those historically bi- or multireligious countries like Germany, which, traditionally seeing that man is by nature a religious animal, have understood that it is the duty of the state not to be neutral toward religion, but to foster it. The goal has not been the reestablishment of some single religion, but the creation of a public order more receptive to religion than that which is found where church and state are strictly separated.[320] In this compromises are worked out between the religions found in each country and then again between the religious population and those who are not religious. While realizing that return to some earlier age is impossible, such an arrangement tries to recapture the high medieval—I hesitate to say "feudal"—understanding of liberty as each sphere of life enjoying its special rights.[321] It tries to avoid the sense, found in the more dysfunctional of multireligious countries, that there is no shared public space in which the various religions share.

An argument of the present chapter has been that we should be prepared to accept a wider spectrum of political regimes than generally the left has been open to, specifically a wider spectrum of hierarchical and non-democratic regimes. The poles of the possible are occupied by the confessional religious state, and by the confessional secular state. Demanded of both poles and of everything between is respect of minority points of view and ways of life. In my judgment this is best done not by aiming at the innocuous, the lowest common denominator, but by encouragement of an attitude of appreciation of legitimate diversity.

320. My former colleague Michael McConnell, using a different set of labels than do I, in describing the various schools of interpretation of the First Amendment to the U.S. Constitution, distinguishes between a separationist position and what he calls a "neutrality interpretation." He does not mean by the latter the liberal understanding of neutrality criticized in the present book, but holds that "the government should deal with religions and churches just as it would with secular institutions." The government should neither favor nor discriminate "against institutions simply because they are religious in nature." McConnell observes that in the United States what has happened until recently is the de facto bribery of religious institutions by the government in which they receive money if they secularize: the quoted phrases are from Shane McCammon, "McConnell Discusses Establishment Clause at Hinckley Institute," *DUC* 110, 43 (October 10, 2000): 1–4.

321. In my view, there have been three particularly important moments in the evolution of *libertas/liberté*. First there was the Augustinian *libertas*, "freedom for," which while precious as an understanding of the condition *(liberum arbitrium)* necessary for man to aim at transcendence, tended historically in the early Middle Ages to theological imperialism, "l'Augustinisme politique" (see Henri-Xavier Arquillière, *L'augustinisme politique: Essai sur la formation des théories politiques du moyen-âge*, 2nd ed. [Paris: J. Vrin, 1955]). Next there was the "Germanic" or "feudal" notion of *libertas* as concrete rights, which saw the role of government especially as protecting the historically evolved rights of each order or sphere of society. Then there was the Enlightenment notion of *liberté*, "freedom from," which is ultimately dissolving of both man's orientation to transcendence and of a shared life in society.

Chapter Three

MODERNISM

To be Greek one should have no clothes:
to be mediaeval one should have no body:
to be modern one should have no soul.

—Oscar Wilde, "A Few Maxims for the
Instruction of the Over-Educated"[1]

Common attribution has André Malraux (1901–76) declaring that the twenty-first century either "will be religious or it will not be at all."[2] Undoubtedly this declaration should be placed with the pronouncements of other great naysayers, the Nietzsches, Kierkegaards, Corteses, and Solzhenitsyns, whom, having said something profound but partial, the age in many ways passes by.[3] Because, as all great spiritual protests, the message of each of these writers is a corrective to its age, an attempt to temper the one-sidedness of some particular worldview; removed from the context of its original appearance, it may seem, or be, one-sided itself.[4] I assume that what Malraux meant in saying that the twenty-first century would be reli-

1. Quoted in Daniel Mendelsohn, "The Two Oscar Wilde's," *NYRB* 49, 15 (October 10, 2002): 18–22 at 20. These words circulate in various forms: Oscar Wilde, *The Complete Works of Oscar Wilde,* ed. J. B. Foreman (London: Book Club 1966), 1203, gives "To be really medieval one should have no body. To be really modern one should have no soul. To be really Greek one should have no clothes."

2. I have been unable to determine that Malraux actually said this. He sometimes said roughly the opposite: Pankaj Mishra, "A Cautionary Tale for Americans," *NYRB* 52, 9 (May 26, 2005): 8–11 at 10.

3. The classic Nietzschean text on the modern European as someone "who makes everything small" is *Thus Spoke Zarathustra*. Robert A. Herrera, *Donoso Cortes: Cassandra of the Age* (Grand Rapids, Mich.: Eerdmans, 1995), is a very good study of what was once taken to be an apocalyptic vision, but remains in fact a diagnosis of the contradictions of modernity. Aleksandr Solzhenitsyn is one of the figures traced by David Walsh, *After Ideology: Recovering the Spiritual Foundations of Freedom* (Washington, D.C.: The Catholic University of America Press, 1995).

4. Peter Henrici, "The Mystery of the Everyday," *Co* 31 (2004): 4–7 at 6. R. R. Reno, "Theology After the Revolution," *FT* 173 (May 2007): 15–21, argues that a number of the thinkers admired in the present book, Henri de Lubac and Hans Urs von Balthasar among them, by

gious or not be at all was that the kind of being that at least the European and American world of the twenty-first century would have without transcendence was a being not worth having. Even post-Christian thinkers like Gianni Vattimo suggest that in the twenty-first century God and religion will again become serious subjects for reflection.[5] Max L. Stackhouse put it this way:

We are just beginning to see the implications of the fall of communism. It was not only the fall of Stalinist centralization, or Leninist power analysis, or Engel's historical materialism, or even Marx's world-historical dialectics. It was the collapse of the entire set of humanist presuppositions that humanity can live without God, that civilization can exist without religion, that humanism can exist without theology.[6]

In the spirit of Malraux, one of the most outspoken theologians of radical orthodoxy, Catherine Pickstock, describes the contemporary city as a necropolis which denies eternity and transcendence.[7] The American thinker Christopher Shannon, who like Dawson insists that the viable goods of the past could only have been preserved as part of a larger spiritual order which modernity has shattered, concludes a study of American social thought: "The bourgeois attempt to construct a rational alternative to tradition has failed."[8] The construction of some such alternative to tradition lay at the heart of what has often been called modernism, which especially in its artistic forms is the subject of the present chapter. In spite of the fact that modernism has been defined in many not always compatible ways, this term has had a primary usage which, better than any other, designates those forms of thought which in turning on the past, exemplify the drive in modern thought to free

---

their (allegedly) intemperate criticism of received scholastic culture pointlessly destroyed much in the theological culture of the Church, including "the theological culture that gave vitality and life to their theological projects."

5. *After Christianity*, tr. Luca D'Isanto (New York: Columbia University Press, 2002).

6. "Humanism After Tillich," *FT* 72 (April 1997): 24–28 at 27.

7. *After Writing: On the Liturgical Consummation of Philosophy* (Oxford: Blackwell Publishers, 1998), 110; see also the review by Richard Cipolla in *Antiphon* 4, 2 (1999): 33–36 at 33. For orientation to radical orthodoxy, see *Radical Orthodoxy: A New Theology*, ed. John Milbank, Catherine Pickstock, and Graham Ward (London: Routledge, 1999), and for criticism, Lawrence Dewan, "On Milbank and Pickstock's *Truth in Aquinas*," *Nova et Vetera*, English edition 1, 1 (2003): 199–212. John Milbank, *Theology and Social Theory: Beyond Secular Reason* (Malden, Mass.: Blackwell, 2006), is a wide-ranging critique of the secular assumptions at the base of much contemporary social and political theory. A Catholic response has been formed by R. R. Reno, *In the Ruins of the Church: Sustaining Faith in an Age of Diminished Christianity* (Grand Rapids, Mich.: Brazos Press, 2002).

8. *Conspicuous Criticism: Tradition, the Individual, and Culture in American Social Thought, from Veblen to Mills* (Baltimore: Johns Hopkins University Press, 1996). For the changing definition of modernity over the last two centuries, see Philippe Bénéton, *Equality by Default: An Essay on Modernity as Confinement* (Wilmington, Del.: ISI Books, 2004), and on the ontology of modernity, choosing the spatial, visual, and written over the temporal, heard, and spoken, see Pickstock, *After Writing*, ch. 3.

humans from God, eternity, and transcendence. The dream of the Enlightenment, consummated in modernism, was that man was moving to maturity, self-direction, and self-perfection. Presumably, if this was true, tradition would no longer be needed and religion itself could be abandoned as a no longer necessary way station to adulthood.[9]

All through the twentieth century in Catholic theology, and from at least Karl Barth on in Protestant theology, there were confrontational theologies which in reasserting the transcendence of both the human person and of God engaged in radical criticism of contemporary culture.[10] Influential philosophers such as Martin Heidegger (1889–1976) expressed their disgust with modernity.[11] And prominent writers such as John Updike in important ways ignored their contemporaries and continued exploration of the "vertical" dimensions of human existence, the sense in which humans live in a cosmos defined by theology.[12] An idiosyncratic thinker such as Eric Voegelin (1901–85), belonging to no institutional religious party, made his life's project the attempt "to shift political science from positivist to transcendental, or 'religious,' foundations."[13] His principal work, the uncompleted *Order and History* (1956–87), was "a five-volume study of the rise and development of human awareness of divine transcendence, and of the resulting order in the soul and society."[14]

Charles Taylor turned an essay to the subject of our disenchanted world.[15] This is the world explored at an earlier stage of its development by William James (1842–1910), a world in which religion, if it survives at all, is defined in a Jamesian way as "the feelings, acts, and experiences of individual men in their solitude, so far as they apprehend themselves to stand in relation to whatever they may consider divine."[16] That is, this is a world oriented to a radical individualism focused on the subjective, almost solipsistic, category "experience," on something inward rather than on tradition, community, or cosmos. These latter categories have been removed from the

9. Peter Gay, *Modernism: The Lure of Heresy: From Baudelaire to Beckett and Beyond* (New York: W. W. Norton, 2008).

10. Some of the principal positions here are nicely described in Rodney A. Howsare, "Trojan Horse in the Catholic Church: On Balthasar's Interpretation of Barth," *FQI* 1 (2001): 275–316.

11. Alexander Nehamas, "Foreword" to Alain Renaut, *The Era of the Individual: A Contribution to a History of Subjectivity*, tr. M. B. DeBevoise and Franklin Philip (Princeton, N.J.: Princeton University Press, 1997), vii.

12. Lorrie Moore, "Home Truths," *NYRB* 50, 18 (November 20, 2003): 16–18 at 16.

13. Glenn Tinder, "The Anti-Gnostic," *FT* 128 (December 2002): 47–51 at 47.

14. Ibid., 48, noting that like Gabriel Marcel, "he understood man's vocation to be the task of entering into the mystery of being," and that the essence of modernity for Voegelin was "a revolt not only against the structure of things but against transcendence itself" (50).

15. *Varieties of Religion Today: William James Revisited* (Cambridge, Mass.: Harvard University Press, 2002).

16. The phrase is quoted from an essay on Taylor's book by Richard John Neuhaus, "While We're At It," *FT* 137 (November 2003): 82–92 at 87.

world as a part of what Mircea Eliade described as profane man's desire to rid or empty himself of the past so that he might be re-created without debt to a sacral universe.[17]

The argument has been made that a range of movements from new age cults to the green movements are linked as popular responses "to the loss of a sense of human connectedness to the cosmos."[18] Malraux's declaration (the twenty-first century "will be religious or it will not be at all") undoubtedly assumed that the religion under discussion was Catholicism, or at least Christianity. William Cavanaugh wonders whether the claims of Christianity to uniqueness, the particularism of the Incarnation, which is not easily assimilated to the homogenizing tendencies visible in much religious syncretism, will not appear increasingly arrogant.[19] Already Hans Urs von Balthasar, envisioning a future which belonged to a "religious man" who would tolerate whatever forms religion might take, had declared that Christianity "demonically questions the unification of the world."[20] This seems the true sense of Malraux's declaration, that the religion of the twenty-first century, to be worth having, must be something specific.

At the end of his life, Balthasar spoke of the modern Western soul as an *anima technica vacua*.[21] David L. Schindler has described our situation in a very arresting way by claiming that homelessness—all the symptoms of a disintegrating society from divorce through fatherless children to the explosion of garbage—is the modern condition.[22] Leon R. Kass rings a variation by describing modern man's desire for perpetual youth and concomitant hostility to having children of his own as an expression of the rejection of even the transcendence which is made possible through procreation.[23] Procreation makes possible a certain transcendence of personal finitude and a recognition of one's own impending death by participation in the work of the genera-

17. *The Sacred and the Profane,* tr. Willard R. Trask (New York: Harcourt, Brace, 1959), 203–4; and see James Hitchcock, *The Recovery of the Sacred* (San Francisco: Ignatius Press, 1995), ch. 4.

18. Stratford Caldecott, "Creation as a Call to Holiness," *Co* 30 (2003): 161–67 at 161.

19. "Balthasar, Globalization, and the Problem of the One and the Many," *Co* 28 (2001): 324–47 at 340.

20. *The von Balthasar Reader,* ed. Medard Kehl and Werner Loser (New York: Crossroad, 1982), 195, quoted in Cavanaugh, "The One and the Many," 340.

21. *Epilog* (Einsiedeln: Johannes Verlag, 1987), 8. Cf. von Balthasar, *Love Alone,* tr. Alexander Dru (New York: Herder and Herder, 1969), 114–15. Von Balthasar was far from rejecting science and technology: he only rejected them insofar as they have developed in terms of a false autonomy of the Baconian sort (knowledge is power) and in terms of a mechanistic understanding of the cosmos. I am guided in all this by David L. Schindler, "Sanctity and the Intellectual Life," *Co* 20 (1993): 652–752, who links these diverse phenomena to a "lack of a sense of being as gift."

22. "Homelessness and the Modern Condition: The Family, Evangelization, and the Global Economy," *Lo* 3, 4 (Fall 2000): 34–56, esp. 36–37.

23. "L'Chaim and Its Limits: Why Not Immortality?" *FT* 113 (May 2001): 17–24 at 23.

tions and devotion to posterity. But modern Western man seems so homeless that he little cares whether he is rooted in the generations or not.

In the past homelessness sometimes stirred a turn to religion. The radical rootlessness of late eighteenth- and early-nineteenth-century American society, for instance, with many people severed from their traditional ties and changing their place of abode every few years, pushed many to seek religious explanations of the bewildering paths their lives had taken, and played into evangelical religion and revivalism.[24] We seem to find something similar today in many postcolonial societies, more generally in traditional societies trying to come to terms with modernity. This is no more poignantly caught than in the novels of R. K. Narayan.[25] It seems evidence that "homelessness," though widely recognized, is far from universally approved and may not necessarily be history's final word.

In a posthumously published book not always clear in its argument, the great art historian E. H. Gombrich observed that periodically in the history of the West we find a mood of "primitivism" in which the achievements of the (in this case artistic) past are deprecated, perversely rejected, or turned from in favor of something less developed or disciplined. Picasso abandons his "blue period" to pursue cubism, pouring into an attack on representation "all the aggression and savagery that was pent up in him."[26] About the same time and striking a note sounded a little earlier by the Italian futurists, one of the leaders of the Dadaists declared that Dada finds its origins in disgust, not art. Though sometimes exhibiting a certain wit, in important ways such movements were little more than howls against the past.[27] As did the Communists, the Dadaists scorned the family, of course even now one of the most fixed ways by which the past retains a grip on the present. Some of the futurists praised the destructiveness of World War I as

24. Gordon S. Wood, "All in the Family," *NYRB* 48, 3 (February 22, 2001): 11–12.

25. Pankaj Mishra, "The Great Narayan," *NYRB* 48, 3 (February 22, 2001): 44–47. Of course for Narayan the "resolution" of this problem is generally unsatisfactory, leaving his Indian characters still caught between the sterility of tradition and a modernity they cannot master, and frequently turning to quasi-religious, dream-like explanations of the world in which they find themselves.

26. Clifford Geertz, "The Last Humanist," *NYRB* (November 26, 2002): 6–10, at 8, citing a 1953 lecture of Gombrich in Geertz's review of Gombrich's *The Preference for the Primitive: Episodes in the History of Western Taste and Art* (London: Phaidon, 2002). Cf. *Antimodernism and Artistic Experience: Policing the Boundaries of Modernity*, ed. Lynda Jessup (Toronto: University of Toronto Press, 2001); *Primitivism and Twentieth-Century Art: A Documentary History*, ed. Jack Flam with Miriam Deutch (Berkeley: University of California Press, 2003); David Cottington, *Cubism in the Shadow of War: The Avant-garde and Politics in Paris 1905–1914* (New Haven, Conn.: Yale University Press, 1998); and *Anxious Modernisms: Experimentation in Postwar Architectural Culture*, ed. Sarah Williams Goldhagen and Rejean Legault (Cambridge, Mass.: MIT Press, 2000).

27. Amelia Jones, *Irrational Modernism: A Neurasthetic History of New York Dada* (Cambridge, Mass.: MIT Press, 2004).

a kind of cleansing, their love of the destructive gesture anticipating some tendencies of Italian fascism.[28]

Today Donald Kuspit goes so far as to argue that the age of art is over because, as the result of such ideas, art no longer has aesthetic import.[29] It has been replaced with "postart," Alan Kaprow's term for the elevation of banality over enigma, scatology over sacrality, and cleverness over creativity. The Poles came up with another term, "neo-oppressionism," for a bundle of modernist ideas taken together. Myron Magnet applies this to one of Christo Javacheff's projects:

For all the cant about the artist as liberator of the human spirit, there is much in contemporary art and especially architecture that seeks to impose upon individuals the artist's vast ego and confine them within it, so that they cannot escape his will. It is this whiff of totalitarianism that makes Polish intellectuals label such architecture "neo-oppressionism."[30]

Javacheff is probably too insignificant a target for such vituperation, but certainly it does apply to much that has gone under the label of modernism.

Sometimes attack on the past has seemed really an attack on so-called high culture itself.[31] The futurists sought the end of museums, libraries, and monuments so that the future could arrive, and, less radically, about the same time Henri Matisse and many of his contemporaries saw their task as the dismantling of the edifice of Renaissance art.[32] Today deconstruction of the works of high culture continues, and there is a marked tendency in so-called cultural studies to concentrate on popular culture, even in the face of the argument that everyone needs transcendence, that is (without denying the possibility of popular culture's opening to transcendence), that everyone needs familiarity with aristocratic culture as an entrance to forms of beauty which explicitly speak of transcendence.[33] Julia Kristeva seems correct in stating that "the defining characteristic of modern art is the absence of a totalizing stylistic profile. Instead, there is a cacophony of multiple and mutually exclusive (or mutually indecipherable) simultaneous

---

28. Charles Simic, "Making It New," *NYRB* 53, 13 (August 10, 2006): 10–13 at 10, for once seems to me too tolerant of nonsense. Very striking is his quotation of Tristan Tzara: "Every product of disgust capable of becoming a negation of the family is Dada . . . *Dada; . . .* [is abolition] *of every social hierarchy . . . Dada; abolition of memory."*

29. *The End of Art* (New York: Cambridge University Press, 2004).

30. "The Gates," *New York Sun,* February 16, 2005, quoted in Richard John Neuhaus, "While We're At It," *FT* 153 (May 2005): 60–68 at 67–68.

31. Cf. Robert B. Pippin, *Modernism as a Philosophical Problem: On the Dissatisfactions of European High Culture,* 2nd ed. (Malden, Mass.: Blackwell, 1999).

32. Simic, "Making It New," 10, and Hilary Spurlling, "Matisse's Pajamas," *NYRB* 52, 13 (August 11, 2005): 33–36 at 34.

33. Tracey Rowland, *Culture and the Thomist Tradition after Vatican II* (London: Routledge, 2003), 168. Aidan Nichols, *Redeeming Beauty: Soundings in Sacral Aesthetics* (Burlington, Vt.: Ashgate, 2007), is on how the arts serve as epiphanies of transcendence.

discourses."[34] This is what we would expect of a period in which cultural consensus has broken down and the past has been attacked but no one thing has replaced it. In a certain way it was inevitable that—in spite of the futurists—modernism seek out the museum, for it had largely forsworn the earlier, more public, places in which art had been located.[35]

Sometimes, as in the case of the iconoclasm and destruction of art that attended both the Protestant Reformation and the French Revolution, the attack has been less on high culture per se than on an entire *ancien régime*.[36] "We rejoice in our abandon and are never so full of the sense of accomplishment as when we have struck some bulwark of our culture a deadly blow."[37] The struggle between tradition and innovation is very old, and probably no period of human history has not been marked by it. Even at a time which most people view as hidebound, the early Middle Ages, always there was a struggle between a Church apprehensive about "novelty" and, say, the individual composer of new liturgy: always new things were produced, and always the question was how these were to be related to existing tradition.[38] In the High Middle Ages sculptors often possessed a lively sense of individual achievement.[39] As we will see, even in modernism understood as the rejection of all tradition, tradition must in one or another way be used and addressed.

The struggle between tradition and innovation also influences the roads modern scholarship takes. Kurt Weitzmann (1904–93), arguably at an opposite pole from the modernist instinct, took the history of art to center on iconography, the search for earlier and lost models on which this or that later work of art was based. Such an approach almost by definition emphasized the ways in which tradition has power over the individual artist and work of art, and especially in the assumption that there must be lost models for later works of art, presumed that innovation was a lesser category in comparison with tradition. Though Weitzmann did not deny that each artwork changed the tradition, in an obvious sense for him tradition was the privileged category.[40] By contrast, Meyer Schapiro, while of course

34. As described by Anna Klosowska, *Queer Love in the Middle Ages* (New York: Palgrave Macmillan 2005), 43.

35. Charles Rosen and Henri Zerner, "Red-Hot MoMA," *NYRB* 52, 1 (January 13, 2005): 18–21 at 19, make it clear that there was no simple development here.

36. John O'Malley, *Four Cultures of the West* (Cambridge, Mass.: Belknap Press, 2004), 231.

37. Richard M. Weaver, *Ideas Have Consequences* (Chicago: University of Chicago Press, 1948; reprint 1984), 11.

38. James Grier, *The Musical World of a Medieval Monk: Adémar of Chabannes in Eleventh-century Aquitaine* (New York: Cambridge University Press, 2006), esp. 209–71.

39. Meyer Schapiro, *Romanesque Architectural Sculpture,* ed. Linda Seidel (Chicago: University of Chicago Press, 2006), 33, 86–87, 146.

40. This paragraph is based on a paper by Herbert L. Kesler, "Kurt Weitzmann: The Merit and Madness of Seeking Lost Models," given at the 2007 annual meeting in Toronto of the Medieval Academy of America.

not opposed as an art historian to studying iconography, thought that the importance of "the genealogy of themes" could easily be overemphasized.[41] His point could be applied to any subject with a historical component. Every time a traditional theme is encountered, it must be reconceptualized, looked at to see what new thing was being said this time.

An especially egregious form of anti-traditionalism was found in the British poet William Empson (1906–84), who saw the poet as an outcast sitting in judgment on his society: the artist in suffering isolation and rejection achieves independence.[42] But the ways in which the past can be attacked and the future hailed into existence are unending. For the last generation, the *ancien régime* being attacked has often been Europe, or Western civilization itself. Commonly in these attacks there has been little awareness that there really has not been a homogenous *ancien régime.* For instance, attacks on Europe have often failed to distinguish between "Europe as the Christian tradition," the special target of the Enlightenment, and "Europe as the commercial and industrial novelties introduced by the Industrial Revolution," the special target of much attack on globalization today.

Rémi Brague has shown how misconceived such attack has been: Europe, as a cumulative culture always understanding itself in some form of subalternship to what has gone before, Jewish, Greek, etc., has been the culture least turned in upon itself.[43] It has been the great assimilator of other cultures. Whereas many great cultures have had a certain contentment about the completeness of their heritage, Europeans have generally known that the pasts they have inherited had riches that had since been lost. This is what has made the concept of "renaissance" so distinctly European: in the West there has always been some element of past culture to be reappropriated.

In *Transformations in Late Eighteenth-Century European Art,* the art historian Robert Rosenblum argued that the modern rage for always new beginnings had an especially important source in neoclassical art, with its desire to purge the past of ostentation and return to simplicity.[44] Thus it anticipated minimalism. Rosenblum thought "the desire to wipe the slate clean" a defining characteristic of modern life, and that this gave a kind of continuity to these movements. It took a long time for the attack on elaboration and decoration to take deep roots, witness much of seventeenth- through

41. Linda Seidel, "Introduction" to Schapiro, *Romanesque Architectural Sculpture,* xxxii.

42. John Gross, "The Genius of Ambiguity," *NYRB* 53, 5 (March 23, 2006): 28–31 at 30, noting the unbalanced character of Empson's fulminations against Christianity.

43. *Eccentric Culture: A Theory of Western Civilization,* tr. Samuel Lester (South Bend, Ind.: St. Augustine's Press, 2002).

44. (Princeton, N.J.: Princeton University Press, 1967); see also Herbert Muschamp, "Iconoclastic Art Historian, Seeing the Old in the New," *NYT,* February 28, 2007, B1–B5, for this and the following quoted phrase.

nineteenth-century architecture, but, often driven by the ideals of scientists and engineers, the valuing of simplicity spread, commonly in association with the idea that simplicity was morally superior.[45] Ove Arup thought of modernism not as a style but as a set of beliefs, some social, some aesthetic, involving ideals of practicality and unpretentiousness.[46]

Probably present in much attack on tradition is youthful idealism and perhaps a sense that destruction is beautiful, as we have noted among the Dadaists and was undoubtedly found in Hitler's Germany (indeed, from one point of view, Nazism is the modernist expression par excellence). Since the fall of the Soviet Union a considerable raucousness has characterized Russian letters. In contrast to the relatively recent past, to Pasternak or Solzhenitsyn, everything is now called into question, almost as if after a Soviet interlude, the origins of modernism had been returned to.[47] Sometimes the ideal of the primitive can make strange bedmates, and Hal Foster has shown how modernism has been simultaneously dominated by ideals of the primitive and of the machine.[48] This should not be surprising. The difficulty in defining modernism at all is one effect of its being what Heidegger called a *Stimmung,* not a clear idea but a pervasive mood, shifting and amorphous.[49] David L. Pike has written of a conservative "high modernism" and an "avant-garde" or radical modernism, each generating its own myths.[50]

There is a historical background here. We might say that the great medieval art forms from the time of the Gothic (the Romanesque is too diverse to make this claim for it), and the Baroque too, were constructed to appeal to all, to express the worldview of all, or a worldview with which all could identify.[51] This is especially so of the architecture and music of Bavaria and Austria and continued past the Baroque, no more so than in Vienna, the city of music. In Vienna not only did people of all classes love the same music, the line between serious and popular music was easily penetrated. Undoubtedly in what was in fact a socially quite rigid Viennese society, music served a certain social function in which "the implicit tenet was that

45. Alison Lurie, "When Is a Building Beautiful?" *NYRB* 54, 4 (March 15, 2007): 19–21 at 20.

46. Witold Rybczynski, "Genius in Concrete," *NYRB* 54, 8 (May 10, 2007): 34–36 at 34. For Rybczynski's larger views, see *The Look of Architecture* (New York: Oxford University Press, 2001).

47. Colm Tóibín, "A Thousand Prayers," *NYRB* 53, 19 (November 30, 2006): 50–53 at 52.

48. *Prosthetic Gods* (Cambridge, Mass.: MIT Press, 2004). For background see J. M. Mancini, *Pre-Modernism: Art-World Change and American Culture from the Civil War to the Armory Show* (Princeton, N.J.: Princeton University Press, 2005).

49. Richard J. Bernstein, *The New Constellation: The Ethical-Political Horizons of Modernity/Postmodernity* (Cambridge, Mass.: MIT Press, 1992).

50. *Passage through Hell: Modernist Descents, Medieval Underworlds* (Ithaca, N.Y.: Cornell University Press, 1997); and see the review by William Franke, *Sp* 74 (1999): 808–11.

51. See esp. Robert Harbison, *Reflections on the Baroque* (Chicago: University of Chicago Press, 2000).

beauty begets pleasure, and pleasure begets contentment."[52] But this was hardly a conscious or cynical prostitution of art:

In fact, it was no policy at all, never having been consciously formulated. The state of the arts in Austria sprang quite naturally from a naively mystic faith—not uncommon in Catholic countries—that aesthetic grace was akin to divine grace and that to invest a country with outward beauty would somehow bestow civic virtues that would hold it together inwardly.[53]

We note the parallel between this civic idea that beauty makes the good citizen, and the Orthodox and Catholic idea that liturgy is meant to make one holy or "beautiful for God."[54] In both cases, the mode of thought is quite distant from what we might call Puritan culture, in which beauty is a suspect category, and the function of liturgy, to the extent that liturgy remains at all, is largely didactic, aimed more at good moral formation than at *theosis* or divinization (the living man evermore manifesting the glory of God). Again, in Austria the Baroque vision of life permeated the culture, and was expressed as much in the cherubs above the gate of a modest house as in the great churches. Finally:

Material possessions alone could not change one's social standing in a fixed-status society, and since the public environment was generally delightful, there was less need for private luxury. Consequently, acquisitive drive, the dominant motivating force in open and industrial societies, rarely inspired the Viennese. Their motivation was not so much material success but satisfaction with the task at hand, or, quite often, simply the leisurely enjoyment of the day.[55]

Of course, when modernism came, some of its most radical advocates came from this same society, as if they had eaten too much *sachertorte* and needed their palates cleansed.[56] And yet many visitors still note today in Bavaria and Austria an attachment to tradition and a reluctance to be modern just for its own sake; a certain similarity of spirit to the Southern Agrarians and communitarians of American history; or a certain rejoicing in craftsmanship for its own sake akin to the Beaux Arts traditions or to Antonio Gaudi

---

52. Hans Fantel, "The Land of the Waltz," a thoughtful essay in *Fodor's 93 Austria* (New York 1992), 47–52 at 49, continuing, "The great cities of imperial Austria . . . owe their splendor to the enduring assumption that civic beauty is the key to civic tranquility."

53. Ibid., 49–50.

54. Alain de Botton, *The Architecture of Happiness* (New York: Pantheon, 2006), shows how buildings can improve lives, and see Lurie, "When Is a Building Beautiful," on the long-standing claim for a close association between architectural beauty and the formation of virtue. Modernists such as Le Corbusier still thought architecture should engage in "character formation," but to the end of appreciating technology, democracy, and science.

55. Fantel, "Land of the Waltz," 52. Though this passage seems idealized, it nevertheless draws an important contrast.

56. Carl E. Schorske, *Thinking with History: Explorations in the Passage to Modernism* (Princeton, N.J.: Princeton University Press, 1998), as at 4, on modernism as the detachment of culture from tradition to create a new autonomous space.

in Spain. It has even been argued—and here there is some similarity to Gaudi's "modernism"—that Vienna's fin de siècle modernism had a significant religious dimension.[57]

In the Middle Ages or the early modern period, or still today in places like Italy and Central or Eastern Europe, art was something to be viewed on site, in a church, house, or the town square. Increasingly some especially fine art was separated from work and ordinary life and sequestered in museums and thought of as high art.[58] Now it was only a matter of time that such art should be seen as elitist, as a form of exploitation of the lower orders to make the leisure of the upper classes more enjoyable. No wonder eventually some artists would turn on the tradition that had produced such art and promote a break with the past.[59] But there was no agreement here. This was related to the fatal ambiguity in the idea of modernity.

There has in fact been no single modernity which can take its assured place in the (alleged) progress of history, that is, that can mark a new and definitive stage of the new, but, rather, various competing modernities, and even the occasional anti-modernity or postmodernity, sometimes anticipating the turn to transcendence studied in the present book.[60] Though for a while quite a few thought that architectural history would end with modernism, that is, they could not envisage a style on the far side of modernism, already in the 1970s there were stirrings against modernist architectural orthodoxy, and then, in the midst of modernism, the birth of postmodernism, allowing once again the use of classical motifs.[61] Most of these tendencies are still in process, but we have no reason to believe that generally they are more than competing ways to obtain the high ground for whatever one's own view is of what the future should be. Sometimes, as in the case of Igor Stravinsky (1882–1971), who lacked much of an idea of the future, modern-

57. Robert Weldon Whalen, *Sacred Spring: God and the Birth of Modernism in Fin de Siècle Vienna* (Grand Rapids, Mich.: Eerdmans, 2007).

58. Cf. the treatment of the relation between art and museums, and of the contemporary museum as the paradigm of modernism, in Douglas Crimp, *On the Museum's Ruins* (Cambridge, Mass.: MIT Press, 1993).

59. Christopher Dawson, *The Dynamics of World History*, ed. John J. Mulloy (New York: Sheed & Ward, 1956), 72.

60. See the reflections of Hans Belting, *Art History after Modernism*, tr. Caroline Saltzwedel and Mitch Cohen (Chicago: University of Chicago Press, 2003). Cf. Hilton Kramer, *The Triumph of Modernism: the Art World, 1987–2005* (Chicago: Ivan R. Dee, 2006). John M. Ganim, "Medievalism, Modernism, and Postmodernism in Contemporary Architecture," in *Postmodern Medievalisms*, ed. Richard J. Utz and Jesse G. Swan (Rochester, N.Y.: D. S. Brewer, 2005), 35–46, has illuminating things to say about the role of architects such as Robert Venturi in the interplay between modernism and postmodernism and the recovery of the local and historical in architectural thinking.

61. Martin Filler, "The Getty: For Better and Worse," *NYRB* 53, 18 (November 16, 2006): 47–54 at 47.

ism was not so much a position as an unrelenting need to keep ahead of the pack. A recent book on Stravinsky has shown the burdens he bore as the exemplary modernist, "a man whose constant fear was obsolescence," always needing to come up with something new.[62] More than a few now see in postmodernism a willingness to accept many widespread criticisms of modernism (too individualistic, too rationalistic, too mechanistic) in favor of a worldview more communal, spiritual, and organic.[63]

A fascinating exhibit at the Guggenheim Museum in New York some years ago, called simply "1900," surveyed the kinds of painting and sculpture being done in many places around the world about 1900.[64] Not surprisingly, there was no dominant style, simply a hodgepodge. There was the nihilist or "to hell with everything" form of modernism, which perhaps achieved its apotheosis in Marcel Duchamp (1887–1968), but continued with Jasper Johns, Robert Rauschenberg, Andy Warhol, and Roy Lichtenstein. This stream has not so much engaged in argument as avoided it, becoming almost impervious to serious criticism.[65] The exhibit "1900" posed a number of central questions, such as how important originality is in art. Though the art historians had often presumed that one group of artists was better than another, the exhibit wondered how much, rather, one group was simply different from another, whether there is, or should be, an artistic equivalent of the Whig narrative of progress. In any case, the exhibit showed the difficulty of identifying "the modern," and of applying the label.

A somewhat parallel difficulty enveloped the poet David Jones (1895–1974), who derived inspiration from a turn to the medieval while also expressing a modernist aesthetic.[66] Similarly Paul Virilio, a theoretician of technology, war, time, space, and the modern city, and a convert to Catholicism, is hard to classify.[67] Some label him a postmodernist and some a hypermodernist. Though he allows for progress, he sees this as impossible without undesirable results: every advance involves some form of "integral accident," an inevitable undesired effect of the claimed advance. Further,

62. Stephen Walsh, *Stravinsky: The Second Exile: France and America, 1934–71* (New York: Knopf, 2006). The quotation is from Michael Kimmelman, "All in the Family," *NYRB* 53, 3 (August 10, 2006): 18–21 at 20.

63. M. Francis Mannion, "Toward a New Era in Liturgical Architecture," *Liturgical Ministry* 6 (Fall 1997): 160–72 at 170.

64. On this and what follows, see Richard Dorment, "The Artistic Bloke," *NYRB* 51, 17 (November 4, 2004): 22–25 at 24.

65. James Panero, "A Man Named Jed," *NR* 58, 9 (May 22, 2006): 55–57 at 57.

66. Paul Robichaud, *Making the Past Present: David Jones, the Middle Ages, and Modernism* (Washington, D.C.: The Catholic University Press, 2007).

67. See for instance his *Art and Fear*, tr. Julie Rose (New York: Continuum, 2003); *City of Panic*, tr. Julie Rose (New York: Oxford University Press, 2005); and *The Paul Virilio Reader*, ed. Steve Redhead (New York: Columbia University Press, 2004).

technology tends to separate us from real time and space, erecting, as in television or video games, a kind of second-order or virtual reality. This makes us less wise, as with others we gaze on not the world as it is, but as it has been remade by technology, and in an obvious sense, as technology speeds up, the race belongs to the swift, not the good or the wise. As Jed Perl has put it in two highly combative histories, modernism has been composed of contradictory constructive and annihilating impulses.[68] Further, and here architecture is a particularly good witness, the same art has sometimes been engaged both in the construction of modernity, and in its critique.[69] An art or architecture may be viewed as liberating, or as a signifier of entrapment, as alluring and deadly at the same time. Alberto Giacometti's (1901–66) "revolt against the recent past" can be read as a questioning of modernity itself.[70]

It has been argued that to the degree that modern European societies are secularized, it is not so much because of the presence of a corrosive rationalism as it is because of the disappearance of the memory which is at the heart of religious existence. A religion like Catholicism must in an obvious sense be traditionalist, because it can orient itself in the present only by reference to its past. If most people have forgotten what the past has been—are amnesiac—or have not been taught this past, they will not only be prey to the kinds of gross distortions which compose the Whig view of history, but will also be deprived of the languages of prayer, liturgy, etc., that are carried by a historical tradition.[71] A contemporary situation in which the arts are antagonistic to religious themes exacerbates the problem of historical memory.[72]

This is not to say that tradition is simply to trump change of every kind, and a foundational Christian thinker like Augustine could not emphasize too much that Christianity is not a religion of the eternal return, but of *reformatio in melius* ("reform to the better"), of ever-increasing God-likeness, of making use of the passage of time.[73] The goal is not recapture of the past but perseverance in time to an end only God knows. The artist

68. *Paris without End: On French Art Since World War I* (San Francisco: North Point Press, 1988); and *New Art City* (New York: Knopf, 2005).

69. Hilde Heynen, *Architecture and Modernity* (Cambridge, Mass.: MIT Press, 1999). Cf. Richard Weston, *Modernism* (London: Phaidon, 1996); and *The Paradox of Contemporary Architecture,* ed. Peter Cook et al. (Chichester: Wiley, 2001).

70. Sanford Schwartz, "The Devil and Giacometti," *NYRB* 49, 1 (January 17, 2002): 22–24 at 22.

71. Daniéle Hervieu-Léger, *Religion as a Chain of Memory,* tr. Simon Lee (New Brunswick, N.J.: Rutgers University Press, 2000).

72. Camille Paglia, "Religion and the Arts in America," *Arion* 15, 1 (2007), available in a long form as a PDF file on the Arion web site, treats the antagonism to religion found in much contemporary art.

73. The issues are set forth in Gerhart Ladner, *The Idea of Reform: Its Impact on Christian Thought and Action in the Age of the Fathers,* rev. ed. (New York: Harper & Row, 1967), and see

is not simply a Hesiod or an Amos, claiming that all that he has to say has been received from on high, but an artificer, bringing forth something new. The privileged image for Augustine is not the artist completely dominated by tradition, but the artist working, ex nihilo, like God himself, bringing forth things unheard.[74] In the Middle Ages and well thereafter musical notation did not indicate all the details of performance: discretion about them was left to the artist, who nevertheless performed within a tradition which at least partly carried the experience of earlier performers. Thus always individual creativity and tradition must somehow be linked.

Everywhere we find disagreement about the nature of the modern and about its inevitability. John Banville summarizes the "High Modernist" characteristics of Aidan Higgins as "obsessive subjectivity, a broad range of allusive references, insistence on formal freedom, a plethora of polyglottal quotations, aristocratic disdain of the audience."[75] This is only one man's modernism, but it probably captures what many mean when they designate Joyce or Proust or Lawrence as modernists. These men share a great self-obsession almost the opposite of Homer, who reveals so little of himself that we are uncertain who he was or when he lived. In considering early modernist Spanish literature, C. Christopher Soufas gives an almost completely opposite definition from Banville's, seeing Spanish modernism as centering on a long-standing Spanish critique of the autonomous thinking subject as conceived in the Cartesian tradition, or as found in self-absorbed English-language modernists such as Joyce.[76]

Few if any modernists have had a program free from internal contradiction, and many in one way or another have combined things others thought incompatible. Thus Donald Justice was both a formalist, as it were was the opposite of Higgins, and, though strongly tied to tradition, thought of himself as a modernist. He viewed his sonatinas as based on prior models, "a sort of Platonic script which he had been elected to transcribe."[77] This was a stance closer to the classical writers than to modernism, as usually understood.[78] But in some ways he dwelt in some middle-earth halfway between ancient objectivity and modern subjectivity: he wanted to diminish or displace the self in his works, but not to eliminate it.[79] And what are

my "Problems with the Contrast between Circular and Linear Views of Time in the Interpretation of Ancient and Early Medieval History," *FQI* 1 (2001): 41–65.

74. Catherine Pickstock, "Music: Soul, City, and Cosmos after Augustine," in *Radical Orthodoxy: A New Theology*, ed. John Milbank et al. (London: Routledge, 1999), 243–77 at 248.

75. "The Missing Link," *NYRB* 51, 19 (December 2, 2004): 55–57 at 55.

76. *The Subject in Question: Early Contemporary Spanish Literature and Modernism* (Washington, D.C.: The Catholic University of America Press, 2007).

77. Charles Simic, "The Memory Piano," *NYRB* 52, 3 (February 24, 2005): 39–41 at 39.

78. Rowan Williams, *Grace and Necessity: Reflections on Art and Love* (Harrisburg, Pa.: Morehouse, 2005), considers the relations of creativity and art.

79. Simic, "Memory Piano," 40, and see 41 for his description of the poet Weldon Kees:

we to say of someone such as Hermann Helmholtz (1821–94) early on, at once freeing music from tradition understood as the received tonal system, but trying to found it on something objective and absolute, mathematics?[80] This is an objectification that would have appealed to some Enlightenment minds, one in which the artist is submissive to an abstract mathematical order rather than to a natural order fitted to his hearing.

Constantin Brancusi has been described as "a modernist against modernism."[81] Though thought of as one of the founders of modernist sculpture, Brancusi's vision arguably was the antithesis of what modernism became. He did not highly value the individual, but was a staunch traditionalist; indeed, like Antonio Gaudi, the tradition in which Brancusi most obviously worked was that of sacred art. His shifting of art from mimesis, the Renaissance tradition of imitation, usually imitation of the natural world, to the attempt to contact reality directly was a return to religious art, indeed to the iconographic tradition of his own Orthodoxy. A similar tradition had existed in the West, and it is becoming increasingly clear that the attempt of many "Whig" generations to impose a progressive and modernizing trajectory on the history of European art, in which for instance the emphasis is on growing realism as we pass from Romanesque to Gothic to Renaissance art, has blinded us to the nature of much medieval art, which in important ways was not developmental and can be seen as "abstract" and not particularly interested in being realistic. Art historians now speak of Romanesque art as caught between historicism and modernism, that is, as working within pictorial traditions, but playfully. Indeed there are now those who view the Gothic not so much as a step toward increasing verisimilitude, but as a kind of medieval modernism.[82] In any case when a "modernist" such as Brice Marden affirms that the problem lying at the heart of modernism is struggle against pictorial illusion, he is taking up an old problem running back into the Middle Ages.[83]

Brancusi has been thought of as an abstractionist, as one who reduced sculpture to simple monadic form. But, like "modernism," "abstractionism" can mean very different things. For many abstractionism is associated with

"The style was almost anonymous and therefore classical. . . . It is clearly not the style of a writer desperate for novelty, as so many current styles seem to me to be."

80. See Matthias Rieger, *Helmholtz Musicus: Die Objektivierung der Musik im 19. Jh. Durch Helmholtz' Lehre von den Tonempfindungen* (Darmstadt: Wissenschaftliche Buchgesellschaft, 2006).

81. The phrase and what follows is from Aidan Hart, "Constantin Brancusi: A Modernist Against Modernism," *SS* 7 (2006): 52–58 at 52.

82. Kirk Ambrose, *The Nave Sculpture of Vézelay: The Art of Monastic Viewing* (Toronto: Pontifical Institute of Medieval Studies, 2006), 62–65.

83. See the interesting discussion by Richard Dorment, "Journey from 'Nebraska,'" *NYRB* 53, 20 (December 21, 2006): 8–14 at 12. See also Kirk Varnedoe, *Pictures of Nothing: Abstract Art since Pollock* (Princeton, N.J.: Princeton University Press, 2006).

departure from reality, as if departure from mimesis necessarily involves departure from reality. The latter was far from Brancusi's goals. Like Kandinsky, his aim was the expression of "objective, metaphysical fact," the essence of a thing.[84] In the long-running battle between those who have thought art to be about copying nature and those who have seen it as engaged in imagination, Brancusi was on the side of inner vision.[85] His art was a "sacred art," "founded on the symbolism inherent in forms: the symbol manifests its archetype."[86] But it shared with some modernists the idea that inner vision might be more important than the world as it appears. Both sculptor and viewer were to resonate with the harmony found in all things and indeed Brancusi understood the work of the artist to be mediatory, to express the cosmic harmonies. He is one of the best examples of David Freedberg's perhaps overbroad thesis that all images have "power," making all art medieval in a way that will be explored in the following chapter, that is, as participating in some reality it embodies.[87] In any case Brancusi is close to that understanding which sees abstractionism as a form of contemplation. One of the rooms exhibiting contemporary art in the Lentos Kunstmuseum in Linz, Austria, is titled "Abstrakte Form—Meditation," suggesting that abstraction, like at least one understanding of meditation, is linked to "looking through" form to apprehend reality, as in the use of icons.

For Brancusi, since "beauty is the face of truth," the artist must work in humility, not "creating" as an individual, but submitting himself to that which is.[88] Some such idea of "anonymous authorship" is found at least as early as Homer and Hesiod, and runs through the tradition, complicating all discussions of "individualism" and of when it first appeared. Already in the ancient world some authors were quite conscious of the issues involved in opting for one or the other stance, some Greeks, for instance, refusing to consider the biblical prophets as authors at all because these prophets saw God, not themselves, as the author of their messages. Josephus (37–ca. 100) and some Jewish scholars, who thought anonymity the mark of a truth-carrying tradition, in their own way agreed, seeing in "authorship" a form

---

84. Hart, "Constantin Brancusi," 53.

85. Charles Simic, "The Powers of Invention," *NYRB* 53, 4 (March 6, 2006): 10–14 at 10, seeing the struggle between imitation and imagination as already under way in the fifteenth century (Bosch, Dürer, Grünewald).

86. Hart, "Constantin Brancusi," 53, following Titus Burckhardt, *Sacred Art in East and West: Its Principles and Methods* (London: Perennial Books, 1967), 8. Didier Maleuvre, *The Religion of Reality: Inquiry into the Self, Art, and Transcendence* (Washington, D.C.: The Catholic University of America Press, 2006), in considering a number of the issues examined in the present book, treats the connection between art and religion, the presence of the spiritual in artistic experience.

87. *The Power of Images: Studies in the History and Theory of Response* (Chicago: University of Chicago Press, 1989); see also Caroline Bynum, "The Presence of Objects: Medieval Anti-Judaism in Modern Germany," *Common Knowledge* 10 (2004): 1–32 at 27 n. 55.

88. Hart, "Constantin Brancusi," 53, and see 58.

of self-seeking egotism or individualism.[89] Today the German filmmaker Werner Herzog is said to "prefer to work anonymously, like a medieval artisan."[90] He seeks not "accountant's truth" but "ecstatic truth":

I'm after something that is more like an ecstasy of truth, something where we step beyond ourselves, something that happens in religion sometimes, like medieval mystics.[91]

Brancusi thought egotism only distorts perception, forcing things rather than letting them be. The matter itself from which a sculpture is composed ought not be wrenched into something else, but

must continue its natural life when modified by the hand of the sculptor. . . . Matter should not be used merely to suit the purpose of the artist, it must not be subjected to a preconceived idea and to a preconceived form. Matter itself must suggest subject and form; both must come from within matter and not be forced upon it from without.[92]

Since the goal is "an art that resonates with the cosmic harmonies," its effect should be joy, and any art that does not result in joy is in some way defective.[93] A defect of Michelangelo and much subsequent Western sculpture, according to this view, is that, aimed at the grandiose, it neither comforts nor heals. Michelangelo's grandiloquence tends to replace wisdom with sophistry.

In the next chapter, we will return to this Orthodox criticism of the artistic patrimony of the West. Brancusi, following certain Westerners such as Rodin who, he thought, had not lost their way, saw himself as engaged in precisely the disengagement of simplicity from grandiloquence. He proposed to liberate European art from a bad turn it had taken with the elevation of genius and the individual in the modern period. Thus early modernism and abstractionism, with their ability to draw out the essence of things, for him provided the way back to beauty and joy and the artistic articulation of the harmony of the world. Novelty was not the goal, but because the essence of a thing can never be fully captured, the quest for essence never ends and thus originality is produced. Such a view—which is also that of the present author—has continued in various venues. In spite

89. Jed Wyrick, *The Ascension of Authorship: Attribution and Canon Formation in Jewish, Hellenistic and Christian Traditions* (Cambridge, Mass.: Harvard University Press, 2004). A very perceptive review of this book by Richard Lim disputes Wyrick's neat division between cultural blocks ("Jews," "Greeks," and "Christians") and notes that the dispute about kinds of authorship was internal to "Hellenistic" culture: *CH* 75 (2006): 880–83.

90. Ian Buruma, "Herzog and His Heroes," *NYRB* 54, 12 (July 19, 2007): 24–26 at 24.

91. Quoted in Buruma, "Herzog and His Heroes," 20.

92. Aphorisms from *This Quarter* 1, 1 (January 1925), 235, quoted in Hart, "Constantin Brancusi," 54, and see 57, on the desirability (actually, necessity, if truth is to shine forth) of the elimination of the ego.

93. Hart, "Constantin Brancusi," 54, on this and the following, with 56–58.

of many missteps as well as successes, the goal of art remains what it has always been, joyful discovery of, or participation in, the "endlessly increasing accumulation of beauty."[94]

The argument has been made that musical modernism actually begins a bit earlier than Arnold Schoenberg's introduction of atonality in 1908: Einstein's theory of relativity taught that time is "not one but many," and this made possible a modernism of multiple time, breaking down a "Whig" or linear history of music, as such histories were being broken down in other fields.[95] Through both modernism and postmodernism there runs the idea of multiple time. Time becomes a labyrinth. The advantage for "modernists" like Brancusi is that, "once again," the artist does not have to stand in some single "art history," but can attend directly to beauty. This is another way of keeping the past alive, "by retraining it, as part of our present. It can also, by what it lacks, show us the future."[96]

Subjectivity, freedom, and disdain for the audience defines much in many peoples' modernism, but not everything in everybody's. As stated, "modernism" is notoriously difficult to define.[97] Two of its most learned exponents, Charles Rosen and Henri Zerner, are very evasive in offering any clear definition. They do agree that modernism at its core is more born of anti-authoritarianism or anti-traditionalism, what they call "the autonomy of art, the idea that art was only accountable to its own principles," than composed of any single artistic view or tradition (inevitably, modernism itself became a tradition to be defended, and then, increasingly in artistic circles from the 1970s, to be attacked).[98] This is but to say that modernism is simply the artistic form of the idea that, freed from tradition and natural

94. Etienne Gilson, *Painting and Reality* (New York: Pantheon Books, 1957), 299, in a chapter entitled "The Significance of Modern Painting." Cf. the views of Karl Rahner, "Theology and the Arts," *Thought* 65 (1990): 385–99. See further on joy the discussion of Constantin Brancusi below. In his letter *To Artists* (Boston: Pauline Books and Media, 1999), Pope John Paul II wrote of artists' search for "new epiphanies of beauty" making God's glory manifest to the world.

95. Joseph Kerman, "Playing in Time," *NYRB* 55, 8 (May 15, 2008): 50–54 at 51, on this and the following.

96. Kerman, ibid., 54, quoting Paul Griffiths, *A Concise History of Western Music* (Cambridge: Cambridge University Press, 2006), 316.

97. See Rebecca L. Walkowitz, *Cosmopolitan Style: Modernism Beyond the Nation* (New York: Columbia University Press, 2006), on the political nature of modernism.

98. Rosen and Zerner, "Red-Hot MoMA," give an informative historical overview, centering on the history of American modernism. They argue that "painting is the greatest triumph of modernism. Listening to extended works of modernist music can still make the unsympathetic lay listener nervous, and reading the long novels and poems of modernist literature may often seem a chore. The visual arts, however, make the least demands on our patience" (20). Rosen and Zerner think that modern paintings need to be exhibited so that they can create "the air of authority that is indispensable for comprehending the artistic language used in any recent innovation" (21), but do not explore the ironies present in building up the authority of anti-authoritarianism. Cf. the opening comments of Meyer Schapiro, "On the Aesthetic Attitude in Romanesque Art," *Romanesque Art* (New York: G. Braziller 1977), 1–27.

law, man is free to define himself. Of whatever form, modernism is open to the query why, granted a meaningless world, it is better to create meaning than not to, and the query whether a residual "Westernism" does not lie in such notions as "creativity" and "autonomy," commonly part of the modernist stance: why is autonomy better than submission, action than passivity, creation than contemplation?

Meyer Schapiro was especially prominent in broadcasting the idea of the autonomy of art central to modernism and to much twentieth-century artistic self-understanding. He viewed abstraction, whether he found it in Romanesque sculpture or in twentieth-century painting, as the last and best expression of autonomy and uninhibited creativity.[99] Schapiro's views were erected on a distinctively American as well as modernist platform. He saw a tension emerging in the West from the twelfth century between sacred and secular categories, and often in studying the Middle Ages seemed to be studying the origins of the things he valued and wished to promote in the twentieth century, such as freedom of the artist. Some movement toward secularism and greater artistic individualism was indeed found in the twelfth century, but Schapiro also claimed that a great deal of art which everyone had taken to be religious in content was secular. He particularly emphasized the idea of "public space," seeing the exteriors of ecclesiastical buildings, the surfaces which faced on town and village, as venues for secular themes.[100] These were stimulating thoughts, which effectively read a kind of "separation of Church and state" onto medieval subject matter, the interior of the church being reserved for "private religion" and the exterior for public or secular themes. Again there was some truth in these claims, though they missed how much Romanesque sculpture is presented in a helter-skelter fashion which evades any simple equation of interior with religion and exterior with secularity, and avoids the fact that almost all the architecture and sculpture Schapiro discussed was created by the Church.[101]

In his critique of artistic primitivism and its attack on tradition, Gombrich viewed a good deal of twentieth-century, modern art as "mere hoax or provocation."[102] According to him, *Guernica* is children's art, its gored horse "something a newspaper cartoonist might also have done."[103] Paul Johnson,

99. Willibald Sauerländer, "The Artist Historian," *NYRB* 54, 11 (June 28, 2007): 55–62 at 55. A goal similar to Schapiro's, to replace religion with art as the ground for life, is found in Harold Bloom's writings: Elizabeth Powers, "The Self in Full," *FT* 97 (November 1999): 21–27 at 22.

100. Sauerländer, "Artist Historian," 61, notes that in his later writings Schapiro is not as certain as he was earlier of his ideas about public space.

101. My "On the Frontiers of Eroticism: The Romanesque Monastery of San Pedro de Cervatos," *MS* 8 (1999): 89–104, adds many other considerations to the discussion. Sauerländer, "Artist Historian," 58, comments of a church for the study of which Schapiro became famous, "What we encounter in the sculptures of Souillac, then, is not an emerging secularism but rather religious art expressed with new ardor and narrative intensity." See also 62.

102. Geertz, "Last Humanist," 8.

103. Quoted in ibid., 10.

a serious painter and the son of a painter, seconds Gombrich's judgment in telling us in his overview of the whole history of art that Johnson's father did not want him to have a career in art because "the future would belong to charlatans such as Picasso."[104] Johnson cedes nothing in hyperbole to his father, and his own history of art judges most twentieth-century art and architecture harshly, describing the decades following Bauhaus as "the three most dismal decades in architecture since the fall of Rome," and suggesting that "in the age of the 'machines for living' . . . glass-walled libraries baked their books, hospitals killed their patients, and the people forced to dwell in glass-and-concrete boxes showed a marked tendency toward homicide."[105] A caricature to be sure, one like Tom Wolfe's famous 1980 essay "From Bauhaus to Our House," but one with its uncomfortable truths. The rationalist idealism of Walter Gropius, chairman of the Bauhaus, did admire and embrace many of the qualities of the machine age, efficient function above all, in a way which largely cut him and his buildings off from the earlier history of architecture. And Adolf Loos (1870–1933) did say "the evolution of culture is synonymous with the removal of ornamentation from objects of everyday use."[106] This playing off of function and ornament, hardly present in, say, the Middle Ages, characterizes a good deal of modern art.[107]

Especially since Victorian times, there has been spirited discussion of the modern city, and then of modernist urban planning and suburbanization. Often this has been a reaction to or rejection of rapid change, and the issue has centered on the relation of individualism to something more communal, perhaps to civic patriotism, or the possibility thereof. If the Victorian city often compromised between old and new, designing Gothic train stations, its frequent nostalgia seems to have had some success:

Its vision of an organic city rebuilt upon faith, with a spirit of community and brotherhood expressed through a stratum of guilds, corporations, fraternities and churches, and reflected in a civic fabric of noble edifices and godly symbols, appealed intuitively to the bewildered inhabitants of Britain's cities.[108]

This is but one expression of recent inclination to reassess the Victorians and acknowledge the complexity of their views. If many praised cities as the

104. John J. Reilly, "Art's Truth," *FT* 141 (March 2004): 49–52 at 49, reviewing Paul Johnson, *Art: A New History* (New York: HarperCollins, 2003).

105. The phrases quoted are from Reilly, "Art's Truth," 52. More ferocious and ad hominem is E. Michael Jones's analysis of Bauhaus architecture, *Living Machines: Bauhaus Architecture as Sexual Ideology* (San Francisco: Ignatius Press, 1995). Cf. Jill Perlman, *Inventing American Modernism: Joseph Hudnut, Walter Gropius, and the Bauhaus Legacy at Harvard* (Charlottesville: University of Virginia Press, 2007).

106. *Ornament and Crime: Selected Essays,* ed. A. Opel, tr. M. Mitchell (Riverside, Calif.: Ariadne Press, 1998).

107. Ambrose, *Nave Sculpture of Vézelay,* 60–63.

108. John Brewer, "City Lights," *NYRB* 53, 8 (May 11, 2006): 18–21 at 18, quoting Tristram Hunt, *Building Jerusalem: The Rise and Fall of the Victorian City* (New York: Henry Holt, 2005).

site of progress, and in the cities especially praised the middle class, some like John Ruskin lived to tame urban life in a way that would preserve an at least imagined social cohesion associated with the past.

If it took until 1980 for Wolfe to reflect on why every school now looked "like a duplicating-machine replacement-parts wholesale distribution warehouse," already in 1914 Geoffrey Scott published *The Architecture of Humanism,* championing the principles of the Renaissance and attacking what he held to be various fallacies of modern architecture.[109] Though the present work does not look chiefly to the principles of the Renaissance for its inspiration, it agrees with the general direction of Scott's criticism. One of the fallacies he attacks, a kind of presence in architecture of the Whig Grand Narrative of progress, is the drawing of an analogy between biological growth and the development of architecture, both seen to pass through such stages as youth, maturity, and decline. For Scott the question is not to place any building in such a progression, but to look at it and judge it for itself. Each building finds its merit in what it is, not in its place in some supposed evolution of architecture.[110]

Thus the art historian Robert Bork argues that though late Gothic architecture is usually presented as inferior to contemporary Renaissance architecture, one could argue the opposite, that Renaissance architecture, with its diminished sense of the transcendent, is the lesser form. But Bork does not actually want to weigh the one against the other in this manner. His argument is that always there is more than one style present, normally each with its own insight into reality, and that therefore an architectural history written as if there is a single story line, the Gothic for instance declining as the Renaissance rises to carry the story of architectural progress, is deeply misleading. Bork compares the fifteenth-century situation with the coexistence of heavy metal and rap today. Heavy metal, a music of transcendence, coexists with rap, a music of human achievement, sex, and material acquisition, that is of immanence. We better describe the historical victory of Renaissance architecture in the histories of architecture as "the displacement of the divine by the human, rather than the displacement of a flawed architectural system by an inherently better one."[111] Either the starkly modernist cube of the Great Arch of La Défense in Paris, so to

---

109. The phrase is from Michael S. Rose, "The Wisdom of Hindsight," *AB* 10, 8 (November 2004): 6–7 at 6.

110. Witold Rybczynski, "The Triumph of a Distinguished Failure," *NYRB* 51, 16 (October 21, 2004): 30–32 at 31. For a history of painting which eschews all narratives of progress, see James Fenton, *School of Genius: A History of the Royal Academy of Arts* (London: Royal Academy of the Arts, 2006).

111. Robert Bork, "Stairways to Heaven: Gothic Architecture, Heavy Metal, and the Aesthetics of Transcendence," *Medieval Academy News* 157 (Spring 2007): 11. It is unclear whether Benedict XVI is familiar with heavy metal, but we will see in the next chapter that his views of what was happening architecturally in the Renaissance have common ground with those of Bork.

speak, stands on its own and can be compared in various ways, including in beauty, to the cathedral of Notre Dame, or it is just one more ugly monument to politics without God.[112]

Although Scott seems to me to have articulated a great truth, he did not, in my opinion, articulate it quite correctly. True, no art should be presented as simply one link in a narrative of progress, but the use in the history of architecture or liturgy of such analogies as those making comparisons to biological growth seems to me inevitable. This is for the simple reason that all art stands in some form of tradition. We can always discover some way in which the present work of art is linked to the past, even if only by denial of that past. Therefore, what should have been said is that, though it is inevitable that any work of music or architecture stands in some tradition, the development of that tradition should not be seen as representing stages of progress, but simply as ways of standing in relation to the beautiful, and perhaps of trying to continue insight into the nature of beauty.

The same can be said of all the arts. An interviewer asked the composer Arvo Pärt (born 1935)

whether he believed in musical progress, in the idea of an avant-garde. He vigorously shook his head. "I do not know what this word 'progress' means, at least in the area of art. Progress in science can certainly be measured and described. But to talk about a particular style or a particular work as progressive or regressive is arbitrary, totally misleading. It reminds me a little of Brueghel's painting of the blind leading the blind. One man is tumbling down, his staff held out like a spear or sword in front of him, and the others are following behind him. They are all making progress, and they are all falling down. The story is found in the Bible. How many painters this word 'progress' has made blind! How many composers this word has made deaf!"[113]

If politics without God is often part of the modern agenda, politics with God also occurs, as, arguably, in Steven Holl's Chapel of St. Ignatius at Seattle University. Holl's real concerns seem to be the phenomenology of space and the investigation of form, material, and reflected light and color. Whether one wants to go so far as to claim that his church is really the continuation of politics without God, now in the form of a church without God, at the least we have a chapel almost completely severed from the Catholic tradition, which communicates virtually no sense of standing in Church history or of being part of some vast communion of saints.[114] Whether it

112. George Weigel, *The Cube and the Cathedral: Europe, America, and Politics Without God* (San Francisco: Basic Books, 2005).

113. Alex Ross, "Musical Events," *NY* (December 2, 2002): 114–116. Ross, some of whose own opinions are close to those of Pärt here, has now written perhaps the most thoughtful study of new music: *The Rest Is Noise: Listening to the Twentieth Century* (New York: Farrar, Straus and Giroux, 2007).

114. Steven Holl, *The Chapel of St. Ignatius* (New York: Princeton Architectural Press, 1999).

expresses a conscious desire to shed the burden of the Catholic past or not, this chapel misconceives or ignores one of the most central characteristics of Catholicism, its acceptance of the organic development of history and consequent deep respect for history. It is as if the widespread mood of rebellion, rejection of the past, and innovation found in the Catholic Church in the wake of Vatican II (1962–66) had achieved artistic expression not in the banal A-frame churches then so common, but in serious architecture. We might say that, especially in ecclesiastical architecture, what is necessary is not that development be progressive, but that it be organic, linked to the past in some way that builds on the past. Holl's church, to the extent it is linked to anything, is linked to modernism, not to the history of Christian worship.[115] It seems raised on what Benedict XVI called a "hermeneutics of discontinuity and rupture between the pre-conciliar and post-conciliar Church."[116]

To explain this claim, a detour is in order, guided first by the reflections of Michael S. Rose on the history of Christian architecture. For Rose the Church since Vatican II has been going through its third age of iconoclasm, the first being that of the time of the Byzantine Emperor Leo III (reigned 717–41), and the second the Protestant Reformation. Rose argues that there are three principles of Catholic architecture: verticality, permanence, and iconography.[117] Each of these helps foster a sense of transcendence, especially a Christian understanding of transcendence, in which God is at once transcendent and immanent. They have been lost in much post–Vatican II

Some have spoken of a conscious attempt by architects to eliminate the sacred: see Alison Lurie, "God's Houses Part II," *NYRB* 50, 12 (July 17, 2003): 41–43 at 43, describing the views of Michael S. Rose. Richard Kieckhefer, *Theology in Stone: Church Architecture from Byzantium to Berkeley* (New York: Oxford University Press, 2004), attempts an even-handed discussion of the classic sacramental church, which he favors, the classic evangelical church, and the modern communal church. For general orientation see R. Kevin Seasoltz, *A Sense of the Sacred: Theological Foundations of Christian Architecture and Art* (New York: Continuum, 2005), and Michael S. Rose, *In Tiers of Glory: The Organic Development of Church Architecture Through the Ages* (Cincinnati: Mesa Folio Editions, 2004).

115. Cf. Alcuin Reid, *The Organic Development of the Liturgy: The Principles of Liturgical Reform and their Relation to the Twentieth Century Liturgical Movement Prior to the Second Vatican Council* (San Francisco: Ignatius Press, 2005). Mark A. Torgerson, *An Architecture of Immanence: Architecture for Worship and Ministry Today* (Grand Rapids, Mich.: Eerdmans, 2007), traces the influence of modernism on church architecture and the decline of transcendence, and makes proposals for the accommodation of modernism and attachment to the past. See also Moyra Doorly, *No Place for God: The Denial of the Transcendent in Modern Church Architecture* (San Francisco: Ignatius Press, 2007).

116. Quotation in "News," *SA* 12 (2006): 8. Cf. the critique and counterproposals found in Philip Bess, *Till We have Built Jerusalem: Architecture, Urbanism, and the Sacred* (Wilmington, Del.: ISI Books, 2006).

117. *Ugly as Sin: Why They Changed Our Churches from Sacred Places to Meeting Spaces—and How We Can Change Them Back Again* (Manchester, N.H.: Sophia Institute Press, 2001), and see also Rose's *Tiers of Glory,* and his web site, www.della.chiesa.com. I am guided in the following by the review of these books by Edmund W. Majewski in *FCSQ* 28, 4 (Winter 2005): 38–40.

ecclesiastical architecture, but the last thing Rose wants is simply a return to what existed before the Council. His goal is not some exercise in archaeology, but the use of the past to inspire present and future buildings. Since the church building is the "new Jerusalem," the place where heaven and earth join, what is essential is the use of architecture to manifest this coming together of earth and heaven. This does not necessitate the use of some particular architectural style. But it is simply not possible to manifest the glory of God very fully if the architectural emphasis is horizontal, that is, is on the church as gathered community or "house of the people" rather than "house of God."

It has been popular since Vatican II to think of the Christian church in essentially sociological terms, (mis)appropriating the term "people of God" used in the documents of Vatican II. Such usage stresses the community or horizontal aspects of the church, makes the church about "me" or "us," to the neglect of the fact that it is first of all a place where God is to be met and worshipped. A strong vertical architectural orientation helps make clear that the church is God's house. I do not understand Rose to be saying that a church must have the almost overwhelming vertical thrust of the tallest of Gothic churches. Many lower-lying Byzantine churches clearly manifest the idea that in them heaven and earth meet. Rose's point rather is that, whatever the style used, certain things must be present including iconography, which is almost completely absent from Holl's church.

Modernism in ecclesiastical architecture has tended to evacuate the idea, found in the earliest Christian basilicas and continuing through the great Baroque churches, that the church is a miniature of the cosmos.[118] The evacuation of this metaphor of the church as cosmos has paralleled an anti-cosmological stance assumed in many fields. Most students of, say, Plato or Aristotle presume that an enlightened reading of them must remove what is still valuable, perhaps their ethics, from what is no longer viable, say the implicit theological and cosmological framework in which this ethics first developed.[119] The idea that the church is indeed a miniature cosmos is one of those orienting metaphors which direct us dwellers in time to our final end, and is closely tied to the idea that a proper ecclesiastical architecture must connect heaven and earth, just as do the Incarnation and Eucharist. As natural law doctrines attempt to show how the world may be a guide to human ethical life, how nature sets the norm, the doctrine of the church as

118. Stanley Samuel Harakas, "Faith Formation in Byzantium," in *Educating People of Faith: Exploring the History of Jewish and Christian Communities,* ed. John Van Engen (Grand Rapids, Mich.: Eerdmans, 2004), 115–31 at 121, describes this in detail for an Orthodox church, and at 121–22, gives a succinct explanation of the purpose of icons to draw one into transcendence.

119. Troels Engberg-Pedersen, *Paul and the Stoics* (Louisville, Ky.: Westminster John Knox Press, 2000), 26, a very good book which nevertheless assumes the necessity of this kind of "enlightenment."

a miniature cosmos attempts to direct us to our final end, doxology or the praise of God.[120]

Insofar as the history of ecclesiastical art and architecture is concerned, the disagreement between Luther, Zwingli, and Calvin over what constitutes a desirable church architecture and liturgy has been of special importance. Luther, here as in so many things, though seeing ceremonies as not at the heart of faith, was much closer to Catholicism, allowing images in church, but with Huldrych Zwingli (1484–1531) there appeared in the Reformed tradition an iconoclasm, an early model of which was Zurich, that broke much more radically with medieval art and liturgy than did Luther.[121] All was ordered to the didactic purpose of communicating and making Scripture clear. The holy purposes of imagination faded. Zwingli thought *Gottesdienst,* worship, not so much a matter of ritual action as of living out one's faith, of never separating belief and action. From certain of the Church Fathers he adopted a Neoplatonic anthropology which saw being human as a struggle between the physical and spiritual. Humans were drawn, mentally and sensually, to the physical, and had to avoid its seductions. But Zwingli did not agree with Luther about the status of ceremonies and images.

Zwingli thought humans could never be freed of the material order around them, so they must pay close attention to it. It was not that traditional ritual, architecture, etc., were to be eliminated: they were to be subject to scrutiny to make sure they were not grounded in an erroneous theology. Thus the religious processions and monstrances dear to the medieval Church were to be eliminated, along with much else. At Zurich began that smashing of altars, sacrament houses, and sculpture; the turning into firewood of retablos, crucifixes, and wood sculptures; the melting down of liturgical objects; the whitewashing of church walls formerly painted with murals that would be carried by Protestantism across Europe and is still visible today in the vandalized sculpture of, say, Saint-Gilles-du-Gard.[122] The pastor replaced the colorful priest's vestments with an austere black scholar's robe.[123] Much of the so-called Counter-Reformation and the development of the Baroque may be seen as a reaction especially to the reducing of Christianity to moral and rational categories by the Reformed churches, to reinvigorate the visual and ritual aspects of medieval Christianity.[124]

---

120. Rémi Brague, *The Wisdom of the World: The Human Experience of the Universe in Western Thought,* tr. Teresa Lavender Fagan (Chicago: University of Chicago Press, 2004); see also my "The Natural Law: The First Grace," *Co* 35 (2008): 354–73.

121. Lee Palmer Wandel, "Zwingli and Reformed Practice," in *Educating People of Faith,* 270–93, at 272–74, on this and the following.

122. For an example of defaced sculpture at Saint-Gilles-du-Gard, unremarked by the author, see Schapiro, *Romanesque Architectural Sculpture,* figure 48.

123. Wandel, "Zwingli and Reformed Practice," 278–79.

124. Philip M. Soergel, "Ritual and Faith Formation in Early Modern Catholic Europe,"

Sometimes, as ultimately in America, the result of the paring down found in many forms of Protestantism has been "beige churches," characterless churches devoid of symbolism and narrative; sometimes the result has been some more demanding form of modernism.[125] Especially because of the variety found in Protestantism, low and high church, in America the story has been very complicated. It is not widely known, for instance, that Reinhold Niebuhr (1892–1971) was as much a critic of the liturgy of what might be called the evangelical wing of Protestantism as he was of the doctrines of liberal Protestantism. He wanted a more traditional liturgy (in his case "traditional" signifying the practices of sixteenth-century Protestantism), which communicated a sense of God's transcendence.[126] A recent author has shown how in the quest for "churches that look like churches" nineteenth-century American anti-Catholicism was quite compatible with Protestant appropriation of Catholic art and architecture.[127]

In most Christian traditions the cosmic sense of the liturgy and of liturgical art is constantly eroded today.[128] Only now is a new traditionalism appearing among youth, demanding the heritage denied them by the "manufacturers of new liturgy."[129] Desired is some recovery of Pope Paul VI's idea that "art is meant to bring the divine to the human world, to the level of the senses, then, from the spiritual insight gained through the senses and the stirring of the emotions to raise the human world to God, to his inexpressible kingdom of mystery, beauty and life."[130]

To return then to the conclusion of Geoffrey Scott's attack on the fallacies of modern art, "Scott's argument against the Biological Fallacy continues to be a rebuke to those who promote architectural novelty on the grounds that the new—and only the new—is a proper reflection of our time."[131] It somewhat overlaps Jonathan Clark's later critique of modernist

---

in *Educating People of Faith,* 314–29 at 316–20, emphasizing how much the Catholic revival was formed from below, was popular, as well as imposed from above.

125. Robert Barron, "Evangelizing the American Culture," *SS* 3 (2002): 26–38 at 36.

126. David R. Bains, "Conduits of Faith: Reinhold Niebuhr's Liturgical Thought," *CH* 73 (2004): 168–94.

127. Ryan K. Smith, *Gothic Arches, Latin Crosses: Anti-Catholicism and American Church Designs in the Nineteenth Century* (Chapel Hill: University of North Carolina Press, 2006).

128. M. Francis Mannion, "Bringing the Cosmos to Liturgy," *Antiphon* 6, 1 (2001): 2–4 at 4. For reaction in sacred architecture in favor of transcendence, see the volumes of Cristiano Rosponi and Giampaolo Rossi, *Reconquistare lo spazio sacro: riscoprire la tradizione nell'architettura liturgica del XX secolo* (Rome: Editrice Il bosco e la nave, 1999), and, with Duncan Stroik, *Reconquistare lo spazio sacro: la chiesa nella città del terzo millennio* (Rome: Editrice Il bosco e la nave, 2000).

129. Brian Van Hove, "Reflections on *Toward Ritual Transformation: Remembering Robert Hovda,*" *FCSQ* 27, 1 (Summer 2004): 3–11 at 8, quoting a book on the new orthodoxy, Colleen Carroll, *The New Faithful: Why Young Adults are Embracing Christian Orthodoxy* (Chicago: Loyola Press, 2002).

130. Quoted in Duncan G. Stroik, "One Step Forward: An Analysis of *Built of Living Stones,*" *SA* 8 (2003): 20–24 at 23.

131. Rybczynski, "Triumph of a Distinguished Failure," 32.

materialism and of the postmodernism with which some seek to replace it.[132] Clark understands that the attempt to emancipate ourselves from history has a certain futility about it, that historical identities lie deep in history and in one way or another reassert themselves. He also understands that much postmodernist criticism is "ultra-idealist," as unalert to or unrealistic about history as the modernism which it wishes to replace.

◦━

Modernism in art is but one aspect of the larger "modernist project" we have been considering ever since we took up the Whig Grand Narrative of history in the last chapter. As already stated, the desire to be free from the past had long been forming, and can be in part found in Michel de Montaigne's late sixteenth-century argument, the result of a growth in historical criticism, that the past was so different from the present that it could not illuminate it; or in René Descartes disparagement, a half-century later, of ancient learning, especially about the physical world.[133] Rousseau—a kind of "postmodernist" before the word, who saw in culture a form of social power oppressing the individual—in turn thought that to become free one would have to destroy inherited civilization and polite manners.[134] The growth of a psychological distance between past and present "paves the way for 'modernism'; since what is merely past is no longer living, it leaves the present isolated and so leads to self-concocted experimentation."[135] Central here were the views of Nietzsche, grounded in his contempt for Christianity and famously expressed in *Also Sprach Zarathustra,* both in Nietzsche's own essay of that name in attempt to raise mankind by will, and in Richard Strauss's symphonic poem of the same title in praise of man's ascent from his original, undeveloped state.

The modernist project was central to Freud's desire to "help modern individuals cast off the tyranny of a past that enslaved them unconsciously."[136] It was perhaps no more remorselessly continued than in the writing of Freud's fellow Austrian Thomas Bernhard (d. 1989), who returned again and again to the theme of the individual hedged in by society and tradi-

132. *Our Shadowed Present.*

133. Anthony Grafton, *Bring Out Your Dead: The Past as Revelation* (Cambridge, Mass.: Harvard University Press, 2001). On the continuing reflection on "the modern," see the essays gathered in "God and the Enlightenment," *AHR* 108 (2003): 1057–1104.

134. Robert Darnton, *George Washington's False Teeth: An Unconventional Guide to the Eighteenth Century* (New York: W. W. Norton, 2003); and see Gordon S. Wood, "The Hidden France," *NYRB* 51, 4 (March 11, 2004): 31–34 at 33.

135. Joseph Ratzinger, "Thoughts on the Place of Marian Doctrine and Piety in Faith and Theology as a Whole," *Co* 30 (2003): 147–60 at 151.

136. Mark Lilla, "The New Age of Tyranny," *NYRB* 49, 16 (October 24, 2002): 28–29 at 28. See John Brenkman, "Freud the Modernist," in *The Mind of Modernism: Medicine, Psychology, and the Cultural Arts in Europe and America, 1880–1940,* ed. Mark S. Micale (Stanford, Calif.: Stanford University Press, 2004).

tion.[137] This modernist project was in turn the object of a savage critique by Philip Rieff in the first volume, *My Life Among the Deathworks,* of his last work.[138] According to Rieff, we are living in the third of three ages. In the first, order was rooted in sacred sources. Various "god terms" organized society. In the second, monotheistic age, God more aggressively organized society, and his warriors tried to bring all under his authority. This age lasted past the Reformation, for both Protestant and Catholic believed in being loyal to sacred order. But now, with no small thanks due to Freud, we live in the third, psychoanalytic or therapeutic age, in which our elites insist that we can live without the sacred authority of the first two ages. We have embarked on what Dawson—and Rieff with him—thought impossible, a culture not founded in sacred order. What psychoanalysis has revealed and practices is the destruction of authority and the sacred. It has discovered that all may be interrogated, and that the very interrogation of authority loosens its grip on us. "An aesthetics of therapy replaces the aesthetics of authority."[139] Or we might say that the new aesthetics is one of anti-authority. The first two ages were full of prohibitions, but now "all is allowed." In our anti-culture—was this not Foucault's message also?—the very study of our genealogy liberates us from it. Rieff hated all this, and his final proposal was that the remaining servants of authority subject the aesthetics of anti-authority to the same analysis that they had used to destroy the sacral sources of life. He did not think that good argument would prevail, but that two can play the game of rending authority risible.

There are many ironies here. One of the "new authorities" Freud proposed for throwing off the tyranny of the past, psychoanalysis, has been described as a secularized form of Kabbala, that is, more something very old than something new.[140] Some consider psychotherapy no science at all, but a kind of religion.[141] Denis Donoghue located something like Freud's later project in the origins around 1840 of an American national literature.[142] Listen to Thoreau in *Walden:* "I have lived some thirty years on this planet,

---

137. Tim Parks, "The Genius of Bad News," *NYRB* 54, 1 (January 11, 2007): 46–49 at 47. As Parks points out, Bernhard does not share the view that the world will change or progress through any criticism he might make. He thus repeatedly restaged the "modern liberal's interminably lost battle with his origins and milieu, which is to say with the human condition."

138. Subtitle: *Illustrations of the Aesthetics of Authority* (Charlottesville: University of Virginia Press, 2006).

139. R. R. Reno, "The End of Criticism," *IR* 42, 1 (Spring 2007): 42–46 at 44, a very useful review of Rieff which I am following, and see Rieff's *Freud: The Mind of the Moralist* (Chicago: University of Chicago Press, 1979).

140. Jeffrey J. Kripal, *Roads of Excess, Palaces of Wisdom* (Chicago: University of Chicago Press, 2001), 273.

141. William H. Epstein, *Psychotherapy as Religion: The Civil Divine in America* (Reno: University of Nevada Press, 2006).

142. Christopher Benfey, "American Jeremiad," *NYRB* 52, 14 (September 22, 2005): 65–67, at 65, for the following quotation from Thoreau.

and I have yet to hear the first syllable of valuable or even earnest advice from my seniors." Such a comment exemplifies why America has been so vulnerable to both the rhetoric of progress and those scenarios of both modernism and postmodernism which hardly can think of change except in revolutionary and emancipatory categories, the language of American origins.[143]

Modernism—of course without at first having had a name—has had a central presence in American history, first in the Revolution and then in the Emersonian strand of American thought. In regard to the former, as Mark Noll has so powerfully shown, America was founded by a Revolution which sought to discredit tradition, hierarchy, and historical precedent.[144] Listen to Thomas Paine (1737–1809):

> The case and circumstances of America present themselves as in the beginning of the world. . . . We have no occasion to roam for information into the obscure field of antiquity, nor hazard ourselves upon conjecture. We are . . . as if we had lived in the beginning of time.[145]

Such sentiment was followed in the national period by narratives of republican liberation. When we come to Ralph Waldo Emerson (1803–82), tradition is held to betray human potential. As Emerson writes in *Nature:*

> The foregoing generations beheld God and nature face to face; we, through their eyes. Why should not we also enjoy an original relation to the universe? Why should we not have a poetry and philosophy of insight and not of tradition, and a religion by revelation to us, and not the history of theirs? . . . There are new lands, new men, new thoughts. Let us demand our own works and laws and worship.[146]

The last sentence could be the banner of most writing in the humanities today, where a careerism built around constant emphasis on novelty and attack on the past reigns. But at least as important is the idea of "an original relation to the universe," implicitly at the heart of the category "experience," the inheritance of especially low church Protestantism's dismantling of tradition in favor of an unmediated relation of the individual to all that is, which is quite different from being related to God the Creator through Church and sacrament.[147] When Emerson became disenchanted with Christianity,

143. J. C. D. Clark, *Our Shadowed Present: Modernism, Postmodernism, and History* (Stanford, Calif.: Stanford University Press, 2004), 146.

144. I am describing the conclusion to *America's God: From Jonathan Edwards to Abraham Lincoln* (New York: Oxford University Press, 2002).

145. Quoted in William Pfaff, "Manifest Destiny: A New Direction for America," *NYRB* 54, 2 (February 15, 2007): 54–59 at 54.

146. Quoted and discussed in Wilfred M. McClay, "Tradition, History, and Sequoias," *FT* 131 (March, 2003): 41–47 at 42.

147. Robert Barron, "Evangelizing the American Culture," *SS* 3 (2002): 26–38 at 31–32,

not knowing he was to be called a "transcendentalist," he early on expressed this disenchantment in terms of unhappiness with the idea of a transcendent God. Was it not the heart that was the true creator?[148] Man must listen to himself, not others.[149]

Scholars such as Max Weber focused on the role of the Protestant Reformation as an especially important moment in the shaking off of the past, but in one respect such a claim may mislead.[150] In the sixteenth century Protestants and Catholics both appealed to the past to justify their views:

Sixteenth-century Christians, both Protestant and Catholic, shared a strong cultural assumption that what is older is better than what is new. That assumption applied not only to religion but to civic and cultural relations, art and architecture, law and custom . . . in short, to the whole range of activities and beliefs that give human society its character. The modern notion that new things are generally better and ought in a well-ordered society to supplant what is older was, on the whole, an idea that had not yet found a home. . . . The cultural bias was in favor of what was sound, tested, ancient, and rooted in the collective experience of generations.[151]

Though in the light of this quotation we must not see the sixteenth century as intending some form of modernism, there clearly *is* a sense in which modernity as a cultural expression or creation owes much to Protestantism. It may have taken a long time for the modernist stance or anti-authoritarianism implicit in Protestantism to work itself out, but certainly Weber was right to link the two. Protestantism taught a good part—arguably the most modernizing part—of Europe how to reject one tradition and constitute itself as a replacement.[152] The pattern has been repeated many times since.

The attack on tradition has taken myriad forms, including rejection of the "traditional" family or advancement of some form of constructionism which, refusing all ideas of the natural, demands moral equivalence for one

---

suggesting that "new age spirituality" and the "talk show" are but late forms of the emphasis on experience and the inner states of the individual.

148. *The Letters of Ralph Waldo Emerson,* ed. Ralph Rusk and Eleanor M. Tilton, 10 vols. (New York: Columbia University Press, 1939–96), vol. 7, 200, used in a very helpful essay by Roger Lundin, "'As if God Were Dead': American Literature and the Question of Scripture," in *The Bible and the University,* ed. David Lyle Jeffrey and C. Stephen Evans (Grand Rapids, Mich.: Eerdmans, 2007), 253–83. Lundin describes Emerson's exchanges with his Aunt Mary, who seems better to have seen the issues than some literary historians have: she called Emerson a "pantheist."

149. *The Journals and Miscellaneous Notebooks of Ralph Waldo Emerson,* ed. William H. Gilman et al., 16 vols. (Cambridge, Mass.: Harvard University Press, 1960–82), vol. 3, 199.

150. Robert N. Bellah, "On Being Catholic and American," in *Fire and Ice: Imagination and Intellect in the Catholic Tradition,* ed. Mary K. McCullough (Scranton, Pa.: University of Scranton Press, 2003), 29–47 at 30.

151. David C. Steinmetz, "Luther and Formation in Faith," in *Educating People of Faith,* 253–69.

152. This is worked out in my "The Two Europes," *The European Legacy: Toward New Paradigms* 14, 1 (2009): 133–48.

or another nontraditional institution.[153] With many the emphasis is on the gullibility of all belief systems which rest on authority, tradition, or revelation. The most radical expression thus far of such a point of view is found in the thought of Peter Singer, whose ethical utilitarianism is a form of rationalism completely dismissive of "tradition, habit, instinct, or anything that smacks of authority, especially religious authority."[154] It is a modern form of the ancient sophistic, "man [or in Singer's case, man and his animal friends, his very good animal friends] is the measure of all things."[155]

We have seen that commonly modernism has been tied to a quest for human autonomy and self-actualization, to articulation of one's own values, and to "egotism in work and art," all of which assume some form of self-creation or self-made man, the opposite of Christian belief in human dependence on the love of God, expressed in awe and humility and an older idea of autonomy as the creature's possession of a law proper to its own nature.[156] This seems to be why the language of "democracy" has become so central, a pure or ideal democracy quite different from any historical democracy. The historical democracies—Athens, for example—were elitist (few could vote) and very much favored those whose families had always lived in the polis (hence the large body of resident aliens). But "democracy" today tends to be a modernist term often used in a Kantian sense, severed from history and all the specifics of language and place, even from the nation itself. The emphasis is on one's rights rather than on some external frame of reference from which our obligations are derived. In the religious form of the liberal Protestantism of, say, a Phillips Brooks (1835–93), this "modernism" ultimately surrenders to the spirit of the times, though it so obfuscates and blunts this surrender that the average person does not notice his slide from confessional faith to common sentiment, from doctrines affirmed to an amorphous religious feeling embracing such categories as "authenticity" or "sincerity," sentiments that had been forming and advocated in a wide variety of literature since Adam Smith's *Theory of Moral Sentiments*.[157]

What was long called the Protestant establishment in the United States,

153. Cf. *Habermas and the Unfinished Project of Modernity: Critical Essays on the Philosophical Discourse of Modernity,* ed. Maurizio Passerin d'Entrèves and Seyla Benhabib (Cambridge, Mass.: MIT Press, 1997).

154. Thus the description of John Richard Neuhaus, "While We're At It," *FT* 141 (March 2004): 61–72 at 71.

155. On Singer I cannot recommend too highly the response of James B. Reichmann, *Evolution, Animal "Rights," and the Environment* (Washington, D.C.: The Catholic University of America Press, 2000).

156. The phrase quoted is a chapter title in Weaver, *Ideas Have Consequences*, 70–91.

157. R. R. Reno, "The Great Delayer," *FT* 145 (August/September 2004): 63–69 at 64 and 69. Cf. William R. Hutchison, *The Modernist Impulse in American Protestantism* (Durham, N.C.: Duke University Press, 1992).

a consensus among many of the socially elite to avoid the hard alternatives of a strict Calvinism or the abandonment of Christianity altogether by adherence to an inclusive but vague Christianity, typified by Episcopalianism, was an elite way station to disbelief, "Unitarianism in vestments."[158] There has also been a populist Roman Catholic form of modernism. This is not so much the modernism of the "modernist controversy" of the late nineteenth and early twentieth centuries as a notion of freedom which has tried to free even Catholics from the past.[159] Theoreticians such as Anscar Chapungco, a leading exponent of inculturation, argued that the Catholic liturgy must be accommodated to the modern mentality: "Liturgy . . . must not impose on culture a meaning or bearing that is intrinsically alien to its nature."[160] Here the Church is no longer in the position of teacher but of student, and what it is being taught is inculturation into modernity, the world as it now is. The liturgist becomes, in the words of a hostile interpreter, a "policeman of the sublime," making sure that liturgy never rises above the mundane.

All these things are linked: the quest for personal autonomy, egotism in work and art, self-creation are all linked in a centuries-long process which moves from a social order organized around family and friends, in which the primary association of sexuality is with reproduction, to a social order in which sexuality is primarily associated with personal intimacy and happiness.[161] The history of marriage illustrates this very well. The pre-Protestant view was that the sacrality of marriage was something objective, depending on its status as a sacrament. But for Luther the status of marriage, no longer considered a sacrament, must depend on the holiness of the partners. One might say this characterization still had its objective elements, but had slipped toward the subjective. With such Protestant poets as Philip Sydney (1554–86) and John Donne (1572–1631) marital love becomes something private and modern rather than social and feudal. But Donne wavers. Sometimes, in an Anglican vein, marriage remains the means for uniting a couple to Christ. Sometimes, rather, he thinks of love as a private erotic refuge.[162]

158. Reno, "The Great Delayer," 68–69. Reno argues that such Protestantism "kept the ugliest forms of modernism at bay in our culture: Emerson's latent Nietzschean mysticism of the will, social Darwinism, raw utilitarianism, Marxism, and more."

159. Peter R. D'Agostino, *Rome in America: Transnational Catholic Ideology from the Risorgimento to Fascism* (Chapel Hill: University of North Carolina Press, 2004).

160. Quoted from Robert Louis Wilken, "The Church's Way of Speaking," *FT* 155 (August/September 2005): 27–31 at 30, and see 31, on what follows.

161. John D'Emilio and Estelle B. Freedman, *Intimate Matters: A History of Sexuality in America* (New York: Harper & Row, 1988), xv–xviii, xx, 4, noting that already Protestantism had tended to emphasize the so-called nuclear family at the expense of kinship and community networks. "Sexual liberalism" is D'Emilio's and Freedman's term for the movement to valuing individual autonomy and pleasure in the sexual area as having a large role in human happiness.

162. For this and the following, see R. V. Young, "The Reformations of the Sixteenth and

With John Milton (1608–74) modern subjectivity expresses itself in tandem with the notion that Christ did not really mean marriage to be indissoluble. The Calvinist idea of inner assurance in election is expanded into an ideal of personal contentment and happiness, and now personal experience becomes the measure of conduct, of right and wrong. The goal of marriage seems to be happiness through dispelling loneliness, and, happiness lacking, we have no true marriage. Divorce is allowed. This is not to be the decision of some outside authority, but of the unhappy person. Such a view tends to equate freedom with personal autonomy, and has largely lost an understanding of freedom as a gift of God given to individuals so that they can realize a form of life or mode of being also given by God.[163] In any case, the category "experience," always vague and infinitely malleable, has largely replaced the notion that human life is to be linked to the objective order of the cosmos. Such a shift was well advanced in America by the 1920s, by which time the sexual ideas of middle-class youth "sounded the death knell for an older marriage ideal. Duty, moral character, personal sacrifice, and spiritual union were fast losing their appeal as the defining characteristics of matrimony and the conjugal relationship."[164]

The modernist project had a long gestation, and the contemporary historian Constantin Fasolt traces it to a historical revolution achieved between Renaissance and Enlightenment.[165] Like Jacob Burckhardt (1818–97) before him, who had tried to create a useful history or ancestry for those who wished a secular or modern life rather than one with religion at its center,[166] Fasolt sees the Middle Ages as dominated by custom and tradition, but also by the universalism which existed before nationalism replaced Christendom. Fasolt does not linger over the ways in which certain aspects of "modernity" are very old and can be traced back into the Middle Ages itself, not just to writers like Joachim of Fiore (c. 1132–1202), but to the increasing approval of change found in many twelfth-century writers.[167]

Seventeenth Centuries," in *Christian Marriage: A Historical Study*, ed. Glenn W. Olsen (New York: Herder and Herder, 2001), 269–301.

163. Reinhard Hütter, *Bound to Be Free: Evangelical Catholic Engagements in Ecclesiology* (Grand Rapids, Mich.: Eerdmans, 2004), works out the differences between the Christian and late modern understandings of freedom.

164. D'Emilio and Freedman, *Intimate Matters*, 265. They go on to describe what they call the "new ethic" of "companionate marriage," forged around emotional compatibility and personal satisfaction (265–67).

165. *The Limits of History* (Chicago: University of Chicago Press, 2004). The following description and critique is dependent on the review of this book by Ernst Breisach, *AHR* 110 (2005): 99. Elizabeth Brient, *The Immanence of the Infinite: Hans Blumenberg and the Threshold to Modernity* (Washington, D.C.: The Catholic University of America Press, 2002), with the review by Walter F. Veit, *Sp* 80 (2005): 196–97, is a valuable discussion of the onset of modernity, the limits of secularization as an ordering idea, and the emergence of "self-assertion."

166. Glenn W. Olsen, "Humanism: The Struggle to Possess a Word," *Lo* 7, 1 (Winter 2004): 97–116 at 101–4.

167. Giles Constable, "Renewal and Reform in Religious Life: Concepts and Realities,"

Argument about the valuation of change was indeed older than the Middle Ages, and though there was in the ancient world a powerful distaste for novelty, thoughtful people sometimes tried explicitly to avoid being cast as simply being in favor of or against change.

Christianity by its very newness stood for important forms of rupture ("You have heard that it was said to the men of old . . . But I say to you . . ." [Matthew 5]), and through the centuries Christian reform movements in various ways disturbed society. The relation of the living to the dead has always been a complex matter, but in traditional cultures around the world this relation has been pious. Especially with the coming of the "new religion" Christianity, with its emphasis on "knowing the truth," this piety did not exclude criticizing tradition or wishing in some way to reform or depart from it. Thus the second-century words of Justin Martyr, written of the willingness of the Christian even to die before relinquishing the truth, and presumably written to help the Romans see piety as including love for truth:

Common sense dictates that they who are truly pious men and philosophers should honor and cherish only what is true and refuse to follow the beliefs of their forefathers, if these beliefs be worthless. For sound reason not only demands that we do not heed those who did or taught anything wrong, but it requires that the lover of truth must do and say what is right, even when threatened with death, rather than save his own life.[168]

Such statements initiated a dialogue between "custom" and "truth" running through Christian history. The living see it as their obligation to take up the legacy of their ancestors, but not necessarily to transmit it unchanged. This was the sense of tradition for which T. S. Eliot argued in his famous essay "Tradition and the Individual Talent."[169] Much modernism wishes to sever this dialogue.

Even in the tenth century, in all of Western history surpassed in its goriness only by the twentieth, a gathering of bishops at Rheims in 909 described their day: "The cities are depopulated, the monasteries ruined and burned, the land is reduced to a solitude. As the first lived without law or constraint, abandoned to their passions, so now every man does what pleases him."[170] The bishops thought that in their day the race had been

---

in *Renaissance and Renewal in the Twelfth Century,* ed. Robert L. Benson and Giles Constable (Cambridge, Mass.: Harvard University Press, 1982), 37–67 at 63–66, with "Bibliographical Note." There are a number of relevant studies in *Tradition, Innovation, Invention. Fortschritts-verweigerung und Fortschrittsbewusstsein im Mittelalter,* ed. Hans-Joachim Schmidt (Berlin: De Gruyter, 2005).

168. *First Apology,* ch. 2, in *The Writings of Saint Justin Martyr,* tr. Thomas B. Falls (Washington, D.C.: The Catholic University of America Press, 1948), 34.

169. See also Eliot's *The Sacred Wood and Major Early Essays* (Mineola, N.Y.: Dover Publications, 1998).

170. *Christianity and European Culture: Selections from the Work of Christopher Dawson,* ed. Gerald J. Russello (Washington, D.C. 1998), 120.

reduced to the lamentable situation of the first men. This implies that for the most part the race had progressed beyond those rude first days. The so-called Gregorian reform of the following century certainly thought that one did not have to accept traditional social norms, but might work to uproot these.

From the second century, part of the standard repertoire of Christian apologists was defense of Christianity against the charge that it must be false because it was new. In the later fourth century, St. Ambrose in the dispute over the Altar of Victory derided Roman veneration of the past, his point being that such veneration could be so blind as to hinder improvement and advance and the embracing of new truth. In his *Letter* 18 he declared that clinging only to the past was a kind of barbarism. Hans-Georg Gadamer located a historical consciousness becoming aware of the historicity of all things in the early modern period, but Ambrose, Augustine, and then a number of twelfth-century writers possessed some such sensibility much earlier. Perhaps medieval people did not yet conclude from their observations about the universality of change to a relativism of the form of Michel de Montaigne's (1533–92), and in this sense Gadamer's characterization of early modernity is safe, but clearly from the time of the so-called Twelfth-Century Renaissance awareness of shift over time increasingly characterized the scholarly elite, who sometimes approved change to the better.[171]

Modernity for Fasolt is defined by the prizing of liberty, self-assertion, and autonomy, whether of individuals or of states (the latter called sovereignty). According to him an unbridgeable gap stands between medieval and modern, and this must henceforth define history. His views are almost the opposite of those postmodernists who use the Middle Ages to criticize all the wrong turns taken since.[172] For Fasolt historians must guard the gates against the reemergence of the past. As a perceptive reviewer has noted, this is voluntarism in its baldest form. No reason is given why one historical "event"—a three-centuries-long event at that—should become normative for all that follows. What is the sense of "a revolution made permanent"? Is it in fact true that the Middle Ages is simply dead? For some, for all? As irrationally or willfully as a Freud, Fasolt insists that we must not go home, that we must be modern.[173]

⟡

171. Hans-Georg Gadamer, "The Problem of Historical Consciousness," in *Interpretive Social Science: A Second Look,* ed. Paul Rabinow and William M. Sullivan (Berkeley: University of California Press, 1987), 89–90, with Peter Seixas, "Collective Memory, History Education, and Historical Consciousness," in *HS* 7, 2 (November/December 2005): 17–19 at 17.

172. Bruce Holsinger, *The Premodern Condition: Medievalism and the Making of Theory* (Chicago: University of Chicago Press, 2005).

173. "The Limits of History: An Exchange," *HS* 6, 5 (May–June, 2005): 5–17, gives a range of criticism of Fasolt's views.

There is a certain superficiality in seeing the modern period as simply engaged in opposition to the past. Certainly most people's views are more complicated and conflicted than that. This has led Darrin M. McMahon to propose that modernity is characterized not by the abandonment of the past, but by a struggle between Enlightenment and Counter-Enlightenment.[174] That is, not only was the Counter-Enlightenment—the resistance to Enlightenment ideals—a central feature of nineteenth-century society, it is and will remain a central feature of modernity. This is because the present is not characterized by an inevitable slide to secularism, but by a continuing, apparently unending struggle between Enlightenment and Counter-Enlightenment, between the advocates and opponents of a world without transcendence. This is the point of view of the present book.

Thinkers like George Grant will presumably continue to appear, attempting to subvert modernity at every step, and continuing a line of criticism going back to the French Counter-Revolutionary tradition itself.[175] Short of some world-transforming catastrophe or the unlikely victory of one party or the other—and here even totalitarianism failed—there can be no end to modernity as thus defined. Though thinkers as different as Bernard Lonergan and Jürgen Habermas have wished for a second Enlightenment, that is, a critical reevaluation of the first Enlightenment, and that is eminently desirable, what in any case we will have is continuing struggle.[176] Apparently the most we can hope for is the appreciation and appropriation by traditionalists and modernists of each other, that is, acknowledgment that neither Enlightenment nor Counter-Enlightenment are homogeneously good, and that partisans of both would be wise to seek out good in the other.

A modernist project characterized the "atheist humanism" of the twentieth century.[177] Both Stalin and Mao, with revolutionary Marxism-Leninism, thought society a tabula rasa which, like man himself, could be given whatever content one wished.[178] Of course the secularism of the Marxist experiment was not the same as that of the liberal West, for Soviet officialdom was

174. *Enemies of the Enlightenment: The French Counter-Enlightenment and the Making of Modernity* (New York: Oxford University Press, 2001).

175. *George Grant and the Subversion of Modernity: Art, Philosophy, Religion, Politics and Education,* ed. Arthur Davis (Toronto: University of Toronto Press, 1996). For a longer list of cultural critics, see *The Superfluous Men: Conservative Critics of Modern Culture, 1900–1945,* edited with a new introduction by Robert M. Crunden (Wilmington, Del.: ISI Books, 1999). See also *Critics of the Enlightenment: Readings in the French Counter-Revolutionary Tradition,* ed. Christopher Olaf Blum (Wilmington, Del.: ISI Books, 2004).

176. *Philosophic Interventions in the Unfinished Project of Enlightenment,* ed. Axel Honneth et al. (Cambridge, Mass.: MIT Press, 1992).

177. The classic study is Henri de Lubac, *The Drama of Atheist Humanism,* tr. Edith M. Riley (New York: Sheed & Ward, 1950).

178. Ian Buruma, "Master of Fear," *NYRB* 51, 7 (May 13, 2004): 4–6 at 5.

at one and the same time modernist in its severing of itself from the social and religious past, and anti-modernist in not approving much that in the arts passed as modernism. It is notoriously difficult to peg someone such as Dmitrii Dmitrievich Shostakovich (1906–75), for some "the last [or most recent] great composer," living his life out in the Soviet environment, sometimes compromising but in other ways "rising above it all," in love with all music "from Bach to Offenbach," and the composer of some of the most transcendent music we have.[179]

Some now go so far as to claim that there is no right to religious education, which, it is said, inculcates reactionary values. According to James Dwyer, the state is obligated to prohibit or monitor such education, even if at home.[180] To be discarded with Freud's tyranny of the past, others say, is the place of the father, that is, the father-son relationship as the model of proper relation to the past.[181] Theodor Adorno's (1903–69) book from 1950, *The Authoritarian Personality*, with its equation of fascism and tradition, was an especially ruthless presentation of this case against the past.[182] The need to be "absolutely modern" has indeed become in some quarters a "terrorist slogan" (Milan Kundera, *Life is Elsewhere*) in service to the obligation to devalue all earlier values.[183]

In the twentieth century the desire to cast off tradition penetrated into the most unexpected cultural corners: in the 1920s the secretary of commerce under Herbert Hoover could declare: "Tradition is the enemy of progress."[184] "Modernity," we might say, had come to represent the "absolute starting point of progress."[185] This was only exacerbated by "the events of 1968 in Paris," which "seemed to signal a natural affinity between political revolution and a post-structuralism on the brink of cultural studies. Everything, it seemed, could be made new."[186] As a kind of response to all this, Jörg Friedrich, though of course lamenting all the dead of World War II, ends a moving book on the destruction of Germany with a lament for all the libraries and archives destroyed, the beautiful old cities in ruin, the contrast between the beauty of the old and the ugliness of what replaced it, the zeal of those who wished to construct—and often succeeded—a mod-

---

179. Jay Norlinger, "DDS at 100," *NR* 58, 8 (May 8, 2006): 54–55 at 54 for the first and third phrases.

180. *Religious Schools vs. Children's Rights* (Ithaca, N.Y.: Cornell University Press, 1998).

181. María Zambrano, *Hacia un saber sobre el alma* (Madrid: Alianza, 2001), 147–48.

182. Christopher Shannon, "Catholicism as the Other," *FT* 139 (January 2004): 46–52 at 51.

183. Olivier Boulnois, "The Modernity of the Middle Ages," *Co* 30 (2003): 234–59 at 236. This article makes response to the ideas of Hans Blumenberg.

184. John Lukacs, *At the End of an Age* (New Haven, Conn.: Yale University Press, 2002), 78 n. 22.

185. Adrian Walker, "Introduction," *Co* 30 (2003): 177–79 at 177, describing Boulnois, "Modernity of the Middle Ages."

186. Paul J. Griffiths, "Christ and Critical Theory," *FT* 145 (August/September 2004): 46–55 at 47.

ern Germany "stripped of history," engaged in a "collective turning away from German history and culture."[187]

A broader form of lament over modernism's turning away from the past can be discerned by the discriminating reader in much of the literature of modernism itself. Thus my colleague Vincent Pecora has cleverly shown nostalgia for an older kind of household and economy running through much of the so-called modernist tradition.[188] Indeed, one might speak of two traditions tracking each other since the French Revolution, one of deep melancholia and regret over the lost past, and one of boosterism for an always-better future.[189] In Paris, the "capital of modernity," one can trace this struggle to the present. The expression of reaction, Sacre Coeur, looks out over such expressions of progress, at least equally vacuous, as Pei's pyramid at the Louvre and the Centre Pompidou.[190]

Milton's immortal characterization of Satan at the beginning of *Paradise Lost*—"Better to reign in Hell, than to serve in Heav'n"—has a certain application to modern self-assertion. Though, as Foucault showed, the cultivation of the self had been taken fairly far by certain of the ancients, it was above all the Age of Reason, the seventeenth and eighteenth centuries, which in its cultivation of the self in such figures as Diderot and Rousseau, drowned the world of Pascal or La Rochefoucauld. The old values of self-denial and self-repression were overwhelmed by self-expression.[191] This is a link between Enlightenment and Romanticism. That is, while the "heart" of Romanticism rebelled against the sterile "reason" of the Enlightenment, the two movements had more in common than is often admitted. Above all, if we leave difficult-to-classify figures such as William Blake (1757–1827) aside, both Enlightenment and Romanticism centered on the self, on the experiencing and creative ego.[192] This is why the Romantics were so "unreliable," so "unstable." They were not necessarily attempting to reassert traditions which the Age of Reason had overridden, perhaps to return to

187. Ian Buruma, "The Destruction of Germany," *NYRB* 51, 16 (October 21, 2004): 8–12 at 12.

188. *Households of the Soul* (Baltimore: Johns Hopkins University Press, 1997).

189. The melancholic half of the story is told by Peter Fritzsche, *Stranded in the Present: Modern Time and the Melancholy of History* (Cambridge, Mass.: Harvard University Press, 2004).

190. David Harvey, *Paris, Capital of Modernity* (London: Routledge, 2003).

191. P. S. Furbank, "Body and Soul," *NYRB* 51, 7 (April 29, 2004): 49–51 at 50–51.

192. The circle of artists who looked to Blake with such reverence that they called him "the Interpreter" used this label because they saw Blake as a prophet receiving messages from God, to which he submitted himself. There may be a romantic notion of genius in this, but the larger point is that Blake saw himself not as creating things, but as interpreting that which had been given to him: James Fenton, "In Samuel Palmer's Garden," *NYRB* 53, 8 (May 11, 2006): 34–36 at 34. Alfonso López Quintás, "Aportación Decisiva del Cristianismo a la Cultura Occidental," *Verbo* 433–34 (March–April 2005): 217–43 at 228, is right to remind us that there is a web of Christian inspiration still found in, say, Wagner, but this detritus of earlier ages, the continuing presence of classical mythology and medieval legend, does not seem to me to undermine the point made here.

a more communitarian Middle Ages. As often as not under the banner of freedom from the old order, many asserted a preference for chaos and the liberated individual.

Obviously, if, say, Beethoven were taken up at this point, further qualifications would be in order. In 1819 Beethoven wrote, "In the world of art, as indeed in the whole of creation, freedom and progress are the main objectives," and it has been observed that by the end he dwelt in "a world of his own making."[193] Thus, in an obvious sense he has a place in the drive to modernism, yet it is not so clear that this is an adequate description. Is the transcendentalism at which his music aimed self-created, or a statement of realities to which he had broken through? Why, all through his life, did he return to the study of Bach? While there is an emphasis on individual genius and liberty in his music and politics, he also appreciated the tradition in which he stood. As E. T. A. Hoffmann insisted, Beethoven was not a wild genius but the soberest of composers, believing that music had a "nature" which the composer had to capture.[194] In composing his *Mass in C Major Op. 86,* first presented in 1808, he, against Haydn, whose masses had become operatic in their disconnection from the underlying liturgy, reasserted the unity of the mass, eliminating solo arias and the separation between *Sanctus* and *Benedictio.* Reprising the music of the opening *Kyrie* at the close of the *Agnus Dei* reinforced the unity of this mass. Beethoven's younger contemporary Felix Mendelssohn (1809–47), less attracted to the cult of creativity and freedom, nevertheless manifested a tension partially parallel to Beethoven's. In Mendelssohn the tension was between reverence for the great masters of the past, and a desire to bring them into the present.[195]

When it came to theory, writers such as Willard Huntington Wright, in his 1916 *The Creative Will,* presented the artist as "an omnipotent god who moulds and fashions the destiny of a new world."[196] The view is that Honoré de Balzac, a true artist-demiurge, is to be preferred to Émile Zola, "a mere copyist of a preexisting reality." Today parallel questions about genius and creativity weigh heavily on Chinese letters as they increasingly come in contact with the West and Western ideas of creativity. In Nell Freudenberger's *The Dissident,* Yuan Zhao calls this "the problem of copying."[197]

193. Both quotations are from Lewis Lockwood, "Beethoven Beyond Classicism," *NYRB* 50, 12 (July 17, 2003): 27–29 at 28.

194. Charles Rosen, "From the Troubadours to Frank Sinatra," *NYRB* 53, 6 (February 23 2006): 41–45 at 43. Cf. the discussion of Mozart in Rosen, "The Best Book on Mozart," *NYRB* 54, 16 (October 25, 2007): 25–27 at 26, and the subsequent "What Mozart Meant: An Exchange," *NYRB* 54, 19 (December 6, 2007): 76–77.

195. Lewis Lockwood, "Which Is the Real Mendelssohn?" *NYRB* 51, 17 (November 4, 2004): 44–46 at 46.

196. J. M. Coetzee, "The Making of William Faulkner," *NYRB* 52, 6 (April 7, 2005): 20–30 at 20, for this and the next quotation.

197. On this and the following see Jennifer Schuessler, "The Terrified Copyist," *NYRB* 53, 16 (October 19, 2006): 18.

Brought up on a discipline of copying, because knowing that "what is original does not come out of air," Yuan Zhao wonders not only whether he
can avoid aping Western art, but whether the very valuing of originality is
not a Western import. Perhaps this puts the general problem of originality
too simply. Yuan Zhao's declaration that the original does not come out
of air expresses a worldwide idea of the relation of tradition to originality.
A "Foreword" to Euripides's *Helen* notes that "at every point, the sensitive
reader will feel the dramatist's delight in his own virtuosity, in his ability
to 'dance in the chains of convention,'" and such "dancing in the chains
of convention" must have been a common experience in many traditional
cultures.[198]

A perceptive American visitor to Spain has understood the difference
between the old values and the new. During a month in Spain, each day attending mass in various parts of the country, she noted that everywhere the
mass was said the same. The manner of the priests everywhere was unvary-
ing: "Their movements were fluid but exact, informed by a deep concentration focused on humbling themselves in an act of surrender."[199] Coming
from a country in which hardly ever are two masses alike, our visitor was
struck by the homogeneity she met. The priests lacked "personality" and
their saying of the mass lacked "dynamism." Something was missing. Even
the churches seemed dark voids. At least as puzzling as this was the fact that,
away from the altar, the priests clearly did not lack personality. As soon as
the mass was over, there they were, smiling and witty. It was just during the
mass that they never smiled, never suggested something of themselves. We
might say that our visitor had discovered that in Spain even today the mass
is still said as if God is its author, and the priest simply an instrument in
God's hands. The priest officiates in humility, effacing himself before Him
who comes in the mass. There is no pride, the priest is not "creative" nor
"original" nor "chummy." The goal is not in any immediate way fostering
community or focusing on the self, but opening up to the transcendent. In
sum, to go to mass in Spain is to experience the supernatural. I, who have
spent more time in Spain than our American visitor and have sometimes
experienced masses that suggest that, there too, creativity sometimes raises
its ugly head, nevertheless assent to her main point.

When the great conductor Carlo Maria Giulini died on June 15, 2005,
he was remembered as seeing himself as "a reverential servant of the great
composers."[200] He did not, as some, view the scores of others as occasions
for centering on his own creativity, but tried to pass on the genius he had

198. William Arrowsmith, "Editor's Foreword," Euripides, *Helen,* tr. James Michie and Colin Leach (Oxford: Oxford University Press, 1981), xi.
199. Carolyn Foster, "Pageantry Over Piety," *AB* 10, 8 (November 2004): 4–5 at 4, on this
and the following.
200. "Italy," *DMN,* June 16, 2005.

received. We can still find explicitly religious expressions of a similar view, as in the movie *Junebug* (2005), in which a North Carolinian "primitive" artist gives a Southern Baptist rendition of his paintings as "sent from God."

Romanticism was built around the idea of the individual who had the gift of special sight. In one of its forms it united a traditional sense of inspiration with the more modern notion of genius, in the process allowing the individual to come to the fore so that he or she was less "handmaid" than "creator." Some such sense of inspiration remains to the present, and is given voice by, say, Bob Dylan. Similarly, the late, deeply religious filmmaker Andrei Tarkovsky thought of himself as having been given an almost unbearable gift to foresee the future.[201] As much as any romantic, he thought of himself as possessing mysterious powers to see into the heart of reality, but unlike the romantics he understood that a greater-than-himself or higher reality was speaking through him. Thus a quite traditional sense of inspiration and transcendence lived into our own day.

~

There may sometimes have been reluctance or bad conscience in the rebellion of the artists: in the words of Leo Steinberg, modernism "invites us to applaud the destruction of values which we still cherish."[202] We find here not so much a reasoned rejection, say of transcendence, as a groundless refusal. Although modern people are not the first to entertain contradictory ideas simultaneously, Orhan Pamuk thinks that part of the modern condition is a perpetual contradicting of oneself, a slipperiness of mind, and of course this can express itself in a certain irrational reaction for its own sake.[203] Hence the common ground between modernism and nihilism as already diagnosed by Nietzsche and Heidegger, and found also in the nihilist streak that ran through Nazism.[204] The economist Timur Kuran has spoken of "preference falsification," making people publicly praise ideas they believe are false by the mobilization of social pressure, and this too seems related to the nihilist phenomena.[205] But there is something more universal here. Students of the Soviet Union have sometimes wondered about the cooperation of so many with slogans and platitudes many knew at least at some level were falsified by reality. Steven Kotkin has written of a "dual reality" in which people lived, at once believing and disbelieving in

---

201. Gabriel F. Giralt, "Andrei Tarkovsky's Adaptation of Motifs Embedded in Leonardo Da Vinci's *The Adoration of the Magi*," *Canadian Journal of Film Studies* 14, 2 (Autumn 2005): 71–83 at 80.

202. Quoted in Michael E. DeSanctis, *Building from Belief: Advance, Retreat, and Compromise in the Remaking of Catholic Church Architecture* (Collegeville, Minn.: Liturgical Press, 2002), 60.

203. "Freedom to Write," *NYRB* 53, 9 (May 25, 2006): 6.

204. David B. Hart, "Christ and Nothing," *FT* 136 (October 2003): 47–56 at 49.

205. *Private Truths, Public Lies: the Social Consequences of Preference Falsification* (Cambridge, Mass.: Harvard University Press, 1995).

what they were told.[206] No doubt this was true of the Soviet Union, but something like this must be the experience of many people in many times, and above all in our times.

To stay with art, some would say, as impressionism and expressionism explored the limits of the sense of sight itself, art turned into experimenting with self-created worlds.[207] This is how Thomas Molnar reads Kandinsky, as someone who no longer affirmed the "good purpose" and harmony of the cosmos, and turned from all forms of representation to weaving endless abstraction.[208] This reading can be disputed, and Robert Lipsey sees in Kandinsky and many of his contemporaries movement toward—but failure to arrive at—an art both contemporary and spiritually alive.[209] This seems the fairer judgment. The turn to self-created worlds undoubtedly describes some artists, but is inapplicable to others. Some American abstractionists, indeed, felt that European modernism failed to confront the sublime.[210] Before them, in the late nineteenth century, George Inness increasingly insisted that the goal of a simply accurate description of the world missed its sacred beauty: for him, art, as an endeavor of the spirit, is the ally of religion, not science.[211]

There have been various reactions against the subjectivism of many early twentieth-century avant-garde movements: some of these were brought together at the Museo Thyssen-Bornemisza in Madrid from October 2005 to January 2006 under the exhibition title "Mimesis: Modern Realism 1918–1945." As already suggested, it is the gravest mistake to equate mimetic or representational art with tradition, and abstract art with modernity.[212]

206. *Magnetic Mountain: Stalinism as a Civilization* (Berkeley: University of California Press, 1995); also see Anne Applebaum, "Pulling the Rug Out from Under," *NYRB* 51, 2 (February 12, 2004): 9–11.

207. Joseph Ratzinger (Benedict XVI), *The Spirit of the Liturgy,* tr. John Saward (San Francisco: Ignatius Press, 2000), 131, and see 145–46. Cf. *Modernity and Modernism: French Painting in the Nineteenth Century,* ed. Francis Frascina et al. (New Haven, Conn.: Yale University Press, 1993).

208. Thomas Molnar, "Tradition, Science and the Centuries," *An* 9 (2003): 171–77 at 171–72, citing the classic works on the disintegration of cosmic harmony; Alexandre Koyré, *From the Closed World to the Infinite Universe* (Baltimore: Johns Hopkins University Press, 1957); and Paul Hazard, *La crise de la conscience européenne (1680–1715)* (Paris: Boivin, 1935).

209. *An Art of Our Own: the Spiritual in Twentieth-Century Art* (Boston: Shambhala, 1988), arguing for religious and philosophical concerns in Cézanne, Picasso, Mondrian, Klee, Matisse, Jackson Pollock, Mark Rothko, and Georgia O'Keefe.

210. Jack Flam, "Space Men," *NYRB* 48, 7 (April 26, 2001): 10–14 at 14, commenting on the paradox that the large-scale painting of people like Pollock resulted in a kind of art often more public than European abstractionism.

211. Andrew Butterfield, "The Genius of George Inness," *NYRB* 55, 14 (September 25, 2008): 8–10 at 8.

212. On many of these issues, see Francesca Aran Murphy, *Art and Intellect in the Philosophy of Étienne Gilson* (Columbia: University of Missouri Press, 2004), and Robert Scholes, *Paradox of Modernism* (New Haven, Conn.: Yale University Press, 2006). José Marín-Medina, "La voluntad de modernidad y la cuestión realista," *El Cultural,* October 13, 2005, 30–31, is on the Madrid exhibit.

Meyer Schapiro long ago noted that much Romanesque art does not display an orderly use of general forms or geometrical abstraction, but is a helter-skelter combination of "archaic primitivism and increasing realism."[213] Romanesque abstraction distorts for expressive ends. Perhaps a better way of putting this would be to say that from the first Christianity produced a different "art of the body." God had become incarnate, but because body is ordered to soul, sensual nudes are ruled out, and in medieval sculpture we generally find a certain "writhing and squirming" in which the body reveals the spiritual tremors below its surface.[214] The Madrid exhibit claimed that modern realism was itself one way of being modern. Some would call both the American social realism of the 1930s and the reaction against it in abstract art after World War II "modern," and on both sides of the Atlantic modernism has wavered between abstractionism and representation.[215]

Neither abstractionism nor representation was new in the twentieth century. It has been said of Raphael that he "eventually resolves every natural shape into ovals; for all their solidity, his figures are also powerfully abstract."[216] The almost barren church interiors of the Dutch painter Pieter Saenredam (1597–1665) seem a form of abstract art.[217] And the genre scenes of Gerard der Borch (1617–81) have also been described as "fundamentally abstract."[218] Olivier Boulnois suggests that medieval concern that art be more than representational, overridden in the early modern centuries, only returns about the beginning of the twentieth century.[219] Vincent van Gogh, dying on the doorstep of modernity, perhaps complicates such a view: at least with him we have far from mimetic landscapes which seem almost to have arrived from another world, endowed with the idea that God uses the objects of everyday life to speak to us.[220]

Similarly, as in earlier periods, we sometimes find at least in the early Picasso and Matisse an attempt to "evoke the sacred through objects of the everyday world."[221] Certainly this is true of Gaudi, central to whose work

213. Quoted from the appreciation of Schapiro by Willibald Sauerländer, "The Great Outsider: Meyer Schapiro," *Romanesque Art: Problems and Monuments,* 2 vols. (London: Pindar, 2004), II, 833–49 at 837, suggesting a link between Schapiro's appreciation of the Romanesque and his defense of modern abstract expressionism. See further on representation and Schapiro, Seidel, "Introduction" to *Romanesque Architectural Sculpture,* xxxvii, xxxix, and 156–59, 160–63.

214. Richard John Neuhaus, "Le Danse Macabre," *FT* 171 (March 2007): 56–57, commenting on Michael J. Lewis, "Body and Soul," *Commentary* 123, 1 (January 2007): 129–33.

215. Paul Wood, *Modernism in Dispute: Art since the Forties* (New Haven, Conn.: Yale University Press, 1993).

216. Ingrid Rowland, "The Magician," *NYRB* 51, 20 (December 16, 2004): 16–20 at 18.

217. Sanford Schwartz, "White Secrets," *NYRB* 53, 2 (February 9, 2006): 8–9 at 8.

218. Sanford Schwartz, "Ladies in Satin," *NYRB* 52, 2 (February 10, 2005): 8–11 at 8.

219. "Modernity of the Middle Ages," 258.

220. John Updike, "Determined Spirit," *NYRB* 52, 19 (December 1, 2005): 13–14 at 13.

221. Jack Flam, "Twin Peaks," *NYRB* 50, 5 (March 27, 2003): 26–28 at 27. Cf. John Golding, *Paths to the Absolute: Mondrian, Malevich, Kandinsky, Pollock, Newman, Rothko, and Still* (Princeton, N.J.: Princeton University Press, 2000), and Mark C. Taylor, *Disfiguring: Art, Archi-*

was his observation as a child of his artisan father's work as a metalsmith. In presenting an alternative to much that he deplored in the modern world, Gaudi brought the forms of nature and of rural Catalonian vernacular into a sacred art full of joy and playfulness.[222] As from 1878 he worked on the Templo Expiatorio de la Sagrada Familia, this work itself effected a conversion in his life, which as he aged became ever more ascetic as he walked the streets, begging for donations to continue the building of his church.[223] He saw God as the true source of his Templo, reportedly remarking, "Man does not create . . . he discovers." If his cause for beatification is successful, he will become the first professional artist ever to be so recognized. Similarly, the wonderful Palau de la Música Catalana in Barcelona, built between 1905 and 1908 by Lluís Domènech I Montaner and often described as one of modernism's great creations, is based largely on natural forms, also incorporating many medieval elements.

The combining of some form of traditionalism and of modernism or radicalism was common in the early twentieth century. In England from the late 1920s the Catholic traditionalist Chelsea group to which Christopher Dawson belonged demanded radically new forms of art. In the words of one of its members, "We were up against, dismayed by, the hideous expressions of modern religion."[224] In America we have Frank Lloyd Wright, at once innovative in his modernist functionalism but rejecting celebration of discontinuity, and deeply attached to the rural and communitarian, somewhat in the manner of the arts and crafts movement. In one way or another, many "modernists" were anti-modern.[225] The singular music of Manuel de Falla (1876–1946), at odds with the world around him, has been labeled "sacred passions."[226]

---

tecture, Religion (Chicago: University of Chicago Press, 1992), on artistic experience as religious experience.

222. Robert Hughes, "For the Love of Gaudi," Condé Nast Traveler (June 2004): 118–27, a sometimes silly and misinformed popular article which nevertheless makes some good points. Hughes so misunderstands Gaudi's religion as to be unable to explain how an emphasis on penitence and disgust with much in modern art could result in an architecture so full of joy. Hughes means it as criticism when he says that the Church of Gaudi's day wanted a new Counter-Reformation, but one might note the parallelism between the exuberance of Counter-Reformation architecture and of Gaudi's (121). On modernism in Catalonia, see Borja de Riquer et al., Modernismo: Architecture and Design in Catalonia (New York: Monacelli Press, 2003).

223. "Holy Architect," AB 10, 7 (October 2004), noting in turn the conversion through working on this church of the Japanese architect Etsuro Sotoo, who began working in 1978 to finish Gaudi's project. Cf. William H. Robinson et al., Barcelona and Modernity: Picasso, Gaudi, Miro, Dali (New Haven, Conn.: Yale University Press, 2006).

224. Tom Burns, The Use of Memory: Publishing and Further Pursuits (London: Sheed & Ward, 1993), 44.

225. Louise Blakeney Williams, Modernism and the Ideology of History: Literature, Politics, and the Past (New York: Cambridge University Press, 2002), and Robert Hughes, "Master Builders," NYRB 54, 14 (September 27, 2007): 46–49 at 46.

226. Carol A. Hess, Sacred Passions: The Life and Music of Manuel de Falla (New York: Oxford University Press, 2004).

As we have seen, in some cases we can speak of "modern art despite modernism," that is, of an anti-modernist impulse that continues in art some think of as modern.[227] Sure judgment is difficult, and some now use a language of postmodernism in art and architecture as elsewhere.[228] Clearly there is a postmodern irony, in which all forms of transcendence are denied and the ironist finds what significance art has in the contingency of history or in impersonal cosmic forces.[229] But there is also postmodernism without irony, what Terry Teachout has described as a renewed quest for beauty, which he finds in the plays of David Ives, the movies of Whit Stillman or John Sayles, the dances of Mark Morris, and in the "new tonalist" composers.[230] And what are we to make of what some are calling neo-Baroque aesthetics, the late twentieth-century tendency to nurture a culture of special effects?[231]

One writer has described the surprise one feels in many art museums on entering the twentieth-century exhibits: it is as if all correlation to or continuity with the past has been lost.[232] For many, "things turn ugly," and there is palpable disappointment or a sense that one is being "put on." Of course there are continuities, but the discontinuities are much more striking.[233] Though David Walsh convincingly argues that specifically modern-

227. Robert Storr, *Modern Art Despite Modernism* (New York: Museum of Modern Art, 2000). For an example of an attempt to sift these issues in regard to one architect, see Sarah Williams Goldhagen, *Louis Kahn's Situated Modernism* (New Haven, Conn.: Yale University Press, 2001), and for praise of Kahn's classicism and criticism of mainstream modernism, see Martin Filler, *Makers of Modern Architecture* (New York: New York Review Books, 2007), and Hughes, "Master Builders."

228. Charles Jencks, *The New Paradigm in Architecture: The Language of Post-Modernism* (New Haven, Conn.: Yale University Press, 2002).

229. William A. Frank, "Western Irreligion and Resources for Culture in Catholic Religion," *Lo* 7, 1 (Winter 2004): 17–44 at 38–39.

230. *A Terry Teachout Reader* (New Haven, Conn.: Yale University Press, 2004).

231. Angela Ndalianis, *Neo-Baroque Aesthetics and Contemporary Entertainment* (Cambridge, Mass.: MIT Press, 2004).

232. Robert R. Reilly, *The Music of the Spheres,* The Thomas Aquinas College Lecture Series, December 2001 (Santa Paula, Calif. 2001), 1. On p. 2 Reilly quotes a prescient anti-Wagnerite predicting the future in 1865: "The music would resemble that of a crazed sculptor, who would do exactly the opposite of what had been done before him; in place of a mouth parallel to the chin, he would chisel a perpendicular mouth. In the place of the nose, he would put a cheek, and in the place of the generally-accepted two eyes, a single eye in the middle of the forehead."

233. Cf. *Modernism: 1890–1930*, ed. Malcolm Bradbury and James McFarlane (New York: Penguin, 1976); T. J. Clark, *Farewell to an Idea: Episodes from a History of Modernism* (New Haven, Conn.: Yale University Press, 1999); *Modernism: An Anthology of Sources and Documents,* ed. Vassiliki Kolocotroni et al. (Chicago: University of Chicago Press, 1998); and the incendiary study by E. Michael Jones, *Dionysos Rising: The Birth of Cultural Revolution out of the Spirit of Music* (San Francisco: Ignatius Press 1994), an unrelenting analysis of modern music as a vehicle of cultural revolution. Jasper Griffin, "The Comedy Murder Case," *NYRB* 49, 12 (July 18, 2002): 35–38 at 38 reminds us that too much can be attributed to modernism: "The period around the first World War was so startlingly innovative that an intimidated public still thinks of it, a cen-

ist enterprises in fields other than art, such as the hermeneutics of suspicion, deconstructionism, and the critique of religion as wish fulfillment, are based on the transcendent principle of desire for truth, and thus that it is not possible to eliminate the transcendent, many people seem practically to have done this.[234] We have moved from a medieval or Byzantine situation, in which in art holy people were presented with a minimum of natural context; through the diminishment of holy figures and the increase of the natural landscape of a Pieter Bruegel the Elder (c. 1520–69); to the suggestion of Romanticism that if landscape is not all we see, the divine is but an invisible presence in nature; to a modernism in which we float free of nature and God.[235]

George Steiner has provocatively asked whether artistic creation is possible without belief in transcendent value.[236] That is, either music and literature have "made-up" meanings, in which "anything goes," or they share in or express transcendent values. In the latter case, always a cosmic view can be recovered; otherwise a cosmic point of view is as arbitrary as any other. Much more than modernism is involved here, for the unsettling discoveries of students of culture would suggest the incompatibility of beauty and democracy.[237] Concentrated power such as we find in monarchies tends to express itself in and thus produce aesthetic structures by which to justify itself: thus the prominence of ritual in the life of the late medieval court or the public ceremonies of the early modern city. Diffuse power such as we find in democracies tends to express itself in and produce functional structures.[238] This does not mean that concentrated power cannot produce great ugliness or democracies objects of beauty, but it does mean that aesthetic considerations will tend to lose out to functional considerations in democracies, creating aimless public spaces. This is one more reason for the lover

---

tury later, as 'modern art.' Terms like 'postmodern' let us evade the recognition that the period was not, after all, decisive. The arts have gone on, and in directions very different from those envisaged by Jarry and Schoenberg and Braque."

234. *Guarded by Mystery: Meaning in a Postmodern Age* (Washington, D.C.: The Catholic University of America Press, 1999). Robert Coles, *The Secular Mind* (Princeton, N.J. 1999), believes the transcendent has largely been excised or tamed by contemporary secular rhythms of life, and that things such as churchgoing are compartmentalized practices within an overwhelmingly secular existence hardly open to transformation: this was Nietzsche's point when he said God was dead.

235. John Updike, "The Thing Itself," *NYRB* 48, 19 (November 19, 2001): 10–12 at 10.

236. *Real Presences* (Chicago 1989).

237. Against those who would adduce the exception of Periclean Athens, I would quote Will Cuppy, *The Decline and Fall of Practically Everybody* (New York: Dorset Press, 1956), 32: "Pericles was the greatest statesman of ancient Greece. He ruled Athens for more than thirty years in its most glorious period. . . . Or, rather, the people ruled, for Athens was a democracy. At least, that's what Pericles said it was. He only told them what to do."

238. This line of thought and further bibliography may be found in C. Stephen Jaeger, *Ennobling Virtue: In Search of a Lost Sensibility* (Philadelphia: University of Pennsylvania Press, 1999), 41–42.

of the good, true, and beautiful to keep a certain reserve in regard to the political values of the day.

Against the modernist situation, whether we are speaking of urban or of ecclesiastical spaces, we now have the spiritual reaction, sometimes of religious inspiration, of the architects themselves, attempting in one way or another, sometimes under the label of "organicism," to reconnect at least with history, specifically with the history of architecture.[239] Gaudi in Sagrada Familia tried to construct a church distinctly of the twentieth century, but synthesizing tradition and innovation.[240] Around 1900 the radical painter Paul Signac feared submitting to pure abstraction, and wished his work linked with history.[241] Joan Miró tried to link Catalan Romanesque art with contemporary painting. As always there are degrees, and we also have such apparent iconoclasts as Mondrian, Kandinsky, and Malevitch.[242] One student has described these latter as in their various ways taking "paths to the Absolute," often the expression of rejection of that materialism at the heart of modernism which denies the primacy of the spiritual.[243] In music the Polish composer Witold Lutoslawski (1913–94), while writing such works as *Concerto for Orchestra* (1954) in a very contemporary idiom, did not want to abandon the values of the past and in the event achieved a beautiful "non-tonal" music.

In literature the difficult-to-classify poet Czeslaw Milosz, Roman Catholic but with his own distinctive view of things, objected to the attempt of modernism to rebel against past literature, and to render life meaningless.[244] For Milosz, writing in occupied Poland, the horrors of his time had been prepared by a whole string of charlatans who had done away with traditional ideas of absolute good and evil and had made basically nihilistic and destructive ideas plausible by presenting them as beautiful or progressive. Truth had been repudiated for action.[245] To the degree that the gods

---

239. Stanford Kwinter, *Architectures of Time: Toward a Theory of the Event in Modernist Culture* (Cambridge, Mass.: MIT Press, 2001).

240. Maria Antonietta Crippa, "A Cathedral for the Twentieth Century: Antoni Gaudi's Project for the Sagrada Familia," *Co* 29 (2002): 762–69.

241. Robert L. Herbert, "An Anarchist's Art," *NYRB* 48, 20 (December 20, 2001): 20–25 at 22. This article also notes Signac's dependence on Pierre Kropotkin's idea that "modern technology was to be decentralized and put at the service of largely autonomous productive units that would be established away from modern industrial cities, which degraded labor and life" (24).

242. Alain Besançon, *The Forbidden Image: An Intellectual History of Iconoclasm,* tr. Jane Marie Todd (Chicago: University of Chicago Press, 2000), part 3.

243. See Golding, *Paths to the Absolute,* and the very helpful review by Flam, "Space Men," 10. More generally, see Kelly Nicholson, *Body and Soul: The Transcendence of Materialism* (Boulder, Colo.: Westview Press, 1997).

244. Charles Simic, "A World Gone Up in Smoke," *NYRB* 48, 20 (December 20, 2001): 14–18 at 16. In addition to the lines from Milosz's "Either-Or," quoted at the beginning of the next chapter below, see his "Secretaries," on the sense in which we are "merely" God's secretaries.

245. Charles Simic, "Salvation Through Laughter," *NYRB* 53, 1 (January 12, 2006): 22–25 at 25.

remain, concerns about the true and the good, because generating dissension and disagreement, have been driven into the private sphere, leaving us with the "thin goods" of liberalism.[246] The self, now conceived as punctual and as defined by discrete actions rather than a history or narrative which makes these actions intelligible, is buried in the particular, and, not seeing itself as dependent on others and on others' narratives for its very existence, hardly senses the loss of or a need for transcendence.[247] Robert Walser expressed this sense of the "I" in his suggestion that his prose writings were chapters in "a long, plotless, realistic story," a "cut up or disjoined book of the self [*Ich-Buch*]."[248]

One of the great Christian medieval contributions to the clarification of human life was conceiving of that life as having "the unity of a narrative quest," as aiming beyond the self to some *telos* or good.[249] But the very concept of exercising a virtue or aiming at a good is only possible within a tradition: "the story of my life is always embedded in the story of those communities from which I derive my identity." Individualism and modernism conceived as deliberate break with the past do not liberate but imprison in a self almost incapable of transcendence. I say "almost" because the last sign of the fact that, as Augustine said, we are ineradicably made for transcendence is our desire to reach out to others or to art or music, to transcend ourselves, in love.[250] The ingenious science fiction writer Richard Powers holds that science "is about reverence, not mastery," thus through the biomole Ressler in *The Gold Bug Variations* rejects the traditional equation of science with the quest for power. The purpose of science, writes Powers,

was not the accumulation of gnostic power, . . . accomplishing the sadistic myth of progress. The purpose of science was to revive and cultivate a perpetual state of wonder. For nothing deserved wonder so much as our capacity to feel it.[251]

The irony is that the more enclosed the self becomes, the more incapable it is of even the meaningful choice on which all love depends.

The papal call in *Fides et Ratio* (1998) for a return to metaphysics was in effect a call for a return to transcendence, to those absolute and immate-

246. Pierre Manent, *Modern Liberty and Its Discontents*, ed. and tr. Daniel Mahoney and Paul Seaton (Lanham, Md.: Rowman & Littlefield, 1998).

247. Alasdair MacIntyre, *After Virtue: A Study in Moral Theory*, 3rd ed. (Notre Dame, Ind.: University of Notre Dame Press, 2007), 204–25 at 214.

248. Quoted in J. M. Coetzee, "The Genius of Robert Walser," *NYRB* 47, 17 (November 2, 2000): 13–16 at 16.

249. MacIntyre, *After Virtue*, 219, and 221 for the following quotation.

250. Louis Dupré, *Symbols of the Sacred* (Grand Rapids, Mich.: Eerdmans, 2000), concludes with a meditation on the capacity of the mind to grasp the transcendent.

251. All quotations are taken from John Leonard, "Mind Painting," *NYRB* 48, 1 (January 11, 2001): 42–48 at 44.

rial values denied during the "epoch of secularization."[252] For the pope the human person has a transcendent dignity, placed within moral absolutes which define the proper use of his will. Without both, it is very difficult to defend any notion of human rights. In *Evangelium Vitae* John Paul II had challenged the state in regard to its claim to be arbiter of the beginning and ending of life, but the larger goal was to tame the claim of the nation-state as it had emerged in modern history to be the "envelope" within which all takes place. "Cultures, when profoundly rooted in the human, bear witness to man's characteristic openness to the universal and to transcendence."[253] Without transcendence, the individual is buried within the limitations of his or her culture and can have no more dignity than that particular culture allows.[254]

Centesimus Annus (1991) had earlier declared that human freedom depends on transcendence and an objective order of truth, and that without these the ability to choose may be little more than the ground of a contest for power. As John Paul II wrote the same year in *Redemptoris Missio* (no. 3), we are faced with "a kind of soulless economic and technical development which only stimulates the search for the truth about God, about man, and about the meaning of life itself."[255] In the words of David Walsh:

The deepest truth of our age is not that the modern world is over but that we have already passed into the transcendent perspective that enables us to view it as limited. The death of the modern project has reawakened us to eternity.[256]

Søren Kierkegaard (1813–55) argued that only the absolute can make man free, and John Paul II's argument was that Christianity supplies the anthropology that modern man needs.[257]

252. For the quoted expression, see Rocco Buttiglione, *Augusto Del Noce. Biografia di un pensiero* (Casale Nonferrato: Piemme, 1991), 203–25. This very interesting treatment of modernity, built around rejection of the idea that there is a monolithic modernity and the argument that there are two Cartesian traditions, is especially recommended to those with a knowledge of the history of philosophy going well beyond the Anglo-American canon. The Winter 2002 issue of *Co* (vol. 29) contained several excellent articles under the general title "Freedom, Transcendence, and the Good."

253. John Paul II, *Encyclical Letter, Fides et ratio, of the Supreme Pontiff John Paul II: to the Bishops of the Catholic Church on the Relationship between Faith and Reason* (Boston: Daughters of St. Paul, 1998), n. 70.

254. John Paul II, "The Globalization of Solidarity" (article composed of extracts from the Message for the World Day of Peace, January 1, 2000, and other statements) *Faith and Culture Bulletin* 8 (2000): 7–9 at 8.

255. Cf. *Encyclical Letter Redemptoris Missio of the Supreme Pontiff John Paul II on the Permanent Validity of the Church's Missionary Mandate* (Boston: Daughters of St. Paul, 1991), 38.

256. *Guarded by Mystery: Meaning in a Postmodern Age* (Washington, D.C.: The Catholic University of America Press, 1999).

257. Pierpaolo Donati, "El desafío universalismo en una sociedad multicultural postmoderna: un planteamiento relacional," *Razón práctica y multiculturalismo: actas del Ier Simposio Internacional de Filosofía y Ciencias Sociales,* ed. Enrique Banús and Alejandro Llano (Pamplona:

For John Paul II the human being was made for transcendence. This is not simply the transcendence achieved by the solitary philosophical or theological thinker. The account of Genesis notes Adam's original solitariness to make the point that he needed another, that he was made for someone. A similar point has been made outside Christianity. Cicero declared in *De officiis* (1.7.22):

We are not born for ourselves alone. . . . Everything that the earth produces is created for our use, and we, too, as human beings are born for the sake of other human beings, that we might be able mutually to help one another; we ought therefore to take nature as our guide and contribute to the common good of humankind by reciprocal acts of kindness, by giving and receiving from one another, and thus by our skill, or industry, and our talents work to bind human society together in peace and harmony.[258]

For John Paul, again deepening ideas anticipated in the pre-Christian world, we exist as social beings with a complementary sexual differentiation to transcend ourselves and learn that we exist to serve the other, for mutual surrender.[259] Man and woman are discovered as gifts to each other: this is the "nuptial meaning of the body." Man has "a primordial awareness of the nuptial meaning of the body from his transcendent likeness to God in as much as he is a gift."[260] Among other things, the very body of man manifests the invisible realities of God: the sexual complementariness of the male and female, their availability for self-donation, expresses the idea of Gift most supremely signified in the Self-donation of the Creator. Specifically within the Christian tradition, Javier Prades has defended the idea that man is more than related to an unknown and transcendent "beyond," of which some philosophers spoke.[261] Incarnation and Eucharist reveal a Presence which opens to transcendence. The uniqueness and singularity of Christ at once bears a universal significance.[262] Though much twentieth-century theology took Incarnation and Eucharist, the sacraments generally, as pointing toward transcendence, the goal of theologians such as Prades, but especially of Marc Ouellet, has been to recover a fuller patristic perspective which views the sacraments as symbols more than signs, as partici-

Centro de Estudios Europeos, Universidad de Navarra, 1999), 1–34 at 16–17, and 30–32 on the "new" or "relational" universalism.

258. Tr. O'Malley, *Four Cultures,* 133.

259. Paula Jean Miller, "The Body: Science, Theology, and *Humanae Vitae,*" *Lo* 3, 3 (Summer 2000): 154–65 at 160.

260. John Paul II, *The Theology of the Body* (Boston: Pauline Books and Media, 1997); the homily cited is from February 20, 1980. See also Mary Shivanandan, "Body Narratives: Language of Truth?" *Lo* 3, 3 (Summer 2000): 166–93 at 187.

261. "'From the Economic to the Immanent Trinity': Remarks on a Principle of Renewal in Trinitarian Theology," *Co* 27 (2000): 240–61 at 254–55.

262. Ibid., 259, quoting *Redemptoris Missio,* no. 6.

pating in that which they signify.[263] Here a rationalist perspective in which the sacraments are a kind of teaching device or memory aid is replaced by an emphasis on eschatology, on the ways the sacraments already participate in the last things, are eschatological. The point never to be forgotten is that through liturgy not only is God glorified but man sanctified, brought to God and made Godlike.[264]

We must not be put off by the prophetic broadsides of a Malraux or a Pickstock. Both are brilliant moralists—and much more than that—whose message nevertheless needs a discriminating reception because the times are never one thing. If the question is the relationship between religion and mass culture, we experience opposing tendencies and contradictory evidence every day.[265] In August 2000, two million young Catholics gathered in Rome to participate in World Youth Day. Three hundred thousand of them went to confession in—a nice touch—the Circus Maximus. One can only guess at what inspired these young people; one can only speculate about the quality of understanding of their faith; and one can only wonder what tenacity of conviction they manifested in a few years' time. Yet, such events as the periodic World Youth Days suggest that in some sense Max Weber's pronouncements on the disenchantment of the world are premature, even for Europe. These young people may in fact be themselves profoundly secularized, in a thousand ways bearing the marks of the utilitarian, rationalizing, and bureaucratizing—now globalizing—processes which were at the heart of Dawson's fears and Weber's analysis. But they seem to be looking for a different world than Weber described, indeed sometimes to be looking for something "not of this world" at all. The International Youth Forum, which prepared the message for World Youth Day, stated that holiness today means going "against the current."[266] The young people in Rome may not have understood this "going against the current" to involve the martyrdom that had been asked of so many in the twentieth century, but they do understand that some form of heroism is asked of them and some of them are willing to be, if not exactly "countercultural," discriminating in their embrace of the world.[267]

263. Marc Ouellet, "Trinity and Eucharist: A Covenantal Mystery," *Co* 27 (2000): 262–83 at 282. In the same issue, on both the reconciliation of immanence and transcendence in the Eucharist and its leading to divinization, see Mario Antonelli, "Trinity and Eucharist in Blondel," 284–99 at 284, 293.

264. Edward E. Schaefer, "The Expressive and Formative Roles of Music: A Search for Balance in Liturgical Reform," *Antiphon* 7, 2 (2002): 21–36 at 21. The argument of this excellent article is that sacred music is both expressive, revealing ourselves before God, and formative, shaping us "into something beyond our present state" (22).

265. William L. Portier, "Americanism and Inculturation: 1899–1999," *Co* 27 (2000): 139–60 as at 141.

266. "World's Young People Revitalize Pope" (Catholic News Service), *IC* 62, 29 (August 25, 2000): 1–4 at 4.

267. See the proposals of Christopher Ruddy, "Heroism, Hospitality, and Holiness: Generational Perspectives on the Church-World Relationship," *Lo* 7, 1 (Winter 2004): 45–62.

It is not simply many of the young who want to hear a different story than Weber's, to live a different life than he described. Throughout the twentieth century many have in effect resisted Weber's prognoses about the present and future, and have insisted that human beings are ordered to transcendence, and that this ordering is a permanent aspect of life, never to be left behind, which will reassert itself if neglected or attacked.[268] Some of their proposals about the shape transcendence might take in societies of the future will be the subject of the final chapter of this book. For now we need simply note that, in the spirit of Bernard Lonergan's suggestion that what is needed is a second Enlightenment, a reexamination of the original Enlightenment not to the goal of its rejection but to the end of a more discriminating reception than the Enlightenment originally received, thinkers like Hugo Meynell set forth criteria for an engagement with postmodernism which will allow transcendental principles a proper place.[269] Before we can turn to these, we must form a more precise sense of the historical forms ideas of transcendence have taken, and of the relative loss of these in the modern period: this is the goal of the next two chapters.

268. Hent de Vries, *Philosophy and the Turn to Religion* (Baltimore: Johns Hopkins University Press, 1999), treats Levinas, Heidegger, and Derrida. See also Donn Welton, *The Other Husserl: The Horizons of Transcendental Phenomenology* (Bloomington: Indiana University Press, 2000). Eugene McCarraher, *Christian Critics: Religion and the Impasse in Modern American Social Thought* (Ithaca, N.Y. 2000), in tracing to about 1975 some of the most important Christian criticism of corporate capitalism, mounts an interesting argument in favor of the enduring importance of theology to the American left that has application elsewhere.

269. *Postmodernism and the New Enlightenment* (Washington, D.C.: The Catholic University of America Press, 1999). See McMahon, *Enemies of the Enlightenment*.

Chapter Four

THE MUSIC OF THE SPHERES

Tell us Poet what you do? "I praise!"
. . . . And the Nameless, beyond guess or gaze
How do you call it, conjure it? "I praise!"

   —Rainer Maria Rilke, "I Praise"

Priesthood should be our calling
Even if we do not wear liturgical garments.
We should publicly testify to the divine glory
With words, music, dance, and every sign.

   —Czeslaw Milosz, "Either-Or"[1]

Add to the artists and thinkers considered in the last chapter such composers as Arvo Pärt, Henryk Górecki, and John Tavener, and we see that
we already have in the arts, above all music, a kind of *fuga mundi nostri,*
a flight from the world as we have received it, but also a way of opening
that world to realities long neglected.[2] This can be viewed either as the in-
breaking into our world of these long-neglected realities or, as in the case of
Pärt's tintinnabuli style (from the Latin for "bells") the beginning of a new
middle ages beyond modernism.[3] In his abandonment of the ego-centered

---

1. David W. Fagerberg, "The Spiritual Animal: Sacramental Nature of Church Art and Architecture," *SA* 13 (2007): 19–23 at 19, and for a variation of the idea that man is a religious
animal: "The first, the basic definition of man is that he is *the priest*." Fagerberg goes on to write
that man's place in the cosmos "turns out to be a liturgical place." The lines from Milosz are
found in *New and Collected Poems 1931–2001* (New York 2001), 540–41 at 540.

2. Tavener was and Pärt is a Russian Orthodox Christian interested in a discipline or prayer
of silence that gives space for union with God: John Tavener, *The Music of Silence: A Composer's
Testament,* ed. Brian Keeble (London: Faber and Faber, 1999), and Paul Hillier, *Arvo Pärt* (Oxford: Oxford University Press, 1997). See also on Pärt, Alex Ross, "Musical Events," *NY* (December 2, 2002): 114–16, observing "his chords silence the noise of the self, binding the mind to
an eternal present."

3. Leopold Brauneiss, "Arvo Pärt's Tintinnabuli Style: Contemporary Music toward a New

voice of much modern music, Pärt recaptures the sense of an everlasting cosmic harmony by embedding the motions of the melodic line in a triadic background running throughout a given piece.[4]

We all know that "you can't go home," that is, recapture some earlier historical situation. But the composers just named generally understand that at all points in history another dimension is present, which we may speak of as ontological or eschatological, or even as immanent transcendence, that is, as the transcendent found at the heart of the created order.[5] One long-standing way of expressing this was to view God as an artificer and man as in his own sphere a creator, and art as something caught between the human and the divine.[6] No more than in the Middle Ages do these artists abandon all individuality, but they have discovered the musical equivalent of the Christian dictum that one must lose oneself to find oneself.[7]

Here we are at the Christological center of being, and virtually everything we need say about the relation of transcendence and immanence is found in the cosmic narrative rooted in the life of the flesh-and-blood Jesus. This fostered the

dual perspective on Jesus Christ that lies at the heart of Christianity. . . . He was, for believers, the "wholly human and visible icon of the wholly transcendent and invisible God"—and the wholly immaterial or bodily being of the one wholly immaterial or incorporeal God. Through what became known as the "incarnation" or "enfleshment" of God's Word or Wisdom, the life of God was communicated to his creatures, so they could be "in touch" with that life. . . . The physical is sanctified as the vehicle of the divine presence, whether it be the actual living and dying of saints and martyrs, who themselves become "types" of Christ or the concrete reality of the Eucharistic bread and wine received in communion.[8]

Middle Ages?" in *Postmodern Medievalisms,* ed. Richard J. Utz and Jesse G. Swan (Rochester, N.Y.: D. S. Brewer, 2005), 27–34.

4. Ibid., 29. The great background study is Leo Spitzer, *Classical and Christian Ideas of World Harmony,* ed. Anna Hatcher (Baltimore: Johns Hopkins University Press, 1963).

5. Adrian Walker, "'Constitutive Relations': Towards a Spiritual Reading of *Physis,*" an article to be published in a festschrift for David L. Schindler, who especially has advanced understanding of the "constitutive relation thesis." Walker's article excellently shows why divine immanence and transcendence should not be opposed. His explanation of the transcendental property of being, the *unum* of the beautiful, good, and true, as appearing in the world but more than the world, is presumably more sophisticated than the understanding of transcendence of any of the named composers, but provides an entrance into the best of contemporary philosophical/theological thought on this subject.

6. E. Østrem, "Deus artifex and homo creator: Art between the Human and the Divine," in *Creations, Medieval Rituals, the Arts, and the Concept of Creation,* ed. Sven Rune Havsteen et al. (Turnhout: Brepols, 2007).

7. An observation made specifically in regard to Pärt by Brauneiss, "Arvo Pärt's Tintinnabuli Style," 30.

8. Frances M. Young, "Prelude: Jesus Christ, Foundation of Christianity," in *The Cambridge History of Christianity: Origins to Constantine,* ed. Margaret M. Mitchell and Frances M. Young (Cambridge: Cambridge University Press, 2006), 34.

From this perspective Christianity has been called a religion of reality, in which the spiritual is understood as active in the artistic experience.[9]

Cosmically put, the idea first is that just as the whole is greater than its parts, there is a wholeness to the cosmos which is greater than the totality of its parts, a unity of form and light, already perceived by Plato, but with Christ incarnated. The transcendentals express the more-than-world discovered within the world.[10] With a number of theologians, above all Hans Urs von Balthasar, the composers mentioned above understand beauty to be God's primary mode of self-disclosure.[11] Of course it is not necessary to respond to a beauty in but more than the world with a sacred art or music—at the least there are degrees here, and the idea of a secular art is intelligible—but the prime interest of the present book is those responses which are sacred, in which some artistic expression is connected to transcendence.[12]

The very language of immanence and transcendence, the ideas of cosmic wholes and of finding something at the "heart" of reality, alert us to the fact that "metaphors are ontology," or—another metaphor—openings into the real: "heaven is an unbordered meadow of meaning," "the metaphor of metaphors."[13] "All descriptions of the creating or sustaining principle in things must be metaphorical, because they must be verbal."[14] A brilliant if sometimes controversial book on Dante postulates that for Dante and other medieval thinkers "the world of space and time does not exist in space or time: it exists in Intellect (the Empyrean, pure conscious being)," and though we should not claim that every medieval thinker using the language of cosmic music had such a view in mind, it is helpful to consider some such idea as often behind the language of the music of the spheres.[15]

9. Didier Maleuvre, *The Religion of Reality: Inquiry into the Self, Art, and Transcendence* (Washington, D.C.: The Catholic University of America Press, 2006).

10. I here adumbrate a subject discussed by Walker, "'Constitutive Relations.'" On the whole as greater than its parts, see also my "The Return of Purpose," *Co* 33 (2006): 666–81.

11. John Milbank et al., *Theological Perspectives on God and Beauty* (Harrisburg, Pa.: Trinity Press International, 2003).

12. The idea of a secular art is particularly defensible if etymologically connected to *saeculum* as used by Hugh of St. Victor to refer to the world in its temporal aspect. Meyer Schapiro, "On the Aesthetic Attitude in Romanesque Art," *Romanesque Art* (New York: G. Braziller, 1977), 1–27, is both a defense of the idea of secular beauty, and a sobering comment on the inadequacy of medieval definitions of beauty for even understanding medieval churches customarily thought beautiful.

13. Jeffrey Burton Russell, *A History of Heaven: The Singing Silence* (Princeton, N.J.: Princeton University Press, 1997). Alain Guerreau, "Stabilità, via, visione: le creature e il Creatore nella spazio medievale," in *Arti e storia nel medioevo*, vol. 3: *Del vedere: pubblici, forme e funzioni*, ed. Enrico Castelnuovo and Giuseppe Sergi (Turin: Einaudi, 2004), 167–97, while not using the language of metaphor, gives orientation to medieval artistic expression of transcendence and such symbolisms as those of light, "oculus cordis" and "videre deum."

14. G. K. Chesterton, *Orthodoxy* (Garden City, N.Y.: Image Books, 1959), 78.

15. Christian Moevs, *The Metaphysics of Dante's Comedy* (New York: Oxford University

The larger fact was a sacramental view of reality, which has been characterized in the following way:

Dante's allegory is not one genre among others, but a habit of viewing the whole
universe and that habit is justified, he would remind us, because in fact the universe itself is one great system of coruscating and interreflecting signs. It is not
that, for example, believers found it convenient to compare the pelican to Christ,
but that one of the reasons why God from all eternity created the pelican was
precisely that it should be a sign of Christ.[16]

According to the *Catechism of the Catholic Church,* no. 2502, sacred art
is true when

its form corresponds to its particular vocation, evoking and glorifying, in faith
and adoration, the transcendent mystery of God—the surpassing invisible beauty
of truth and love visible in Christ, who "reflects the glory of God and bears the
very stamp of his nature," in whom "the whole fullness of deity dwells bodily."[17]

Sacred art may guide us from seeing to contemplation to adoration. Christian sacred art is rooted in the fact that the incarnated Christ is the icon of
God: "Christ is the image *(eikon)* of the invisible God" (Col 1:15). As the
Catechism, no. 1073, says of liturgical catechesis or mystagogy, it "aims to ini-
tiate people into the mystery of Christ by proceeding from the visible to the
invisible, from the sign to the thing signified, from the 'sacraments' to the
'mysteries.'"[18] Sacred architecture may be spoken of as a "pre-sacrament," a
word applied by John Paul II to the Sistine Chapel. Architecture in general
is a built form of ideas, and sacred architecture is a built form of theology in
which the church building signifies theological realities.[19]

Two of the composers mentioned above, Pärt and Górecki, come from
Eastern Europe, and the third was an English convert to Russian Orthodoxy (Tavener, who after two decades left Orthodoxy).[20] George Weigel
has spoken of a Slavic view of history, not really much more than a Christian view of history, in which rupture with the past in its Jacobin sense, de-
lineated above in chapter 2, is rejected, and true revolution entails recovery

---

Press, 2005), 8, arguing in chapter 1 that, using Aristotle's definition of matter as the principle of
unintelligibility, Dante alone saw that the Empyrean must be completely immaterial. There is a
helpful review of this book by Warren Ginsberg, *Sp* 82 (2007): 467–70.

16. Dante, *The Inferno,* tr. Anthony M. Esolen (New York: Modern Library, 2002), 408.

17. Quoted and discussed in Jem Sullivan, "The Beauty of Faith: Sacred Architecture and
Catechesis," *SA* 11 (2006): 12–14 at 12, and see also 14, for the following quotations.

18. Whereas at points in the present book an overly didactic use of liturgy is criticized, we
note that the idea of liturgical catechesis, instruction in worship and proper adoration of God,
brings together teaching and worship.

19. Denis McNamara, "Built Form of Theology: The Natural Sympathies of Catholicism
and Classicism," *SA* 12 (2006): 20–24 at 20.

20. All three are considered by Wilfrid Mellers, *Celestial Music? Some Masterpieces of European Religious Music* (Rochester, N.Y.: Boydell Press, 2002).

of lost spiritual values.[21] Polish Romantic writers such as Adam Mickiewicz (1798–1855) embodied this tradition, but so does a "low-profile" (from the point of view of Christianity) writer like Václav Havel, and a "high-profile" writer such as Aleksandr Solzhenitsyn (1918–). For all these men, the deepest currents of history are spiritual and cultural, not political and economic. They tend to be suspicious of the nihilism and scientism of the West, but also of Eastern despotism.[22]

Though they are not all anti-bourgeois, these thinkers tend to share with a powerful twentieth-century stream of anti-bourgeois sentiment the thought that all the forms of materialism from Marxism to capitalism tend to get lost in the here and now. In one way or another these critics write on behalf of recovering a symbolic or liturgical universe. We might almost speak of them as New Platonists, because, with the Neoplatonists of late antiquity and the early Middle Ages, their interest is "immaterial materiality," the revelation of the immaterial symbolically.[23] The ancient idea of cosmic harmony had expressed itself in the idea that various things, such as music and liturgy, may express the harmony or order that constitutes the world. Central was the idea of glory: "Glory is the axis which connects the increate to the created nature and which, in the old traditions, used to be symbolically represented by the Cosmic Tree or the Mountain in the centre of the world."[24]

Each of those composers and thinkers in his own way identifies with the famous words of the emissaries sent out in 988 by Prince Vladimir of Kiev to find the true religion. Having seen a liturgy in Hagia Sophia in Constantinople, the emissaries could only exclaim: "We knew not whether we were in heaven or on earth, for surely there is no such splendor or beauty anywhere upon earth. . . . God dwells there among men, and . . . their service surpasses the worship of all other places. For we cannot forget its beauty."[25] This is a constant theme in Christianity: in the liturgy things always true and beautiful not only present themselves for new appropria-

---

21. "Europe's Problem—and Ours," *FT* 140 (February 2004): 18–25 at 21.

22. James H. Billington, *Russia in Search of Itself* (Washington, D.C.: Woodrow Wilson Center Press, 2004), is excellent on the Russian thinkers, and see Daniel J. Mahoney, "Traducing Solzhenitsyn," *FT* 145 (August/September 2004): 14–17 at 16.

23. Michael Harrington, *Sacred Place in Early Medieval Neoplatonism* (New York: Palgrave Macmillan, 2004), 2 and 201, and see especially chapters 3 and 4, on Dionysius the Areopagite. For orientation, see Barbara Obrist, *La cosmologie médiévale. Textes et images,* vol. 1: *Les fondements antiques* (Florence: SISMEL/Edizioni del Galluzzo, 2004).

24. Robert Lazu, "Crisis of the Symbolic Universe," *SS* 7 (2006): 6–8 at 6. See N. H. Petersen, "Ritual and Creation: Medieval Liturgy as Foreground and Background for Creation," in *Creations,* ed. Havsteen. Peter Vergo, *That Divine Order: Music and Visual Arts from Antiquity to the Eighteenth Century* (New York: Phaidon, 2005), surveys the link between the mathematical order of music, the physical order of the universe, and the moral order of society.

25. Serge Schmemann, "Gorbachev and Church: Soviet Leader's New Tolerance Recognizes the 1000 Year Grip Is Not Easily Broken," *NYT,* June 16, 1988, A12.

tion, but are actualized.[26] The eschatological orientation of the Scriptures is expressed above all in the liturgy. That is, it is in the liturgy that the end times break into time. In the words of Benedict XVI: "In the celebration of the liturgy, the Church moves toward the Lord; liturgy is virtually this act of approaching his coming. In the liturgy the Lord is already anticipating his promised coming. Liturgy is anticipated Parousia."[27] In every liturgy we find Christ's "second coming."

We can speak of Christianity as historically engaged in a sanctification of time and place. The Christian version of the cosmic story is that the whole material order was created good and pure, as the stage on which freedom, angelic and human, was to be played out. Had the Fall not taken place, time and place would not have had to be sanctified, for that is how they were created. But since the Fall a terrible (= awe-inspiring) drama has been working itself out, involving ultimately the question of whether creatures with free will will freely return to God and return the temporal and spatial order they have so seriously harmed to God. It is in this context that we can speak of Christianity as engaged in the sanctification of time and place, in the ordering of these dimensions in the light of the Kingship of Christ. Already in St. Athanasius's late-fourth-century *Life of St. Antony,* the first monastic life, a geography of sanctity is fully present in which the monks are "soldiers of Christ" fighting on the front line against Satan and pushing the demons ever further into the desert. Antony's own single-mindedness and holiness is shown by his ever further penetration of the desert, and his setting up in it of "mountains of God," places where monks congregate at once to recapture the life of Eden and of the first Christians at Jerusalem, while anticipating heaven.[28] In the early Middle Ages the cult of the saints spread from valley to valley, in time claiming the geography of Europe for Christianity and the saints, and placing the land under the saints' protection. This continued all through the Middle Ages and, in Catholic areas, past the Reformation. Indeed, as suggested in the last chapter, one can draw striking contrasts even today between a less sacralized (Protestant) north of Europe and a still-sacralized Catholic south.[29]

---

26. Gregory Wolfe, *Intruding upon the Timeless: Meditations on Art, Faith and Mystery* (Baltimore: Johns Hopkins University Press, 2003), has been one of the most prominent American thinkers addressing the importance of religion for art. See also Philip Sherrard, *The Sacred in Life and Art* (Ipswich, England 1990).

27. Joseph Ratzinger (Benedict XVI), *A New Song for the Lord: Faith in Christ and Liturgy Today,* tr. Martha M. Matesich (New York: Crossroad, 1996), 129.

28. An entrance to my studies on these themes is provided by my "The *Ecclesia Primitiua* in John Cassian, the Ps. Jerome *Commentary* on Mark, and Bede," in *Biblical Studies in the Early Middle Ages,* ed. Claudio Leonardi and Giovanni Orlandi (Florence: SISMEL/Edizioni del Galluzzo, 2005), 5–27.

29. William A. Christian Jr., "Priests, Mountains, and 'Sacred Space' in Early Modern Europe," *CHR* 93 (2007): 84–103, a fascinating survey of recent scholarship on "sacred space" (see

The liturgy of Hagia Sophia which so impressed Vladimir's emissaries was a product of the long process of the sanctification or transfiguration of this world undertaken by the Church in order to anticipate here and now the ceaseless praise of the age which is coming. This is the true *theologia prima,* aiming at the liturgical fulfillment of creation.[30] The liturgy of the hours, of Matins, Vespers, and Vigils, developing over the centuries, is special witness to this process.[31] Like Sunday itself, though it may be put to social and political uses, this liturgy has no purpose beyond itself. It is as useless as art (as useless as art not bent to politics), and exists simply for itself, the way by which every created thing may become transparent to God and joy flourish.[32] In one way or another such composers as Pärt, Górecki, and Tavener recognize the perils of the loss of this liturgical world, and aim at some form of recovery of it.[33]

Christianity, so far as the doctrine of God is concerned, speaks in the light of the Incarnation.[34] *Pace* some earlier scholars, there never was a period in which Christianity was aniconic, that is, was indisposed to use the visual to image God, since, as the Book of Wisdom 13:5 (Jerusalem version) already draws the basis for such a view, "through the grandeur and beauty of the creatures we may, by analogy, contemplate their Author."[35] This is the ground of a Christian understanding of transcendence. As Plotinus intimated, art allows for participation in the reality to which the image points. Virtually from the beginning—that is, from the time there was a Christian material culture—we find seeds of what became the Orthodox position on icons. This position did not hold that God could be seen, but that there was a "salvific vision" or "non-physical seeing 'face to face.'"[36] Specifically,

p. 103 for Christian's explanation of why he prefers the expression "sacred place" to "sacred space").

30. David Fagerberg, *Theologia Prima: What Is Liturgical Theology?* (Chicago: Hillenbrand Books, 2004).

31. Robert F. Taft, *The Liturgy of the Hours in East and West: the Origin of the Divine Office and Its Meaning for Today* (Collegeville, Minn.: Liturgical Press, 1993).

32. Robert F. Taft, *Beyond East and West: Problems in Liturgical Understanding,* 2nd ed. (Rome: Edizioni Orientalia Christiana, Pontifical Oriental Institute, 2001); Alexander Schmemann, *For the Life of the World: Sacraments and Orthodoxy* (Crestwood, N.Y.: St. Vladimir's Seminary Press, 1982).

33. Cf. James Hitchcock, *Recovery of the Sacred* (San Francisco: Ignatius Press, 1995), and see the treatment of music in Aidan Nichols, *Scattering the Seed: A Guide Through Balthasar's Early Writings on Philosophy and the Arts* (Washington, D.C.: The Catholic University of America Press, 2006).

34. Herbert L. Kessler, *Spiritual Seeing: Picturing God's Invisibility in Medieval Art* (Philadelphia: University of Pennsylvania Press, 2000), introduces the patient reader to all the issues.

35. Robin M. Jensen, "Towards a Christian Material Culture," in *Cambridge History of Christianity: Origins,* is a splendid treatment of the origins of Christian art and architecture.

36. Robin M. Jensen, *Face to Face: Portraits of the Divine in Early Christianity* (Minneapolis: Fortress Press, 2005), takes the story back to the Roman catacombs about A.D. 200. The quoted phrases are from a review of this book by James A. Francis, *JECS* 13 (2005): 405–6 at 405. Ann

Christ as "the image of the invisible God" makes possible a seeing God "face to face" which is "the sum and substance of being truly alive."[37] We might say of especially the Byzantine tradition that its interest was not so much in "pure art," but in devotional objects which made manifest the relationship between divine and human.[38] Isidore of Seville (c. 560–636), in *Etymologiae* (19, 16, 1), summarized this tradition as it stood in the last days of the Western Empire in a chapter, *"De pictura,"* which considered such questions as the fictive aspect of images, and later writers continued this discussion.[39] In the Carolingian period this theme was treated theologically, especially under the heading of Present Absence.

Paschasius Radbertus of Corbie (ca. 790–ca. 860) took the traditional trope present/absence to present "the human being's connatural assimilation to God."[40] Present/absence was "one of the themes associated with the emotive figure known as *evidentia,* which is a vivid depiction of an object through the accumulation of a number of real or invented observable details." The goal was through a verbal image "to draw listeners into the presence of the thing." An absent person became virtually present through a letter: a letter could unite the minds of sender and recipient in a way that minimized the distance between them. Though Radbertus thought a graphic image might make something absent present, for him words were superior to manufactured objects in doing this. An icon painter or guardian of a saint's relic might disagree, but the larger point was that something physical may invoke the presence of something absent.[41] One might speak of thus dwelling mentally in heaven. An "illusion" created by rhetoric may direct us to a true presence beyond sensation. When the virtue of the dead is imitated, one shares in their undying moral beauty. The rational soul may seek God beyond the visible, but so far as sensation and imagination are concerned, they require shapes and figures. In the Incarnation the visible and invisible join, and a certain calibration between God and man takes place in which the God-man provides an access to that which is above sensation and imagination.

R. Meyer, *Medieval Allegory and the Building of the New Jerusalem* (Rochester, N.Y.: D. S. Brewer, 2003), part 1, is on Plotinian ideas of the relationship between the visible and invisible.

37. Jensen, *Face to Face,* 99.

38. Glenn Peers, *Sacred Shock: Framing Visual Experience in Byzantium* (University Park: Pennsylvania State University Press, 2004).

39. Isidore of Seville, *Etimologias,* ed. Jose Oroz Reta and Manuel A. Marcos Casquero, 2 vols. (Madrid: Editorial Católica, 1982–83), vol. 2, 450–52.

40. I am following the wonderful article of my former student David Appleby, "Present Absence: From Rhetorical Figure to Eucharistic *Veritas* in the Thought of Paschasius Radbertus," *FQI* 3 (2003): 139–71 at 142, from which the two following quotations come.

41. Ibid., 145, and see 148, 150–62, on what follows. One might go so far as to see in Radbertus's belief that especially hagiographic narrative makes the dead present a foreshadowing of the Western turn (relatively speaking) from an iconic to a narrative church decoration, discussed below in regard to the thought of Joseph Cardinal Ratzinger (Pope Benedict XVI). Kessler, *Spiritual Seeing,* esp. 104–48, treats the ability of images to make things present.

This calibration, which is a way of talking about man as microcosm, implies the possibility of a certain human attunement to or consonance with God, a Godlikeness in man.[42] Just as the Logos is the sun at the center of the cosmos, so the heart is at the center of man the microcosm.[43] Radbertus is one of those Carolingian writers who surprise us with the depth to which they have penetrated the Christian mystery. His ideas about Christ are neither those of his surrounding Germanic warrior culture, nor, simply, those of the classical world, and they burst classical aesthetic notions. He presents Christ as glorified in abasement, self-emptying, descent, abandonment, and suffering in ways that little agree with classical notions of beauty, balance, or harmony, or Germanic ideas of exaltation through one's own strong right arm. In the *Vita Adalhardi* Radbertus assimilates his subject, the abbot Adalhard, to Christ's sacrifice, granting Adalhard a glory in suffering far from the traditional anachronistic portrayals of Carolingian humanism as if it were simply an anticipation of Renaissance humanism in all its—from a Christian point of view—unadventuresomeness.[44] Though in none of this was Paschasius explicitly addressing the Iconoclastic Controversy which was still tearing the East apart in his day, in all of it we find a Western position with many similarities to the Eastern defenders of images.

Hans Belting showed that in the Middle Ages paintings and sculptures had something of the quality of relics.[45] They shared in the holiness of the thing portrayed. Harald Kleinschmidt has since mounted the provocative argument that in the early Middle Ages a kind of collective thinking dominated, in which perception and action were not separated, as they have been since roughly the twelfth century.[46] In the earlier period group-centered identities dominated, and goals were set by leaders and pursued by the group. Action was understood as a process an individual participated in more than as oriented toward a goal the individual set. Though Kleinschmidt's sugges-

42. Hans Urs von Balthasar, *The Glory of the Lord: A Theological Aesthetics*, vol. 1: *Seeing the Form*, tr. Erasmo Leiva-Merikakis, ed. Joseph Fessio and John Riches (San Francisco: Ignatius Press, 1982), 241–57; and see David Appleby, "'Beautiful on the Cross, Beautiful in His Torments': The Place of the Body in the Thought of Paschasius Radbertus," *Traditio* 50 (2005): 1–46 at 5, and see p. 6 for a description of the harmony between siblings on earth in musical terms, and then as an anticipation of celestial harmony.

43. Appleby, "'Beautiful on the Cross,'" 11. One recalls that for many ancient and medieval people, the heart was the center of the human being, including the reason (Logos): Glenn W. Olsen, "John of Salisbury's Humanism," in *Gli Umanesimi Medievali*, ed. Claudio Leonardi (Florence: SISMEL/Edizioni del Galluzzo, 1998): 447–68.

44. Appleby, "'Beautiful on the Cross,'" 7.

45. *Likeness and Presence: A History of the Image Before the Era of Art*, tr. Edmund Jephcott (Chicago: University of Chicago Press, 1994); see also Caroline Bynum, "The Presence of Objects: Medieval Anti-Judaism in Modern Germany," *Common Knowledge* 10 (2004): 1–32 at 23–24.

46. *Perception and Action in Medieval Europe* (Rochester, N.Y.: Boydell Press, 2005).

tion has the potential for illuminating more than early medieval Germanic culture, it needs working out, and in any case presumably does not fully apply to a learned thinker such as Paschasius.[47] As we have just seen in the case of Paschasius, learned people distinguished between an image and the reality it represented.[48] Yet, not only were some icons thought literally to have derived from a vision or to have come from heaven, but pictures tended to be thought of as holy matter in the way Belting suggests.[49]

In a more general sense, the education found in the West in the early Middle Ages was in some degree iconic, with the cathedral master the icon. This education was built around imitation of the master in all his aspects, his gait, his amiability, and the radiance of his countenance, as well as the actual contents of his teaching. Of course students did not "look through" the master in the manner that the believer "looked through" an icon to enter into the mystery it represented, but still there were parallels. In a time when education above all was charismatic, the goal was for the student to be transformed both internally and externally by what he saw in the master, by the master's charisma. This was a kind of liturgical understanding of learning itself, in which virtue was not just a body of maxims gained by memorization and moral exertion, but part of a larger project in which the goal—something like Plato's goal—was reformation achieved by attention to the beautiful object. It depended for its efficacy on there being some truth in the idea, again older than Plato but especially prominent in the Orthodox understanding of liturgy, that attention to beauty can actually make us more Godlike; that we are not so flawed that such reformation is impossible.[50] Benedict XVI has noted that, though normally thought precedes word, in the case of the liturgy it is the other way around. God provides the words and through the liturgy teaches us to pray.[51]

In the West the organization of clerical and monastic life around such charismatic and iconic categories was reduced by the rise of scholasticism around 1200. Especially before that time, education was more education of man as an embodied animal than it was the education of a disembodied intellect to which scholasticism subsequently tended to direct itself.[52]

47. Sean L. Field, Review, *AHR* 112 (2007): 566–67.

48. Jeffrey Hamburger, "Seeing and Believing: The Suspicion of Sight and the Authentication of Vision in Late Medieval Art," in *Imagination und Wirklichkeit: Zum Verhältnis von mentalen und realen Bilder in der Kunst der frühen Neuzeit,* ed. Alessandro Nova and Klaus Krüger (Mainz: Philipp von Zabern, 2000), 47–70.

49. Bynum, "Presence of Objects," 24.

50. Timothy Garton Ash, "The Stasi on Our Minds," *NYRB* 54, 9 (May 31, 2007): 4–8 at 8, discusses a pivotal scene in the movie *The Lives of Others,* in which Lenin's question is raised whether one can be unchanged by hearing beautiful music. Some form of this question runs through the history of philosophy: see W. K. C. Guthrie, *The Sophists* (Cambridge: Cambridge University Press, 1971), 250–60.

51. *Jesus of Nazareth* (New York: Doubleday, 2007), 131.

52. I have developed these ideas from a reading of C. Stephen Jaeger, *The Envy of Angels:*

Though, as already suggested, the idea of transformation of the human being by attention to the liturgy may be thought to be a special emphasis of Orthodoxy, even in Latin scholasticism after the earlier charismatic form of education had in some degree retreated, Thomas Aquinas thought of liturgy as "a complex of signs which express and at the same time bring about the sanctification of man by God."[53] By it the Christian is transformed into a new creation (2 Cor 5:17).

Perhaps no one in the Middle Ages explored the question of the power of the beautiful object to draw forth love more profoundly than Aquinas's contemporary St. Bonaventure. This was a part of his rendition of the common Neoplatonic and Christian idea of the fecundity of the Good. As Aquinas did, Bonaventure held that there was a theological imperative for diversity and individuality, since no one species of created being can reflect all that God is.[54] Both the production of creatures and their goodness are rooted in the diffusion of Good within the inter-Trinitarian procession. Bonaventure sees that "the created world is like a book that reflects, represents and describes the creative trinity."[55] He uses the metaphor of "the music of creation" to talk of the new music of creation which arises following upon Christ's death.[56] This is a favored metaphor to describe Trinitarian creativity, the "overflow" of goodness into the created order. The creation is a living book legible both macrocosmically, in the cosmos taken as a whole, and microcosmically, in the human soul.[57] As an infinite sphere, the center of this cosmos is everywhere, so close are macro- and microcosm. A half-century later, Dante, according to an interpretation introduced above, held that as unlimited Being is approached and the self joins its Source, time and space are seen as fictive and the center as everywhere.[58]

Augustine had thought that the cosmos was not a "thing" but an assemblage of relations, and this idea runs through learned tradition: hence the appropriateness in thinkers such as Bonaventure of referring to reality as a

Cathedral Schools and Social Ideals in Medieval Europe, 950–1200 (Philadelphia: University of Pennsylvania Press, 1994).

53. L. J. Elders, "St. Thomas Aquinas and the Liturgy," *FCSQ* 29, 4 (Winter 2006): 9–13 at 10.

54. Michael Dirda, "Dante: The Supreme Realist," *NYRB* 54, 1 (January 11, 2007): 54–58 at 55.

55. *Breviloquium* 2.12 (v. 230), cited in Peter J. Casarella, "Trinity, Simultaneity, and the Music of Creation in St. Bonaventure," an unpublished paper Prof. Casarella kindly made available to me, which I have used in the following.

56. On the following see also Peter J. Casarella, "Carmen Dei: Music and Creation in Three Theologians," *Theology Today* 62 (2006): 484–500.

57. Ann W. Astell, *Eating Beauty: The Eucharist and the Spiritual Arts of the Middle Ages* (Ithaca, N.Y.: Cornell University Press, 2006), studies Bonaventure's attempt to restore macrocosmic and microcosmic beauty: see the probing review of this book by Jeffrey Hamburger, *Sp* 82 (2007): 679–81.

58. Moevs, *Metaphysics of Dante's Comedy.*

song, a modest image promising articulation of relations from some particular perspective rather than an Olympian view of "everything at once."[59] All humans must perceive "from inside" the relations which constitute the cosmos, because all humans are finite: no one can view the whole as whole. For Bonaventure particularly, the creation could be described as a well-ordered song, but the beauty of this song can only be seen by directing one's view to the whole, even if finally this eludes one. Bonaventure speaks of degrees of beauty. The fabric of the world has great beauty, but above this is the beauty of the Church, an eschatological beauty, and higher again is the beauty of the heavenly Jerusalem, expressed most fully in the Trinity.[60]

In explaining his remark that in mechanical art the artificer would "if it were in his power . . . produce an effect which would know and love him," Bonaventure drew an analogy with the Incarnation.[61] There is an analogy between God's motive in the Incarnation and the motive of the artist. Bonaventure posits an

ideal situation in which, if an artist had it in his power to make a supremely personal work of art, this work would actually reciprocate the knowledge and love of the artist. In order to accomplish this, the work must come to know its maker through the similitude according to which it was made. Moreover, if the work were unable to grasp the similitude, then the similitude would have to lower itself to the level of the work. Herein we see the necessity of the Incarnation made manifest in the production of artifacts: "And since by sin the rational creature had dimmed the eye of contemplation, it was most fitting that the Eternal and Invisible should become visible and take flesh that He might lead us back to the Father." The divine similitude generated in the mind of the divine Artist is the model of all created "works of art," including the rational creature.[62]

This is all possible because the second person of the Trinity is the perfect image of God. He is at once the "image of the invisible God" of Colossians 1:10 and the image by which, according to Genesis 1:26, man is created. The final goal of all art is to express the Father's love and to lead us back to Him. In this "era before the era of art," in which images participated in the reality they represented, we are very far from a self-conscious Renaissance playing with illusion, which calls attention to the fact that the image is "just an image," and no longer something hailing from another world.[63]

59. Catherine Pickstock, "Music: Soul, City, and Cosmos after Augustine," in Radical Orthodoxy: A New Theology, ed. John Milbank et al. (London: Routledge, 1999), 243–77 at 247.

60. Casarella, "Trinity, Simultaneity, and the Music of Creation."

61. De Reductione Artium ad Theologiam, tr. Emma Therese Healy (St. Bonaventure, N.Y.: The Franciscan Institute, Saint Bonaventure University, 1955), 12, quoted in John P. Bequette, "Illumination, Incarnation, and Reintegration: Christian Humanism in Bonaventure's De Reductione Artium ad Theologiam," FQI 2, 1 (2003): 63–85 at 74.

62. Bequette, "Illumination, Incarnation, and Reintegration," quoting De Reductione Artium, 12.

63. Bynum, "Presence of Objects," 26, referring to Belting.

We also find in Bonaventure a further specification of human artistic creation. In following Augustine in identifying the *carmen universitatis* or music of the universe with six types of number, Bonaventure with Augustine writes that the sixth type, judicial numbers, includes *numeri artificiales,* man-made numbers. Bonaventure makes these into a seventh kind of musical number, seeing the artist as creating these numerical forms. Peter Casarella finds in this a greater attunement to the aesthetics of creation by Bonaventure than Augustine, who nevertheless had already held that number has a human dimension in that humans are naturally ordered to or have a natural endowment for numbers.[64] The songs and early forms of polyphony being composed by Bonaventure's Franciscan brothers were a continuation of the fecundity of the triune God.[65]

Orthodoxy, despite flirtation with iconoclasm along the way, understands the instinct to portray God visually very well, but a contemporary turn to transcendence in most Christian traditions is acknowledgment of what lies at the Christian core. As the Roman Catholic liturgist M. Francis Mannion has put it, "Transcendence does not mean divine remoteness from the communal, but the embodiment of divine glory in communal events."[66] To speak of the composers, throughout much of the twentieth century Oliver Messiaen (1908–92) wrote from a perspective captured in the title of his last large work, "Illuminations of the Beyond." Messiaen, who thought God present everywhere, is famous for having found in birdsong the most sublime possibilities of nature for expressing religious mystery. Using the inspiration already found in the natural world, his music explores the grip of the beyond on us. His "Quartet for the End of Time," based on the statement of the book of Revelation that "there should be time no longer" and written in a World War II prisoner-of-war camp, depicts eternity.[67] A journey to see the natural wonders of Utah in 1973 resulted in his "Des canyons aux étoiles (From the Canyons to the Stars)," the expression of the idea that we journey from the deserts to the heavens.[68] We may debate our reactions to the distinctive musical language he developed to communicate his vision, the quality of meditation found in his work, but who can doubt that this language centers on a faith, hope, and charity irradiating our world from beyond?[69] Though words may play some role, like

64. Casarella, "Carmen Dei," 485.

65. "Trinity, Simultaneity, and the Music of Creation." For Augustine see *Augustine on Music: An Interdisciplinary Collection of Essays,* ed. Richard R. La Croix (Lewiston, N.Y.: Edwin Mellen Press, 1988), and Pickstock, "Music," 244–55, on cosmic music.

66. "Beyond Environment and Art in Catholic Worship," *Antiphon* 4, 2 (1999): 2–4 at 4.

67. For background see W. Verbaal, "Invocatio musae: Inspired by the Muse, the Inescapable Reality," in *Creations,* ed. Havsteen, and Elizabeth Eva Leach, *Sung Birds: Music, Nature, and Poetry in the Later Middle Ages* (Ithaca, N.Y.: Cornell University Press, 2007).

68. Jeff Bram, "Speaking in Bird Tongues," in *Tempo* (Spring/Summer 2007): 3.

69. Michael C. Jordan, "Preface," *Lo* 7, 1 (Winter 2004): 5–15 at 7–9, and see Peter Hill and Nigel Simeone, *Messiaen* (New Haven, Conn.: Yale University Press, 2005).

all art and performance, music takes us beyond this world to a point where language fails.[70]

⌒

So far as music is concerned, the ancestry of the turn to transcendence involves the whole history of Western music and liturgy.[71] Pythagoras's view of the mathematical construction of the cosmos was one expression of the ancient idea, found especially among the philosophical elite, that beauty lies in the order of the universe.[72] The larger vision, shared by most, was of the gods and humanity living together more or less harmoniously in a rationally ordered cosmos.[73] This could be developed in various ways, the Aristotelians seeing the cosmos enveloped by the divine presence, the Stoics the cosmos as filled with the divine, and the Middle Platonists the cosmos as emanation of the One.[74] All in one way or another acknowledged that the fit between man and the cosmos is not perfect, specifically that in some way man is out of harmony with the cosmos. Even without the Christian doctrine of original sin, the idea that humans simultaneously are part of a larger whole and offend against that whole is commonplace.

If in various forms of the Platonic tradition God and the soul engage in a "face-to-face" dialogue, in Aristotelianism, especially in its medieval forms, "deiformity requires passage by way of the cosmic order, known in the philosophical sciences that human reason constructs."[75] The details of the description of the cosmos vary from writer to writer, but continuing is

70. John W. O'Malley, *Four Cultures of the West* (Cambridge, Mass.: Belknap Press, 2004), 179–80, 182–83, 189–90.

71. Cf. Giovanni Comotti, *Music in Greek and Roman Culture,* tr. Rosaria V. Munson (Baltimore: Johns Hopkins University Press, 1989), and *Music and the Muses: The Culture of Mousike in the Classical Athenian City,* ed. Penelope Murray and Peter Wilson (New York: Oxford University Press, 2004).

72. Christiane L. Joost-Gaugier, *Measuring Heaven: Pythagoras and His Influence on Thought and Art in Antiquity and the Middle Ages* (Ithaca, N.Y.: Cornell University Press, 2006). See also Hans Urs von Balthasar, *Cosmic Liturgy: The Universe According to Maximus the Confessor* (San Francisco: Ignatius Press, 2003).

73. Kathy L. Gaca, *The Making of Fornication: Eros, Ethics, and Political Reform in Greek Philosophy and Early Christianity* (Berkeley: University of California Press, 2003), 69–70, is useful for early Stoic cosmology, which (along with many writers such as Homer) has greater agonistic and sexual elements than the language of harmony might suggest, and see 102–3 n. 19, for Pythagorean cosmology. For the Middle Ages see E. Edson and E. Savage-Smith, *Medieval Views of the Cosmos* (Oxford: Bodleian Library, University of Oxford, 2004). See more generally Rémi Brague, *The Wisdom of the World: The Human Experience of the Universe in Western Thought,* tr. Teresa Lavender Fagan (Chicago: University of Chicago Press, 2004).

74. Appleby, "Present Absence," 150. On Aristotle's organic thought, which conceived society by analogy to an organism, and the cosmos by analogy to society, always placing individuals in some larger framework so that "they come into their own precisely as participants in the community of the universe," see Walker, "'Constitutive Relations.'"

75. Wayne J. Hankey, "Self and Cosmos in Becoming Deiform: Neoplatonic Paradigms for Reform by Self-knowledge from Augustine to Aquinas," in *Reforming the Church before Modernity: Patterns, Problems and Approaches,* ed. Christopher M. Bellitto and Louis I. Hamilton (Burlington, Vt.: Ashgate, 2005), 39–60 at 46.

the idea that humans perfect themselves through conformity to an encompassing order. A number of classical texts still read in the Middle Ages, such as Ovid's *Metamorphoses* (1:84–86), expressed the idea that humans had an upright stance so that they—by contrast to the animals—might contemplate the heavens. This merged with the Christian idea that part of Adam's dignity was his being created to stand upright, and all this was part of the idea that, again, man was "fit" to understand the cosmos.[76]

There was a long and partially parallel development in Hebrew tradition from polytheism to henotheism to a God of history to a God of nature, and finally to a transcendent God. The opening hymn of Colossians 1:18 expressed a Christian summation of this development, "in him everything continues in being."[77] Homer's Golden Chain combined with Genesis and found its continuation in Origen's view of salvation history as a cosmic course from the creation of the first light to Christ's return in glory.[78] The idea of transcendence took various forms. In most of the pre-Christian systems, though a distinction was made between God and the world, the distance between God and man was not as radical as it tended to be in Judaism and Christianity, especially when framed around an ex nihilo idea of creation and the insights of negative theology. Put in terms of art, the realness and immediacy of much classic Roman art, and its goal of housing the perfect soul in the perfect body, gave way to the profound transcendence or otherworldliness of much early Christian art, its greater abstractness or tendency to simplify, with its goal of asserting the importance of soul over body.

Speaking specifically of music, Plato observed: "God has produced in man the natural inclination to produce harmony and rhythm, not at random, but ultimately in imitation of spiritual harmony."[79] For Plato there were many ways in which man and the cosmos are fitted to each other. God himself is *Deus geometria,* the source of ordered beauty.[80] Music might be viewed as man's "principal means of communicating with the gods," and Plotinus insists that music's "ulterior purpose is to bear the listener beyond nature, to the highest beauty, whereby the soul, being beautified, becomes like God."[81] About the same time the Christian Origen has it that just as

---

76. Kirk Ambrose, *The Nave Sculpture of Vézelay: The Art of Monastic Viewing* (Toronto: Pontifical Institute of Medieval Studies, 2006), 25–27, with my "Return of Purpose."

77. Appleby, "Present Absence," 151.

78. Friedrich Ohly, *Sensus Spiritualis: Studies in Medieval Significs and the Philology of Culture,* ed. Samuel P. Jaffe, tr. Kenneth J. Northcott (Chicago: University of Chicago Press, 2005), xvi.

79. *Ion,* 534D, quoted in F. C. Lehner, "Music (Philosophy)," in *The New Catholic Encyclopedia,* 16 vols. (New York: McGraw-Hill, 1967), vol. 10, 89–91.

80. Ohly, *Sensus Spiritualis.*

81. The first phrase is from Steven Mithen, *The Singing Neanderthals: The Origins of Music, Language, Mind and Body* (London: Weidenfeld & Nicolson, 2006), quoted in John McNeill, "Beyond Words," *NYRB* 53, 7 (April 27, 2006): 26–28, at 26. The second phrase is from *Enne-*

the Logos holds the cosmos together, so It makes present in the human subject the transcendent attributes of God.[82] Like the Scriptures, the cosmos is "a text authored by God to provide a locus for spiritual transformation."[83]

These were themes developed by a host of Christian writers. In the West, Augustine, in reflecting on inwardness and the fact that humans have the possibilities of interior as well as exterior histories, was a great explorer of transcendence and of life as a pilgrimage toward God.[84] Somewhat later (the matter is disputed), the great Christian thinker Denys the Areopagite viewed theology as "holy celebration," more a hymn about the glory that fills the universe than a spoken word.[85] Maximus the Confessor (580–662) deepened the discussion by viewing the Christian liturgy as a symbol of the cosmic mystery in which the whole world is being drawn into Christ's hypostatic union.[86] In Western Neoplatonism from Augustine to Aquinas the very notion of reform involved both self and cosmos becoming deiform.[87] In a general way we may speak of the chant of the Christian Church, East and West, as a synthesis of those tendencies in the Hebrew and Greek worlds to the musical embodiment of the ideas of peace and equilibrium.[88] Still in the eighteenth century Giuseppe Tartini's study of harmony developed against a Neoplatonic background.[89]

If not the case with Augustine or Denys the Areopagite, implicit for most in this was the idea, which continued past the time of Newton, that time itself is objective, something absolute which takes our measure.[90] Though—witness Genesis 1—the Jewish tradition was careful to insist that only God, not the cosmos, was divine, and that therefore the sun, moon, and stars were not to be worshipped, all considered the structure of the universe to "speak to man." The Psalmist (19:2) declared: "The heavens proclaim the glory of God, and the firmament makes known the work of his

ads, tr. Stephen MacKenna, 4th ed. (London: Faber and Faber, 1969), 1.6.6. Cf. Stephen Gersh, "Plotinus on Harmonia. Musical Metaphors and Their Uses in the Enneads," in *Agonistes: Essays in Honour of Denis O'Brien,* ed. John Dillon and Monique Dixsaut (Burlington, Vt.: Ashgate, 2005), 181–92.

82. Endre von Ivánka, *Plato Christianus. Übernahme und Umgestaltung des Platonismus durch die Vater* (Einsiedeln: Johannes Verlag, 1964), 309–85; see also Appleby, "Present Absence," 151.

83. Joseph W. Trigg, Review, *JECS* 10 (2002): 424–26 at 426.

84. Brian Stock, *Augustine the Reader: Meditation, Self-Knowledge, and the Ethics of Interpretation* (Cambridge, Mass.: Belknap Press, 1996), 2.

85. Balthasar, *Glory of the Lord,* vol. 2: *Studies in Theological Style: Clerical Styles,* 144–210 at 172–77.

86. Balthasar, *Cosmic Liturgy.*

87. Hankey, *Self and Cosmos.*

88. Alfonso López Quintás, "Aportación Decisiva del Cristianismo a la Cultura Occidental," *Verbo* 433–34 (March–April 2005): 217–43 at 220.

89. Pierpaolo Polzonetti, *Giuseppe Tartini e la musica secondo natura* (Lucca: LIM, 2001).

90. Peter Galison, *Einstein's Clocks and Poincaré's Maps: Empires of Time* (New York: W. W. Norton, 2003); see also Donald A. Yerxa, "Einstein's Clocks, Poincaré's Maps: An Interview with Peter Galison, Part I," *HS* 5, 2 (November 2003): 5–9 at 8.

hands." We might speak of artistic culture, especially music, as originating in *cultus,* in liturgy and worship, and as in varying degrees maintaining this relation well into the modern period.[91] There seems to be an analogical relation between the forms of nature, the forms of culture, and the forms of religious ritual.[92]

The early Christian writer Clement of Alexandria wrote of God in his *Protrepticos,* 1: "Truly he has embellished the universe with melody and drawn the dissonance of the elements into the unity of order, so that the whole world might become harmony in his presence."[93] From the late Roman world Christian music became especially the *universa laus* or *laus perennis* of both the daily liturgy and of monasticism, chant or continual prayer across the course of the day.[94] In the words of the seventh-century Spanish *Regula Monastica Communis,* "The Catholic Church celebrates un-ceasingly these canonical hours from east to west."[95] Whatever the setting, the goal was liturgy as a kind of alignment in which the optimistic hope was that "the *ordo* of heaven become the *ordo* of earth."[96] "Music is a prin-ciple whereby man can know, analogously, the harmony of God's govern-ment."[97] This was Boethius's view in *De institutione musica,* written about 510, transmitted throughout the Middle Ages in teaching music as part of the *quadrivium.*[98]

In light of the ancient background, it is no surprise that in the early Middle Ages, music typically centered on mathematics and theory, some-times even expressing a disdain for performance. In identifying music with number, a late-ninth-century handbook of liturgical instruction went so far as to say, "Notes pass away quickly; numbers, however, though stained by the corporeal matter of voices and moving things, remain."[99] From a Christian point of view, this showed a danger in too close an association of

---

91. O'Malley, *Four Cultures,* 19–22, 179–233, though O'Malley emphasizes the links be-tween antique visual culture and Western art and architecture.

92. Hans van der Laan, *The Play of Forms: Nature, Culture, and Liturgy* (Leiden: Brill, 2005).

93. Translation found in Johannes Quasten, *Music and Worship in Pagan and Christian An-tiquity,* tr. Boniface Ramsey (Washington, D.C.: National Association of Pastoral Musicians, 1983), ii. For the Christianization of ancient cosmology, see Hervé Inglebert, *Interpretatio Chris-tiana: Les mutations des saviors, cosmographie, géograpie, ethnographie, histoire, dans l'Antiquité chrétienne, 30–630 après J. C.* (Paris: Institut d'études augustiniennes, 2001).

94. Emilio Rey García, "Algunos Aspectos de la Vida Musical Hispánica en la Edad Me-dia," in *Vida Cotidiana en la España Medieval* (Aguilar de Campóo: Fundación Sta. María la Real, Centro de Estudios del Románico, 1998), 85–106 at 91.

95. My modification of *Regula Monastica Communis,* 10 (attributed to Fructuosus of Bra-ga), tr. Claude W. Barlow, *Iberian Fathers,* vol. 2: *Braulio of Saragossa and Fructuosus of Braga,* The Fathers of the Church, 63 (Washington, D.C.: The Catholic University of America Press, 1969), 191.

96. Robert Barron, "Evangelizing the American Culture," *SS* 3 (2002): 26–38 at 37.

97. Augustine, *Epistulae,* 166.5.13, quoted in Lehner, "Music (Philosophy)."

98. The first book of *De institutione musica* is devoted to Pythagorean theory.

99. *Musica et Scholica enchiriadis,* 113–14, tr. Bruce W. Holsinger, *Music, Body, and Desire in*

music with mathematics, which could reduce music simply to idea and impugn "corporeality" itself. One scholar has written of Hrotswitha of Gandersheim's (935?–after 973) discussion of music in the next century that it was "unmitigatedly theoretical . . . with no performance," as it often still was at Paris three hundred years later.[100] Hrotswitha began her *Paphnutius* with a discussion between the monk Paphnutius and his disciples about the harmony of the world, which led to a brief discussion of mathematics, which in turn led to a discussion of music. Paphnutius divides music into three kinds: celestial, human, and instrumental. The disciples ask why the music of the spheres and planets cannot be heard, and Paphnutius responds that many reasons are given, such as that men have become so accustomed to it that it is no longer heard. Hrotswitha's plays embody the traditional teaching that "life's goal was to reunite the soul with the divine": her understanding of music is that its harmonies provide the context in which this reunion takes place.[101]

"Medieval rituals were performed inside an encapsulating cosmology that gave them meaning," and especially in the twelfth century there was a great flourishing of cosmic themes among the learned.[102] Hildegard of Bingen, the author of *Symphonia armoniae celestium revelationum,* in seeing music as part of the cosmic order and her own abilities and songs as God-given rather than the result of her own ingenuity, asserted that Adam's and the race's first state was singing.[103] She claimed to have heard (presumably in a vision) a "celestial concert . . . when the heavens were open to her" in praise of the "celestial hierarchy."[104] Many illuminated manuscripts from this time show King David accompanied by various musicians and dancers. These represent both the order of the universe and praise of God (see Psalm 150).[105] Related ideas are found all through Renaissance *cosmopoiesis.*[106] In the fifteenth century Nicolas of Cusa declared: "'The science of praise

Medieval Culture (Stanford, Calif.: Stanford University Press, 2001), 4–10 for current discussion, at 4 for quotation.

100. O'Malley, *Four Cultures,* 94, and see Anna Maria Busse Berger, *Medieval Music and the Art of Memory* (Berkeley 2005), chs. 4–5.

101. Timothy J. Reiss, *Mirages of the Selfe: Patterns of Personhood in Ancient and Early Modern Europe* (Stanford, Calif.: Stanford University Press, 2003), 271–72 at 271, and see 282 on Hildegard of Bingen.

102. See Thomas A. Boogaart II, "Our Saviour's Blood: Procession and Community in Late Medieval Bruges," in *Moving Subjects: Processional Performance in the Middle Ages and the Renaissance,* ed. Kathleen Ashley and Wim Hüsken (Amsterdam: Rodopi, 2001), 69–116, at 75. See also Brian Stock, *Myth and Science in the Twelfth Century: A Study of Bernard Silvester* (Princeton, N.J.: Princeton University Press, 1972).

103. See esp. Barbara Newman, *Saint Hildegard of Bingen: Symphonia* (Ithaca, N.Y.: Cornell University Press, 1988), 18.

104. Ibid., 7.

105. Jesús Herrero Marcos, *Arquitectura y Simbolismo del Románico de Cantabria* (Madrid: Ars Magna, 1995): 115–17.

106. Giuseppe Mazzotta, *Cosmopoiesis: The Renaissance Experiment* (Toronto: University of Toronto Press, 2001).

is naturally born' in beings capable of knowledge, because the creaturely mind, reflecting on its nature, must think of itself as a ray of the glory of God, and therefore indeed is called to imitation of what is praiseworthy."[107]

⌒

Already before Augustine, as much as in philosophy and theology, in theorizing about music Platonic and Pythagorean views struggled with Christian incarnationalism.[108] Thus the preponderance of Platonic-Pythagorean thinking in the late Roman and medieval worlds is not the whole story. One scholar has said of early Christian music theory that there was "not an overweening desire to escape the flesh, but . . . the challenge of reconciling the pleasures of musical embodiment with the incarnational religiosity they practice."[109] The task of coming to terms with the pleasure music gives was important to Augustine's ever-developing thought. Particularly important is *Confessions* 9.7.16, which chapter, according to the same scholar, "registers the author's initial realization that the beauty and power of music lie not in the transcendence of materiality in favor of a sublime geometry 'free of all body,' but in the stimulation and vivification of the flesh."[110] Though Augustine's aversion to enjoying the world for its own sake might lead one to moderate this language of "stimulation and vivification," some inclination for enjoyment perhaps lies behind the emergence of polyphonic music later, with its greater sensuousness and lesser austerity, in comparison to chant.[111] Such was present already in the Winchester troper of about 1000.[112] Yet Gregorian chant itself should not be simply identified with asceticism, simplicity, and purity, for, as Pärt came to see in our own day after his break with serialism, there is also embellishment in chant.[113] Up to the sixteenth century most polyphony retained both the simplicity of chant and the pleasures of elaboration by the use of a *cantus firmus,* a pre-existent melody, usually in plain song.[114] We should not be surprised that still today some living Chris-

107. *Excit. Lib.* 6, quoted in Balthasar, *Glory of the Lord,* vol. 5: *The Realm of Metaphysics in the Modern Age,* 218, and see 220–22.

108. Holsinger, *Music,* 1–83, gives a provocative, if not always closely reasoned, overview of developments in the late antique period, nicely emphasizing that there was no single Christian view. Cf. Richard Sorabji, *Emotion and Peace of Mind: From Stoic Agitation to Christian Temptation* (New York: Oxford University Press, 2000), as at 81–92, 130–32, on ancient understanding of music and, 83–84, 405–6, its possible association with lust.

109. Holsinger, *Music,* 30.

110. Ibid., 72. Holsinger's treatment is both stimulating and exasperating: what he calls "inconsistency" and "disingenuousness" in Augustine (75–76), I would call "uncertainty" and "honesty."

111. Guillaume Gross, "Chanter en polyphonie à Notre-Dame de Paris sous le règne de Philippe Auguste: un art de la magnificence," *Revue Historique* 308 (2006): 609–34.

112. For context see William T. Flynn, *Medieval Music as Medieval Exegesis* (Lanham, Md.: Scarecrow Press, 1999).

113. Brauneiss, "Arvo Pärt's Tintinnabuli Style," 28.

114. Ibid., 32.

tian composers such as Pärt, in attempting a flight from the world they have received, seek not flight per se, but some new incarnationalism which gives earth its due but, in a way the music of the modernist, laicist, and Communist experiments failed to do, ties it to heaven, gives heaven also its due.

"Getting incarnationalism right" has taken a long time, witness the Iconoclastic Controversy of the eighth and ninth centuries and the debate—between Cathar, Waldensian, Wycliffite or Hussite, and Catholic in the thirteenth, fourteenth, or fifteenth centuries, and between Calvinism and Catholicism in the Reformation and Baroque periods—as to what the proper relation is of the sensuality of this world to that which is invisible.[115] Presumably historically there would not have been extended argument about the difference between *dulia* (veneration) and *latria* (worship) of images, if people had not been engaging in image-worship, and it is clear from various medieval legends and *exempla* that some did see images as wonder-working and animated in ways that a learned theologian was likely to disapprove.[116] In the seventeenth century people could remark with astonishment on the different aesthetics of the Friends' meeting houses, all light, white, and pictureless, in comparison with Catholic churches.[117] One may view the tremendous destruction of Catholic churches, monasteries, and religious art both in the Reformation and the French Revolution as a form of iconoclasm.[118]

"Getting incarnationalism right" may involve much more than usually falls under the heading of the historical quarrels over iconoclasm. Iconoclasts typically defend the transcendent by throwing all materiality and sensuality under suspicion, and iconodules defend a measured use of materiality. But before the Counter-Reformation and development of the Baroque, the problem of another way of losing transcendence had hardly presented itself, namely losing transcendence through what we might call the categories of the lachrymose or cloying, of unmodulated sentiment, even of a certain morbid attention to the Crucified One, as in many early modern,

115. O'Malley, *Four Cultures,* 195–99, 208–33. Charles Barber, *Figure and Likeness: On the Limits of Representation in Byzantine Iconoclasm* (Princeton, N.J.: Princeton University Press, 2002), considers especially the theological questions concerning the ability of images to portray the divine. Alain Besançon, *The Forbidden Image: An Intellectual History of Iconoclasm,* tr. Jane Marie Todd (Chicago: University of Chicago Press, 2000), is an ambitious survey of the whole Western tradition. On the use of images to counter Catharism, see Arturo Carlo Quintavalle, "Il viaggio, l'immagine, l'eresia: la trasformazione del sistema simbolico della Chiesa fra Riforma gregoriana ed eresia catara," in *Arti e storia nel medioevo,* vol. 3: *Del vedere: pubblicii,* ed. Castelnuovo and Sergi, 593–669 at 659–69. On the question of the relation between the Catholic and Protestant liturgical traditions, see the articles gathered in *Worship in Medieval and Early Modern Europe: Change and Continuity in Religious Practice,* ed. Karin Maag and John D. Witvliet (Notre Dame, Ind.: University of Notre Dame Press, 2004).

116. Kathleen Kamerick, *Popular Piety and Art in the Late Middle Ages: Image Worship and Idolatry in England, 1350–1500* (New York: Palgrave, 2002), esp. ch. 2.

117. Christian, "Priests, Mountains and 'Sacred Space,'" 99–100.

118. Henry Kraus, *The Living Theatre of Medieval Art* (Bloomington: Indiana University Press, 1967), 163–82.

especially German, crucifixes. There certainly is something to the idea that the lachrymose sweetness of a good deal of later Counter-Reformation, especially Marian, piety from the seventeenth century onward represents a loss of transcendence in which the majesty of God is buried in sentiment or at least in the Baroque envelope of, say, the *Stabat Mater* of Pergolesi (1710–36).[119] This is a complicated question, but the Baroque, while expressing the glory of God and thus presumably his transcendence, also emphasized that God could be found in all things, and thus was open to a sentimentalization and histrionics far from the Gospel portrayal of the Incarnate One. In any case at various times since, there have been factors within the Church, as well as pressures coming from the larger society, which sometimes have led to a muffling of transcendence. The kind of charismatic spirituality sometimes found in some of the new Catholic movements can be as sentimental and infantile as the worst Baroque excess.

At heart always has been the question of the adequacy of any portrayal of the ineffable, and the relation between such portrayal and the thing in itself. Already in a famous letter sent to the Second Council of Nicea of 787, Pope Hadrian I seems to have achieved a certain balance. Referring to visible images of the face of Christ, Hadrian wrote:

By means of a visible face, our spirit is carried away by a spiritual attraction towards the invisible majesty of the divinity by contemplating the image in which is represented the flesh that the Son of God deigned to take for our salvation.[120]

This was to remain the dominant Orthodox and Catholic position, and in the twelfth century Suger of St. Denis wrote of the ability of the material culture of this world to carry him into another world.[121] Similarly his contemporary, Richard of St. Victor (d. 1173), a contemplative on the threshold of scholasticism, used the traditional expression *per visibilia ad invisibilia* to express his idea of a theological method which begins in an attempt to understand the visible world and then in contemplation penetrates the mysteries of the invisible world, moving in ascent to a vision of God.[122]

A kind of generic iconoclasm remained a threat, and a classic study by

---

119. Anna Klosowska, *Queer Love in the Middle Ages* (New York: Palgrave Macmillan, 2005), 34–36. Klosowska goes on to interpret Mary's silence in the *Stabat Mater* as passivity (36–37), for once perhaps falling into a liberal mode of presentation: arguably Mary's suffering, like her silence, is not passive but contemplative, an expression of expectation and great alertness.

120. O'Malley, *Four Cultures,* 197, and see 198–99, on the centrality of John Damascene, on whom see also Andrew Louth, *St. John Damascene: Tradition and Originality in Byzantine Theology* (New York: Oxford University Press, 2004). More definitive on II Nicea is Hans Georg Thümmel, *Die Konzilien zur Bilderfrage im 8. und 9. Jarhhundert: Das 7. Ökumenische Konzil in Nikaia 787* (Paderborn: Ferdinand Schöningh, 2005).

121. O'Malley, *Four Cultures,* 201–2.

122. See Paul Rorem, review of D. M. Coulter, *"Per visibilia ad invisibilia": Theological Method in Richard of St. Victor (d. 1173)* (Turnhout 2006), in *Sp* 83 (2007): 973–74. The brilliant and revisionary Thomas F. X. Noble, *Images, Iconoclasm, and the Carolingians* (Philadelphia: University of Pennsylvania Press, 2009), was only received when the present book was in press.

Gunter Bandmann has since argued that, if the articulation of a symbolic universe in church architecture is one's goal, someone like Bernard of Clairvaux, with his attack on all distracting church decoration, represents a secularization—Bandmann's word—within twelfth-century Catholicism itself, in which a certain didacticism threatened all that was cosmic and symbolic.[123] By using the word "secularization" Bandmann meant to indicate that in attacking Romanesque decoration, Bernard was attacking the inherited symbolic and liturgical universe in favor of a more austere art and architecture less capable of articulating mystery and thus less capable of pointing to that which is beyond the *saeculum*. It was not just the distracting animals and monsters of Romanesque sculpture that Bernard threatened, but the whole inherited cosmic order. Obviously even in a pared down Cistercian church the cosmic order remained in the liturgy itself, and Cistercian illustrated manuscripts continued whimsical decoration, but Bandmann's is a useful perspective for viewing the much later secularizations of Christianity found in the "iconoclasm" of Jansenism or of that "iconoclastic" or "secularizing" interpretation of Vatican II which stripped so many churches of their inherited architecture and expressed a didacticism hostile to all that is polyvalent and symbolic.[124] Bandmann's is not a comprehensive treatment of Bernard himself, and others have pointed out that there is a theological aesthetic in Bernard which centers on a loving relation with the Word expressed in all areas of life.[125]

Charles Rosen argues that from the first there was in Western music a specific alliance between music and philosophy, which in the modern period has been expressed in the idea that score and "the theoretical structure of pitch and rhythm" are so central that "the score may be beautiful irrespective of my realization."[126] From this perspective we might say that "cosmic music" had never been so much something heard as something seen in the

123. Gunter Bandmann, *Early Medieval Architecture as Bearer of Meaning*, tr. Kendall Wallis (New York: Columbia University Press, 2005), which sees the Cistercian search for architectural simplicity, and that of the mendicants later, as forms of secularization and the victory of reason over symbol standing in a tradition of rejection of art running from Plato to the Quakers (237–41). Cf. Conrad Rudolph, *The "Things of Greater Importance": Bernard of Clairvaux's Apologia and the Medieval Attitude toward Art* (Philadelphia: University of Pennsylvania Press, 1990), and "La resistenza all'arte nell'Occidente," in *Arti e storia nel medioevo*, vol. 3: *Del vedere*, ed. Castelnuovo and Sergi, 49–84. Astell, *Eating Beauty*, thinks Bernard's iconoclasm has been much exaggerated.

124. Glenn W. Olsen, *Beginning at Jerusalem: Five Reflections on the History of the Church* (San Francisco: Ignatius Press, 2004), 40, 54–65. Meyer Schapiro, *Romanesque Architectural Sculpture*, ed. Linda Seidel (Chicago: University of Chicago Press, 2006), 151–53, gives examples of Cistercian manuscript decoration. Of David Freedberg's various studies of especially Protestant iconoclasm in the modern period, see *Iconoclasts and their Motives* (The Hague: Schwartz, 1985).

125. Pierluigi Lia, *L'estetica teologica di Bernardo di Chiaravalle* (Florence: Edizioni del Galluzzo per la Fondazione Ezio Franceschini, 2007).

126. "The Future of Music," *NYRB* 48, 20 (December 20, 2001): 60–65 at 64. Pickstock, "Music," 259–60, introduces further considerations.

mind. This notion of an objective or ideal structure was wonderfully expressed visually in pre-Romanesque Spanish manuscript illumination. Especially through such images as the Lamb on Mount Sion, the Woman and the Dragon (Apocalypse 12:1–18), or the Adoration (Apocalypse 19:1–10), the Spanish Beatus manuscripts (tenth through sixteenth centuries) present a hierarchy of temporal and transcendent realms, of heaven and earth.[127] One of their themes is the celestial liturgy.[128] In turn, Spanish Romanesque sculpture, especially along the road to Santiago, expressed the idea that the liturgy is a symbolic image of the universe and of God's creative and salvific activity.

The genius of particularly Latin liturgy is its synthesis of cosmic or atemporal and historical reality. We might say—Romano Guardini said— that first of all the liturgy is play.[129] Before we are speakers or doers, we are hearers and listeners. As a kind of dance, liturgy elevates its participants from the so-called "real world" of ordinary time into a more real world, "out of time." Better, it brings that more real world into our ordinary world. The Eucharist itself is from this perspective a kind of spiritual art making beauty present.[130] Liturgy is cosmic or atemporal, circling around God in praise. The building in which it takes place may be described as the new Jerusalem or as a replica of the court of heaven.[131] In a monastic environment, this liturgical space of the church building might "spill out" and engulf the cloister, itself becoming both Eden and a pre-figuration of Paradise.[132] In the thirteenth century, William Durandus expressed the idea that a church is more than the material out of which it is made: "For the material church, wherein the people assemble to set forth God's holy praise, symbolizes that

127. Mireille Mentré, *Illuminated Manuscripts of Medieval Spain,* tr. Jenifer Wakelyn (London: Thames and Hudson, 1996), 170–92, with beautiful illustrations. See also the sections "La percepción del espacio 'cosmico'" and "Espacio y tiempo sagrados," in Francisco Javier Fernández Conde, *La Religiosidad Medieval en España,* vol. 1: *Alta Edad Media (s. VII–X)* (Oviedo: Universidad de Ovieda, 2000), 363–81, 525–29.

128. Mentré, *Illuminated Manuscripts,* 193–96.

129. *The Spirit of the Liturgy,* tr. Ada Lane (New York: Crossroad, 1998), 66: "The liturgy creates a universe brimming with fruitful spiritual life, and allows the soul to wander about in it at will and to develop itself there. . . . The liturgy has no purpose, or at least, it cannot be considered from the standpoint of purpose. It is not a means which is adapted to attain a certain end—it is an end in itself. This fact is important, because if we overlook it, we labor to find all kinds of didactic purposes in the liturgy. . . . When the liturgy is rightly regarded, it cannot be said to have a purpose, because it does not exist for the sake of humanity, but for the sake of God. In the liturgy man is not so much intended to edify himself as to contemplate God's majesty."

130. Astell, *Eating Beauty.*

131. Claude Carozzi, "Dalla Gerusalemme celeste alla chiesa: testo, immagini, simbolli," in *Arti e storia nel medioevo,* vol. 3: *Del vedere,* ed. Castelnuovo and Sergi, 145–66. In the same volume see Quintavalle, "Il viaggio," 627–42.

132. *Claustros Románicos Hispanos,* ed. Joaquin Yarza Luaces and Gerado Boto Varela (León: Edilesa, 2003), frontispiece quoting Honorius of Autun, *De Gemma animae,* I, CXLIX, on the cloister as pre-figuration, and 20–25, on the cloister as liturgical space.

holy church that is built in Heaven with living stones."[133] Many of the famous converts to Catholicism living at the time of Vatican II were sorely tested by the liturgical innovations coming out of the Council precisely because their conversions had been in part occasioned by discomfort with the modern world, and they saw at least some of these innovations as a capitulation to all that was banal in that world.[134]

Though the liturgy may teach, it is not in its essence didactic. Perhaps this is why, when the conversion of Constantine brought so many people into the Church that a need was felt to explain the elaborate liturgical ceremonies, resort was most commonly made not to historical interpretations, but to allegorical and mystical interpretations.[135] As Guardinii stated, the liturgy might be said to exist not for mankind's sake, but for God's sake. But the liturgy also declares the great events of salvation history. Liturgy is rooted at once in the events of salvation history, having a narrative dimension, but also in the cosmos, giving it a cosmological dimension which goes out (turns East) to meet the Lord (the Son/Sun) who is to come again. The cosmos already spoke of this Christ, and in Him cosmos and history are united.[136] We find this also in the architecture which envelopes the liturgy.[137] In the synthesis of the Roman Catholic priest Robert Sokolowsi:

As we say the Eucharistic canon, we join the angels and saints and take part in the celestial Eucharist, the glory given to the Father by the Son who redeemed the world. . . . Our worldly Eucharist joins with the celestial. . . . The celestial Eucharist is beyond time and world history. It touches history because the saving action of the Son of God took place in time, but his action was not just a temporal event. . . . The celestial Eucharist is the eternal aspect of the death of Christ; it is not just a memorial or reminder of that event. . . . It is not simply the worldly substance of the body and blood of the Lord that are present in the Eucharist, but his glorified body and blood, which share in the eternity of the ce-

133. Quoted in O'Malley, *Four Cultures*, 205.

134. Adam Schwartz, *The Third Spring: G. K. Chesterton, Graham Greene, Christopher Dawson, and David Jones* (Washington, D.C.: The Catholic University of America Press, 2005), as at 27–28.

135. O'Malley, *Four Cultures*, 189–91, who, 190, gives the following seventh-century Byzantine example, from St. Germanus, patriarch of Constantinople: "The holy table [the altar] is the place where Christ was buried, and on which is set forth the true bread from heaven, the mystic and bloodless sacrifice, i.e., Christ. . . . It is also the throne upon which God who is borne up by the cherubim, has rested. At this table, too, Christ sat down at his last supper in the midst of his apostles. . . . It was prefigured by the table of the Law on which was the manna that comes down from heaven." See also my *Beginning at Jerusalem*, 42–55.

136. Benedict XVI (Joseph Cardinal Ratzinger), *The Spirit of the Liturgy*, tr. John Saward (San Francisco: Ignatius Press, 2000), esp. part 2, 74, 94. See also I. Marchesin, "Cosmologie et musique au moyen âge," in *Moyen Âge: entre ordre et désordre*, ed. Marion Challier and Bernadette Caille (Paris 2004). C. S. Lewis, *The Discarded Image: An Introduction to Medieval and Renaissance Literature* (Cambridge: Cambridge University Press, 1994), is a classic treatment of late medieval cosmological assumptions.

137. Santiago Sebastian, *Mensaje Simbólico del Arte Medieval. Arquitectura, Liturgia e Iconografía* (Madrid: Encuentro Edidiones, 1994).

lestial Eucharist. The bread and wine are now the vehicles for the presence of the eternal Christ. . . . The Christian tradition of the East, with its strong focus on the celestial liturgy, encounters less difficulty with the Real Presence of Christ in the sacrament than does the West, precisely because of this focus and the correlative belief in the eucharistic presence of the glorified Christ. We in the West tend to think primarily in terms of human psychology and worldly history, and these concerns make us raise problems that may be less likely to arise in the East. . . . The redemptive action of the Son is eternally present to the Father, and this action is carried out by the person of the Son in the Eucharist.[138]

Even a style as massive as the Romanesque was used to articulate the translucent kingdom of heaven and the way in which this world may be an antechamber of Heaven.[139] The door of the individual church was the door by which one enters eternal life (see Jn 10:9). Especially Romanesque porch archivolts expressed the harmonies of the universe and cycles of the seasons, sometimes through the vehicle of carvings or, as in the Pantheon at Saint Isidro in León, through paintings of the activities specific to the twelve months, or by a new use of the signs of the Zodiac.[140] Christ is not only Pantocrator, Lord of the Universe, but Chronocrator, the Lord of Time.[141] At Paris in the time of Hugh of St. Victor, we find one of the most elaborate correlations of macro/microcosmic harmony in Hugh's *The Mystic Ark* (ca. 1125–30).[142]

The exquisite representation of King David playing a cithern on a column at Revilla de Collazos in Palencia, and the magnificent sculptures of the 24 Elders of the Apocalypse, instruments in hand, on the south portal of Moissac (c. 1125–30) and all along the road to Santiago, embody the idea of an eternal, cosmic liturgy, of a supra-terrestrial beauty which still finds its voice in this world.[143] Singing and praying is participation in the cosmic

138. "The Eucharist and Transubstantiation," *Co* 24 (1997): 867–80 at 869–71.

139. Christine Smith et al., *Before and After the End of Time: Architecture and the Year 1000* (New York: Harvard Design School/George Braziller, 2000).

140. Jesús Herrero Marcos, *Arquitectura y Simbolismo del Románico Palentino*, 2nd ed. (Madrid 1995), gives many examples, stressing that the interest of much so-called fertility symbolism in Romanesque sculpture is in expression of the cosmic and solar cycles.

141. For eleventh- through thirteenth-century examples, see Herrero Marcos, *Arquitectura y Simbolismo del Románico Palentino*, 75, 77, and Viviane Minne-Sève and Hervé Kergall, *Romanesque and Gothic France: Architecture and Sculpture*, tr. Jack Hawkes and Lory Frankel (New York: Abrams, 2000), 67.

142. Conrad Rudolph, *"First, I Find the Center Point": Reading the Text of Hugh of Saint Victor's The Mystic Ark* (Philadelphia: American Philosophical Society, 2004).

143. Herrero Marcos, *Arquitectura y Simbolismo del Románico Palentino*, 128–29, with picture, and see p. 139 for a "cosmic" interpretation of two dancers between musicians found on a series of porch capitals of twelfth-century Moarves de Ojeda. God is the Grand Musician, the creator of the melody which sustains the cosmic order. For a picture of the portal at Moissac, see Minne-Sève and Kergall, *Romanesque and Gothic France*, 45, and see 30, 91. See also the articles gathered in *El Códice Calixtino y la música de su tiempo*, ed. José López-Calo and Carlos Villanueva (A Coruña: Fundación Pedro Barrié de la Maza, 2001), esp. Thomas H. Connolly, "The Tuning of Heaven: The Aesthetic of the Pórtico de la Gloria," 95–110.

liturgy, and the great expression of this is the angels. In spite of the challenges to the Neoplatonic underpinnings of this view of cosmic liturgy a revived Aristotelianism presented from the thirteenth century, it survived into the modern period, witness the title of a modern book about music in early English religious drama, Richard Rastall's *The Heavens Singing*.[144]

But of course things did change and toward the end of the eighteenth century, alongside continuing emphasis on art or poetry as mimetic, there developed an emphasis on imagination.[145] As we have seen, the older idea had been that artistic production was largely inspired, a gift coming to the artist from outside. We might say that in this there was no "distance" between message and messenger, that the latter was swallowed up by the former. Of course the artist or architect in some sense knew himself to be the workman bringing forth beauty, but, as Procopius declared of Hagia Sophia, "whenever anyone enters this church to pray, he understands at once that it is not by human power or skill but by the influence of God that this work has been so finely turned out."[146]

We must not draw distinctions too clearly here: by the late Middle Ages, in many spheres of life, we find self-consciousness competing with the idea that God speaks through the artist, prophet, saint, or mystic. Thus in the fifteenth century the illiterate Margery Kempe in complicated fashion simultaneously claimed "religious authority, yes, but also sacred awe, a delighted satisfaction with her own sainthood, the pride of an artist who has mastered a difficult craft, . . . and sheer wonder at what it is possible for a human being to know of God."[147] Alistair J. Minnis has claimed that from the twelfth through the fifteenth century compilation was the master pattern of authorship.[148] The author was to be both the source of *auctoritates* and fallible, and his book was often composed of fragments of earlier works. This is to say that some idea of the creativity of the author was known, but in one way or other the author or artist remained a servant and reconstitutor of tradition.

～

144. Subtitle: *Music in Early English Religious Drama*, vol. 1 (Cambridge: Brewer, 1996). On the challenges of the thirteenth and fourteenth centuries, specifically on the rethinking of the problem and reinterpretation of the Neoplatonic universe by Nicole Oresme, see Gabriela Ilnitchi, "*Musica mundana*, Aristotelian natural philosophy and Ptolemaic astronomy," *Early Music History* 21 (2002): 37–74.

145. On this and the following, see John Lukacs, *At the End of An Age* (New Haven, Conn.: Yale University Press, 2002), 27.

146. Translation found in O'Malley, *Four Cultures*, 183.

147. Barbara Newman, "What Did It Mean to Say 'I Saw'? The Clash between Theory and Practice in Medieval Visionary Culture," *Sp* 80 (2005): 1–43 at 33. Newman goes on to discuss the threat that various late medieval developments presented to "the theology of spontaneous divine intervention" (34).

148. *Medieval Theory of Authorship: Scholastic Literary Attitudes in the Later Middle Ages* (Philadelphia: University of Pennsylvania Press, 1988), 3–4; and see Klosowska, *Queer Love*, 71–72.

I am not sure that Martin Jay is right in his claim that Greek thought had an "oracularcentric bias," which distinguished between subject and object and always kept a distance between the two.[149] Looking beyond simply the visual, it seems to me that sometimes there was distance, sometimes not. For instance, running back at least as far as the Delphic oracle were two traditions, one which aimed at self-knowledge, and one which tried to lose the self in something greater.[150] When Christian monasticism first appeared, some monks scrutinized themselves intensely, while others thought it sinful to be preoccupied with the self when one was to lose oneself in God. From the twelfth century, as some sense of Augustine's idea that we are the sum of the choices we have made over our life's course began to revive, an early step on the long road to modern individualism, a German mystic such as Mechthild of Magdeburg (ca. 1212–ca. 1281), who sometimes has been viewed as silenced by misogyny, marks a reverse development and slowly disappears from her writings. Mechthild developed a form of writing which deemphasized the author in favor of placing direct dialogue with God at the forefront (thus obtaining another kind of authority).[151] That said, Jay is right in thinking that there was a medieval model of visuality in which subject and object were fused.[152] I am inclined to think that much more than vision was involved here, and that the basic distinction should be between looking out on the world as a participant in it, as part of it, and looking at it in the manner of the modern scientist, dispassionate, distanced, and apart.[153] The point then would be that the older classical-Christian view of man's relation to the cosmos saw man in any act of creation as an instrument for communicating something greater than himself, something that had overwhelmed him and become one with him.

We see something parallel to this classical-Christian view still in the seventeenth-century Republic of Letters. Isaac Newton (1642–1727) grew up in this republic:

an international society of men, and later, women, dedicated to the pursuit of knowledge rather than of personal gain. They organized collective inquiries, sent each other news of discoveries . . . in the hope of establishing the simple truth.

149. *Downcast Eyes: The Denigration of Vision in Twentieth-Century French Thought* (Berkeley: University of California Press, 1993); see also Emma Campbell and Robert Mills, "Introduction," in *Troubled Vision: Gender, Sexuality, and Sight in Medieval Text and Image,* ed. Emma Campbell and Robert Mills (New York: Palgrave Macmillan, 2004), 1–14 at 7–8.

150. The great guide to the tradition of self-knowledge is Pierre Courcelle, *Connais-toi toi-même, de Socrate à Saint Bernard,* 3 vols. (Paris: Institut d'études augustiniennes, 1974–75).

151. Sara S. Poor, *Mechthild of Magdeburg and Her Book: Gender and the Making of Textual Authority* (Philadelphia: University of Pennsylvania Press, 2004). Poor has interesting things to say about Romanticism's continuing hold on scholarly treatment of the mystical tradition.

152. See Suzannah Biernoff, *Sight and Embodiment in the Middle Ages* (New York: Palgrave Macmillan, 2002); also Campbell and Mills, "Introduction," 8.

153. Cf. Suzanne Conklin Akbari, *Seeing through the Veil: Optical Theory and Medieval Allegory* (Toronto: University of Toronto Press, 2004).

As citizens of this republic, they professed that they did not care about rank or gain, only about the truth—to the point that some of their new periodicals did not give the names of authors.[154]

It was as if the best aspects of the life of the mind in the Middle Ages were still alive, but this was not to last. By the end of Newton's life, traditional etiquette had been burned away, and the various nationalities were claiming that one of their own had been the first to discover this or that. The Republic of Letters gave way to a Hobbesian war of all against all:

These ferocious writers liked nothing better than to wound their opponents, and they paid little heed to the old rules of unselfishness and generous recognition of others' accomplishments when they did so. . . .

In these debates, a basic principle of modern science took shape: what matters is not simply arriving at the truth, but arriving there first. Modern scientists . . . establish their ownership of a fact or a principle only by publishing it before anyone else.

Raging individualism and a cult of genius came to replace an older order in many fields. Newton was a fast learner here, and his younger habit of concealing his discoveries for years was replaced with the expression of public contempt for his rivals, the stacking of a commission called to adjudicate the controversy between himself and Leibnitz over calculus, and a general seeking of credit for his discoveries.[155]

If behind every mistaken practical idea there is a mistaken theological idea, Newton's seems to have been his un-Trinitarian voluntarism.[156] A transitional early modern idea was that the artist is "divine," both filled with divine inspiration, and filled with genius.[157] Then in turn a newer and more modern emphasis was on imagination, on art as the product of creative genius. The composer became an inventor, a Promethean personage. Inspiration involved the assumption of separation between observer and observed. Imagination put the observer to the fore. If the ancient-medieval view typically had about it a naiveté which overlooked what later centuries would call epistemological questions, the newer view sometimes beggared credulity with its unreserved views of genius.

The older view assumed that the artist works within a tradition, and that discipline precedes freedom. In St. Francis of Assisi's words, "In self-forgetfulness we find our true selves."[158] This older view was but an artistic

---

154. Anthony Grafton, "The Ways of Genius," *NYRB* 51, 19 (December 2, 2004): 38–40 at 39, on this and the following.

155. Ibid., 40.

156. Simon Oliver, "Motion According to Aquinas and Newton," *MT* 17, 2 (2001): 163–99, and *Philosophy, God, and Motion* (New York: Routledge, 2005), 153–82.

157. Patricia A. Emison, *Creating the "Divine" Artist: From Dante to Michelangelo* (Leiden: Brill, 2004).

158. Quoted in David Clayton, "The Way of Beauty," *SS* 4 (2003): 19–26 at 23.

expression of the communion of saints, that is, of the idea that tradition itself is an everlasting conversation in which the generations discourse back and forth. This was already the idea behind Romanesque portrayal of the twenty-four elders of the Apocalypse engaged in holy conversation. The idea also is found in Fra Angelico's (c. 1395–1455) treatment of the Madonna and Child. Before Angelico the Madonna and Child had been placed on altarpieces in compartments separated from the saints. Angelico placed them altogether in a throne room, united in meditation.[159] Over time, this early form of the *sacra conversazione* expanded into a variety of Sacred Conversations showing people who were not contemporaries in solemn conversation—there are fine examples in the Regional Museum in Palermo, where Thomas Aquinas (c. 1225–74) and Emperor Charles V (1500–88) become contemporaries, and in the Accademia in Venice.

The newer view of genius placed the ego at the center of artistic creation. In alliance with the views of the universe developing in the thought of Galileo and Newton, a universe governed by mathematical laws and increasingly an object of research, less and less emphasis was placed on veneration of the cosmos.[160] Already in 1543 *(On the Revolutions of the Heavenly Spheres),* Copernicus's language about God ("the Best Workman") and "the machinery of the world" anticipates Newton's "loveless," mechanical universe, and is at the greatest remove from Dante's "Love that moves the sun and the other stars." This was Blake's insight in drawing Newton "as one of his typical perverse antiheroes, beautiful, muscular, yet imprisoned by the numbers that framed his lifeless technical world."[161]

It took a long time for the old view completely to fade away. Goethe still alluded to cosmic liturgy in his idea that man's music, if it is to be beautiful, must conform to the rhythms and harmonic principles of the universe.[162] One of the beliefs of French classicism virtually into our own day has been that music is more science than art, and dance a subset of music. There is a "most apt" way to present, say, the human foot. Though as noted in the last chapter he became an exemplar of modernism, when Igor Stravinsky first came to France, he entered into this tradition with great enthusiasm. Good music and dance expressed the objective order of the world.[163] Little wonder that Stravinsky's coreligionist Tavener, who also thought that one entered into a Tradition more than left Tradition behind,

159. Andrew Butterfield, "The Pious Revolutionary," *NYRB* 53, 1 (January 12, 2006): 10–13 at 12.

160. Jacques Servais, "Finding God in All Things," *Co* 30 (2003): 260–81 at 262–63.

161. Grafton, "Ways of Genius," 40.

162. Ratzinger, *Spirit of the Liturgy,* 136–56 at 152–54.

163. Jennifer Homans, "Geniuses Together," *NYRB* 49, 20 (December 19, 2002): 32–35, is a very instructive piece on the religious dimensions of George Balanchine's and Stravinsky's dance.

was to find so much to approve in Stravinsky's views. George Balanchine, too, asked his dancers to "submit to the ordered laws of ballet and music, cosmic and physiological."[164]

Only with Hegel's idea that music is an expression of the subject, and, especially, Schopenhauer's idea that music is the primal expression of will, do we have the groundwork laid for "modern music" understood as a repudiation of such cosmic laws and order.[165] There is perhaps no better expression of the new view, and of the way it became attached to perpetual immaturity, than in a letter of W. B. Yeats's father describing his famous son's talents:

A man of genius should be like a young boy who is never, never and never will be a grown up. He must have a new style & new methods. Not for fashion's sake, but because he has outgrown the old ways.[166]

Thus we move from medieval culture's valuing of memory over creativity, and its use of writing to enhance memory, especially its use of techniques which allow the interiorization of sacred texts, to a modern situation in which thought centers on the creating self.[167] The heavens increasingly close and many live within an immanent secular horizon.

St. Paul and the early Church Fathers had seen the whole cosmos as involved in a struggle that God might be all in all. God was in His creation, but could not be equated with it: He transcends all that is. Fathers such as St. Basil spoke of roses having no thorns before Adam's disobedience. For them the cosmos itself, originally pure and whole, was involved in man's first sin and was, with man, now standing in need of redemption. That is, they awaited cosmic renewal. Though surviving in parts of the Orthodox world, such an idea has been almost completely lost to inhabitants of the Western modern world. For these, except in a romantic mood, the mate-

164. Ibid., 35. John Mason Hodges, "Windows into Heaven: The Music of John Tavener," *Image* 10 (Summer 1995): 88–94, discusses Tavener's love of harmonic music, rejection of modernist techniques, in favor of tonality, and use of repetition.

165. Ratzinger, *Spirit of the Liturgy*, 154. Hegel's idea is much more complicated than indicated here, and must be understood in the context of, for instance, his rehabilitation, after Kant, of the proofs for God, now seen as establishing the mind's ability to rise to infinity. Cf. the interesting study by Allen Shawn, *Arnold Schoenberg's Journey* (New York: Farrar, Straus and Giroux, 2002); and the trenchant remarks of Charles Rosen, "Should We Adore Adorno?" *NYRB* 49, 16 (October 24, 2002): 59–66. No doubt, Schopenhauer did not see in his definition of music as the expression of will Norman Mailer's contention that "jazz is orgasm, it is the music of orgasm," but everyone needs his American interpreter: John D'Emilio and Estelle Freedman, *Intimate Matters: A History of Sexuality in America* (New York: Harper & Row, 1988), 275–76, for quotation.

166. Quoted in John Banville, "The Rescue of W. B. Yeats," *NYRB* 51, 3 (February 26, 2004): 12–14 at 12.

167. See Mary Carruthers, *The Book of Memory: A Study of Memory in Medieval Culture* (New York: Cambridge University Press, 1990), and *The Craft of Thought: Meditation, Rhetoric, and the Making of Images, 400–1200* (New York: Cambridge University Press, 1998).

rial order is not alive with God, but mere matter in motion. Any language about the creation praising God must be taken as highly figurative. There is no meaningful sense in which it can be said that the created order worships or rejoices in God. It is this conclusion that prepared the way for the psychology of modernity, which suggests that, the world not being alive with God, it can be manipulated endlessly by man. One notes what a difficult time the minority opinion of, say, Emile Mersch and certain theologians of *la nouvelle théologie* to the present have had in insisting that even the sub-intentional world, with its laws and patterns, might be spoken of, of course by analogy, as giving glory to God, of suggesting that "religion" is part of the structure of nature.[168]

We have noted the tremendous shrinking of memory attendant on the modern situation, now much accelerated in a generation raised on the Internet by teachers who wish to avoid all that is "rote." A society that does not practice the Catholic daily examination of conscience, an examination which aims at understanding how one has forged one's life through one's choices, is not likely to be composed of individuals with a strong sense of their former selves. The past is not very present in such "individuals," and they have a difficult time viewing themselves as part of some larger community, let alone *sub specie aeternitatis*.

⌒

Christian liturgy is in its origins overwhelmingly cosmic.[169] In it we do not "make up tunes" or will a world into existence. We join our voices with the angels in praise of a cosmos ordered by and to the Word. "The Heavens declare the glory of God, and the firmament showeth his handiwork." "For the invisible things of Him, from the creation of the world, are clearly seen, being understood through the things that are made: His eternal power also and divinity."[170] This is an *imago* or exemplarist theology in which the world both hides and reveals God, so beautifully expressed still in the nineteenth century by Cardinal Newman in his sermon "The Invisible World":

Bright as is the sun, and the sky, and the clouds; green as are the leaves and the fields; sweet as is the singing of the birds; we know that they are not all, and we will not take up with a part for the whole. They proceed from a centre of love and goodness, which is God himself; but they are not his fullness; they speak of heaven, but they are not heaven; they are but as stray beams and dim reflections of His Image; they are but crumbs from the table. We are looking for the coming of the day of God, when all this outward world, fair though it be, shall perish;

---

168. Emile Mersch, *Morale et corps mystique* (Paris: Desclée de Brouwer, 1955), chs. 1–3; see also David L. Schindler, "The Significance of World and Culture for Moral Theology," *Co* 31 (2004): 111–42 at 126 n. 26.

169. Balthasar, *Cosmic Liturgy*, is one of the great studies.

170. Graham Carey, "What Symbolism Is," *SS* 5 (2004): 39–48, begins by quoting these verses from Psalms and Romans.

when the heavens shall be burnt, and the earth melt away. We can bear the loss, for we know it will be but the removing of a veil. We know that to remove the world which is seen, will be the manifestation of the world which is not seen.[171]

There is a necessarily objective character to the liturgy, rooted in the idea that it expresses the Logos behind all things. As the single most widely read work of Orthodoxy, compiled in 1782, the *Philokalia* ("love of the beautiful"), understands it, the beautiful is the transcendent source of life.[172] By contrast to this, as the heirs of a world created by Protestantism and liberal individualism, as people who tend—if we think of it at all—to think of salvation as something individual, it is easy for us to miss the social and cosmological character of Christianity itself, all the ways in which it is incompatible with the world that liberal modernity has created. Thus Harry Blamires argues that if a Christian mind is to be recovered in the midst of modernity, it will involve not just taking a supernatural orientation seriously, but acquiring a sacramental cast of thinking.[173]

Initially the Christian hope was the redemption of the entire creation, and this is of what ancient Christian music sings. The Christian awaits—or used to await—the salvation of the world.[174] Many medieval writers closely connected music, peace, and friendship: the way in which music brings people to like-mindedness and removes discord recalls Eden and anticipates Heaven.[175] It is this perspective that much of the new Christian music tries to reiterate. A fair amount of recent church music has itself taken on the flavor of subjectivity and willfulness, has become modern, but arguably whenever people remember what the liturgy is, they will flee these categories. Thus, as we have noted, Orthodox composers have had a large presence in the current turn to transcendence, which in long perspective can often be seen as a new stage of the tradition of "hesychasm," the form of contemplation characteristic of much Byzantine religious life.[176] As with hesychasm, this development is not simply a flight to the transcendent. Although there are differences that ought not be glossed over, thinkers turning from the world as it has become, East and West, agree that what is wanted is not "the

171. *Parochial and Plain Sermons,* new ed., 8 vols. (London: Longmans, Green, 1894), 4:211–18; see also Alan Bray, *The Friend* (Chicago: University of Chicago Press, 2003), 297–98, 303–4.

172. Tr. and ed. G. E. H. Palmer, Philip Sherrard, and Kallistos Ware, 4 vols. (London: Faber and Faber. 1979).

173. *The Christian Mind: How Should a Christian Think?* (Ann Arbor, Mich.: Servant Books, 1978). See also Terence L. Nichols, *The Sacred Cosmos: Christian Faith and the Challenge of Naturalism* (Grand Rapids, Mich.: Brazos Press, 2003).

174. Jean Daniélou, *Essai sur le mystère de l'histoire* (Paris: Éditions du Seuil, 1953), 340.

175. This is a theme running through C. Stephen Jaeger's *Envy of Angels,* and *Ennobling Love: In Search of a Lost Sensibility* (Philadelphia: University of Pennsylvania Press, 1999), as at 55.

176. See Dirk Krausmüller, "The Rise of Hesychasm," in *The Cambridge History of Christianity,* vol. 5: *Eastern Christianity,* ed. Michael Angold (Cambridge: Cambridge University Press, 2006).

bad faith of transcendence," that is, a turn to transcendence at the expense of the material, immanent, and embodied.[177] What is wanted is a heaven and earth that are both distinct and intertwined. Thus Tavener attempts to reunite heaven and earth, to return to prelapsarian innocence, to restore the cosmos, and to forge a music suitable to the vision of the earthly church building as already paradise.[178] Though the music is very different, like Mozart's it speaks of a creation both prelapsarian and resurrected.[179]

As (for two decades) an Orthodox believer living in the West, Tavener's goal was a recapturing, after all the disasters of the Enlightenment, of the Orthodox vision of the liturgy as the place where earth and heaven are transparent to one another.[180] As the Orthodox theologian Alexander Schmemann said, the liturgy both makes the universe transparent to God and raises the Church up to heaven.[181] A monk of the Byzantine Catholic (Ruthenian) Eparchy puts it thus: "The life we live right now and the life we will live for eternity are in some mysterious way one and the same. 'The darkness is passing away,' says St. John, 'and the true light is already shining' (I John 2:8)."[182] This St. John, not accidentally, is for both East and West St. John the Divine, that is, an especially full instance of *theosis* or the divinization of man, of man as a living image and embodiment of the divine.[183]

As we have noted in various ways, in Eastern Christianity the emphasis is less on the believers' imitation of Jesus through moral choice than it is on the believers' participation in the life of Christ and incorporation into God through the Eucharist.[184] Here the common Western view of recent centuries that "values" are expressed in art is reversed. It is not so much that good men express their goodness in icons or beautiful churches, but that the use of icons and the presence of beautiful churches make men Godlike.

177. The phrase of Edward and Kate Fullbrook is quoted in Amy Hollywood, *Sensible Ecstasy: Mysticism, Sexual Difference, and the Demands of History* (Chicago: University of Chicago Press, 2002), 121.

178. John Tavener, *The Music of Silence: A Composer's Testament,* ed. Brian Keeble (London: Faber and Faber, 1999), with the review by Dale J. Nelson, "Metaphysical Music," *Touchstone* 14, 4 (May 2001): 45–47.

179. Hans Urs von Balthasar, "Tribute to Mozart," *Co* 28 (2001): 398–99.

180. Khaled Anatolios, "Heaven and Earth in Byzantine Liturgy," *Antiphon* 5, 3 (2000): 21–28, an article with a better understanding of Byzantine liturgy than Tavener's. Robert F. Taft, "'Eastern Presuppositions' and Western Liturgical Renewal," *Antiphon* 5, 1 (2000): 10–22, is a riveting account of Western misperceptions of Orthodox liturgy, and Orthodox inability to develop a strategy for facing modernity.

181. *The Eucharist: Sacrament of the Kingdom* (Crestwood, N.Y.: St. Vladimir's Seminary Press, 1987), 165, and *For the Life of the World,* and see Peter Galadza, "Liturgy and Heaven in the Eastern Rites," *Antiphon* 10 (2006), 239–61.

182. Maximos Davies, "Celibacy in Context," *FT* 128 (December 2002): 13–15 at 13.

183. Jeffrey F. Hamburger, *St. John the Divine: the Deified Evangelist in Medieval Art and Theology* (Berkeley: University of California Press, 2002).

184. Ralph C. Wood, "Ivan Karamazov's Mistake," *FT* 128 (December 2002): 29–36 at 33.

There was a similar idea in the West before the modern period. A historian of the thirteenth-century English parish remarks how for people of all social classes religion was not simply a matter of doctrine or the intellect, but a way of life which brought them into contact with the powers of the universe, in which liturgy and ritual were very important.[185] Something like his idea continued in the "Letter of Pope John Paul to Artists," issued on Easter Sunday, 1999. Section 16 of this letter, "The Beauty That Saves," takes its title from Dostoyevsky's idea that "beauty will save the world" (*The Idiot,* III, 5). John Paul presents beauty as both an entrance to mystery and a call to transcendence.

The understanding of the liturgy as transformative, as aiming at *theosis,* is therefore also Western.[186] To stay for a moment with the specific issue of church buildings, Alison Lurie observes it to be a widespread belief among (even) contemporary American architects that "their building will influence the people who use them. They see architecture as a cause of human action, rather than an effect."[187] Thus an ancient belief, in part accounting for the beauty of great cities already in the ancient world, lives on. Still in the Renaissance the city was to be a "built environment" shaping the lives of its citizens. Humanist sensibility insisted that there was a sacred order in which the city found its place, of which it was a microcosm, and that the city should express shared aspiration.[188] Philip Rieff went so far as to claim that all the marks of culture—books, prayers, parades, architecture, dancing—originated in and only thrive in such a sacred environment.[189] It is not just that pragmatic and shoddy cities fail humans. It is doubtful that there can be great cities without shared ideals and a shared transcendental orientation.

Though not surprisingly the influence of architecture on people expected in Lurie's American Protestant context seems to be essentially moral, traditional Catholic architecture, with all its differences, is closer to Orthodoxy. Baroque architecture aimed more at ontological than simply moral transformation. Though almost all Protestant thinkers have conceded to progressive categories of thought, seeing history itself as linear, some Cath-

185. Joseph Goering, "The Thirteenth-Century English Parish," in *Educating People of Faith: Exploring the History of Jewish and Christian Communities,* ed. John Van Engen (Grand Rapids, Mich.: Eerdmans, 2004), 208–22 at 217.

186. Vladimir Lossky, *In the Image and Likeness of God,* ed. John H. Erickson and Thomas E. Bird, with an introduction by John Meyendorff (Crestwood, N.Y.: St. Vladimir's Seminary Press, 1974), is a classic study of deification; and see now Norman Russell, *The Doctrine of Deification in the Greek Patristic Tradition* (Oxford: Oxford University Press, 2005), and Nancy J. Hudson, *Becoming God: The Doctrine of Theosis in Nicholas of Cusa* (Washington, D.C.: The Catholic University of America Press, 2006), esp. ch. 3.

187. "God's Houses," *NYRB* 50, 11 (July 3, 2003): 30–32 at 30.

188. David Mayernik, *Timeless Cities: An Architect's Reflections on Renaissance Italy* (Boulder, Colo,. 2003); see also Philip Bess, "The Old Urbanism," *FT* 141 (March 2004): 39–43.

189. As described by Bess, "Old Urbanism," 42.

olics still stand beside their Orthodox brethren in protesting the view of time and human development which has come to dominate the West. According to this now regnant view, time must take either a cyclical or a linear form, the latter presumptively being the Jewish and Christian preference because expressing the idea that salvation has a history. But the view of the Church Fathers and of medieval thinkers such as St. Bonaventure was much more sophisticated than this. The fullness which had come in Christ was not something that would be surpassed, one stage in a tale of progress, but something available for acceptance or rejection in all historical moments. History, at least so far as a human can chronicle, does not have one narrative line for the simple reason that some accept Christ, some close in on themselves. Thus there is not one linear and irreversible direction in which the story of salvation, or human history itself, moves. All moments stand equally before God, and in them God's will is both being done and not being done. A great naysayer of the Western tradition, Giambattista Vico, partly saw this when, in rejecting the Enlightenment view that history means progress, he mounted as an alternative a kind of cyclical view.[190]

The Orthodox Romanian student of religion Mircea Eliade, in the very act of thinking of himself as vindicating the distinctiveness of a supposedly Christian preference for linear views of time, fell into the trap of accommodating to the secularized Western notion that the Christian story is a progressive story.[191] It is hard to say whether Christianity here was a central cause of the secularization of the West, or whether the secularization of the West remade Latin Christianity. To say that the Christian story or the human story is linear and progressive is ironically tantamount to removing God from history, for it gives a narrative story line such integrity and visibility that anyone can chronicle it. In the old view, the mystery of the drama of the struggle between good and evil, the drama of salvation, continued until the end of time, and had no clear outcome within history. In the new view as the eighteenth century developed it, there was visible a story almost a fool could write, a story which made sense of secular experience and gave it an integrity apart from God.[192]

Although Tavener would not like the suggestion, the Baroque, especial-

---

190. *The New Science of Giambattista Vico,* tr. from the 3d ed. (1744) by Thomas Goddard Bergin and Max Harold Fisch (Ithaca, N.Y.: Cornell University Press, 1948).

191. I explore these issues more fully in "Problems with the Contrast between Circular and Linear Views of Time in the Interpretation of Ancient and Early Medieval History," *FQI* 1 (2001): 41–65. David B. Hart, "Christ and Nothing," *FT* 136 (October 2003): 47–56, is a profound piece showing that some Eastern Orthodox theologians have a view of time which is neither cyclical nor progressive.

192. Paul Zahner, *Die Fülle des Heils in der Endlicheit der Geschichte: Bonaventuras Theologie als Antwort auf die franziskanischen Joachiten* (Werl: D.-Coelde-Verlag, 1999), makes the argument, not always very clearly, that thinkers like Joachim of Flora, with the idea that salvation history itself has stages, furthered the secularization of the world.

ly in architecture, itself was an attempt to use matter and material splendor to express the ongoing drama of salvation understood as the Logos of the world, to at once fall down before the transcendent Lord and to find Him in all things.[193] In the long view, in spite of powerful currents that have sometimes led to flight from the world, Catholicism has been "inspired by an intense faith in the boundless powers of assimilation which the Christian faith possessed and which made it a unitive principle in life and thought," and this confidence that Catholicism could assimilate even the forces of what was then modern life was nowhere more present than in Baroque architecture.[194] We find this already fully expressed in the late-medieval, pre-Baroque German painter Albrecht Dürer, who in spite of some sympathy for Lutheran reform ideas, stood at an opposite pole from the tendency toward iconoclasm of Catholic humanists such as Erasmus. For Dürer the beautiful forms of paganism, even of the pagan gods, could be assimilated and transformed by Christianity.[195]

Christopher Dawson aptly described humans as the Metaxy, the bridge between material and spiritual.[196] But in the fifteenth century a number of thinkers moved away from the vision of man as union of spirit and flesh to focus on human enfleshment. The Baroque reversed this unfortunate development, to reassert a world at once fleshly and spiritual. Bold would be the person who could draw an easy line between Protestantism and Catholicism here—the very existence of Bach and Mozart warn us against all such enterprises—but it has been argued that nevertheless we can observe certain divides appearing between, say, a Protestant and a Catholic repertory.[197] Tavener did not understand much of this and unfortunately had the narrow-mindedness of a person who, having discovered something wonderful, the musical traditions of the Orthodox world and Eastern civilizations generally, tended to deprecate the world from which he had come.

At the opposite pole from Tavener's aversion to polyphony, let alone the Baroque, is the Orthodox theologian David Hart's appreciation of Bach as "the greatest of Christian theologians. . . . No one as compellingly demonstrates that the infinite is beauty and that beauty is infinite."[198] But from

193. Giles Dimock, "Revisiting the Baroque," *Antiphon* 5, 3 (2000): 8–10, and Jeffrey Chipps Smith, *Sensuous Worship: Jesuits and the Art of the Early Catholic Reformation in Germany* (Princeton, N.J.: Princeton University Press, 2002). *Worship in Medieval and Early Modern Europe,* ed. Maag and Witvliet, is a demanding study of the continuity and changes in late medieval and early modern liturgy, Catholic and Protestant.

194. Christopher Dawson, *Religion and World History: A Selection from the Works of Christopher Dawson,* ed. James Oliver and Christina Scott (Garden City, N.Y.: Doubleday, 1975), 291.

195. O'Malley, *Four Cultures,* 213.

196. "The Nature and Destiny of Man," in *God and the Supernatural: A Catholic Statement of the Christian Faith* (London: Sheed & Ward, 1936), 57–84 at 57–59.

197. Alexander J. Fisher, *Music and Religious Identity in Counter-Reformation Augsburg, 1580–1630* (Burlington, Vt.: Ashgate, 2004).

198. David Bentley Hart, *The Beauty of the Infinite: The Aesthetics of Christian Truth* (Grand

the viewpoint of *communio* theology, there is an even greater point to be made here. Tavener completely missed the fact that the life of God and of the Church centers on *communio,* on a community of dialogue, and this polyphony in particular is placed to articulate. Bach is the greatest of composers because the "communional" structure of his polyphony speaks of the Trinitarian dialogue at the heart of reality.[199] His music reflects the structure of being, and he sees himself in medieval fashion as more an artisan than a creative genius.[200] By the time of Palestrina (1525?–94), a century and a half earlier, polyphony had been able to articulate both individual voices and a choral unity, and this was Bach's inheritance. In his music different persons speak of a common theme in a conversation. His music is not self-expression but communication, voices addressed to one another, dialogue shared. One of his goals is the synthesis and balancing of earlier stylistic tendencies, the reception and development of received tradition. This continued a long-standing practice, going deep into the Middle Ages, of memorizing vast bodies of musical matter.[201]

The English composer Frederick Stocken, younger and less published than Tavener, clearly would side with Hart against Tavener on the question of the merit of polyphony, though in other matters he shares much common ground with Tavener.[202] A convert to Catholicism, Stocken identifies strongly with the tradition running from Josquin des Pres to Bruckner. He won notoriety in 1994 by being one of the hecklers protesting at a performance of Harrison Birtwistle's *Gawain,* and he has had scathing things to say about such modernists as Pierre Boulez.[203] Stocken, noting that music was undeveloped before the appearance of Christianity and that it thenceforth developed in tandem with Catholic Europe, calls music "the most Christian of the arts."[204] He does not mean to remark something incidental, a mere chronological coincidence in Christianity and "chordal progression or several voices singing together in different parts" appearing at the

Rapids, Mich.: Eerdmans, 2003), quoted in Geoffrey Wainwright, "A Farther Horizon," *FT* 141 (March 2004): 36–39 at 36–37. Presumably Sir Thomas Beecham did not agree. Asked why he did not like Bach, he replied, "It's counterpoint, and even worse, it's Protestant counterpoint." Cf. Jaroslav Pelikan, *Bach among the Theologians* (Philadelphia: Fortress Press, 1986), and see Frederick Stocken, "Music as a Christian Art," *SS* 5 (2004): 55–59 at 55.

199. Adrian Walker, "Introduction," *Co* 31 (2004): 1–3 at 3; see also Jonah Lynch, "Community and Dialogue: A Reading of Bach's Solo Violin Works," 168–75, in the same issue.

200. Lynch, "Community and Dialogue," 168, and 169, 171, on the following.

201. Berger, *Medieval Music.*

202. Those wishing orientation to the long debate about the merits of polyphony might refer to Edward E. Schaefer, "The Expressive and Formative Roles of Music: A Search for Balance in Liturgical Reform," *Antiphon* 7, 2 (2002): 21–36.

203. See the websites www.musicweb.uk.net/SandH/2000/feb00/stocken.htm, www.musicweb.uk.net/SandH/2000/feb00/stocken.htm, and www.geocities.com/dcjarviks/Idler/vIIn13.html.

204. "Music as a Christian Art," 55–58, for this and the following phrases. Stocken goes on to make very interesting comments about the need to keep imagination under control.

same time, but something necessary. Music and religious experience are beyond words, "less representational than visual art. . . . Music lends itself to
expressing transcendence better than other art forms." Stocken goes so far
as to claim that what we get from the late Middle Ages is a kind of "music
made flesh" paralleling the Christian doctrine of the Incarnation. Music,
like the Word, is something both immanent and transcendent.

Stocken emphasizes the musical continuity of the half-millennium up
to Bruckner, and the stark break thereafter typified by Schoenberg and atonality. Stocken paints with a wide brush, and it is unclear what he would
do with works such as—to the present writer—the beautiful "Transfigured
Night" by Schoenberg. Indeed, he sees the decline of music after Schoenberg as in tandem with the decline of Christian belief. In the one case the
laws of music were rejected, in the other case the laws of God. Bad music
is a kind of false doctrine. Stocken does not argue for timidity in composi-
tion, but for recognizing the awful mistakes atonality and modernism were,
and for going back to that point just before they appeared to return to
development of the previous five-hundred-year tradition in some way that
does not abandon the past. Critical is the one thing all had agreed on, "that
there were timeless laws of music that could be adapted to every age. . . .
The whole background of a culture steeped in the Catholic faith allowed
composers to accept both the order and freedom that tonality brings with a
'religious' faith, even if they never stopped to think of it in those terms." Finally, paying attention—perhaps what another thinker might call contemplation—is of the essence: "The listener who pays close attention to music
almost becomes the music whilst it is playing. If love is at the centre of the
Christian message then perhaps music, fostering, as it does, our capacity for
attention, has a unique mission in the fostering of this divine love."

Though much nineteenth-century music is egocentric in the extreme,
Anton Bruckner's vast Symphony No. 8, in which the heart of God stands
pounding at the heart of a cosmic vision, shows that even the Wagnerian
tradition could be overcome and placed in service of transcendence.[205] Just
as with the history of painting, there was no one development of music in
the nineteenth century. There were many countercurrents, and, as a coun-
terpresence to the cult of genius, we find the old tradition, running back
into the Middle Ages, of leaving the determination of dynamics to the performer replaced by the practice of specifying accents, thus hedging in the
choices of the performer.[206] By the time we get to twentieth-century elec-

205. The most redemptive readings of Wagner are by Fr. M. Owen Lee, *Wagner's Ring:
Turning the Sky Round* (New York: Summit Books, 1990), and *Wagner: The Terrible Man and His
Truthful Art* (Toronto: University of Toronto Press, 1999).

206. Cf. on the anachronism present in any attribution to the Middle Ages of a distinction
between written and oral music, Leo Treitler, "Written Music and Oral Music: Improvisation

tronic music, everything regarding performance will be specified, and the performer will have disappeared, except in such avant-garde programs as those of Mills College, in which no scores need be written, and every performance of the composer/performer is new. Here we have, or can have, at one and the same time, the disappearance and triumph of the performer's freedom.[207]

In the nineteenth century everything was complicated by "new" musical instruments such as the piano, just as they were once again to be complicated by synthesizers in the twentieth century. One might almost say that the piano, a solo instrument if ever there was one, most easily was put in service of the individualism from which it had sprung, just as today the synthesizer is often in the service of solipsism, a music so private that it often speaks almost entirely to its own composer. But working in another direction was a different aspect of much of Romanticism. Though typically Romanticism in music, as in literature, exalted the creative individual, it also commonly sought out the past, including earlier forms of music. One cannot speak of music for the first time acquiring a historical sense, but a sense of what the history of music had been, and a valuing of elements of the past, was highly prized. Frédéric Chopin models his preludes on Bach's *Well-Tempered Clavier,* and Johannes Brahms models his preludes and choral motets on the preludes of Bach's *Orgelbüchlein* and Bach's choral motets.[208]

One could argue that much of the Roman Catholic liturgical movement to the present, associated with a succession of figures beginning with Prosper Guéranger and Solesmes in the mid-nineteenth century, has tried liturgically to reunite the matter and spirit separated first by Descartes, and then by the whole development of a materialistic civilization which has divided life into a secular sphere and an increasingly marginalized otherworldly sphere.[209] These liturgical thinkers have tried in one way or another to reverse the Cartesian view of the world as an assemblage of matter in motion, to return to some form of the ancient-medieval idea of the music of the spheres, of an organic universe. Against the marked tendency of Christians themselves habitually now to live in a secular time shaped by society and the state, the goal of writers such as Msgr. Peter J. Elliott

---

in Medieval Performance," in *Códice Calixtino,* ed. López-Calo and Villanueva, 113–34, with Berger, *Medieval Music.*

207. Charles Rosen, "From the Troubadours to Sinatra: Part II," *NYRB* 53, 4 (March 9, 2006): 44–48 at 45.

208. Schaefer, "Expressive and Formative Roles of Music," 26. Rosen, "From the Troubadours to Sinatra," 45, writes of Beethoven, "No composer studied his predecessors so intensely and borrowed more from them."

209. M. Francis Mannion, one of the most important figures in the contemporary American Catholic liturgical movement, has given an overview in "Liturgy and Culture: A Failed Connection," *Antiphon* 5, 3 (2000): 2–4 at 2.

has been to recall them to liturgical time, to a sense of time formed by the liturgical year.[210]

As stated above, critics of the present Catholic liturgy often point to an unfortunate development following Vatican II in which the liturgy was viewed (in Protestant fashion) primarily as a teaching instrument rather than an expression of God's glory and our incorporation into that glory.[211] This development had in fact been much longer in preparation than many of the critics realized, and in some ways, paradoxically, reaches back to the origins of the liturgical movement in Enlightenment thought.[212] But to stay with recent developments, in regard to the Catholic liturgy in America, the Congregation for Divine Worship has along these lines become one of its most severe critics. In its "Observations on the proposed retranslation of the 1975 *Missale Romanum,*" of March 16, 2002, the Congregation noted that "a focus on transcendent realities in the Latin prayers too often shifts in the English prayers to a focus on the interior dispositions and desires of those who pray."[213] Further, "in an already secularized culture, it is difficult to see what legitimate purpose could be served by a deliberate desacralization of religious terminology." A certain anthropocentrism in some forms of the liturgical movement, an elevation of ethical over religious values, a Kantian favoring of religion within the bounds of reason, and the ideal of noble simplicity all have their Enlightenment roots.[214]

⌒

Before becoming Pope Benedict XVI, Joseph Cardinal Ratzinger developed a reading of the whole Christian tradition which took into account the distinctive glories of Orthodoxy and of Roman Catholicism, while arguing that in large degree the factors that make them distinctive are complementary.[215] Ratzinger sees Christianity as synthesizing cosmos and history, as rooted in salvation history while praying toward the East.[216] He follows the Orthodox theologian Paul Evdokimov in arguing that the Orthodox the-

210. See especially the introduction to Peter J. Elliott, *Ceremonies of the Liturgical Year* (San Francisco: Ignatius Press, 2000).

211. Thus David Torevell, *Losing the Sacred: Ritual, Modernity, and Liturgical Reform* (Edinburgh: T & T Clark, 2000).

212. Waldemar Trapp, *Vorgeschichte und Ursprung der liturgischen Bewegung: vorwiegend in Hinsicht auf das deutsche Sprachgebiet* (Würzburg: R. Mayr, 1939); and see Aidan Nichols, *Looking at the Liturgy: A Critical View of Its Contemporary Form* (San Francisco: Ignatius Press, 1996).

213. Printed in *AB* 8, 4 (June 2002): 4–5 at 4.

214. Jeremy Driscoll, "Rethinking Ritual," *FT* 73 (May 1997): 52–53 at 53.

215. Eamon Duffy's paper "Pope Benedict XVI and the Liturgy," given at a 2006 colloquium of the Centre International des Études Liturgiques and surveying the development of Ratzinger's liturgical thought, is summarized in Shawn Tribe, "'The Genius of the Roman Liturgy': CIEL Colloquium 2006," in *Antiphon* 10 (2006): 314–22 at 316–17.

216. *Spirit of the Liturgy,* ch. 3, considers prayer toward the East in Judaism, Christianity, and Islam.

ology of icons views the cosmos especially according to the iconography of the Pantocrator, which presumes a Platonic or Neoplatonic background and was the common inheritance of the Greek East and the Latin West in the late antique period and the early Middle Ages.[217] This point should be stressed, because Rémi Brague has since presented a Byzantium to which the idea of renaissance was foreign, because never seeing itself as separated from its cultural origins; and a West defined by the idea of renaissance, that is by a sense of separation from, but also of recurrent appropriation or reappropriation of, its origins.[218] This, at least on the Western side, seems an oversimplification. Better to see the West as essentially "Orthodox" or "Eastern" until the Carolingian period, when a sense developed amongst certain of the clergy that, indeed, the past had been partially lost and needed to be recovered. From that time, originally under a language of *correctio* and then under a language of *reformatio,* the West was periodically touched by a series of renaissances, Carolingian, Twelfth-Century, and Italian. Arguably, it was in this period that the West became more "linear" than the East, witness Hugh of St. Victor's twelfth-century interest in the *saeculum* as the temporal aspect of the world. Christopher Dawson long ago observed that it was in the Renaissance and Reformation that the West lost contact with the East and its contemplative tradition, to develop the specifically extrovert characteristics of subsequent Western history, centered on material organization.[219] In analyzing Romanesque sculpture, Meyer Schapiro distinguished between two types of imagery, one of "themes of state," hierarchical and used for the portrayal of such things as Christ in Judgment, and one of "themes of action," narrative and in some way showing movement.[220] We might expand Ratzinger's view of things by noting that "themes of state" had characterized early Christian and Byzantine art, while "themes of action" or narrative had an increasing presence in Western art from about 1100.

According to Ratzinger a great shift occurred when in the Latin world of the twelfth and thirteenth centuries an Aristotelian background replaced the previous Neoplatonic background. By a Neoplatonic background is meant the view that the visible is a shadow of the eternal, that we are meant

217. Paul Evdokimov, *The Art of the Icon: A Theology of Beauty,* tr. Steven Bigham (Redondo Beach, Calif.: Oakwood Publications, 1990), as studied by Ratzinger in the chapter "A Question of Images," in his *Spirit of the Liturgy,* also printed as "Art, Image and Artists," *AB* 8, 1 (March, 2002), 1–8, on which the following paragraphs depend. See also Ratzinger's *The Feast of Faith: Approaches to a Theology of the Liturgy* (San Francisco: Ignatius Press, 1986).

218. *Eccentric Culture: A Theory of Western Civilization,* tr. Samuel Lester (South Bend, Ind. 2002), as at 124–25.

219. "The Revolt of the East and the Catholic Tradition," *The Dublin Review* 183 (Winter 1928): 1–14.

220. *Romanesque Architectural Sculpture,* ed. Seidel, lectures 4–5, with the warning on p. 123 that the distinction can be drawn too sharply.

to rise from and via the former to the latter. This is a very complicated question, but the argument is that whereas Orthodox thought and prayer, rooted in the icon, continued to look toward Easter and a resurrection we do not clearly see, and toward the Eighth Day, our final eschatological status, such a stance was increasingly overridden in the West from about the time of the appearance of the Gothic. More and more the Latin emphasis became incarnational, the crucified Lord replacing the Pantocrator.[221] The icon as a means to see what cannot be seen, of looking through an image to see beyond this world, was increasingly replaced with the telling of the story of the Passion. Historical narrative came to the fore, and the liturgy itself was increasingly conceived not so much as that which restores the cosmos, or as the beginning of the final hymn of thanksgiving, or as a looking toward the East, where the risen Lord has gone ahead, but as a reproduction of the central event of the narrative of salvation, the death of the suffering savior.[222] Since Ratzinger wrote, Jean Wirth has noted that the Latin world distinguished between *imago,* used as *eikôn* in the East normally to designate the picture of a person, and *historia* or *pictura,* used to designate a narrative image.[223]

Karl Barth's way of putting this was to say that the West "has a decided inclination towards the *theologia crucis,*" while the East "inclines towards the *theologia gloriae.*"[224] The contrast can be overdrawn, and, to use Chartres cathedral as an example, at the same time the pilgrim views the whole narrative of salvation (the Western emphasis) in this church, he or she is "inserted into a sacramental present fully realized in the liturgy" (the Eastern emphasis).[225] This said, it could be argued that while the Latin West still largely existed within a sacred cosmos, a certain disenchantment of this world or secularization was taking place, a small symbol of which was the gradual displacing of Eden and the East from the top of maps to indicate their importance and centrality as the theological center of the world, to, in

221. Tendencies Ratzinger associates with the Gothic developed centuries earlier. Kenotic themes and the centrality of the Crucifixion were well developed in Carolingian Christianity: Glenn W. Olsen, "One Heart and One Soul (Acts 4:32 and 34) in Dhuoda's *Manual*," *CH* 61 (1992): 23–33, and Celia Chazelle, *The Crucified God in the Carolingian Era: Theology and Art of Christ's Passion* (New York: Cambridge University Press, 2001).

222. Benedict XVI, "The Joy Born of Faith," *SA* 14 (2008): 28–30 at 30, reminds us, however, that Gothic cathedrals are highly complex and use harmonious proportions to symbolize the unity of creation, that is, to present a unified cosmic vision. Cf. Jules Lubbock, *Storytelling in Christian Art from Giotto to Donatello* (New Haven, Conn.: Yale University Press, 2006).

223. "Il culto delle immagini," in *Arti e storia nel medioevo,* vol. 3: *Del vedere,* ed. Castelnuovo and Sergi, 3. The discussion of Paschasius Radbertus above suggests that Wirth's generalization does not fully convey the variety of linguistic usage.

224. *Dogmatics in Outline,* tr. G. T. Thompson (New York: Harper and Brothers, 1959), 114, insisting that these two emphases need each other.

225. Jem Sullivan, "The Beauty of Faith: Sacred Architecture and Catechesis," *SA* 11 (2006): 12–14 at 13.

modern fashion, orient maps to the North (where the Europeans live).[226]

Clearly there are both similarities and important differences in emphasis between East and West. An anonymous Ukrainian Catholic Byzantine monk puts the matter the following way. From deep in the ancient Church there were two architectural alternatives. One, the Western, derived from the Roman basilica, had a rectangular axial nave, with an entrance at the western end, and an altar toward the east. Visually one's sight was compelled to progress down the nave to the apse. Here there was a latent emphasis on movement or pilgrimage, west to east, highlighted especially from the time of the Romanesque. In the East, by contrast, we find from even before the time of Justinian's construction of the Church of Holy Wisdom in Constantinople in the sixth century a relatively centralized organization of space, with a round, square, octagonal, or small cruciform floor plan, covered by a broad ceiling or dome. Here we have little sense of movement, and the eye is drawn upward rather than forward. And of course the eye goes upward to encounter a great Pantocrator, Christ the Ruler of All. Here one is less on pilgrimage than at one's goal. There is perhaps a greater sense of being in the midst of mystery than there is in the West. This is underlined in time by things such as the growth of an iconostasis separating the layman from the Holy of Holies, the altar area and sole preserve of the clergy.[227] We might make the contrast theologically by saying that whereas in the founder of Western thought, Augustine, ascent to God is through the intellect, in Greek Christianity ascent is theurgic or sacramental.[228] But we then must add that in the West from the time of Anselm it was common to combine what earlier had been distinct forms of Neoplatonism. Crucially, Aquinas placed his "Aristotelian turn to the sensible within a Christian ascent to God."[229]

We must be careful with our terminology. It is a commonplace that for the early Greek Fathers the bond between Eucharist and Incarnation was very close. The Eucharist re-presents the Incarnation. If the bond between Eucharist and Incarnation is our subject, it is inadequate to speak of a growing incarnationalism in the West from the twelfth century. The truth, from a Greek perspective, was more the reverse. In the West an emphasis on the bond between Eucharist and Passion replaced an emphasis on the bond between Eucharist and Incarnation.[230] But it must not be forgotten that at the same time, say in the thought of Thomas Aquinas, the idea of grace became

226. Alan Jacobs, "In Search of Eden," *FT* 170 (February 2007): 26–30 at 29.

227. The foregoing is a summary of "Holy Transfiguration Skete: A Pilgrim's View," *SA* 11 (2006): 17–18.

228. Hankey, "Self and Cosmos," 50.

229. Ibid., 52.

230. Michael Figura, "The Eucharist as Sacramental Incarnation," *Co* 30 (2003): 39–56, is an excellent exposition.

much more "Greek," something which transforms and renews man, Christifies him, by communicating the Divine Life. "It is not merely a power that moves the will but a *light* that illuminates the mind and transfigures the whole spirit."[231]

It is very difficult to take the full measure of this question. One can overemphasize the difference between Greeks and Latins. Patriarch Nikephoros (758–828), for instance, in asserting that icons are less effective than narrative presentations in teaching the faith, seems to appreciate the latter in a way commonly associated with Western Christianity.[232] On the other hand, what does one make of the growing emphasis in the Gothic on verticality as well as on a long processional aisle? Does the former not represent a movement toward transcendence, rather than the incarnationalism to which the Gothic is so commonly reduced? More fundamentally, is the contrast between a Neoplatonic East and an Aristotelian West the whole story? Leaving aside the debates between specialists over whether the overall shape of Aquinas's thought is not at least as much Neoplatonic as Aristotelian, what of all the scholarship on a claimed Neoplatonic spirit which forms the Gothic from its first twelfth-century manifestation at St. Denis?[233] Many see a Platonic "light mysticism" at work at St. Denis, especially of course in the stained glass that would be so prominent throughout the Gothic. In a different medium than that of the Greek icon, this also tries to go through the material to the immaterial, though perhaps less insistently. The material world is to be seen as connected to God. Most scholars believe Abbot Suger, the man behind St. Denis, had read Pseudo-Dionysius's *The Celestial Hierarchy* in John Scottus Eriguena's translation, and with his commentary.[234] However, the view of Erwin Panofsky that Suger himself was the source of the light mysticism of the early Gothic has been challenged by Conrad Rudolph, who, rather, thinks that Suger simply took these ideas over from Hugh of St. Victor, and that they are at least as much Augustinian as Dionysian.[235] In either case, whether creatively or derivatively, Suger thought of light as not simply something physical, but

231. Christopher Dawson, *Medieval Essays* (New York: Sheed & Ward, 1952), 101–2.

232. Henry Maguire, *Art and Eloquence in Byzantium* (Princeton, N.J.: Princeton University Press, 1981), 11.

233. *Abbot Suger: On the Abbey Church of St. Denis and Its Art Treasures,* ed. Erwin Panofsky (Princeton, N.J.: Princeton University Press, 1946), as at 23, 73–75.

234. Ibid., 18.

235. *Artistic Change at St.-Denis: Abbot Suger's Program and the Early Twelfth-Century Controversy over Art* (Princeton, N.J.: Princeton University Press, 1990), 32–35. 56. Lindy Grant, *Abbot Suger of St. Denis: Church and State in Early Twelfth-Century France* (New York: Longman, 1998), 23–24, believes that historians have overemphasized the influence of Pseudo-Dionysius on Suger, which she takes to have been unexceptional. Peter Kidson, "Panofsky, Suger and St. Denis," *Journal of the Warburg and Courtauld Institutes* 50 (1987): 1–17 at 4–6, called into question Suger's knowledge of Pseudo-Dionysius, and Suger's ability to construct the theories of light attributed to him.

in terms of that which it illuminated: the physical world thus reflects God's higher world.[236] In *De Administratione* he wrote:

When—out of my delight in the beauty of the house of God— . . . worthy meditation has induced me to reflect, transferring that which is material to that which is immaterial . . . then it seems to me that I see myself dwelling, as it were, in some strange region of the universe which neither exists entirely in the slime of the earth nor entirely in the purity of Heaven.[237]

Thus Suger expressed the ancient idea that the church building anticipates the Heavenly Jerusalem.[238]

Whatever the exact influences on Abbot Suger, the border between what was Greek and what Latin constantly shifted, and on important issues commonalities remained. One could argue that the Baroque idea of grace is much closer to Orthodoxy than it is to Augustinian Protestantism. There were other exceptions and shadings. Fourteenth- and fifteenth-century Umbrian art still shows its Byzantine heritage in presenting a calm crucifixion with just enough blood to remind the viewer of the price paid when the world was reborn through the cross. Similarly, late medieval Tuscan altarpieces, as at Siena, in their attempt to link the viewer immediately with the subject viewed, Christ or the Virgin, maintain the Eastern function of the icon.[239] And "Raphael's paintings sometimes look as if no one painted them at all. Like those Greek icons described as *archeiropoêtoi,* 'not made by hand,' they seem to have sprung into being of their own volition, or by divine decree."[240] They still belong to a world in which the artist is an instrument in God's hands.[241] They still belong to a world not of secular communes, but of cities in which most people were socialized by the liturgy: "Thirteenth-century Italians worshiped in a world of sacred spaces and sacred rites."[242] So did Raphael.

Both emphases, cosmic and incarnational, express something central to Christianity, and therefore are found in East and West. Sometimes one has to look a bit, and Ratzinger suggests that Gothic stained glass, even with its Latin narrative emphasis on showing the history of salvation, especially the history of the last week of Christ's life, performs something of the function

---

236. *Abbot Suger,* tr. Panofsky, 20.

237. Ibid., 63–65.

238. Hanns Peter Neubauer, "Die Kirchenweihbeschreibungen von Saint-Denis," in *Mittelalterliches Kunsterleben nach Quellen des II. bis 13. Jahrhunderts,* ed. Andreas Speer and Günther Binding (Stuttgart-Bad Cannstatt: Frommann-Holzboog, 1994), 183.

239. Ingrid Rowland, "Eastern Glory," *NYRB* 51, 9 (May 27, 2004): 23–25 at 24.

240. Ingrid Rowland, "The Magician," *NYRB* 51, 20 (December 16, 2004): 16–20 at 16.

241. Rowland, "Magician," 20, writes that Raphael has a "radically different sensibility" from the modernist ethos, "a sensibility that hides not only the physical toil of painting, but also the social maneuverings by which this personable young man set up a stable of creators, a circle of patrons, a whole aesthetic climate in which he presided almost invisibly."

242. Augustine Thompson, *Cities of God: The Religion of the Italian Communes, 1125–1325* (University Park: Pennsylvania State University Press, 2005), 343.

of the Greek iconostasis.[243] In any case, there is a good measure of agreement that with the coming of the Renaissance, the West largely lost the sense of "looking through" the icon to the greater reality of which it was the shadow. This is commonly, if imprecisely, expressed by saying that earlier artists turned their eyes heavenward, the artists from the Renaissance on more to the earth.[244] A more philosophical way of expressing this is to say that about the thirteenth century in the West "the noetic or intuitive faculty of man was eclipsed in favor of the rational. . . . Art begins to emphasize three-dimensional space and depth perspective at the expense of metaphysical space and perspective. By the Renaissance and the Baroque period Western culture is effectively anthropocentric rather than theocentric."[245]

A new aesthetic sense developed in which beauty was no longer something always beyond the visible, but rather something caught by the thing seen. From this point of view El Greco, in the sixteenth century, with his training as a maker of icons, failure to provide high-Renaissance perspective, attenuated anatomy, and compressed space, was something of a throwback.[246] One can see the point of Ratzinger's view of Western developments, though the contrast between East and West can be overstated. Change there certainly was, but again and again, from Giotto to Bernini, we find earthly beauty used to articulate a sense of the mystery which envelops all, a participation of human in divine artifice, in spite of the new estimates of human genius. We might say that art's physical presence, its immanence, was explored at the expense of diminishment of a sense of transcendence, but that such a sense was not lost.

The Baroque, commonly maligned today in East and West, had as a chief goal not the restoration of the ancient perspective, but a new form of it.[247] Consider the following quotation from St. John Damascene, one of the great Greek thinkers with a large following in the West:

---

243. *Reading Images and Texts. Medieval Images and Texts as Forms of Communication,* ed. Marielle Hageman et al. (Turnhout: Brepols, 2005), introduces many further considerations in regard to how images are to be perceived and read, and the interplay of text and image, as in ritual.

244. Olivier Boulnois, "The Modernity of the Middle Ages," *Co* 30 (2003): 234–59 at 242–43. David Brown, *God and Enchantment of Place: Reclaiming Human Experience* (Oxford 2004), compares iconic transcendence and Renaissance immanence.

245. Aidan Hart, "Constantin Brancusi: A Modernist against Modernism," *SS* 7 (2006): 52–58 at 58.

246. John Updike, "Singular in Everything," *NYRB* 50, 17 (November 6, 2003): 14–18 at 14. Sometimes, as on Crete, where we have the mysticism of the East and the physicality and perspectivism of the Renaissance, East and West meet in ways which shatter the generalizations: Rowland, "Eastern Glory," 25. Something similar might be said of the fourteenth-century Church of the Pantokrator at Decani, in Kosovo, which combines Byzantine and Romanesque elements: Bratislav Pantelic, *The Architecture of Decani and the Role of Archbishop Danilo II* (Wiesbaden: Reichert, 2002).

247. Evonne Levy, *Propaganda and the Jesuit Baroque* (Berkeley: University of California, 2004), considers the "propagandistic" goals of the Baroque, often at the center of criticism of it.

I worship the Creator of matter, who became matter for me, taking up his abode in matter, and accomplishing my salvation through matter. . . . I salute matter and I approach it with reverence, and I worship that through which my salvation has come. I honor [matter], not as God, but because it is full of divine grace and strength.[248]

The Iconoclast Controversy of which this statement was one product took place in a historical situation very different from the world of the Baroque, but these words would be completely at home above the entrance to any Baroque church. Of course important changes had occurred! Now the altar was the icon, the window through which God comes to us and we view the divine realities. But praise of God, thanksgiving, in a Greek Eucharistic sense, remains central. So, though by the sixteenth century the artistic traditions had taken very different roads, East and West, something of the same understanding remained for those with eyes to see.

In Ratzinger's view it was positivism, the belief that there is nothing more than the verifiable, that destroyed all these earlier ways of seeing through the visible to something greater but invisible. It is the true enemy of worship. It undermines art itself, which increasingly becomes an experiment with self-created worlds, creativity to no purpose beyond itself, and no object. One wonders whether many of the living composers of sacred music who rebel against a world without transcendence could not come to some form of common ground built on such a reading of what has happened to music and liturgy. More than a half-century ago the Thomist Étienne Gilson, a champion of the idea that beauty lies in the beautiful object, and a critic of the romantic view of the artist, argued against just the representational art that Ratzinger saw destroying the earlier, "iconic," ways in which art had been a window through which one peered into a reality greater than itself.[249] Gilson approved the fact that nonrepresentational art, the art of Manet and Cezanne, had restored art's true dignity.[250] Thus some of the modernists such as Georges Rouault found new ways to express ancient truth in a contemporary idiom.

Hans Urs von Balthasar's great seven-volume work, *The Glory of the Lord,* is built around the (especially Latin) tradition that hearing is from the viewpoint of theology the central act of perception.[251] There is much

248. *On Divine Images: Three Apologies against Those Who Attack the Divine Images,* tr. David Anderson (Crestwood, N.Y.: St. Vladimir's Seminary Press, 1980), II, 14; see also William A. Frank, "Western Irreligion and Resources for Culture in Catholic Religion," *Lo* 7, 1 (Winter 2004): 17–44, at 44 n. 31.

249. *The Arts of the Beautiful* (New York: Scribner, 1965), and see Gilson's *Forms and Substances in the Arts* (New York: Scribner, 1966).

250. *Painting and Reality* (New York: Pantheon Books, 1957); see also Gregory Wolfe, "Modernism, Science, and Spirituality," *FT* 134 (June/July 2003): 38–41 at 41.

251. Subtitle: *A Theological Aesthetics,* tr. Erasmo Leiva-Merikakis, ed. Joseph Fessio and

to be said in favor of this idea, though especially Gothic artists thought the one could be expressed in the other, music in pictures or images of music.[252] Sight, to stay with Balthasar, requires distance, hearing beckons us to unsystematized wonder and participation. Both allow us to take in the glory of God in the world, but especially hearing is open and vulnerable to the transcendent. Already in the twelfth century St. Bernard taught "in matters of faith and in order to know the truth, hearing is better than sight." Bernardine architecture sought acoustic perfection because not only silence was valued, but also the human voice praising God reverberating and magnified by the vaults of a church.[253]

The American Catholic theologian Peter Casarella very much agrees. He, so to speak, begins where Nietzsche in his announcing of the twilight of cosmic theophany left off. Nietzsche observed that the world is no longer a cipher for transcendence.[254] The Orthodox thinker Dumitru Staniloae agrees, and argues that the greatest problem facing Orthodoxy is the reconciliation of the cosmic theology of the Fathers with the conclusions of modern science.[255] Few see the world's forms as God's footprints. This not in the comparatively trivial sense of finding God in babbling brooks, but in finding kenosis, death to self, the Cross, as a rhythm or pattern built into the whole cosmos, aimed at its transfiguration. God's funeral has been prepared in his believers' blindness to his disappearance from the cosmos in this sense, in their no longer viewing the cosmos as cruciform. What has been called "the mechanization of the world picture," the reduction of it to mathematics and mechanics, makes very difficult any sense that the world is a cipher for transcendence.[256] In any case, telescopes seem to reveal an

John Riches (San Francisco: Ignatius Press, 1983–91). The point is disputed. Robin M. Jensen, *The Substance of Things Seen: Art, Faith, and the Christian Community* (Grand Rapids, Mich.: Eerdmans, 2004), argues that the verbal and visual are finally the same, reinforcing one another. Many art historians have claimed a late medieval privileging of sight over the other senses: Newman, "What Did It Mean to Say 'I Saw'?" 16–18.

252. Björn R. Tammen, *Musik und Bild im Chorraum mittelalterlicher Kirchen, 1100–1500* (Berlin: Reimer, 2000), on *Musikdarstellungen*. This book has rich discussions of such things as classical theories of instruments and tones and scholastic debate about the relative value of modes of sensory perception. For the argument that the auditory can be translated into the visual, see Elizabeth Martin, *Architecture as a Translation of Music* (New York: Princeton Architectural Press, 1994).

253. Minne-Sève and Kergall, *Romanesque and Gothic France*, 55. Cf. David C. Appleby, "The Priority of Sight according to Peter the Venerable," *Mediaeval Studies* 60 (1998): 123–57.

254. "Waiting for a Cosmic Christ in an Uncreated World," *Co* 28 (2001): 230–64 as at 246. Not all agree that we must begin with Nietzsche's dictum: George L. Murphy, *The Cosmos in the Light of the Cross* (Harrisburg, Pa. 2003), both physicist and theologian, attempts a synthesis.

255. See in general Alexei V. Nesteruk, *Light from the East: Theology, Science, and the Eastern Orthodox Tradition* (Minneapolis: Fortress Press, 2004), and specifically Charles Miller, *The Gift of the World: An Introduction to the Theology of Dumitru Staniloae* (Edinburgh: T & T Clark, 2000), on the cosmic scope of Orthodoxy.

256. E. J. Dijksterhuis, *The Mechanization of the World Picture* (Oxford: Clarendon Press,

incompleteness or chaos in the universe, and microscopes (if the naked eye were not sufficient) a violent natural world; and it is not at all clear how all this can be an expression of cosmic theophany.

Taking his lead from Pauline eschatology, Casarella has turned to the extraordinarily difficult task of relating Christ to an "a-cosmic" modern cosmology, that is, to a view of the world which, while denying almost all the terms of traditional Christian cosmology, especially the themes tied to the Pauline, patristic, and Orthodox Cosmic Christ and cosmic theophany, still carries a cosmology, but now speaking the language of infinity, vacuity, coldness, and purposelessness.[257] In William Butler Yeats's words, "Things fall apart; the centre cannot hold." There seems nothing transcendent of which the visible order can be a cipher. Man is not only metaphysically homeless, but since man is no more than an element subject to the same impersonal laws as everything else in nature, the death of God involves the death of man as understood by Christianity, man as in and above nature and as oriented to transcendence. Man can no longer be a microcosm of the real. Casarella does not explicitly take up the point, but for hundreds of years it has been assumed that the earth is not the center of the universe—the universe has no center, and no defining story. It would be very interesting to see him address the thesis that John Lukacs has been developing over many books, that, contrary to received opinion, the earth is the center of the universe, the only universe we can know.[258] Lukacs stresses that man is the only creature capable of historical consciousness, and thus by definition is at the center of the universe. We will return to this in the last chapter.

Casarella thinks the time is premature for a synthesis between theology and science, and rather is interested in the conditions which must be present for a dialogue to be fruitful. From the viewpoint of theology, these center, in his judgment, on the idea that the form of Christ is the form of the world. The idea itself is unfamiliar to many modern people, for, as will be noted in the next chapter, a pronounced tendency within Christianity itself since the late medieval world has been in the direction of a religion of "God and the soul," in which the way to the transcendent is conceived of as inward and subjective rather than outward and through the cosmos. Even many Christians look at the cosmos under the categories of modern mechanism and reductionism, rather than under the heading of gift, let alone of the idea of Romans 8:22 that all creation is groaning toward transfiguration. The notion of the cosmos as gift is of course an expression of the idea that it is created, but the whole form of modern a-cosmic cos-

---

1961), is still well worth reading. Among the seminal studies of Alexandre Koyré, see *From the Closed World to the Infinite Universe* (Baltimore: Johns Hopkins University Press, 1957).

257. "Waiting for a Cosmic Christ," at 231, and see 246–47, on the following.

258. See esp. Lukacs, *At the End of an Age,* esp. 94ff.

mology implies an uncreated world, leaving the Christian who would join science and religion as they now stand in the place of trying to put Humpty Dumpty back together, but with some of the parts missing.[259] The situation is constantly in flux. One writer, in noting growing dissatisfaction with the warfare metaphor used to characterize the relation of science and religion, which he takes to be one aspect of the Whiggish story of progress, has concluded that as long as we do not recognize how much both Christianity and science have changed over time, discussion of their relationship is doomed.[260] Another writer, noting that the Book of Genesis itself was "a polemic against pagan superstition" and tried to portray sun and moon as mere heavenly lamps rather than objects of worship, suggests how far we have to go in understanding all the ways in which Christianity has both enchanted and disenchanted the world.[261]

Casarella has given a good indication of how extraordinarily difficult a synthesis of theology and science now is.[262] If in agreeing I may complicate the problem even further, the modern historian, tutored in a "hermeneutic of suspicion," tends to view all proposals that music or architecture expresses cosmic harmonies, from Pythagoras to Tavener, as rather the responses of some person or group to their own historical predicament. To give an example and put the issue sharply, the Baroque had a kind of grandiloquence which both despaired of and expressed the irrationalism of early modern thought, the apparent inability of Protestant or Catholic to win "the battle for Christendom" through disciplined argument, and decided to win the cultural issue through spectacle. One could argue that similarly Tavener in the two decades he was Russian Orthodox represented an Orthodoxy which is profoundly displaced in the modern world and seems to be one of the great historical losers, and that what he really proposed was the abandonment of the whole modern situation in favor of a comprehensive ideology in which Orthodoxy would have recovered its centrality. I myself believe the issues are much more complicated than this, but the point is that we now can hardly view discussions about cosmic harmony, whether we are for or against this harmony, as at least not partly one more aspect of the culture

---

259. Casarella, "Waiting for a Cosmic Christ," 230–31. In the following pages Casarella turns to Bonaventure and the sapiential tradition for alternatives.

260. John Hedley Brooke, *Science and Religion: Some Historical Perspectives* (New York: Cambridge University Press, 1991), with Jon H. Roberts, "'The Idea That Wouldn't Die': The Warfare between Science and Christianity," *HS* 4, 3 (February 2003): 21–24 at 22.

261. Stephen M. Barr, "Retelling the Story of Science," *FT* 131 (March 2003): 16–25, arguing that contemporary science itself has largely debunked the materialist "story of science" scientists themselves formerly followed and in specific ways is returning to ancient preoccupation with the beauty of the structure of the cosmos.

262. Cf. Stephen M. Barr, *Modern Physics and Ancient Faith* (Notre Dame, Ind.: University of Notre Dame Press, 2003).

wars which fill our time.[263] To be for or against such harmonies is a way of taking sides in the battle over how "modern" our culture should be.

A hermeneutic of suspicion has limitations. In a very interesting critique of the life's work of the historian Peter Brown, Paul Antony Hayward, while praising Brown for having laid bare how the ancient saints of the Church and their cult served to legitimate various elites, criticizes him for seeing his sources as "propaganda for a uniform religious ethos." Rather, "far from being the product of a highly ordered society, the hagiographical idea of cosmic order was the fantasy of an elite threatened by violence and competition."[264] A very shrewd reviewer, in turn suggests that Hayward's position is just as subject to criticism as Brown's.[265] That is, both of these readings of ancient holy men rest on the same evidentiary basis, of which each historian has emphasized certain aspects. Hayward emphasizes instability and self-interest, Brown stability and consensus. None of this means that there is no objective cosmic harmony to be expressed or recovered, but it does mean that proposals like Tavener's or Schmemann's may too easily try to put together what the modern experience has undone, simply rejecting modernity and learning no lessons from it. I hasten to add that Schmemann was much more aware than Tavener of Orthodoxy's predicaments today, and went so far as to observe that, lacking a crisis of the magnitude of the Enlightenment, Eastern Orthodoxy has ossified to such a degree that it does not know how to engage modernity.[266]

One wonders, even at the aesthetic level, whether this rejection of modernity is wise. It is just as short-sighted to reject the new because it is new as to accept it for the same reason. If change and growth are central and

263. Similarly, Philipp Buc has argued that whereas ethnologists and sociologists formerly considered rituals that are "sacred, orderly, and deeply believed" to be "good" ritual expressing the nature of the communities which practice them, such ritual can now be seen as "a partisan stance." These phrases are from Geoffrey Koziol, "Review Article: The Dangers of Polemic: Is Ritual Still an Interesting Topic of Historical Study?" *EME* 11 (2002): 367–88 at 370.

264. Paul Antony Hayward, "Demystifying the Role of Sanctity in Western Christendom," in *The Cult of Saints in Late Antiquity and the Early Middle Ages: Essays on the Contribution of Peter Brown,* ed. James Howard-Johnston and Paul Antony Hayward (New York: Oxford University Press, 1999), 127, 130–31. In various essays and reviews, Warren Treadgold has been much harsher in his judgment of Brown's reading of religious motives as other than religious, as "political, cultural, psychological, or sexual" (this phrase is from a Reply in the Letters section of *HS* 4 [2002]: 36). See Treadgold's "Imaginary Early Christianity," *International History Review* 15 (1993): 535–45, and "Taking Sources on their Own Terms and on Ours: Peter Brown's Late Antiquity," *Antiquité Tardive* 2 (1994): 153–59. Peter Brown, *A Life of Learning,* ACLS Occasional Paper, No. 55 (New York: American Council of Learned Societies, 2003), if acknowledging that Augustine's authority may have been more fragile than Brown originally portrayed it, does not respond to his critics and is unrepentant: "If each age gets the historical methodology that it deserves, then the Christian writers of late antiquity, skilled rhetors that they were and impenitent producers of powerful and self-serving 'representations' of the world around them, have got what they richly deserved: a stringent dose of post-modern 'hermeneutical suspicion'" (17–18).

265. Megan McLaughlin, Review, *CH* 70 (2001): 775–77 at 776.

266. George Sim Johnston, "After the Council: Living Vatican II," *IC,* December 17, 2004.

unavoidable in life, then always what is called for is discernment, neither uncritical acceptance nor rejection. At some level Tavener certainly knows this, for despite his fierce adherence to tradition, he is the most inventive of composers.

John Nelson, the artistic director of Soli Deo Gloria ("To God Be the Glory"), has spoken of his enterprise as anti-Nietzschean.[267] Such a view is now spreading among composers turning from the modernist views which filled so much of the twentieth century. Schoenberg's famous remark that he was "cured of the delusion that the artist's aim is to create beauty" now has become in some quarters contemptible.[268] Some reassert in at least a Neo-Pythagorean sense the roots of music in nature, insisting that consonance and harmony are not simply conventions.[269] As we have seen, often there has been a religious dimension to the *fuga mundi nostri,* or a restlessness about a perceived banality in modern life. This has taken very different paths, from "holy minimalism" to Nelson's Neo-Romanticism. Elaine Scarry, in insisting that beauty is not a distraction from injustice, has fought to prevent the severing of beauty, goodness, and truth from each other.[270] In some agreement, Peter Berger and Thomas Dubay point to beauty as the primary "signal of transcendence."[271] While sympathetic to all these attempts, I would warn that they have not fully considered the question unless they have asked whether it is simply a recovery of cosmic harmony we should seek, some return to a past order rooted in resistance to the change time always brings; or whether the harmony we seek is eschatological, something of which we have a foretaste in history but the fullness of which lies beyond history. If the world really is broken, this has implications for how we conceive the music of the spheres and its relation to our world.

267. Robert R. Reilly, "John Nelson: To God Be the Glory," *Crisis* 18, 4 (April 2000): 52–55 at 53–54.

268. Ibid., 54, and Reilly, *Music of the Spheres,* 3, 8–13, on this and the following, quoting Pierre Boulez's remark, "Once the past has been got rid of, one need only think of one's self" (9); and see Wendy Steiner, *Venus in Exile: The Rejection of Beauty in Twentieth-Century Art* (New York: Free Press, 2001).

269. Reilly, *Music of the Spheres,* 3–7. Reilly makes interesting remarks about Steve Albert's, Nicholas Maw's, John Adams's, and George Rockberg's problems with serialism, Rockberg calling it "the denial of memory" (9–12).

270. *On Beauty and Being Just* (Princeton, N.J.: Princeton University Press, 1999).

271. Thomas Dubay, *The Evidential Power of Beauty: Science and Theology Meet* (San Francisco: Ignatius Press, 1999).

Chapter Five

THE LOSS OF TRANSCENDENCE

Halfway from modernity is not far enough.

—Stephen J. Tonsor, "Why I Too Am Not a Neoconservative"[1]

All religions make cosmological claims, claims about the structure, nature, and purposes of the cosmos, but, like Judaism before it, Christianity from the beginning was of its essence cosmological, seeing human life
both as dramatic, centered on a struggle to achieve a proper use of freedom,
and as eschatological, receiving its orientation from beyond history. All was
viewed against a cosmic background articulated in Scripture and preserved
in the liturgy. The previous chapter described the abundant variety of expressions of transcendence, both the transcendence of the philosophers and
that of the theologians, found in ancient Christianity and to the eve of the
Enlightenment, indeed, at least in reaction to powerful secularizing trends,
until today. This chapter describes the loss of a sense of transcendence, the
loss of a sense that there is a reality beyond the visible, beginning in the late
Middle Ages and continuing to the present, and relates this loss to such
things typical of modernity as the growth of forms of individualism which
tend to remove individuals from larger contexts, social or cosmological. The
argument is that humans are of their nature oriented to transcendence, and
that to allow transcendence to shrivel is not just in general to impoverish
life, but to threaten Christianity's very survival.

To express his sense of the loss of transcendence, the poet Friedrich
Hölderin (1770–1843) declared, "Once Gods walked among humans, but,
friends, we have come too late! The Gods are . . . up there in another world."[2]
Understanding of our present situation is not possible without some history

---

1. *Equality, Decadence, and Modernity: The Collected Essays of Stephen J. Tonsor*, ed. Gregory
L. Schneider (Wilmington, Del.: ISI Books, 2005).

2. Didier Maleuvre, *The Religion of Reality: Inquiry into the Self, Art, and Transcendence* (Washington, D.C.: The Catholic University of America Press, 2006), is a meditation on these lines.

of the fate and loss of transcendence in the modern period.[3] This must concern itself more with general issues than with the unending, sometimes not assimilable, detail of lived life in all the regions and nations of Europe and the Americas, let alone of the world. We have seen that the ancient and medieval worlds were ordered to, or at least found a generous place for, many forms of transcendence. This was part of a synthesis of ideas about God and man that could be more or less taken for granted. In the twelfth century this synthesis informed the *Sentences* of Peter Lombard (ca. 1100–60), of which distinctions 2–34 of book 1 treat God in His transcendence, and the remainder God's attributes as they are manifest in His actions toward creatures.[4]

Martin Heidegger famously compared the meditative knowledge of medieval figures such as St. Bernard of Clairvaux, aimed at the transformation of our being in the light of our destiny, with the calculative thinking of the modern world, aimed at acquiring tools of action.[5] This latter Adriaan Peperzak has written of as "rationality without receptivity," thinking without "admiration, gratitude, and compassion, but rather . . . [based on] celebration of human intelligence, possession, engineering, and mastery."[6] Passage from medieval to modern involves attenuation of the contemplative dimension, with an accompanying loss of transcendence and growth of the calculative dimension, the latter at least largely oblivious to transcendence.

One of the most important ideas concerning transcendence in early Christian thought was Gregory of Nyssa's (ca. 335–ca. 394) understanding of becoming as an eternal stretching out *(epektasis)* of the soul into the infinity of God.[7] Man's orientation is not finally to death, but in ecstasy to God. In the High Middle Ages, and especially in the thought of Thomas Aquinas, this took a specific form which we have, a bit anachronistically, called *communio* theology (Augustine had already used the word in regard to the role of the Holy Spirit).[8] This was a theology of the participation of

3. For an explanation of the difference between a medieval and a Kantian understanding of the transcendentals themselves (unity, truth, goodness, and beauty), which in important ways mimics the shift from medieval "moderate-realism" to modern "nominalism," see Jan Aertsen, *Medieval Philosophy and the Transcendentals: The Case of Thomas Aquinas* (New York: E. J. Brill, 1996). For beauty see Armand A. Maurer, *About Beauty: A Thomistic Interpretation* (Houston, Tex. : Center for Thomistics Studies, University of St. Thomas, 1983).

4. Peter Lombard, *The Sentences: Book 1: The Mystery of the Trinity,* tr. Giulio Silano (Toronto: Pontifical Institute of Medieval Studies, 2007).

5. See Charles Dumont, *Pathway of Peace* (Kalamazoo, Mich.: Cistercian Publications, 1999), 72.

6. Quoted by John Sullivan, "Reading Habits, Scripture and the University," in *The Bible and the University,* ed. David Lyle Jeffrey and C. Stephen Evans (Grand Rapids, Mich.: Zondervan, 2007), 216–39 at 236.

7. See the letter of David B. Hart in *FT* 139 (January 2004): 3–4, on this and the following.

8. I am being anachronistic in my use of labels in order to highlight the links between contemporary *communio* theology, with its emphasis on communion as the defining context of all singularity, and discussion going back to the scholastic and patristic writers: Adrian J. Walker, "Personal Singularity and the *Communio Personarum,*" *Co* 31 (2004): 457–80, esp. 458–62. For

the creature in the life—the act-of-being—of the Creator.[9] In this theology all creatures are also related to each other, not·in the trivial sense of standing in exterior relations to each other, but in the sense of participating in the one, overall work of the Creator, both a hierarchy of being and a historical work in progress.

This theology of participation was radically undermined by late medieval nominalism and voluntarism, which had been long forming in a tradition of Augustinian interpretation already found in Gottschalk in the ninth century.[10] In this a univocal idea of being replaced the idea of participation. Here both God and creature were seen as belonging to the overarching category "being." Both God and creatures were instances of the category being, rather than, as in Thomas's view, creatures being, by participation and analogy, "in God," having a being which is God's. The *Summulae de Dialectica* of John Buridan (1300–1358) is one systematic exposition of this nominalism.[11] With Buridan we are on that long road leading to the mechanistic idea that we only know the natural world by distancing ourselves from what is to be understood.[12]

In the early modern period a certain idea of indeterminacy, common among medieval thinkers, slowly gave way before what finally became the Newtonian view. In showing how Aquinas took up Moses Maimonides's theory of contingency, Amos Funkenstein put the matter as follows.[13] For both Maimonides and Aquinas there is an objective indeterminacy in nature. As under God's *potentia ordinata,* that is, as something willed by God, it could have been otherwise, and we can speculate on this otherwise, but to no conclusion because to say that it could have been otherwise is already to articulate an indeterminacy in the nature of things. There is enough order in nature for us to describe it as ordered, but this order is one of "heteroge-

---

Augustine, *De Trinitate,* VI, 10, see Walker, "'Constitutive Relations': Towards a Spiritual Reading of *Physis,*" an article to be published in a festschrift for David L. Schindler. For Aquinas on transcendence, see Peter A. Kwasniewski, "Transcendence, Power, Virtue, Madness, Ecstasy—Modalities of Excess in Aquinas," *Mediaeval Studies* 66 (2004): 129–81, esp. 131–43.

9. There is a chasm between interpretation of Aquinas in the analytical and continental traditions: see Philipp W. Roseman, Review, *Sp* 80 (2005): 246–47.

10. Louis Bouyer, *The Spirit and Forms of Protestantism* (Westminster, Md.: Newman Press, 1956), is a classic study of the role nominalism played, for good and ill, in the Reformation. Stephen J. Grabill, *Rediscovering the Natural Law in Reformed Theological Ethics* (Grand Rapids, Mich.: Eerdmans, 2006), as at 54–57, is representative of a new scholarship challenging much that has been written about nominalism and voluntarism. Bonnie Kent, *Virtues of the Will: The Transformation of Ethics in the Late Thirteenth Century* (Washington, D.C.: The Catholic University of America Press, 1995), is an excellent study.

11. Tr. with a philosophical introduction by Gyula Klima (New Haven, Conn.: Yale University Press, 2001).

12. Morris Berman, *The Reenchantment of the World* (Ithaca, N.Y.: Cornell University Press, 1981).

13. "Maimonides: Political Theory and Realistic Messianism," *Miscellanea Mediaevalia* 9 (1977): 81–103 at 89.

neous elements which of themselves do not demand or imply this particular order."[14] Thus the medievals had a view of the divine economy which granted man and human evolution only a relative autonomy. Excluded was the kind of "Newtonian" granting to human history of an absolute autonomy as part of a necessary objective order. Gone in the latter view, for those with eyes to see, was miracle and any category which would deny the iron laws that now governed the universe, and in place we eventually have Adam Smith's (1723–90) "invisible hand" or Immanuel Kant's (1724–1804) *"geheimer Plan der Natur."*

Whereas in Thomas's view all creatures participate analogically in the "to be" of God, for thinkers like William of Ockham (ca. 1287–1347) both God and creatures sit beside one another as discrete existents.[15] The participation of God in creatures is denied, and therefore the connections between creatures attenuated. Individuals and the material order stand out, while universals and transcendentals recede, the result of which is a shift in what is considered real. From the denial of universals follows, as night the day, the denial of transcendentals, which philosophically are but the highest form of universals. Ineluctably what the intelligence understands is replaced by what the senses perceive, and we are on the way to modern empiricism. The idea that the world was created for a purpose—for humans freely to cooperate with and imitate God—recedes before the idea that we are tinkerers trying to discover how the world works, its secrets, to the goal of domination.[16] To reformulate one of Alasdair MacIntyre's ideas, life is less and less medieval, the dramatic story of a quest, and more and more modern and exploitive, the story of a conquest. Contemplation recedes in the face of busyness, practice replaces theory, will trumps reason. Here, *in nuce,* we have the appearance of the isolated or disassociated, what is now called the "unencumbered," individual.[17] In the modern world the spread of this individualism tracked the spread of the isolated God of deism: as a sense of the Trinitarian or communitarian interior life of God receded, and God himself came to be thought of as a monad, so did man. Only in non-European parts of the world where older and more communal definitions of what man is still dominated, as in much of Africa even today, could man clearly be seen as socially defined by his membership in various communities.[18]

⌒

14. Ibid., 90, and see 93 on what follows.

15. For orientation, see Matthias Kaufmann, *Begriffe, Sätze, Dinge: Referenz und Wahrheit bei Wilhelm von Ockham* (Leiden: E. J. Brill, 1994), and Armand Maurer, *The Philosophy of William of Ockham in the Light of Its Principles* (Toronto: Pontifical Institute of Medieval Studies, 1999).

16. Richard M. Weaver, *Ideas Have Consequences* (Chicago: University of Chicago Press, 1948), 2–7.

17. Robert Barron, "Evangelizing the American Culture," *SS* 3 (2002): 26–38 at 29–30.

18. Timothy Radcliffe, *What Is the Point of Being a Christian?* (London: Burns & Oates, 2005), 134–37.

Surveying the disasters of the modern age, Christopher Dawson thought that if one begins with a seriously flawed view of God and man which emphasizes will over all other categories, one should not be surprised to end with a politics that does the same.[19] Many people do not understand how far modern individualism has departed from an earlier Christian view of things. Though the early Christians differed significantly among themselves, even the "optimistic" Origen insisted that humans do not have unbridled choice in this life.[20] The "pessimistic" Augustine traced with great relish all the ways our choices are determined by what has gone before, all the ways we are hedged in and not free to do what we please. The paradoxical "voluntarist rationalism" developing in late medieval scholasticism and in Machiavelli and then in René Descartes (1596–1650) and Thomas Hobbes (1588–1679), increasingly departed from such views, achieving its fullness in the contemporary idea that "how we should live together is nothing but a construction of human will rather than an apprehending by reason."[21] Granted Duns Scotus's (ca. 1266–1308) voluntarism and his claim that we can only know God's *voluntas ordinata,* that is, that God is so free that he could have done the opposite of what he has done, and we not only have the God of classical Protestantism, untethered from reason and the analogy of being, a "totalitarian God" shared with Islam, but we have a model of a politics also built on will.[22]

The Dominican Servais Pinckaers has seen all this very well.[23] Pinckaers's special interest is that Christian morality be viewed not simply as a

19. I assume that Dawson did not mean that, for instance, Protestantism ineluctably leads to totalitarianism, but that there is a common thread between Luther's or Calvin's view of God, Luther's insistence that the good Christian obey political authority, and totalitarianism. In each case the natural law has fallen away. God does not have to be faithful to Himself as good, and man's obedience is not limited by things that cannot be done.

20. Elizabeth Ann Dively Lauro, *The Soul and Spirit of Scripture within Origen's Exegesis,* The Bible in Ancient Christianity, vol. 3 (Boston: Brill, 2005), 88–91.

21. Gary Glenn, "Words That Sound Alike but Have Different Meanings: Christian 'Natural Rights' and Kantian Inspired 'Human Rights,'" *CSSR* 9 (2004): 21–28 at 21. David C. Schindler, "Toward a Non-Possessive Concept of Knowledge: On the Relation between Reason and Love in Aquinas and Balthasar," *MT* 22, 4 (October 2006): 577–607, argues that Balthasar goes beyond Aquinas's insistence that the will and intellect include each other to hold that there is a kind of third principle here, beauty, which connects truth and goodness.

22. I am expanding a brief remark made by Benedict XVI in his Regensburg lecture of September 12, 2006, "Faith, Reason and the University: Memories and Reflections." Consult *Duns Scotus on the Will and Morality,* ed. Allan B. Wolter, tr. William A. Frank (Washington, D.C.: The Catholic University of America, 1997). Calvin and Melancthon, of course, tried to "retether" God and reason, but it seems to me that the damage had already been done by Luther's and Calvin's denial of natural knowledge of God and of the analogy of being. For a tracing of the ontology of modernity to Scotus, see Catherine Pickstock, "Transition," in *After Writing: On the Liturgical Consummation of Philosophy* (Oxford: Blackwell Publishers, 1998).

23. For orientation, see Servais Pinckaers, *The Sources of Christian Ethics,* tr. Mary Thomas Noble (Washington, D.C.: The Catholic University of America Press, 1995), and *The Pinckaers Reader: Renewing Thomistic Moral Theology,* ed. John Berkman and Craig Steven Titus (Washington, D.C.: The Catholic University of America Press, 2005).

body of obligations and laws, but as a way of life. He sees Catholic moral thought as caught in the modern period between *eudemonism,* an ethic of happiness, and an ethic of obligation. Ockham is the source of the latter. In the late medieval voluntarism found in Ockham, the virtues and vices came to be conceived as dispositions of the will, the result of acts of free choice.[24] Instead of the will being of its nature ordered to the good, to something "above" itself, the will is the source of the good. In the modern period, according to Pinckaers, such a view almost overwhelmed the morality inherited from St. Paul, the Fathers, and Aquinas, which had held that a good life must correspond to our yearning for happiness. In this earlier, and Pinckaers thinks proper, view, morality must be a response to or correlated to our natural desires, and thus finally to God as both formal cause and final object.[25]

As it develops historically, a powerful stream of modern liberalism, by contrast, inclines to a "freedom of indifference" in which, at the most, the will aims at some good but is not constituted by the good. That is, in the typical sketch of freedom drawn in the modern period, especially from the mid-nineteenth century, the good is not seen as an anterior condition of the will itself, as something ordering the will, but as something exterior, something the will latches on to. Willing does not begin in a contemplative moment, but is from the first "pure action."[26] The conscience is not "God's invitation to embrace His law as free subjects," but our freedom to judge as we see best.[27] Increasingly freedom becomes purely autonomous, separated from communal categories, indeed from the sense that "man is part of a shared existence and his freedom is shared freedom."[28] Nietzsche, who perfected the line of thought that will is pure action, ended *On the Genealogy of Morality* with the words "man would much rather will *nothingness* than

24. Bonnie Kent, "On the Track of Lust: *Luxuria,* Ockham, and the Scientists," in *In the Garden of Evil: The Vices and Culture in the Middle Ages,* ed. Richard Newhauser (Toronto: Pontifical Institute of Medieval Studies, 2005), 349–70, at 349.

25. Cf. James Alison, *The Joy of Being Wrong: Original Sin Through Easter Eyes,* foreword by Sebastian Moore (New York: Crossroad, 1998), 151 n. 13, who, having given Aquinas's commentary on Romans 7:20 in *Super Epistolam ad Romanos Lectura,* writes, "St. Thomas thinks . . . that real freedom consists precisely in being moved from within by God, who is not 'another' in any normal sense, precisely because there is no rivalry between the Creator and any of his creatures; thus they can occupy the same 'space' (for instance, a human will) without displacing each other."

26. Pinckaers, *Sources of Christian Ethics,* 327–53, as read by David L. Schindler, "The Significance of World and Culture for Moral Theology," *Co* 31 (2004): 111–42 at 129–30, and see 135–38.

27. George Cardinal Pell, "The Inconvenient Conscience," *FT* 153 (May 2005): 22–26 at 22, asserting the primacy of truth rather than conscience.

28. Pinckaers attempts to get to the heart of what is involved in modern ideas of the will. Of course the reality is much messier, with, typically, liberal causes such as sexual freedom or gender equality asserted as if they were absolutes binding on all. Benedict XVI, *Jesus of Nazareth* (New York: Doubleday, 2007), 204.

not *will*," and though we may doubt the universal truth of this observation, it rather aptly summarizes the emphasis on will going back to Ockham, and found in raw form in the Nazi naked will, and in gloved form in the notion of the U.S. Supreme Court, to which we will return, that we each find or create our own life's meaning.[29]

If the good is first of all an object of choice, not something that precedes the will and orders it, little wonder that there can no longer be a cosmic music, for one condition for such music is that it be always understood as naturally correlated to what humans are. Just as humans, if they are properly human, cannot write just any music they wish but must be the voice of something greater than themselves, something to which by their nature they respond, so if the giftedness of being, the fact that everything, music included, is received from "on high" is forgotten, all we have left is the noise, the arbitrary willfulness, of modernity and self-centeredness. If it is forgotten that man is first a contemplative being, set in motion by God and ordered to receive His gifts, and only then to develop them in cooperation with God, the ego of man swells until it makes man a creative genius, the center of the universe.

To be free, rather, is not something negative ("freedom from") or simply the absence of wrongdoing. To be free is to be "free for" human excellence. Ockham and his disciples, however, "prioritize the moral act over the moral actor, and will over reason."[30] They conceive freedom as the ability of an indifferent will to choose between alternatives. Combined with a shift then under way from qualitative to quantitative categories in the measurement of reality, this thought is already modern.[31] In time a mechanistic science essentially technological in nature rises in tandem with a "politics of modernity," both characterized by emptying nature of teleology.[32] Further, if Mi-

---

29. Subtitle: *A Polemic*, tr. M. Clark and A. J. Swensen (Indianapolis: Hackett, 1998), 118.

30. I am all along following the review by E. Christian Brugger, *FCSQ* 27, 1 (Spring 2004): 26–27, here at 26, of Servais Pinckaers, *Morality: The Catholic View*, preface by Alasdair MacIntyre, tr. Michael Sherwin (South Bend, Ind.: St. Augustine's Press, 2001).

31. Alfred W. Crosby, *The Measure of Reality: Quantification and Western Society, 1250–1600* (New York: Cambridge University Press, 1997), and *Écrire, compter, mesurer. Vers une histoire des rationalités pratiques*, ed. N. Coquery, F. Menant, and F. Weber (Paris: Rue d'Ulm, 2006). With Ockham we are also on the road to modernity in the sense that he, like others before him, places his pen in the service of the monarchy, attacking the immunities of the Church: *Political Thought in Early Fourteenth-Century England: Treatises by Walter of Milemete, William of Pagula, and William of Ockham*, ed. and tr. Cary J. Nederman (Tempe: Arizona Center for Medieval and Renaissance Studies, 2002).

32. See both Walker, "'Constitutive Relations,'" and my "The Return of Purpose," *Co* 33 (2006): 666–81. Philip Sherrard, "The Desanctification of Nature," in *Sanctity and Secularity: The Church and the World*, ed. Derek Baker (Oxford: Blackwell, 1973), 1–20, is a probing reflection on how nature came to be desanctified in the West. The most impressive attempt of which I am aware to imagine an alternative to mechanistic science is David L. Schindler, "The Meaning of the Human in a Technological Age: *Homo Faber, Homo Sapiens, Homo amans*," *Co* 26 (1999): 80–104. Schindler develops Aristotle's distinction between nature, understood as

chael Gillespie is right, we have in Ockham and the nominalists the point of origin of that tradition of nihilism which gathers force in the thought of Descartes, Fichte, the German Romantics, the Russian nihilists, and finally in Nietzsche himself.[33] Ockham already held that God could delude and deceive the human senses, as by making an absent object seem present.[34] His follower Robert Holkot (d. 1349) declared that the Bible reveals God as often practicing deception.[35]

Fair treatment of the slightly earlier Scotus shows how difficult judgment of these developments is.[36] By placing the essences of things outside God's divine knowledge, the nominalist tradition seems an early form of secularization. Pickstock sees in Scotus's replacement of the analogy of being with univocity a flattening out of being which prepares the way for the spatialization attendant on the birth of modern science. Worse, she thinks, his idea of the action of the Eucharist tends to make it less the action of the medieval sacred city—God's kingdom come on earth—than a bald miracle, the work of God's sovereignty, without analogies elsewhere. The idea of the Church as formed by the Eucharist will subsequently wither. Finally, Scotus's idea of freedom prepares the way for Cartesian voluntarism and a political order dominated by practical reason. In all kinds of ways, according to Pickstock, a society liturgically organized by love was being replaced by one organized by will.[37]

Pickstock's reading of Scotus has been challenged on a number of points.[38] Particularly of interest to us is the view of some that the "secularization" or "laicization" we find in him, a work of theologians, not of philosophers, is analogous to Aquinas's earlier giving back to the philosophers questions such as the existence of God, which were of their nature philosophical, and should never have been considered a part of revealed theology. To elaborate, despite the Neoplatonic framework still visible in Aquinas's great synthesis, his turn to Aristotle was in many respects decisive.

---

unmanufacturable in principle, and artifice to set a limit to technology. Paul Feyerabend, *Conquest of Abundance: A Tale of Abstraction versus the Richness of Being*, ed. Bert Terpstra (Chicago: University of Chicago Press, 1999), is on the cost to experiential richness of the victory of the scientific worldview.

33. *Nihilism Before Nietzsche* (Chicago: University of Chicago Press, 1995). For criticism of Descartes, see Richard A. Watson, *The Breakdown of Cartesian Metaphysics* (Atlantic Highlands, N.J.: Humanities Press International, 1987), and *The Failure of Modernism: The Cartesian Legacy and Contemporary Pluralism*, ed. Brendan Sweetman (Mishawaka, Ind.: American Maritain Association, 1999).

34. Barbara Newman, "What Did It Mean to Say 'I Saw'? The Clash between Theory and Practice in Medieval Visionary Culture," *Sp* 80 (2005): 1–43 at 35.

35. Ibid., 35–36.

36. *Duns Scot à Paris, 1302–2002*, ed. Olivier Boulnois (Turnhout: Brepols, 2005), describes the state of research.

37. Pickstock, "Transition."

38. See the very helpful review by Robert Sokolowski, "Theology and Deconstruction," *Telos* 110 (Winter 1998): 155–66 at 166.

Henceforward the natural world was increasingly to stand forth.[39] Considerable apophaticism remained in Aquinas's theology and in that of his day, but in comparison with the negative theology of the Greek tradition, the world arguably more came into view. This was Erich Auerbach's point in calling Dante a little later "poet of the secular world."[40] Dante was at once the poet of the Christian cosmos, and a man acutely observant of the everyday world around him. He saw humans as the link between the worlds of change and eternity, both generated by seed and created by God.[41]

The argument of some of Pickstock's critics is that when speaking of Scotus's view, we should by analogy to Aquinas's achievements speak more of "de-theologizing" than of secularization:

It therefore makes more sense to see here a "de-theologizing" operated by the theologians themselves, in order to rid themselves of representations unworthy of God in his absolute transcendence. What this history shows us, then, is not so much a secularization (from the outside) as an emancipation of reason demanded by theological rationality (however ambiguous).[42]

By the fifteenth century we find a slow fading of what Hans Urs von Balthasar called "the cosmological method," the previous viewing of all being within a cosmological framework.[43] Increasing "cosmological disinterest" accompanied the "turn to the subject" already developing in the *devotio moderna* and encouraged by Protestant pietism. More and more the interest was anthropological rather than cosmological.[44] All this said, we can see the truth in Pickstock's analysis of Scotus: she has made plausible linkages between Scotus's thought and later, world-changing developments. There might be something parallel to what Pickstock finds in the process, detailed for Castile by Teofilo F. Ruiz for the period from 1150 to 1350, by which attitudes toward the spiritual world became more practical, quantitative,

39. Though I would not put every point the way he does, Christopher Dawson, *Progress and Religion* (Garden City, N.Y. 1952), 138–41, and *Medieval Religion and Other Essays* (London: Sheed & Ward, 1934), 60–83, strikingly catches these developments.

40. *Dante, Poet of the Secular World,* tr. Ralph Manheim (Chicago: University of Chicago Press, 1961).

41. Patrick Boyde, *Dante: Philomythes and Philosopher: Man in the Cosmos* (Cambridge: Cambridge University Press, 1981).

42. Olivier Boulnois, "The Modernity of the Middle Ages," *Co* 30 (2003): 254–89 at 250. The issues seem to me more complicated than Boulnois indicates. *Ästhetik und Säkularisierung,* vol. 1: *Von der Renaissance zur Romantik,* ed. Silvio Vietta and Herbert Uerlings (Munich: Wilhelm Fink, 2008), gives an idea of the many ways secularization and sacralization occurred in tandem from the Middle Ages into the modern period.

43. *Love Alone: The Way of Revelation* (London: Burns & Oates, 1968), 11–24; and Peter Casarella, "Solidarity as the Fruit of Communion," *Co* 27 (2000): 98–123 at 120–21. See also Peter Casarella, "Waiting for a Cosmic Christ in an Uncreated World," *Co* 28 (2001): 230–64 at 248–49.

44. M. Francis Mannion, "Bringing the Cosmos to Liturgy," *Antiphon* 6, 1 (2001): 2–4 at 3, and *Entdeckung des Ich: Die Geschichte der Individualisierung vom Mittelalter bis zur Gegenwart,* ed. Richard van Dülmen (Cologne: Böhlau, 2001).

and secular.[45] But we are warned about all generalizations on such subjects: against very influential writers such as Max Weber and R. H. Tawney, who argued for an essential link between Protestantism and capitalism, Kurt Samuelsson delinks Christianity and capitalism.[46]

Nominalism deeply influenced Luther and Calvin, and despite all the communal themes also present in their thought, recast their renditions of both transcendence and the individual. We have already noted the claim that the divorce of faith from reason in their thinking contributed to modern nihilism. They saw God's transcendence as radical. God was infinite and holy; man finite and sinful, utterly corrupt in Calvin's view. Man no longer participated in God, and all that had mediated between God and man in medieval Catholicism, especially the sacramental order, was either rejected or radically attenuated. To put this in categories developed by David Tracy, in Catholicism we find an analogical imagination which emphasizes the analogies, connections, and similarities between things, and in Protestantism a dialectical imagination which emphasizes the dissimilarities between things, and tends to draw strong dichotomies between sacred and secular, with a highly transcendent notion of God.[47] Protestantism generally, though more in the Calvinist and Anabaptist traditions than in the Lutheran, turned against "ceremonies" and "idolatry," and tended toward a didactic understanding of all church services. Liturgy understood as iconic, as entrance into God's presence and participation in His life, tended to recede in favor of an understanding of church services as occasions for instruction and moral formation.[48] The center of attention shifted from altar to pulpit.

Differences in aesthetic as well as religious sensibilities developed between Protestant and Catholic Europe. Yet even in Catholicism, witness the success of the *Imitation of Christ,* there was some tendency to make Christianity less a sacramental religion, to turn from what was visible and sensual in the Church, and to make Christianity more a religion centering on interiority or "experience," on the individual rather than the group. The Christian humanism of Erasmus, which tended to think of ceremonies as "trivial little rituals," aimed at simplicity of worship and an interiorized

45. *From Heaven to Earth: The Reordering of Castilian Society, 1150–1350* (Princeton, N.J.: Princeton University Press, 2004). Cf. the remarks on the "bureaucratic spirit" found in the English twelfth-century *Dialogue concerning the Exchequer*, 36–65.

46. *Religion and Economic Action: The Protestant Ethic, the Rise of Capitalism, and the Abuses of Scholarship,* tr. E. Geoffrey French, ed. D. C. Coleman (Toronto: University of Toronto Press, 1993).

47. *The Analogical Imagination: Christian Theology and the Culture of Pluralism* (New York: Crossroad, 1981).

48. Though there were significant differences among the reformers, even Luther emphasized the teaching function of hymns: Robin A. Leaver, *Luther's Liturgical Music: Principles and Implications* (Grand Rapids, Mich.: Eerdmans, 2007).

religion to which many creedal points and theological distinctions were un-important. Arguably, the spread of a culture of the printed book from the middle of the fifteenth century accelerated thinking about religion as more practiced through reading than through gesture.[49] "Ceremonies" could be attacked under the other code words of "ignorance" and "superstition." This attack was not simply intellectual. As noted in the previous chapter, across Europe, in varying degrees, Protestants pursued a new iconoclasm: some-times, as at Souillac, literally attacking Catholic churches and monasteries to smash and destroy their art and sculpture; sometimes, as at Regensburg, just rendering formerly Catholic churches simpler by removing many of their sacred objects.[50] We might call this the "first modernism," for it often was a conscious attempt to destroy and break with the old regime, to reject the authority of Christendom and Catholicism in favor of a reformed and up-to-date way of life. Where Protestant iconoclasm succeeded it "usually marked a point of no return regarding the old faith," just as in our day vari-ous attacks on the classics, the Great Books, and the Western canon have produced generations with many quite cut off from what their parents or grandparents knew, read, and valued.

Though there were important degrees of difference here, with Luther much more appreciative of the place of the senses in worship, Andreas Karl-stadt (1486–1541), Ulrich Zwingli (1484–1531), and John Knox (ca. 1514–72) saw sensuality in worship as defilement of the purity and singularity of God's Word. From a Catholic point of view the most radical of them, Karl-stadt, avoided the implications of the Incarnation almost entirely, writing of images in church as violations of the First Commandment (as we saw in the previous chapter, the Christian argument already in the ancient world had been that because God in Christ had taken on flesh, material represen-tation of Christ did not violate the First Commandment: Karlstadt's posi-tion is closer to Judaism or Islam than it is to earlier Christianity).[51]

Protestant thinkers in varying degrees tried to remove all barriers and distractions between the individual and God. At most the *communio*/par-

49. See Hans-Joachim Griep, *Geschichte des Lesens: Von den Anfängen bis Gutenberg* (Darm-stadt: Wissenschaftliche Buchgesellschaft, 2005), and Stephan Füssel, *Gutenberg und seine Wirkung*, 2nd ed. (Darmstadt: Wissenschaftliche Buchgesellschaft, 2004).

50. John O'Malley, *Four Cultures of the West* (Cambridge, Mass.: Belknap Press, 2004), 208–12. O'Malley goes on to discuss Erasmus's making light of the intercessory powers of the saints, another form of "detranscendentalizing" the world, of disconnecting this world from the next, and remarks that Erasmus seems to have no sense of how the presence of Christ "might be effected by an icon" (212). O'Malley notes that at St. Gall, the attack on the cathedral produced "forty-six wagons of rubble" and that the devastation in Scotland was so universal that "virtually nothing would remain of the artistic heritage of the nation" (215). He also describes the shift from altar to pulpit (218), and see 215 for what follows.

51. Ibid., 64, 213–16, noting that Luther and Melancthon opposed the removal at Witten-berg of all images, to which Karlstadt had persuaded the city council, and also noting Luther's more moderate position(s).

ticipation framework of Catholic thought became secondary: "The attack was ultimately an attack on the sacramental principle of the invisible being mediated through visible objects and performance."[52] The non-sacramental (by Catholic definition) Christianity of Calvin especially, which denied the imagination its holy function, prepared the way for the disenchantment of the world. The doctrine of the Real Presence of Christ in the Eucharist had kept the visible and invisible worlds connected in pre-Protestant thought, for literally in the Eucharist each world was present to the other. This denied, disenchantment and secularization seem inevitable.

Over the modern centuries Christian anthropology continuously changed. There was a drift from Augustine's sense of the will, free to choose but at every step predisposed by that which lies outside it—Monica's nagging, for instance—to the Enlightenment sense of an autonomous will, seemingly altogether floating free from history, just as the "enlightened ones" thought the present could be freed from the past.[53] Critical here was Descartes's separation of mind from matter. No longer were human beings one thing, a union of form and matter, as they were for Aquinas, but two things, accidentally joined as it were. In Descartes's separation was present the thought, to be worked out by later generations, that the body, all material nature, is pre-moral, mechanistic, raw material to be molded this or that way. There is nothing in the body's structure capable of dictating what human life should be, no bodily nature that must be respected, and thus a basis for the destruction—that is, unlimited refashioning—of nature is at hand.[54]

With the replacement of the idea that the soul is essentially the form of the body with the idea of a mind constructing reality as it wishes, modernity in one of its most common meanings is on the horizon.[55] The self-grounded moral rules toward which much of Enlightenment thought is ordered tend to replace a received morality grounded in man's bodily nature. These self-grounded moral rules are a kind of ethical parallel to the political fiction of the state of nature, used in the social sphere to ground a regimen that assumes the priority of the individual, thus denying the Aristotelian idea that humans are by nature social. According to a very influential form of this fiction of the state of nature, first there was the sovereign individual, and then only by agreement or convention was the state constructed and did popular sovereignty appear.

52. Ibid., 216, and 218–20.

53. Carol Harrison, *Augustine: Christian Truth and Fractured Humanity* (Oxford: Oxford University Press, 2000), 92. Jonathan I. Israel, *Enlightenment Contested: Philosophy, Modernity, and the Emancipation of Man* (Oxford: Oxford University Press, 2006), is a comprehensive history of the intellectual movements of the period.

54. Schindler, "Significance of World and Culture," 118–19.

55. Cf. Jennifer Michael Hecht, *The End of the Soul: Scientific Modernity, Atheism, and Anthropology in France* (New York: Columbia University Press, 2003).

Of course, as more than one Counter-Enlightenment critic was to point out, it never actually happened this way historically.[56] Aristotle was much closer to the truth when he said first came the family, into which the individual was born, dependent on others in every way, not sovereign. The contractualist view reversed all this, giving the individual such priority that, for instance, marriage, less and less seen as serving the common good, disintegrates under the pressure that it serve the individual. Some have alleged that all political orders are grounded in some fiction, whether it be divine right or the state of nature.[57] If this means that no origin story, Genesis included, is a blow-by-blow account of historical events as they actually took place, this may well be true. But a great distinction should be made between fictions which are in their overall claim possible—such as that kings receive their authority from God—and fictions which never could have been true, such as the picture of human origins in the form John Locke (1632–1704) gave it, on which so much Anglo-Saxon political thought is grounded, that the race started as autonomous individuals—proto-liberals—who by common assent gave up some of their individual autonomy to allow the state to appear.[58] Here all the ways in which history and our ancestors have shaped us is elided in favor of a conception of society based on human relations as essentially chosen.

This fiction leads in turn to many other fictions and denials that fill recent liberal and utopian thought, such as that sexual acts between consenting adults are of no concern to anyone else. Clearly the aggregate acts of consenting adults do have a great influence on other individuals and society as a whole. If sex is reconceived under the heading of self-fulfillment, we should not be surprised to see a culture of sexual self-fulfillment appear.[59] The willfulness and deep irrationalism of such thought, present in John Mill's (1806–73) dismissal at the beginning of *On Liberty* of any need for

---

56. *Critics of the Enlightenment: Readings in the French Counter-Revolutionary Tradition,* ed. and tr. Christopher Olaf Blum (Wilmington, Del.: ISI Books, 2004), and see my "John Rawls and the Flight from Authority: The Quest for Equality as an Exercise in Primitivism," *In* 21 (1994): 419–36.

57. Garry Wills, "Lessons of a Master," *NYRB* 51, 11 (June 24, 2004): 12–14 at 14, noting that the fiction of popular sovereignty has become plausible by the use of politics to make the world look like the myth.

58. Janet Coleman, "Are There Any Individual Rights or Only Duties? On the Limits of Obedience in the Avoidance of Sin according to Late Medieval and Early-Modern Scholars," in *Transformations in Medieval and Early-Modern Rights Discourse,* ed. Virpi Mäkinen and Petter Korkman (Dordrecht: Springer, 2006), 3–36 at 25–30, excellently summarizes the nature of the Lockeian and Hobbesian selves. In the same volume, Brian Tierney, "Dominion of Self and Natural Rights before Locke and After," 173–203, continues, properly, to insist on the gradual emergence of the autonomous self from its medieval background. Peter Augustine Lawler, "Orestes Brownson and the Truth About America," *FT* 128 (December 2002): 23–28 at 26, attempts to show that Locke's thought, with its contract theory and belief "that political reality is created out of nothing by sovereign human beings," is destructive of all government.

59. Mary Ann Glendon, "Principled Immigration," *FT* 164 (June/July 2006): 23–26 at 24.

him to deal with the question of free will, or Karl Marx's (1818–83) insistence that God must not exist, is remarkable. One would have thought that a treatise on liberty would have first to ascertain the possibility and nature of freedom, or that treatises claiming to understand the movement of history and promising a utopian future would have had to nail down the non-existence of God, His non-interference with history and all utopian plans. But Mill in a chilling modern manner refuses to talk about "metaphysics"; and Marx's point is not that he has a contribution to make to the classical discussion of God's existence, but that for his views to be possible, there must be no God, therefore he will not even enter into discussion of the matter.

In the Augustinian view freedom *(libertas)* does not primarily signify the ability to choose *(liberum arbitrium* = free will), which ability is merely the necessary precondition for freedom, as eyes are for vision. Freedom, to live in freedom, is adhesion to the good, the "ability to live that choice as a wholehearted personal embrace of a destiny that shines through and gives meaning to all the particulars of one's life."[60] We get a kind of conclusion of the shift from Augustine's identification of freedom with settled adhesion to God's will to the modern association of freedom with autonomous choice in the recent manufacture by the United States Supreme Court of a theory of individual autonomy quite at odds with previous constitutional tradition, but very much in agreement with a liberal understanding of human autonomy as it has now evolved.[61] As Harold Bloom argued, the "American religion" has become a new gnosticism, in which all are in search of the original self, something which requires absolute freedom from all authority.[62]

In *Eisenstadt v. Baird* (1972) the U.S. Supreme Court defined marriage not as "an independent entity with a mind and heart of its own, but as an association of two individuals each with a separate intellectual and emotional make-up."[63] That is, the legal fiction of liberalism that we begin in a state of nature where individuals rule autonomously was expanded to marriage, which therefore no longer could be a natural institution or a covenant, composed of two people united in their differences or complementarity. Now they were two autonomous individuals, only united by contract.

---

60. Adrian Walker, "Introduction," *Co* 30 (2003), 177–79 at 178, describing José Noriega Bastos, "The Origin and Destiny of Freedom," 282–336, in the same issue.

61. Michael M. Uhlmann, "The Supreme Court Rules," *FT* 136 (October 2003): 26–35 at 28. We might also describe this development as a final exercise in Protestant nominalism, because in it, like God, we are free to create our own natures: David B. Hart, "Christ and Nothing," *FT* 136 (October 2003): 47–56 at 53.

62. *The American Religion: The Emergence of the Post-Christian Nation* (New York: Simon & Schuster, 1992).

63. John Haas, "The Contemporary World," in *Christian Marriage: A Historical Study,* ed. Glenn W. Olsen (New York: Herder and Herder, 2001), 332–59 at 334–35.

In all cases, one makes up the meaning of one's life, rather than receiving it. At the present not everyone, of course, accepts such a view, and we might describe the "postmodern" situation as containing both diffuse or flexible notions of the self, and coherent selves, communicating in a situation of widespread instability.[64] Writers such as Pierre Manent try to defend a realistic notion of freedom, navigating between the Scylla of an unfettered or utopian freedom, and the Charybdis of a retreat from politics that is the almost inevitable result of the failure of utopian expectations. What, with Hobbes, he especially fears is a kind of triumph of the logic of democracy and liberalism in which the nation is replaced with a kind of "virtual reality" or "mere concourse of wills" that has "long been a dream of the democratic mind."[65]

In the midst of the developments just described, the cosmic Christ, personal and involved in all things human, came to be replaced with theism, the reduction of God to an impersonal principle linked to the world as first cause but otherwise uninvolved in daily life. Certain thinkers, such as Jonathan Edwards (1703–58) in America, though sometimes themselves in one way or another implicated in the Newtonian universe, mightily resisted important assumptions behind this theism. Unacceptable was any writing of history which eliminated God as an active actor in historical events.[66] For Edwards, on the contrary, history depends entirely on God's redemptive activity, manifested in periodic evangelical revivals. Human agency is not at the center of history, but God's initiatives. In many ways Edwards was close to traditional Catholicism. In the words of one of his best interpreters, for Edwards

the starting point for all thought must be the recognition that the universe is essentially personal. All being originates in the interpersonal relationships of the Trinity and the very purpose of creation is to express God's redemptive love. Hence all of created reality is a text or language about the love and beauty of God, epitomized ultimately in the sacrificial love of Christ for the undeserving. In all that is around them, whether in stunning landscapes, ordinary objects, or other people, believers can see the beauty of a loving God revealed as "Images, or Shadows, of Divine Things."[67]

64. A. David Napier, *The Righting of Passage: Perceptions of Change after Modernity* (Philadelphia: University of Pennsylvania Press, 2004).

65. These phrases are taken from Russell Hittinger's review, "Dissecting a Democratic Illusion," *IR* 41, 2 (Fall 2006): 50–54 at 51.

66. I have treated some of the issues here in "Christian Philosophy, Christian History: Parallel Ideas?" in *Eternity in Time: Christopher Dawson and the Catholic Idea of History*, ed. Stratford Caldecott and John Morrill (Edinburgh: T & T Clark, 1997), 131–50.

67. George Marsden, "Can Jonathan Edwards (and His Heirs) Be Integrated into the American History Narrative?" *HS* 5, 6 (July/August 2004): 13–15 at 15. More generally see Patricia U. Bonomi, *Under the Cope of Heaven: Religion, Society, and Politics in Colonial America*, updated ed. (New York: Oxford University Press, 2003).

We might speak of Edwards as Alexandrian rather than Eusebian, for he wrote history not from the point of view of the worldly success and expansion of the Church, but from God's point of view, that is, as about the divine work of redemption in the world, and the manifestation of the glory of God in time.[68] Yet in an English or American context even most Evangelicals, like other Christians, in accepting a Newtonian account of the universe, allowed limits to be placed on God. Religion might come to center on pietist categories such as "experience" and "the heart," which for the average person implied a God still very much present in history, but God himself had to operate within limits which were moving in the direction of Kant's "religion within the bounds of reason alone."[69] Moreover, by tending to center religion on individual subjectivity, Evangelicalism conspired with theism to loosen what influence religion had had over, say, the shape of economic or political life.

Catholic theologians who attempted in subsequent centuries to show the limitations of the world sealed by Descartes and Newton commonly failed to see the depths of the problem.[70] Even now, when postmodern science for more than a generation has been calling into question the mechanistic assumptions of the modern period, those assumptions still reign in many quarters.[71] However, John Lukacs is certainly right in arguing that we live at the end, in many ways stagnant, of an age characterized by a mechanical view of causality and a philosophical dualism of subject and object which is no longer believable, though still regnant in many quarters. Witness the continued influence of Marx, Darwin (the prime exhibit of the discredited mechanical causality), Freud, and Einstein (in his rejection of quantum theory).[72] Werner Heisenberg himself noted that the mechanics of Newton and classical physics assumed that God can and must be bracketed as a preface to any description of the world. This was part of a larger assumption that the object of natural science was somehow independent of

---

68. Avihu Zakal, *Jonathan Edward's Philosophy of History: The Re-Enchantment of the World in the Age of Enlightenment* (Princeton, N.J.: Princeton University Press, 2003); and see Zakal's "Jonathan Edwards's Vision of History," *HS* (June 2003): 28–30. "Alexandrian" and "Eusebian" are of course not absolutely opposed categories, but Eusebius's interests are in *ecclesiastical* history, Edwards's in the work of the spirit in time.

69. Margaret Bendroth, "Wheaton Jeremiad," *JHS* 3 (Summer/Fall 2003): 439–44 at 440.

70. Michael Buckley, *At the Origins of Modern Atheism* (New Haven, Conn.: Yale University Press, 1987), 363; see also Casarella, "Waiting for a Cosmic Christ," 249, and my "Return of Purpose."

71. Current criticism was already anticipated by David Bohm, *Causality and Chance in Modern Physics* (Philadelphia: University of Pennsylvania Press, 1957). More current is Jean Guitton, Grichka Bogdanov, and Igor Bogdanov, *Dieu et la science. Vers la métaréalisme* (Paris: B. Grasset, 1991); see also Casarella, "Waiting for a Cosmic Christ," 250f., at 251. The very interesting debate being conducted by historians about whether there was a "scientific revolution" reveals much about how science has been conceived in the modern period: *Rethinking the Scientific Revolution,* ed. Margaret J. Osler (New York: Cambridge University Press, 2000).

72. *At the End of an Age* (New Haven, Conn. 2002), at 178–80.

its observer, a failure to recognize that any explanation involves an inter-play between what is being explained and the person doing the explaining. There is a legitimate sense in which God as first cause must be bracketed to discover the secondary causation at work in any separate science, but denial of this presumably was not what Heisenberg had in mind. His con-cern, rather, was to insist that man the observer and interpreter of necessity stands at the center of physics as much as of any form of knowledge.[73]

David L. Schindler argues that the assumptions involved in a theistic understanding of God—that is, in an understanding of God as simply the monad of much modern philosophy and the cosmos as simply matter in motion—already carry secularism with them.[74] Both nature and human nature are emptied of any intrinsic relationship to God. God, nature, and the individual likely remain in the thought of the theist or deist, but as standing only in external relations to each other: neither man nor nature is understood as being substantively what they are because of a constituting relation to God the Creator, especially a relation of love. With such the-ism we are here not far from the atheism "sitting unnoticed at the heart of American religiosity."[75] By contrast to a medieval symbolic or sacramental understanding of the world, in which all creatures speak of God and stand in an asymmetrical relation to Him which is a creaturely participation in the asymmetric but mutual relations of the Trinitarian persons to one an-other, theism typically speaks of God in a unitarian manner, and thus does not find in the created order relations imitating those internal to the Trinity itself. Nature becomes external to God, and God external to nature, and the relations between all things are external. God is transcendent to, but not immanent in, nature. All worldly relations become "mechanical," as if the universe were a vast machine. The constituting parts have no more interiority than machine parts. If one views creation in an Augustinian or medieval way as the "footprints of God," each thing will also be a symbol of something beyond itself, finally of God; not arbitrarily, not because we assign it that meaning, but really, because God has made it that way. If one views creation in a merely theistic way, there are no inter-Trinitarian rela-tions to be repeated analogously elsewhere, and the cosmos becomes simply mathematical and mechanical, Cartesian and Newtonian, and a "grey on-tology" reigns.[76]

73. Ibid., 179–80.
74. "Creation and Nuptiality: A Reflection on Feminism in Light of Schmemann's Liturgi-cal Theology," *Co* 28 (2001): 265–95. Michael Sean Winters, "The Struggle within American Catholicism," *NeR* 221, 9 (August 30, 1999): 39–44, is an uneven but useful explanation of the importance of Schindler within the spectrum of American Catholic thought.
75. Walker, "'Constitutive Relations,'" gives an excellent exposition of these points and is the source of the phrase quoted.
76. Schindler, "Creation and Nuptiality," 284. Simon Oliver, "Motion according to Aqui-

Schindler believes that Western liberalism, with or without belief in God, carries with it this secularized view of man and nature. It has come to teach a false view of human autonomy, and specifically privileges the masculine as the carrier of this false autonomy. Feminism, while quite properly reacting against such "paternalism," often merely democratizes it, spreading it to women as well as men. All become interchangeable, and asymmetrical relations, mutual or not, are removed from the world.[77] This is Mary Ann Glendon's point in holding that feminism bears prime responsibility for a radical departure from earlier legal norms in which the "right to privacy . . . substitutes the individual for the couple or the family."[78] In the Supreme Court's holding that men have no right to participate in their wives' decision regarding abortion, "we are being asked to concede the very notion of the human person as necessarily connected to others."[79]

According to the Orthodox theologian Alexander Schmemann, secularism is "above all a negation of worship."[80] A sacramental view of life, an understanding that God is love and that therefore love is at the center of all created being, can only be recovered by attending to the liturgy, that is, by recovery of those dimensions of life most neglected in the busy "external" life of secular liberal man. Schindler speaks of a "way of Love" which integrates what is important in both ancient and modern thought by taking seriously the idea that God is love, and that loving relations constitute the world.[81] For Schindler, following John Paul II, the nuptial relation, mutual but asymmetric, is central to understanding the relation between God and the world, and the liturgy especially articulates this. In speaking of the order of the universe, the ranks of angels and other created beings, this liturgy presents a hierarchical creation, every rank in an asymmetrical relation to God. This is implicitly denied in the drive for human equality commonly advocated by liberalism and the drive for interchangeability of parts advocated by mechanistic theory (a stem cell is simply one possible configuration of its matter).

---

nas and Newton," *MT* 17, 2 (2001): 163–99, and *Philosophy, God, and Motion* (London: Routledge, 2005), 153–82, establishes the links between Newton's un-Trinitarian voluntarism, Arianism, and nominalism and his conception of matter and motion. Oliver shows that following Newton relation becomes an extrinsic category governed by force, and things are understood as constituted in relation to themselves, so to speak, in their solitude. Jean-Luc Marion, "Descartes and Onto-Theology," in *Post-Secular Philosophy: Between Philosophy and Theology*, ed. Phillip Blond (London: Routledge, 1998), 97 n. 1, uses the phrase "grey ontology."

77. Schindler, "Creation and Nuptiality," 285–94, esp. 290–91.

78. Described by Elizabeth Fox-Genovese, "Feminism and the Unraveling of the Social Bond," *Voices* 19, 3 (2004): 9–14 at 12. Fox-Genovese's general position was that women's complaints are often justified, but that the solutions feminism proposes are often unjust.

79. Ibid., 13, suggesting that abortion is "the ultimate objectification" of the person.

80. *For the Life of the World* (Crestwood, N.Y.: St. Vladimir's Seminary Press, 1998 [1963]), the book at the center of Schindler, "Creation and Nuptiality." See also the essays of Schindler and Robert Slesinski in *Co* 29 (2002): 606–14.

81. Walker, "'Constitutive Relations,'" gives an overview of Schindler's thought.

Though normally addressing only the alleged equality of human beings, such notions tend toward a flattened universe which throws into the shadows any created hierarchical diversity of the world as understood by, say, Dante ("In my father's house there are many mansions" [Jn 14:21]).[82]

⌒

Learned early modern Europeans almost invariably continued to take it for granted that public life must be under God and somehow aim at the great transcendentals of the good, true, and beautiful. As in the medieval Church's resistance to usury, indeed to what we may describe as many elements of early capitalism, it was not a foregone conclusion that human beings must adjust to and accept all new economic possibilities. Certainly the pressures of what Joel Kaye has called the monetization of society, the growth of monetary consciousness and coinage from the thirteenth century, were real.[83] But, as we noted above in chapter 2, one writer, taking the large view, terms the late twelfth through early fourteenth century central, and understands northern Italian communes as "cities of God" reminding us that urban environments were still packed with expressions of religion.[84] Marsilius of Padua (1275/80–1342/43) was one of the first to sever the good order of the political community from any more comprehensive theory of the good, but it took centuries for the implications of this and a purely secular view of the state to work themselves out.[85] Machiavelli (1469–1527) quite accurately noted that political thought, ancient and medieval, had first been about what man ought be, and then only secondarily about what he is. He is often presented as denying the first idea and being only concerned with the latter, but it is probably more correct to say that he combines traditional ideas in a novel way. He does not deny the idea that morality is absolute, but he lays more emphasis on the traditional notion that *necessitas non habet legem* ("necessity knows no law") than had either the

---

82. Susan R. Kramer and Caroline W. Bynum, "Revisiting the Twelfth-Century Individual: The Inner Self and the Christian Community," in *Das Eigene und das Ganze: Zum Individuellen im mittelalterlichen Religiosentum,* ed. Gert Melville and Markus Schürer (Münster: Lit, 2002), 57–85 at 59. Bynum has written a book that makes vividly clear the undemocratic nature of heaven itself in Christian thought: *Fragmentation and Redemption: Essays on Gender and the Human Body in Medieval Religion* (New York: Zone Books, 1990). See also her *The Resurrection of the Body in Western Christianity, 200–1336* (New York: Columbia University Press, 1995).

83. *Economy and Nature in the Fourteenth Century: Money, Market Exchange, and the Emergence of Scientific Thought* (Cambridge: Cambridge University Press, 1998), esp. chs. 1–3.

84. Augustine Thompson, *Cities of God: The Religion of the Italian Communes, 1125–1325* (University Park: Pennsylvania State University Press, 2005).

85. Annabel S. Brett, "Politics, Right(s) and Human Freedom in Marsilius of Padua," in *Transformations,* ed. Mäkinen and Korkman, 95–116. Francesco Maiolo, *Medieval Sovereignty: Marsilius of Padua and Bartolous of Saxoferrato* (Delft: Eburon Academic, 2007), assesses Marsilius's contribution to the justification of popular government. George Garnett, *Marsilius of Padua and the Truth of History* (Oxford: Oxford University Press, 2006), dissents from the idea that Marsilius's is an early advocacy of a secular state, but agrees that he held that all priests should be under the coercive authority of the prince (ch. 3).

ancient or medieval lawyers.[86] For him the ruler is often obliged to act out of necessity, ignoring the good as traditionally understood. This has the effect of making human life appear to lack a transcendental orientation.

The self-sufficiency at which man aims, according to thinkers such as Marsilius, was conceived "purely in biological and material terms."[87] With them we are on the path to the elimination of "soul" as a term of discourse, and have a first instance of an enclosed, non-transcendental political order.[88] In previous thought man and the state had been held up to a transcendental measure. The medieval idea that theology is the "queen of the sciences" was but one expression of the idea that the whole world can be viewed in the light of sacred teaching without taking away the specific differences, the secularity, of each thing.[89] Marsilius, without the invocation of any particular moral principle, wrenched man from this larger, transcendental context. By so stressing the fact that the state must first ensure its own security and that in this necessity knows no law, Machiavelli in effect followed him, and that is why Leo Strauss thought Machiavelli so central to the abandonment of the whole tradition of natural right and the birth of the modern situation.[90]

With Machiavelli, interested in religion not as something true but only in its possible usefulness in achieving various temporal political goods, we are on the road to the vision of Hobbes, Locke, Montesquieu, Constant, and Turgot, the destruction of the transcendent in any religious or political form so that a liberal commercial society might flourish.[91] As Nietzsche so well understood, to forsake the final ordering of all under God, the theological analogue of turning on the *ancien regime,* was to reject the idea of ordered unity itself. All science is based on a pre-scientific apprehension, at once aesthetic and moral, of formal, meaningful wholes. Either such unity finally finds its source in God, or it must be imposed irrationally through power. Thus does late medieval voluntarism run its course. The Christian universe had been built on the belief that every thought somehow was also

86. Gaines Post, *Studies in Medieval Legal Thought: Public Law and the State, 1100–1322* (Princeton, N.J.: Princeton University Press, 1964), 241–309.

87. Cary J. Nederman, "The Meaning of 'Aristotelianism' in Medieval Moral and Political Thought," *JHI* 57 (1996): 563–85 at 583–84, on Marsilius's departure from Aristotle.

88. Hecht, *End of the Soul.*

89. John Montag, "Revelation: The False Legacy of Suarez," in *Radical Orthodoxy: A New Theology,* ed. John Milbank et al. (London: Routledge, 1999), 38–63.

90. *Natural Right and History* (Chicago: University of Chicago Press, 2000); see also Mark Lilla, "The Closing of the Straussian Mind," *NYRB* 51, 17 (November 4, 2004): 55–59 at 56, on this and the following.

91. Timothy Burns, "The Liberal Uses of Religion," *FT* 113 (May 2001): 25–31 at 27. Cf. the analysis of Pierre Manent, *The City of Man,* tr. Marc LePain (Princeton, N.J.: Princeton University Press, 1998). Jeremy Waldron, *God, Locke, and Equality* (New York: Cambridge University Press, 2002), argues that Locke's thought has Christian foundations which cannot be eliminated without removing the ground for equality.

in the mind of God. Now either no universe survived, or it was willfully constructed by man.

Locke in particular replaced the "friendship" and kinship so central to binding traditional society together with the abstract category "civil society," which has remained to the present in the Anglo-Saxon world and beyond.[92] An ancient insight, especially present in Greek and Roman literature, had been that the dead give us our communities, that is, what gives coherence to present life is the continuing presence in it of our dead, our remembrance of them and sense of being in continuity with them. Edmund Burke (1729–97) and T. S. Eliot (1888–1965) had particularly strong senses of this "community of the dead," which each generation joins. This community had nourished the kinship and friendship so important to traditional society. But long before Burke or Eliot all this had disappeared from Locke's thought, replaced with the individual and civil society, neither much rooted in any past. The individualism of the forming liberal tradition actually turned its eyes from the fact of death itself. The insight that death and mortality must be at the center of political reflection all but disappeared from the thought of most of the moderns, only to be retained by explicitly Counter-Enlightenment thinkers.[93] Even Hobbes, intent on establishing the grimness of the first human condition, missed the chance for reflection on the place of death in politics.

Such developments perhaps reflected how much movements we associate with the Enlightenment had already changed England in the century after the Reformation. When Locke went up to Oxford in 1652, it was already abuzz with the new experimental philosophy, with chemistry, mathematics, and astronomy, and placed great hope on the rational reordering of all spheres of life.[94] More and more the state was to determine what is to be done on the basis of what is best for itself: it replaces the "natural power of contracting marriage" with its own determination of what is fit.[95] The Christian covenant is made subservient to the "original contract" of civil society. We are on the road to Kant and the notion that society is founded

---

92. Alan Bray, *The Friend* (Chicago: University of Chicago Press, 2003), must be read in full to appreciate his brilliant comments about Locke, 212–13, 216. Bray stresses that in traditional society the categories of kinship and friendship overlap, the latter being one way of forming or entering "family." See also the illuminating comparisons drawn by Boyd Hilton, *A Mad, Bad, and Dangerous People? England 1783–1846* (Oxford: Clarendon Press, 2006), and the opening essays on Maitland and Alan Macfarlane in Stephen D. White, *Re-Thinking Kinship and Feudalism in Early Medieval Europe* (Burlington, Vt.: Ashgate, 2006).

93. Joseph Bottum, "Death & Politics," *FT* 174 (June/July 2007): 17–29.

94. Bray, *Friend*, 208–9, with very interesting comments, 209–12, on the changes in the configurations of the great houses which accompanied this, decreasing bodily intimacy and the mixing of the social classes, and the recasting of service as menial and degrading. The kiss is replaced by the handshake.

95. Ibid., 215, on the shift from marriage being *"in facie ecclesiae,"* or "before God," to being a contract of civil society.

on universal benevolence rather than face-to-face friendship.[96] Further, in consummation of a millennia-long tendency to expand the "time of Man" at the expense of the "time of the gods," evident already in Herodotus and Thucydides, with Locke (see especially the *Second Treatise,* 21) and others of similar mind there is the "deist" insistence that God does not intervene in the affairs of man.[97] In the eighteenth and nineteenth centuries, a multitude of factors tended to replace the "communitarian" ways of life of earlier centuries with the greater individualism already evident in Locke's championing of the rights of children, especially in the matter of consent, against paternal authority. In America all this was to be accelerated by the settling of lands in outlying areas, out of the reach of family and church; the gradual disestablishment of the Protestant churches in the wake of the American Revolution with a concomitant decrease in their moral authority; and a growing "Enlightenment" belief in the goodness of sexual happiness and pleasure detached from procreation.[98]

It is always difficult to sweep out the demons. With Locke, political theory, in quest of a civil society distinct from the Church and from the "irrational" bonds of traditional family and friends, became more mythical than it had been, a tale about an originally autonomous man driven by necessity into society. No matter that the notion of an original autonomy is about as far as we can get from what the early forms of human life look like to historians. As Tolstoy wrote in the second epilogue to *War and Peace,* of all forms of political thought grounded in the idea that there had been a transference of some collective will to some sovereign government: "The theory seems irrefutable just because the act of transference of the people's will cannot be verified, for it never occurred."[99]

Compared to the richness and historical depth into the twentieth century of, say, Spanish or Italian thought about the origins of the state, Locke's thought is extraordinarily abstract and ahistorical.[100] But his theory, mightily resisted as it may have been by those who wanted or want a more traditional and communal life, a different modernity or no modernity at all, is

96. Bray, *Friend,* 213, 226, 259.

97. For what Locke's God can and cannot do, see Waldron, *God, Locke, and Equality:* God's communication is limited to what man's reason can understand through nature. On Pierre Vidal-Naquet's distinction between *"le temps des dieux"* and *"le temps des hommes,"* see my "Problems with the Contrast between Circular and Linear Concepts of Time in the Interpretation of Ancient and Early Medieval History," *FQI* 1 (2001): 41–65 at 46.

98. John D'Emilio and Estelle Freedman, *Intimate Matters: A History of Sexuality in America* (New York: Harper & Row, 1988), 40.

99. Tr. Louise and Aylmer Maude (New York 1942), 1328.

100. Juan Bms. Vallet de Goytisolo, "Las Diversas Clases de Pactismos Históricos, su Puesta en Relación con el Concepto Bodiniano de Soberanía," *An* 9 (2003): 15–33. Kirstie M. McClure, *Judging Rights: Lockean Politics and the Limits of Consent* (Ithaca, N.Y.: Cornell University Press, 1996), raises probing questions about the liberalism and the rights-based theories of politics flowing from Locke.

what was needed to ground Whig economic individualism. Spinoza (1632–77), Locke's almost exact contemporary, while articulating a somewhat different early form of liberalism, arguably accomplished for Judaism something quite similar to Locke's refashioning of Christian society and political thought. Some have gone so far—the matter is disputed—as to argue that modern Judaism, for the most part individualistic and centered on a private identity consonant with liberal individualism, is Spinozist.[101] In any case, for the Whig tradition, with Locke the "friend" of traditional society disappeared; and, especially with Immanuel Kant a rational or civil ethic in which friendship became undifferentiated benevolence appeared.[102] An undefined and abstract egalitarianism, always experienced as a thing of the surface, advanced at the expense of the concrete forms of friendship, the deep things, that from time immemorial had defined the actual societies of village and neighborhood. Traditional friendship, one form of which could be marriage, had been based not on equality, but on complementarity, the suitability for society of natural differences, the ways in which natural differences urge and advance social cooperation. Now, the claim was, all are equal, all interchangeable.

Part of the rampant illogic of the Enlightenment, what one writer has called the Endarkenment, of thinkers like Jean-Jacques Rousseau (1712–78) and then of the French Revolution, was to make equality and fraternity coordinates.[103] Rousseau's version of the myth of an original state of nature was, if anything, more preposterous than Locke's, positing, as it did, an original liberty (where is Hobbes when one really needs him?) and equality, two intrinsically incompatible concepts held together only by the belief also in an original benevolence and peacefulness. In the traditional society of "the friend," one could, within limits, select one's friends; now in Enlightenment society—Rousseau, with his idea that primitive man lives so much in the moment that he has little relationship to others, aside—one was to be a friend to all. This of course was because Rousseau like so many others aimed at a civic religion in which Christianity was placed in the service of

<hr />

101. Joseph B. Soloveitchik, "Majesty and Humility," *Tradition* 17 (Spring 1978): 25–37. See also Avishai Margalit, "The Lessons of Spinoza," *NYRB* 54, 6 (April 12, 2007): 71–74, treating Spinoza's views on commerce (desirable to divert the masses' interest from religion), civil religion (controlled by the state), and transcendence (there is none).

102. Bray, *Friend*, 258–59.

103. Weaver, *Ideas Have Consequences*, 41–42, noting how this foreshadows modern political campaigns, in which all can be promised, no matter how incompatible; and the ways in which equality, except before the law, is a "disorganizing concept." Fareed Zakaria, *The Future of Freedom: Illiberal Democracy at Home and Abroad* (New York: W. W. Norton, 2003), makes the brave argument that too much democracy threatens liberty, i.e., that the whole tradition of seeing these two things as complementary typically avoids the hard questions. On Régine Pernoud's language of "Endarkenment," see my "Stubborn Myths," *The University Bookman* 42, 4 (2003): 5–9.

strengthening national unity. It has been insufficiently remarked that, in another historical context than Locke's, Nietzsche and Marx share a common ground in trying to replace a gift economy, the economy of friends, with utilitarian exchange, the economy of those who are not friends.[104]

Protestantism's role in the secularization of life and growth of individualism has been observed more than once. For instance, in the wake of Kant, in the Protestant north of Germany particularly, we find, especially in the upper-middle class, a civic religion shared by Reformed Jew and Lutheran.[105] Or again, an irony of American history has been that often the most fervent religious currents have in the end been secularizing and the promoters of individualism. Thus the Great Awakening of the mid-eighteenth century encouraged fervor at the expense of the established churches and clergy, often cutting people loose from their traditional religious ties, as once again the evangelical revival of the late twentieth century has. Revivalist preachers of the eighteenth century encouraged trust in "self-examination," even asserting the "absolute Necessity for every Person to act singly . . . as if there was not another human Creature upon Earth."[106] No communion of saints there!

The English workers' trade unionism of the 1830s, with its rhetoric of the poor, a combined, often Methodist, language of socialism and the Bible still present in the twenty-first century in Prime Minister Tony Blair, shows that not all were convinced of the superiority of the world ushered in by the Whigs. Not for these workers was Locke's civil society. They much preferred traditional, intimate, even village, life. No matter that many were agricultural unionists, and many found their living in mining or some other job participating in the new Industrial Revolution. All shared

a fierce contempt for the economic individualism of the Whigs. Civil society had not entered their soul. Possessed of a traditional view of religion's role, they stubbornly continued to stand outside the "civil" view of the world and defied it. . . . [In this we see] the continuing vitality of that traditional religion into the nineteenth century.[107]

This was one expression of an anti-modernism that offers itself to the religious man until the present, an anti-modernism which in myriad forms continues to protest Enlightenment and liberalism. Religion, after all,

104. Vincent Pecora, *Households of the Soul* (Baltimore: Johns Hopkins University Press, 1997).
105. Amos Elon, "The Triumph of a Double Life," *NYRB* 53, 16 (October 19, 2006): 26–29 at 26. Jonathan Elukin, *Living Together, Living Apart: Rethinking Jewish-Christian Relations in the Middle Ages* (Princeton, N.J. 2007), 2–3, has interesting observations on the relations between Zionism and the modernization of Judaism.
106. Revivalist preacher quoted in Gordon S. Wood, "American Religion: The Great Retreat," *NYRB* 53, 10 (June 8, 2006): 60–63 at 60.
107. Bray, *Friend*, 287.

teaches one—or should do so—how to be a failure, that is, that life is not at heart about the Whig categories of progress and success, and one of the most worrisome things about the demise of religion in the modern world is the loss of a sense of loss.[108] The lack of this sense of loss in some forms of evangelical Christianity—but thank God for Johnny Cash!—is a measure of their inauthenticity as religion.

John Stuart Mill was a complicated figure with evolving ideas and is not easy to place in this story. Students have been unable to agree about how much Mill is a Romantic (it is clear that as his thought developed, he gave more weight to history as the necessary context for understanding society), and how much open to religious faith. But a plausible argument can be made that he is the apostle of personal autonomy, and thus a very important figure in the liberal tradition. The enemy was a corrupt aristocracy and thinkers like Edmund Burke, who idealized the past and failed to criticize the inefficacy of past institutions. Progress was to be through Parliament and the rational middle classes. In one more form of modernism, Mill portrayed our ancestors as less wise than we. What was wanted today, according to him, was a new aristocracy, now of spiritual and intellectual excellence. But what is most important for our purposes is Mill's continuation in *On Liberty* of the tradition of John Milton's *Areopagitica* (1644) in praise of free speech and thought above all, now placed in service of the ideal of personal development formed by Goethe and Humboldt. This was not so much the "do one's own thing" of contemporary culture, but "be as excellent as you can be." There are deep contradictions in Mill's thought and it is not clear that his utilitarianism, his belief that happiness is the test of right and wrong, is at all compatible with his devotion to individual freedom. One does not have to affirm the Christian doctrine of Original Sin to think that here, in his most central belief, Mill is wrong and promotes the utopianism criticized in chapter 2 above. Gertrude Himmelfarb is here his most incisive critic.[109]

Enlightenment and the early stages of liberalism, like Romanticism after them, turn out to have been but way stations until someone drew the inevitable conclusion from Marsilius's premises, namely, that everything is permitted. In retrospect one can then describe the classical economists of the eighteenth century, while they claimed to find an order within nature, as in fact having subordinated nature to a quantitative mode of thought in which the movement of money is the true reality. The classical economists still find laws in nature, laws which in a certain sense must be obeyed, but these laws are no longer the command to preserve natural justice of earlier

---

108. Roger Scruton, "Regaining My Religion," in his *Gentle Regrets: Thoughts from a Life* (New York: Continuum, 2005).

109. Alan Ryan, "Freedom Fighter," *NYRB* 52, 5 (March 26, 2005): 40–43.

thought. In any case, they treat social relations as abstract and commodified, not as personal and historical.

For the flourishing of liberal commercial society, religion had to be privatized and "made rational," given a Kantian existence within the bounds of reason alone.[110] Kant hardly averted to religion's great insight that not only is man mortal, but that all human communities keep the dead alive among them and thus achieve their identity: there is no mention of death or mortality in Kant's 1784 essay "What Is Enlightenment?"[111] In Kant there is an epistemology at work in which reason is held to be the sole source of knowledge, against all religious claims for Revelation as another source. Religious faith is to be "consistently 'improved' by becoming increasingly reasonable, tolerant, irenic, and humane."[112] As Adolf von Harnack was around 1900 to recast Lutheranism, worship too was to be jettisoned in favor of a humanitarian moral message. Given these assumptions, secularization was inevitable. This logic has in good measure been followed in the West, and today also has its supporters in the Islamic world. The Moroccan philosopher Abdou Filali-Ansari, disenchanted with dogma, urges that it be replaced with the ethical principles underlying it: "Faith becomes a matter of individual choice and commitment, not an obligation imposed on the community."[113]

There was an obvious flaw in Kant's position from the first, one perhaps flowing from his inadequate understanding of the history of philosophy. In his famous *Essay on the Development of Christian Doctrine,* completed about forty years after Kant's death, Cardinal Newman declared, "There never was a time when reason was unaided."[114] Historically, one can never find an "unaided" or "pure" form of reason. Always reason has worked in consort with other things—theology, cosmology, mythology, science—and there simply are no examples of a reason isolated from and not bearing the mark of some historical context.[115] Aristotle had made the important observation that because things might be distinguished in principle does not mean that they can be separated in fact, and Kant seems to have forgotten this. Almost all forms of liberalism subsequently depend on the isolation of reason from history, as if reason was something one could unproblematically de-link from historical context. This is the ground of the idea of a purely secular life. Down this path lay not simply the impossible idea of "religion within the bounds of reason alone," but the constant proliferation of rights

110. Barron, "Evangelizing the American Culture," 31.

111. Bottum, "Death and Politics," 20.

112. Christine Caldwell Ames, "Does Inquisition Belong to Religious History?" *AHR* 110 (2005): 11–37 at 38.

113. "Muslims and Democracy," *Islam and Democracy in the Middle East,* ed. Larry Diamond, Marc F. Plattner, and Daniel Brumberg (Baltimore: Johns Hopkins University Press, 2003), 193–207 at 203.

114. (New York, D. Appleton, 1845), 40.

115. See my "Christian Philosophy?"

formally ungrounded but always surreptitiously called into existence by, and dependent for their being on, some particular historical situation. The attenuation or elimination of religion in favor of reason has been one liberal or secular agenda to the present, witness Richard Rorty's belief that the "'highest achievements of humanity' are incompatible with traditional religion."[116] Central is the belief that significant human improvement is possible, especially under the aegis of science.[117] In *Modernity's Wager,* Adam B. Seligman speaks of the attempt to liberate the individual from external authority, whether social or religious, in favor of a rational self which is its own moral authority.[118]

Religion did not travel a single road in the modern period, and alongside the developments we have been tracing there was also Jean-Jacques Rousseau's protest against the elimination of the transcendent, but acknowledgment that its ancient forms were irrecoverable. Rousseau believed that though we have an "eros for wholeness" or longing for transcendence, this could only be exercised in a modern form.[119] Indeed, his was a form of modernism. Nature was not to be followed but broken with in order to develop a wholly autonomous culture in which transcendence was expressed in the human power to create and legislate. Politics came to be the vehicle for the elimination of evil—now seen to lie in society rather than the individual—from human life. Specifically the origin of human evil lay in domination. This was the first sin.[120] Instead of expressing man's search for union with God, transcendence now expressed or aimed at a kind of self-divinization within a worldly sphere. Rousseau reversed almost every aspect of the earlier understanding of transcendence.

In the early modern period, in spite of many foreshadowings of modern conditions of life and thought of the type found in Marsilius and Machiavelli, and in spite of the willfulness of various popes, kings, and emperors, the law of both Church and state existed in a wider context which continued to assume that positive law was to be an application of the eternal law

116. Quoted in the exposition of various positions by James Hitchcock, "The Enemies of Religious Liberty," *FT* 140 (February 2004): 26–29 at 27.

117. In the *Atlantis,* partially paralleling Thomas More's discussion in *Utopia,* but to opposite effect, Bacon imagines a kingdom in which primary loyalty is given to one's nation, rather than to one's religion: love of the state replaces love of God, and toleration rules.

118. Subtitle: *Authority, the Self, and Transcendence* (Princeton, N.J.: Princeton University Press, 2000). Cf. Alain Renaut, *The Era of the Individual: A Contribution to a History of Subjectivity,* tr. M. B. DeBevoise and Franklin Philip, with a foreword by Alexander Nehamas (Princeton, N.J.: Princeton University Press, 1997), and Donn Welton, *The Other Husserl: The Horizons of Transcendental Phenomenolgy* (Bloomington: Indiana University Press, 2000).

119. The phrase and analysis are from an anonymous review of Richard L. Velkely, *Being After Rousseau: Philosophy and Culture in Question* (Chicago: University of Chicago Press, 2002), in *FT* 126 (October 2002): 79–80 at 79.

120. Luigi Amicone, "Event as Encounter: The Battle Against Utopia," *Traces* 5, 5 (May 2003): 16–17 at 16.

of God.[121] The two, God's sacred law and man's worldly approximation thereof, were linked, the law finding its foundation in norms beyond itself. The competing jurisdictions of Church, state, and the orders of society were decisively reorganized in the French Revolution, with its democratic fostering of the centralized state, which dissolved any basis for the law beyond the law itself. But religion partly recovered in the nineteenth century, and there is something to J. Budziszewksi's claim, following Lord Acton, that even at the beginning of the twentieth century "most people believed in . . . the moral law, written . . . on the 'tablets of eternity.'"[122] Though in America the tradition of Locke was strong, the tradition of Montesquieu, with its combination of covenantal and contractarian jurisprudence, still survived.[123] Until the present, the social tractarianism of Locke has competed with Edmund Burke's sense that "men are together because of their past and their future and that such togetherness had nothing to do with any voluntary contractual agreement."[124]

Into the early modern period the state was generally viewed as under the natural law, under a transcendental criterion of action. In spite of the tendencies of the national monarchs and of thinkers such as Marsilius and Machiavelli to advocacy of an autonomous state, at the end of the Middle Ages a transcendental rule of judgment was still widely accepted: the state was subject to, rather than the origin of, the definition of good. There were—and always had been—cracks in the cosmic picture which supported this idea, but as Romano Guardini (1885–1968) suggested, when all was said and done, humans still felt at home in a hierarchical nature and cosmos, part of a cosmic harmony, or of Catherine Pickstock's liturgical city.[125] All coherence was not yet gone. The ideal of universal humanity, that beneath all particularity all humans share in a common humanity, already found in the ancient world in such institutions as the law of nations and the idea of the natural law, remained.[126]

121. This and the following are an incapsulation of Paolo Prodi, *Una storia della giustizia; Dal pluralismo dei fori al moderno dualism tra coscienza e diritto* (Bologna: Il Mulino, 2000), which, while not always perfectly informed about the medieval Church, is a brilliant, Tocquevillian account of the secularization of law over the centuries, its loss of transcendent Christian standards and thence of all moral foundation.

122. J. Budziszewski, "The Compassionate Amoralist," *FT* 114 (June/July 2001): 58–61 at 58.

123. Paul O. Carrese, "The Single-Minded Constitution," *FT* 145 (August/September 2004): 59–63 at 61–62. In the same issue see Richard John Neuhaus, "To Be American," 93–97 at 94, approving the argument of Samuel P. Huntington, *Who Are We? The Challenges to America's National Identity* (New York: Simon & Schuster, 2004), against placing too much weight on the Lockean origins of American values.

124. Peter Munz, "Past and Present Cross-Fertilized," *HS* 5, 5 (May/June 2004): 26–28 at 26.

125. Romano Guardini, *The End of the Modern World*, intro. Frederick D. Wilhelmsen, foreword Richard J. Neuhaus (Wilmington, Del.: ISI Books, 1998); Pickstock, *After Writing*, 169–70.

126. Alain Finkielkraut, *In the Name of Humanity: Reflections on the Twentieth Century* (New

Then, as Louis Dupré has argued, in late medieval nominalism and the individualism celebrated in the early Renaissance there began a splitting of the self from the cosmos. Before there had been a sense of the inter-connectedness of all things, afterward many separations, such as between subject and object and nature and transcendence.[127] This revealed itself in a hundred ways. Around 1500 the sculptor Tilman Riemenschneider's large male figures express a spirituality with a heightened sense of the individual, but the haloes are gone. That is, this Catholic sculptor is enough a man of his age that, though his figures express an interior faith, they less and less manifest an embodied one.[128]

A host of thinkers—Nicolaus Cusanus (c. 1400–64), Ignatius Loyola (1491–56), Giordano Bruno (1548–1600), Francis de Sales (1567–1622)—at-tempted to reunite the human and the cosmic, with varying degrees of suc-cess, but time was on the side of an increasingly anthropocentric culture. We have noted a certain anti-sacramentalism and iconoclasm lying at the heart of most forms of Protestantism: this was intimately tied to historic Protestant rejection of patristic and medieval modes of biblical exegesis.[129] Briefly, in ancient and medieval Christianity the Scriptures were viewed analogically or symbolically as a vast garden, as having an interconnected network of references rising from the literal or historical sense to various spiritual senses. This expressed an interconnected cosmos in which words referred to objects, and objects were signs referring to and in relation with other objects. This cosmos broke down in the Protestant insistence that there was only one, literal, sense of Scripture, which left material objects incapable of signifying and incarnating spiritual realities, for most chang-ing the sacraments from being signs and means of salvation to being ways to recollect the plain word of Scripture:

York: Columbia University Press, 2000), sketches the slow passage from vertical to horizontal ideas about the relations of humans to each other.

127. *Passage to Modernity: An Essay in the Hermeneutics of Nature and Culture* (New Haven, Conn.: Yale University Press, 1993); and Randolph Starn, review of *Passage to Modernity*, *AHR* 101 (1996): 154–55 at 155. See also Dupré's *The Enlightenment and the Intellectual Foundations of Modern Culture* (New Haven, Conn.: Yale University Press, 2004), and *Religion and the Rise of Modern Culture* (Notre Dame, Ind.: University of Notre Dame Press, 2008), on the nature of modernity. Cf. the account of the emergence of the modern self throughout Alasdair Ma-cIntyre, *After Virtue: A Study in Moral Theory*, 3rd ed. (Notre Dame, Ind.: University of Notre Dame Press, 2007), as at 205.

128. John Updike, "A Wistful Master," *NYRB* 47, 6 (April 13, 2000): 18–20 at 19–20. See further Julien Chapuis, *Tilman Riemenschneider: Master Sculptor of the Late Middle Ages* (Wash-ington, D.C.: National Gallery of Art, 1999). Of course, witness the subsequent development of the Baroque, Riemenschneider's was only one path to the future.

129. In some Protestant circles there is today an openness to earlier forms of exegesis: see my "The Spiritual Sense(s) Today," in *The Bible and the University*, ed. David Lyle Jeffrey and C. Stephen Evans (Grand Rapids, Mich.: Zondervan, 2007), 116–38, originally given at Baylor University before a largely Protestant audience.

The Protestant Reformation, by promoting the culture of the literal word, effected a dramatic contraction of the sphere of the sacred, forcibly stripping objects, natural and artificial, of the roles they had once played as bearers of meaning.[130]

The Catholic category of mystery, a reality not discernible by the senses, tended to disappear from many forms of Protestantism, making Protestantism vulnerable to the rationalism and reductionism of early modern science.[131]

Alan Jacobs, a Protestant, has articulated a further dimension of what was involved in the passage from Catholic to Protestant ways of reading the Bible. Jacobs takes up Hans-Georg Gadamer's (1900–2002) observation that the modern notion of objectivity is rooted in the stance taken by Protestantism in regard to the Scriptures. Having to defend their approach to the Bible against traditional Catholic habits of reading, which placed the interpreter within Catholic tradition,

the Reformers found themselves obliged by their polemical situation to show that they could specify a set of reliable safeguards against error—safeguards which would serve a similar liminal function to the concept of "tradition" in the Roman Catholic Church—and this need to provide safeguards and eliminate error came to dominate the hermeneutical tradition for the next several centuries. The chief goal of theological hermeneutics naturally, then, comes to be associated more closely with "getting it right" than with a deepening of understanding or a growing in love.[132]

Jacobs's argument is that whereas the ancient Christian understanding of reading, embodied in Augustine's *De Doctrina Christiana,* was that the text must be read with love, we are with classical Protestantism on the road to a Cartesian hermeneutic in which the reader must be distanced from the text rather than in love with it. Jacobs of course does not mean that Luther and Calvin did not read with love, but that over the generations an original emphasis on the literal sense as the only valid sense of Scripture led to a scholarly stance in which, as a kind of substitute for the abandoned

130. Peter Harrison, *The Bible, Protestantism, and the Rise of Natural Science* (Cambridge: Cambridge University Press, 1998), 117, quoted in the review by James Altena, "Secular Hermeneutics," *Touchstone* 14, 6 (July/August 2001): 51–55 at 52, on which my exposition depends. Cf. Wendell Berry, "Life Is a Miracle," *Co* 27 (2000): 83–97, elucidating and criticizing these developments.

131. Altena, "Secular Hermeneutics," 54–55.

132. Alan Jacobs, *A Theology of Reading: The Hermeneutics of Love* (Boulder, Colo.: Westview Press, 2001), on which see Richard John Neuhaus, "The Hermeneutics of Love," *FT* 124 (June/July 2002): 85–88 at 86. I suspect that the culprit in view here is less the sixteenth-century Protestant, with his or her great love of the Scriptures, than the nineteenth-century Protestant exegete, ever more giving his first loyalty to scientific rather than ecclesiastical principles. By similar token, the Catholic magisterium on its side was concerned with "getting it right." Lorraine Daston and Peter Galison, *Objectivity* (New York: Zone Books, 2007), is at once a history of objectivity and of the scientific self.

Catholic magisterium, a true understanding of Scripture was secured by a scientific approach to reading in which the interpreter had, as any good scientist, to distance himself from the text, to be a dispassionate scientist rather than a passionate lover. Robert Louis Wilken, an adult convert from Lutheranism to Catholicism, agrees with Jacobs.[133] His observation is that what we call modern thought is marked by "a posture of critical distance in the interpretation of sacred texts" foreign to the Fathers.[134] The whole story is an example of how Protestantism in particular was in the modern period to be refashioned from within by assumptions taken from developing modernity.

The separation of the self from the cosmos was further exacerbated by classical Protestantism's attack on nature and natural law which, by denying the analogy of being, tended to place man in such a sinful and darkened state that talk of cosmic harmonies must fall away.[135] Man becomes, in Lutheran fashion, a citizen of two kingdoms, one earthly and one divine, with quite different laws. For many the implications of this development were hidden from view by the forceful retention of national unity and a shared national life by theocratic or divine-right monarchs. Noting that the Reformation was centered in lands outside those that had been part of the Roman Empire, many have suggested that the sixteenth-century differences in religion owed much to political and economic factors. Christopher Dawson went so far as to describe Protestantism as "a Nordic revolt against Latin traditions," a revolt against the union of classical and northern culture which had been the achievement of the Middle Ages.[136] In these areas Paul was "now to be taken without his Hellenism and Augustine without his Neoplatonism."[137]

It would have been hard at the time to predict the opening Luther's sharp distinction between the two kingdoms presented for the emergence of theism or deism, with its effective removal of God from the world.[138] Such factors seem somewhat neglected in David Tracy's nevertheless brilliant account of the origins of deism.[139] Deism, conceiving of God as a

133. *The Spirit of Early Christian Thought: Seeking the Face of God* (New Haven, Conn.: Yale University Press, 2003).

134. These are the words of an appreciation by Richard John Neuhaus, "In Lieu of Memoirs," *FT* 135 (September 2003): 61–64 at 62.

135. My "Natural Law: The First Grace," *Co* 35 (2008): 354–73, treats the attempt by some Protestants today to recover a form of natural law.

136. James Hitchcock, "Christopher Dawson and the Demise of Christendom," *HS* 5, 1 (September 2003): 23–25 at 24, describing Dawson.

137. Ibid., again describing Dawson.

138. Craig M. Gay, *The Way of the (Modern) World: Or, Why It's Tempting to Live As If God Doesn't Exist* (Grand Rapids, Mich.: Eerdmans, 1998), considers many of the topics explored in the present book, such as how technology decreases the awareness of God, the intrinsic secularity of much economic development, and the growth of a "worldly self."

139. *Analogical Imagination.*

"clock-maker" who created the world but now pretty much allows it to run according to its own laws without interference, developed at various paces and in various forms in the seventeenth and eighteenth centuries. As we have seen, its roots lay earlier, in the separation of nature from God present in some late medieval thought. But it took a modern form with Lord Herbert of Cherbury (1583–1648), who held Revelation unnecessary. The idea originally was that the primary truths of God's existence, the moral law, and a retributive future life could be known by reason alone, which was sufficient for salvation. Some retained a bit more traditional belief: Newton believed in biblical prophecy but rejected the Trinity and Incarnation.[140]

When Benjamin Franklin, one of the most prominent of the early American deists, died in 1790, he was vilified by the Federalists as "one of our first Jacobins, the first to lay his head in the lap of French harlotry; and prostrate the christianity and honour of his country to the deism and democracies of Paris."[141] At the end of the eighteenth century, at least the more aristocratic party in America was not ready for the fullness of Enlightenment religion or radical democracy, but, especially in the person of Jefferson, deism importantly influenced the American founding, witness the language of the Declaration of Independence itself, with its "laws of Nature and of Nature's God."[142] In preparing the so-called Jefferson Bible, Jefferson, who thought the religion of Jesus so simple a child could understand it, omitted all references to the miraculous and presented Jesus as a preacher of benevolence, and His message as no more than moral doctrine.[143] In time deism, America's civil religion, has been revealed as "a halfway house on the road to atheism."[144] Perhaps the popularity of Freemasonry, a kind of "Deism with rituals" for the masses, in a country in which ten of thirteen governors of Virginia between 1786 and 1819 were Masons, hid the fact of how much Christianity was being refashioned.[145]

We may in the modern situation continue to speak of "God and the soul," but less and less of man and the cosmos. Important here was the

---

140. The nature of Newton's religion is under debate: see Avery Cardinal Dulles, "The Deist Minimum," *FT* 149 (January 2005): 15–30 at 25, and the exchange generated by this article, *FT* 152 (April 2005), 8–9. Cornelio Fabro, *God in Exile: Modern Atheism from Its Roots in the Cartesian "Cogito" to the Present Day,* tr. Arthur Gibson (Westminster, Md.: Newman Press, 1968), 215–357, is a classic treatment of deism.

141. John Brewer, "Big Ben," *NYRB* 51, 12 (July 15, 2004): 36–39 at 39. David L. Holmes, *The Faiths of the Founding Fathers* (New York: Oxford University Press, 2006), usefully differentiates the varieties of American deism.

142. Dulles, "Deist Minimum," 26. Wood, "American Religion," 62–63.

143. Thomas Jefferson, *The Jefferson Bible,* with the annotated commentaries on religion of Thomas Jefferson, intro. Henry Wilder Foote, foreword Donald S. Harrington, ed. O. I. A. Roche (New York: C. N. Potter, 1964); also see Dulles, "Deist Minimum," 27.

144. Dulles, "Deist Minimum," 28.

145. Walter A. McDougall, *Freedom Just Around the Corner: A New American History, 1585–1828* (New York: HarperCollins Publishers, 2004).

abandonment of monasticism by Protestantism, which initially threw religion back on the family, making it more private and domestic.[146] Similarly important was the lessening over time of the medieval Church's suspicion of the mercantile life. Many factors had composed this suspicion, but none had been more important than the observation that merchants sought private advantage, and this created strong inducement to lying. When Catholic writers like Michael Novak today praise the virtues of the entrepreneur, his initiative and derring-do, they hardly comment on Christ's warnings to rich men: their life is hardly possible without deceit and dissimulation. Henry James is a more helpful guide to what eventually became "New World" or "New York" money when he writes of "the black and merciless things that are behind the great possessions."[147] The high medieval Church's insistence on the doctrine of the "just price" was an attempt to avoid the pollution of urban life by greed and deceit. In most quarters it is now a quaint relic of the past.

Art historians have noted the paradoxical play of iconic and iconoclastic tendencies in Reformation religious imagery, as in the work of Lucas Cranach.[148] Though thinkers such as Cusanus, Bruno, and Ignatius of Loyola, and the artistry and vision of the Baroque attempted to reunite the human and the cosmic, the disintegrating tendencies set loose by Renaissance humanism and fostered by myriad material factors, which we may loosely bring together under the label commercial capitalism, continued apace. Even Ignatius's "finding God in all things" could only take place in sixteenth-century terms, on the basis of a sixteenth-century self. Ignatius had no choice but to occupy the anthropocentric space to which the culture had shifted and was shifting. The Baroque self was a highly self-conscious, busy, operatic self, rather than a still, "medieval," monastic/contemplative self, receptive before and aiming at union with the object of its contemplation.[149] Always the Baroque self was in danger of what has now often happened, becoming so extroverted as to be absorbed in technique.[150] The Baroque from its first expression in Il Gesù (1587) in Rome was the attempt of a very self-conscious self to articulate a world which is both ordered and pulsing with energy and movement, created at once by God and by man. This self looks forward to the Romantic self. The Romantic self, while more than classicism recognizing that only a relative stasis is possible in time, and

146. Dawson, *Progress,* 277.

147. Quoted in Alan Hollinghurst, "On 'The Ivory Tower,'" *NYRB* 51, 4 (March 11, 2004): 26–28 at 26.

148. Joseph Leo Koerner, *The Reformation of the Image* (Chicago 2004).

149. For this contrast, see my "Lay Spirituality *ad majorem Dei gloriam,*" *Co* 6 (1979): 405–12.

150. Christopher Dawson, "Religion and Mass Civilization—The Problem of the Future," *The Dublin Review* 214 (January 1944): 1–8 at 5.

that all of man's works are imperfect, continues to hold that nevertheless humans may find their bearings in this world.

After Descartes, Pascal (1623–62), and Bishop Berkeley (1685–1753), it was impossible for the philosophically aware to recover the "naïve" objectivism of the ancients, to be selves unproblematically linked to the objects of their knowledge. As Pascal insisted, we must accept the fact that once for whatever reason the self has been separated from its larger collective contexts, it must in an important sense be forever disoriented in the universe.[151] What followed from Descartes's use of the subject rather than the world as the point of departure for the intellect—can we call this the Higher Naïveté?—was that like-minded men could no longer have recourse to the world as an orienting point, though of course many scientists, philosophical babes in the woods, have continued to pursue a naïve empiricism to the present. The sealing of the senses against nature in the Third Meditation meant that man must undertake the structuring of the world, which can never be more than something posited through an act of will. Thus Heidegger's observation that, Christianity removed, a nihilistic core standing at the heart of philosophy is revealed.[152] Again, we are on the road to Kant and man the maker of values. How striking the paradox in Kant's thought by which the human mind is denied a Godlike vision, but is seen to constitute the world![153] Thus modern philosophy's oscillation between rationalism and empiricism. In the tradition flowing from Descartes, God and the world may be illusions, and the entire burden weighing on the mind is by its own powers or ideas to pierce through to anything outside itself. Hence one form of the "transcendental ego" taken in some modern philosophy.[154]

European thought henceforth fluctuated between the primitivist affirmation, as in Romanticism, that there were original unities of body, soul, and cosmos, and the anti-primitivist assertion that none of these ever existed, that they merely express an unjustified nostalgia for a unity that had never been.[155] The Baroque had been one attempt to help man recover not stasis but a point of orientation suitable to the self as it had become. Another, Calvinist, route was taken by Jonathan Edwards, who, as we have

---

151. Jacques Barzun, *Classic, Romantic and Modern,* 2nd ed. (Boston: Little, Brown, 1961), 16–17, on this and the following, with his ch. 2. On the philosophical character of the Enlightenment, see *Modern Enlightenment and the Rule of Reason,* ed. John C. McCarthy (Washington, D.C.: The Catholic University of America Press, 1998). Roger L. Emerson, "How Not to Deal with Enlightenments," *HS* 3, 3 (February 2002): 5–6, deals with historiographical issues.

152. Hart, "Christ and Nothing," 53.

153. It should be noted, however, that contemporary autonomy-liberalism goes beyond Kant, who still believed in objective morality.

154. Thomas Prufer, "A Protrepic: What is Philosophy?" *Co* 30 (2003): 337–58 at 350–52, with 352–55.

155. This latter is today the special thought of certain forms of feminism and deconstruction: Françoise Meltzer, *For Fear of the Fire: Joan of Arc and the Limits of Subjectivity* (Chicago: University of Chicago Press, 2001).

seen, a century later attempted to overthrow the Enlightenment and reassert a theocentric point of view.[156] Pascal's emphasis on grace and will, and some of the Romantics' later frank, perhaps too eager, acknowledgment that man must now create whatever orders and harmonies there are to be, are two further responses to the anthropocentric reordering of the world that had taken place.

Ancient skepticism, especially ethical skepticism, had a second birth with Thomas Hobbes, who asserted that the good is no more than our name for what we desire, and has no existence in itself. As already Glaucon had argued in Plato's *Republic,* for Hobbes there is nothing objectively good: good is simply what an individual or group decides to call good. David Hume (1711–76) followed in this tradition, but though he is properly associated with the growth of skepticism and the undermining of metaphysics, he is as much the source of the dismissal of everything, above all miracles, not satisfying the criteria of science as he understood them.[157] Thus the last paragraph of his *Enquiry Concerning Human Understanding:* "If we take in our hand any volume of divinity or school metaphysics . . . let us ask, *Does it contain any abstract reasoning concerning quantity or number?* No. *Does it contain any experimental reasoning concerning matter of fact and existence?* No. Commit it then to the flames: for it can contain nothing but sophistry and illusion."[158] Hume is more an apologist for emerging commercial society, which he goes so far as to present as changing people so that they become less aggressive and more polite, than a true skeptic. Men's minds are to be turned against Christianity by reiterating the harmful things it has done historically, but they are at the same time to be made to believe in the future a thriving commercial life makes possible.[159] Like the Scottish Enlightenment itself, his so-called commitment to reason already moves in the direction of the cult of sentiment found full-blown in the writings of Adam Smith. Only an analytic philosopher could think Hume's thought stands on its own, rather than as wounded at every step by the goal of providing a rationale for a modernizing Edinburgh.[160]

156. Zakai, *Jonathan Edwards's Philosophy of History,* and "Jonathan Edwards's Vision of History."

157. John Earman, *Hume's Abject Failure: The Argument Against Miracles* (Oxford: Oxford University Press, 2000). See also *Early Responses to Hume's Writings on Religion,* ed. James Fieser, 2 vols. (Bristol: Thoemmes Press, 2001). John M. Rist has mounted a powerful defense of Christian thought against the prime figures of the Enlightenment, especially Hume, and Kant: *Real Ethics: Rethinking the Foundations of Morality* (Cambridge: Cambridge University Press, 2002). See also William A. Wallace, *Causality and Scientific Explanation,* 2 vols. (Ann Arbor: University of Michigan Press, 1972–74), vol. 2, 217–37, "The Anti-Humean Turn."

158. Quoted in Rodney Delasanta, "Hume, Austen, and First Impressions," *FT* 134 (June/July 2003): 24–29 at 24.

159. Russell Hittinger, "The Two Cities and the Modern World: A Dawsonian Assessment," *MA* 28, 2/3 (1984): 193–202 at 193.

160. James Buchan, *Crowded with Genius: The Scottish Enlightenment, Edinburgh's Mo-

Kant's parallel exercise, caught in the title of his *Religion within the Boundaries of Reason Alone* (1793), was a paradigm of the drive to place all public discourse within the boundaries of the immanent.[161] Religion was to be reduced to moral categories from which the transcendent had been excised.[162] Sacraments are no longer instrumental means of communicating grace, but at most symbols of the conscience.[163] Kant's notion that religion should only be allowed to inhabit a territory bounded by reason had been centuries in formation. It had been built on a legitimate enterprise found, for instance, in Plato's subjection of received myth to rational analysis, an analysis, however, which with Plato had aimed only at purifying "myth" (narrative stories about the nature of the world), not at eliminating it.[164] In the Middle Ages Averroes had gone much further and proposed that only philosophy is unconditionally true: however, revealed theology—philosophy for the non-philosophical—could be allowed a continued existence as a palliative for the masses. Marsilio Ficino (1433–99) in turn claimed a substantive equivalence for religion and philosophy, and Giordano Bruno, advancing a new form of Averroism, taught a religion for philosophers superior to the superstition of the masses.[165] All this came to term in Kant.

Listen to the viciousness of Kant's language, the way in which his liberalism bludgeons the religious man to give up his life: "Striving for what is supposed to be communion with God is religious *fanaticism*. . . . The fanatical religious illusion . . . is the moral death of reason."[166] The "su-

---

ment of the Mind (New York: HarperCollins, 2003), and John Brewer, "Breaking with the Past," *NYRB* 51, 5 (March 25, 2004): 14–16, are both good on the tensions and contradictions of the Scottish Enlightenment.

161. Cf. Benedict XVI, Regensburg lecture of September 12, 2006 (modified official translation of the Holy See), "Faith, Reason and the University: Memories and Reflections," on Kant's anchoring of "faith exclusively in practical reason, denying it access to reality as a whole." The pope speaks of the "modern self-limitation of reason" as classically represented by the *Critiques*. J. Judd Owen, *Religion and the Demise of Liberal Rationalism: The Foundational Crisis of the Separation of Church and State* (Chicago: University of Chicago Press, 2001), considers current criticisms of the entire liberal tradition in this matter. See also Hent de Vries, *Philosophy and the Turn to Religion* (Baltimore: Johns Hopkins University Press, 1999), for an attempt to rethink the secular Enlightenment.

162. H. Tristram Engelhardt, Jr., "Life & Death After Christendom: The Moralization of Religion & the Culture of Death," *Touchstone* 14, 5 (June 2001): 18–26 at 24. On Hume's parallel project (to Kant's) to eliminate the possibility of miracles, see Earman, *Hume's Abject Failure*.

163. Gerhard Ludwig Müller, "Can Mankind Understand the Spirit of the Liturgy Anymore?" *Antiphon* 7, 2 (2002): 2–5 at 3.

164. Paul O'Callaghan, "Is Christianity a Religion? The Role of Violence, Myth and Witness in Religion," *FCSQ* 29, 4 (Winter 2006): 13–28 at 21; and see the excellent book by Julien Ries, *Il mito e il suo significato* (Milan: Jaca Book, 2005, tr. of French original), 41.

165. On these figures see O'Callaghan, "Is Christianity a Religion?" 17.

166. Immanuel Kant, *Religion Within the Limits of Reason Alone,* tr. T. M. Greene and H. H. Hudson (New York: Harper Torchbooks, 1960), 162–63, quoted with further passages in Engelhardt, "Life and Death after Christendom," at 26. Cf. the brilliant essay of Alfonso Carrasco Rouco, "History and Revelation: Critical Access to the Figure of Jesus Christ," *Co* 30 (2003): 130–46. On the evolution of liberalism and the contingency of its assumptions, see Richard Bellamy, *Liberalism*

perstitious belief of divine worship" is to be rejected, and with it, in the words of a perceptive interpreter of Kant, "holiness ceases to be union with the transcendent and comes instead to mean . . . conformity to the moral law."[167] The goal is "eternal peace," that is, that all submit uniformly to a universal order of rights aiming not at the Augustinian idea of peace, a well-ordered or just society, but at the absence of violence so prized by bourgeois and commercial society.[168] Whether Hume's dismissal of theology as meaningless, or Kant's dismissal of the possibility of Revelation is followed, we are close to Voltaire's *écraser l'infâme*, "crush the infamous thing, Christianity."[169] Hegel (1770–1831) had only to add that not only does philosophy surpass religion, but with the appearance of philosophy there is a "speculative Good Friday" on which the God of religion dies and the Absolute Spirit of philosophy arises.[170]

Europeans, and after them much of the world, have now in significant measure come to live fractured, Cartesian lives. The anthropocentric ordering of life forming in the early modern period only diminished in the twentieth century in the face of "mass man," that is, man made anonymous by a totalitarian state or by the conditions of industrial labor or by drugs or by a music which blocks reflection and self-consciousness. Here we have the "hollow man" and "global youth culture" which is one possibility of modernity, a turn from the individualism which characterized the earlier modern period toward something less personal. With this the fracture of the cosmos becomes even more profound, because it involves not only the loss of a

---

and Modern Society: A Historical Argument (University Park: Pennsylvania State University Press, 1992).

167. The first quotation is from Kant, *Religion Within the Limits of Reason,* 109, the second from Engelhardt, "Life and Death after Christendom," 25.

168. Volker Gerhardt, *Immanuel Kants Entwurf 'Zum ewigen Frieden'. Eine Theorie der Politik* (Darmstadt: Wissenschaftliche Buchgesellschaft, 1995). The rather impious (or impish) Eastern Orthodox theologian David B. Hart, "The Laughter of the Philosophers," *FT* 149 (January 2005): 31–37 at 31, writes of "the sublime spiritual sterility of the texts of Kant's philosophical maturity." As the next chapter should make clear, I would not want to attack all forms of the idea that there are universal human rights, but the idea has caused problems since antiquity: see G. E. R. Lloyd, *Ancient Worlds, Modern Reflections: Philosophical Perspectives on Greek and Chinese Science and Culture* (New York: Oxford University Press, 2004), 155–68, "Human Nature and Human Right."

169. Delasanta, "Hume, Austen, and First Impressions," 27. Hart, "Laughter of the Philosophers," 34, recalls Baudelaire's view in his *Journaux intimes* that Voltaire was no more than a "pastor to the concierges." Though of course not working at the level of Hume or Kant, in one way the shared mission of these men—hardly ever discussed in the histories of philosophy—was to make straight the path for the life they found around them by attack on tradition.

170. O'Callaghan, "Is Christianity a Religion?" 17. Hegel was not always such a "Whig." In his treatment of art, he sensibly argued that the history of medieval art should not be measured by the degree to which it embraced or departed from classical principles, but according to its own principles and conventions: Conrad Rudolph, "A Sense of Loss: An Overview of the Historiography of Romanesque and Gothic Art," in *A Companion to Medieval Art,* ed. Conrad Rudolph (Oxford: Blackwell, 2006), 295–313.

shared history and vision of the world, a shared context in which to live, but also a shrinking of the ego itself attendant on loss of memory.[171]

The paradox, not widely recognized, is that the emphasis on creativity in recent centuries, fed in movements such as modernism by a certain disdain for past achievement, is now reversing course, revealing what always was the logical result of attack on the past, a shrinking of memory and then of the ego that modern individualism had so prized. Gadamer, who tried to show why the modern drive for the autonomy of especially theory from tradition was bound to fail, recalled his contemporaries not to the naïve realism of the Greeks but to a hermeneutic awareness that all reflection begins and remains within a tradition that was in place before reflection began. Thus in the early modern period, still supported by various traditions, the ego expanded as the locus of creativity. Now in many circles, because it cannot survive without memory, it is contracting. Of course this is being mightily aided by the electronic revolution, which shrinks vocabulary, memory, and important forms of attention, above all those founded in contemplation and silence.

Though in one sense Kant and his form of liberalism raised the individual to the status of a sovereign, apparently expanding the domain of the ego and that which it judges, this same individual, set free from tradition, has come to float in a vacuum as the lord of a landscape with no clear boundaries.[172] Martin Buber (1878–1965) said that the I-thou or personal relation of the self to God and the world of previous religious culture was being or had been replaced with an I-it or impersonal relation between an autonomous self and all else. But now we can see this autonomous self, precisely because autonomous and less and less marked by any specific historical tradition, is becoming anonymous and losing consciousness.[173] If we take postmodernism seriously, with its insistence that the person is only a social construct, we should not be surprised to see the "I" disappear.

The further we move into the lands of Orthodoxy and Islam, the less serious the fracture of the cosmos sometimes has been, and the less pronounced the anthropocentrism, but few, for good or ill, at present can avoid its effects. In much of the West, these effects involve both the fracturing of old worldviews and the emergence of new ones. For example, for

171. Mary Carruthers, *The Craft of Thought: Meditation, Rhetoric, and the Making of Images, 400–1200* (New York: Cambridge University Press, 1998), compares a Middle Ages in which writing was used to aid memory, with a contemporary situation in which it replaces memory. In the background stands Walter J. Ong, *Orality and Literacy: The Technologizing of the Word* (New York: Methuen, 1982).

172. This is one theme treated by Russell Hittinger, *The First Grace: Rediscovering the Natural Law in a Post-Christian World* (Wilmington, Del.: ISI Books, 2003).

173. *I and Thou*. A new translation with a prologue, "I and You," and notes by Walter Kaufmann (New York: Scribner, 1970).

many, even those aware of the devastating attacks launched on Freudianism for now more than a generation, the language of Freud has become a surrogate religion in a world from which revealed religion has been removed. Indeed, Ludwig Wittgenstein observed that Freudianism, with its promise of deep meaning, restores a certain mystery to a secularized world.[174] Although presumably Freud would role over in his grave at the suggestion, from one point of view Freudianism presents us a more modern cosmos, resacralized in its own way, to replace what we have lost.

The fracture of the cosmos and loss of the self can be mitigated or shown to have desirable outcomes in various ways. Rather than fight a constantly shifting modernity all down the line, John Paul II tried to enlist the modern turn to the self and subjectivity itself, which seemed to him permanent, in service of a phenomenological examination of human interior experience, especially of freedom.[175] This was to capitalize on the modern turn to the self so as to understand more about the nature of humans than previously possible. That said, especially from the viewpoint of the relatively optimistic anthropologies of the Orthodox tradition, the splintering of the cosmos is much to be regretted.[176] From the viewpoint of Catholicism, and in some ways of classical Protestantism, assessment of the cosmic splintering is more complicated than most of Orthodoxy suggests, and is at once regrettable and unregrettable. For Catholicism especially, although modern Western man probably possesses a false view of the self which for shorthand purposes we can label punctual or Cartesian, the idea that the cosmos is fractured and at least much coherence gone does, as said above, correspond to the human situation after the Fall, in which man is a being capable of great good and great evil living in a world fractured by sin.

From this point of view, especially the early Greek Christian thinkers too easily approved the cosmic harmonies of pagan thought and paganism's optimistic reading of what man is. Conversely, they underappreciated the radicalness of the Pauline declaration (Rom 7:18, Jerusalem version) "instead of doing the good things I want to do, I carry out the sinful things I do not want." Augustine was then a necessary corrective to earlier Christian

174. Lee Patterson, "Chaucer's Pardoner on the Couch: Psyche and Clio in Medieval Literary Studies," *Sp* 76 (2001): 638–80, is at once a serious survey of the question, and very amusing: see here 638–40. See also the very interesting reflections on Wittgenstein's ideas about aesthetics and aesthetic response in Thomas H. Connolly, "The Tuning of Heaven: The Aesthetic of the Pórtico de la Gloria," in *El Códice Calixtino y la música de su tiempo*, ed. José López-Calo and Carlos Villanueva (A Coruña: Fundación Pedro Barrié de la Maza, 2001), 95–110, at 96, 103–9.

175. Francis Cardinal George, "The Anthropological Foundations of John Paul II's Social Thought," *CSSR* 5 (2000): 11–15 at 12.

176. Paul Valliere, *Modern Russian Theology: Bukharev, Soloviev, Bulgakov: Orthodox Theology in a New Key* (Grand Rapids, Mich.: Eerdmans, 2000), is a study of the Russian school of theology, which tries to restore a cosmic dimension to Christianity. See also *Sergii Bulgakov: Towards a Russian Political Theology*, ed. Rowan Williams (Edinburgh: T & T Clark, 1999).

acceptance of a flattering but false view of human nature. He warned that the race is always *in peregrinatio* and always lives fractured lives. He in turn was appropriately corrected or completed by the Baroque sense that there is a certain irreducible theatricality or provisionality in any human drawing of the cosmos. The point then is that all the visions of cosmic harmony are about our first and last state, about the degree to which we walk by faith and hope, and about the degree to which, even as fallen creatures in a disordered world, we can anticipate what it will mean to live forever with God.

Added to the dividing of Europe over the question of "true religion" symbolized by the Peace of Westphalia of 1648 was its subsequent division between the parties of religion and irreligion.[177] Especially in Catholic Europe, an old Church, formerly at the center of society and deeply involved in all aspects of life, though often under royal domination rather than free to pursue its own purposes, was from the late eighteenth century confronted by a laicism intent on driving it to the margins of life, if not eliminating it altogether. Deeply resented as an integral part of an *ancien regime* from which the revolutionary wished to be freed, the Church seemed a natural enemy. Many saw in the subsequent Russian Revolution a continuation of the ideas of the French Revolution, and still in the mid-twentieth century many on the European and American left insisted that the Soviet Union was a force for progress. Outside explicitly Counter-Enlightenment and Counter-Revolutionary writers, who often attempted more a rejection than a weighing of the Enlightenment, rare has been a critique aiming at delineation of the limits of the Enlightenment, rather than simply praise or blame.[178] As Hans Urs von Balthasar insisted, we must not forget that along with the decline of an older synthesis of God and man and the appearance of ahistorical notions of the nature of human reason and the individual in the modern period went advances in understanding the human subject, especially and precisely as a historical being.[179]

---

177. Darrin M. McMahon, *Enemies of the Enlightenment: The French Counter-Enlightenment and the Making of Modernity* (New York: Oxford University Press, 2001), traces the thought of critics of the Enlightenment, and see *The Barbarism of Reason: Max Weber and the Twilight of Enlightenment*, ed. Asher Horowitz and Terry Maley (Toronto: University of Toronto Press, 1994), and Keith Michael Baker and Peter Hanns Reill, *What's Left of Enlightenment? A Postmodern Question* (Stanford, Calif.: Stanford University Press, 2001). It is common to observe the diversity of Enlightenment thought: Jonathan I. Israel, *Radical Enlightenment: Philosophy and the Making of Modernity 1650–1750* (New York: Oxford University Press, 2001). On these issues, see my "The Two Europes," *The European Legacy: Toward New Paradigms. Journal of the International Society for the Study of European Ideas* 14, 1 (2009): 133–48.

178. Leon Chai, *Jonathan Edwards and the Limits of Enlightenment Philosophy* (New York: Oxford University Press, 1998). Cf. Hugo Meynell, *Postmodernism and the New Enlightenment* (Washington, D.C.: The Catholic University of America Press, 1999).

179. Aidan Nichols, *Scattering the Seed: A Guide through Balthasar's Early Writings on Philosophy and the Arts* (Washington, D.C.: The Catholic University of America Press, 2006).

The story and pace of secularization and the driving of religion from public life has varied from country to country.[180] The Kantian idea of the rational state was central: if the norm by which government is to be judged is efficiency and "reason," kings will seem less and less divine or God-connected and more and more human and fallible.[181] In France well before the Revolution the monarchy accelerated secularization, though not always with a full understanding of the likely impact of its actions. Thus Robert Darnton saw an important step in secularization occurring in 1739, when, rather than abandon his mistress Mme. De Mailly, Louis XV refused to undergo the traditional Easter confession, penance, and communion.[182] This deprived him of the royal touch, the ability to heal scrofula, for only a king in a state of grace could perform this ritual. Whereas in 1722 at his coronation Louis had touched more than two thousand of the diseased, by 1749 he had lost his place as mediator between God and his people. All ranks criticized him and expressed fear of God's wrath on the kingdom because of his refusal to confess. Louis had, so to speak, disconnected the monarchy from God.

Louis's act was more the result of personal weakness than a consciously desired secularization of life. Not so with the Jacobins later in the century, who, viewing themselves as the bearers of a bright, de-Christianized future, consciously tried to remove traditional religion from public life, presenting themselves in this as the embodiment and instrument of the general will. In a kind of parody of the earlier Christian sacramentalization of time, they eventually replaced the seven-day week and festivals of Christianity with a "rational" ten-day week, redefining *homo adorans,* man the adorer of God, as a being just of this world.[183] From the Jacobins of the late eighteenth century there is a fairly direct descent to, in a hard form, the party rule of Communism, or, in a softer form, the maintenance of the lay, secularizing, tradition at Brussels.[184] All these are a form of "the struggle for moder-

---

180. Cf. David Torevel, *Losing the Sacred: Ritual, Modernity and Liturgical Reform* (Edinburgh: T & T Clark, 2000).

181. Paul Kléber Monod, *The Power of Kings: Monarchy and Religion in Europe 1589–1715* (New Haven, Conn.: Yale University Press, 1999).

182. "Paris: The Early Internet," *NYRB* 47, 11 (June 29, 2000): 42–47 at 44 and 46, for this and the following.

183. Josef Pieper, *In Tune with the World: A Theory of Festivity,* tr. Richard and Clara Winston (New York: Harcourt, Brace & World, 1965).

184. Nicolas Sarkozy joked at a European Union meeting, "I'm the only non-Socialist in the delegation": Elaine Sciolino, "Socialist Quits French Left to Join Right," *NYT,* July 19, 2007. In addition to my "The Quest for a Public Philosophy in Twentieth Century American Political Thought," *Co* 27 (2000): 340–62, see François Furet, *The Passing of an Illusion: The Idea of Communism in the Twentieth Century,* tr. Deborah Furet (Chicago: University of Chicago Press, 1999), 63–64, for the argument that the Bolsheviks added science and the logic of history to the Jacobinism they had received from the French Revolution.

nity."[185] In Germany with time we have the *Kulturkampf* against Catholicism, which in the event far from succeeded.[186]

Though Konrad Adenauer had considerable truth on his side when he judged that a Europe of national states had become irrelevant to the post–World War II situation, and that Western Europe had to be integrated into something like a United States of Europe, as it turned out the European Union became captive to the lay tradition.[187] Today in all kinds of ways the European Union continues to impose on Europe the vision of the lay party, for instance, in the controversy over whether the religion entry may remain on identity cards in Greece.[188] Here the Socialists as a part of efforts to follow EU trends in regard to privacy and civil rights, confronted the Greek Orthodox Church in a classic replay of the struggle between the lay and religious parties. The policy of the former has been to insist that only a liberal state and society in which religion is not a part of national identity is compatible with membership in the European Union. The goal of the latter has been to retain a traditional form of life with an established national religion that allows citizens to order public life by something other than liberalism. Whatever side one takes, one can hardly deny "the bad 'fit' between Orthodox Greece, NATO, and the EU," and this is but one part of a much larger story being written all over Europe.[189] On July 3, 2002, the Strasbourg parliament adopted a report of one of its committees demanding that abortion be made "legal, safe and accessible to all," and easy abortion a condition for membership in the European Union.[190]

While most of us have been sensitized to view the position of the Greek Orthodox Church as intolerant, or rather to view its form of intolerance as bad, we much less commonly recognize that the position of the European Union is equally intolerant, and not at all neutral about what goods can publicly be recognized.[191] Americans sometimes forget that much of

185. Eli Sagan, *Citizens and Cannibals: The French Revolution, the Struggle for Modernity, and the Origins of Ideological Terror* (Lanham, Md.: Rowman & Littlefield, 2001).

186. Ronald J. Ross, *The Failure of Bismarck's Kulturkampf: Catholicism and State Power in Imperial Germany, 1871–1887* (Washington, D.C.: The Catholic University of America Press, 1998).

187. Gordon A. Craig, "Founding Father," *NYRB* 48, 117 (November 1, 2001): 17–21 at 17.

188. "Greece's Plan to Drop Religion from ID Card Causes Uproar" (Associated Press), *DN*, September 2, 2000, used in the following, notes that 97 percent of the Greek population is baptized in the Greek Church. Though not specifically about religion, the attempt of the European Union to sanction Austria for allowing a far-right party into the government is another example of the EU continuation of the Jacobin tradition: see the New York Times Service article "Panel Clears Way to End Sanctions on Austria," *DN*, September 9, 2000.

189. Victoria Clark, *Why Angels Fall: A Journey Through Orthodox Europe from Byzantium to Kosovo* (New York: St. Martin's Press, 2000), with the review by Walter D. Connor, "The Burdens of History," *FT* 115 (August/September 2001): 59–61 at 59, for the phrase quoted.

190. "Report Demands Abortion Access," *IC*, 64, 26 (July 12, 2002): 2.

191. A. J. Conyers, *The Long Truce: How Toleration Made the World Safe for Power and Profit*

the European elite do not believe in democracy, and that the European Union often proceeds on the premise that things should be done without informing or involving the people, this nowhere more than in the case of religion.[192] Very much the same issues found in regard to the Greek Orthodox Church are found in Turkey in the question of whether there can be any compromise of the secularist tradition of Atatürk with resurgent Islam, a question again debated with one eye to the European Union.[193] A harder case, leaving Europe altogether, is Afghanistan, over which this time UNESCO and at least some spokesmen of traditional society are at loggerheads over such basic questions as whether women's education is desirable.[194]

In the United States not many years ago, former Chief Justice of the Supreme Court William Rehnquist wrote that one ruling on public prayer by his colleagues "bristles with hostility to all things religious in public life."[195] The Anti-Defamation League, a Jewish organization committed to the complete exclusion of religion from public life, asked the first American Jewish candidate for vice presidential office to stop expressing his religious beliefs in his campaign speeches, and specifically rebuked his comment that he would like to reinstate "a place for faith in America's public life."[196] According to Andrew J. Glass, this expressed a continuing "struggle between tradition-minded 'Orthodox' Jews and modern 'progressive' Jews, whose forebears were strongly influenced by the European Enlightenment and who have generally sought to assimilate themselves into the mainstream culture."[197] One combatant in this struggle, David Novak, thinking specifically of Israel, wrote in defense of transcendent religious criteria by which the state is to be both judged and inspired.[198]

(Dallas: Spence, 2001), gives a decent account of the history of toleration, and the spread of the notion that public life belongs to the state.

192. Joseph S. Lucas, "Interview with David Brooks," *HS* 4, 4 (April 2003): 37–39 at 38.

193. Christopher de Bellaigue, "Turkey's Hidden Past," *NYRB* 48, 4 (March 8, 2001): 37–40.

194. Pankaj Mishra, "The Afghan Tragedy," *NYRB* 49, 1 (January 17, 2002): 43–49 at 44.

195. William Rehnquist in dissent from the June 2000 declaration of the Supreme Court against student prayer before public-school football games, as quoted in Jene Kartchner, "Judge's Warning Is Scary," *DN*, August 29, 2000. Public prayer is to many liberal Americans what the veil is to laicist Frenchmen or Turks of the left, a sign that the lay party does not have complete hegemony over public space. I realize that in Europe the lay party so dominates public space that the whole American discussion of whether there can be prayer before public-school events seems quaint. Control over "public time" is a bit different, and in Germany and Poland one still has serious arguments about the status of Sunday.

196. "Lieberman Urged to Tone Down Religious Talk" (Associated Press), *DN*, August 29, 2000. Gustav Niebuhr, "Can U.S. Allow More Religion in Politics?" (New York Times News Service), *DN*, September 2, 2000, places the debate in longer historical perspective, as does Charles Krautheimer, "Lieberman's Religiosity Has Demos over a Barrel," *DN*, September 10, 2000.

197. "Lieberman Fights Bias from His Fellow Jews" (Cox News Service), *DN*, September 3, 2000.

198. "What's Best for the Jews?" *FT* 110 (February 2001): 37–42 at 42.

The nineteenth and twentieth centuries were torn between various authoritarianisms of the right and left. Though some have espied the nation-state's demise—we have already met various views on the issue—the nation-state in fact fared rather well, continuing its centuries-old struggle for hegemony over society.[199] The putatively most obvious alternative to the Continental authoritarianisms, liberalism in its nineteenth-century English form, offered itself as at least a partial alternative, based in individual rights and the limited state, to the logic of a state-secured hegemony over life, whether in alliance with or opposed to religion. Originally, like Protestantism before it, classical liberalism could afford to exalt the individual and freedom because it inhabited a fairly uniform society living off the legacy of the past. It did not have particularly to worry about the logic of exalting freedom and individualism—that is, about the potential of such emphasis for the destruction of social consensus—partly because one of the legacies of the past was the doctrine of natural rights, an attenuated form of natural law thought which still carried a notion of transcendence which limited the possible actions of the state.

Liberalism and liberal democracy in especially the second half of the twentieth century revealed their potential for social dissolution, and indeed especially late-twentieth-century American liberalism commonly presented itself as not about shared notions of the good at all, but as a form of government which is neutral and procedural and leaves each to pursue the good as he or she conceives it within civil society. There could be no social consensus about "the highest things" in such a situation, and pragmatic positions which defied logic were common, such as the simultaneous exaltation of the individual and of the common good.[200] Whatever one thinks of François Furet's autumnal reflections on the follies he shared with the twentieth century, he made a good case for the responsibility of nineteenth-century liberalism in the destruction of the social fabric and the formation of the bourgeois self-loathing that underlay so much twentieth-century tragedy.[201] Although this does not appear to have been its intention, a recent book about the first generation after the Declaration of Independence inadvertently traces the origins of this contradictory blend of individualism and civic piety.[202] The book's argument is that a kind of liberal consen-

199. James Traub, "Sierra Leone: The Worst Place on Earth," *NYRB* 47, 11 (June 29, 2000): 61–66 at 65.

200. Thinkers such as Jürgen Habermas speak at one and the same time of a neutral constitutional order and of orientation to the common good, redefining the common good to mean not something universally good for man but what through discussion a group of citizens determine to be their good: "Pre-political Foundations of the Democratic Constitutional State?" in Joseph Ratzinger and Jürgen Habermas, *Dialectics of Secularization: On Reason and Religion,* ed. Florian Schuller, tr. Brian McNeil (San Francisco: Ignatius Press, 2007), 24–28, 30, 43.

201. Furet, *Passing of an Illusion,* and see the review of Eric D. Weitz in *AHR* 105 (2000): 884–85 at 884.

202. Joyce Appleby, *Inheriting the Revolution: The First Generation of Americans* (Cambridge,

sus appeared in the first generation of the American Republic, organized around individualism and free enterprise.

Louis Menand, describing America a good half-century later, observed that what in America has been called pragmatism was a specific response to the way in which high moral and religious conviction led to the ghastly bloodiness of the American Civil War.[203] Alexis de Tocqueville had noticed a strong tendency to pragmatism deeply rooted in America, but what Menand had his eye on was what we might call the "higher pragmatism" of learned people such as Oliver Wendell Holmes, William James, and John Dewey, which built on and attempted to justify the American de facto pragmatism noted by de Tocqueville.[204] This higher pragmatism often aimed at weaning Americans from religious and ideological conviction, though in the case of William James it took the form of approval of religion as long as it was useful or "worked," making one perhaps more generous or self-sacrificing.[205] Transcendent imperatives were to be renounced. Just as in Europe the liberal tradition had laid the blame for the awful wars of the seventeenth century on religion, the pragmatists took the Civil War as exemplifying the dangers religion presents for public peace. In the case of Dewey, the category "experience" loomed large, and in an Emersonian fashion cut the ground from under any educational imperative to study ancient and foreign languages and more generally to master past tradition: indeed, education was to aim at challenging the core beliefs of the civilization. In the United States since Dewey's day, many educational "reforms" have been one or another form of revolt: against a canon, against religious values, now against even grammar and memorization.[206]

The argument has been that this, relatively speaking, freed the individual from age-old social bonds and hierarchies, and freed economic practice from the judgment of God and universal rules of justice. As we have noted, in America the emphasis on *libertas* sat in company with—was in some degree kept in check by—a civil religion organized around devotion to America itself.[207] We might speak of a Jeffersonian tradition in continuing

---

Mass.: Belknap Press, 2000). See the review of this book by Gordon S. Wood, "Early American Get-Up-and-Go," *NYRB* 47, 11 (June 29, 2000): 50–53.

203. *The Metaphysical Club* (New York: Farrar, Straus and Giroux, 2001); and see Alan Ryan, "The Group," *NYRB* 48, 9 (May 31, 2001): 16–20.

204. Holmes has stood high in the American legal tradition to the present, which remains overwhelmingly pragmatic, but see his treatment by the thoughtful Joseph W. Dellapenna, *Dispelling the Myths of Abortion History* (Durham, N.C.: Carolina Academic Press, 2005).

205. Garry Wills, "An American Hero," *NYRB* 54, 12 (July 19, 2007): 43–44 at 44.

206. Henry T. Edmonson III, *John Dewey and the Decline of American Education* (Wilmington, Del.: ISI Books, 2006).

207. Glenn W. Olsen, "American Culture and Liberal Ideology in the Thought of Christopher Dawson," *Co* 22 (1995): 702–20, and "Religion, Politics, and America at the Millennium," *FR* 22 (1996): 285–315.

struggle with an Adamic tradition, the latter named after John Adams. In the former, actually a quite minor position at the beginning which has only come to full fruition since the 1940s, the goal was the privatizing of religion and the secularizing of politics in the fashion of European lay politics. The latter, Adamic, tradition, which does not believe it possible to achieve a state neutral in matters of public policy or religion understood as a set of common values, has responded with an attempt to balance the various religions, thought of as private, against one public religion, the latter an historically ever-changing amalgam of shared beliefs we can call civil religion. We might say that Adams's belief was in a "tempered" religious freedom, built on an established (civic) religion. For more than the last half century, the Supreme Court has been on the side of the Jeffersonian view, and has cut off many of the traditional ways in which the state had participated in and patronized religion. Some argue that decisions since the mid-1980s suggest that the Court is backing off its more radically separationist views in favor of protecting both private and public forms of religion.[208] In any case, after a long period of dominance of liberal Supreme Court justices, George W. Bush significantly moved the Court to the right.

Historically evolved American public or civil religion has tended toward the non-transcendental or horizontal, replacing especially liturgical and contemplative categories with such things as veneration of the founding constitutional documents and flag, and celebration of national holidays such as the Fourth of July. This has favored the formation of a people enclosed in a world of work, enterprise, and money-making, and the formation of a religion centered on such non-contemplative categories as the doing of good deeds. Of course the United States was from the first a largely Protestant country, and in some degree these developments merely reflect ways in which Protestantism had already changed Christianity elsewhere. In any case, when liberals and communitarians debate in the present, liberals tend to reveal an individualism which trumps all other social values. Seen in this perspective, the term "civil society" is a kind of reduction of what formerly social life was thought to be about to categories of civility and enlightened discussion. In such liberalism the individual now stands severed not only from the cosmos, but from any large idea of a common

208. I am following the terminology and analysis of John Witte Jr., "Publick Religion: Adams v. Jefferson," *FT* 141 (March 2004): 29–34. Witte's "public religion" might be described as a part-surrogate for "natural law," one alternative in a (Protestant) tradition which has little idea of natural law. Witte cites article 2 of the Massachusetts Constitution of 1780 as an embodiment of Adam's principles: "It is the right as well as the duty of all men in society, publickly, and at stated seasons to worship the Supreme Being, the great Creator and preserver of the Universe" (31). Witte acknowledges that the religion approved by the recent Court is often no more than "ceremonial deism," but it is unclear why he thinks that a public religion in a pluralist society could be more than this, could avoid a "crass" reading of religion of the form of Sandra Day O'Connor's (32–33).

good. Civil society is conceived after the order of a very large debating society engaged in an unending Habermannian dialogue from which such
transcendentals as the simply true tend to be excluded in principle, though
in fact certain values probably are treated as self-evidently true and unde-
batable.[209]

The large question is whether liberalism and liberal democracy represent an attack on man himself, or a forgetfulness of what man is. There
always has existed in Western society a powerful anti-democratic tradition,
in which most of the principal thinkers of the ancient, medieval, and early modern worlds stood along with dissenters to the present.[210] One can
wonder whether modern democratic theory more circumvents the classical
objections to democracy than responds to them. That is, a good argument
can be made that humans are by nature social and religious animals and
are naturally oriented not to self-fulfillment but to flourishing in relations
with others, relations first to family, then to community, nature, God, and
the transcendentals. And while liberalism seriously fails in nourishing these
basic human orientations, much democratic theory is utopian, forcing us
in quest of equality to level distinctions rooted in the order of things such
as natural human inequality. Fair observation leads to the conclusion that
humans are by nature unequal, but liberal and democratic theory urges the
opposite, and thus must sponsor an "attack on nature," in the name of its
own soft utopianism.

From this point of view, though in many respects the Enlightenment
achieved genuine critical advances in human understanding, there was
something instinctively right about much Romantic hostility toward it,
though Romanticism was in turn in some of its representatives as unbalanced about what man is as had been the "enlightened ones."[211] We must
sympathize with Giacomo Leopardi's (1798–1837) turn to the ancient Greek
fables as

the mysterious remnants of a world where reason hadn't yet been able to unleash
the full effects of its lethal power, "a power that 'renders all objects to which it

209. Alan Ryan, "The Power of Positive Thinking," *NYRB* 50, 1 (January 16, 2003): 43–46,
is an exposition of Jürgen Habermas's thought which helpfully compares him to American pragmatism.

210. Jennifer Tolbert Roberts, *Athens on Trial: The Antidemocratic Tradition in Western
Thought* (Princeton, N.J.: Princeton University Press, 1996). The depth of this tradition is sometimes obscured today by such goofy attempts as that by Martha C. Nussbaum to make Aristotle
into a liberal democrat.

211. For orientation to recent discussion and criticism of Enlightenment ideas about the
range of reason and human psychology, see John Gray, *Enlightenment's Wake: Politics and Culture
at the Close of the Modern Age* (New York: Routledge, 1995). Neil Postman, *Building a Bridge to
the Eighteenth Century: How the Past Can Improve Our Future* (New York: Knopf, 1999), is an
attempt to evaluate and reappropriate certain of the values of the Enlightenment, as is Meynell,
Postmodernism.

turns its attention small and vile and empty, destroys the great and the beautiful and even, as it were, existence itself.'"[212]

A host of Russian and Orthodox writers may have been unable to separate the wheat from the tares here, but there is something profoundly human, if narrow, in Dostoevsky's (1821–81) reaction to what reason had become in the West.[213] Unleashed, as in Comte, Nietzsche, Feuerbach, and Marx, it had become a prime source of atheism, even, at one stage, for Dostoevsky's own doubts. Dostoevsky used such characters as Roskolnikov and Stavrogin to portray what the consequences of this atheism were, and then, on the other side of atheism, Alyosha and Fr. Zosima as exemplars of the transcendent beauty, goodness, and sanctity which can emerge in the midst of life.[214]

⌒

Just as there was something instinctively right about Romanticism, there was something profoundly human not so much in party-Fascism as in the ideas which led many to be sympathetic in the 1920s and 30s to some of the things that Fascism stood for as a reaction to the intense individualism, modernism, and technologization of twentieth-century life.[215] From Nietzsche to postmodernism, there has been a certain romance with the ideas that formed Fascism.[216] During the Weimar period a "longing for community" had developed which continued aspects of Romantic universalism. Even many Catholics, who in Germany had long been subject to the pres-

212. Charles Simic, "Paradise Lost," *NYRB* 48, 14 (September 20, 2001): 62–64 at 62.

213. Cf. Dale Pesmen, *Russia and Soul: An Exploration* (Ithaca, N.Y.: Cornell University Press, 2000), part 5, on Dostoevsky and love. Dostoevsky is one of the four thinkers who found means of overcoming secular messianism considered by David Walsh, *After Ideology: Recovering the Spiritual Foundations of Freedom* (Washington, D.C.: The Catholic University of America Press, 1995).

214. Henri de Lubac, *The Drama of Atheist Humanism,* foreword by Hans Urs von Balthasar (New York: Sheed & Ward, 1950).

215. Roger Eatwell, *Fascism: A History* (New York: Allen Lane, 1996), is particularly interested in the development of fascism as a body of thought, as is Mark Neocleous, *Fascism* (Minneapolis: University of Minnesota Press, 1997). Mark Lilla, *The Reckless Mind: Intellectuals in Politics* (New York: New York Review Books, 2001), has useful things to say about such thinkers as Carl Schmitt, and see Adrian Lyttelton, "What Was Fascism?" *NYRB* 51, 16 (October 21, 2004): 33–36. Kevin Repp, *Reformers, Critics, and the Paths of German Modernity: Anti-Politics and the Search for Alternatives, 1890–1914* (Cambridge, Mass.: Harvard University Press, 2000), is a survey of the wide range of German responses to modernity. Ruth Ben-Ghiat, *Fascist Modernities: Italy, 1922–1945* (Berkeley: University of California Press, 2001), argues that fascism was a new model of modernity for many Italian Fascists, allowing modern economic development without obliterating traditional social boundaries and values. Robert O. Paxton, *The Anatomy of Fascism* (New York: Knopf, 2004), shows that fascism tended to abandon its early radical positions, what we might call its cultural critique, as it succeeded by making alliances with more conservative institutions and traditional elites, and that it only succeeded in coming to power where liberalism and democracy seemed incapable of handling social crisis.

216. Richard Wolin, *The Seduction of Unreason: The Intellectual Romance with Fascism: From Nietzsche to Postmodernism* (Princeton, N.J.: Princeton University Press, 2004).

sures of Prussian/Protestant conditioning, abandoned the cosmopolitanism of Rome in favor of a folkish populism. Thus the Hungarian-American historian John Lukacs observed that ultimately the principal fault of German Catholics during the Second World War was not that they were too Catholic, that is, loyal to Rome and a transnational point of view, but that they were too German, that is, nationalistic.[217] Nazism, like Communism, can be understood as, for some, commitment to an apocalyptic myth as the way of righting the times. While in some respects reactions to modernity, in other respects Communism and the various Nazi and Fascist movements expected imminent historical rupture and were forms of modernism which saw themselves ushering in a new world.[218]

A. James Gregor argues in regard to the Italian form of communitarian sentiment that it was no more irrational—faint consolation—than other revolutionary ideologies of the time.[219] For those with eyes to see, the failure of various forms of materialism by the 1930s had created a great vacuum which, one way or another, would be filled.[220] In part Fascism was a "youth movement" which, like modernism generally, encouraged the young to revolt against their elders and create a "new man." Futurism laced Italian Fascist propaganda.[221] And yet, the invocation of such propaganda was also often on behalf of the preservation of many traditional national and social identities and boundaries. Mussolini himself early on attacked authority in all its extant forms, while trying to center it on himself.[222] He may have been as irrational as many modernizers of our own day, who attempt a similar project, but he can be viewed as seeing Fascism as a way of allowing modern economic development within the context of the retention of traditional social values.[223]

Indicative here is the treatment of religion by Fascism. At one level this simply continued the long-standing attempt by the state to control religion. At another, also a long-standing phenomenon, Fascism joined with

217. *Remembered Past: John Lukacs on History, Historians, and Historical Knowledge: a Reader*, ed. Mark G. Malvasi and Jeffrey O. Nelson (Wilmington, Del.: ISI Books, 2005), 515. Christopher Clark, *Iron Kingdom: The Rise and Downfall of Prussia, 1600–1947* (Cambridge, Mass.: Belknap Press, 2006), emphasizes the place of "Prussian values" in Nazism.

218. John Gray, "The Moving Target," *NYRB* 53, 15 (October 5, 2006): 22–24 at 23; Claudio Fogu, *The Historic Imaginary: Politics of History in Fascist Italy* (Toronto: University of Toronto Press, 2003); and Martin Rhonheimer, "The Holocaust: What Was Not Said," *FT* 137 (November 2003): 18–27.

219. *Mussolini's Intellectuals: Fascist Social and Political Thought* (Princeton, N.J.: Princeton University Press, 2005). There is a school of thought that considers Italian Fascism more a style of government than a stable ideology: Amos Elon, "A Shrine to Mussolini," *NYRB* 53, 3 (February 23, 2006): 33–35 at 35. Perhaps the best of the comparative histories is Stanley Payne, *A History of Fascism: 1914–1945* (Madison: University of Wisconsin Press, 1995).

220. Lukacs, *End of an Age*, 183–84.

221. Lyttelton, "What Was Fascism?" 35.

222. Tim Parks, "The Illusionist," *NYRB* 52, 6 (April 7, 2005): 54–58 at 54.

223. Ben-Ghiat, *Fascist Modernities*.

the secularizing tendencies of modern European history in placing religious values in service to nationalist and racial goals.[224] But a case can be made that in both Fascism and Nazism we find a kind of sacralization of politics, in which a new politics formed a new religion around the nation.[225] For those who could believe, politics became a surrogate religion. Here one might speak more of "metamorphosis of the sacred" than of secularization, and this process could in some ways intensify religious sentiment through rallies, etc.[226] Already in the 1930s writers such as Eric Voegelin and Raymond Aron identified Fascism as "political religion."[227] Voegelin saw the totalitarian systems of that day as embodying a kind of reverse religious cosmology, with symbols that were "simulacra of traditional and civic religion."[228] These symbols did not express transcendence, but were "world immanent," turned toward the world and a linear progressive passage of time for their completion or satisfaction.[229]

Many Catholics, especially those who had taken to heart the "corporatist" approach to society of Leo XIII's *Rerum Novarum* (1891) and Pius XI's *Quadragesimo Anno* (1931), felt sympathy for the attempt to put this teaching into practice in Italy, Spain, and Portugal.[230] In England, Catholic intellectuals such as Graham Greene, G. K. Chesterton, and Christopher Dawson, faced by the alternative of a Marxism which a priori excised religion from life, could initially wonder about the possibility of some kind of modus vivendi between Christianity and Fascism.[231] As the many Catholics who supported Franco without enthusiasm, they could at least hope for a degree of respect for their rights as believers absent from Marxism.[232] Even if the Dutch bishops in 1934 warned of the dangers of Fascism, and in 1936 told Catholics that they would risk excommunication if they sup-

224. Lyttelton, "What Was Fascism?" 36. See also Karla Poewe, *New Religions and the Nazis* (London: Routledge, 2006).

225. Emilio Gentile, *The Sacralization of Politics in Fascist Italy,* tr. Keith Botsford (Cambridge, Mass.: Harvard University Press, 1996), and *Politics as Religion,* tr. George Staunton (Princeton, N.J.: Princeton University Press, 2006).

226. Emilio Gentile, "The Sacralization of Politics," in *Totalitarian Movements and Political Religions* (electronic resource) 1, 2 (Summer 2000), 28; also see M. A. Casey, "Democracy and the Thin Veneer of Civilisation," *FCSQ* 29 (Winter 2006): 3–9 at 6.

227. *Politische Religion? Politik, Religion und Anthropologie im Werk von Eric Voegelin,* ed. Michael Ley, Heinrich Neisser, and Gilbert Weiss (Munich: Fink, 2003).

228. The quoted phrase is from Russell Hittinger, "The Churches of Earthly Power," *FT* 164 (June/July, 2006): 27–32 at 27.

229. See especially *The Political Religions* in the collection of his writings, *Modernity without Restraint: The Political Religions, The New Science of Politics and Science, Politics, and Gnosticism,* ed. Manfred Henningsen (Columbia: University of Missouri Press, 2000).

230. In 1935 (August 22) a poorly informed reviewer for the *Times Literary Supplement* wrote of "Papal encyclicals which have a definitely Fascist ring." It would have been more accurate to refer to "Fascist ideas which have a definitely Papal ring."

231. Adam Schwartz, "Swords of Honor: The Revival of Orthodox Christianity in Twentieth-Century Britain," *Lo* 4, 1 (2001): 11–31 at 20, and see 22–25.

232. Ibid., 20–21.

ported Fascist organizations, it is easy to forget that in the 1920s and '30s, prestigious journals such as the *Times Literary Supplement,* if suspicious of Hitler, had many favorable things to say about Mussolini and Italian Fascism, which, among other things, appealed to those of anti-monarchic and anti-clerical views.[233] W. B. Yeats, who throughout his life condemned democracy for both good and bad reasons, combining the serious objections of many nineteenth-century thinkers with a snobbery and consciousness of social class particularly his own, was only one of many intellectuals in the 1930s who saw Fascism as much the lesser evil when compared to socialism, "that mechanical eighteenth-century dream."[234]

We can now view writers such as Joseph Roth (1894–1939) "a socialist but no 'modernist,'" with his deep dislike for "the horrific triumph of technology over humanity;" or moviemakers such as Fritz Lang (1890–1976) in *Metropolis* (1927), as protesting against what the world was becoming in ways with which strains of Fascism could sympathize.[235] Even today the German filmmaker Werner Herzog is accused of "Romanticism" and Nazi affinities because of his loathing for technological civilization and consumer culture and his yearning for ecstasy and the sacred.[236] Both Romanticism and Fascism tried to re-situate human beings who had become alienated from the cosmos and doubtful about the merits of unrestricted human freedom in a more ordered and authoritarian social structure than they had known.[237]

Though liberal writers may now criticize the intense nostalgia for community found in much Fascist thought—but also in Communism and in devotion to one's local sports team—it is not clear that liberal thought has come to terms with the deep human desire for group identity to offer some viable position more respectful of community than the philosophy of "lucid individuality."[238] Richard Wolin is correct, in the light of postmodernism's

233. Ronald J. Rychlak, "Goldhagen v. Pius XII," *FT* 124 (June/July 2002): 37–54 at 50; David Lodge, "Happy Birthday," *NYRB* 49, 9 (May 23, 2002): 48–53 at 50. Lucia Scherzberg, *Kirchenreform mit Hilfe des Nationalsozialismus: Karl Adam als kontextueller Theologe* (Darmstadt: Wissenschaftliche Buchgesellschaft, 2001), gives some sense of how complex the issues were.

234. W. B. Yeats, *Autobiographies* (London: Macmillan, 1955), 537; also see John Banville, "The Rescue of W. B. Yeats," *NYRB* 51, 3 (February 26, 2004): 12–14 at 14.

235. Neal Ascherson, "Goodbye to Berlin," *NYRB* 50, 6 (April 10, 2003): 22–26 at 22, who notes Roth's inconsistency and praise of the city (in contradistinction to the praise of the soil common in Nazism). In the same issue see Julian Barnes, "Holy Hysteria," 32–34 at 33–34.

236. Ian Buruma, "Herzog and His Heroes," *NYRB* 54, 15 (July 19, 2007): 24–26 at 25. Corinna Treitel, *A Science for the Soul: Occultism and the Genesis of the German Modern* (Baltimore: Johns Hopkins University Press, 2004), provides entrance into recent historiography, which shows how complicated the question of the origins of Nazi ideology is: see especially for the criticism of "machine science" before Nazism, Ann Harrington, *Reenchanted Science: Holism in German Culture from Wilhelm II to Hitler* (Princeton, N.J.: Princeton University Press, 1996).

237. Mark Lilla, "Inside the Clockwork," *NYRB* 49, 7 (April 25, 2002): 43–45 at 44–45.

238. The phrase of Tim Parks, "Soccer: A Matter of Love and Hate," *NYRB* 49, 12 (July 18, 2002): 38–40 at 39.

infatuation with Fascism, to question its claim to stand in the inheritance of the left, but it is not so clear that it is adequate to label this infatuation simply as "the seduction of unreason."[239] But Wolin is instructive in showing a lineage running from Fascism to postmodernism.

Zeev Sternhell of the Hebrew University in Jerusalem has attempted a friendly correction to George L. Mosse's treatment of Fascism by arguing:

> The fascist ideology was simply the hard core and the most radical variety of a far more widespread, far older phenomenon: a comprehensive revision of the essential values of the humanistic, rationalistic, and optimistic heritage of the Enlightenment.[240]

Sternhell developed his views in earlier study of Fascist ideology during the Vichy years in France, in which he argued that it was neither of the right nor the left.[241] According to him, French Fascism united anti-bourgeois, anti-liberal nationalism, and syndicalist thought in opposition to eighteenth-century politics.

Sternhell himself believes that the late nineteenth-century rejection of the Enlightenment was a catastrophe, but goes on to remark:

> Fascism appealed to people's imagination because it was concerned with a real problem: the nature of social relationships. Fascism provided attractive answers to some of the questions that preoccupied people in the last two centuries: first of all, what makes a group of humans into a society? . . . What constitutes a nation? Is it a freely expressed option of individuals with equal rights, as the French Revolution in its first years maintained, or history, culture, religion, the ethnic group? . . . What, precisely, is the nature of the common factor that enables people to develop the minimum of solidarity which makes life together possible? What gives life in society a meaning?

Fascism may have been even more unbalanced than Romanticism as a response to the Enlightenment, and there is something to François Furet's view that Fascism continued the revolutionary traditions of Europe rather than opposed them, but the point is that both Romanticism and Fascism raised questions which will not go away.[242]

The Fascist or Nazi state organized vertically around a centralized government directing the various groups in society through their official unions, whether developed then in Germany, or now in Egypt, clearly was a disaster,

239. *Seduction of Unreason.*

240. Review, *AHR* 105 (2000): 882–83 at 883. Cf. Zeev Sternhell, with Mario Sznajder and Maia Asheri, *The Birth of Fascist Ideology: From Cultural Rebellion to Political Revolution,* tr. David Maisel (Princeton, N.J.: Princeton University Press, 1994), and the exchange of letters between Sternhell and Adrian Lyttelton in *NYRB* 52, 8 (May 12, 2005): 52–53.

241. *Neither Right nor Left: Fascist Ideology in France* (Berkeley: University of California Press, 1986).

242. Furet, *Passing of an Illusion.* Tim Parks, "The Non-Conformist," *NYRB* 47, 14 (September 21, 2000): 30–35, is an interesting reading of the internal contradictions of Italian Fascism.

especially the attempt by the state to monopolize public discourse and the attempt by a state bureaucracy to form one national voice.[243] No better a response to the "problems which will not go away" was the nihilist intellectual stance of Isaiah Berlin, in which reason opposed all totalitarian unities but was itself incapable of resolving the deep conflict between values people felt.[244] Similarly, the "phyletist" tradition of Orthodox Europe, in which religion and nationality tend to merge and nurse a profound sense of victimhood rooted in the remote past (1453? 1204?), cannot be a point of departure for any serious reflection on the future of Eastern Europe.[245] This phyletist tradition—always remembering the evil done to it, always forgetting the evil done to others, always, as in the case of Vladimir Putin, aimed at the restoration of past glories—may very well understand where the West has gone astray, but has hardly engaged in the hard work of creating a viable contemporary alternative to the West. The easy way is rather to join the West as it is. But Orlando Figes is wise when he writes of the future of Russia that it would be wrong to try to produce there a replica of Western democracy.[246]

A generation ago Jacques Barzun defended the cultural renovation at which the Romantics aimed by calling attention to their "attempt to reconcile personal freedom with the inescapable need of collective action."[247] This seems to me to have been a worthy, if itself too narrow, goal. The later appearance of Fascism and now the various communitarian movements suggests that many people—and precisely those embodying the fullest humanity—will be discontent until the autonomous individual of much of liberal thought is placed into a fuller social, natural, and cosmic setting. The traditions of the left must become more generous in their treatment of social, cultural, and religious questions than they have hitherto generally been. Both right and left must abandon their uncritical attachment to progress and an ever-growing economy. Undoubtedly much of the turn to transcendence will involve a turn from the left. Such turns have their own great dangers, as Fascism warns us. The left must be convinced of its bigotries and blind spots, its narrow-mindedness, but without relinquishing all in the Enlightenment of which it is a carrier.

243. Max Rodenbeck, "Witch Hunt in Egypt," *NYRB* 47, 19 (November 16, 2000): 39–41.

244. John Gray, *Isaiah Berlin* (Princeton, N.J.: Princeton University Press, 1996). Although Berlin has been the darling of journals such as the *NYRB,* he has been intensely criticized elsewhere: see Hart, "Laughter of the Philosophers," 35.

245. Clark, *Why Angels Fall,* has much to say on this.

246. Orlando Figes, "In Search of Russia," *NYRB* 50, 16 (October 23, 2003): 37–39 at 39.

247. *Classic, Romantic and Modern,* 137, and esp. ch. 2. For my comments on Barzun here and below, see Roger Shattuck, "Decline and Fall?" *NYRB* 47, 11 (June 29, 2000): 55–58 at 55. I do not accept the contrast between "classical" and "romantic" Barzun sketches in *Classic, Romantic and Modern,* ch. 3. I find it odd that he does not introduce discussion of the Baroque; he does not seem to realize that the Baroque was an attempt, largely successful in my opinion, to overcome what Barzun views as eternal oppositions. It is the architectural form which above all unites transcendence and immanence.

A great German historian, Ernst Nolte, before he got into a great German *Historikerstreit,* called Fascism most fundamentally "resistance to transcendence."[248] On the face of it, this seems almost the reverse of calling Fascism an ideology functioning as a religion. But what Nolte meant to indicate was that Fascism was attached to the local, partial, and historically and spatially specific.[249] All through the modern period states had understood quite well that a firmly held transcendent religion was the greatest barrier to their ambitions, and Fascism from this point of view was just the latest attempt to disallow the kind of transcendence and universality that, especially, Christianity presented. As Paul Ricoeur subsequently articulated the problem, a general predicament in which modern people find themselves is that history has meaning to the degree it approaches universality, but this meaning empties to the degree that it eliminates the singularity of individual life and experience.[250]

Fascism is in this perspective an insistence on the meaning found in particularity. Thus it did resist transcendence, but this was the vacuous utopian universalism of the Enlightenment tradition. Contra Nolte, one could argue that Fascism was or could be a criticism of "false transcendentalism," that is, of the way the Enlightenment had conceived universal categories so as to ignore history.[251] The imposition on Europe of the Napoleonic Code or of Wilsonian notions of national rights are examples of an unhelpful universalism which ignores history. Secondly, one could argue that Fascism was criticism of one's age by either the standards of other ages or simply by transcendental standards. An example here is the Fascist criticism of "godless Communism." It is in this sense that a description of Fascism as a movement toward transcendence seems most helpful, and François Furet wrote in reply to Nolte that both Communism and Fascism were themselves utopian efforts at overcoming the spiritual dissatisfactions generated by liberal modernity.[252] Of course, as Pius XII pointed out in *Mit brennende Sorge,* Nazism had its special false transcendentalism in its elevation of race to transcendental status. This said, it evades the most profound questions facing twenty-first-century man to see such movements as simply aberrations or the result of mad men. To repeat, the very appearance of Fascism was a response to a hollowness that many had found in modern life.

248. Ernst Nolte, *Three Faces of Fascism: Action Française, Italian Fascism, National Socialism,* tr. Leila Vennewitz (New York: Holt, Rinehart and Winston, 1966), 429. See also the exchange between François Furet and Ernst Nolte, *Fascism and Communism,* tr. Katherine Golsan (Lincoln: University of Nebraska Press, 2001), and Ryan, "Power of Positive Thinking," 44–45.

249. Nolte, *Three Faces,* 429–54 at 430–31.

250. *History and Truth,* tr. with an introduction by Charles A. Kelbley (Evanston, Ill.: Northwestern University Press, 1965).

251. I use this expression by analogy to the "false Romanticism" (the separation of man from his soul consequent on mechanistic materialism) Jacques Barzun found in *Darwin, Marx, Wagner: Critique of a Heritage,* 2nd ed. (Garden City, N.Y.: Doubleday, 1958).

252. *Fascism and Communism.*

There is a paradox here. Liberalism, above all in its Rawlsian form, has come to use a Kantian language of universal rights to create an enclosed political order from which any notion of a common good raised on a universal idea of the good has been increasingly excluded, thus leaving the societies it creates profoundly specific or non-transcendental in Nolte's sense. Fascism, in spite of all its horrors and dehumanizations, sometimes, especially in its early stages, tied profound attachment to one's own culture to critique of one's age by transcendental standards. It was thus addressed to a central problem of human life which liberalism tends to turn its eyes away from, whether man can still "be at home" in the world. Clearly *"homo economicus"* can still be at home if he lives in the right part of the modern world, but can all that man is still express itself in a shared life or must we reduce things either to private realities or to some common denominator so low that even the European Union might embrace it? If, as some say, liberal democracy represents "the end of history," that toward which history all along has been moving, and beyond which there will be no radically different order, then the danger is that what we have at the end is a very impoverished humanity, a humanity about as impoverished, if not as brutalized, as if some form of Fascism had proved to be the twentieth-century victor.[253] The great political question is the possibility of constructing a life in society more generous to humans' transcendental orientations than liberalism and generally politics of the left have been, and more respectful of the mystery of grace—that is, of the fact that we profoundly differ—than politics of the right generally have been.

253. Since Plato and Aristotle seem right in holding that all political orders decay, the belief that liberal democracy would somehow avoid this seems mere wishful thinking: Robert Nisbet, *Twilight of Authority* (New York: Oxford University Press, 1975).

Chapter Six

ALTERNATIVES

Nobody is obliged to participate in the crisis of his time.
He can do something else.

    —Eric Voegelin[1]

The previous two chapters traced the history of the practice and expression of a sense of transcendence, and the diminishment of an orientation to transcendence in recent centuries. Earlier, the third chapter gave some idea of the role of the arts in both fostering and diminishing the place of transcendence in life. This final chapter considers thinkers and movements outside the arts who have rebelled against the diminishment of transcendence and have proposed various alternatives as to how the transcendent dimension of life might be expressed today.

In 1893 Maurice Blondel (1861–1949) published *L'Action,* with its central idea that human desire is unsatisfied by the immanent: there is something about us, he thought, which imperiously aspires beyond all things immanent. "The supernatural is at home with our nature," the natural and supernatural penetrate each other, and human desire is integrative and sacramental.[2] About the same time that Blondel was forming these thoughts, Martin Heidegger came to a conclusion others had, and which we met in the last chapter, that the "voluntarist" tradition had brought the West to nihilism, expressed in a wide range of modern beliefs, fascism, communism, democracy, and technology. All these placed the will at the center of human life, and thought of human existence as essentially action. The alternative was some kind of recovery of a contemplative mode of existence. Heidegger thought a good deal about transcendence, seeing it not as a realm set apart

---

1. *Conversations with Eric Voegelin,* ed. R. Eric O'Connor (Montreal: Thomas More Institute, 1980), 33.

2. Graham McAleer, review of Maurice Blondel, *The Letter on Apologetics and History and Dogma,* tr. Alexander Dru (Grand Rapids, Mich. 1994), in *NOR* 66, 9 (October 1999): 43–44 at 44.

from common human experience, but as coming to light in the world. He saw modern man as living on a precipice from which he could either fall into complete forgetfulness of Being, or could recover the meaning of Being.[3]

Rebellion against the loss of transcendence coursed through the twentieth century. Eric Voegelin began the fourth volume (1974) of his *Order and History* with the admission that to that point, in thinking of history as on a single narrative line that the historian could capture, he had been on the wrong track.[4] He now realized how mysterious history is: the hermetic language of the mystics, who had seen that history is "an open field where the divine and human meet," was what was appropriate, and the great division is not between liberal and conservative, but between materialists and those who acknowledge a transcendental order.[5] The idea that the historian—implicitly anyone who would understand the nature of reality—must approach life as a mystic was so far from modern assumptions that few followed Voegelin, or could even understand him. But a claustrophobic sense of life in a world without transcendence arguably grew, especially in the closing years of the century.

Today the turn to transcendence and to the transcendentals of truth, goodness, and beauty continues to take many forms.[6] There seems to be a certain common ground on which many emphasize that the human person has an objective dignity which cannot be overridden by government or law. Although for non-religious people the origins of this dignity may be unclear, for Christians it is seen as a gift, something given by Creator to created and the source of our capacity for transcendence. At least in the thought of John Paul II, this dignity of the individual was not to be confused with a "self-congratulating anthropocentrism," because the individual is seen as always in community.[7] Religious people often ground this view of human dignity in the idea that man is made in the image and likeness of God, but secular people such as Jürgen Habermas, acknowledging the historical dependency on Christianity of ideas central to a secular humanism, consciously retain this "Christian" idea.[8]

---

3. Mark Lilla, "The Perils of Friendship," *NYRB* 46, 19 (December 2, 1999): 25–29 at 25.

4. *The Ecumenic Age* (Baton Rouge: Louisiana State University Press, 1974).

5. Mark Lilla, "Mr. Casaubon in America," *NYRB* 54, 11 (June 28, 2007): 29–31 at 31.

6. James E. Faulconer, *Transcendence in Philosophy and Religion* (Bloomington: Indiana University Press, 2003), and José Granados, "Love and the Organism: A Theological Contribution to the Study of Life," in *Love Alone Is Credible: Hans Urs von Balthasar as Interpreter of the Catholic Tradition*, vol. 1, ed. David L. Schindler (Grand Rapids, Mich.: Eerdmans, 2008), 141–75.

7. This is the phrase of James Hanink, quoted in Mark and Louise Zwick, "New Biography of John Paul II," *HCW* 19, 7 (December 1999): 7–9 at 8.

8. See especially the opening essays in *Recovering Self-Evident Truths: Catholic Perspectives on American Law*, ed. Michael A. Scaperlanda and Teresa Collett (Washington, D.C.: The Catholic University of America Press, 2006).

Benedict XVI has compared our situation to ancient Greece, which experienced its own Enlightenment

in which a divinely based law lost its obviousness, and it became necessary to look for deeper justifications of the law. This led to the idea that in the face of a positive law that can in reality be injustice, there must be a law that derives from the nature, from the very being, of man himself.[9]

It would seem that any turn to transcendence today, whatever else it might be, must involve something like the ancient Greek turn to nature, which for those capable of this turn, as the Stoics, was based not specifically on religious revelation but on the idea that humans have an ontology, an objective structure that is knowable by reason.

Any recovery of transcendence in life, if thought through to foundations, would seem to entail not just a recovery of the natural law tradition, but a teaching for the first time to most people of that tradition and of the idea that the universe has been structured by a rational God. This is not only necessary if life is to regain a transcendent dimension, but also if things many secularists wish to flourish, such as a universal human law transcending all actual legal systems and binding all humans as humans, is to be grounded in reason, rather than simply will. And we should not forget that the idea of natural law is as much a check on religious fanaticism, on the pathologies specific to religion, as it is a check on a form of secularism, one of reason's pathologies, which claims "all is permitted."[10] This is because natural law positions teach that the good, or rather part of it, is knowable by reason alone, and that since this knowledge is potentially universal, open to every human, even the claims of revelation, should they conflict with natural law, must be judged at reason's bar. If someone claims that God has commanded him to kill me, I have the right to inquire what injustice, as determined by reason, I have done to deserve this. Reason is a check on false religion or a false claim to revelation, claims that sanction breaking the natural law, which, grounded in reason, is logically prior for humans to revelation.[11]

≈

One of the more unexpected turns toward transcendence comes from paleontology, in which debate about the criteria for defining the origins of humanity has centered on consciousness as a sure index of the appearance of man. There are no graves in the animal world; only man constructs

9. Joseph Ratzinger, "That Which Holds the World Together," in Joseph Ratzinger and Jürgen Habermas, *Dialectics of Secularization: On Reason and Religion,* ed. Florian Schuller, tr. Brian McNeil (San Francisco: Ignatius Press, 2006), 67–68, at 67 for the quotation.

10. Ibid., 77.

11. I have studied this at greater length in "Separating Church and State," *FR* 20 (1994): 403–25.

them. But graves are an indication that man has understood that he will die, is conscious of his finiteness. He has grasped the fact that humans have limitations, and he can in some way measure this sense of finiteness against some idea of infinity.[12] Anthony O'Hear pursues this line of analysis, and notes that humans have a reason that at least partly understands that we are caught between finitude and infinity, and in this measure have the capacity to transcend ourselves.[13] This is the origin of any turn to transcendence.

The higher animals can use tools, but only man can transcend himself. This was already Pascal's point in his famous "man is a thinking reed" passage (*Pensées,* 346):

But, if the universe were to crush him, man would still be more noble than that which killed him, because he knows that he dies and the advantage which the universe has over him; the universe knows nothing of this.[14]

To anyone who knows Giambattista Vico's *The New Science* (1744), our paleontologists' observations are not completely new. Vico's views became the base from which Robert Pogue Harrison launched a contemporary reflection on burial of the dead, and the relation of the dead to the living. Harrison is essentially in agreement with the paleontologists: humanity "is not a species (*Homo sapiens* is a species); it is a way of being mortal and relating to the dead. To be human means above all to bury."[15] Humans have about them a "history-making mortality," the aboriginal sign of which is the grave marker.[16] All this, the sense of man's finiteness and that he will die, permeates Western classical literature, and is found in Homer, Greek drama, and Virgil. We noted in the last chapter that it is only in the modern period, especially in the classical political thinkers of the English and French Enlightenments, that the centrality of death in constructing political community itself was lost. The Enlightenment traditions are from one point of view continuing attempts to sever us from our dead and to deny that we die.[17]

Harrison's reflections are very much in agreement with a line of thought developed by John Lukacs, who has been arguing in a series of books that scientific materialism has it completely backwards. It is not matter that pro-

12. Cf. the study of human origins through "prehistoric" cave paintings by J. Wentzel van Huyssteen, *Alone in the World? Human Uniqueness in Science and Theology* (Grand Rapids, Mich.: Eerdmans, 2007); also see *The Evolution of Rationality: Interdisciplinary Essays in Honor of J. Wentzel van Huyssteen,* ed. F. LeRon Shults (Grand Rapids, Mich.: Eerdmans, 2005), and Terence L. Nichols, *The Sacred Cosmos: Christian Faith and the Challenge of Naturalism* (Grand Rapids, Mich. 2003).

13. *Beyond Evolution* (Oxford: Oxford University Press, 1997).

14. Translation found in John Lukacs, *At the End of an Age* (New Haven, Conn.: Yale University Press, 2002), 208.

15. *The Dominion of the Dead* (Chicago: University of Chicago Press, 2003), quoted in W. S. Merwin, "You Can Take it With You," *NYRB* 51, 6 (April 8, 2004): 63–67 at 67.

16. Ibid., 64.

17. Joseph Bottum, "Death & Politics," *FT* 174 (June/July 2007): 17–29.

duces mind, but human consciousness that shapes everything. It is non-sense to talk about humans as anything but at the center of reality. Matter itself has no center or lack of center: it is indifferent to such categories. It is humans, and if we exclude God and the angels, only humans, who are conscious and can speak of centers. And humans have no choice as conscious beings other than to be at the center. In showing the many limitations of Darwinism, Lukacs goes further than some of the paleontologists, arguing for the incoherence of the application of the idea of evolution ever further backwards in time, one result of which has been the claim that humans existed as much as a million years ago. The hidden assumption here is the materialist one that matter preceded human mind, mind only gradually appearing. Lukacs has no patience with this "dribs and drabs" theory, and rejects the very idea of a "pre-historic" man.[18] Man is defined by the fact that he is a historic or conscious being, a conscious being oriented in time. He has no pre-history, only history.

A more theologically and philosophically sophisticated form of Lukacs's leading ideas can be found in the thought of Robert Sokolowski, who distinguishes three ways of relating matter and spirit.[19] The first is that found in Darwinism and in most cognitive science, in which spirit is but an epiphenomenon of matter. The second, what we may call the complementarity of matter and spirit, is Aristotelian or Stoic, and holds that in the universe matter and spirit are mixed. Neither can be reduced to the other. The third is biblical and creationist, holding that the spiritual or personal precedes the material. Here the spiritual brings the material into being (God creates *ex nihilo*), the eternal in some sense preceding and causing the temporal.

Sokolowski's is a eucharistically oriented thought, and he illustrates his point by reference to the Eucharist:

The Eucharist itself, because it would not be possible except against the background of this understanding of spirit and matter, is a perpetual reminder of the transcendence and power of God, which manifested themselves most fully not by spectacular cosmic effects but by the life, Death, and Resurrection of Jesus the Lord.

The Real Presence in the Eucharist is therefore not just the concealed presence of one worldly substance under the appearances of another, but the presence of the full mystery of God's being and his work, the mystery hidden from all ages and now made manifest to us, the point of the universe and of creation.[20]

18. *End of an Age*, 8, 120–21. This book rests on Lukacs's *Historical Consciousness: Or, the Remembered Past* (New York: Harper & Row, 1968).

19. "The Eucharist and Transubstantiation," *Co* 24 (1997): 867–80 at 872–73, on this and the following.

20. Ibid., 873. Sokolowski has also written important essays on political philosophy in *The God of Faith and Reason: Foundations of Christian Theology*, with a new preface (Washington, D.C.: The Catholic University of America Press, 1995), and in *Christian Faith and Human Un-*

Thus:

> The Eucharist . . . is a perpetual reminder of the transcendence of God, . . . when it is celebrated and overcomes the confinements of time and history by reenacting in the present the sacrifice of Christ. . . . By revealing the mystery of Creation, the Eucharist reveals the divine nature as transcendent to the world and yet acting in it, both giving it being and recreating it through the mystery of Christ.[21]

This both deepens Lukacs's point, and makes clear why an adequate doctrine of the Eucharist is central to any Christian recovery of transcendence.

From such materials Michael Schulz brilliantly constructs a countercultural position. The common wisdom is that the development of science has shown that the earth is a minor planet, not the center of the universe, and that nothing about what is happening in the universe centers on man. Against such a view, Schulz argues that none of this terminology, "cosmos" or "universe," makes any sense other than as expressed by a human. It is indeed true that the earth is a minor planet, and that in a physical sense the universe has no center. But statements such as these are not possible without the human who makes them. In this sense, as the surveyor of reality, man is its center.[22] Time is a convention, Albert Einstein and Henri Poincaré insisted, and the only time we have is our time.[23] This is also Lukacs's point, who notes that because historical consciousness centers on human beings, the very notion of history must be human-centered.[24] "We did not *create* the universe," he writes in a provocative formulation. "But the universe is our *invention*."[25] The universe only exists qua universe, a mental invention, in a human mind. What Copernicus was understood to have done, expelled humans from the center of the universe, has now been undone by Neils Bohr and the insistence that man is at the center of any description of the world.

Schulz is a Catholic theologian whose goal is to show that it is the rela-

---

derstanding: Studies on the Eucharist, Trinity, and the Human Person (Washington, D.C.: The Catholic University of America Press, 2006).

21. "Eucharist and Transubstantiation," 874, 879.

22. Cf. David Novak, *Natural Law in Judaism* (Cambridge: Cambridge University Press, 1998), 147–48, arguing that natural law, the "recognition of the normative significance of the limits of nature," arises "when humans realize that all their historical acts have limits just as human life itself has an outer limit. Only with this recognition can the world be cosmos."

23. Peter Galison, *Einstein's Clocks and Poincaré's Maps: Empires of Time* (New York: W. W. Norton, 2003); and Donald A. Yerxa, "Einstein's Clocks, Poincaré's Maps: An Interview with Peter Galison, Part I," *HS* 5, 2 (November 2003): 5–9 at 8.

24. Lukacs, *End of an Age*, 109, has some fun at the expense of the physicist Steven Weinberg, and see 112–13, 203–4, 223–25.

25. Lukacs, *End of an Age*, 204, and see 206–14. Part of Lukacs's analysis depends on the "Duhem-Quine thesis" that scientific theories cannot, strictly speaking, be tested empirically. On this see John H. Zammito, *A Nice Derangement of Epistemes: Post-Positivism in the Study of Science from Quine to Latour* (Chicago: University of Chicago Press, 2004), with the review of Theodore M. Porter, *AHR* 109 (2004): 1194.

tion between God and man that elicits the very categories cosmos or universe, and that

whatever occurs between man and God is always a cosmic event. . . . When we speak of the relationship between God and man we are considering a relation than which no more encompassing relation can be thought. For finite reality first comes to itself in man; it is presented to itself and as such recognized. Only within man's relation to an infinite God can we succeed in grasping finitude. Finitude's coming to itself through a human relation to God's infinity is also the presupposition for there actually being a free relationship between God and creation. From this point of view, the whole of finite reality is gathered up in man. The world thus arises precisely within man's relation to God; this is the locus in which the world receives its determination.

Further:

One does not become more objective by attempting to gain a neutral perspective from which to view finitude in abstraction from the human knower, which in any event is epistemologically impossible. If the cosmos can be grasped as cosmos only in man, and if independently from man it does not even exist (at least as cosmos), then the most objective view of the world is given within the horizon of man's orientation to God. . . . If the ultimate meaning of the essence of the cosmos is dependent upon the reality of man, then the cosmos with man is qualitatively more than it is without him.[26]

Only by standing in a relation with God can man talk of such things as the unity of the world, of categories such as infinity and finiteness.

For our purposes we only need look at one aspect of Schulz's analysis, which he pursues in defense of a traditional view of how sin affects the creation. On the presumption that the theory of evolution is correct, Schulz explores the question of the origin of (human) consciousness, on which we have seen the very existence of a known cosmos depends:

Evolution . . . testifies to the anthropocentric character of the cosmos. . . . Evolutionary development ends up with ever more complex structures. The more the complexity grows, the more we are able to distinguish between an interior and an exterior in a living being, and the more the form of subjectivity takes shape.[27]

Hence we come to the debate among the paleontologists about the origins of human consciousness and the criteria of human existence already alluded to: "According to them, consciousness (which is characterized by relation to transcendence) counts as the sure index for human existence."[28] Graves allow us to deduce that

26. Michael Schulz, "'Fallen' Nature: How Sin Affects the Creation," Co 29 (2002): 490–505 at 490, 497–98, for this and the following quotation.

27. For a current Catholic consideration of evolution, see Józef Zycinski, God and Evolution: Fundamental Questions of Christian Evolutionism, tr. Kenneth W. Kemp and Zuzanna Maslanka (Washington, D.C.: The Catholic University of America Press, 2006).

28. Schulz, "'Fallen' Nature," 499, for the following quotations.

a certain population had developed a consciousness of death. One can attain a consciousness of death only if one grasps the limitations of one's life and finitude within the horizon of the infinite. It is not necessarily with the use of tools that human existence begins, but rather with metaphysics.

Thus Schulz comes to a conclusion similar to that of many of the first philosophers and early Christian Fathers—human existence begins in wonder and contemplation, in spiritual transcendence of finite realities. Man is "not bound up with the things of this world in an absolute way like the animals. Man is . . . a creature of transcendence; this creature is the window through which the cosmos 'sees' its origin." This was Christopher Dawson's point in his insistence that in even the most primitive religions, there is a sense of the transcendent.[29]

Schulz's analysis is complemented by that of Javier Prades. In the first chapter of this volume, the argument was that religion cannot be eliminated from human life. Just when we think it has been eliminated and the world thoroughly disenchanted, religion appears in new garb. Prades, concerned with the relation between religion and anthropology, asks of our times the question "Is God at the center of life?"[30] The answer in Weberian terms would obviously have to be no. But Prades's argument is that the strong position has passed from anthropology to religion. Today religion is recovering and anthropology, our understanding of the nature of man, is in crisis. Postmodernity, Prades thinks, has kept the "exaltation of the subject" found in modernity, the idea that man is subject to nothing above himself. In its most egregious form we find the idea that in principle man can know everything and there are no limits on what he may do, especially in the sense that no limits should be placed on science and technology. A certain "subjectivist juridicism" is found round the world, in which freedom is so exalted that rights are demanded absolutely, including the right of the individual to make up his own meaning of life. Rights language is extended to more and more aspects of life, lifestyle choices being made into universal human rights, and rights coming to include such things as the "right not to be born."[31]

Against such views, Prades introduces Norberto Bobbio's idea of the "impotence of the subject."[32] We cannot in fact do whatever we want. We cannot define reality however we want. We have the most severe limitations.

---

29. Cf. Huston Smith, *Essays on World Religion* (New York: Paragon House, 1992), on the centrality of transcendence in human life.

30. *Co* 30 (2003): 180–208 at 182, and for the following phrases, 183–86.

31. Ibid., 185, for the quoted phrase, coined in the United States in regard to "wrongful birth" lawsuits. Pierre Manent, *A World beyond Politics? A Defense of the Nation-State* (Princeton, N.J.: Princeton University Press, 2006), treats the making of lifestyle choices into human rights in several chapters.

32. Prades, "Is God at the Center?" 187–91, on this and the following.

No amount of knowledge and technology can eliminate human suffering. Alongside our belief in an unending immanent secular progress stand the most substantial doubts, and a sense of abject powerlessness. Can globalization be contained at all? Are we condemned to a world of terrorism? In the face of such questions, what possibly can it mean to speak of our being free? Thinking of man instrumentally, as the subject of unlimited technological advance, has not given him peace or certainty in facing life. The conclusion follows that man is not self-sufficient, and thus the question of religion reappears, paradoxically first religion as consolation, and then as an insistence that we never allow our hope for a better world, whether here or hereafter, to disappear. Religion's gift of eschatology, of insisting on something beyond what we see, of transcendence, may here receive new appreciation. Thus the proposal that we aim at a transmodern self, which acknowledges meaning and purpose transcending the self while rejecting the polar delusions of unlimited autonomy and cosmic meaningless.[33]

We arrive at the fact that though the exaltation of the subject has survived modernity into postmodernity and can be expressed in a very strong fashion, the experience of the self for many—and in much postmodern theory—is of a weak self, an "I" that hardly exists, is insecure, and can be endlessly reconstructed. Early in the twentieth century G. K. Chesterton, as if seeing the postmodernism that was coming, remarked, "You cannot call up any wilder vision than a city in which men ask themselves if they have any selves": we may not yet have cities of such men, but we certainly have university departments with people who describe things thus.[34] The conclusion of the religious man is that he is a mystery, even to himself, and lives in a mystery, or is defined by relation to Mystery. But, *pace* those who think that humans make up their lives' meanings, the *anima technica vacua* or *homo technicus* tends not to ask the most obvious of questions: "What is the meaning of my life?" As a "neutral" observer, he tends to be separated from all life, including his own.[35]

Prades proposes the alternative stance of "gratitude," acknowledgment of our reason and freedom as dependent. Our life—a proper anthropology—finds its origin in dependency, not assertion. "The point is to show that the typically human dynamisms of reason and freedom are realized if, instead of enclosing them in an immanent anthropology, they are recognized as open to a good, transcendent origin, whose historical mode of realization is a sonship." Freedom is not properly understood as unbounded or self-determined, but after the model of the relation of a son to a father,

33. *The Self: Beyond the Postmodern Crisis,* ed. Paul C. Vitz and Susan M. Felch (Wilmington, Del.: ISI Books, 2005).

34. *Orthodoxy* (Garden City, N.Y.: Image Books, 1959), 37.

35. Prades, "Is God at the Center?" 191–208, for this and the following.

as filial and trusting. Thus Prades comes to a specifically biblical and patristic view of man as *homo vivens,* made in the *imago Dei.* Knowing must not depend simply on the reason of science, striving for neutrality and isolated from what it observes. It is the whole man, not reason in its limited scientific definition, who knows the truth or engages with reality. That which is central, say, the love in a mother's smile, cannot be reduced to geometric-mathematical judgment. When the subject bears on the meaning of life, on anything personal or social, we must become "co-natural" with the object examined, not distanced and neutral observers, but empathetic and involved.

Prades lays special weight on the specifically Jewish and Christian idea that the paternal love of God is unlimited: this, a love without limit, is the true transcendent and the norm of Jesus' mission. Prades's thought here closely parallels Hans Urs von Balthasar's, which insists ("God is Love") that love as the meaning of being is the ground of all the transcendentals.[36] This is a more personal way of putting the point, but also agrees with the analysis of the Orthodox theologian David Bentley Hart, who argues that one can truly think transcendence only if one begins with *creatio ex nihilo.*[37] The primal contrast is between that which in no sense is its own origin, the creature, and that which is the origin of all, which has brought everything from nothing, the Creator. That contrast marks a full notion of transcendence.[38]

❧

Maurice Cowling's (b. 1926) has been a lonely but searing voice. A fellow of Peterhouse, Cambridge, and the author of a massive three-volume history of the secularization of England—of England's intellectual classes—over the last century and a half, Cowling is an absolute disbeliever in progress and modernity. He is conservative in the sense that he is a ferocious critic of ideology in every form, and therefore has no ideology of his own to propose. He is simply a partisan of the concrete, of an English way of life as it was when Church and Crown supported one another. In the sense that Edmund Burke was an "integralist," so is Cowling. For social life to be worth living, there must be social solidarity and the restraint of individual passion. Church and state must cooperate in achieving this. From the point of view of society, religion and politics are part of one whole, so that reli-

36. D. C. Schindler, "Does Love Trump Reason? Towards a Non-Possessive Concept of Knowledge" (unpublished), observes that whereas for Aquinas the transcendentals govern the soul's relation to being, for Balthasar they also analogously govern the relation of each thing to every other thing.

37. *The Beauty of the Infinite: The Aesthetics of Christian Truth* (Grand Rapids, Mich.: Eerdmans, 2003), 125–51.

38. Henri de Lubac, *The Mystery of the Supernatural,* tr. Rosemary Sheed (New York: Herder and Herder, 1967), 53–100.

gion, whatever else it is, must be "civic," a shared project of Church and state aimed at "crowd control and social solidarity."[39] Here is the common bond between the English and French right, English and French integralism, even if a man like Burke is not easily so classified. In the wake of the French Revolution the desire for social order was so great that virtually all the forms of Christianity came to the defense of the thrones of Europe, the pope asking the Poles to obey the Tsar, who had plundered their church, and the Patriarch commanding the same of the Greeks in regard to the Ottomans, who had similarly devastated their church.[40]

Perhaps it is fair to say that Cowling speaks in defense of a late stage of that order of things, present by the eleventh century, in which "all men were considered to be Christian and discipline had been relaxed in order to hold the weakest brother within the community."[41] As such, he is different from most of the radical religious critics of the contemporary world, who, like the present writer, tend to have the self-consciousness of the convert. Most history of Church reform is written by critics who at least implicitly reject an ideal such as Cowling's. Augustine is approved for having tried to untie, especially at the psychological level, Christianity's destiny from Rome's, for insisting on a certain distance between *Romanitas* and *Christianitas*.[42] Approved are Gregory the Great's attacks on those "who confess Christ because they see everyone else is a Christian," that is, Gregory's attacks on the nominal Christians produced by an established Christianity.[43] The problem for those of views similar to Gregory's is the nominal, lukewarm Christianity produced by "a society in which Christians were no longer made, but born." In this situation assimilation to the received values of society was a constant danger, along with temptation to dull or obliterate the radical instincts basic to Christianity. "What was at stake was the visible holiness of the Christian people, threatened by its assimilation to the prevailing standards of the secular world around it." Presumably, as Gregory of Tours (538–94) and the Venerable Bede (673–735) each saw in turn, some degree of assimilation to the larger society was inevitable, but one of the

39. In the words of the trenchant analysis by Russell Hittinger, "The Churches of Earthly Power," *FT* 164 (June/July, 2006): 27–32 at 28.

40. Ibid., noting that this collaboration of throne and altar was swept away by mid-century by the next round of revolutions.

41. Frank Barlow, *The English Church 1066–1154* (London: Longman, 1979), 146.

42. Robert A. Markus, "Church Reform and Society in Late Antiquity," in *Reforming the Church before Modernity: Patterns, Problems and Approaches,* ed. Christopher M. Bellitto and Louis I. Hamilton (Burlington, Vt.: Ashgate, 2005), 3–19 at 15, going on to admit that Augustine's radicalness had little future in comparison with Gelasius's "compromise," which allowed a close cooperation between Church and state.

43. *Homiliae in Evangelia,* ed. Raymond Etaix (*Corpus Christianorum, Series Latina* 141; Turnhout: Brepols, 1999), II.3, tr. Markus, "Church Reform and Society," 13, with 14–15, 17, for the following quotations.

functions of the early medieval councils and goals of early medieval pastoral practice was to ensure that this did not go too far.

Cowling will have none of this. His ideal is not a world of self-conscious Christians, but a world of instinctive Christians, not the mentality of the first-generation Christian, but of the second-generation Christian:

A religion ought to be habitual and ought not to involve the self-consciousness inseparable from conversion. What Christianity requires is a second-generation sensibility in which . . . struggle has ceased to be of Christianity's essence. This is not a situation which can easily be achieved in the contemporary world; indeed, the religions which can most easily avoid self-consciousness in the contemporary world are the secular religions which are absorbed at the mother's knee or from the mother's television set.[44]

Cowling's is a sensibility like that of Jane Austen (1775–1817), less interested in the exploration of Christian doctrine than in the texture of everyday life in a society populated by Christians, and in the contrast between modern individualism and a traditional society in which people have and accept—grow into—roles. Coming from a very different direction, he wants something partly similar to those poststructuralist thinkers who acknowledge that identity does not exist in isolation, but is constituted by a web of relationships, to which each is in debt.[45] Like Austen, Cowling traces uncontrolled individualism to "the marginalization of the Church in the life of England, the failure of clergy to be the makers of English manners, and the consequent intrusion of other forces as the maker of manners."[46] The individualists in Austen's account are those addicted to novelty, who have no memories and want no past. They do not in a meaningful sense live in a community.[47]

We have seen that this latter point has been made by many critics of liberal regimes as they have evolved since Austen's day. In America, though an emphasis on individualism and a certain instrumentalism were present from the beginning, we have noted that society nevertheless generally saw itself as "under God" and affirmed the moral law in various forms. Americans believed that virtuous and selfless public servants were necessary to any experiment in self-government, and often had reservations about democracy. Arguably they would have been astonished by an evolution in which

44. I am quoting Cowling from a brilliant analysis of him I am following, by David B. Hart, "A Most Partial Historian," *FT* 138 (December 2003): 34–40 at 39. On the study of "minimal Christianity," see Norman Tanner and Sethina Watson, "Least of the Laity: The Minimum Requirements for a Medieval Christian," *Journal of Medieval History* 32 (2006): 395–423.

45. Noëlle McAfee, *Habermas, Kristeva, and Citizenship* (Ithaca, N.Y.: Cornell University Press, 2000). *Recovering Self-Evident Truths,* ed. Scaperlanda and Collett, has a number of relevant articles.

46. See the excellent Peter J. Leithart, "Jane Austen, Public Theologian," *FT* 139 (January, 2004): 28–37, at 29, for the phrase describing Austen.

47. Ibid., 33.

much contemporary liberalism has come to insist, for instance, on abortion rights. Those who now consider themselves neo-liberal or neo-conservative, including most of the Catholic neo-liberals, commonly continue to hold the beliefs of the older liberalism, and fear democracy in ways it did. Often their view is that the earlier liberalism was increasingly corrupted or lost at some time later in the nineteenth century, or even in the twentieth.

Just as the regimes of evolving liberalism increasingly, especially in the twentieth century, have undone social consensus, we have seen that they have long tended to destroy the forms of divine and natural hierarchy on which all community depends, and of which Cowling so approves. At the divine level, the sanction of the ruler by God was already undermined by the appearance of republicanism, and this undermining advanced as democracy advanced; at the natural level the same process increasingly threatens the distinctions between parents and children, wise and foolish, etc. More provocatively, if we accept the analysis of Hans Jonas (1903–93), this leveling process has even given us our present-day science, with all its limitations.[48]

The general observation, not specific to Jonas, is that in the long run most cultures have a certain internal consistency in which, if they hold a certain view on one point, they tend to look at other matters from the same point of view. This is one of the reasons for the great tensions in American Catholicism, which tries to tie together an essentially hierarchical religion to a democratic politics. Jonas did not wish to pursue the obvious, that a democratic age tends to level all things, but to apply this insight to an area most do not apply it to, science. He observed that pre-modern science was essentially hierarchical, as pre-modern society was. Now even science has become democratic. In pre-modern science it was assumed that there was a great chain of being in which everything found its place and there was an ordering according to the nature of each thing, that is, a teleological ordering according ultimately to final causation, the purpose for which each thing existed. In modern science we have a materialist "heap" in which everything is "egalitarian," just one more way of putting matter together.

Since Francis Bacon's time, the universe has lost its hierarchical character, and has become composed of interchangeable common matter. Whatever dignity survives lies not with things, but with the scientist's commanding mind, which can now do to nature whatever he will: there is no "hierarchical" nature to be respected. The leading human activity is not contemplation, but the wielding of power. Jonas notes that if hierarchy is abolished, so is transcendence of whatever kind, for we can no longer speak of anything as higher than man. Indeed, since man is the wielder of power,

48. *The Phenomenon of Life: Toward a Philosophical Biology* (New York 1966), 191–207, for the following quotations and discussion.

implicitly the objects he studies are lower than him. Practical use defines science, and thus science becomes at heart technological. "The aristocracy of form is replaced by the democracy of matter." Wholes become mere sums of their parts, whereas in classical science generally the whole was more than its parts.

If the whole is the sum of its parts, it follows that explanation lies in those parts, that is, in the reduction of things to their parts. The world has become thoroughly nominalistic. Further, whereas infinity in Greek science lay in the everlasting character of *theoria,* the infinity found in modern science is that of an interminable process in which tentative hypotheses are forever revised and absorbed into new integrations: the idea of unending progress thus becomes as essential to modern science as it is to modern technological civilization. I have elsewhere tried to show that it is not possible to know the world except under the category of final causation.[49] If I am correct in this, then even the science of a democratic world is radically deficient.

The undermining of natural hierarchy has usually been aided by the incompetence or evil of the hierarchy being undermined. Nothing can isolate us from human folly, whether our life be hierarchical or egalitarian. The most that can be done, as in the best of the American constitutional tradition, is to construct barriers which make folly less dangerous, less capable of undoing public goods. But before one sets about trying to limit human folly in some given historical situation, there is a prior question of whether in principle it is better for society to be hierarchical or egalitarian. If it is better for it to be hierarchical, this means that, despite all the mischief brought about by historical hierarchies, it is still better for human life to be modeled on the idea that we naturally complement each other in our differences, than to think of ourselves as all the same.[50] There is a marked tendency for the aristocratic ideal of excellence and the acknowledgment of superiority gradually to fade and *machinisme* and democracy (equality in mediocrity) to advance. A "tempo of life too fast for anyone's good" results.[51] Eventually few feel themselves inferior to others, and self-understanding disappears. Therapeutic notions that everyone should feel good about themselves often work in tandem with the spread of egalitarianism; and of course egalitarianism is a notion especially popular with the least perceptive.

49. "The Return of Purpose," *Co* 33 (2006): 666–81.

50. Steven Pinker, *How the Mind Works* (New York: Norton, 1997), argues not only that there are distinct male and female natures, but that because such things as freedom and equality cannot simultaneously be pursued without limits, most ideologies realize that there are tradeoffs between such categories: see on this Edward T. Oakes, "The Blind Programmer," *FT* 81 (March 1998): 35–42 at 40.

51. Robert Beum, "The Divinization of Democracy," *MA* 49, 2 (Spring 2007): 120–29 at 121–22, 124. Cf. Loren J. Samons II, *What's Wrong with Democracy? From Athenian Practice to American Worship* (Berkeley: University of California Press, 2004).

Cowling seems correct that there always is a congruence between the shape of one's society and the shape of one's religion. This is why it is so difficult to maintain, not just Catholicism, but any monotheistic religion, in a liberal, egalitarian society. Monotheism is the religion naturally suited to a hierarchical society. The religion naturally suitable to a modern, liberal, multicultural society, with its "conflicting spheres of activity and value," is polytheism.[52] Just as the old gods fought about and parceled out their various activities, the new gods among whom we now live each rule over this or that aspect of life, but no one rules the whole. The god of consumption and his followers duke it out with the god of environmental protection and his followers, but there is now no God of the universe. The liturgical sign of this latter, the loss of God, is informal worship. Where one God is believed in, worship tends to be solemn and dignified; where God is a fading presence, replaced perhaps by such gods as "community" and "self-affirmation," there is nothing to be solemn about, no overarching Reality which transcends the present.

Of course it takes time for the mutual destructions of modernity to work themselves out, and we have seen that some people have long been aware of the dangers against which Cowling warns. The papal encyclicals of the nineteenth and twentieth centuries, with the decline of all forms of monarchy and aristocracy in view, warn that even if the system be democratic, the people are to understand that the person chosen by them receives his authority not from them, but from God.[53] The general idea had long been understood. In 1645 Governor John Winthrop addressed the General Court of Massachusetts: "The questions that have troubled the country have been about the authority of the magistracy and the liberty of the people. It is you who have called us unto this office; but being called, we have our authority from God."[54] This was precisely the understanding of authority rejected in the American Declaration of Independence. Here authority was not merely resisted but destroyed, and government was based not on some mythical social contract placed in an unlocatable past, but on present consent. Thus, logically, all subordination was dissolved, though not all the Revolutionaries admitted this.[55] This paralleled the spread of the ideal of *fraternité*, more obvious in the French Revolution than in the American, which by making

52. The phrase is from M. A. Casey, "Democracy and the Thin Veneer of Civilisation," *FCSQ* 29, 4 (Winter 2006): 6, who notes that the idea of the return of polytheism goes back to Max Weber, who held that when the gods return to a modern, disenchanted world, they return as impersonal forces, not as Mercury but as ever-faster communications.

53. See especially Leo XIII, *Immortale Dei* (1885), and, on the limitations of the American constitutional order, *Longinqua Oceani* (1895).

54. Quoted in Richard M. Weaver, *Ideas Have Consequences* (Chicago: University of Chicago Press, 1948), 76.

55. Edmund S. Morgan, "The Other Founders," *NYRB* 52, 14 (September 22, 2005): 41–43 at 43.

everyone brothers undermined the various forms of natural inequality or authority marked by the relations between fathers and sons, and between the generations. Breaking the links of transmission through the generations inevitably diminishes the idea of history itself—this is the true "end of history"—and leaves all afloat in a rootless present.

Hierarchy, whether divinely or naturally sanctioned, depends on shared assumptions about ends, but not only is life in liberal regimes reduced to procedure, the drive for equality destroys the natural distinctions between humans on which any notion of natural authority is based.[56] This is one of Harvey Mansfield's points in his defense of "manliness," of the idea that there are natural differences between the sexes.[57] And, since Plato and Aristotle were right in their observation that people are in every empirical sense by nature unequal, justice—to give each his due—becomes impossible where the natural distinctions between people are ignored. The churches even begin to pray for an ever-increasing equality, for instance of material circumstance, and think of themselves as "just" in so doing. Almost forgotten is the thought that both knowledge and virtue depend on some transcendent standard (self-discipline, rightly understood, is submission to some Other).

Liberal societies tend to replace transcendent standards with material standards, and thus the transcendent dimensions of life dim, and with them any basis for mutual affection within society. For the affections that hold people together to flourish, they must agree on many things. "Modern democracy replaced the traditional bonds of mutual affection and obligation with the abstract principles of consent and contract; freeing the individual from traditional constraints, modern society also denied him traditional supports and protections."[58] This was Saul Bellow's point in his first novel of 1944, *Dangling Man,* in which Joseph the journal-keeper writes, "Goodness is achieved not in a vacuum, but in the company of other men, attended by love."[59] Something very like this is present in Benedict XVI's observation that "the coming clash will be between this radical emancipation of man and the great historical cultures."[60] That is, it will be clearer

---

56. Weaver, *Ideas Have Consequences,* ch. 2, "Distinction and Hierarchy."

57. *Manliness* (New Haven, Conn.: Yale University Press, 2006).

58. Christopher Shannon, "Catholicism as the Other," *FT* 139 (January, 2004): 46–52 at 48.

59. Quoted by J. M. Coetzee, "Bellow's Gift," *NYRB* 51, 8 (May 27, 2004): 4–8 at 4. Coetzee, writing of the isolation which attends individualism, summarizes, "by enthroning Man at the center of the universe, the Enlightenment, particularly in its Romantic phase, imposed impossible psychic demands on us, demands that work themselves out not just in petty fits of violence . . . or in such moral aberrations as the pursuit of greatness through crime (*vide* Dostoevsky's Raskolnikov) but perhaps in war." Cf. in the same issue, 12–16 at 14, the description of John Lennon's (of the Beatles) vision of terror as a potential outgrowth of freedom: Andrew O'Hagan, "Back in the US of A."

60. *Christianity and the Crisis of Cultures* (San Francisco: Ignatius Press, 2006), 44.

and clearer to those with eyes to see that the individual is meaningless except standing in a historical culture. Mansfield's "womanly nihilism," that is, radical feminism's attempt to move society in the direction of an undefinable and always receding freedom (to clearly state one's goal, to make freedom definite, is no longer to be free: this was one of Michel Foucault's main points), is the opposite of this.[61]

What Cowling wants is actually very close to some forms of traditional Catholicism, which, while promoting heroic spiritual lives for those who were able, was very conscious about not losing the many and aimed at saving the "mediocre man," the man of middling goals and self-consciousness, Jean Cardinal Danielou's "poor," not so much the materially poor as those without much sense of their own dignity and prospects.[62] What was needed for these was not an elaborate theory, but an emphasis on good practice. Paul Claudel was convinced that human imperfection is such that we are more designed to ward off defeat than to obtain victory, and this is the premise of Cowling's view. Augustine had declared that "we are the times, what we are the times will be"; Pascal had added that we do not so much have to plan a good culture as to begin acting as we should. Still, without discounting the obvious truth of Augustine's or Pascal's "just do it," one can with Romano Guardini wonder if a "second-generation" Catholicism which does not have the form of the life of the martyrs or of most of the saints is still open to us. Guardini, writing in the middle of the twentieth century, thought the coming world would be ever more dangerous for the Christian, and that the Christianity it demanded would have to be almost the opposite of Cowling's.

Volume 2 of Cowling's *magnum opus* concludes with analysis of those Christian writers with whom the present book began, thinkers like Christopher Dawson, who tried to halt the spread of secularization. Cowling does not think any of these made sufficient reply to the forces arrayed against them. In volume 3 he traces both the latitudinarian tradition of accommodationism, those who have tried to adjust Christianity to secularist doctrine, and those more traditional English Christian thinkers who have opposed this doctrine. The conclusion Cowling draws is that since secularism is a religion, an expression of man's nature as a religious animal, it too will pass in favor of some other religious expression. The situation could be recaptured by Christianity.[63]

⌒

The basic question of the merit of democracy and of the understanding of "rights" as found in liberal democracies is much contested. Philosophers

61. Charles S. Kesler, "The Male Calling," *NR* 58, 8 (May 8, 2006): 45–46.
62. See my "'You Can't Legislate Morality': Reflections on a Bromide," *Co* 2 (1975), 148–62.
63. Hart, "Most Partial Historian," 37–40.

such as Charles Taylor have seen in transcendence a ground for things they value in modernity, things that modernity has given us, such as the primacy of rights.[64] This primacy Taylor sees as foundational for an ethic of unconditional love, an ethic based on our being in the image of God. His view, like that of John Paul II, is that we must write and work from within modernity and develop a "Catholic modernity," but this view is far from unchallenged. It has been provocatively explored in a striking book by Robert P. Kraynak, which argues against Christianity's relatively recent embrace of the idea that a rights-based form of democracy is the best form of political life: "Constitutional monarchy under God" is in principle much preferable.[65]

Kraynak marshals much traditional thought on his behalf, and we could easily introduce further materials. Two recent studies of the early Jesuits show that, though they disagreed amongst themselves on many things, most assumed that monarchy and hierarchy were naturally suited to humans.[66] The arguments to this conclusion are as old as Plato's observation that humans are by nature unequal and Aristotle's consideration of the question what should be done if a person superior to everyone else appears in society. Dante in turn assimilated Virgil's rendition of the providential mission of Rome into a vision of an earthly order mirroring the divine, but this was common coin in the medieval period. Further, well into the modern period virtually all held that toleration—doing nothing to suppress evil if one had the possibility of so doing—was disastrous for the individual soul and the political order itself.[67] Thus Pedro de Ribadeneira argued in 1595 in his *Christian Prince* that heresy caused civil unrest and concomitant social disintegration.

64. Charles Taylor, *A Catholic Modernity? Charles Taylor's Marianist Lecture,* ed. James L. Heft (New York: Oxford University Press, 1999); and the review by Thomas Landy, *Collegium* 1, 10 (April 2000): 5–6 at 6, on this and the following. See also Taylor's *A Secular Age* (Cambridge, Mass.: Harvard University Press, 2007).

65. *Christian Faith and Modern Democracy* (Notre Dame, Ind.: University of Notre Dame Press, 2001), 232. I have found particularly helpful the reflections on this book found in "Robert P. Kraynak's Christian Faith and Modern Democracy: A Symposium," ed. Kenneth L. Grasso and Cecilia Rodriguez Castillo, in *CSSR* 9 (2004): 13–95. See here Grasso's "Introduction," 14. The discussion continues in *In Defense of Human Dignity: Essays for Our Times,* ed. Robert Kraynak and Glenn Tinder (Notre Dame, Ind.: University of Notre Dame Press, 2003). Francis Oakley, *Kingship: The Politics of Enchantment* (Malden, Mass.: Blackwell, 2006), argues that kingship as the most common form of government over the ages represents a wisdom that does not have to let modern secular discourse set the political agenda.

66. Robert Birely, *The Jesuits and the Thirty Years War: Kings, Courts, and Confessors* (Cambridge: Cambridge University Press, 2003), and Harro Höpfl, *Jesuit Political Thought: The Society of Jesus and the State, c. 1540–1630* (Cambridge: Cambridge University Press, 2004). Here and in the following I am following a useful review of these books by John M. Vella, "The Jesuits and Political Power," *MA* 48, 2 (Spring 2006): 158–163, here at 158–59.

67. Brad Gregory, *Salvation at Stake: Christian Martyrdom in Early Modern Europe* (Cambridge, Mass.: Harvard University Press, 1999). On the historical meaning of "toleration" see my "Setting Boundaries," and "The Middle Ages in the History of Toleration: A Prolegomena," *MS* 16 (2008): 1–20.

It was not just that monarchy was accepted as the form of government most natural to man, because replicating God's rule of the universe and the desirable place of the father within the family; it was assumed that there should be a congruence between the rule of the universe by God, the rule of the Church by the pope, and the rule of the political order by the king. It is all very well to claim, as in America, that a hierarchical Church is compatible with a democratic society, but in our moments of passing lucidity we must acknowledge that the Jesuits were right. What has actually happened in American Catholic history is that habits of authority originally brought to America from a variety of sources, everything from the dominance of the parish priest in traditional Irish village life to European monarchism, have with time been undermined in tandem with parental authority by habits brought into the Church and the family from the larger "democratic" society. Anti-Catholicism and ethnic ghettoes initially shielded the American Catholic population from the more radical tendencies of egalitarianism, but, especially since the "opening to the world" in the wake of Vatican II, the gates have been down.

Kraynak is of course not the first fundamentally to call into question the desirability of what seems to most the political givens of the age, republican freedom, self-government, popular sovereignty, democracy, individual rights, and, more generally, rights theory: such a counter-cultural stance is present in the writings, for instance, of Oliver and Joan Lockwood O'Donovan.[68] And we have noted that earlier in American history there were present much more limited understandings of democracy than those generally found today, Abraham Lincoln, for instance, holding that humans are only equal in their right to the results of their own labor.[69] But arguably Kraynak has thought his position through more thoroughly.

Kraynak's proposal is that we "sever the Christian-democrat connection."[70] Since he acknowledges that "some version of democracy is the only practical option in the present age for the ordering of temporal affairs," I take him to mean that the Christian should not say that democracy is the best form of government per se, or that it is what Christianity concludes to, but that it is at present the only viable form for us, a form we must always work to tame in a non-liberal way.[71] The dominant American Catholic be-

---

68. The O'Donovans' extremely helpful *From Irenaeus to Grotius; A Sourcebook in Christian Political Thought, 100–1625* (Grand Rapids, Mich.: Eerdmans, 1999) is complemented by the essays in their *Bonds of Imperfection: Christian Politics, Past and Present* (Grand Rapids, Mich.: Eerdmans, 2004), and see Oliver O'Donovan, *The Desire of the Nations: Rediscovering the Roots of Political Theology* (New York: Cambridge University Press, 1996). See also Michael Hoelzl, *Religion and Political Thought* (New York: Continuum, 2006), and Hugh Heclo et al., *Christianity and American Democracy* (Cambridge, Mass.: Harvard University Press, 2007).

69. David Bromwich, "How Lincoln Won," *NYRB* 53, 16 (October 19, 2006): 46–49 at 48.

70. *Christian Faith,* 183; Grasso, "Introduction," 14.

71. *Christian Faith,* 244. In reply, Kenneth L. Grasso, "Democracy, Modernity and the

lief that there is an intrinsic compatibility between Catholicism and the American constitutional tradition, indeed that America has found the best solution yet to such questions as the relation of Church to state, is mistaken: there are intrinsic tensions and incompatibilities between Catholicism and any form of democracy.

There is perhaps some overlap between Kraynak's opinions and some of Pope Benedict XVI's subsequent remarks on democracy. Having stated that "the guarantee of a shared collaboration in the elaboration of the law and in the just administration of power is the basic argument that speaks in favor of democracy as the most appropriate form of political order," Benedict takes notice of the serious problems in forming a democratic will. The most common sense of "democratic" in recent papal encyclicals has been "following the rule of law and having a fixed constitutional order," but here Benedict seems to be thinking of democracy as more than this, as a specific form of political system.[72] Thinkers such as Habermas have taught us to have special concern for achieving public consensus, but Benedict reminds us that nothing guarantees that a majority will be right. The majority principle may establish laws, but it cannot establish their goodness. I suppose the basic fact, so far as the United States is concerned, is that from the beginning there was a plurality of religions which became central to the history of the country and which must reasonably be assumed to be a permanent feature of American life.

Kraynak believes that the theory of so many, including Jacques Maritain and John Courtney Murray, that there is a natural "harmony or convergence between Christianity and liberal democracy" is mistaken.[73] Again, the basic fact is that things such as the American practice of religious toleration are rooted first not in some theoretical position, but in the desire for public tranquility. That is, the American separation of Church and state was not the result of the implementation of some best constitutional arrangement, but a pragmatic response to the question of how political union is possible, granted a variety of religions.

Kraynak is not the first to deny that there is a natural convergence between Christianity and liberal democracy; Michael Baxter, to whom we will turn later, has written eloquently against Americanism, which he defines as "the belief that the American government and its principles were benign to and even supportive of the aims of the Catholic Church, and that the United States was a providential instrument to aid the Church in bringing salva-

---

Catholic Human Rights Revolution: Reflections on Christian Faith and Modern Democracy," *CSSR* 9 (2004): 37–45 at 38–39, points out that Catholic social teaching has never held that democracy is the only acceptable form of government, but that thinkers like Jacques Maritain do argue that it is the best form of government.

72. Ratzinger, "That Which Holds the World Together," 59–60, at 59 for quotation.

73. "About Christian Faith and Modern Democracy," *CSSR* 9 (2004): 17–19, at 17.

tion to the world."[74] For Baxter, who sees the Americanism condemned by Leo XIII in 1899 as in fact the foundation of American civil theology up to the present, this simply is not true, and he deplores a situation in which while, "both liberal and conservative Catholics have different conceptions of Catholicism, and different conceptions of America, . . . they both believe there exists a fundamental harmony between the two."[75]

For Kraynak belief in a natural convergence between Christianity and liberal democracy is a relatively recent aberration in Christian thought, above all the result of the importation into Christian thought of Kant's views about the nature of freedom and his approach to human rights. Catholic thinkers have seen the benefit of the use of this theory in defense against tyranny, but, according to Kraynak, have not appreciated sufficiently the negative side of rights theory, its subversion of traditional forms of authority and the notion of hierarchy itself, and its promotion of an uncontrollable notion of human autonomy.[76] Kraynak uses very strong language here, speaking of current emphasis on rights as a "spiritual lobotomy" which cuts out "the highest part of the human soul, the part that longs for eternity and for spiritual transcendence."[77]

Kraynak sees himself as continuing the views of Augustine about the relation of the Two Cities. Here, although this is not fatal to much that he wishes to say, he seems to misunderstand Augustine, for in fact on this critical point he seems closer to Luther than Augustine.[78] Kraynak repeatedly writes as if Augustine equated the City of God with the Church, and the City of Man with the state.[79] But for Augustine the City of God was composed of all those who have done, are doing, or will do the will of God, and the City of Man of all those who do the Devil's will.[80] No historical or

74. "Lectures," in *EC* (Spring 2005): 9, describing the Schmitt Lecture, "Seeking Another City: Beyond Liberal and Conservative Catholicism in the United States," given at the Notre Dame Center for Ethics and Culture, April 13, 2005.

75. Ibid., 9.

76. "About Christian Faith," 18.

77. *Christian Faith*, 270; and see Gregory Beabout, "Personhood as Gift and Task: The Place of the Person in Catholic Social Thought," *CSSR* 9 (2004): 67–75 at 70.

78. Jeanne Heffernan, "Making the Christian Case for Democracy: A Response to Kraynak's Criticism," *CSSR* 9 (2004): 29–35, esp. 29–31, at 30, recognizes the "Lutheran" (Two Kingdoms) reading of the Two Cities found in Kraynak. Kraynak's response to his critics evidences a shaky knowledge of patristic and medieval thought about the Two Cities, "The Illusion of Christian Democracy," *CSSR* 9 (2004): 87–95 at 89–92. I do think Kraynak is right when he says all his critics in this particular symposium avoid some of his main points, such as "the hostility of democracy to the concept of hierarchy which is so important for the Church and for the perfection of the human soul" (90–91).

79. Robert Dodaro, *Christ and the Just Society in the Thought of Augustine* (Cambridge: Cambridge University Press, 2004), with the review by Paul Weithman in *JECS* 14 (2006): 245–47, raising a number of interesting issues.

80. In "About Christian Faith," 18–19, Kraynak continues to say that his hope is "to recover the traditional Christian doctrine of the Two Cities—the distinction between God's realm and Caesar's realm, or between the city of God and the earthly city—and apply it to the modern

visible community may be identified with either city. The Church has in it many who say "Lord, Lord," but do not the will of God; and Caesar's realm may have in it those who have never heard of Christ but who attempt to do God's will. This said, it does seem to me that Kraynak is right in insisting that Christianity is not tied to any specific form of government. This, that there are a plurality of legitimate forms of government was, after all, the position of Leo XIII. That one can show that monarchy is in principle the best form of government does not make it suitable to every historical experience.

Arguably a great insight of the most perceptive political thinking since the sixteenth century, against the tendency of ancient and medieval thought to speak primarily of the best state, has been a certain realism which insists that no one escapes their history: that history is always a limit on what is possible. This was briefly discussed in chapter 2. Aristotle in his criticisms of Plato's political thinking already understood this, but before Machiavelli most thought had been of an "ought" hardly constrained by one's history. We here face the most difficult of choices. On the one side stands the universalism of Roman law and all its descendants in the Latin lands, but also of Kant and all thought in quest of some universal best law. All these instincts to find a best law have something noble about them, and in their drive for a single, all-embracing civilization a great confidence in human reason. On the other hand we have the instinct of some at least of the Romantics, but also of certain forms of multiculturalism today. These luxuriate in and celebrate the differences between peoples and cultures, and do not believe a single worldwide civilization possible or desirable. The choice between these two alternatives is as agonizing as any made in the political sphere, for it involves a decision about how rational humans are, and how much in control of their destinies. Kraynak—with the present writer—thinks that we will always be caught between these two options, capable of envisioning a universal order, but incapable of achieving it. We should therefore be content with a multiplicity of constitutionalisms, each of which works well enough within a given history, and not throw this over in favor of a best form of life.

In any case, for Kraynak the Church teaches "constitutionalism without liberalism": any constitutionally limited government under God is legitimate, but the best such governments are mixed regimes which combine hierarchy and democracy.[81] The forms and structures of all societies are

---

age." Most of the scholars who respond to Kraynak in this symposium do not notice his basic misunderstanding of Augustine. This misunderstanding is common in Protestant exegesis, but was pointed out as wrong more than a half-century ago by, among others, Etienne Gilson in his introduction to *Saint Augustine: The City of God* (Garden City, N.Y.: Doubleday, 1958). Besides Heffernan, David S. Crawford, "Christianity, a Culture of Love, and Kraynak's Critique," *CSSR* 9 (2004): 77–85 at 77 and 85 n. 12, does note Kraynak's mistaken exegesis.

81. "About Christian Faith," 18–19. For the history of mixed forms of government, see Alois

constantly changing, and while at a given point, for instance, bourgeois society may have a certain form of public sphere, over time this will certainly
change.[82] Further, it is clear, if we cling to the nineteenth-century English
understanding of liberalism, that though today the language of liberalism is
all around us, we much more live in managerial than liberal states.[83]

His critics seem right in pointing out that Kraynak tends to speak of all
rights as Kantian in nature when in fact there was a "natural rights" tradition going back into the Middle Ages which was not autonomy-based.[84] In
fact, there was lively discussion in the late Middle Ages of, for instance, the
limits of obedience, that is, of whether only duties exist, and no individual
rights.[85] As W. Norris Clarke has shown, in the medieval tradition human
dignity was not founded simply on human freedom, but on man's status in
the universe as *imago Dei,* as possessing a soul and being capable of obedience to God in achieving God's end for him.[86] This was not a "dumb obedience," but cooperation as a co-creator with God, exercising providential
direction over one's own life in a manner analogous to God's providential direction of the universe. That is, though human dignity is more than
human freedom, the fact that man is free is essential to what is asked of
him. He is asked voluntarily to become Godlike. So, though there is a pre-
Kantian form of rights discourse, the emphasis in pre-Kantian Christian
thought is not on rights, but on obligations to God and one's fellows freely
embraced.

At a less theological or philosophical level, a number of scholars have
been building on the contributions of Brian Tierney to the elucidation of
medieval natural rights thought.[87] These scholars have shown the appearance in twelfth-century canon law of discussion of rights and their cor-

---

Riklin, *Machtteilung: Geschichte der Mischverfassung* (Darmstadt: Wissenschaftliche Buchgesellschaft, 2006).

82. Jürgen Habermas, *The Structural Transformation of the Public Sphere: An Inquiry into a
Category of Bourgeois Society,* tr. Thomas Burger (Cambridge, Mass.: MIT Press, 1989).

83. Paul Gottfried, *After Liberalism: Mass Democracy in the Managerial State* (Princeton,
N.J.: Princeton University Press, 1999).

84. Gary Glenn, "Words That Sound Alike but Have Different Meanings: Christian 'Natural Rights' and Kantian Inspired 'Human Rights,'" *CSSR* 9 (2004): 21–28 at 21. Glenn's argument is that a pre-Kantian understanding of rights is useful, and should not have fallen under Kraynak's general censure (23). For Glenn it is "human rights" and "democratic human
rights"—that is, any notion of an unconditional right—that should be censured, not "rights."
See also Francis Oakley, *Natural Law, Laws of Nature, and Natural Rights: Continuity and Discontinuity in the History of Ideas* (New York: Continuum, 2005).

85. Janet Coleman, "Are There Any Individual Rights or Only Duties? On the Limits of
Obedience in the Avoidance of Sin according to Late Medieval and Early-Modern Scholars," in
Transformations in Medieval and Early-Modern Rights Discourse, ed. Virpi Mäkinen and Petter
Korkman (Dordrecht: Springer, 2006), 3–36, is one of several relevant studies in this volume.

86. "Freedom, Equality, Dignity of the Human Person: The Roots of Liberal Democracy,"
CSSR 9 (2004): 61–66 at 61 and 63–64.

87. Of Tierney's various writings, see *The Idea of Natural Rights: Studies on Natural Rights,
Natural Law, and Church Law, 1150–1625* (Atlanta: Scholars Press, 1997).

responding obligations. For instance, a body of law about marriage took up the patristic idea that men and women are moral and spiritual equals, but not necessarily equal in authority within the family or society. This law talks about the rights and responsibilities of spouses to one another, to their families of origin, and to their children. The goal was the balancing of these various rights against one another, but with the assumption that the end in view was the protection of marriage as sacramental and as part of a larger community.[88] The whole framework of thought was quite different from a modern liberal or secular idea of rights, for the center of thought was not the individual, but marriage itself as a community worth protecting.[89]

In a limited degree the medieval understanding of natural rights survives in the American Declaration of Independence, where we find a notion of natural rights and nature which is partly traditional, partly born of the Enlightenment.[90] As Kraynak himself notes without seeming fully to see the significance of this observation, long before Kant thinkers such as Suarez (1548–1617) affirmed that humans have natural rights "embedded in the social nature of man" in a schema in which the common good is primary, that is, in which the individual is not autonomous but placed under the common good.[91] Just as in the case of modernism, there is no necessity that we accept the Kantian revolution in the understanding of rights: we can always insist that we remain in continuity with the pre-Kantian Christian natural rights tradition and build on it. This, it can be argued, is precisely what especially John Paul II did. In this tradition man is not "born free" in a liberal sense, but always into a manifold and hierarchical social situation, and it is acknowledged that no two people were ever "born equal." Justice is not the promotion of ever-greater equality, but the ordering of society around the differences or natural inequalities found among all individuals (the liberal employs politics to attack the hierarchies or differences found in nature; the Catholic, actually anyone who respects the structures of nature, employs politics to construct a society ordered around those differences).

Kraynak's larger analysis is for the most part correct. In Kantian discourse rights define the person, but in pre-Kantian discourse this definition was derived from the hierarchy of ends in which the person participated, we might say by community in its largest sense. Ancient Greek Republican thought had little place for freedom understood as non-dependency, and

---

88. Charles J. Reid Jr., *Power Over the Body, Equality in the Family: Rights and Domestic Relations in Medieval Canon Law* (Grand Rapids, Mich.: Eerdmans, 2004), 4–5.

89. Ibid., 2–3.

90. Glenn, "Words That Sound Alike," 26.

91. *Christian Faith*, 122–23. Cf. Nicholas Wolterstorff, *Justice: Rights and Wrongs* (Princeton, N.J.: Princeton University Press, 2008), for treatment of many of the issues discussed by Kraynak, arguing that human rights are inadequately grounded either in a purely secular account of human dignity or in ancient eudaimonism.

saw no value per se in political participation.[92] In pre-Kantian discourse, because the temporal communities within which the individual found himself—his family, village, class, or state—were all intrinsically limited in their goals, so were his rights; but if rights be viewed in Kantian fashion as equally applying to all, and to be gathered by each in the name of all as a part of the very definition of their humanity, there is no limit to their expansion.[93] A good example of this is the invention by the Supreme Court in the 1940s of "civil liberties," which ever since have expanded with virtually no attention to an earlier understanding of either duty or natural law, and very little attention to the common good.

All communities, that is, anything historically specific, are threatened by rights' universalizing tendencies. The authority of parents or teachers, for instance, tends to dissolution in the face of children as rights-bearers, little instances of universal humanity ("the right of humanity in our own person," Kant says), smaller but as persons substantially their parents' equals.[94] "Right" itself is understood primarily as "freedom," independence from constraint insofar as this is compatible with everyone else's freedom. Such language is intrinsically subversive and skeptical of anything standing in the way of the individual, and thus tends to undermine all authority, including that of religion. To the degree it advances, a shared idea of the common good and thus a shared life in society becomes impossible. Any religion using this language is asking for trouble.[95] As several of those who have made rejoinders to Kraynak point out, what he has really demonstrated is the incompatibility of Catholicism and a Kantian understanding of freedom. Some other understanding of freedom, particularly some earlier understanding, may not be vulnerable to his criticisms. With the Catholic tradition we can choose to think of freedom as "freedom for the good," rather than as something autonomous, self-sufficient and self-explanatory, not ordered to things beyond itself.[96] We conclude that Kraynak has not proved that Catholicism and democracy are incompatible, only that if democracy is to be compatible with Catholicism, it must be built on a nonliberal anthropology, one which in principle preserves hierarchy and an orientation to transcendence.[97]

⟜

92. Eric Nelson, *The Greek Tradition in Republican Thought* (Cambridge: Cambridge University Press, 2004).

93. Glenn, "Words That Sound Alike," 22, and also 25, on the following. Both Kraynak and Glenn realize Kant is not consistent, and sometimes understands rights in more traditional fashion than he does at other times.

94. Ibid., 22, citing Immanuel Kant, *The Science of Right* III, 222, 25, 28.

95. Ibid., 23; Clarke, "Freedom, Equality, Dignity of the Human Person," 65.

96. Clarke, "Freedom, Equality, Dignity of the Human Person," 65.

97. Heffernan, "Making the Christian Case for Democracy," 32, proposing the thought of Yves Simon as a model.

Of recent years, many have noted the "turn to religion" in Continental philosophy.[98] Hent de Vries has suggested that a turn to religion already manifest among philosophers is an anticipation of a larger cultural shift.[99] He sees in thinkers such as Theodor Adorno (1903–69) and Emmanuel Levinas (1906–95) a "theology in pianissimo," religious echoes of the transcendent.[100] Perhaps more basic is the growing number of philosophical and theological voices rising in defense of metaphysics understood in one or another of its classical or realist forms. Against the tendency of especially positivist, pragmatic, and deconstructionist philosophical positions to, allegedly, dispose of metaphysics altogether, these voices defend several propositions: 1) that man is not autonomous in the Cartesian or Rawlsian sense, but dependent for language and meaning on both social context and historical tradition, 2) that man cannot form intelligible statements without some at least implicit orientation to universal standards such as truth, goodness, and beauty, and 3) that man is of his nature therefore transcendentally oriented.

It is not just philosophers and theologians who have come to the defense of metaphysics traditionally understood. Even in sociology we sometimes find disenchantment with a disenchanted world and discipline. Walter Benjamin (1892–1940) was one of the Frankfurt School theorists who early on suspected that the road to madness lies in a purely secular reason, and many sociologists have returned to something like Christopher Dawson's view not just that culture should be a central sociological category, but that social forms express religious or theological ideas.[101] Kiernan Flanagan has written a book, *The Enchantment of Sociology,* invoking Max Weber's fear that a disenchanted modernity would lock humans in an "iron cage" of disenchantment.[102] Flanagan sees in postmodernity's criticism of linear technical rationality, its openness to play, and its use of the apophatic the paradox that "the form that effects disbelief can also actuate belief."[103] This was also the argument of Philip Rieff, who thought the very pervasiveness of an aesthetics of anti-authority in contemporary culture could be turned on the house of cards which is modernity.[104] Just as modernity had de-

98. *Rethinking Philosophy of Religion: Approaches from Continental Philosophy,* ed. Philip Goodchild (New York: Fordham University Press, 2003); Dominique Janicaud et al., *Phenomenology and the "Theological Turn"* (New York: Fordham University Press, 2000).

99. *Philosophy and the Turn to Religion* (Baltimore: Johns Hopkins University Press, 1999), and see Philip Blosser, "God Among the Philosophers," *NOR* 66, 9 (October 1999): 39–42.

100. *Minimal Theologies: Critiques of Secular Reason in Adorno and Levinas,* tr. Geoffrey Hale (Baltimore: Johns Hopkins University Press, 2005).

101. John A. Coleman, "Review," in *Theological Studies* 58 (1997): 375–77 at 376; Eric Jacobson, *Metaphysics of the Profane: The Political Theology of Walter Benjamin and Gershom Scholem* (New York: Columbia University Press, 2003).

102. Subtitle: *A Study of Theology and Culture* (London: Macmillan, 1996).

103. Ibid., 143.

104. *My Life Among the Deathworks. Illustrations of the Aesthetics of Authority* (Charlottes-

stroyed the sacral sources of life, the authority of modernity could be rendered risible in preparation for something beyond itself.

There are other reasons for the turn to religion, or at least the resources of religion, witness the thought of Terry Eagleton, only one of a number of cultural theorists now appropriating various aspects of Christianity. A cradle Catholic and adult Marxist, Eagleton is "a post-Catholic Marxist" with strong Christian yearnings.[105] He believes cultural theory is in severe decline: "The Babylon of the market has captured cultural theory, and . . . the nation-state and the university are now hostage to the corporation," so that the only "intellectual tradition with sufficient resources and independence" for cultural theory to turn to is religion. In Paul J. Griffiths's words, Eagleton views capitalism as committed "to the idea that humans are infinitely plastic, that our appetites can be shaped into ever-new forms without constraint by nature. The market requires such a view so that it can educate our desires into inexhaustibly new patterns of need and consumption." The empty formalism of liberalism, Eagleton thinks, is the ally of such views, and his attack on capitalism and liberalism comes close to the strictures of John Paul II on these same phenomena.

One of John Paul II's signal contributions to contemporary thought—in part a return to a pre-Cartesian way of viewing things—was his idea that both the human body and the world have a sacramentality which reveals invisible realities.[106] John Paul insisted that man is his body and that this body expresses human mystery and transcendence. For him the created order, coming as a gift from a personal God who is love, may be spoken of analogically as in communion with God, as forming a community with God. The physical, while itself neither spiritual nor personal, is open to the organic-human, has an interior order, form, and finality which make it apt for "integration into the organic-human."[107] It cannot be viewed as the "dead matter" technological reason wishes endlessly to manipulate.

In an attempt to elucidate the subjective dimension or interiority of all beings, persons or not, this line of thought has been developed by the Catholic philosophers Kenneth Schmitz and W. Norris Clarke. Such a line of thought, which uses such ideas as interiority analogously of non-personal beings, which of course are not deliberative, is very far removed from the analytic tradition

---

ville: University of Virginia Press, 2006). See also Rieff's *Sacred Order/Social Order*, vol. 2: *The Crisis of the Officer Class, the Decline of the Tragic Sensibility* (Charlottesville: University of Virginia Press, 2007), on modernity and postmodernity.

105. Paul J. Griffiths, "Christ and Critical Theory," *FT* 145 (August/September 2004): 46–55 at 48–49, for this and the following quotations.

106. See for instance "The Original Unity of Man and Woman," in *The Theology of the Body: Human Love in the Divine Plan* (Boston: Pauline Books and Media, 1997), 76–77.

107. David L. Schindler, "The Significance of World and Culture for Moral Theology," *Co* 31 (2004): 111–42 at 128, commenting on Wojtyla.

which has formed much English-language philosophy. Schmitz has proposed a Thomism developed by personalism in which freedom becomes

one of the transcendental attributes of being itself, analogously understood, of course, alongside of one, true, good, and (for many) beautiful. . . . At the lowest level of being he insists on a certain amount of "spontaneity" that cannot be fully captured by any formal, mathematical laws. . . . He does have quantum physics on his side, according to which it is impossible to predict the behavior of any single subatomic particle, like a photon of light. The laws here are only statistical averages over large numbers.[108]

A person is simply the highest form of being, which in itself is relational. Aristotle is wrong that the highest perfection is solitary self-sufficiency, as with the Prime Mover; the highest perfection, *actus purus,* is persons-in-communion. Analogously, this is what we find throughout all being: "The personalization of being has taken place!"[109]

Schmitz urged an overcoming of the Cartesian separation of mind from matter and an overcoming of a consequent modern epistemology that divides everything into subject and object. What is wanted is "a stance that is both trans-objective and trans-subjective," the understanding "already implicit in pre-modern thought."[110] Thus Schmitz, while valuing very much the insights of modern thought into human subjectivity, interiority, or subjecthood, also proposed the recovery of the insight that man is a microcosm, of course the very insight on which traditional views of transcendence were built. He wanted to defend the view that, always analogously, non-intellectual beings may be spoken of as free, as having "a certain qualified autonomy." He insisted that such language is more than metaphor. The modern identification of freedom with choice

makes the attribution of freedom to things seem extravagant, and . . . it can easily be made to appear absurd. But the attribution is meant to free things from their confinement as objects standing over against a human subject, so that their whole being is then reduced to that relation, either for purposes of experience, control, or utility. . . . Insofar as things are grasped in their being, they are freed from the modern dichotomy of determinism and indeterminism and released to the freedom to be themselves in accordance with their nature.

The technological view logically culminates in what John Paul II called "the culture of death," the conclusion that if matter has no intrinsic meaning, human life has no intrinsic value. People may be viewed as objects, as obstacles that stand in one's way.[111] This is the opposite of the view that the

---

108. W. Norris Clarke, "The Integration of Person and Being in Twentieth-Century Thomism," *Co* 31 (2004): 435–46 at 439, describing Schmitz.

109. Ibid., 444.

110. "To Father Norris Clarke in Appreciation," *Co* 31 (2004): 447–56 at 451–53, for the following quotations.

111. Elizabeth Fox-Genovese, "Feminism and the Unraveling of the Social Bond," *Voices* 19, 3

physical is something God-given ordered to the organic and human.[112] The cosmology of this latter view, on which a transcendent liturgy depends, can only be recuperated through an ontology of giftedness. No field of knowledge, not physics and biology nor anthropology and economics, can be viewed simply materialistically. As *Gaudium et Spes,* the Pastoral Constitution on the Church in the Modern World of Vatican II, declared, man "can fully find his true self only in the sincere gift of self."[113] We discover ourselves more in self-giving than in self-assertion, more in relationship than in autonomy.

All must be seen as, of course analogically, ordered to the distinctively human and personal.[114] When John Paul's successor, Benedict XVI, said that modern Enlightenment philosophy is replacing the Christian roots of Western society, this is what he had in mind: Christianity is about self-giving; the Enlightenment is about autonomous individuals piling up rights.[115] The tragedy of the latter is that, typically, while rights are accumulated, life itself is evacuated of meaning. This was a special concern of Benedict's first encyclical, *Deus Caritas Est.* Here Benedict tried to specify the ways in which the Church's mission of social justice is different from the state's. Both often aim at the same thing, but the state pursues justice juridically and institutionally, while for the Church this is something that flows from the Eucharist. That is, for the Church the mission to justice is a dimension of the communion of saints wherein those who communicate in the Eucharist are compelled by that fact to the mission of directly bringing justice into the world of their everyday lives. The example of Mother Teresa is apposite here. The Christian approves the attempt of the state to build up a more just social order, but, however that attempt stands, Christians by the fact of their participation in the Eucharist and the communion of saints are bound directly to live justly.

In an address to the United Nations General Assembly, in 1995, John Paul II brought together many of the themes treated in the present book. Observing that the human person always finds himself between both universal and particular values, the pope insisted that cultures must acknowledge the person's rights and dignity, thus limiting their own right to demand allegiance. That said, cultures must also defend themselves and their own particularity, because in particularity God's richness is revealed. The

---

(2004): 9–14 at 11, discussing, 12, the relentless war of feminism on institutions which curtail women's autonomy, and therefore as the "cutting edge" of all that is most destructive in modernity.

112. Adrian J. Walker, "On 'Rephilosophizing' Theology," *Co* 31 (2004): 143–67 at 158–59.

113. Quoted and commented on by George Sim Johnston, "After the Council: Living Vatican II," *IC*, December 24, 2004, 3.

114. Schindler, "Significance of World," 135, for further bibliography.

115. Joseph Ratzinger, *Christianity and the Crisis of Cultures* (San Francisco: Ignatius Press, 2006). For Ratzinger's "political theology," see also his *Values in a Time of Upheaval* (San Francisco: Ignatius Press, 2006).

diversity of cultures points to the transcendence of God, the many ways in which culture can reveal and be related to God. Cultural diversity is a good which encourages continuing exchange between the universal and the particular.[116]

Benedict XVI developed these themes when he in turn addressed the United Nations General Assembly in 2008. His particular interest was "to restore a proper understanding of human rights."[117] Acknowledging that "human rights are increasingly being presented as the common language and the ethical substratum of international relations," Benedict reminded his audience that human rights are "grounded and shaped by the transcendent nature of the person" and are "based on the natural law inscribed on human hearts and present in different cultures and civilizations." Finally, noting that religious dialogue must never be suppressed, he stated that "religious liberty . . . has to give due consideration to the public dimension of religion."

As John Paul II remarked in 1999 in *Ecclesia in America:* "The Church which . . . can in no way be confused with the political community nor tied to any political system, is both a sign and safeguard of the transcendent character of the human person."[118] Benedict XVI continued this line of thought in *Deus Caritas Est,* 28, by stating that though

the State may not impose religion, . . . it must guarantee religious freedom and harmony between the followers of different religions. For her part, the Church, as the social expression of Christian faith, has a proper independence and is structured on the basis of her faith as a community which the State must recognize. The two spheres are distinct, yet always interrelated.[119]

This is quite different from a tradition of a "high wall" separating Church and state.

Throughout the twentieth century there were voices trying to conceive our life in society differently. This happened in many fields, especially, as we know, in the arts. Such lament often resulted in an unreflective rejection of the new, but what the more serious critics of modernism targeted, say, in church architecture, was an architecture which had forgotten its purpose. The goal of much "modern" ecclesiastical architecture seemed to be the creation of an abstract space so denuded of iconic connections with the past that the church building evokes more a sense of puzzlement than of mystery.

116. See the letter of Derek S. Jeffreys, "Which Diversity," in *FT* 142 (April 2004): 6.

117. This and the following are from Susan Yoshihara, "Pope's UN Address Urges Proper Understanding of Human Rights, UN Role," C-FAM.

118. Para 27, cited in Peter J. Casarella, "Solidarity as the Fruit of Communion," *Co* 27 (2000): 98–123 at 110, and see 111, on the eschatological standard.

119. Vatican translation, Libreria Editrice Vaticana 2005.

Many decried the creation of prosaic liturgical spaces. Thus in an article in the March 24, 2000, issue of *Commonweal,* Sidney Callahan lamented the sterility and lack of mystery and sacramentality of many contemporary (American) churches:

In a real cathedral or church my spirit expands if there are dim corners where worshippers can pray privately before illuminated icons and banks of vigil lights. . . . Without this transcendent eschatological dimension of worship, fully embodied in art, music, beauty, ritual, and sacred space, Cromwell wins. . . . Habitual exposure to the stripped-down aesthetic of a school cafeteria or supermarket presents peculiar difficulties for the spirit.[120]

The theologians gathered around John Milbank and Catherine Pickstock, interested in prodding the imagination to reconsider what life in society might be capable of, wondered if some form of non-integralist re-enchantment was not possible. Pickstock's special interest has been "the liturgy as a way of life," which she sees as being at great risk from anti-ritual modernity.[121] Her goal is challenging all in the contemporary world which is inimical to liturgical life, which means challenging pretty much everything. She begins with a radical claim, but in making it shows that Plato held something similar: "Language exists primarily, and in the end only has meaning as, the praise of the Divine."[122] The medieval, liturgical city was "avowedly semiotic . . . entirely and constitutively articulate through the signs of speech, gesture, art, music, figures, vestment colour, fire, water, smoke, bread, wine and relationality," speaking constantly of eternity.[123] By contrast, the modern city/necropolis denies eternity. Nominalism has been so victorious in it that its denizens no longer participate in that of which they speak.

Pending the overthrow of such a state of affairs, Pickstock proposes that a liturgy be devised that refuses "to be enculturated in our modern habits of thought and speech."[124] The Christian of the twenty-first century is at every point to challenge all in modern culture which obscures proper worship of God.[125] If this is done, even spatial categories can be seen to express God's

120. Quoted and discussed in "Back to Mystery?" *AB* 6, 3 (May 2000): 7.

121. Pickstock, "Medieval Liturgy and Modern Reform," *Antiphon* 6, 1 (2001): 19–25 at 21, and see Mayna Rivera Rivera, "Radical Transcendence? Divine and Human Otherness in Radical Orthodoxy and Liberation Theology," in *Interpreting the Postmodern: Responses to "Radical Orthodoxy,"* ed. Rosemary Radford Ruether and Marion Grau (New York: T & T Clark, 2006), 119–38.

122. *After Writing: On the Liturgical Consummation of Philosophy* (Oxford: Blackwell Publishers, 1998), xiii, parts 1, and 2; and see the review by Richard Cipolla in *Antiphon* 4, 2 (1999): 133–36 at 33, which I am using in the following. Plato's claim was mentioned in the Introduction above in regard to the observation that man is by nature a religious animal.

123. *After Writing,* 169–70; also see Cipolla, "Review," 33.

124. *After Writing,* 172.

125. Pickstock, "Medieval Liturgy and Modern Reform," 20. Pier Angelo Sequeri, *L'estro di Dio: saggio e estetica* (Milan: Glossa, 2000), deals with many of Pickstock's themes in more Balthasarian mode.

transcendence. As creator He may be spoken of as situating sites, of preoccupying them before they were.[126] Pickstock is a partisan of the traditional Roman rite as it was before the changes of Vatican II which led to the *Novus Ordo* of 1969. For her the traditional Roman rite embodies a language of gift and sacrifice transcending the modern dichotomies of "orality and writing, time and space, gift and given, subject and object, active and passive, life and death."[127] The *Novus Ordo* does not, she thinks, challenge contemporary society. The scholars who composed it failed to understand that the old rite had been "embedded in a culture which was ritual in character."[128] Disastrously, their revision followed the secular language of contemporary society. This is something everyone who knows Latin will have to judge for themselves, but the present author's opinion is that it is more the translations of the *Novus Ordo* into various languages, especially English, which are to be lamented, not the Order itself. It seems to me still quite awe-inspiring said in Latin, Italian, or Spanish.

Though literal recovery of the medieval liturgy is not possible, the reforms following Vatican II have been devastating, in Pickstock's opinion, because they have been so tone-deaf to the magnificent "stuttering" apophaticism of the medieval liturgy, with its strong sense of the distance of God from man, which the twentieth-century reformers tended to replace with linear didacticism.[129] Instead of the repetitions and constant re-beginnings of the medieval liturgy, which highlighted God's transcendence, post–Vatican II reforms typically used contemporary secular language and patterns of expression.

Many think of churches as mere parts of some larger culture, but Pickstock and likeminded thinkers reverse the relation. In the words of David Yeago, the [Catholic] Church is "a culture in its own right and is not simply a function of the cultures of the nations among which it dwells. . . . [It is a] public reality . . . the civic assembly of the eschatological city."[130] An adage about the saints suggests that "it is the paradox of history that each generation is converted by the saint who contradicts it most," and the radical orthodox do not seek to ingratiate themselves by saying pleasant things, but to speak the truth.[131] They continue to represent a "new generation" dissatisfied with the compromises of the past. Though this writer is deeply

126. *After Writing*, 229.

127. Ibid., 169, and Cipolla, "Review," 34.

128. *After Writing*, 170, and Cipolla, "Review," 34.

129. See also on this my *Beginning at Jerusalem: Five Reflections on the History of the Church* (San Francisco: Ignatius Press, 2004), index under "liturgy."

130. "Messiah's People: The Culture of the Church in the Midst of the Nations," *Pro Ecclesia* 6 (Spring 1997), 150, quoted in Robert Louis Wilken, "Angels and Archangels: The Worship of Heaven and Earth," *Antiphon* 6, 1 (2001): 10–18 at 17.

131. David Paul Deavel, "Francis De Sales: A Patron Saint of Our Age," *SS* 7 (2006): 9–18 at 9.

sympathetic to what Pickstock wants, radical orthodox like her raise in an acute form the problem of catholicity, of whether their proposals do not simply pass most Christians by. But clearly their idea that at the heart of Christianity is the liturgy, and that therefore any restoration of transcendence must come through the liturgy, is very attractive, reversing as it does all the programs of assimilation which have for so long been followed.

An American analogue to the level of discontent with the modern world found among the English radical orthodox can be found—but generally without either the philosophic or aesthetic underpinnings—among especially some younger Catholics disgusted with a "progressive Catholicism" which has accepted the Protestantization and Americanization of Catholicism as the price that had to be paid for social acceptance of Catholics. The hope of many at the time of the Second Vatican Council was that finally Catholicism and modern culture would be reconciled. This hope is what "progressivism" most commonly designates. Arguably the hope was always very naïve, but it seduced many, and as Tracey Rowland, an Australian Catholic who studied with the radical orthodox faculty at Cambridge University, has shown, progressives seem not in general to have taken the measure of the modernity they wished to embrace.[132] Mistakes have been made all around, Rowland suggests, even, so to speak, by the right side. That is, some of the attempts by the Church itself "to transpose ecclesiastical culture into the idioms of modernity" have been "ill-advised and premature."[133]

Rowland has turned to the cultural issue that some of the radical orthodox have neglected. According to her, the Thomist tradition that dominated Catholic intellectual life before the Second Vatican Council has been in crisis because it has an "undeveloped account of the role of culture in moral formation."[134] Rowland sees the Second Vatican Council, especially *Gaudium et Spes,* as having failed to provide either a theological hermeneutic of culture or a systematic account of how the Church is to be related to modern culture. Rowland believes there was a certain "extrinsicism" at the Council which saw no intrinsic relation between Church and culture, but accepted a view of culture which was essentially Kantian and presumed that culture is self-governing and autonomous. This tended to replace an older "integralism."

For Rowland, who in a general way is the follower here of Henri de Lubac and the *communio* theologians, both these positions were built on a misunderstanding of the relation of nature and grace. For her the two orders

---

132. *Culture and the Thomist Tradition after Vatican II* (London: Routledge, 2003).

133. This is from an anonymous review in *SS* 4 (2003): 70.

134. *Culture and the Thomist Tradition,* 3, but in what follows I am also using the review of Rowland's book by Daniel McInerny in *FCSQ* 28, 1 (Spring 2005): 22–25.

of nature and grace are to be distinguished but not separated. The inadequacy of the extrinsicism of Vatican II on the cultural issue was to think of, for instance, the arts and sciences as found in contemporary secular culture as autonomous. To put this in the language of our treatment of modernism above, Vatican II at least half-accepted the modernist view of culture as independent from tradition. One can debate whether Vatican II was consistent enough to attribute to it the view Rowland does, but she seems right in holding that the idea of an exterior worldly culture to which the Church must adjust was rather naïvely proposed, and not very thoroughly examined, by the Council.

Vatican II, indeed *Gaudium et Spes,* 22, did have the potential for rethinking these issues, provided by the famous reference to the mystery of man being illuminated by the mystery of the incarnation of Christ, an idea at the center of the thought of John Paul II. This idea "means that, while the natural and social sciences and the arts may be 'autonomous' in the sense that they are not the subject of ecclesiastical governance, they are not 'autonomous' in the sense of having their own frames of reference external to the theology of the Incarnation."[135] Thus John Paul II's critiques of liberal modernity, especially in *Evangelium Vitae.* No sphere of culture is autonomous, all must be open to transformation by the Gospel. This is the sense of John Paul's idea that Christians must work to change the "culture of death" into a "culture of life." In the latter culture of love, priority would "be given to doxology over work, to being over doing."[136] And so we are brought back to the problem with which the first chapter of the present book began, the fact that unless we have a basic cultural reorientation in which work is not pursued in itself but only as a means to personal and cultural flourishing, we will be unable to halt the kind of "lives of their own" that such fields as biomedical technology are now set on.

Rowland seems right on some central issues, especially in her desire to open culture to the transcendentals of truth, beauty, and goodness as seen in the light of Christ. Clearly she is proposing transformation of culture, not retreat from or mute acceptance of it. But a criticism of her can be made similar to that made of Kraynak above. Though she is undoubtedly right in her criticism of the "Whig Thomists," thinkers like John Finnis, who try to accommodate the Thomist natural law to liberal notions of rationality, the question remains of whether it is not necessary in some way to use modern language, language that those outside the Church understand, to address cultural issues. How can liberal secularism be addressed at all but in a language secular liberals understand? It would seem that John Paul was right in his prudential decision to speak the language of rights and democ-

---

135. *Culture and the Thomist Tradition,* 37.
136. Ibid., 107.

racy, in spite of all the misunderstandings to which use of such language is open. We do not need Whig Thomists, thinkers who recast the substance of Thomas into Kantian categories, but we do need twenty-first-century Thomists, thinkers who can use their mastery of contemporary thought to show how theology can redirect culture. The resources of Thomism are very valuable here precisely because of the Thomist confidence in reason, in a natural order open in some degree to common understanding by Christian and non-Christian, on the basis of which understanding a common conversation can begin. "What the modern age most requires is a renewed sense that talk of the transcendent is not a mere matter of subjective desire or of religious faith, but a discourse that is available to all human intellects *by nature.*"[137]

Assimilation to modernity can now be seen as having produced myriad problems, not least bishops (but also parents) unwilling to stand up to cultural mores. The American radical orthodox take heart in those few bishops who are willing to discipline public figures defiant of Church teaching.[138] They have no expectations that a faithful Catholicism can ever be easily reconciled with or fit into society, British, American, or other. They may even think that Pius IX was close to the truth when he gave as the last condemned proposition of the *Syllabus of Errors* (1864), "The Roman Pontiff can, and ought, reconcile himself and come to terms with progress, liberalism, and modern civilization."[139] They may also sympathize with the anti-modernism of Pius X (1903–14). Indeed they may do the until recently almost unthinkable and approve the Catholic judgment from 1850 to 1950 that all solutions of "the problem of modernity" from Descartes to Hegel had been failures.

Further, they may approve Leo XIII's advocacy of Thomism (*Aeterni Patris,* 1880) as providing the always needed theological common culture upon which the legitimately new can be built.[140] They may see the popes as motivated not by some irrational "fear of modernity," but by a perfectly rational judgment on the inadequacy of especially the canonical philosophers of the modern period, and note that Bernard Lonergan early on said as much.[141] Though the suggestion that there should be a blanket condemna-

---

137. McInerny, Review, 25.

138. Richard John Neuhaus, "To Be American," *FT* 145 (August/September 2004): 93–97 at 96–97.

139. Quoted in Hittinger, "Churches of Earthly Power," 30. Michael Burleigh, *Earthly Powers: The Clash of Religion and Politics in Europe from the French Revolution to the Great War* (New York: HarperCollins, 2005), argues that the great story of recent centuries is how the Church stood up to the secular state.

140. R. R. Reno, "Theology After the Revolution," *FT* 173 (May 2007): 15–21, at 16.

141. Ibid., and see the comments on de Lubac's claim to have found in neo-scholasticism a covert form of modernism (17). Neil Postman, well known for his critique of modern technology, calls for a reassessment to the end of appropriation of some of the chief Enlightenment val-

tion of modern civilization may be a bit much even for a traditionalist, the popes now seem to have been onto something in their grave reservations as to how the world was turning out.

With Marxism removed from the European field but with no wish for an authoritarian or nostalgic state of the right, the radical orthodox in part continue the unmasking of liberalism, especially of the tendency of liberalism to drive religion to the margins of life. In important ways, especially in their stand against "the spirit of the age," they continue the work of the Oxford Movement. For them the central question is how to achieve a society more generous toward the transcendental orientations of human beings. As Philippians 3:20 states, the Christian's citizenship is in heaven, which radical orthodoxy takes to mean that the Christian's first loyalty or membership is in the Church, not the state.[142]

One might almost suggest the existence of a law according to which the more clearly the transcendent and "vertical" orientations of life are present, the more one is not inclined to assimilation, but the more the emphasis is put on "horizontal" orientations, the more one is inclined to become like the surrounding culture. An address given by the Belgian Jan Cardinal Schotte illustrates this very well. Having remarked that many people today look to the Church primarily for its activity on behalf of the poor or oppressed, Cardinal Schotte remarked on how this "horizontal" activity could lead to downplaying the Church's transcendent dimension. As composed of sinners redeemed in the blood of Christ, the Church is first of all a people dedicated to praise of God, to the vertical, and then a people dedicated to the service of others, the horizontal.[143]

⌒

Lines of analysis similar to those of radical orthodoxy have been applied to the American context by Michael Baxter, a kind of third-generation descendant of radical orthodoxy through Stanley Hauerwas of Duke University.[144] Baxter is especially alert to the dangers nationalism or national loyalties present to Christian life, and he is particularly hard on all claims for Ameri-

---

ues in *Building a Bridge to the Eighteenth Century: How the Past Can Improve Our Future* (New York: Knopf, 1999), and Hugo Anthony Meynell, *Postmodernism and the New Enlightenment* (Washington, D.C.: The Catholic University of America Press, 1999), engages in Lonerganian fashion with the heritage of the Enlightenment, as well as the challenge of postmodernism.

142. Some of the American disciples of this school have provocative essays in *God Is Not . . . Religious, Nice, "One of Us," an American, a Capitalist,* ed. D. Brent Laytham (Grand Rapids, Mich.: Eerdmans, 2004).

143. Commencement address at Thomas Aquinas College, California (*Thomas Aquinas College Newsletter,* Summer 1999), described by James V. Schall, "Structures of Evil—Structures of Good: On the Centrality of Personal Sin," *FCSQ* 32, 1 (Winter 2000): 7–14 at 8–9.

144. "The Unsettling of Americanism: A Response to William Portier," *Co* 27 (2000): 161–70, esp. 163–66, in which Baxter does a fine job of showing how, twist and turn as it might, nineteenth-century Catholicism was captive to the nation-state, nowhere more than in America, where to the present many have not had the eyes even to see this captivity for what it is.

can exceptionalism, that is, claims that America is an elect nation, chosen above all the others. For most American Catholics and virtually all historians of American Catholicism, the story of Catholicism in America has been a success story in which Catholicism has ended up fitting into the American Way of Life. It is only Catholics like Baxter who criticize such Catholic intellectuals as Fr. John Courtney Murray (1904–67) or Fr. John Tracy Ellis (1905–92) for having tended to the view that there need be no conflict between Catholicism and this American Way of Life. For most it was Rome that was misguided in the Americanist controversy. For Baxter, Rome was right and Catholicism in America wrong. Only thinkers like Baxter have the "gall" to reveal writers like Fr. Murray as the neo-Constantinians (or neo-Eusebians) they were or are.[145]

Some elaboration is in order before we can pursue Baxter's thought further. In a book taken note of earlier, John McGreevy argued that though historically American Catholics and non-Catholics may have shared a common vocabulary in their use of words such as "freedom," these words were understood differently.[146] In a subsequent book in praise of early-twentieth-century American Catholic intellectual opposition to the shape modernity took in pragmatism ("philosophic Protestantism") and progressivism, Thomas E. Woods Jr. has pursued this insight.[147] Woods shows how poorly understood the Progressive Era has been, particularly by historians who have thought that because Catholics sometimes agreed politically with their progressive counterparts, they shared the same positions. In Woods's description during the late nineteenth century, American Catholicism, specifically American Catholic intellectuals, confronted the ideals of the Progressive Era. Part of this confrontation was debate about what then was called theological modernism, condemned in 1907 by Pius X. In many ways the debate about theological modernism paralleled the debate about modernism in art going on at the same time. Catholic leaders in America, while generally affirming the superiority of Catholic teaching, tended in fact to pick and choose between progressive doctrines.

What had become a dominant philosophical position among secular thinkers (but in some ways, as Alexis de Tocqueville noted in the nine-

145. Richard John Neuhaus, "Religion within the Limits of Morality Alone," *FT* 72 (April 1997): 58–61 at 59–60, describing an article by Baxter. William Portier, "Here Come the Evangelical Catholics," *Co* 31 (2004): 35–66 at 61–65, has an interesting section on the Americanist controversy. Kenneth R. Craycraft Jr., "The Ambivalence of John Courtney Murray," *Crisis* 12, 3 (March 1994): 54–56, seems to me correct in stressing the deep ambivalence, ambiguity, and non-systematic nature of Murray's thought, and therefore its susceptibility to being placed in the service of many camps.

146. *Parish Boundaries: The Catholic Encounter with Race in the Twentieth-Century Urban North* (Chicago: University of Chicago Press, 1996).

147. *The Church Confronts Modernity: Catholic Intellectuals and the Progressive Era* (New York: Columbia University Press, 2004).

teenth century, this had always been the American inclination), pragmatism, "that odd assemblage of rationalism, technocratic solutions, and a romanticized ideal of democracy," attracted the ire of many Catholic thinkers.[148] They noted pragmatism's lack of interest in discussing truth or the ends of conduct in themselves, and therefore saw this position as not useful for discussion of the traditional questions of political philosophy. The educational theories pragmatism spawned, with their goal of value-free education, seemed both philosophically unsophisticated and irreconcilable with any faith position. In economics, however, a field rarely held back by working from false premises, much common ground could be found, and there was much to be praised in progressive notions of desirable social reform. Even here, however, the preference of progressives for technocratic solutions and state control caused Catholic discomfort. As Protestants generally, the progressives had little understanding of or appreciation for natural law arguments.

Historically all this, especially the pragmatist tendency to avoid categories of universal truth, has made America itself—that is, the current state of American public opinion—into a kind of authority of last resort for its citizens, an authority which claims of the Christian an allegiance that he is supposed to give only to the Church. For the most part Catholics "follow the crowd," replicating the fashions of public opinion in the moral and social positions they take. Baxter prefers the perspective of the second century *Letter to Diognetus,* with its insistence that the Christian is nowhere at home in this world, everywhere a resident alien.[149] The ideal expressed in the *Letter to Diognetus,* as Augustine's later, was centered on the idea that the Christian is on perpetual pilgrimage. The Christian does not abandon the world, but lives within it by the law of "another city."

In some ways what Baxter has to say meshes with what many European theologians, less in thrall to their various nation-states at the beginning of the twenty-first century than they were at the beginning of the twentieth, have been saying.[150] Benedict XVI himself seems to envisage his task as "a

---

148. Gerald J. Russello, reviewing Woods in *FT* 149 (January 2005): 54–55 at 55. I am following this review here and in what follows. Russello does not like Woods's assessment of the Church under John Paul II, but it seems to me rather accurate.

149. This and the following is based on Baxter's "Why Catholics Should be Wary of 'One Nation Under God,'" *HCW* (January–February 2005): 8–13, earlier published as "God Is Not American: Or, Why Christians Should Not Pledge Allegiance to 'One Nation Under God,'" in *God Is Not . . . ,* ed. Laytham, 55–75. Christopher Bryan, *Render to Caesar: Jesus, the Early Church, and the Roman Superpower* (Oxford: Oxford University Press, 2005), while also stressing Christian critique of the culture in which they live, is more moderate.

150. There is an interesting chapter on the struggle with modernity arguing that the twentieth century was an age of great theological creativity, by Adrian Hastings, "The Twentieth Century," in *Christianity: Two Thousand Years,* ed. Richard Harries and Henry Mayr-Harting (New York: Oxford University Press, 2001).

confrontation with modern culture in order to assert the primacy of the Gospel."[151] Instead of practicing the endless accommodation to modernity that many continue to urge, which can have no good issue, he accepts the necessity of confrontation. What he says of the Roman emperor in *Jesus of Nazareth* presumably can be said of all states:

"Render to Caesar the things that are Caesar's, and to God the things that are God's" (Mk 12:17) . . . is a way of expressing the essential compatibility of two spheres. But when the imperial power interprets itself as divine, . . . then the Christian has to "obey God more than men" (Acts 5:29). It is then that Christians become "martyrs," witnesses of Christ.[152]

Perhaps Benedict looks back to the heroism and counter-culturalism of Pius X, who in the wake of the abrogation in France in 1905 of the Concordat of 1801 and the dissolution of the religious orders and consequent closure of Catholic schools, insisted on the independence of the Church, refusing to join the associations suggested by the state to control Church property. Some scholars suggest that, rather than marking the death of Catholicism in France, the pope's action lay behind "thirty glorious years for Catholicism" in France from 1930 to 1960.[153] Pius's "counter-culturalism" expressed a militancy which revived the French church.

Whereas most Americans understand the *aggiornamento,* or "updating," asked for at Vatican II to be an embrace of the larger culture, thinkers like Baxter ask what point there is in embracing a culture which, already in the 1960s, was "in a state of terminal disintegration."[154] Baxter is willing to talk about fundamental problems from which most Christians turn their eyes. Especially since the French Revolution, all Christians have had to decide the desired stance in the face of a culture actively antagonistic to Christianity. It is very superficial to criticize, say, Christians or popes of the later nineteenth century for having a "ghetto mentality." In the face of armies trying to destroy the Church and of political movements aimed at removing the influence of the Church from society in whatever ways possible, it is unclear what alternatives were available. Joe Holland seems to be right in arguing that, overall, the so-called Leonine popes from 1878 to 1958 did not reject liberal bourgeois society root and branch, but tried to reform it while loosening the historic ties of the Church to old elites and strengthening the ties of the Church to

---

151. James Hitchcock, "Pope Benedict XVI," *Voices* 20, 2 (2005): 14–15 at 14.

152. Tr. Adrian Walker (New York 2007), 12.

153. *Histoire religieuse de la France contemporaine,* ed. Gérard Cholvy and Yves-Marie Hilaire, 3 vols. (Toulouse: Privat, 1985–88); see also Hugh McLeod, "Introduction," in *The Decline of Christendom in Western Europe, 1750–2000,* ed. Hugh McLeod and Werner Ustorf (Cambridge: Cambridge University Press, 2003), 19; Hugh McLeod, *Secularization in Western Europe 1848–1914* (London: St. Martin's Press, 2000), 69.

154. To use Richard John Neuhaus's words: "The Bishops Get Their Report Card," *FT* 141 (March 2004): 57–61 at 60.

labor and a vaguely defined "Christian democracy."[155] Modernity and a mitigated capitalism were not givens to be overturned, but the framework for re-
Christianization. Still it is true that in important respects Vatican II did represent an opening to a world that until yesterday had been viewed suspiciously.

The question is whether this larger world had overnight become more
nurturing of Christian life, or had Christians just tired of the fight? Much in
progressive Catholicism could be viewed as capitulation to and absorption by
this larger culture. Cardinal Francis Stafford thus rightly stated in an interview that "the crisis in the Church will continue until the Catholic Church
comes to a deeper awareness and consciousness—and above all judgment—
about the compatibility of elements within modern culture and the Catholic
faith."[156] To descend abruptly from the general to the specific, John Paul II,
for instance, said that knowledge of Latin is the "indispensable condition for
a proper relationship between modernity and antiquity, for dialogue among
culture, and for affirming the identity of the Catholic priesthood," but what
parents see that their children learn Latin, and what bishops insist that the
seminaries their future clergy attend, let alone their diocesan schools, impart
a working knowledge of Latin?[157] By everything they fail to do, parents and
the clergy communicate their own lack of seriousness.

Baxter was especially critical of the late Richard John Neuhaus's "Americanism." For Neuhaus, according to Baxter, the nation, especially the United
States, is the political body through which God's will is accomplished. Instead of seeing the drama of our time as centered on the competition of the
nation-state with the Church for the Christian's loyalty, Neuhaus's story line
was the old one of fundamental harmony between the two. The *Letter to
Diognetus* had seen Christians as hated for opposing the world's pleasures,
and had presumed ongoing conflict between Christianity and the state, but
Neuhaus's hope, in spite of his frequent acknowledgment of society's failures, was for continuing support by Church of nation-state. Though opposed to the way in which the Supreme Court has imposed a liberal regime
on the United States, especially through the Casey decision of 1992, with its
famous "mystery clause" making religion and morality into wholly private
matters, Neuhaus was from Baxter's point of view in a more general way
overly solicitous not to endanger the lowest-common-denominator consensus embodied in his understanding of natural law in the fashion of John
Courtney Murray. Here a kind of civil religion called "Judaeo-Christianity"
presents itself as a "Judaeo-Christian" agreement that all that the natural law
teaches must be adhered to in the public life of the nation.

155. *Modern Catholic Social Teaching: The Popes Confront the Industrial Age 1740–1958* (New
York: Paulist Press, 2003); see also the review by Paul Misner, *CHR* 90 (2004): 520–21, on this
and the following.
156. Quoted in Tracey Rowland, "John Paul II and Vatican II," *SS* 5 (2004): 5–14 at 12.
157. Quoted in ibid., 14.

Though I think whatever natural law consensus there was in Murray's day largely has broken down, and that therefore the views of both Murray and Neuhaus are somewhat passé, I myself share Neuhaus's concerns as to the place of natural law in life. If one may doubt how much natural law understanding was ever present among American Jews or Protestants, and to that doubt one must now add doubt about one's fellow Catholics, there is nevertheless no road to a more just society than through the natural law. That said, Baxter seems right in his criticism of Neuhaus's emphasis on the compatibility and harmony of Church and state in an American context, rather than on the continuing story of the competition between these two entities.

Baxter's Catholics, like those in the *Letter to Diognetus*, do not fit in. They differ from those around them in how they marry and have children. Tensions are perpetually present between them and the larger society, and they are the subject of persecution. Whereas thinkers like Neuhaus seem to have accepted the Erasmian notion that civil peace is worth almost any price, more generally that what must not be replicated in America is the Wars of Religion of the old world, Baxter, while of course not wishing discord for its own sake, seems resigned to the fact that the Christian's lot in America is not likely to be happy. Baxter does not want a naked public square either—that is, a public life in which religion has no place—but since his religion is not "religion" but Catholicism, and he is unwilling to trim his Catholicism to a form acceptably "Judaeo-Christian," he would prefer that Christians be fully Christian, and take the consequences.

Perhaps it is unfair to observe that even Baxter has not explored the depths of the question of the Christian's lot in this world. We all know that small states, say the states of Eastern Europe, do not dictate this world's terms. This does not necessarily make their societies better than those of the larger and more powerful states, but one wonders what the logic of Christianity demands here. History does in some obvious ways seem to belong to the victors. Does the more "radically Christian" one becomes dictate an increasing powerlessness, both for states and individuals? A number of the radically orthodox are pacifists, but have not, to my knowledge, addressed in sustained fashion the question of whether their position implies no attempt to evangelize the public square by anything beyond witness. If the modern urban space is a necropolis, are the only proper responses lamentation, withdrawal, or twittering the Roman rite just off the square? If the Christian may scrap for a presence in and influence on this public square, may this influence take the form of legislation, say privileging Sunday as a holy day?[158]

⸻

158. See the discussion of Robert L. Wilken's thought below.

The times have changed. In America the immigrant Catholic subculture, largely European, which once buffered Catholics from anti-Catholicism and the most undesirable effects of life in a voluntary religious culture has all but dissolved into the suburbs.[159] In the early and mid-twentieth century, as their economic status improved, many Catholics wanted the fruits of their labor, that is, to be liberated from a Catholic ghetto and to play on a larger stage. This was one of the reasons that Vatican II was interpreted the way it was in America, as providing an entrance to this larger stage. Granted, just at the moment the older immigrants had emptied their ghettos, new immigrants appeared, Hispanic, Vietnamese, Eastern European, African. One wonders whether their story will be different. Will these groups, now often at the edge of mainstream culture, be able to find something between melting pot and ghetto, a Christianity in but not completely of the United States?[160] Or, especially in the case of many Hispanic immigrants, with their continuing close ties to their native lands and language, will the new immigrants, or some of them, simply take a bit longer to assimilate?

It is probably fair to say that few American bishops before the end of World War I thought of themselves as prophetic, as challenging the deepest political and social assumptions of the larger society. As leaders of an immigrant Church intent on avoiding persecution, they deemed civic campaigns addressed to the larger society unwise. Resist this society, especially from the 1930s in their defense of sexual morality, they sometimes did, especially in furtherance of what they saw as their main task, the *ad intra* building up of the Church by attention to internal discipline in such matters as marriage, family, and religious education.[161] Here they had striking successes, and a book hostile to Catholic teaching on contraception but written by a fair-minded historian has acknowledged, for instance, the large number of Catholics who tried to live in full accord with Catholic teaching, and followed a procreative sexual ethic.[162]

Until the 1960s parish missions often discussed contraception, and a

159. William L. Portier, "'The Eminent Evangelist from Boston': Father Thomas A. Judge as an Evangelical Catholic," *Co* 30 (2003): 300–319 at 300–301, and "Here Come the Evangelical Catholics," 45–48.

160. Mark Griffin and Theron Walker, *Living on the Borders: What the Church Can Learn from Ethnic Immigrant Cultures* (Grand Rapids, Mich.: Eerdmans, 2004).

161. John D'Emilio and Estelle Freedman, *Intimate Matters: A History of Sexuality in America* (New York: Harper & Row, 1988), 281.

162. Leslie Woodcock Tentler, *Catholics and Contraception: An American History* (Ithaca, N.Y.: Cornell University Press, 2004); and see the useful review by Janet E. Smith, *FT* 155 (August/September 2005), 47–49, used in the following. Presumably refusing to practice contraception was some indication of how seriously one took one's religion, and has some bearing on the question of the comparative religiosity of America and Europe. What then do we make of the fact that by the end of the century America had the highest rate of annulment in the universal Church? See R. H. Vasoli, *What God Has Joined Together: The Annulment Crisis in American Catholicism* (New York: Oxford University Press, 1998).

fair number of young people aspired to a domestic sanctity in compliance with a strict sexual discipline. But from about this time a widespread Catholic synthesis of official teaching and popular practice, expressed both in large families and in the acknowledgment that indulgence in contraception was a confessional matter, faltered and then collapsed. It was not so much that popular practice changed, for many who thought of themselves as Catholics had practiced contraception, but that popular Catholic belief collapsed, and many of the rank and file—with many of their priests—no longer thought contraception a matter of grave sin.[163] Actually, in the years following Vatican II many of them thought frequent confession outdated. One could argue that confession is the most counter-cultural of the sacraments, because it encourages one to think of conformity to God's will as the great imperative, this in turn encouraging throwing a cold eye on one's historical surroundings. Perhaps contemporary infrequency of confession is one sign of how much Catholics have become conformed to the world.

To repeat, most of the bishops were descendants of John Carroll, worried first of all about the Church's internal life, and concerned, in this country in which anti-Catholicism was the deepest bias, not to be taken as anti-American.[164] Now most of this is a memory.[165] Largely gone is a "thick" shared Catholic religious culture, partly because of economic and demographic changes verging on the inevitable and having to do with Catholic success on the American economic ladder, and partly because of the cooperation of many "assimilationist" bishops in the abandonment of such defining Catholic practices as the keeping of a full calendar of days of obligation. Many now (bishops and laity) are reluctant to identify themselves with a full Catholicism and many at least nominally Catholic institutions, especially colleges and hospitals, are more concerned to meet the standards of the secular institutions around them than to be faithful to the more difficult or counter-cultural points of Catholic doctrine.

Even among young "evangelical" Catholics, those twenty- or thirty-something Catholics identified with the "ascendance of orthodoxy," maybe as much as a third of the younger Catholic population, who like being Catholic and agree with core doctrinal beliefs, commitment to the institutional Church often is weak and has little ecclesial dimension.[166] Many are

163. I am following the summary of Tentler's argument in a review by James P. McCartin in *Collegium* 1, 18 (Fall 2005): 16–17 at 16.

164. Timothy M. Dolan, "The Bishops in Council," *FT* 152 (April 2005): 20–25 at 21, and see 22 on Arthur Schlesinger Sr.'s famous observation about "the deepest bias in American culture."

165. *The Church Confronts Modernity: Catholicism since 1950 in the United States, Ireland, and Quebec,* ed. Leslie Woodcock Tentler (Washington, D.C.: The Catholic University of America Press, 2007).

166. Portier, "Here Come the Evangelical Catholics," 49, 55–60, explaining that the evan-

ill-prepared to cope with the larger culture. In important ways the products of John Paul II's pontificate, these younger Catholics do recognize that Catholicism is "a hard faith," and many of them are taken with the adventure of being Catholic, some even repopulating convents which had almost emptied, but often they really do not understand the nature of the larger contractual and utilitarian culture that surrounds them and at every step draws them into its web.[167] In deciding such issues as whether to support stem-cell research using human embryos or not, it is unclear whether these younger Catholics will understand what is at issue between Catholicism and an approach to life that defines things by the criterion of usefulness.[168] There is a parallel situation in Europe, where despite many signs of Catholic revival, especially in association with the new movements or, say, the efforts of the Polish church to re-missionize Europe, institutional weakness remains.

Historically, one name for a vital Catholicism flourishing under the pluralistic conditions of a state in which religion is voluntary is "evangelical." Today this seems an appropriate label for much of Southern Catholicism in the United States, which, because of both Hispanic immigration and the movement of Northerners into especially the Southeast, is growing by leaps and bounds and generally has a greater commitment to the teachings of the Church than that of older Catholic regions.[169] In many ways this evangelical Catholicism fulfills the hope expressed in the U.S. bishops' 1983 pastoral letter that intensifying Hispanic immigration would revive, even save, the Church in the United States.[170]

"Evangelical" indicates a form of voluntary religion centered on personal conversion and public witness.[171] In a Catholic form it assumes the stance of John Paul II, simultaneously affirming religious liberty and the necessity of the evangelization of culture. It probably admires the things John Paul stood for, and has some sense of the Church as a universal institution, perhaps nurtured by occasional attendance at a World Youth Con-

---

gelicals, never having experienced pre–Vatican II Church life, are generally neither "conservative" nor restorationist. See also Peter Boyer, "A Hard Faith," *NY* 81, 13 (May 16, 2005): 54–66, a well-researched article on the resurgence of Catholic orthodoxy, and Robert Wuthnow, *After the Baby Boomers: How Twenty- and Thirty-Somethings are Shaping the Future of American Religion* (Princeton, N.J.: Princeton University Press, 2007), arguing that above all the post-boomers want community.

167. Kelli Kennedy, "Convents See Increase in Applicants," *DMN,* April 21, 2007, E3.

168. David M. McCarthy, "Shifting Settings from Subculture to Pluralism: Catholic Moral Theology in an Evangelical Key," *Co* 31 (2004): 85–110 at 93.

169. Tim Padgett, "Bible-Belt Catholics," *Time,* February 14, 2005, 44–46. Cf. John L Allen Jr., "Canada's Evangelical Catholics," *National Catholic Reporter* 7, 27 (May 30, 2008).

170. Padgett, "Bible-Belt Catholics," 46.

171. Portier, "'Eminent Evangelist,'" 301. See also Portier's "Here Come the Evangelical Catholics."

gress.[172] It may turn Feuerbach and Marx on their heads, and use religion as "the premise of all social critique."[173] A good argument can be made that, in an American context, this will be the vital Catholicism of the future.[174] This prognostication, however, is complicated by the fact, already noted, that even many of the young, enthusiastic Catholics have a weak ecclesial sense. They also, like most Americans, are often quite religiously illiterate.[175] It has been observed that an evangelical Catholicism, too, needs to form a kind of subculture. That is, living in a larger utilitarian culture, in order to flourish it needs a framework of authority, law, and obligation able to resist the larger culture. The Church still had this in the *Kulturkampf* of the nineteenth century, but it is less clear that it has it today.[176] The threats showered by such as the American Civil Liberties Union on the Ave Maria community in Naples, Florida, should the town actually pursue a life publicly ordered by Catholicism, shows that the problems involved in vigorous entrance into the public square at all are immense.

Though in America evangelicalism has been more associated with Protestantism, it has had its Catholic forms. One would not expect that many would live the life of, say, Fr. Thomas A. Judge (1868–1933), of Dorothy Day and the Catholic Worker communities, of some Communion and Liberation groups, or of L'Arche communities, but these seem to bear some resemblance to the form of daily life for which radical orthodoxy asks, and which Pope Benedict XVI seems to think is possible for contemporary Europe especially.[177] On this last point, Benedict has spoken with some regularity of "creative minorities." In the light of what Ignatius of Loyola did with "a few good men," Benedict's hopes for these creative minorities do not seem unfounded. Without rejecting more traditional ideas of a shared, public, religious culture, he seems to think that such is not likely to be the main form of life in the foreseeable future, at least in Europe. Therefore, what is needed are groups of truly faithful, practicing, and witnessing Catholics.[178] Some groups already are not afraid to witness in a public way,

172. Portier, "Here Come the Evangelical Catholics," 57.

173. McCarthy, "Shifting Settings," 107.

174. Portier, "Here Come the Evangelical Catholics," 53.

175. Stephen Prothero, *Religious Literacy: What Every American Needs to Know—And Doesn't* (San Francisco: HarperSanFrancisco, 2007), reveals most Americans, including those such as evangelicals who are usually assumed to be the most religiously knowledgeable, as knowing very little.

176. McCarthy, "Shifting Settings," 103–04.

177. In general on the place of religious communities in both the Church and the world, see Fabio Ciardi, *Koinonia: Spiritual and Theological Growth of the Religious Community* (Hyde Park, N.Y.: New City Press, 2000), and Michael A. Hayes, *New Religious Movements in the Catholic Church* (New York: Burns & Oates, 2005). Mark and Louise Zwick, *The Catholic Worker Movement: Intellectual and Spiritual* (New York: Paulist Press, 2005), read the Catholic Worker Movement as a radical alternative to public theology built around person-to-person witness rather than attempting to influence public policy.

178. This follows the analysis of Peter Colosi as found in an interview by Emily Stimpson,

to have their members think of themselves as apostles and evangelists, as members of a missionary family, and to engage in such public practices as Marian processions. They may want to be fully Catholic, maintaining the bond between orthodoxy and social justice.

The large question is whether evangelical Catholicism—or any other form of American Catholicism—will be able to avoid the perils and internal contradictions of life in a pluralistic or multicultural society.[179] For while pluralism makes evangelicalism possible, and sometimes offers interesting possibilities for dialogue and learning from others, it deforms all forms of Christian (or religious) life and makes a full Catholic ecclesiology virtually impossible:

> Modern notions of tolerance tend to domesticate both the gospel that is being preached and the form of life it entails by treating them as simply one among many possible private "religions." Soon religious pluralism transforms from a providential fact into a theoretical good, a natural state of things best left undisturbed.[180]

Further, pluralism typically involves a decrease in shared symbolism, and this affects life all along the line, but especially the liturgy.[181]

The movement from an ad hoc to a de jure pluralism seems already to have occurred in the thinking of Richard Neuhaus, who wrote, "The great and audaciously new thing in the American founding is that for the first time in world history a state was established with the explicit provision that the religious beliefs and practices of the people are not the business of the government." Neuhaus clearly believed that this was a good thing, but he left most unclear the relationship between government and the reign of Christ.[182] Kenneth Grasso calls such a view as Neuhaus approved a "monism of pluralism," and wonders "is it possible to call such a political arrangement a 'society' at all?"[183]

Obviously the freedom of the Church demands that it not fall under the control of the state, but does this mean also that the state has no obligation

---

"Civilization in Crisis: The Loss of Faith in Western Europe," *Franciscan Way* (Autumn 2006): 14–15 at 15.

179. Here and in what follows I am using and reflecting on the analysis of Portier, "Here Come the Evangelical Catholics," as at 38–39, 41–44, 51.

180. Ibid., 43.

181. Eamon Duffy, "The Stripping of the Altars and the Modern Liturgy," *Antiphon* 2, 3 (Winter 1997): 3–12 at 11.

182. Cf. Daniel Bell Jr., "The Insurrectional Reserve: Latin American Liberationists, Eschatology, and the Catholic Moment," *Co* 27 (2000): 643–75, critiquing Neuhaus's notion of transcendence, and in the process arguing his project is distinctly Protestant.

183. In Craycraft, "Ambivalence of John Courtney Murray," 55. Craycraft goes so far as to conclude that, on the question of "whether American democracy is compatible with Catholicism," "Murray himself, despite the mountains of proof-texts that one may produce to the contrary, sadly concluded that the answer is 'No'" (56).

to advance religion?[184] Such a position as Neuhaus's, which does indeed fly in the face of much Catholic history and thought, needs a much more formal grounding than Neuhaus ever gave it. One can appreciate skepticism about what mischief a government might cause if it interests itself in religion, but if humans are by nature religious (not Catholic or Protestant, but religious), then is not the flourishing of religion a natural good which the state is obliged to promote? Again, all arrangements may be abused, and one rightly fears the possibility of the state imposing undesirable things on the Church should it have a hand in, say, Catholic education, but in principle it is better to have a state which acknowledges its responsibilities to religion than one that does not. One is free to reject the aid thus offered.

I have commented on the problems with Neuhaus's ideas about pluralism elsewhere, and have tried to draw out the implications of some of the things he held.[185] I do not want to dwell on an old debate, but it is important to state the central points of my criticism. Behind what Neuhaus held lies a common American misunderstanding of Vatican II's teaching on religious freedom, to which I have already referred. Neuhaus believed that *Dignitatis Humanae,* the Declaration on Religious Liberty of the Council, broke with former Catholic approval of confessional states.[186] This is not

184. One of John Courtney Murray's more influential writings here is a 1954 piece, "The Problem of Pluralism," republished in *Thought* 65 (1990): 323–58. Michael Novak, "Running Into a Wall," *FT* 166 (October 206): 44–47 at 46, believes that though Church and state should be separated, government should "support religion." I have considered this question at some length in "Separating Church and State."

185. "The Catholic Moment?" *Co* 15 (1988): 474–87. One of the things Neuhaus continued to do over the years was to portray especially European history as a struggle between "monism" and "pluralism." Thus his "Religion and Politics: 'The Great Separation,'" *FT* 179 (January 2008): 59–63 at 63: "From Constantine to modernity, the Church in Christendom sometimes made monistic claims, equating itself with society and claiming that temporal powers received their authority from God as mediated through the Church. Remember the Investiture Controversy. . . . Of all the things that were new in the *novus ordo seclorum* of the American founding, none is more important than its resistance to the monistic impulse. . . . This is the pluralism that is built into our constitutional order." Neuhaus went on to portray pluralism as a check on the ambitions of the modern state and on totalitarianism. One hardly knows where to begin! I would term the oldest and most pervasive system of European government "theocratic monarchy," a system in which the ruler claims to rule all society (including religion) on behalf of God. This, whether in the time of Charlemagne, Henry IV of Germany, Henry VIII of England, or Peter the Great has almost always been a lay form of government, and should be distinguished from, say, the kind of dualism we find in Gelasius I (492–96), which, while claiming that ultimately the Church has a higher authority than the state, does not translate this into the Church's becoming the governor of society: the state retains its proper jurisdiction, and normally governs by its own best light. To say that temporal government receives its authority mediated by the Church does not mean that the Church rules society, but, as intrinsically the higher authority, that the Church has a general power of superintendence, most commonly expressed negatively in interference with the state if the state gravely violates the natural law or the teachings of the Church.

186. "Catholic Moment?" 476–77. Avery Cardinal Dulles, "*Dignitatis Humanae* and the Development of Catholic Doctrine" in *Catholicism and Religious Freedom: Contemporary Reflections on Vatican II's Declaration on Religious Freedom,* ed. Kenneth L. Grasso and Robert P. Hunt

so, and though the point seems moot so far as American history is concerned, the establishment of religion is not disallowed by Vatican II. On the contrary, *Dignitatis Humanae, 6*, specifically comments: "If in view of peculiar circumstances obtaining among peoples, special civil recognition is given to one religious community in the constitutional order of society, it is at the same time imperative that the right of all citizens and religious communities to religious freedom should be recognized."[187] Thus the Council is not unequivocally on the side of the American First Amendment, and does not give religious pluralism or some American understanding of the separation of Church and state the high ground. It is incorrect to present the Council as belatedly recognizing and adopting for the Church universal the constitutional arrangements discovered by the Americans.

In my earlier response to Neuhaus's ideas I noted his equivocal use of the word pluralism: "Neuhaus uses few words more equivocally, to refer to almost anything from the multiplicity of the world, to what the social encyclicals have called the intermediary institutions in society, to legitimate religious pluralism."[188] One of his usages was to indicate diverse forms of obedience to the Gospel (a plurality of churches), and I would agree with him that such could be called a healthy pluralism. But he went further and held that since pluralism is an effect of the incompleteness of historical existence, we should not struggle to reduce it. This does not seem to me to follow. I would think reducing religious pluralism or not would depend on exactly how much one or another denomination actually understands reason and revelation correctly. More generally, to accept pluralism, either of a specifically religious form or not, as a reality does not mean that one cannot work to limit it. To take a stance on any moral issue implies that one wishes pluralism—the views of one's opponents—limited. To say that the state should intervene on the side of children in cases of child abuse limits someone's "pluralism." Neuhaus did not discuss directly in this regard the question of what is to be done if one form of "obedience to the Gospel" concludes to the right to abortion, while another holds that abortion is a serious sin and crime. He did not tell us how irreconcilable worldviews can be part of a desirable pluralism. We can all praise the superficial cultural pluralism of, say, the existence of a variety of ethnic foods, but what of a situation in which various incompatible worldviews must live cheek-by-jowl in one society? What of "deep pluralism"? Pluralism in America, reli-

---

(Lanham, Md.: Rowman & Littlefield, 2006), 43–67 at 46, 52–56, gives a much more precise reading.

187. Glenn W. Olsen, "The Meaning of Christian Culture: A Historical View," in *Catholicism and Secularization in America*, ed. David L. Schindler (Notre Dame, Ind.: Communio Books, 1990), 98–130 at 115 for analysis and quotation.

188. "Catholic Moment?" 478.

gious or not, often does make any substantial sharing in truth impossible for large numbers of people.

My earlier critique of Neuhaus suggested that his idea of pluralism "seems sometimes to be put in the service of the actual religious pluralism which exists, and then to introduce into the ecclesiastical realm an analogy to the secular myth 'e pluribus unum.'"[189] The hope seems to be that in a pluralistic situation truth will be attained through dialogue. I would not deny that this can happen, but my jaded observation of history suggests that this is not often the case. More to the point, there is a deep paradox here. If pluralism really aims at a situation in which there can be growing consensus about the truth, it aims at its self-destruction, and pluralism is not the goal, but social consensus in the truth. E pluribus unum hides this fact under cover of the idea that one can have it both ways, have one's pluralism and have one's social consensus. Presumably all agree that the question of "how much consensus" is possible has a considerable prudential dimension, but it really will not do to affirm that religious pluralism is a higher value than agreement in true religion.

David M. Gallagher has written:

> It would be better, all things considered, to have unanimity among the body politic on the ultimate questions, and if there were such agreement, a number of matters consequent upon the shared comprehensive doctrine could enter into political life. Public life would be richer, would produce more good for its citizens, if it included aspects of the transcendent. But if there is not unanimity, if there is factual plurality, then it seems that the liberal approach is needed: if we cannot agree on ultimate matters, let us, instead of constantly fighting about them, make them private and keep for the public domain only those things we can agree upon, things like security from criminals and from foreign powers. . . .
>
> But if we accept . . . the unity of reason, the matter is otherwise. If I am convinced that my comprehensive doctrine is true and is true for all even if they do not admit that, then it does not seem that I can responsibly refrain from introducing that view and its practical consequences into public discussion.[190]

This would seem to be true whether we are speaking of natural or revealed truths. Obviously prudence would have to determine what could be introduced helpfully into public discussion and legislation, but in principle if reason is unified, then there is a common body of truths which, because

---

189. Ibid. Robert D. Putnam, *E Pluribus Unum: Diversity and Community in the Twenty-First Century* (Malden, Mass.: Blackwell, 2007), argues that everyone is negatively affected by increasing diversity, which tends to discourage civic engagement. Peter Wood, *Diversity: The Invention of a Concept* (San Francisco: Encounter Books, 2003), studies the shift from nineteenth-century interest in diversity, understood as fascination with humanity's variety, to current egalitarian interest in diversity, understood as the prescription of racial and ethnic outcomes.

190. "Rawls, Liberalism, and the Unity of Reason," in *Is a Culture of Life Still Possible in the U.S.?* ed. Anthony Mastroeni (South Bend, Ind.: St. Augustine's Press, 1999), 45–47.

they are true, we each have responsibility to urge on others. If I understand Neuhaus correctly, though he believed in the natural law he also thought that a constitutional situation of continuing pluralism, an implicitly deep pluralism (though Neuhaus seems to have thought that we can somehow control pluralism, perhaps limit it to two or three religions in society so that we can avoid its logic), is superior to the traditional Catholic view that one of the aims of government is where possible to bring humans to the truth, both the truth of the natural law and the truth of the Church.

The logic of Catholicism leads to witness to the ends of the earth and the desire to give all life a Catholic form. The limit, finally part of the mystery of God's action in time but presumably beyond human capacity to achieve, is that all enter the Church. Christ sent the Apostles to preach "everywhere," and there is even a certain *compelle intrare* ("give them no choice but to come in," Lk 14:23) in which Christians are to participate, even if this be understood to involve preaching an irresistible Gospel rather than using force or violence.[191] As Pius X understood and stated, restoring all things in Christ must refer not simply to the salvation of individuals, but to the obligation of Christians to construct a Christian civilization.[192] Good Catholics have always fairly doubted that this would, this side of the eschaton, happen in any large measure, but the logic of Catholicism is to work until all be one. This "one" receives a quite specific form in Pickstock's idea that individuals and societies can only thrive if they have doxology, presumably a common form of worship.[193] This both takes the discussion to a much more profound level than it has had in the United States, and does seem to imply an established religion as the ordering idea or *telos*.

Presumably there will always be various forms of pluralism in society, some of them healthy and to be encouraged. The issue is so important that we may explore it a bit further through a moving argument, made by George Weigel. Weigel recounts the following story with which Michael McConnell concluded a paper:

In 1789, there was a great public feast in Philadelphia . . . to celebrate the ratification of the Constitution. The feast included a fitting symbol of the new nation's attitude toward religious diversity: a special table where the food conformed to Jewish dietary laws. This was a fitting symbol because it included Jewish Americans in the celebration without requiring that they sacrifice their distinctiveness as Jews.

191. Paul O'Callaghan, "Is Christianity a Religion? The Role of Violence, Myth and Witness in Religion," *FCSQ* 29, 4 (Winter 2006): 13–28 at 22.

192. See quotation in Christopher Dawson, *Judgment of the Nations* (London: Sheed & Ward, 1943), 99. O'Donovan, *Desire of the Nations,* details the tension between present and eschaton without losing sight of the Christian mission: see esp. his ch. 6 on the idea of Christendom as a Christian order which knows itself to be passing.

193. Robert Sokolowski, "Theology and Deconstruction," *Telos* 110 (Winter 1998): 155–66 at 166.

A few years later, in France, Napoleon summoned the leaders of the Jewish community to a "Great Sanhedrin." Their task was to make modifications in the Jewish law so that Jewish people could be integrated into the French nation. In a gesture no less revealing than the kosher table in Philadelphia, Napoleon's Minister of the Interior scheduled the first session to be held on Saturday, (i.e., the Jewish Sabbath, a day reserved for religious observance).

Here we see the alternatives. Under the old regime, Jews would be excluded from the celebration, for they could not be citizens. Under the secular state, Jews would be welcome to attend, but they would be expected to eat the same food that other citizens ate. If they wanted to keep kosher, they could do it at home, in private, at their own expense.

Under the pluralist vision, multiple tables are provided to ensure that all citizens can participate in the commonwealth, and that their religious differences would be protected and respected. The French Revolution created a secular establishment. The American Revolution presupposed that religion is consistent with liberal democracy and protected religion by making it free.[194]

Chapter two above commented unfavorably on the lay French notion of nationalism, which inevitably leads to secularization. If the choice is between it and American pluralism, rather idealistically portrayed by McConnell and Weigel in the passage just quoted, we should prefer the American solution. However, hard-headed analysis forces two comments. This "solution" works best when there is relatively little religious diversity present in a country, two or three religions. Second, this solution, because prudential and pragmatic at its core, while an example of a kindly toleration, does obscure the nature of the life in society at which the Christian aims, the ways in which what we do in this world is eschatological, connected to the Kingdom which, even now, is forming ("thy kingdom come on earth as in heaven").

The logic of Catholicism is incarnational, finding God in all things, and, when and where possible, moves in the direction of a public Church and a shared culture that is informed by Christianity. The world was created to be a place of loving, free, and obedient response to God. Even before the Exodus the Israelites struggled for freedom of worship. The Promised Land was a space given them for their own liturgy, and a place of obedience to God, who as the true owner of the world, had everything at His disposal. This land was to be freed from idolatry. In the Diaspora, Israel scattered and the idea of the land shifted its meaning from national possession to restatement of the universality of God's claim to the earth. Already Zechariah saw that the land (of Israel) was not simply a nation-state, but was to be a universal kingdom of peace, something that overcame national boundaries.

In Christianity the king of peace reigns in the Eucharist, and the Church itself is a "preliminary sketch" of a world ordered by peace. In the words of the Orthodox theologian Olivier Clement, "in its deepest understanding,

194. George Weigel, "One Banquet Many Tables," *IC,* August 11, 2000.

the Church is nothing other than the world in the course of transfiguration."[195] The Kingdom of God begins in time in the degree to which God's will is done, but is only completed beyond time. All this means that we cannot declare a priori how far the Kingdom is to come this side of the end of time. We must not do anything to block its arrival, and one mark of this arrival is a land ordered to worship of the one, true God.[196] Since the Kingdom of God is composed of all those who do the will of God, it at least partially dissolves previous social orders, such as that of the Jews. But Christ with his disciples forms a new Israel and a new family, bringing the God of Israel to the nations. This new Israel or Church cannot bring the historical order of Israel in all its specificity to all the nations—this was Paul's point—for the Church, by contrast to the old Israel, is universal.

The birth of Christianity represents a kind of secularization because men are left free to discover what social arrangements best accord with the idea of the Kingdom of God, with a universal communion in God's will. At least in much of the West, the modern world has transformed this secularization which Christianity initiated into an absolute form which denies any orientation to God or communion with Jesus. What the Christian works for is a non-theocratic order (a new Israel, not the old Israel), which allows such enduring concrete realities as the family to flourish, and so far as possible extends universal communion in the will of God, never escaping inherited history. The model here is more old Christendom than the modern nation-state, a "universal" communion in faith and culture, but a communion without the kind of governing or political center characteristic of the nation-state, and therefore probably including many political centers.

The logic of pluralism and of Neuhaus's notion that it is the Americans who have found a better constitutional arrangement than any found earlier in the history of Christendom is that a constitutional barrier, the First Amendment, is allowed to place a limit on the work of God in time. This declares that in America it is against the law that there ever be a (religious) "one." All must remain voluntary, and religion implicitly must be private and relatively disembodied, though streets may be blocked off so that Corpus Christi processions may proceed. One can understand perfectly well that if the premise be that thirteen colonies with various types of established religion needed to form one federal order, it was necessary to disestablish all religion; but from this it does not follow at all that this is the best constitution for all mankind.

⁓

There is a serious problem around which we have hitherto tiptoed: most of us find it easier to offer our allegiance to a system that sustains our sense

195. *The Roots of Christian Mysticism* (New York: New City Press, 1996), 95.
196. Benedict XVI, *Jesus of Nazareth* (New York: Doubleday, 2007), 82–84, 100–101, and see 111–22, on what follows.

of ourselves than to live a counter-cultural life.[197] This was one "fact of human nature" arguing in favor of Maurice Cowling's views above. One of the reasons why the notion of a two-level universe, one of nature and one of grace, was so popular in pre–Vatican II American thought was that it made possible a "public theology" founded in the natural law, about the nature of which most—Catholic, Protestant, and Jew—could agree. Whatever their disagreements about revealed theology, most—not just intellectuals, but the average person—could agree that there was a set of common moral principles grounded in reason and open to all rational beings. Sometimes this shared heritage was called the Jewish-Christian tradition, though of course the whole point was that there was nothing specifically Jewish or Christian about it. Indeed exemplary of this tradition was the fact that the Ten Commandments stood at its center. While the Commandments are found in all the religions of the Book, they are not distinctive to any of these religions, and are a form of what Judaism calls the Noahide Laws (because given to Adam and Noah before the revelation of the Commandments to Moses), a law of universal application to all mankind.[198]

This body of common truths could make most feel that they had some part in the American experiment, just as expressions like "Judaeo-Christian" suggested that one (political) tradition could be made of two (religious) traditions. While Americans disagreed at the level of revelation, they could more or less agree about what reason or nature demanded. Arguably, for Catholics this fostered a certain optimism about Catholic engagement with the larger culture which prepared the way for an optimistic reading of *Gaudium et Spes* when it appeared in the 1960s.[199] Only relatively recently has it become clear that in such a "public theology" not only is revealed theology indefinitely bracketed from political life so that we can live a peaceable shared existence, but also that this bracketing is essentially acceptance of a low-church Protestant definition of religion as private.[200] What stands revealed is the deep hope that a counter-cultural life is no longer necessary, that we can all be Americans without anything substantively Christian or Jewish getting in the way.[201]

Robert Wilken thinks such a view mistaken. To the goal of advocating

197. Mathew Kuefler, *The Manly Eunuch: Masculinity, Gender Ambiguity, and Christian Ideology in Late Antiquity* (Chicago: University of Chicago Press, 2001), 288. Cf. *The Church as Counterculture,* ed. Michael L. Budde and Robert W. Brimlow (Albany: State University of New York Press, 2000), and Robert F. Gotcher, "New Ecclesial Movements and Communities: a Pastoral and Theological Challenge to the Local Church," *FQI* 2 (2002): 55–90 at 69–70.

198. See my "Setting Boundaries."

199. Eugene McCarraher, "Remarks on John McGreevy's Catholicism and American Freedom," *HS* (September/October 2004): 28–31 at 31, referring to the analysis of Rowland, *Culture and the Thomist Tradition.*

200. Olsen, "Separating Church and State."

201. Frederick Christian Bauerschmidt, "Confessions of an Evangelical Catholic: Five Theses Related to Theological Anthropology," *Co* 31 (2004): 67–84 at 75.

not Christian adjustment to the larger culture, but Christian work to make that larger culture supportive of Christian life, Wilken has insisted that the average Catholic person needs a sustaining Christian culture, not a high culture of Bach or Caravaggio, but T. S. Eliot's "total harvest of thinking and feeling."[202] For Wilken it is superficial to rail against "Constantinianism," for Christians in all ages must work for the Christianization of their society, albeit in ways that embody fair politics. Wilken holds it is good that "in 321 Constantine made Sunday a public holiday," implicitly extending the time of the Church to society.[203] Presumably in an imperial situation such an act was politically proper, for people had always received normative rules from their emperor. Though in a democracy this same act may not be possible (this depends on the particular democracy and its rules), the Christian remains under an obligation to argue for an impress of religion on the whole of life. He will want this for himself and his children, and if he is one of the chosen few, more conscious about the issues than the average mediocre Christian, he will have on him a special obligation to work for this impress of Christianity on all life. Of course this is not a command to imprudence, and it may be that wise judgment decides that this or that moral disorder cannot reasonably be removed from a given society. Writers like Peter J. Leithart and Oliver O'Donovan argue that though a new Christendom is not likely, it is not to be excluded a priori.[204]

At the least, within his own community of the Church, the Christian must always remember that the real (or more real) time is the time of the Church, not the time of the state; a time ordered around "feast days and sacred seasons," not around the Fourth of July and Memorial Day.[205] Minimally, the state must encourage public religious expression:

If Christ is culture, let the sidewalks be lit with fire on Easter Eve, let traffic stop for a column of Christians waving palm branches on a spring morning, let streets be blocked off as the faithful gather for a Corpus Christi procession. Then will others know that there is another city in their midst, another commonwealth, one that has its face, like the faces of angels, turned toward the face of God.[206]

Always one must judge the times, but once again we arrive at the point that an incarnational Christianity aims not in principle at the American separation of Church and state or any idea that in principle liberal democracy is

---

202. "The Church as Culture," *FT* 142 (April 2004): 31–36 at 32.

203. Ibid., 34. Wilken is one of a number of writers who attack the anti-Constantinianism of thinkers such as Stanley Hauerwas in *God, Truth, and Witness: Engaging Stanley Hauerwas,* ed. L. Gregory Jones, Reinhard Huetter, and C. Rosalee Velloso Ewell (Grand Rapids, Mich.: Brazos Press, 2005).

204. Peter J. Leithart, *Against Christianity* (Moscow, Idaho: Canon Press, 2003), and of the books of O'Donovan see, with Joan Lockwood O'Donovan, *Bonds of Imperfection.*

205. Wilken, "Church as Culture," 34.

206. Ibid., 36.

the best regime, but at that politics which most allows the temporal order to be supportive of all that is good, true, and beautiful, whether finding its source in reason or revelation. From a Christian point of view, the best politics is especially solicitous of the poor, not just the materially poor but those who are numbered among the mediocre.

What the Cambridge theologians of radical orthodoxy and others of similar mind ask is that Christians' sense of themselves be sustained first by their Church, especially their local church, rather than by their national culture. Implicitly such a position believes that the mediocre can no longer be supported by the larger culture, that they will simply lose their way in that culture, and that therefore the Church, especially the local church, must become their point of reference. One's immediate response to such a proposal might be that such thinkers must not have spent much time in a local church, but I do not take their position to express a roseate view of how things are at the level of either the local or the universal Church, but the simple conclusion "we have no choice." However we work this out, the first truth remains "here we have no lasting city, but we are looking for the city that is to come" (Heb 13:14).[207]

Paul Griffiths has pointed to some hard realities which must be faced if we speak of the Church as possibly providing a counter-culture to the larger society. According to Griffiths, there are only three international institutions with enough power to provide "translocal habits of being: nation-states, corporations, and churches."[208] Griffiths observes, correctly, that our patterns of life now come primarily from economic institutions, and secondarily from political institutions. The Church is in a distant third place:

We have become consumers who occasionally think of ourselves as citizens. Any tattered remnants of religious habits of being are now subservient to (indeed, usually understood precisely in terms of) habits of consumption.

This means that nation-states and corporations are now the principal determinants of everyone's character and action.

Nevertheless, Griffiths notes growing discontent with this situation:

As the bankruptcy and corruption of the corporate promise begins slowly to become evident, people turn again to the churches, and with renewed passion. And so we have resurgent Islam across the world, the explosive growth of Christianity in much of Africa and parts of East Asia, and the increasing evidence of inchoate desires on the part even of jaded and sophisticated European and American Catholic Christians for a habit of being that is truly Catholic, truly all-embracing.[209]

207. Bauerschmidt, "Confessions of an Evangelical Catholic," at 80.
208. "What Can We Reasonably Hope For?" *FT* 99 (January 2000): 24–25 at 24, and for the following quotation.
209. Ibid., 25.

Griffiths's conclusion is that for Christians who read the times correctly, the future is full of Christian opportunity. The radical orthodox are not wrong in pointing us away from nation and corporation and to the Church.

The question of how counter-cultural and how accommodating the Church must be to whatever culture it finds itself in is perennial. Arguably there is no one answer, certainly no precise answer. Common sense would suggest that in principle the Church should be neither simply counter-cultural nor simply supportive, but must forever judge cases, or discern the times. Bryan Hehir makes an important point here, seconded by Christopher Ruddy, that the stance of *Gaudium et Spes* is that the Church is "in" the world, not, per se, "against" it. Ruddy quotes Gerhard Lohfink:

It is the will of God to have a people in the world so that one can clearly see, by looking at that people, how God proposes that human society should be, so that the world can see the unanimity and peace that is possible in such a people and thus come to peace for itself.[210]

"The church ... exists to remind the world of its true story." Cardinal George of Chicago, precisely because the Church is called to love the world, has expressed a dislike for describing the Church as "countercultural."[211] Obviously in varying measures the Church always is counter-cultural, and the present author has no decisive objection to the use of that word. However, especially for those not very familiar with Christianity, perhaps it is not helpful to make counter-culturalism their first introduction.[212] In sum, although a kind of sectarianism in which some Christian groups, like the ancient monks, are set apart from society is acceptable, for most Christians the universal Church as made concrete in their local church should be their first point of reference, but in a way that does not despair of bringing all things to God, and thus always strives for an increasing imprint of Christianity on society as a whole.

☞

David L. Schindler, the dean of the John Paul II Institute at The Catholic University of America and one of contemporary liberalism's most persistent and perceptive critics, is sympathetic to much in radical orthodoxy, but himself develops a position closer to that of John Paul II (as noted, by origins radical orthodoxy is Anglican and tends to a not-always-appreciative view of the papacy). Above all, as an advocate of *communio* theology and

---

210. Christopher Ruddy, "Heroism, Hospitality, and Holiness: Generational Perspectives on the Church-World Relationship," *Lo* 7, 1 (Winter 2004): 45–62 at 47, for this and the following quotation.

211. Ibid., 52.

212. The language of "culture war" is very common: James Davison Hunter, *Culture Wars: The Struggle to Define America* (New York: Basic Books, 1991), shows that the deepest faults in society do not run along the lines of race or ethnicity, but between rival worldviews or cosmologies.

of the thought of Hans Urs von Balthasar, Schindler has an especially full understanding of transcendence and of beauty, and his is a position toward which the present book has been moving.[213] But first to Schindler's understanding of the *saeculum* and the lay state.

Schindler begins with the 1988 declaration of *Christifideles Laici,* 16, that the laity are defined both by their new life in baptism, and by their "secular character."[214] This latter means that the laity live their lives within the *saeculum* or present age: the world is the place in which the laity exercise their specific character, "to restore to creation all its original value" through Christ and the Eucharist "so that God might be all in all" (cf. 1 Cor 15:28; Jn 12:32).[215] I would go a bit further, especially following Augustine, but also a number of the Eastern fathers, and say that the goal of human life, lay or not, is not simply to restore the creation to its original value, but to complete Adam's task of *reformatio in melius,* "reform to the better," unending imitation of God in this life and the next leading to ever fuller *theosis* or divinization.[216] Adam was meant for a life of perfect conformity to God's will. He fell. The task of fallen humanity is not simply to restore the creation or recover Adam's first state, but to continue the task Adam left incomplete. This is, as a creature, forever to become more Godlike while remaining a creature. So far as the lay state is concerned, "the proper identity—and mission—of the lay faithful . . . consists in *being* a eucharistic presence at the heart of the 'secular.'"[217] With Benedict XVI we may describe the Eucharist as "the enactment within history of the new politics for which the human heart yearns."[218] This is at the furthest remove from a purely private piety, and brings all the foregoing discussion into a focus it does not have if we, with MacIntyre, simply stand "waiting for Benedict [the monk].'"

Several things stand out. With the Jesuits Schindler finds God in all things, and sees the lay task as remaining in the world and trying to bring all in it to God. This rules out any ultimate despair about the age we live in, or flight from the world. The layman, rather, is compelled to dialogue with the world and redemption of the times. Though working with particularly faithful or charismatic groups or movements is acceptable, sectarianism as

213. Throughout the following discussion I am using an unpublished paper by Schindler, "Beauty, Transcendence, and the Face of the Other: Religion and Culture in America," a summary of which appeared in *Co* 26 (1999): 915.

214. David L. Schindler, "Toward a Culture of Life: The Eucharist, the 'Restoration' of Creation, and the 'Worldly' Task of the Laity in Liberal Societies," *Co* 29, 1 (2002): 679–90 at 680.

215. *Christifideles Laici* 15 and Schindler, "Toward a Culture of Life," 680.

216. The classic study is Gerhart Ladner, *The Idea of Reform: Its Impact on Christian Thought and Action in the Age of the Fathers,* rev. ed. (New York: Harper & Row, 1967).

217. Schindler, "Toward a Culture of Life," 680.

218. Richard Neuhaus, "The Public Square," *FT* 163 (May 2006): 59–64 at 63, describing *Deus Caritas Est.*

usually understood is also ruled out in the name of a Catholic ecclesiology which aims at the salvation of all and nurtures the poor and mediocre. Schindler's is a view that ties immanence and transcendence together by giving a proper evaluation to the created order as "aimed" at God:

> The creaturely act is characterized at once by *immanence* and *transcendence*. Immanence, in the sense that the relation to God and others that is constitutive of the creature presupposes the creature's capacity to receive the other *within itself*, and the creature is so far marked by *interiority*. Transcendence in the sense that the relation to God and others that is constitutively (hence continuously) *given to* and *received by* the creature presupposes the creature's openness to an other who is always already "beyond" the self. Immanence and transcendence in the creature cannot be dissociated: they are dual aspects of the same act.

The interpenetration of immanence and transcendence is most profoundly found in the Eucharist, God present in the midst of the age.[219]

An earlier chapter discussed the idea that the liturgy makes us beautiful, and alluded to Dostoevsky's idea that beauty will save the world. Schindler's way of putting this is to insist that experience of transcendence—openness to the infinite—is only possible within the context of experience of beauty. He thinks that liberal societies push beauty, and thus the experience of transcendence, to the margins. For America the paradox is that widespread religiosity accompanies a lack of genuine transcendence. Central to Schindler's critique is his understanding of beauty in a Balthasarian way, as the manifestation of the other as gift. This is quite removed from any of the pre-Christian understandings of beauty, which, in whatever form, saw beauty as a natural aesthetic category. Schindler's "beauty" is that of Christ and of the arc of Christ's life, sent from on high to die on a cross and descend into the netherworld, and from death on a cross to return to the Father in glory.[220] This beauty turns conventional ideas on their head, upsetting all pre-Christian ideas of beauty, and of course also all the post-Christian ideas we find around us. Christ is for the Christian pure gift. More generally, since we are creatures, all is for us pure gift. This giftedness of being, in its supreme form the gift of the Son for the world, gives beauty its content.

Beauty and transcendence are related. Beauty may be a signal of the ecstatic nature of relation to the other. Plato was only one of many before Christianity to see that humans are constituted for self-transcendence. He commonly considered this to be the work of *eros,* of desire for the other—whether another human being or an idea. This desire for something outside oneself was not for him, as it is for the modern liberal, as much an exercise

---

219. David L. Schindler, "The Given as Gift: Creation and Disciplinary Abstraction in Science," to appear in *Communio*.

220. See also Nicholas J. Healy, *The Eschatology of Hans Urs von Balthasar: Being as Communion* (Oxford: Oxford University Press, 2005).

of the will in which the self chooses something for itself—to add to itself—as the opposite, a self-transcendence in which the self is left behind to cling to another. This was a foretaste of Christian insight. To transcend oneself is to discover another as meaningful and lovable, precisely because not oneself, because drawing one out of oneself. "In a word, the self achieves transcendence only in and through the gift of the other."[221] Schindler concludes that for transcendence "aesthetics" comes before "ethics." This is what was meant by saying that the liturgy is first to make us beautiful, and only secondarily to be a didactic exercise. Obviously these are not unrelated categories, but the emphasis, against hundreds of years in which especially Calvinism has encouraged a Christianity so centered on the moral life as almost to abandon the category of beauty, is on the restoration of beauty and glory to the heart of theology and Christian life in the world.

Transcendence is not something which enters or is allowed to flourish only in the few empty spaces remaining in a society dominated by consumerism and technocracy. Because God is at once transcendent and immanent, he is everywhere, "inside" everything, not just in certain interstices left to Him until life becomes completely "busy" and "noisy." Because God is everywhere, we are meant to find him everywhere, simultaneously pursuing, if we may use this language, the heights and depths of being. Schindler appropriates Wendell Berry's distinction between our present economy and what Berry calls the Great or Loving Economy. This latter needs some religious tradition to support it, and in Christian terms may be called the Kingdom of God, an economy or way of life in which God sees every sparrow fall, and whose primary aim is not possession, consumption, or power, but maximum well-being for all, the ability of each to embody a beauty appropriate to him or it. "The purpose of the Great Economy above all . . . is to promote the maximum of beauty: by subordinating oneself to the service of God and all the others, thus transcending oneself."[222] The ability to receive and give are primary in each created being as that which makes relation to the other possible, and the primacy of relations implies the primacy of beauty. "In the genuine experience of transcendence, the beauty of the other and the glory of God stand and fall together": this is why it is so difficult for self-absorbed modern culture to see the Glory of God.[223]

One of Schindler's specific missions has been the criticism of neo-liberal or neo-conservative pleading on behalf of a quite unfettered capitalism. Of course generally neo-conservatives do not hold a purely laissez-faire economics, and most do see moral and religious principles as higher than econom-

221. Quoted from Schindler, "Beauty, Transcendence" (unpublished manuscript).
222. Ibid.
223. Quoted from David L. Schindler, "Which Ontology Is Necessary for an Adequate Anthropology?" (unpublished paper).

ics, and in some sense as guiding economic life. But differences of degree here can be marked, and Schindler has been described by someone favorable to his criticism as struggling "to save the social thought of Pope John Paul II from a Wall Street takeover."[224] Many do view the neo-conservatives as tending to co-opt papal teaching to their own advocacy of democracy and capitalism. Probably those open to criticism of the neo-conservatives have been appalled by the brutal "ethics" of large business especially common from the 1990s and typified by the Enron scandal, the intentional laying off of workers in profitable industries because cheaper labor exists in some other country, and the permanent disequilibrium flowing from concentration on corporate takeovers and the replacement of "owners' capitalism" with "managers' capitalism."[225] Most of this is not new—some of the textile industries the American South has been losing to foreign countries today came to the South from the North as part of an earlier quest for cheap labor; and the story is not one of unremitting greed and irresponsibility—Costco flourishes as well as Wal-Mart—but there is much to promote the belief that big business has little concern for the common good or sense of public responsibility.

When Catholic neo-conservatives such as Michael Novak celebrate the entrepreneurial spirit they do not much discuss all that is dark in the chiaroscuro of the contemporary business climate. Business historians such as Louis Uchitelle, on the other hand, note how much contemporary labor practices are "a lot like those of the nineteenth-century robber barons"—who of course also do not figure very prominently in Novak's paeans to capitalism.[226] It is difficult for the non-specialist to know where the truth lies between such diverse interpretations, and certainly there are today both virtuous and exploitative employers. But everyday experience suggests that the neo-conservatives, preoccupied with promoting the liberty on which they see the entrepreneurial spirit depending, tend to gloss over much that is "out of control" in current economic life. It is not that writers such as Novak do not acknowledge weaknesses in American democratic liberalism, but that, these acknowledgments having been made, they proceed as if none of this touches the heart of what we are.

224. Portier, "Here Come the Evangelical Catholics," 37.

225. James Lardner, "The Specter Haunting Your Offices," *NYRB* 54, 10 (June 14, 2007): 62–65 at 64. On manager's capitalism see Alfred D. Chandler Jr., *The Visible Hand: The Managerial Revolution in American Business* (Cambridge, Mass.: Harvard University Press, 1977), and, with Herman Daems, *Managerial Hierarchies: Comparative Perspectives on the Rise of the Modern Industrial Enterprise* (Cambridge, Mass.: Harvard University Press, 1980). See also Richard R. John, "Elaborations, Revisions, Dissents: Alfred D. Chandler Jr.'s *The Visible Hand* after Twenty Years," *Business History Review* 71 (1997): 151–200, and Jeff Madrick, "Time for a New Deal," *NYRB* 55, 14 (September 25, 2008): 65–70.

226. The quoted phrase is from a review of recent books in business history: Lardner, "Specter Haunting Your Offices," 62. Glenn Porter, *The Rise of Big Business*, 2nd ed. (Wheeling, Ill.: Harlan Davidson, 1992), is excellent in guiding the reader through the disagreements among business historians about topics such as the robber barons.

Novak's "Catholic social thought" is very far from, say, G. K. Chesterton's unblinking assessment: "The rich man is bribed; he has been bribed already. That is why he is a rich man."[227] Even in the case of Chesterton, it is not that money-making is itself condemned, but that, as for such thinkers as Charles Péguy, a certain artisan ideal is to be aimed at in which the good of making must continue to be valued above the good of money-making.[228] The so-called free market is often in neo-liberal circles "a euphemism for letting the private sector set its own rules."[229] A post–World War II social contract which tried to keep businesses rooted in specific places and encouraged a sense of obligation on the part of businessmen for the welfare of their employees and communities has now largely disappeared, with few corporate leaders showing "respect for our non-material and non-individualistic selves." Against all this Schindler, with the radical orthodox, protests.

∽

The conclusion to which this book has been leading has many similarities to Schindler's analysis. The civilization, the world, and the very possibility of thinking about a cosmos began in contemplation, in human reflection about human destiny. It expressed itself in powerful metaphors of cosmic harmony and the music of the spheres, which were ways of enunciating the place of humans in a larger reality. As Aristotle already saw, man is first of all a "theoretical" animal, a being for whom contemplation *(theoria)* is ontologically prior to action. This was a continuing insight of the learned all through the ancient and medieval worlds, and meant that these worlds assumed humans are of their nature oriented to transcendence, to rising above and passing out of themselves. The understanding of transcendence was deepened by the coming of Christianity, which, through the doctrine of the incarnation, insisted on an intimate link between transcendence and immanence. The transcendent is found at the heart of the life of the *saeculum,* above all in the Eucharist.

In the late medieval world the ancient and medieval cosmos began to crumble. With the passage of time life became increasingly oriented around punctual individuals, individuals who saw themselves as autonomous, in isolation, not as part of larger communities of God, angels, saints, ancestors, and other humans. Though the timelines of this development varied widely, even the most intimate communities, those of the family, neighbor-

227. *Orthodoxy,* 118. The force of Chesterton's moralizing would be much reduced if he stopped to make every desirable qualification every time he made such statements, but it might be observed here that in such lines as those quoted he is harsher than the Gospel, which, though deeply skeptical of the ability of the rich man to enter into the Kingdom of God, "only" stated that such entrance would be more difficult than a camel going through the eye of a needle.

228. Charles Péguy, *Oeuvres en prose,* II (Paris: Gallimard, 1957), 1050 f.; also see Adrian J. Walker, "The Gift of Simplicity: Reflections on Obedience in the Work of Adrienne von Speyer," an unpublished essay kindly sent to me.

229. This and the next quotation is from Lardner, "Specter Haunting Your Offices," 65.

hood, or village, eventually lost their cohesiveness wherever modern conditions of life spread. There is a significant way in which, in this world, one can never return home, and the rise of punctual individuals who repeated their own separation from the cosmos in other separations such as of objects from subjects meant that the world could never be as whole as it once had been. From one point of view this was a loss, but it also was a gain, for the very emphasis on epistemology in modern thinking following Descartes revealed a naïveté in the old view, which had been uncritical about the way in which an observer frames the world he observes. Naïve realism was no longer possible, and neither was a stance which simply wanted to return to some first condition such as contemplation or wholeness. Augustine and Aquinas had both observed that for embodied creatures the contemplation central to life is not for its own sake, but is to be oriented to action. Humans are social creatures, and both heaven and the Trinity are forms of *communio.* The Christian doctrine of original sin ruled out any wholeness in this life, any rendering of the parts into a stable whole or any stopping of time. As Kierkegaard was eventually to say, there is a profound sense in which we are left with "fragments."

From especially the time of the Enlightenment, individualism expressed itself in attack on the past itself, in an attempt to separate oneself from tradition. This continues until the present. The ideas that humans are embodied souls, and that because this world is created, soul or spirit must be the logically prior category to body or matter, were very commonly replaced with some form of materialism, which denied the very idea of transcendence. Against this there was always protest, and after or as a result of the brutal materialisms of the nineteenth and twentieth centuries, these often took the form of flight from the world as it had become and turn to transcendence.

The question is what we can now expect of life. Politically the argument of this book has been cautionary, warning against all forms of progressivism and utopianism, and, while admitting that such classical questions as that of "the best form of government" are still worth discussing, urging that the role of history in making us what we are is much more decisive than the ancient theorists or modern ideologues have understood. There are reasons, natural and revealed, for doubting that either democracy or the American separation of Church and state is some best arrangement for all humans. There are reasons for thinking that history is so central to what people are that it is foolish to try to give them a radically new history, to, for instance, try to make them democrats if they have no tradition of democracy. It should be enough to work for certain arrangements always beneficial to humans, such as an articulated constitutional order and law, or a just judiciary, within what they have received from the past.

In terms of what is most central to us, we are to work for a proper expression of the relation of time and eternity, immanence and transcendence. Rather than flee the world, we are to continue the Ignatian program of finding God in all things. If we receive a tawdry and banal ecclesiastical architecture, we are to reassert the idea that the Church must both express—say, in images of the communion of saints in which we stand—the fact that we are on pilgrimage and have no abiding place; but that here in this place the Lord of the universe is truly present. Whether in church or not, we are to oppose a music or art that is lost in noisiness or busyness, in being caught up in a mindless urge to change for its own sake, with a music or art which either helps bring another world to us, or us to another world. Finally, we are to realize that our first home is the Church, not any other community. Though political duties or politics are not to be neglected, our principal effort must be to build up the life of the Church. In doing this we are uniting earth and heaven, anticipating in this life the world to come.

WORKS CITED

Abrams, Elliott. "Judaism or Jewishness." *FT* 74 (June/July 1997): 18–25.

Abulafia, David, ed. *The New Cambridge Medieval History,* vol. 5: *C. 1198–c. 1300.* Cambridge: Cambridge University Press, 1999.

Ackerman, Bruce, and James S. Fishkin. *Deliberation Day.* New Haven, Conn.: Yale University Press, 2004.

Aertsen, Jan. *Medieval Philosophy and the Transcendentals: The Case of Thomas Aquinas.* New York: Brill, 1996.

After Secularization, an issue of *The Hedgehog Review* (Spring/Summer 2006).

"*AHR* Conversation: Religious Identities and Violence." *AHR* 112 (2007): 1433–79.

Akbari, Suzanne Conklin. *Seeing through the Veil: Optical Theory and Medieval Allegory.* Toronto: University of Toronto Press, 2004.

al-Marrakushi, 'Abd al-Wahid. *The Admirable in Abridgment of the News of the West,* translated by John A. Williams. In *Medieval Iberia: Readings from Christian, Muslim, and Jewish Sources,* edited by Olivia Remie Constable, 185–89. Philadelphia: University of Pennsylvania Press, 1997.

Alison, James. *The Joy of Being Wrong: Original Sin Through Easter Eyes.* Foreword by Sebastian Moore. New York: Crossroad, 1998.

Altena, James. "Secular Hermeneutics." *Touchstone* 14, 6 (July/August 2001): 51–55.

Althoff, Gerd. *Otto III.* Translated by Phyllis G. Jestice. University Park: Pennsylvania State University Press, 2003.

Alvarez, A. "A Double Bind." *NYRB* 51, 20 (December 16, 2004): 76–77.

Ambrose, Kirk. *The Nave Sculpture of Vézelay: The Art of Monastic Viewing.* Toronto: Pontifical Institute of Medieval Studies, 2006.

Ames, Christine Caldwell. "Does Inquisition Belong to Religious History?" *AHR* 110 (2005): 11–37.

Amicone, Luigi. "Event as Encounter: The Battle Against Utopia." *Traces* 5, 5 (May 2003): 16–17.

"An Alternative Future: An Exchange." *NYRB* 50, 19 (December 4, 2003): 57–61.

Anatolios, Khaled. "Heaven and Earth in Byzantine Liturgy." *Antiphon* 5, 3 (2000): 21–28.

Anderson, Margaret Lavinia. "The Limits of Secularization: On the Problem of the Catholic Revival in 19th-Century Germany." *HR* 38 (1995): 647–70.

Andrews, Cory L. "The Metaphor as Wrecking Ball." *IR* 39, 1–2 (Fall 2003/Spring 2004): 66–69.

Angell, Marcia. "The Truth About the Drug Companies." *NYRB* 51, 12 (July 15, 2004): 52–58.

Antonelli, Mario. "Trinity and Eucharist in Blondel." *Co* 27 (2000): 284–99.

Appiah, Kwame Anthony. "You Must Remember This," *NYRB* 50, 4 (March 13, 2003): 35–37.

———. *Cosmopolitanism: Ethics in a World of Strangers.* New York: W. W. Norton, 2006.

Applebaum, Anne. "Pulling the Rug Out from Under." *NYRB* 51, 2 (February 12, 2004): 9–11.

Appleby, David. "Sign and Church Reform in the Thought of Jonas of Orléans." *Viator* 27 (1996): 11–33.

———. "The Priority of Sight according to Peter the Venerable." *Mediaeval Studies* 60 (1998): 123–57.

———. "Present Absence: From Rhetorical Figure to Eucharistic *Veritas* in the Thought of Paschasius Radbertus." *FQI* 3 (2003): 139–71.

———. "'Beautiful on the Cross, Beautiful in His Torments': The Place of the Body in the Thought of Pascasius Radbertus." *Traditio* 50 (2005): 1–46.

Appleby, Joyce. *Inheriting the Revolution: The First Generation of Americans.* Cambridge, Mass.: Belknap Press, 2000.

Armstrong, Colin. "English Catholicism Under Mary Tudor." *CHR* 93 (July 2007): 588–93.

Arquillière, Henri-Xavier. *L'augustinisme politique: Essai sur la formation des théories politiques du moyen-âge.* 2nd ed. Paris: J. Vrin, 1955.

Arrowsmith, William. "Editor's Foreword." In Euripides, *Helen.* Translated by James Michie and Colin Leach. Oxford: Oxford University Press, 1981.

Asad, Talal. *Genealogies of Religion: Discipline and Reasons of Power in Christianity and Islam.* Baltimore: Johns Hopkins University Press, 1993.

———. *Formations of the Secular: Christianity, Islam, Modernity.* Stanford, Calif.: Stanford University Press, 2003.

Ascherson, Neal. "Goodbye to Berlin." *NYRB* 50, 6 (April 10, 2003): 22–26.

———. "In the Black Garden." *NYRB* 50, 18 (November 20, 2003): 37–40.

Ashford, Robert, and Rodney Shakespeare. *Binary Economics; the New Paradigm.* Lanham, Md.: University Press of America, 1999.

Astell, Ann W. *Eating Beauty: The Eucharist and the Spiritual Arts of the Middle Ages.* Ithaca, N.Y.: Cornell University Press, 2006.

Aston, Nigel. *Religion and Revolution in France, 1780–1804.* Washington, D.C.: The Catholic University of America Press, 2000.

Atwood, Margaret. "Arguing Against Ice Cream." *NYRB* 50, 10 (June 12, 2003): 6–10.

Auerbach, Erich. *Dante, Poet of the Secular World.* Translated by Ralph Manheim. Chicago: University of Chicago Press, 1961.

Aurell, Martin. *The Plantagenet Empire 1154–1224.* Translated by David Crouch. New York: Pearson Education, 2007.

Austin, Greta. "Jurisprudence in the Service of Pastoral Care: The *Decretum* of Burchard of Worms." *Sp* 79 (2004): 929–59.

Bacevich, A. J. "Who Are You?" *FT* 73 (May 1997): 40–45.

———. "The Seed of the Church." *FT* 74 (June/July 1997): 53–55.

———. "Does Empire Pay?" *HS* 4, 4 (April 2003): 32–33.

"Back to Mystery?" *AB* 6, 3 (May 2000): 7.

Bains, David R. "Conduits of Faith: Reinhold Niebuhr's Liturgical Thought." *CH* 73 (2004): 168–94.

Baker, Keith Michael, and Peter Hanns Reill. *What's Left of Enlightenment? A Postmodern Question.* Stanford, Calif.: Stanford University Press, 2001.

Bambach, Charles. "German Philosophy and the Ethical Life." *MA* 48, 1 (Winter 2006): 85–89.

Bandmann, Gunter. *Early Medieval Architecture as Bearer of Meaning.* Translated by Kendall Wallis. New York: Columbia University Press, 2005.

Banús, Enrique. "¿Desde o Hacia el Multiculturalism? Un Concepto y su Plasmación en la Unión Europea y el Consejo de Europa." In *Razón Práctica y multiculturalismo.* Edited by Enrique Banús and Alejandro Llano, 258–77. Pamplona: Centro de Estudios Europeos, Universidad de Navarra, 1999.

———, ed. *Subsidiariedad: historia y aplicación.* Pamplona: Universidad de Navarra, Centro de Estudios Europeos, 2000.

Banville, John. "The Rescue of W. B. Yeats." *NYRB* 51, 3 (February 26, 2004): 12–14.

———. "The Missing Link." *NYRB* 51, 19 (December 2, 2004): 55–57.

———. "Executioner Songs." *NYRB* 54, 3 (March 1, 2007): 14–17.

Barber, Benjamin R.. *Jihad vs. McWorld.* New York: Ballantine Books, 1996.

Barber, Charles. *Figure and Likeness: On the Limits of Representation in Byzantine Iconoclasm.* Princeton, N.J.: Princeton University Press, 2002.

Barlow, Frank. *The English Church 1066–1154.* London: Longman, 1979.

Barnes, Julian. "Holy Hysteria." *NYRB* 50, 6 (April 10, 2003): 32–34.

———. "Flaubert, C'est Moi." *NYRB* 53, 9 (May 25, 2006): 12–15.

Barr, Stephen M. *Modern Physics and Ancient Faith.* Notre Dame, Ind.: University of Notre Dame Press, 2003.

———. "Retelling the Story of Science." *FT* 131 (March 2003): 16–25.

Barron, Caroline, and Jenny Stratford, eds. *The Church and Learning in Late Medieval Society: Studies in Honour of Professor R. B. Dobson.* Donington, England: Shaun Tyas/Paul Watkins, 2002.

Barron, Robert. "Evangelizing the American Culture." *SS* 3 (2002): 26–38.

Barth, Karl. *Dogmatics in Outline.* Translated by G. T. Thompson. New York: Harper and Brothers, 1959.

Barton, Anne. "The Romantic Survivor." *NYRB* 52, 20 (December 15, 2005): 24–26.

Barzun, Jacques. *Darwin, Marx, Wagner: Critique of a Heritage.* 2nd ed. Garden City, N.Y.: Doubleday, 1958.

———. *Classic, Romantic and Modern.* 2nd ed. Boston: Little, Brown, 1961.

Bauerschmidt, Frederick Christian. *Julian of Norwich and the Mystical Body Politic of Christ.* Notre Dame, Ind.: University of Notre Dame Press, 1999.

———. "Confessions of an Evangelical Catholic: Five Theses Related to Theological Anthropology." *Co* 31 (2004): 67–84.

Bauman, Zygmunt. *Globalization: The Human Consequences.* New York: Columbia University Press, 1998.

Baxter, Michael. "The Unsettling of Americanism: A Response to William Portier." *Co* 27 (2000): 161–70.

———. "Why Catholics Should be Wary of 'One Nation Under God.'" *HCW* (January–February 2005): 8–13. Earlier and more fully published as "God Is Not American: Or, Why Christians Should Not Pledge Allegiance to 'One Nation Under God.'" In *God Is Not . . . Religious, Nice, "One of Us," an American, a Capitalist,* edited by D. Brent Laytham, 55–75. Grand Rapids, Mich.: Eerdmans, 2004.

———. "Lectures." *EC,* Spring 2005.

Beabout, Gregory. "Personhood as Gift and Task: The Place of the Person in Catholic Social Thought." *CSSR* 9 (2004): 67–75.

Beales, Derek. *Prosperity and Plunder: European Catholic Monasteries in the Age of Revolution, 1650–1815.* New York: Cambridge University Press, 2003.

Bell Jr., Daniel. "The Insurrectional Reserve: Latin American Liberationists, Escha-tology, and the Catholic Moment." *Co* 27 (2000): 643–75.

———. "The Resumption of History in the New Century." In Daniel Bell, *The End of Ideology: On the Exhaustion of Political Ideas in the Fifties,* xi–xxviii. Cam-bridge, Mass.: Harvard University Press, 2000.

Bell, David A. *The Cult of the Nation in France: Inventing Nationalism, 1680–1800.* Cambridge, Mass.: Harvard University Press, 2001.

Bellah, Robert N. "On Being Catholic and American." In *Fire and Ice: Imagination and Intellect in the Catholic Tradition,* edited by Mary K. McCullough, 29–47. Scranton, Pa.: University of Scranton Press, 2003.

Bellamy, Richard. *Liberalism and Modern Society: A Historical Argument.* University Park: Pennsylvania State University Press, 1992.

Belting, Hans. *Likeness and Presence: A History of the Image Before the Era of Art.* Translated by Edmund Jephcott. Chicago: University of Chicago Press, 1994.

———. *Art History after Modernism.* Translated by Caroline Saltzwedel and Mitch Cohen. Chicago: University of Chicago Press, 2003.

Ben-Ghiat, Ruth. *Fascist Modernities: Italy, 1922–1945.* Berkeley: University of Cali-fornia Press, 2001.

Bendroth, Margaret. "Wheaton Jeremiad." *JHS* 3 (Summer/Fall 2003): 439–44.

Benedict XVI (Joseph Ratzinger). *The Feast of Faith: Approaches to a Theology of the Liturgy.* San Francisco: Ignatius Press, 1986.

———. *A New Song for the Lord: Faith in Christ and Liturgy Today.* Translated by Martha M. Matesich. New York: Crossroad, 1996.

———. *The Spirit of the Liturgy.* Translated by John Saward. San Francisco: Ignatius Press, 2000.

———. "Thoughts on the Place of Marian Doctrine and Piety in Faith and Theol-ogy as a Whole." *Co* 30 (2003): 147–60.

———. "Introduction to Christianity: *Yesterday, Today, and Tomorrow.*" *Co* 31 (2004): 481–95.

———. *Deus Caritas Est.* Vatican City, 2005.

———. *Christianity and the Crisis of Cultures,* with Marcello Pera. San Francisco: Ignatius Press, 2006.

———. *Values in a Time of Upheaval.* San Francisco: Ignatius Press, 2006.

———. *Europe Today and Tomorrow: Addressing the Fundamental Issues.* San Fran-cisco: Ignatius Press, 2007.

———. *Jesus of Nazareth.* New York: Doubleday, 2007.

———. "The Joy Born of Faith." *SA* 14 (2008): 28–30.

Benfey, Christopher. "American Jeremiad." *NYRB* 52, 14 (September 22, 2005): 65–67.

Bequette, John P. "Illumination, Incarnation, and Reintegration: Christian Human-ism in Bonaventure's *De Reductione Artium ad Theologiam.*" *FQI* 2, 1 (2003): 63–85.

Berger, Peter L., ed. *The Desecularization of the World: Resurgent Religion and World Politics.* Grand Rapids, Mich.: Eerdmans, 1999.

Bergmann, Sigurd. *Geist, der Natur befreit: Die trinitarische Kosmologie Gregors von Nazianz im Horizont einer ökologischen Theologie der Befreiung.* Mainz: Matthias-Grünewald-Verl, 1995.

Berkowitz, Peter. "The Styles of Modern Politics." *FT* 72 (April, 1997): 38–42.

Berlin, Isaiah. *The Magus of the North: J. G. Hamann and the Origins of Modern Irrationalism.* Edited by Henry Hardy. New York: Farrar, Straus and Giroux, 1994.

———. *The Roots of Romanticism.* Edited by Henry Hardy. Princeton, N.J.: Princeton University Press, 1999.

———. *Three Critics of the Enlightenment: Vico, Hamann, Herder.* Edited by Henry Hardy. Princeton, N.J.: Princeton University Press, 2000.

———. *Political Ideas in the Romantic Age: Their Rise and Influence on Modern Thought.* Edited by Henry Hardy, introduction by Joshua L. Cherniss. Princeton, N.J.: Princeton University Press, 2006.

Berman, Morris. *The Reenchantment of the World.* Ithaca, N.Y.: Cornell University Press, 1981.

Bernard, G. W. *The King's Reformation: Henry VIII and the Remaking of the English Church.* New Haven, Conn.: Yale University Press, 2005.

Bernstein, Richard J. *The New Constellation: The Ethical-Political Horizons of Modernity/Postmodernity.* Cambridge, Mass.: MIT Press, 1992.

Berrigan, Daniel, and Robert Coles. *The Geography of Faith: Underground Conversations on Religious, Political, and Social Change.* Woodstock, Vt.: Skylight Paths, 2001.

Berry, Wendell. "Life Is a Miracle." *Co* 27 (2000): 83–97.

———. *Life Is a Miracle: An Essay Against Modern Superstition.* Washington, D.C.: Counterpoint, 2000.

Bertelli, Sergio. *The King's Body: Sacred Rituals of Power in Medieval and Early Modern Europe.* Translated by R. Burr Litchfield. University Park: Pennsylvania State University Press, 2001.

Besançon, Alain. *The Forbidden Image: An Intellectual History of Iconoclasm.* Translated by Jane Marie Todd. Chicago: University of Chicago Press, 2000.

Bess, Philip. "The Old Urbanism." *FT* 141 (March 2004): 39–43.

———. "After Urbanism: The Strange Bedfellows of Neo-Traditional Architecture and Town Planning." *EC* (Fall 2006): 4.

———. *Till We have Built Jerusalem: Architecture, Urbanism, and the Sacred.* Wilmington, Del.: ISI Books, 2006.

Besslich, Barbara. *Wege in den 'Kulturkrieg': Zivilisationskritik in Deutschland 1890–1914.* Darmstadt: Wissenschaftliche Buchgesellschaft, 2000.

Best, Joel. *Flavor of the Month: Why Smart People Fall for Fads.* Berkeley: University of California Press, 2006.

Beum, Robert. "The Divinization of Democracy." *MA* 49, 2 (Spring 2007): 120–29.

Bianchi, S., et al., eds. *I manoscritti datati del Fondo Conventi Soppressi della Biblioteca Nazionale Centrale di Firenze.* Florence: SISMEL: Edizioni del Galluzzo, 2002.

Biddick, Kathleen. "Translating the Foreskin." In *Queering the Middle Ages,* edited by Glenn Burger and Steven F. Kruger. Minneapolis: University of Minnesota Press, 2001.

Biernoff, Suzannah. *Sight and Embodiment in the Middle Ages.* New York: Palgrave Macmillan, 2002.

Bilinkoff, Jodi. "Introduction," *Colonial Saints: Discovering the Holy in the Americas, 1500–1800.* Edited by Alan Greer and Jodi Bilinkoff. New York: Routledge, 2003.

Billington, James H. *Russia in Search of Itself.* Washington, D.C.: Woodrow Wilson Center Press, 2004.

Birely, Robert. *The Jesuits and the Thirty Years War: Kings, Courts, and Confessors.* Cambridge: Cambridge University Press, 2003.

Bissoondath, Neil. "I Am Canadian." *Saturday Night* (October 1994): 11–22.

———. *Selling Illusions: The Cult of Multiculturalism in Canada.* Toronto: Penguin Books, 1994.

Bivins, Jason C. *The Fracture of Good Order: Christian Antiliberalism and the Challenge to American Politics.* Chapel Hill: University of North Carolina Press, 2003.

Blamires, Harry. *The Christian Mind: How Should a Christian Think?* Ann Arbor, Mich.: Servant Books, 1978.

Blight, James G., and Janet M. Lang, eds. *The Fog of War: Lessons from the Life of Robert S. McNamara.* Lanham, Md.: Rowman & Littlefield, 2005.

Bloom, Harold. *The American Religion: The Emergence of the Post-Christian Nation.* New York: Simon & Schuster, 1992.

Blosser, Philip. "God among the Philosophers." *NOR* 66, 9 (October 1999): 39–42.

Blum, Christopher Olaf, ed. *Critics of the Enlightenment: Readings in the French Counter-Revolutionary Tradition.* Wilmington, Del.: ISI Books, 2004.

Bobbitt, Philip. *The Shield of Achilles: War, Peace and the Course of History.* New York: Knopf, 2002.

Bogle, Joanna. "Ufton Court: A Reminder of Catholic Heritage." *Voices* 22, 1 (2007): 21–22.

Bohm, David. *Causality and Chance in Modern Physics.* Philadelphia: University of Pennsylvania Press, 1957.

Bonaventure. *De Reductione Artium ad Theologiam.* Translated by Emma Therese Healy. St. Bonaventure, N.Y.: The Franciscan Institute, Saint Bonaventure University, 1955.

Bonomi, Patricia U. *Under the Cope of Heaven: Religion, Society, and Politics in Colonial America.* Revised edition. New York: Oxford University Press, 2003.

Boogaart II, Thomas A. "Our Saviour's Blood: Procession and Community in Late Medieval Bruges." In *Moving Subjects: Processional Performance in the Middle Ages and the Renaissance,* edited by Kathleen Ashley and Wim Hüsken, 69–116. Amsterdam: Rodopi, 2001.

Bork, Robert. "Stairways to Heaven: Gothic Architecture, Heavy Metal, and the Aesthetics of Transcendence." *Medieval Academy News* 157 (Spring 2007): 11.

Bottum, Joseph. "Death & Politics." *FT* 174 (June/July 2007): 17–29.

Boulnois, Olivier. "The Modernity of the Middle Ages." *Co* 30 (2003): 234–59.

———, ed. *Duns Scot à Paris, 1302–2002.* Turnhout: Brepols, 2005.

Boureau, Alain. *La Religion de l'État: La construction de la république étatique dans le discours théologique de l'occident médiéval (1250–1350).* Paris: Belles Lettres, 2006.

Bouyer, Louis. *The Spirit and Forms of Protestantism.* Westminster, Md.: Newman Press, 1956.

Bowers, C. A. *Let Them Eat Data: How Computers Affect Education, Cultural Diversity, and the Prospects of Ecological Sustainability.* Athens: University of Georgia Press, 2000.

Boyde, Patrick. *Dante: Philomythes and Philosopher: Man in the Cosmos.* Cambridge: Cambridge University Press, 1981.

Bradbury, Malcolm, and James McFarlane, eds. *Modernism: 1890–1930.* New York: Penguin, 1976.

Brague, Rémi. *The Wisdom of the World: The Human Experience of the Universe in*

Western Thought. Translated by Teresa Lavender Fagan. Chicago: University of Chicago Press, 2004.

Bram, Jeff. "Speaking in Bird Tongues." *Tempo* (Spring/Summer 2007): 3.

Brauneiss, Leopold. "Arvo Pärt's Tintinnabuli Style: Contemporary Music toward a New Middle Ages?" In *Postmodern Medievalisms,* edited by Richard J. Utz and Jesse G. Swan, 27–34. Rochester, N.Y.: D. S. Brewer, 2005.

Bray, Alan. *The Friend.* Chicago: University of Chicago Press, 2003.

Brenkman, John. "Freud the Modernist." In *The Mind of Modernism: Medicine, Psychology, and the Cultural Arts in Europe and America, 1880–1940,* edited by Mark S. Micale. Stanford, Calif.: Stanford University Press, 2004.

Brett, Annabel S. "Politics, Right(s) and Human Freedom in Marsilius of Padua." In *Transformations in Medieval and Early-Modern Rights Discourse,* edited by Virpi Mäkinen and Petter Korkman, 95–116. Dordrecht: Springer, 2006.

Brewer, John. "The British Empire and Globalization: A Forum." *HS* 4, 4 (April 2003): 21–39.

———. "Breaking with the Past." *NYRB* 51, 5 (March 25, 2004): 14–16.

———. "Big Ben." *NYRB* 51, 12 (July 15, 2004): 36–39.

———. "City Lights." *NYRB* 53, 8 (May 11, 2006): 18–21.

———. "Selling the American Way." *NYRB* 53, 19 (November 30, 2006): 58–61.

Brient, Elizabeth. *The Immanence of the Infinite: Hans Blumenberg and the Threshold to Modernity.* Washington, D.C.: The Catholic University of America Press, 2002.

Brockway, George P. *The End of Economic Man: An Introduction to Humanistic Economics.* 4th ed. New York: W. W. Norton, 2001.

Bromwich, David. "How Lincoln Won." *NYRB* 53, 16 (October 19, 2006): 46–49.

Brooke, John Hedley. *Science and Religion: Some Historical Perspectives.* New York: Cambridge University Press, 1991.

Brown, Peter. "Gibbon's Views on Culture and Society in the Fifth and Sixth Centuries." *Daedalus* (Spring 1976): 73–86.

———. *A Life of Learning.* ACLS Occasional Paper, No. 55. New York: American Council of Learned Societies, 2003.

Bruce, Steve. *Choice and Religion: A Critique of Rational Choice Theory.* Oxford: Oxford University Press, 1999.

Brugger, E. Christian. Review. *FCSQ* 27, 1 (Spring 2004): 26–27.

Bryan, Christopher. *Render to Caesar: Jesus, the Early Church, and the Roman Superpower.* Oxford: Oxford University Press, 2005.

Buber, Martin. *I and Thou.* Translated, with a prologue and notes, by Walter Kaufmann. New York: Scribner, 1970.

Buchan, James. *Crowded with Genius: The Scottish Enlightenment, Edinburgh's Moment of the Mind.* New York: HarperCollins, 2003.

Buckley, Michael. *At the Origins of Modern Atheism.* New Haven, Conn.: Yale University Press, 1987.

Budde, Michael L., and Robert W. Brimlow, eds. *The Church as Counterculture.* Albany: State University of New York Press, 2000.

Budziszewski, J. *The Revenge of Conscience: Politics and the Fall of Man.* Dallas: Spence, 1999.

———. "The Compassionate Amoralist." *FT* 114 (June/July 2001): 58–61.

Burckhardt, Titus. *Sacred Art in East and West: Its Principles and Methods.* London: Perennial Books, 1967.

Burgwinkle, William E. *Sodomy, Masculinity, and Law in Medieval Literature: France and England, 1050–1230.* Cambridge: Cambridge University Press, 2004.

Burleigh, Michael. *Earthly Powers: The Clash of Religion and Politics in Europe from the French Revolution to the Great War.* New York: HarperCollins, 2005.

———. *Sacred Causes: the Clash of Religion and Politics, from the Great War to the War on Terror.* New York: HarperCollins, 2007.

Burns, Timothy. "The Liberal Uses of Religion." *FT* 113 (May 2001): 25–31.

Burns, Tom. *The Use of Memory: Publishing and Further Pursuits.* London: Sheed & Ward, 1993.

Buruma, Ian. "Master of Fear." *NYRB* 51, 7 (May 13, 2004): 4–6.

———. "The Destruction of Germany." *NYRB* 51, 16 (October 21, 2004): 8–12.

———. "The Indiscreet Charm of Tyranny." *NYRB* 52, 8 (May 12, 2005): 35–37.

———. "Herzog and His Heroes." *NYRB* 54, 12 (July 19, 2007): 24–26.

———, and Avishai Margalit. "Occidentalism." *NYRB* 49, 1 (January 17, 2002): 4–7.

———. "Seeds of Revolution." *NYRB* 51, 4 (March 11, 2004): 10–13.

Butterfield, Andrew. "The Pious Revolutionary." *NYRB* 53, 1 (January 12, 2006): 10–13.

———. "The Genius of George Inness." *NYRB* 55, 14 (September 25, 2008): 8–10.

Buttiglione, Rocco. *Augusto Del Noce. Biografia di un pensiero.* Casale Monferrato: Piemme, 1991.

Bynum, Caroline Walker. *Holy Feast and Holy Fast: the Religious Significance of Food to Medieval Women.* Berkeley: University of California Press, 1987.

———. *Fragmentation and Redemption: Essays on Gender and the Human Body in Medieval Religion.* New York: Zone Books, 1990.

———. *The Resurrection of the Body in Western Christianity, 200–1336.* New York: Columbia University Press, 1995.

———. "The Presence of Objects: Medieval Anti-Judaism in Modern Germany." *Common Knowledge* 10 (2004): 1–32.

Caldecott, Stratford. "Creation as a Call to Holiness." *Co* 30 (2003): 161–67.

———. "Chesterton for Today: A Tribute to *The Chesterton Review*." *SS* 7 (2006): 69–72.

Calin, William. *The French Tradition and the Literature of Medieval England.* Toronto: University of Toronto Press, 1994.

Callahan, Daniel. "Visions of Eternity." *FT* 133 (May 2003): 28–35.

Callam, Daniel. "Jane Austen's Catholic Sensibility." *SS* 5 (2004): 22–29.

Canals Vidal, Francisco. "Por Qué Descristianiza el Liberalismo?" *Verbo* 439–40 (November–December 2005): 817–28.

Caputo, John D., Mark Dooley, and Michael J. Scanlon, eds. *Questioning God.* Bloomington: Indiana University Press, 2001.

Carey, Graham. "What Symbolism Is." *SS* 5 (2004): 39–48.

Carrasco Rouco, Alfonso. "History and Revelation: Critical Access to the Figure of Jesus Christ." *Co* 30 (2003): 130–46.

Carrese, Paul O. "The Ironies of American Power." *FT* 135 (September 2003): 39–42.

———. "The Single-Minded Constitution." *FT* 145 (August/September 2004): 59–63.

Carroll, Colleen. *The New Faithful: Why Young Adults are Embracing Christian Orthodoxy.* Chicago: Loyola Press, 2002.

Carroll, Michael P. *The Penitente Brotherhood: Patriarchy and Hispano-Catholicism in New Mexico.* Baltimore: Johns Hopkins University Press, 2002.

Carruthers, Mary. *The Book of Memory: A Study of Memory in Medieval Culture.* New York: Cambridge University Press, 1990.

———. *The Craft of Thought: Meditation, Rhetoric, and the Making of Images, 400–1200.* New York: Cambridge University Press, 1998.

Carter, Stephen L. *The Culture of Disbelief: How American Law and Politics Trivialize Religious Devotion.* New York: Basic Books, 1993.

———. *God's Name in Vain: The Wrongs and Rights of Religion in Politics.* New York: Basic Books, 2000.

Caryl, Christian. "Tyrants on the Take." *NYRB* 49, 6 (April 11, 2002): 27–30.

———. "Window on Russia." *NYRB* 50, 9 (May 29, 2003): 26–29.

———. "Why They Do It." *NYRB* 52, 14 (September 22, 2005): 28–32.

———. "Ice Capades." *NYRB* 54, 14 (September 27, 2007): 60–63.

Casarella, Peter J. "'Modern Forms Filled with Traditional Spiritual Content': On Louis Dupré's Contribution to Christian Theology." In *Christian Spirituality and the Culture of Modernity: The Thought of Louis Dupré,* edited by Peter J. Casarella and George P. Schner, 276–86. Grand Rapids, Mich.: Eerdmans, 1998.

———. "Solidarity as the Fruit of Communion." *Co* 27 (2000): 98–123.

———. "Waiting for a Cosmic Christ in an Uncreated World." *Co* 28 (2001): 230–64.

———. "Carmen Dei: Music and Creation in Three Theologians." *Theology Today* 62 (2006): 484–500.

Casey, M. A. "How to Think About Globalization." *FT* 126 (October 2002): 47–56.

———. "Democracy and the Thin Veneer of Civilisation." *FCSQ* 29, 4 (Winter 2006): 4–9.

Catechism of the Catholic Church. 2nd ed. San Francisco: Ignatius Press, 2003.

Cavanaugh, William T. "'A Fire Strong Enough to Consume the House': The Wars of Religion and the Rise of the State." *MT* 11 (1995): 397–420.

———. "The City: Beyond Secular Parodies." In *Radical Orthodoxy,* edited by John Milbank, Catherine Pickstock, and Graham Ward, 182–200. New York: Routledge, 1999.

———. "Balthasar, Globalization, and the Problem of the One and the Many." *Co* 28 (2001): 324–47.

———. *The Theopolitical Imagination: Christian Practices of Space and Time.* Edinburgh: T & T Clark, 2003.

———. *Being Consumed: Economics and Christian Desire.* Grand Rapids, Mich.: Eerdmans, 2008.

Chace, James. "TR and the Road Not Taken." *NYRB* 50, 12 (July 17, 2003): 35–38.

———. "The Winning Hand." *NYRB* 51, 4 (March 11, 2004): 17–20.

———. "Empire, Anyone?" *NYRB* 51, 15 (October 7, 2004): 15–18.

Chai, Leon. *Jonathan Edwards and the Limits of Enlightenment Philosophy.* New York: Oxford University Press, 1998.

Chandler, Jr., Alfred D. *The Visible Hand: The Managerial Revolution in American Business.* Cambridge, Mass.: Harvard University Press, 1977.

———, with Herman Daems. *Managerial Hierarchies: Comparative Perspectives on the Rise of the Modern Industrial Enterprise.* Cambridge, Mass.: Harvard University Press, 1980.

Chang, Jung, and Jon Halliday. *Mao: The Unknown Story.* New York: Knopf, 2005.

Chapuis, Julien. *Tilman Riemenschneider: Master Sculptor of the Late Middle Ages.* Washington, D.C.: National Gallery of Art, 1999.

Charles, J. Daryl. *Retrieving the Natural Law: A Return to Moral First Things.* Grand Rapids, Mich.: Eerdmans, 2008.

Chazelle, Celia. *The Crucified God in the Carolingian Era: Theology and Art of Christ's Passion.* New York: Cambridge University Press, 2001.

Chernow, Ron. *Alexander Hamilton.* New York: Penguin, 2004.

Chesterton, G. K. *Orthodoxy.* Garden City, N.Y.: Image Books, 1959.

Cholvy, Gérard, and Yves-Marie Hilaire, eds. *Histoire religieuse de la France contemporaine.* 3 vols. Toulouse: Privat, 1985–88.

Christian Jr., William A. "Priests, Mountains, and 'Sacred Space' in Early Modern Europe." *CHR* 93 (2007): 84–103.

Christofferson, Michael Scott. *French Intellectuals against the Left: The Antitotalitarian Moment of the 1970's.* New York: Berghahn Books, 2004.

Chua, Amy. *World on Fire: How Exporting Free Market Democracy Breeds Ethnic Hatred and Global Instability.* New York: Doubleday, 2003.

Ciardi, Fabio. *Koinonia: Spiritual and Theological Growth of the Religious Community.* Hyde Park, N.Y.: New City Press, 2000.

Cladis, Mark S. *Public Vision, Private Lives: Rousseau, Religion, and 21st-Century Democracy.* New York: Oxford University Press, 2003.

Clark, Christopher. *Iron Kingdom: The Rise and Downfall of Prussia, 1600–1947.* Cambridge, Mass.: Belknap Press, 2006.

———, and Wolfram Kaiser, eds., *Culture Wars: Secular-Catholic Conflict in Nineteenth-Century Europe.* New York: Cambridge University Press, 2003.

Clark, James G. *A Monastic Renaissance at St. Albans: Thomas Walsingham and His Circle c. 1350–1440.* New York: Clarendon Press, 2004.

———, ed. *The Religious Orders in Pre-Reformation England.* Rochester, N.Y.: Boydell & Brewer, 2002.

Clark, Michael D. *The American Discovery of Tradition, 1865–1942.* Baton Rouge: Louisiana State University Press, 2005.

Clark, T. J. *Farewell to an Idea: Episodes from a History of Modernism.* New Haven, Conn.: Yale University Press, 1999.

Clark, Victoria. *Why Angels Fall: A Journey Through Orthodox Europe from Byzantium to Kosovo.* New York: St. Martin's Press, 2000.

Clarke, W. Norris. "Freedom, Equality, Dignity of the Human Person: The Roots of Liberal Democracy." *CSSR* 9 (2004): 61–66.

———. "The Integration of Person and Being in Twentieth-Century Thomism." *Co* 31 (2004): 435–46.

Clayton, David. "The Way of Beauty." *SS* 4 (2003): 19–26.

Clement, Olivier. *The Roots of Christian Mysticism.* New York: New City Press, 1996.

Coakley, John W. *Women, Men, and Spiritual Power: Female Saints and Their Male Collaborators.* New York: Columbia University Press, 2006.

Coetzee, J. M. "The Genius of Robert Walser." *NYRB* 47, 17 (November 2, 2000): 13–16.

———. "Bellow's Gift." *NYRB* 51, 8 (May 27, 2004): 4–8.

———. "The Making of William Faulkner." *NYRB* 52, 6 (April 7, 2005): 20–30.

———. "Sleeping Beauty." *NYRB* 53, 3 (February 23, 2006): 4–8.

Cohen, Daniel. *Globalization and Its Enemies.* Cambridge, Mass.: MIT Press, 2006.

Cohen, Ed. "Legislating the Norm: From Sodomy to Gross Indecency." *South Atlantic Quarterly* 88, 1 (Winter 1989), 181–217.

Cohen, Eric. "Rival Immortalities." *FT* 149 (January 2005): 38–41.

Cohen, G. A. *If You're an Egalitarian, How Come You're So Rich?* Cambridge, Mass.: Harvard University Press, 2000.

Coleman, Janet. "Are There Any Individual Rights or Only Duties? On the Limits of Obedience in the Avoidance of Sin according to Late Medieval and Early-Modern Scholars." In *Transformations in Medieval and Early-Modern Rights Discourse,* edited by Virpi Mäkinen and Petter Korkman, 3–36. Dordrecht: Springer, 2006.

Comotti, Giovanni. *Music in Greek and Roman Culture.* Translated by Rosaria V. Munson. Baltimore: Johns Hopkins University Press, 1989.

Concilium Parisiense 829. In *Monumenta Germaniae Historica, Concilia,* 1, 2: *Concilia aevi Karolini.* 2 vols., 2nd ed., edited by Albert Werminghoff. Hannover: Hahn, 2003.

Condic, Maureen L. "The Science of Wishful Thinking." *FT* 145 (August/September 2004): 69–74.

Connolly, Thomas H. "The Tuning of Heaven: The Aesthetic of the Pórtico de la Gloria." In *El Códice Calixtino y la música de su tiempo,* edited by José López-Calo and Carlos Villanueva, 95–110. A Coruña: Fundación Pedro Barrié de la Maza, 2001.

Connor, Walter D. "The Burdens of History." *FT* 115 (August/September 2001): 59–61.

Constable, Giles. "Renewal and Reform in Religious Life: Concepts and Realities." In *Renaissance and Renewal in the Twelfth Century,* edited by Robert L. Benson and Giles Constable, 37–67. Cambridge, Mass.: Harvard University Press, 1982.

Conyers, A. J. *The Long Truce: How Toleration Made the World Safe for Power and Profit.* Dallas: Spence, 2001.

Cooper, Tim. *The Last Generation of English Catholic Clergy: Parish Priests in the Diocese of Coventry and Lichfield in the Early Sixteenth Century.* Rochester, N.Y.: Boydell & Brewer, 1999.

Coquery, N., F. Menant, and F. Weber, eds. *Écrire, compter, mesurer. Vers une histoire des rationalités pratiques.* Paris: Rue d'Ulm, 2006.

Cottington, David. *Cubism in the Shadow of War: The Avant-garde and Politics in Paris 1905–1914.* New Haven, Conn.: Yale University Press, 1998.

Courcelle, Pierre. *Connais-toi toi-même, de Socrate à Saint Bernard.* 3 vols. Paris: Institut d'études augustiniennes, 1974–75.

Craig, Gordon A. "Founding Father." *NYRB* 48, 117 (November 1, 2001): 17–21.

Crampton, Richard. "Myths of the Balkans." *NYRB* 48, 1 (January 11, 2001): 14–18.

Crawford, David S. "Christianity, a Culture of Love, and Kraynak's Critique." *CSSR* 9 (2004): 77–85.

Crimp, Douglas. *On the Museum's Ruins.* Cambridge, Mass.: MIT Press, 1993.

Crippa, Maria Antonietta. "A Cathedral for the Twentieth Century: Antoni Gaudí's Project for the Sagrada Familia." *Co* 29 (2002): 762–69.

Crosby, Alfred W. *The Measure of Reality: Quantification and Western Society, 1250–1600.* New York: Cambridge University Press, 1997.

Crunden, Robert M., ed. *The Superfluous Men: Conservative Critics of Modern Culture, 1900–1945.* Wilmington, Del.: ISI Books, 1999.

Cuppy, Will. *The Decline and Fall of Practically Everybody.* New York: Dorset Press, 1956.

Dagron, Gilbert. *Décrire et peindre: Essai sur le portrait iconique.* Paris: Gallimard, 2007.

Dallas, Gregor. *1945: The War That Never Ended.* New Haven, Conn.: Yale University Press, 2005.

Daniélou, Jean. *Essai sur le mystère de l'histoire.* Paris: Éditions du Seuil, 1953.

Dante. *The Inferno.* Translated by Anthony M. Esolen. New York: Modern Library, 2002.

Darnton, Robert. "Paris: The Early Internet." *NYRB* 47, 11 (June 29, 2000): 42–47.

———. "A Euro State of Mind." *NYRB* 49, 3 (February 28, 2002): 28–30.

———. *George Washington's False Teeth: An Unconventional Guide to the Eighteenth Century.* New York: W. W. Norton, 2003.

Daston, Lorraine, and Peter Galison. *Objectivity.* New York: Zone Books, 2007.

Davies, Maximos. "Celibacy in Context." *FT* 128 (December 2002): 13–15.

Davis, Arthur, ed. *George Grant and the Subversion of Modernity: Art, Philosophy, Religion, Politics and Education.* Toronto: University of Toronto Press, 1996.

Dawson, Christopher. "The Revolt of the East and the Catholic Tradition." *The Dublin Review* 183 (Winter 1928): 1–14.

———. *Medieval Religion and Other Essays.* London: Sheed & Ward, 1934.

———. "The Nature and Destiny of Man." In *God and the Supernatural: A Catholic Statement of the Christian Faith,* 57–84. London: Sheed & Ward, 1936.

———. *Religion and the Modern State.* New York: Sheed & Ward, 1936.

———. *Judgment of the Nations.* London: Sheed & Ward, 1943.

———. "Religion and Mass Civilization—The Problem of the Future." *The Dublin Review* 214 (January 1944): 1–8.

———. *Medieval Essays.* New York: Sheed & Ward, 1952.

———. *Progress and Religion.* Garden City, N.Y.: Doubleday, 1952.

———. *The Dynamics of World History,* edited by John J. Mulloy. New York: Sheed & Ward, 1956.

———. *Understanding Europe.* Garden City, N.Y.: Doubleday, 1960.

———. *The Dividing of Christendom.* New York: Sheed & Ward, 1965.

———. *The Gods of Revolution.* London: Sidgwick & Jackson, 1972.

———. *Religion and World History: A Selection from the Works of Christopher Dawson,* edited by James Oliver and Christina Scott. Garden City, N.Y.: Doubleday, 1975.

De Bellaigue, Christopher. "Turkey's Hidden Past." *NYRB* 48, 4 (March 8, 2001): 37–40.

De Botton, Alain. *The Architecture of Happiness.* New York: Pantheon Books, 2006.

De Grazia, Victoria. *Irresistible Empire: America's Advance through Twentieth-Century Europe.* Cambridge, Mass.: Belknap Press, 2005.

De Jong, Mayke. "The Empire as *Ecclesia*: Hrabanus Maurus and Biblical *Historia* for Rulers." In *The Uses of the Past in the Early Middle Ages,* edited by Yitzhak Hen and Matthew Innes, 191–226. Cambridge: Cambridge University Press, 2000.

De Lubac, Henri. *The Drama of Atheist Humanism.* Translated by Edith M. Riley. New York: Sheed & Ward, 1950.

———. *The Mystery of the Supernatural.* Translated by Rosemary Sheed. New York: Herder and Herder, 1967.

De Vries, Hent. *Philosophy and the Turn to Religion.* Baltimore: Johns Hopkins University Press, 1999.

———. *Minimal Theologies: Critiques of Secular Reason in Adorno and Levinas.* Translated by Geoffrey Hale. Baltimore: Johns Hopkins University Press, 2005.

Deane-Drummond, C., B. Szerszynski, and R. Grove-White, eds. *Re-Ordering Nature: Theology, Society and the New Genetics.* New York: T & T Clark, 2003.

Deavel, David Paul. "Francis De Sales: A Patron Saint of Our Age." *SS* 7 (2006): 9–18.

Delasanta, Rodney. "Hume, Austen, and First Impressions." *FT* 134 (June/July 2003): 24–29.

Delbanco, Andrew. "Colleges: An Endangered Species." *NYRB* 52, 4 (March 10, 2005): 18–20.

———. *Melville: His World and Work.* New York: Knopf, 2005.

Dellapenna, Joseph W. *Dispelling the Myths of Abortion History.* Durham, N.C.: Carolina Academic Press, 2005.

D'Emilio, John, and Estelle B. Freedman. *Intimate Matters: A History of Sexuality in America.* New York: Harper & Row, 1988.

DeMott, Benjamin. "It's a Wonderful Life." *NYRB* 46, 15 (October 7, 1999): 16–18.

Derrida, Jacques, and Gianni Vattimo, eds. *Religion.* Stanford, Calif.: Stanford University Press, 1998.

DeSanctis, Michael E. *Building from Belief: Advance, Retreat, and Compromise in the Remaking of Catholic Church Architecture.* Collegeville, Minn.: Liturgical Press, 2002.

Dewan, Lawrence. "On Milbank and Pickstock's *Truth in Aquinas.*" *Nova et Vetera,* English edition 1, 1 (2003): 199–212.

Diggins, John Patrick. *Ronald Reagan: Fate, Freedom, and the Making of History.* New York: W. W. Norton, 2007.

Dijksterhuis, E. J. *The Mechanization of the World Picture.* Oxford: Clarendon Press, 1961.

Dimock, Giles. "Revisiting the Baroque." *Antiphon* 5, 3 (2000): 8–10.

Dirda, Michael. "Dante: The Supreme Realist." *NYRB* 54, 1 (January 11, 2007): 54–58.

"The Disturbing Light of Reality: Sin and Redemption in the Writing of Graham Greene and Evelyn Waugh." *EC* (Spring, 2005), 3–5 (anon.)

Ditchfield, Simon. "Martyrs Are Good to Think With: Review Essay." *CHR* 88 (2001): 470–73.

Dively Lauro, Elizabeth Ann. *The Soul and Spirit of Scripture within Origen's Exegesis.* The Bible in Ancient Christianity, vol. 3, edited by D. Jeffrey Bingham. Boston: Brill, 2005.

Dodaro, Robert. *Christ and the Just Society in the Thought of Augustine.* Cambridge: Cambridge University Press, 2004.

Dolan, Timothy M. "The Bishops in Council." *FT* 152 (April 2005): 20–25.

Donati, Pierpaolo. "El desafío universalismo en una sociedad multicultural postmoderna: un planteamiento relacional." In *Razón práctica y multiculturalismo,* edited by Enrique Banús and Alejandro Llano, 1–34. Pamplona: Centro de Estudios Europeos, Universidad de Navarra, 1999.

Donohue, Kathleen G. *Freedom from Want: American Liberalism and the Idea of the Consumer.* Baltimore: Johns Hopkins University Press, 2003.

Doorly, Moyra. *No Place for God: The Denial of the Transcendent in Modern Church Architecture.* San Francisco: Ignatius Press, 2007.

Dorment, Richard. "The Artistic Bloke." *NYRB* 51, 17 (November 4, 2004): 22–25.

——. "Journey from 'Nebraska.'" *NYRB* 53, 20 (December 21, 2006): 8–14.

Douthat, Ross. "Lost and Saved on Television." *FT* 173 (May 2007): 22–26.

Driscoll, Jeremy. "Rethinking Ritual." *FT* 73 (May 1997): 52–53.

Drury, Marjule Anne. "Anti-Catholicism in Germany, Britain, and the United States: A Review and Critique of Recent Scholarship." *CH* 70 (2001): 98–131.

Dubay, Thomas. *The Evidential Power of Beauty: Science and Theology Meet.* San Francisco: Ignatius Press, 1999.

Duerr, Peter. *Nudité et pudeur: Le mythe du processus de civilisation.* Préface by André Burguiéere, translated from the original German by Véronique Bodin. Paris: Maison des sciences de l'homme, 1998.

Duffy, Eamon. "The Stripping of the Altars and the Modern Liturgy." *Antiphon* 2, 3 (Winter 1997): 3–12.

——. *The Voices of Morebath: Reformation and Rebellion in an English Village.* New Haven, Conn.: Yale University Press, 2001.

——. *The Stripping of the Altars: Traditional Religion in England, 1400–1580.* 2nd ed. New Haven, Conn.: Yale University Press, 2005.

——. "The Holy Terror." *NYRB* 53, 16 (October 19, 2006): 41–45.

Dulles, Avery Cardinal. "Postmodernist Ecumenism." *FT* 136 (October 2003): 57–61.

——. "The Deist Minimum." *FT* 149 (January 2005): 15–30.

——. "*Dignitatis Humanae* and the Development of Catholic Doctrine." In *Catholicism and Religious Freedom: Contemporary Reflections on Vatican II's Declaration on Religious Freedom,* edited by Kenneth L. Grasso and Robert P. Hunt, 43–67. Lanham, Md.: Rowman & Littlefield, 2006.

Dupré, Louis. *Passage to Modernity: an Essay in the Hermeneutics of Nature and Culture.* New Haven, Conn.: Yale University Press, 1993.

——. *Symbols of the Sacred.* Grand Rapids, Mich.: Eerdmans, 2000.

——. *The Enlightenment and the Intellectual Foundations of Modern Culture.* New Haven, Conn.: Yale University Press, 2004.

——. *Religion and the Rise of Modern Culture.* Notre Dame, Ind.: University of Notre Dame Press, 2008.

Dwyer, James. *Religious Schools vs. Children's Rights.* Ithaca, N.Y.: Cornell University Press, 1998.

Dyson, Freeman. "The Tragic Tale of a Genius." *NYRB* 52, 12 (July 14, 2005): 10–13.

——. "The Dream of Scientific Brotherhood." *NYRB* 54, 8 (May 10, 2007): 47–52.

Earman, John. *Hume's Abject Failure: the Argument Against Miracles.* Oxford: Oxford University Press, 2000.

Eatwell, Roger. *Fascism: A History.* New York: Allen Lane, 1996.

Eck, Diana L. *A New Religious America: How a "Christian Country" Has Now Become the World's Most Religiously Diverse Nation.* San Francisco: HarperSanFrancisco, 2002.

Edmonson III, Henry T. *John Dewey and the Decline of American Education.* Wilmington, Del.: ISI Books, 2006.

Edson, E., and E. Savage-Smith. *Medieval Views of the Cosmos.* Oxford: Bodleian Library, University of Oxford, 2004.

Elders, L. J. "St. Thomas Aquinas and the Liturgy." *FCSQ* 29, 4 (Winter 2006): 9–13.

Eliade, Mircea. *The Sacred and the Profane.* Translated by Willard R. Trask. New York: Harcourt, Brace, 1959.

Eliot, T. S. *The Sacred Wood and Major Early Essays.* Mineola, N.Y.: Dover Publications, 1998.

Elliott, J. H. "Barbarians at the Gates." *NYRB* 53, 3 (February 23, 2006): 36–38.

Elliott, Peter J. *Ceremonies of the Liturgical Year.* San Francisco: Ignatius Press, 2000.

Elon, Amos. "A Shrine to Mussolini." *NYRB* 53, 3 (February 23, 2006): 33–35.

———. "The Triumph of a Double Life." *NYRB* 53, 16 (October 19, 2006): 26–29.

Emerson, Ralph Waldo. *The Letters of Ralph Waldo Emerson,* edited by Ralph Rusk and Eleanor M. Tilton, 10 vols. New York: Columbia University Press, 1939–96.

———. *The Journals and Miscellaneous Notebooks of Ralph Waldo Emerson,* edited by William H. Gilman et al., 16 vols. Cambridge, Mass.: Harvard University Press, 1960–82.

Emerson, Roger L. "How Not to Deal with Enlightenments." *HS* 3, 3 (February 2002): 5–6.

Emison, Patricia A. *Creating the "Divine" Artist: From Dante to Michelangelo.* Leiden: Brill, 2004.

Engberg-Pedersen, Troels. *Paul and the Stoics.* Louisville, Ky.: Westminster John Knox Press, 2000.

Engelhardt, H. Tristram, Jr. "Life & Death After Christendom: The Moralization of Religion & the Culture of Death." *Touchstone* 14, 5 (June 2001): 18–26.

Engerman, David C. *Modernization from the Other Shore: American Intellectuals and the Romance of Russian Development.* Cambridge, Mass.: Harvard University Press, 2003.

Enright, Michael. "The Second Most Important Question." *SA* 8 (2003): 25–27.

Epstein, William H. *Psychotherapy as Religion: The Civil Divine in America.* Reno: University of Nevada Press, 2006.

Erkens, Franz-Reiner, ed. *Das Frühmittelalterliche Königtum. Ideelle und religiöse Grundlagen.* Berlin: De Gruyter, 2005.

Esposito, John L., and Azzam Tamimi, eds. *Islam and Secularism in the Middle East.* New York: New York University Press, 2000.

Evans, R. J. W. "Mighty Prussia: Rise and Fall." *NYRB* 54, 14 (September 27, 2007): 64–67.

Evdokimov, Paul. *The Art of the Icon: A Theology of Beauty.* Translated by Steven Bigham. Redondo Beach, Calif.: Oakwood Publications, 1990.

Fabro, Cornelio. *God in Exile: Modern Atheism from Its Roots in the Cartesian "Cogito" to the Present Day.* Translated by Arthur Gibson. Westminster, Md.: Newman Press, 1968.

Fagerberg, David W. *Theologia Prima: What is Liturgical Theology?* Chicago: HillenbrandBooks, 2004.

———. "The Spiritual Animal: Sacramental Nature of Church Art and Architecture." *SA* 13 (2007): 19–23.

Fantel, Hans. "The Land of the Waltz." In *Fodor's 93 Austria.* New York: Fodor's Travel Publications, 1992.

Farrow, Douglas. "Three Meanings of Secular." *FT* 133 (May 2003): 20–23.

Fasolt, Constantin. *The Limits of History.* Chicago: University of Chicago Press, 2004.

Faulconer, James E. *Transcendence in Philosophy and Religion.* Bloomington: Indiana University Press, 2003.

Fenton, James. "In Samuel Palmer's Garden." *NYRB* 53, 8 (May 11, 2006): 34–36.

———. *School of Genius: A History of the Royal Academy of Arts.* London: Royal Academy of the Arts, 2006.

Fernández-Armesto, Felipe. *Civilizations: Culture, Ambition, and the Transformation of Nature.* New York: Free Press, 2001.

Feyerabend, Paul. *Conquest of Abundance: A Tale of Abstraction versus the Richness of Being.* Edited by Bert Terpstra. Chicago: University of Chicago Press, 1999.

Fieser, James, ed. *Early Responses to Hume's Writings on Religion.* 2 vols. Bristol: Thoemmes Press, 2001.

Figes, Orlando. "In Search of Russia." *NYRB* 50, 16 (October 23, 2003): 37–39.

———. "Murder, Russian Style." *NYRB* 51, 6 (April 8, 2004): 52–55.

———. "What a Disaster!" *NYRB* 51, 19 (December 2, 2004): 41–43.

———. "Islam: The Russian Solution." *NYRB* 53, 20 (December 21, 2006): 74–77.

Figura, Michael. "The Eucharist as Sacramental Incarnation." *Co* 30 (2003): 39–56.

Filali-Ansari, Abdou. "Muslims and Democracy." In *Islam and Democracy in the Middle East,* edited by Larry Diamond, Marc F. Plattner, and Daniel Brumberg, 193–207. Baltimore: Johns Hopkins University Press, 2003.

Filler, Martin. "The Getty: For Better and Worse." *NYRB* 53, 18 (November 16, 2006): 47–54.

———. *Makers of Modern Architecture.* New York: New York Review Books, 2007.

Finkielkraut, Alain. *In the Name of Humanity: Reflections on the Twentieth Century.* Translated by Judith Friedlander. New York: Columbia University Press, 2000.

Finocchiaro, Maurice A. *Retrying Galileo, 1633–1992.* Berkeley: University of California Press, 2005.

———. "The Church and Galileo." *CHR* 94 (2008): 260–83.

Fischer, David Hackett. *Liberty and Freedom.* Oxford: Oxford University Press, 2005.

Fisher, Alexander J. *Music and Religious Identity in Counter-Reformation Augsburg, 1580–1630.* Burlington, Vt.: Ashgate, 2004.

Fisher, Anthony. "Bioethics and the Culture of the Family." *SS* 4 (2003): 12–17.

Flam, Jack. "Space Men." *NYRB* 48, 7 (April 26, 2001): 10–14.

———. "Twin Peaks." *NYRB* 50, 5 (March 27, 2003): 26–28.

Flam, Jack, with Miriam Deutch, eds. *Primitivism and Twentieth-Century Art: A Documentary History.* Berkeley: University of California Press, 2003.

Flanagan, Kiernan. *The Enchantment of Sociology: A Study of Theology and Culture.* London: Macmillan, 1996.

Flynn, William T. *Medieval Music as Medieval Exegesis.* Lanham, Md.: Scarecrow Press, 1999.

Fogu, Claudio. *The Historic Imaginary: Politics of History in Fascist Italy.* Toronto: University of Toronto Press, 2003.

Foster, Carolyn. "Pageantry Over Piety." *AB* 10, 8 (November 2004): 4–5.

Foster, Hal. *Prosthetic Gods.* Cambridge, Mass.: MIT Press, 2004.

Foucault, Michel. *The History of Sexuality: An Introduction.* Vol. 1, translated by Robert Hurley. New York: Vintage Books, 1978.

———. *Discipline and Punish.* Translated by Alan Sheridan. New York: Vintage Books, 1979.

———. "Omnes et Singulatim: Towards a Critique of Political Reason." In *Tanner*

Lectures on Human Values, ed. Sterling McMurrin, 224–54. Salt Lake City: University of Utah Press, 1981.

Fox-Genovese, Elizabeth. "Feminism and the Unraveling of the Social Bond." *Voices* 19, 3 (2004): 9–14.

Frank, Isnard Wilhelm. *A Concise History of the Medieval Church.* Translated by John Bowden. New York: Continuum, 1995.

Frank, William A. "Western Irreligion and Resources for Culture in Catholic Religion." *Lo* 7, 1 (Winter 2004): 17–44.

Frascina, Francis, et al., eds. *Modernity and Modernism: French Painting in the Nineteenth Century.* New Haven, Conn.: Yale University Press, 1993.

Fredrickson, George M. "They'll Take Their Stand." *NYRB* 53, 9 (May 25, 2006): 34–36.

"Free Trade and Modern History: A Forum." *HS* 5, 3 (January 2004): 17–30.

Freedberg, David. *Iconoclasts and their Motives.* The Hague: Schwartz, 1985.

———. *The Power of Images: Studies in the History and Theory of Response.* Chicago: University of Chicago Press, 1989.

Fritzsche, Peter. *Stranded in the Present: Modern Time and the Melancholy of History.* Cambridge, Mass.: Harvard University Press, 2004.

Frobock, Fred M. *Public Reason: Mediated Authority in the Liberal State.* Ithaca, N.Y.: Cornell University Press, 1999.

Fructuosus of Braga. *Regula Monastica Communis,* translated by Claude W. Barlow. *Iberian Fathers,* vol. 2: *Braulio of Saragossa and Fructuosus of Braga.* The Fathers of the Church, 63. Washington, D.C.: The Catholic University of America Press, 1969.

Fukuyama, Francis. *The End of History and the Last Man.* New York: Free Press, 1992.

Fumaroli, Marc. *L'État culturel: Une religion moderne.* Paris: Editions de Fallois, Libraire générale française, 1991.

Funkenstein, Amos. "Maimonides: Political Theory and Realistic Messianism." *Miscellanea Mediaevalia* 9 (1977): 81–103.

Furbank, P. S. "Body and Soul." *NYRB* 51, 7 (April 29, 2004): 49–51.

———. "The Scientific Takeover." *NYRB* 52, 9 (May 26, 2005): 39–40.

Furet, François. "Vendée." In *A Critical Dictionary of the French Revolution,* edited by François Furet and Mona Ozouf, 169. Cambridge, Mass.: Harvard University Press, 1989.

———. *The Passing of an Illusion: The Idea of Communism in the Twentieth Century.* Translated by Deborah Furet. Chicago: University of Chicago Press, 1999.

——— and Ernst Nolte. *Fascism and Communism.* Translated by Katherine Golsan. Lincoln: University of Nebraska Press, 2001.

Füssel, Stephan Thompson. *Gutenberg und seine Wirkung.* 2nd ed. Darmstadt: Wissenschaftliche Buchgesellschaft, 2004.

Gaca, Kathy L. *The Making of Fornication: Eros, Ethics, and Political Reform in Greek Philosophy and Early Christianity.* Berkeley: University of California Press, 2003.

Gadamer, Hans-Georg. "The Problem of Historical Consciousness." In *Interpretive Social Science: A Second Look,* edited by Paul Rabinow and William M. Sullivan. Berkeley: University of California Press, 1987.

Galadza, Peter. "Liturgy and Heaven in the Eastern Rites." *Antiphon* 10 (2006), 239–61.

Galison, Peter. *Einstein's Clocks and Poincaré's Maps: Empires of Time.* New York: W. W. Norton, 2003.

Gallagher, David M. "Rawls, Liberalism, and the Unity of Reason." In *Is a Culture of Life Still Possible in the U.S.?* edited by Anthony Mastroeni, 39–49. South Bend, Ind.: St. Augustine's Press, 1999.

Gamble, Richard M. *The War for Righteousness: Progressive Christianity, the Great War, and the Rise of the Messianic Nation.* Wilmington, Del.: ISI Books, 2003.

Ganim, John M. "Medievalism, Modernism, and Postmodernism in Contemporary Architecture." In *Postmodern Medievalisms,* edited by Richard J. Utz and Jesse G. Swan, 35–46. Rochester, N.Y.: D. S. Brewer, 2005.

García Avilés, Alejandro. *El Tiempo y los Astros: Arte, Ciencia y Religión en la Alta Edad Media.* Murcia: Universidad de Murcia, Servicio de publicaciones, 2001.

Garnett, George. *Marsilius of Padua and the Truth of History.* Oxford: Oxford University Press, 2006.

Garry, Patrick M. *Wrestling with God: The Courts' Tortuous Treatment of Religion.* Washington, D.C.: The Catholic University of America Press, 2006.

Garton Ash, Timothy. "Kosovo: Was It Worth IT?" *NYRB* 47, 14 (September 21, 2000): 50–60.

———. "Odd Man Out." *NYRB* 48, 17 (November 1, 2001): 49–51.

———. "Islam in Europe," *NYRB* 53, 15 (October 5, 2006): 32–35.

———. "The Stasi on Our Minds." *NYRB* 54, 9 (May 31, 2007): 4–8.

Gay, Craig M. *The Way of the (Modern) World: Or, Why It's Tempting to Live As If God Doesn't Exist.* Grand Rapids, Mich.: Eerdmans, 1998.

Gay, Peter. *Modernism: The Lure of Heresy: From Baudelaire to Beckett and Beyond.* New York: W. W. Norton, 2008.

Geary, Patrick J. *Phantoms of Remembrance: Memory and Oblivion at the End of the First Millennium.* Princeton, N.J.: Princeton University Press, 1994.

———. "Land, Language, and Memory in Europe, 700–1000." *Transactions of the Royal Historical Society,* 6th ser., 9 (1999): 169–84.

———. *The Myth of Nations: The Medieval Origins of Europe.* Princeton, N.J.: Princeton University Press, 2002.

Geertz, Clifford. "The Last Humanist." *NYRB* (November 26, 2002): 6–10.

———. "Which Way to Mecca? Part II." *NYRB* 50, 11 (July 3, 2003): 30–39.

Genet, Jean-Philippe. *La genèse de l'état moderne. Culture et société politique en Angleterre.* Paris: Presses universitaires de France, 2003.

Gentile, Emilio. *The Sacralization of Politics in Fascist Italy.* Translated by Keith Botsford. Cambridge, Mass.: Harvard University Press, 1996.

———. "The Sacralisation of Politics." *Totalitarian Movements and Political Religions* (electronic resource) 1, 1 (Summer 2000).

———. *Politics as Religion.* Translated by George Staunton. Princeton, N.J.: Princeton University Press, 2006.

George, Francis Cardinal. "The Anthropological Foundations of John Paul II's Social Thought." *CSSR* 5 (2000): 11–15.

Gerhardt, Volker. *Immanuel Kants Entwurf 'Zum ewigen Frieden'. Eine Theorie der Politik.* Darmstadt: Wissenschaftliche Buchgesellschaft, 1995.

Gersh, Stephen. "Plotinus on Harmonia. Musical Metaphors and their Uses in the Enneads." In *Agonistes: Essays in Honour of Denis O'Brien,* edited by John Dillon and Monique Dixsaut, 181–92. Burlington, Vt.: Ashgate, 2005.

Geuss, Raymond. *Public Goods, Private Goods.* Princeton, N.J.: Princeton University Press, 2001.

Giddens, Anthony. *Consequences of Modernity.* Stanford, Calif.: Stanford University Press, 1990.

Gillespie, Michael Allen. *Nihilism Before Nietzsche.* Chicago: University of Chicago Press, 1995.

Gilson, Étienne. *Painting and Reality.* New York: Pantheon Books, 1957.

———. "Introduction," *Saint Augustine: The City of God.* Garden City, N.Y.: Doubleday, 1958.

———. *The Arts of the Beautiful.* New York: Scribner, 1965.

———. *Forms and Substances in the Arts.* New York: Scribner, 1966.

Giralt, Gabriel F. "Andrei Tarkovsky's Adaptation of Motifs Embedded in Leonardo Da Vinci's *The Adoration of the Magi.*" *Canadian Journal of Film Studies* 14, 2 (Autumn 2005): 71–83.

Glendon, Mary Ann. "Principled Immigration." *FT* 164 (June/July 2006): 23–26.

Glenn, Gary. "Words That Sound Alike but Have Different Meanings: Christian 'Natural Rights' and Kantian Inspired 'Human Rights.'" *CSSR* 9 (2004): 21–28.

Glenny, Misha. *The Balkans: Nationalism, War and the Great Powers.* New York: Viking, 2000.

"God and the Enlightenment." *AHR* 108 (2003): 1057–1104.

Goering, Joseph. "The Thirteenth-Century English Parish." In *Educating People of Faith: Exploring the History of Jewish and Christian Communities,* edited by John Van Engen, 208–22. Grand Rapids, Mich.: Eerdmans, 2004.

Goethe, Johann Wolfgang. *Faust.* Translated by David Luke. Oxford: Oxford University Press, 1987.

Goldhagen, Sarah Williams. *Louis Kahn's Situated Modernism.* New Haven, Conn.: Yale University Press, 2001.

——— and Rejean Legault, eds. *Anxious Modernisms: Experimentation in Postwar Architectural Culture.* Cambridge, Mass.: MIT Press, 2000.

Golding, John. *Paths to the Absolute: Mondrian, Malevich, Kandinsky, Pollock, Newman, Rothko, and Still.* Princeton, N.J.: Princeton University Press, 2000.

Gombrich, E. H. *The Preference for the Primitive: Episodes in the History of Western Taste and Art.* London: Phaidon, 2002.

Gonzalez Calleja, Eduardo. *La España de Primo de Rivera. La modernización autoritaria: 1923–1930.* Madrid: Alianza Editorial, 2005.

Goodchild, Philip, ed. *Rethinking Philosophy of Religion: Approaches from Continental Philosophy.* New York: Fordham University Press, 2003.

Gorski, Philip S. *The Disciplinary Revolution: Calvinism and the Rise of the State in Early Modern Europe.* Chicago: University of Chicago Press, 2003.

Gotcher, Robert F. "New Ecclesial Movements and Communities: a Pastoral and Theological Challenge to the Local Church." *FQI* 2 (2002): 55–90.

Gottfried, Paul. *After Liberalism: Mass Democracy in the Managerial State.* Princeton, N.J.: Princeton University Press, 1999.

Gow, A. "Challenging the Protestant Paradigm: Bible Reading in Lay and Urban Contexts of the Later Middle Ages." In *Scripture and Pluralism. Reading the Bible in the Religiously Plural Worlds of the Middle Ages and Renaissance,* edited by T. J. Heffernan and T. E. Burman. Boston: Brill, 2005.

Grabill, Stephen J. *Rediscovering the Natural Law in Reformed Theological Ethics.* Grand Rapids, Mich.: Eerdmans, 2006.

Grafton, Anthony. "Over the Rainbow." *NYRB* 47, 19 (November 30, 2000): 4–6.

———. *Bring Out Your Dead: The Past as Revelation.* Cambridge, Mass.: Harvard University Press, 2001.

———. "The Ways of Genius." *NYRB* 51, 19 (December 2, 2004): 38–40.

———. "Stoppard's Romance." *NYRB* 54, 9 (May 31, 2007): 30–33.

Granados, José. "Love and the Organism: A Theological Contribution to the Study of Life." In *Love Alone is Credible: Hans Urs von Balthasar as Interpreter of the Catholic Tradition,* vol. 1, edited by David L. Schindler, 14–75. Grand Rapids, Mich.: Eerdmans, 2008.

Grant, Lindy. *Abbot Suger of St. Denis: Church and State in Early Twelfth-Century France.* New York: Longman, 1998.

Grasso, Kenneth L. "Democracy, Modernity and the Catholic Human Rights Revolution: Reflections on Christian Faith and Modern Democracy." *CSSR* 9 (2004): 37–45.

——— and Cecilia Rodriguez Castillo, eds. "Robert P. Kraynak's Christian Faith and Modern Democracy: A Symposium." *CSSR* 9 (2004): 13–95.

Gray, John. *Enlightenment's Wake: Politics and Culture at the Close of the Modern Age.* New York: Routledge, 1995.

———. *Isaiah Berlin.* Princeton, N.J.: Princeton University Press, 1996.

———. *False Dawn: The Delusions of Global Capitalism.* New York: New Press, 1998.

———. *Two Faces of Liberalism.* New York: New Press, 2000.

———. *Al Qaeda and What it Means to be Modern.* New York: New Press, 2003.

———. "The World Is Round." *NYRB* 52, 13 (August 11, 2005): 13–15.

———. "The Mirage of Empire." *NYRB* 53, 1 (January 12, 2006): 4–8.

———. "The Global Delusion." *NYRB* 53, 7 (April 27, 2006): 20–23.

———. "The Moving Target." *NYRB* 53, 15 (October 5, 2006): 22–24.

Greenblatt, Stephen. "Me, Myself, and I." *NYRB* 51, 6 (April 8, 2004): 32–36.

———. "Who Killed Christopher Marlowe?" *NYRB* 53, 7 (April 6, 2006): 42–46.

———. "Shakespeare and the Uses of Power." *NYRB* 54, 6 (April 12, 2007): 75–82.

Greenfeld, Liah. *The Spirit of Capitalism: Nationalism and Economic Growth.* Cambridge, Mass.: Harvard University Press, 2001.

———. "Speaking Historically about Globalization and Related Fantasies." *HS,* 5, 3 (January 2004): 23–28.

Gregor, A. James. *Mussolini's Intellectuals: Fascist Social and Political Thought.* Princeton, N.J.: Princeton University Press, 2005.

Gregory the Great. *Homiliae in Evangelia,* edited by Raymond Etaix. *Corpus Christianorum, Series Latina* 141. Turnhout: Brepols, 1999.

Gregory, Brad. *Salvation at Stake: Christian Martyrdom in Early Modern Europe.* Cambridge, Mass.: Harvard University Press, 1999.

Grew, Raymond. "Liberty and the Catholic Church in 19th Century Europe." In *Freedom and Religion in the Nineteenth Century,* edited Richard Helmstadter. Stanford, Calif.: Stanford University Press, 1997.

Griep, Hans-Joachim. *Geschichte des Lesens: Von den Anfängen bis Gutenberg.* Darmstadt: Wissenschaftliche Buchgesellschaft, 2005.

Grier, James. *The Musical World of a Medieval Monk: Adémar of Chabannes in Eleventh-century Aquitaine.* New York: Cambridge University Press, 2006.

Griffin, Jasper. "The Comedy Murder Case." *NYRB* 49, 12 (July 18, 2002): 35–38.

Griffin, Mark, and Theron Walker. *Living on the Borders: What the Church Can Learn from Ethnic Immigrant Cultures.* Grand Rapids, Mich.: Eerdmans, 2004.

Griffiths, Paul. *A Concise History of Western Music.* New York: Cambridge University, Press, 2006.

Griffiths, Paul J. "What Can We Reasonably Hope For?" *FT* 99 (January 2000): 24–25.

———. "Proselytizing for Tolerance, Part I." *FT* 127 (November 2002): 30–34.

———. "Christ and Critical Theory." *FT* 145 (August/September 2004): 46–55.

Grosby, Steven. "The Biblical 'Nation' as a Problem for Philosophy." *HPS* 1, 1 (Fall 2005): 7–23.

Gross, Guillaume. "Chanter en polyphonie à Notre-Dame de Paris sous le règne de Philippe Auguste: un art de la magnificence." *Revue Historique* 308 (2006): 609–34.

Gross, John. "The Genius of Ambiguity." *NYRB* 53, 5 (March 23, 2006): 28–31.

Gross, Michael B. *The War against Catholicism: Liberalism and the Anti-Catholic Imagination in Nineteenth-Century Germany.* Ann Arbor: University of Michigan Press, 2004.

Guardini, Romano. *The End of the Modern World.* Introduction by Frederick D. Wilhelmsen, foreword by Richard J. Neuhaus. Wilmington, Del.: ISI Books, 1998.

———. *The Spirit of the Liturgy.* Translated by Ada Lane. New York: Crossroad, 1998.

Guénon, René. *The Crisis of the Modern World.* Translated by Arthur Osborne. London: Luzac, 1942.

Guerreau, Alain. "Stabilità, via, visione: le creature e il Creatore nella spazio medievale." In *Arti e storia nel medioevo,* vol. 3: *Del vedere: pubblici, forme e funzioni,* edited by Enrico Castelnuovo and Giuseppe Sergi, 167–97. Turin: Einaudi, 2004.

Guillén, Mauro. *The Taylorized Beauty of the Mechanical: Scientific Management and the Rise of Modernist Architecture.* Princeton, N.J.: Princeton University Press, 2006.

Guitton, Jean, Grichka Bogdanov, and Igor Bogdanov. *Dieu et la science. Vers la métaréalisme.* Paris: B. Grasset, 1991.

Guthrie, W. K. C. *The Sophists.* Cambridge: Cambridge University Press, 1971.

Gutmann, Amy, and Dennis Thompson. *Democracy and Disagreement.* Cambridge, Mass.: Belknap Press, 1996.

Guy, John. *Tudor England.* Oxford: Oxford University Press, 1988.

Haas, John. "The Contemporary World." In *Christian Marriage: A Historical Study,* edited by Glenn W. Olsen, 332–59. New York: Herder and Herder, 2001.

Habermas, Jürgen. *The Structural Transformation of the Public Sphere: An Inquiry into a Category of Bourgeois Society.* Translated by Thomas Burger. Cambridge, Mass.: MIT Press, 1989.

——— and Joseph Ratzinger (Pope Benedict XVI). *The Dialectics of Secularization: On Reason and Religion.* San Francisco: Ignatius Press, 2007.

Hacker, Andrew. "Patriot Games." *NYRB* 51, 11 (June 24, 2004): 28–31.

Haddad, Yvonne Yazbeck, and John L. Esposito, eds. *Muslims on the Americanization Path?* New York: Oxford University Press, 2000.

Hageman, Marielle, et al., eds. *Reading Images and Texts: Medieval Images and Texts as Forms of Communication.* Turnhout: Brepols, 2005.

Hamburger, Jeffrey. "Seeing and Believing: The Suspicion of Sight and the Authentication of Vision in Late Medieval Art." In *Imagination und Wirklichkeit: Zum Verhältnis von mentalen und realen Bilder in der Kunst der frühen Neuzeit,* edited Alessandro Nova and Klaus Krüger, 47–70. Mainz: Philipp von Zabern, 2000.

———. *St. John the Divine: The Deified Evangelist in Medieval Art and Theology.* Berkeley: University of California Press, 2002.

Hamburger, Philip. *Separation of Church and State.* Cambridge, Mass.: Harvard University Press, 2002.

Hampshire, Stuart. "The Pleasure of Iris Murdoch." *NYRB* 48, 18 (November 15, 2001): 24–26.

Hankey, Wayne J. "Self and Cosmos in Becoming Deiform: Neoplatonic Paradigms for Reform by Self-knowledge from Augustine to Aquinas." In *Reforming the Church before Modernity: Patterns, Problems and Approaches,* edited by Christopher M. Bellitto and Louis I. Hamilton, 39–60. Burlington, Vt.: Ashgate, 2005.

Hansen, Ron. "Art and Religion: Hopkins and Bridges." *Lo* 7, 1 (Winter 2004): 78–96.

Hanson, Neil. *The Confident Hope of a Miracle: The True History of the Spanish Armada.* New York: Knopf, 2003.

Harakas, Stanley Samuel. "Faith Formation in Byzantium." In *Educating People of Faith: Exploring the History of Jewish and Christian Communities,* edited by John Van Engen, 115–31. Grand Rapids, Mich.: Eerdmans, 2004.

Harbison, Robert. *Reflections on the Baroque.* Chicago: University of Chicago Press, 2000.

Harding, Alan. *Medieval Law and the Foundations of the State.* New York: Oxford University Press, 2002.

Harries, Richard, and Henry Mayr-Harting, eds. *Christianity: Two Thousand Years.* New York: Oxford University Press, 2001.

Harrington, Ann. *Reenchanted Science: Holism in German Culture from Wilhelm II to Hitler.* Princeton, N.J.: Princeton University Press, 1996.

Harrington, Michael. *Sacred Place in Early Medieval Neoplatonism.* New York: Palgrave Macmillan, 2004.

Harrison, Carol. *Augustine: Christian Truth and Fractured Humanity.* Oxford: Oxford University Press, 2000.

Harrison, Peter. *The Bible, Protestantism, and the Rise of Natural Science.* Cambridge: Cambridge University Press, 1998.

Harrison, Robert Pogue. *The Dominion of the Dead.* Chicago: University of Chicago Press, 2003.

Hart, Aidan. "Constantin Brancusi: A Modernist Against Modernism." *SS* 7 (2006): 52–58.

Hart, David Bentley. *The Beauty of the Infinite: The Aesthetics of Christian Truth.* Grand Rapids, Mich.: Eerdmans, 2003.

———. "Christ and Nothing." *FT* 136 (October 2003): 47–56.

———. "A Most Partial Historian." *FT* 138 (December 2003): 34–40.

———. Letter. *FT* 139 (January 2004): 3–4.

———. "The Laughter of the Philosophers." *FT* 149 (January 2005): 31–37.

Harvey, David. *Paris, Capital of Modernity.* London: Routledge, 2003.

Haskell, Thomas L. *Objectivity is Not Neutrality: Explanatory Schemes in History.* Baltimore: Johns Hopkins University Press, 1998.

Haslam, Jonathan. *No Virtue Like Necessity: Realist Thought in International Relations Since Machiavelli.* New Haven, Conn.: Yale University Press, 2002.

Hastings, Adrian. "The Twentieth Century." In *Christianity: Two Thousand Years,* edited by Richard Harries and Henry Mayr-Harting. New York: Oxford University Press, 2001.

Hauerwas, Stanley. Interview. *Traces* 5, 5 (May 2003): 22.

Hayes, Michael A. *New Religious Movements in the Catholic Church.* New York: Burns & Oates, 2005.

Hayward, Paul Antony. "Demystifying the Role of Sanctity in Western Christendom." In *The Cult of Saints in Late Antiquity and the Early Middle Ages: Essays on the Contribution of Peter Brown,* edited by James Howard-Johnston and Paul Antony Hayward. New York: Oxford University Press, 1999.

Hazard, Paul. *La crise de la conscience européenne (1680–1715).* Paris: Boivin, 1935.

Healy, Gene. "What's So Conservative about the Pledge of Allegiance?" *SLT,* October 23, 2003.

Healy, Nicholas J. *The Eschatology of Hans Urs von Balthasar: Being as Communion.* Oxford: Oxford University Press, 2005.

Hecht, Anthony. "Knowing the Score." *NYRB* 49, 19 (December 5, 2002): 54–57.

Hecht, Jennifer Michael. *The End of the Soul: Scientific Modernity, Atheism, and Anthropology in France.* New York: Columbia University Press, 2003.

Heclo, Hugh, et al. *Christianity and American Democracy.* Cambridge, Mass.: Harvard University Press, 2007.

Heffernan, Jeanne. "Making the Christian Case for Democracy: A Response to Kraynak's Criticism." *CSSR* 9 (2004): 29–35.

Henrici, Peter. "The Mystery of the Everyday." *Co* 31 (2004): 4–7.

Herbert, Robert L. "An Anarchist's Art." *NYRB* 48, 20 (December 20, 2001): 20–25.

Herlihy, David, ed. *The History of Feudalism.* New York: Harper & Row, 1970.

Herrera, Robert A. *Donoso Cortes: Cassandra of the Age.* Grand Rapids, Mich.: Eerdmans, 1995.

Herrero Marcos, Jesús. *Arquitectura y Simbolismo del Románico Palentino.* 2nd ed. Madrid: Ars Magna, 1995.

———. *Arquitectura y Simbolismo del Románico de Cantabria.* Madrid: Ars Magna, 1996.

Hervieu-Léger, Daniéle. *Religion as a Chain of Memory.* Translated by Simon Lee. New Brunswick, N.J.: Rutgers University Press, 2000.

Herzstein, Robert E.. "Judgment and Restitution: Goldhagen, the Catholic Church, and Anti-Semitism." *JHS* 3, 3–4 (Summer/Fall 2003): 471–92.

Hess, Carol A. *Sacred Passions: The Life and Music of Manuel de Falla.* New York: Oxford University Press, 2004.

Heyd, David, ed. *Toleration: An Elusive Virtue.* Princeton, N.J.: Princeton University Press, 1996.

Heynen, Hilde. *Architecture and Modernity.* Cambridge, Mass.: MIT Press, 1999.

Hill, Peter, and Nigel Simeone. *Messiaen.* New Haven, Conn.: Yale University Press, 2005.

Hillier, Paul. *Arvo Pärt.* Oxford: Oxford University Press, 1997.

Hilton, Boyd. *A Mad, Bad, and Dangerous People? England 1783–1846.* Oxford: Clarendon Press, 2006.

Himmelfarb, Gertrude. *The Roads to Modernity: The British, French, and American Enlightenments.* New York: Knopf, 2004.

Hitchcock, James. *The Recovery of the Sacred.* San Francisco: Ignatius Press, 1995.

———. "Bureaucracy—a Force for Change." *Voices* 17, 2 (2002): 29.

———. "Christopher Dawson and the Demise of Christendom." *HS* 5, 1 (September 2003): 23–25.

———. "The Enemies of Religious Liberty." *FT* 140 (February 2004): 26–28.

————. *The Supreme Court and Religion in American Life.* 2 vols. Princeton, N.J.: Princeton University Press, 2004.

————. "Pope Benedict XVI." *Voices* 20, 2 (2005): 14–15.

Hittinger, Russell. "The Two Cities and the Modern World: A Dawsonian Assessment." *MA* 28, 2/3 (1984): 193–202.

————. "Christ and the Sanctification of the *Saeculum*." *Magnificat* 22 (September 2000): 5–7.

————. *The First Grace: Rediscovering the Natural Law in a Post-Christian World.* Wilmington, Del.: ISI Books, 2003.

————. "The Churches of Earthly Power." *FT* 164 (June/July 2006): 27–32.

————. "Dissecting a Democratic Illusion." *IR* 41, 2 (Fall 2006): 50–54.

Hobsbawm, Eric. *The Age of Extremes: A History of the World, 1914–91.* New York: Vintage Books, 1994.

Hodges, John Mason. "Windows into Heaven: The Music of John Tavener." *Image* 10 (Summer 1995): 88–94.

Hoelzl, Michael. *Religion and Political Thought.* New York: Continuum, 2006.

Hoffmann, Stanley. "The Foreign Policy the US Needs." *NYRB* 53, 13 (August 10, 2006): 60–64.

Holl, Steven. *The Chapel of St. Ignatius.* New York: Princeton Architectural Press, 1999.

Holland, Joe. *Modern Catholic Social Teaching: The Popes Confront the Industrial Age 1740–1958.* New York: Paulist Press, 2003.

Hollinghurst, Alan. "On 'The Ivory Tower.'" *NYRB* 51, 4 (March 11, 2004): 26–28.

Hollywood, Amy. *Sensible Ecstasy: Mysticism, Sexual Difference, and the Demands of History.* Chicago: University of Chicago Press, 2002.

Holmes, David L. *The Faiths of the Founding Fathers.* New York: Oxford University Press, 2006.

Holsinger, Bruce. *Music, Body, and Desire in Medieval Culture.* Stanford, Calif.: Stanford University Press, 2001.

————. *The Premodern Condition: Medievalism and the Making of Theory.* Chicago: University of Chicago Press, 2005.

"Holy Architect." *AB,* 10, 7 (October 2004).

"Holy Transfiguration Skete: A Pilgrim's View." *SA* 11 (2006): 17–18.

Holzem, Andreas, ed. *Normieren, Tradieren, Inszenieren: Das Christentum als Buchreligion.* Darmstadt: Wissenschaftliche Buchgesellschaft, 2004.

Homans, Jennifer. "Geniuses Together." *NYRB* 49, 20 (December 19, 2002): 32–35.

Honneth, Axel, et al., eds. *Philosophic Interventions in the Unfinished Project of Enlightenment.* Cambridge, Mass.: MIT Press, 1992.

Höpfl, Harro, ed. *Luther and Calvin on Secular Authority.* Cambridge: Cambridge University Press, 1993.

————. *Jesuit Political Thought: The Society of Jesus and the State, c. 1540–1630.* New York: Cambridge University Press, 2004.

Horner, Patrick, J., ed. and trans. *A Macaronic Sermon Collection from Late Medieval England.* Toronto: Pontifical Institute of Medieval Studies, 2006.

Horowitz, Asher, and Terry Maley, eds. *The Barbarism of Reason: Max Weber and the Twilight of Enlightenment.* Toronto: University of Toronto Press, 1994.

Horton, Richard. "The Dawn of McScience." *NYRB* 51, 4 (March 11, 2004): 7–9.

Howard, Thomas Albert. "A 'Religious Turn' in Modern European Historiography?" *HS* 5, 4 (June 2003): 24–26.

Howsare, Rodney A. "Trojan Horse in the Catholic Church: On Balthasar's Interpretation of Barth." *FQI* 1 (2001): 275–316.

Hudson, Nancy J. *Becoming God: The Doctrine of Theosis in Nicholas of Cusa.* Washington, D.C.: The Catholic University of America Press, 2006.

Hughes, Robert. "Master Builders." *NYRB* 54, 14 (September 27, 2007): 46–49.

Hughes, Thomas P. *Human-Built World: How to Think about Technology and Culture.* Chicago: University of Chicago Press, 2004.

Humbert of Silva Candida. "Priesthood and Kingship." Translated in Brian Tierney, *The Crisis of Church and State 1050–1300,* 41–42. Englewood Cliffs, N.J.: Prentice-Hall, 1964.

Hunt, Tristram. *Building Jerusalem: The Rise and Fall of the Victorian City.* New York: Henry Holt, 2005.

Hunter, James Davison. *Culture Wars: The Struggle to Define America.* New York: Basic Books, 1991.

Huntington, Samuel P. *The Clash of Civilizations and the Remaking of World Order.* New York: Simon & Schuster, 1996.

———. *Who Are We?: The Challenges to America's National Identity.* New York: Simon & Schuster, 2004.

Hutchison, William R. *The Modernist Impulse in American Protestantism.* Durham, N.C.: Duke University Press, 1992.

Hütter, Reinhard. *Bound to Be Free: Evangelical Catholic Engagements in Ecclesiology.* Grand Rapids, Mich.: Eerdmans, 2004.

Ilnitchi, Gabriela. "*Musica mundana,* Aristotelian natural philosophy and Ptolemaic astronomy." *Early Music History* 21 (2002): 37–74.

Inglebert, Hervé. *Interpretatio Christiana: Les mutations des saviors, cosmographie, géograpie, ethnographie, histoire, dans l'Antiquité chrétienne, 30–630 après J. C.* Paris: Institut d'études augustiniennes, 2001.

"Institute Continues International Outreach with Amsterdam Conference." *Acton Notes: The Newsletter of the Acton Institute* 12, 10 (October 2002): 3.

Isidore of Seville. *Etimologias.* Edited by Jose Oroz Reta and Manuel A. Marcos Casquero, 2 vols. Madrid: Editorial Católica, 1982–83.

Israel, Jonathan I. *Radical Enlightenment: Philosophy and the Making of Modernity 1650–1750.* New York: Oxford University Press, 2001.

———. *Enlightenment Contested: Philosophy, Modernity, and the Emancipation of Man.* Oxford: Oxford University Press, 2006.

Ivereigh, Austen, ed. *The Politics of Religion in an Age of Revival: Studies in Nineteenth-Century Europe and Latin America.* London: Institute of Latin American Studies, 2000.

Iyer, Pico. "Passage to Bombay." *NYRB* 49, 16 (October 24, 2002): 30–31.

Jaccard, Roland. *L'Exil Intérieur: Schizoïdie et Civilisation.* Paris: Éditions Seuil, 1975.

Jacobs, Alan. *A Theology of Reading: The Hermeneutics of Love.* Boulder, Colo.: Westview Press, 2001.

———. "In Search of Eden." *FT* 170 (February 2007): 26–30.

Jacobson, Eric. *Metaphysics of the Profane: The Political Theology of Walter Benjamin and Gershom Scholem.* New York: Columbia University Press, 2003.

Jaeger, C. Stephen. *The Envy of Angels: Cathedral Schools and Social Ideals in Medieval Europe, 950–1200.* Philadelphia: University of Pennsylvania Press, 1994.

———. *Ennobling Love: In Search of a Lost Sensibility.* Philadelphia: University of Pennsylvania Press, 1999.

James, Henry. *The Ivory Tower.* Introduction by Alan Hollinghurst, with an essay by Ezra Pound. New York: New York Review Books, 2004.

Janicaud, Dominique, et al. *Phenomenology and the "Theological Turn."* New York: Fordham University Press, 2000.

Jardine, Murray. *The Making and Unmaking of Technological Society: How Christianity Can Save Modernity from Itself.* Grand Rapids, Mich.: Brazos Press, 2004.

Jarnut, Jörg, and Matthias Wemhoff, eds. *Vom Umbruch zur Erneuerung? Das 11. Und beginnende 12. Jahrhundert—Positionen der Forschung.* Munich: Fink, 2006.

Jay, Martin. *Downcast Eyes: The Denigration of Vision in Twentieth-Century French Thought.* Berkeley: University of California Press, 1993.

Jayyusi, Salma Khadra. "Andalusi Poetry: The Golden Period." In *The Legacy of Muslim Spain,* 2 vols., edited by Salma Khadra Jayyusi, I, 317–66. Leiden: Brill, 1994.

Jefferson, Thomas. *The Jefferson Bible,* with the annotated commentaries on religion of Thomas Jefferson, introduction by Henry Wilder Foote, foreword by Donald S. Harrington. Edited by O. I. A. Roche. New York: C. N. Potter, 1964.

Jeffreys, Derek S. "Which Diversity." *FT* 142 (April 2004): 6.

Jencks, Charles. *The New Paradigm in Architecture: The Language of Post-Modernism.* New Haven, Conn.: Yale University Press, 2002.

Jencks, Christopher. "Who Should Get In?" *NYRB* 48, 19 (November 29, 2001): 57–63.

Jenkins, Philip. "A New Religious America." *FT* 125 (September 2002): 25–28.

———. *God's Continent: Christianity, Islam, and Europe's Religious Crisis.* New York: Oxford University Press, 2007.

———. *The Next Christendom: The Coming of Global Christianity.* New York: Oxford University Press, 2007.

Jensen, Robin M. *The Substance of Things Seen: Art, Faith, and the Christian Community.* Grand Rapids, Mich.: Eerdmans, 2004.

———. *Face to Face: Portraits of the Divine in Early Christianity.* Minneapolis: Fortress Press, 2005.

———. "Towards a Christian Material Culture." In *The Cambridge History of Christianity: Origins to Constantine,* edited by Margaret M. Mitchell and Frances M. Young. Cambridge: Cambridge University Press, 2006.

Jessup, Lynda, ed. *Antimodernism and Artistic Experience: Policing the Boundaries of Modernity.* Toronto: University of Toronto Press, 2001.

John Buridan. *Summulae de Dialectica.* Translated by Gyula Klima. New Haven, Conn.: Yale University Press, 2001.

John Damascene. *On Divine Images: Three Apologies against Those Who Attack the Divine Images.* Translated by David Anderson. Crestwood, N.Y.: St. Vladimir's Seminary Press, 1980.

John Paul II. *Encyclical Letter Redemptoris Missio of the Supreme Pontiff John Paul II on the Permanent Validity of the Church's Missionary Mandate.* Boston: Daughters of St. Paul, 1991.

———. *The Theology of the Body.* Boston: Pauline Books and Media, 1997.

———. *Encyclical Letter, Fides et ratio, of the Supreme Pontiff John Paul II: to the Bishops of the Catholic Church on the Relationship between Faith and Reason.* Boston: Daughters of St. Paul, 1998.

———. *To Artists.* Boston: Pauline Books and Media, 1999.

———. "The Globalization of Solidarity." *Faith and Culture Bulletin* 8 (2000): 7–9.

John, Richard R. "Elaborations, Revisions, Dissents: Alfred D. Chandler Jr.'s *The Visible Hand* after Twenty Years." *Business History Review* 71 (1997): 151–200.

Johnson, James Turner. "Just War, As It Was and Is." *FT* 149 (January 2005): 14–24.

Johnson, Paul. *Art: A New History.* New York: HarperCollins, 2003.

———. "The Almost-Chosen People." *FT* 164 (June/July 2006): 17–22.

Johnston, George Sim. "After the Council: Living Vatican II." *IC,* December 17, 2004.

Jonas of Orléans. *De institutione laicali. PL,* vol. 106.

———. *De institutione regia ad Pippinum regem. PL,* vol. 106.

Jonas, Hans. *Philosophical Essays: From Ancient Creed to Technological Man.* Englewood Cliffs, N.J.: Prentice-Hall, 1974.

Jones, Amelia. *Irrational Modernism: A Neurasthetic History of New York Dada.* Cambridge, Mass.: MIT Press, 2004.

Jones, E. Michael. *Degenerate Moderns: Modernity as Rationalized Sexual Misbehavior.* San Francisco: Ignatius Press, 1993.

———. *Dionysos Rising: The Birth of Cultural Revolution out of the Spirit of Music.* San Francisco: Ignatius Press, 1994.

———. *Living Machines: Bauhaus Architecture as Sexual Ideology.* San Francisco: Ignatius Press, 1995.

Jones, L. Gregory, Reinhard Huetter, and C. Rosalee Velloso Ewell, eds. *God, Truth, and Witness: Engaging Stanley Hauerwas.* Grand Rapids, Mich.: Brazos Press, 2005.

Joost-Gaugier, Christiane L. *Measuring Heaven: Pythagoras and His Influence on Thought and Art in Antiquity and the Middle Ages.* Ithaca N.Y.: Cornell University Press, 2006.

Jordan, Michael C. "Preface." *Lo* 7, 1 (Winter 2004): 5–15.

Jordan, William Chester. *The French Monarchy and the Jews: From Philip Augustus to the Last Capetians.* Philadelphia: University of Pennsylvania Press, 1989.

———. *Unceasing Strife, Unending Fear: Jacques de Thérines and the Freedom of the Church in the Age of the Last Capetians.* Princeton, N.J.: Princeton University Press, 2005.

Joshi, Vijay, and Robert Skidelsky. "One World?" *NYRB* 51, 5 (March 25, 2004): 19–21.

Judt, Tony. "The French Difference." *NYRB* 48, 6 (April 12, 2001): 15–22.

———. "Its Own Worst Enemy." *NYRB* 49, 13 (August 15, 2002): 12–17.

———. "Israel: The Alternative." *NYRB* 50, 16 (October 23, 2003): 8–10.

———. "Dreams of Empire." *NYRB* 51, 17 (November 4, 2004): 38–34.

———. "Europe vs. the US." *NYRB* 52, 2 (February 10, 2005): 37–41.

———. "A Story Still to be Told." *NYRB* 53, 5 (March 23, 2006): 11–15.

Justin Martyr. *First Apology.* In *The Writings of Saint Justin Martyr,* translated by Thomas B. Falls. Washington, D.C.: The Catholic University of America Press, 1948.

Kagan, Robert. *Of Paradise and Power: America and Europe in the New World Order.* New York: Knopf, 2003.

———. *Dangerous Nation.* New York: Knopf, 2006.

Kamen, Henry. *The Spanish Inquisition: A Historical Revision.* New Haven, Conn.: Yale University Press, 1998.

Kamerick, Kathleen. *Popular Piety and Art in the Late Middle Ages: Image Worship and Idolatry in England, 1350–1500.* New York: Palgrave, 2002.

Kane, Harold, ed. *Prickynge of Love.* Salzburg: Institut für Anglistik und Amerikanistik, Universität Salzburg, 1983.

Kant, Immanuel. *Religion Within the Limits of Reason Alone.* Translated by T. M. Greene and H. H. Hudson. New York: Harper Torchbooks, 1960.

Kaplan, Benjamin J. *Divided by Faith: Religious Conflict and the Practice of Toleration in Early Modern History.* Cambridge, Mass.: Harvard University Press, 2007.

Kass, Leon R. "L'Chaim and Its Limits: Why Not Immortality?" *FT* 113 (May 2001): 17–24.

Kaufmann, Matthias. *Begriffe, Sätze, Dinge: Referenz und Wahrheit bei Wilhelm von Ockham.* Leiden: Brill, 1994.

Kaye, Joel. *Economy and Nature in the Fourteenth Century: Money, Market Exchange, and the Emergence of Scientific Thought.* Cambridge: Cambridge University Press, 1998.

Keefe, Patrick Radden. "Quartermasters of Terror." *NYRB* 52, 2 (February 10, 2005): 33–36.

Kekes, John. *The Illusions of Egalitarianism.* Ithaca, N.Y.: Cornell University Press, 2003.

Kelly, Aileen. "The Secret Sharer." *NYRB* 47, 4 (March 9, 2000): 33–37.

———. "In the Promised Land." *NYRB* 48, 19 (November 15, 2001): 45–48.

———. "The Two Dostoevskys." *NYRB* 50, 5 (March 27, 2003): 23–25.

Kennedy, Emmet. "Simone Weil: Secularism and Syncretism." *JHS* 5 (2005): 203–25.

Kennedy, Paul. "The Modern Machiavelli." *NYRB* 49, 17 (November 7, 2002): 52–55.

———. "Mission Impossible?" *NYRB* 51, 10 (June 10, 2004): 16–19.

Kedward, Rod. *France and the French: A Modern History.* Woodstock, N.Y.: Penguin, 2006.

Kent, Bonnie. *Virtues of the Will: The Transformation of Ethics in the Late Thirteenth Century.* Washington, D.C.: The Catholic University of America Press, 1995.

———. "On the Track of Lust: *Luxuria,* Ockham, and the Scientists." In *In the Garden of Evil: The Vices and Culture in the Middle Ages,* edited by Richard Newhauser, 349–70. Toronto: Pontifical Institute of Medieval Studies, 2005.

Kerman, Joseph. "Playing in Time." *NYRB* 55, 8 (May 15, 2008): 50–54.

Kessler, Herbert L. *Spiritual Seeing: Picturing God's Invisibility in Medieval Art.* Philadelphia: University of Pennsylvania Press, 2000.

Kidson, Peter. "Panofsky, Suger and St. Denis." *Journal of the Warburg and Courtauld Institutes* 50 (1987): 1–17.

Kieckhefer, Richard. *Theology in Stone: Church Architecture from Byzantium to Berkeley.* New York: Oxford University Press, 2004.

Kilroy, Gerard. *Edmund Campion: Memory and Transcription.* Burlington, Vt.: Ashgate, 2005.

Kimmelman, Michael. "All in the Family." *NYRB* 53, 3 (August 10, 2006): 18–21.

Kleinschmidt, Harald. *Perception and Action in Medieval Europe.* Rochester, N.Y.: Boydell Press, 2005.

Klosowska, Anna. *Queer Love in the Middle Ages.* New York: Palgrave Macmillan, 2005.

Kohut, Andrew, John C. Green, Scott Keeter, and Robert C. Toth. *The Diminishing Divide: Religion's Changing Role in American Politics.* Washington, D.C.: Brookings Institution Press, 2000.

Kolakowski, Leszek. "The Revenge of the Sacred in Secular Culture." In *Modernity on Endless Trial,* 63–74. Chicago: University of Chicago Press, 1990).

———. "What Is Left of Socialism?" *FT* 136 (October 2002): 42–46.

———. *My Correct Views on Everything.* South Bend, Ind.: St. Augustine's Press, 2005.

Kolocotroni, Vassiliki, et al., eds. *Modernism: An Anthology of Sources and Documents.* Chicago: University of Chicago Press, 1998.

Kotkin, Steven. *Magnetic Mountain: Stalinism as a Civilization.* Berkeley: University of California Press, 1995.

Koyré, Alexandre. *From the Closed World to the Infinite Universe.* Baltimore: Johns Hopkins University Press, 1957.

Koziol, Geoffrey. "Review Article: The Dangers of Polemic: Is Ritual Still an Interesting Topic of Historical Study?" *EME* 11 (2002): 367–88.

Kramer, Hilton. *The Triumph of Modernism: the Art World, 1987–2005.* Chicago: Ivan R. Dee, 2006.

Kramer, Susan R., and Caroline W. Bynum. "Revisiting the Twelfth-Century Individual: The Inner Self and the Christian Community." In *Das Eigene und das Ganze: Zum Individuellen im mittelalterlichen Religiosentum,* edited by Gert Melville and Markus Schürer, 57–85. Münster: Lit, 2002.

Kraus, Henry. *The Living Theatre of Medieval Art.* Bloomington: Indiana University Press, 1967.

Krausmüller, Dirk. "The Rise of Hesychasm." In *The Cambridge History of Christianity,* 5: *Eastern Christianity,* edited by Michael Angold. Cambridge: Cambridge University Press, 2006.

Kraynak, Robert P. *Christian Faith and Modern Democracy: God and Politics in the Fallen World.* Notre Dame, Ind.: University of Notre Dame Press, 2001.

———. "About Christian Faith and Modern Democracy." *CSSR* 9 (2004): 17–19.

———. "The Illusion of Christian Democracy." *CSSR* 9 (2004): 87–95.

——— and Glenn Tinder, eds. *In Defense of Human Dignity: Essays for Our Times.* Notre Dame, Ind.: University of Notre Dame Press, 2003.

Kripal, Jeffrey J.. *Roads of Excess, Palaces of Wisdom.* Chicago: University of Chicago Press, 2001.

Kristof, Nicolas. "Wretched of the Earth." *NYRB* 54, 9 (May 31, 2007): 34–36.

Kselman, Thomas. *European Religion in the Age of the Great Cities, 1830–1930.* London: Routledge, 1995.

Kuefler, Mathew. *The Manly Eunuch: Masculinity, Gender Ambiguity, and Christian Ideology in Late Antiquity.* Chicago: University of Chicago Press, 2001.

Kuran, Timur. *Private Truths, Public Lies: The Social Consequences of Preference Falsification.* Cambridge, Mass.: Harvard University Press, 1995.

Kuspit, Donald. *The End of Art.* New York: Cambridge University Press, 2004.

Kwasniewski, Peter A. "Transcendence, Power, Virtue, Madness, Ecstasy—Modalities of Excess in Aquinas." *Mediaeval Studies* 66 (2004): 129–81.

Kwinter, Stanford. *Architectures of Time: Toward a Theory of the Event in Modernist Culture.* Cambridge, Mass.: MIT Press, 2001.

La Croix, Richard R., ed. *Augustine on Music: An Interdisciplinary Collection of Essays.* Lewiston, N.Y.: Edwin Mellen Press, 1988.

Ladner, Gerhart. *The Idea of Reform: Its Impact on Christian Thought and Action in the Age of the Fathers.* Rev. ed. New York: Harper & Row, 1967.

Lahey, Stephen E. *Philosophy and Politics in the Thought of John Wyclif.* Cambridge: Cambridge University Press, 2003.

Laqueur, Thomas W. *Solitary Sex: A Cultural History of Masturbation.* New York: Zone Books, 2003.

Lardner, James. "The Specter Haunting Your Offices." *NYRB* 54, 10 (June 14, 2007): 62–65.

"Last Things." *SS* 4 (2003): 79–80.

Laurence, Jonathan, and Justin Vaisse. *Integrating Islam: Political and Religious Challenges in Contemporary France.* Washington, D.C.: Brookings Institution Press, 2006.

Laursen, John Christian, and Cary J. Nederman, eds. *Beyond the Persecuting Society: Religious Toleration Before the Enlightenment.* Philadelphia: University of Pennsylvania Press, 1998.

Laven, David. *Venice and Venetia under the Habsburgs, 1815–1835.* Oxford: Oxford University Press, 2002.

Laytham, D. Brent, ed. *God Is Not . . . Religious, Nice, "One of Us," an American, a Capitalist.* Grand Rapids, Mich.: Brazos Press, 2004.

Lazu, Robert. "Crisis of the Symbolic Universe." *SS* 7 (2006): 6–8.

Leach, Elizabeth Eva. *Sung Birds: Music, Nature, and Poetry in the Later Middle Ages.* Ithaca, N.Y.: Cornell University Press, 2007.

Lears, Jackson. *No Place of Grace: Antimodernism and the Transformation of American Culture 1880–1920.* New York: Pantheon Books, 1981.

Leaver, Robin A. *Luther's Liturgical Music: Principles and Implications.* Grand Rapids, Mich.: Eerdmans, 2007.

Lee, M. Owen. *Wagner's Ring: Turning the Sky Round.* New York: Summit Books, 1990.

———. *Wagner: the Terrible Man and His Truthful Art.* Toronto: University of Toronto Press, 1999.

Lehmann, Hartmut, ed. *Säkularisierung, Dechristianisierung, Rechristianisierung im neuzeitlichen Europa.* Göttingen: Vandenhoeck & Ruprecht, 1997.

Lehner, F. C. "Music (Philosophy)." In *The New Catholic Encyclopedia,* 16 vols. New York: McGraw-Hill, 1967.

Leithart, Peter J. *Against Christianity.* Moscow, Idaho: Canon Press, 2003.

———. "Jane Austen, Public Theologian." *FT* 139 (January, 2004): 28–37.

Lekan, Thomas M. *Imagining the Nation in Nature: Landscape Preservation and German Identity, 1885–1945.* Cambridge, Mass.: Harvard University Press, 2003.

Leonard, John. "Mind Painting." *NYRB* 48, 1 (January 11, 2001): 42–48.

Lerner, Michael. *Spirit Matters.* Charlottesville, Va.: Hampton Roads, 2000.

Levy, Evonne. *Propaganda and the Jesuit Baroque.* Berkeley: University of California Press, 2004.

Lewis, C. S. *The Discarded Image: An Introduction to Medieval and Renaissance Literature.* Cambridge: Cambridge University Press, 1994.

Lewis, Michael J. "Body and Soul." *Commentary* 123, 1 (January 2007): 129–33.

Ley, Michael, Heinrich Neisser, and Gilbert Weiss, eds. *Politische Religion? Politik, Religion und Anthropologie im Werk von Eric Voegelin.* Munich: Fink, 2003.

Lia, Pierluigi. *L'estetica teologica di Bernardo di Chiaravalle.* Florence: Edizioni del Galluzzo per la Fondazione Ezio Franceschini, 2007.

Lilla, Mark. "The Perils of Friendship." *NYRB* 46, 19 (December 2, 1999): 25–29.

———. *The Reckless Mind: Intellectuals in Politics.* New York: New York Review Books, 2001.

———. "Inside the Clockwork." *NYRB* 49, 7 (April 25, 2002): 43–45.

———. "The New Age of Tyranny." *NYRB* 49, 16 (October 24, 2002): 28–29.

———. "The Big E." *NYRB* 50, 10 (June 12, 2003): 46–47.

———. "The Closing of the Straussian Mind." *NYRB* 51, 17 (November 4, 2004): 55–59.

———. "Slouching Toward Athens." *NYRB* 52, 11 (June 23, 2005): 46–48.

———. "Mr. Casaubon in America." *NYRB* 54, 11 (June 28, 2007): 29–31.

———. *The Stillborn God: Religion, Politics, and the Modern West.* New York: Knopf, 2007.

Limentani, Caterina Virdis, and Mari Pietrogiovanna. *Great Altarpieces Gothic and Renaissance.* New York: Vendome Press, 2002.

"The Limits of History: An Exchange." *HS* 6, 5 (May–June, 2005): 5–17.

Lindsey, Brink. "The Origins and Progress of the Industrial Counterrevolution." *HS* 5, 3 (January 2004), 17–21.

Lipsey, Robert. *An Art of Our Own: the Spiritual in Twentieth-Century Art.* Boston: Shambhala, 1988.

Little, Lester K. "Cypress Beams, Kufic Script, and Cut Stone: Rebuilding the Master Narrative of European History." *Sp* 79 (2004): 909–28.

Lloyd, G. E. R. *Ancient Worlds, Modern Reflections: Philosophical Perspectives on Greek and Chinese Science and Culture.* New York: Oxford University Press, 2004.

Lockwood, Lewis. "Beethoven Beyond Classicism." *NYRB* 50, 12 (July 17, 2003): 27–29.

———. "Which Is the Real Mendelssohn?" *NYRB* 51, 17 (November 4, 2004): 44–46.

Lodge, David. "Happy Birthday." *NYRB* 49, 9 (May 23, 2002): 48–53.

López-Calo, José, and Carlos Villanueva, eds. *El Códice Calixtino y la música de su tiempo.* A Coruña: Fundación Pedro Barrié de la Maza, 2001.

Löwith, Karl. *Meaning in History: The Theological Implications of the Philosophy of History.* Chicago: University of Chicago Press, 1949.

Loomie, Albert J. "Oliver Cromwell's Policy Toward the English Catholics: The Appraisal by Diplomats, 1654–1658." *CHR* 90 (2004): 29–44.

Loos, Adolf. *Ornament and Crime: Selected Essays.* Edited by A. Opel, translated by M. Mitchell. Riverside, Calif.: Ariadne Press, 1998.

Lossky, Vladimir. *In the Image and Likeness of God.* Edited by John H. Erickson and Thomas E. Bird, with an introduction by John Meyendorff. Crestwood, N.Y.: St. Vladimir's Seminary Press, 1974.

Louth, Andrew. *St John Damascene: Tradition and Originality in Byzantine Theology.* New York: Oxford University Press, 2004.

Lubbock, Jules. *Storytelling in Christian Art from Giotto to Donatello.* New Haven, Conn.: Yale University Press, 2006.

Lucas, Joseph S. "Interview with David Brooks." *HS* 4, 4 (April 2003): 37–39.

Lukacs, John. *Historical Consciousness: or, the Remembered Past.* New York: Harper & Row, 1968.

———. *At the End of An Age.* New Haven, Conn.: Yale University Press, 2002.

———. *Democracy and Populism: Fear and Hatred.* New Haven, Conn.: Yale University Press, 2005.

———. *Remembered Past: John Lukacs on History, Historians, and Historical Knowledge: a Reader.* Edited by Mark G. Malvasi and Jeffrey O. Nelson. Wilmington, Del.: ISI Books, 2005.

Lundin, Roger. "'As If God Were Dead': American Literature and the Question of Scripture." In *The Bible and the University,* edited by David Lyle Jeffrey and C. Stephen Evans. Scripture and Hermeneutics Series, vol. 8, 253–83. Grand Rapids, Mich.: Zondervan, 2007.

Luria, Keith P. *Sacred Boundaries: Religious Coexistence and Conflict in Early-Modern France.* Washington, D.C.: The Catholic University of America Press, 2005.

Lurie, Alison. "God's Houses, Parts I and II." *NYRB* 50, 12 (July 3 and 17, 2003): 30–32, 41–43.

———. "When Is a Building Beautiful?" *NYRB* 54, 4 (March 15, 2007): 19–21.

Lynch, Jonah. "Community and Dialogue: A Reading of Bach's Solo Violin Works." *Co* 31 (2004): 168–75.

Lyttelton, Adrian. "What Was Fascism?" *NYRB* 51, 16 (October 21, 2004): 33–36.

McAfee, Noëlle. *Habermas, Kristeva, and Citizenship.* Ithaca, N.Y.: Cornell University Press, 2000.

McCarraher, Eugene. "Remarks on John McGreevy's Catholicism and American Freedom." *HS* (September/October 2004): 28–31.

McCarthy, David M. "Shifting Settings From Subculture to Pluralism: Catholic Moral Theology in an Evangelical Key." *Co* 31 (2004): 85–110.

McCarthy, John C., ed. *Modern Enlightenment and the Rule of Reason.* Washington, D.C.: The Catholic University of America Press, 1998.

McClay, Wilfred M. "The Continuing Irony of American History." *FT* 120 (February 2002): 20–25.

———. "Tradition, History, and Sequoias." *FT* 131 (March, 2003): 41–47.

McCloskey, Deirdre. *The Bourgeois Virtues: Ethics for an Age of Commerce.* Chicago: University of Chicago Press, 2006.

McClure, Kirstie M. *Judging Rights: Lockean Politics and the Limits of Consent.* Ithaca, N.Y.: Cornell University Press, 1996.

McDougall, Walter A. *Freedom Just Around the Corner: A New American History, 1585–1828.* New York: HarperCollins, 2004.

McGrade, Arthur Stephen. "Right(s) in Ockham: A Reasonable Vision of Politics." In *Transformations in Medieval and Early-Modern Rights Discourse,* edited by Virpi Mäkinen and Petter Korkman, 63–94. Dordrecht: Springer, 2006.

McGrath, Alister. *The Twilight of Atheism: The Rise and Fall of Disbelief in the Modern World.* New York: Doubleday, 2004.

McGreevy, John T. *Parish Boundaries: The Catholic Encounter with Race in the Twentieth-Century Urban North.* Chicago: University of Chicago Press, 1996.

———. "Catholicism and American Freedom." *HS* (September/October 2004): 25–26.

McGurn, William. "Bob Casey's Revenge." *FT* 149 (January 2005): 6–8.

MacIntyre, Alasdair. *Whose Justice? Which Rationality?* Notre Dame, Ind.: University of Notre Dame Press, 1988.

———. *Three Rival Versions of Moral Enquiry: Encyclopaedia, Genealogy, and Tradition.* Notre Dame, Ind.: University of Notre Dame Press, 1990.

———. *Dependent Rational Animals: Why Human Beings Need the Virtues.* Chicago: Open Court, 1999.

———. *After Virtue: A Study in Moral Theory.* 3rd ed. Notre Dame, Ind.: University of Notre Dame Press, 2007.

McLeod, Hugh, and Werner Ustorf, eds. *The Decline of Christendom in Western Europe, 1750–2000.* Cambridge: Cambridge University Press, 2003.

McKibben, Bill. *Enough: Staying Human in an Engineered Age.* New York: Times Books, 2003.

———. "Crossing the Red Line." *NYRB* 51, 10 (June 10, 2004): 32–38.

———. "The Coming Meltdown." *NYRB* 53, 1 (January 12, 2006): 16–18.

McMahon, Darrin M. *Enemies of the Enlightenment: The French Counter-Enlightenment and the Making of Modernity.* New York: Oxford University Press, 2001.

McLaren, Anne. "Gender, Religion, and Early Modern Nationalism: Elizabeth I, Mary Queen of Scots, and the Genesis of English Anti-Catholicism." *AHR* 107 (2002): 739–67.

McLeod, Hugh. *Secularisation in Western Europe, 1848–1914.* New York: St. Martin's Press, 2000.

———. "Introduction." In *The Decline of Christendom in Western Europe, 1550–2000,* edited by Hugh McLeod and Werner Ustorf. Cambridge: Cambridge University Press, 2003.

McNamara, Denis. "Built Form of Theology: The Natural Sympathies of Catholicism and Classicism." *SA* 12 (2006): 20–24.

McNaspy, C. J. "A Chat with Christopher Dawson." *America* (October 28, 1961): 122.

McNeill, William H. "Bigger and Better?" *NYRB* 51, 16 (2004): 61–63.

———. "Beyond Words." *NYRB* 53, 7 (April 27, 2006): 26–28.

———. "Man Slaughters Man." *NYRB* 55, 6 (April 12, 2008): 43–48.

Maag, Karin, and John D. Witvliet, eds. *Worship in Medieval and Early Modern Europe: Change and Continuity in Religious Practice.* Notre Dame, Ind.: University of Notre Dame Press, 2004.

Mack, Michael. *German Idealism and the Jew: the Inner Anti-Semitism of Philosophy and German Jewish Responses.* Chicago: University of Chicago Press, 2003.

Madrick, Jeff. "The Power of the Super-Rich." *NYRB* 49, 12 (July 18, 2002): 25–27.

———. "The Way to a Fair Deal." *NYRB* 53, 1 (January 12, 2006): 37–40.

———. "Time for a New Deal." *NYRB* 55, 14 (September 25, 2008): 65–70.

Magnou-Nortier, Elisabeth. "L'*Admonitio generalis:* Etude critique." In *Jornades internacionals d'estudi sobre el bishe Feliu d'Urgell.* Barcelona, 2000.

Maguire, Henry. *Art and Eloquence in Byzantium.* Princeton, N.J.: Princeton University Press, 1981.

Mahoney, Daniel J. "A Noble Failure." *FT* 139 (January 2004): 57–61.

———. "Traducing Solzhenitsyn." *FT* 145 (August/September 2004): 14–17.

Maier, Hans, ed. *Totalitarismus und Politische Religionen: Konzepte des Diktaturvergleichs.* 3 vols. Paderborn: Ferdinand Schöningh, 1996–2003. Translated as *Totalitarianism and Political Religions.* 3 vols. London: Routledge, 2004–8.

Maiolo, Francesco. *Medieval Sovereignty: Marsilius of Padua and Bartolous of Saxoferrato.* Delft: Eburon Academic, 2007.

Mäkinen, Virpi, and Petter Korkman, eds. *Transformations in Medieval and Early-Modern Rights Discourse.* Dordrecht: Springer, 2006.

Maleuvre, Didier. *The Religion of Reality: Inquiry into the Self, Art, and Transcendence.* Washington, D.C.: The Catholic University of America Press, 2006.

Mancini, J. M. *Pre-Modernism: Art-World Change and American Culture from the Civil War to the Armory Show.* Princeton, N.J.: Princeton University Press, 2005.

Manent, Pierre. *The City of Man.* Translated by Marc LePain. Princeton, N.J.: Princeton University Press, 1998.

———. *Modern Liberty and Its Discontents.* Edited and translated by Daniel Mahoney and Paul Seaton. Lanham, Md.: Rowman & Littlefield, 1998.

————. *A World Beyond Politics? A Defense of the Nation-State.* Princeton, N.J.: Princeton University Press, 2006.

Mannion, M. Francis. "Toward a New Era in Liturgical Architecture." *Liturgical Ministry* 6 (Fall 1997): 160–72.

————. "Beyond Environment and Art in Catholic Worship." *Antiphon* 4, 2 (1999): 2–4.

————. "Liturgy and Culture: A Failed Connection." *Antiphon* 5, 3 (2000): 2–4.

————. "Bringing the Cosmos to Liturgy." *Antiphon* 6, 1 (2001): 2–4.

Mansel, Philip. *Paris Between Empires: Monarchy and Revolution, 1814–1852.* New York: St. Martin's Press, 2003.

Mansfield, Harvey. *Manliness.* New Haven, Conn.: Yale University Press, 2006.

Marcel, Gabriel. *Men against Humanity.* London: Harvill Press, 1952.

Marchesin, I. "Cosmologie et musique au moyen âge." In *Moyen Âge: entre ordre et désordre,* edited by Marion Challier and Bernadette Caille. Paris: Cité de la Musique, 2004.

Margalit, Avishai. "The Lessons of Spinoza." *NYRB* 54, 6 (April 12, 2007): 71–74.

Marion, Jean-Luc. "Descartes and Onto-Theology." In *Post-Secular Philosophy: Between Philosophy and Theology,* edited by Phillip Blond. London: Routledge, 1998.

Markus, Robert A. "Church Reform and Society in Late Antiquity." In *Reforming the Church before Modernity: Patterns, Problems and Approaches,* edited by Christopher M. Bellitto and Louis I. Hamilton, 3–19. Burlington, Vt.: Ashgate, 2005.

Marsden, George. "Can Jonathan Edwards (and His Heirs) Be Integrated into the American History Narrative?" *HS* 5, 6 (July/August 2004): 13–15.

Marshall, Robert L., and Charles Rosen. "What Mozart Meant: An Exchange." *NYRB* 54, 19 (December 6, 2007): 76–77.

Marsilius of Padua. *Marsilius of Padua: The Defender of the Peace.* Edited by Annabel S. Brett. Cambridge: Cambridge University Press, 2005.

Martin, David. *Does Christianity Cause War?* New York: Oxford University Press, 1997.

————. "Living in Interesting Times." *FT* 124 (June/July 2002): 61–64.

Martin, Elizabeth. *Architecture as a Translation of Music.* New York: Princeton Architectural Press, 1994.

Massa, Mark S. *Anti-Catholicism in America: The Last Acceptable Prejudice.* New York: Crossroad, 2003.

Mastnak, Tomaz. *Crusading Peace: Christendom, the Muslim World, and Western Political Order.* Berkeley: University of California Press, 2002.

Maurer, Armand. *About Beauty: A Thomistic Interpretation.* Houston, Tex.: Center for Thomistic Studies, University of St. Thomas, 1983.

————. *The Philosophy of William of Ockham in the Light of Its Principles.* Toronto: Pontifical Institute of Medieval Studies, 1999.

Mayernik, David. *Timeless Cities: An Architect's Reflections on Renaissance Italy.* Boulder, Colo.: Westview Press, 2003.

Mazur, Eric Michael. *The Americanization of Religious Minorities: Confronting the Constitutional Order.* Baltimore: Johns Hopkins University Press, 1999.

Mazzotta, Giuseppe. *Cosmopoiesis: The Renaissance Experiment.* Toronto: University of Toronto Press, 2001.

Meddeb, Abdelwahab. *The Malady of Islam.* Translated by Pierre Joris and Ann Reid. New York: Basic Books, 2003.

Meilaender, Peter C. *Toward a Theory of Immigration.* New York: Palgrave, 2001.

———. "Immigration: Citizens & Strangers." *FT* 173 (May 2007): 10–12.

Mellers, Wilfrid. *Celestial Music? Some Masterpieces of European Religious Music.* Rochester, N.Y.: Boydell Press, 2002.

Meltzer, Françoise. *For Fear of the Fire: Joan of Arc and the Limits of Subjectivity.* Chicago: University of Chicago Press, 2001.

Melzer, Arthur M., et al., eds. *History and the Idea of Progress.* Ithaca, N.Y.: Cornell University Press, 1995.

Memmi, Dominique. "Verso una confessione laica? Nuove forme de controllo pubblico dei corpi nella Francia contemporanea." In *Corpi e storia: Donne e uomini dal mondo antico all'età contemporanea,* edited by Nadia Maria Filippini, Tiziana Plebani, and Anna Scattigno, 229–49. Rome: Viella, 2002.

Menand, Louis. *The Metaphysical Club.* New York: Farrar, Straus and Giroux, 2001.

Mendelsohn, David. "The Two Oscar Wildes." *NYRB* 49, 15 (October 10, 2002): 18–22.

Mentré, Mireille. *Illuminated Manuscripts of Medieval Spain.* Translated by Jenifer Wakelyn. London: Thames and Hudson, 1996.

Merriman, John. *The Stones of Balazuc: A French Village in Time.* New York: W. W. Norton, 2002.

Mersch, Emile. *Morale et corps mystique.* Paris: Desclée de Brouwer, 1955.

Merwin, W. S. "You Can Take It With You." *NYRB* 51, 6 (April 8, 2004): 63–67.

Meyer, Ann R. *Medieval Allegory and the Building of the New Jerusalem.* Rochester, N.Y.: D. S. Brewer, 2003.

Meynell, Hugo. *Postmodernism and the New Enlightenment.* Washington, D.C.: The Catholic University of America Press, 1999.

Milbank, John. *Theology and Social Theory: Beyond Secular Reason.* Malden, Mass.: Blackwell, 2006.

——— et al. *Theological Perspectives on God and Beauty.* Harrisburg, Pa.: Trinity Press, International, 2003.

———, Catherine Pickstock, and Graham Ward, eds. *Radical Orthodoxy: A New Theology.* London: Routledge, 1999.

Miller, Charles. *The Gift of the World: An Introduction to the Theology of Dumitru Staniloae.* Edinburgh: T & T Clark, 2000.

Miller, Maureen. "Religion Makes a Difference: Clerical and Lay Cultures in the Courts of Northern Italy, 1000–1300." *AHR* 105 (2000): 1095–1130.

Miller, Paula Jean. "The Body: Science, Theology, and *Humanae Vitae.*" *Lo* 3, 3 (Summer 2000): 154–65.

Minne-Sève, Viviane, and Hervé Kergall. *Romanesque and Gothic France; Architecture and Sculpture.* Translated by Jack Hawkes and Lory Frankel. New York: Abrams, 2000.

Minnis, Alastair J. *Medieval Theory of Authorship: Scholastic Literary Attitudes in the Later Middle Ages.* Philadelphia: University of Pennsylvania Press, 1988.

Mishra, Pankaj. "The Great Narayan." *NYRB* 48, 3 (February 22, 2001): 44–47.

———. "The Afghan Tragedy." *NYRB* 49, 1 (January 17, 2002): 43–49.

———. "The Empire Under Siege." *NYRB* 51, 12 (July 15, 2004): 33–35.

———. "The Neglected Majority Wins!" *NYRB* 51, 13 (August 12, 2004): 30–37.

———. "A Cautionary Tale for Americans." *NYRB* 52, 9 (May 26, 2005): 8–11.

———. "Massacre in Arcadia." *NYRB* 52, 15 (October 6, 2005): 8–11.

―――. "The Misunderstood Muslims." *NYRB* 52, 18 (November 17, 2005): 15–20.

―――. "Impasse in India." *NYRB* 54, 11 (June 28, 2007): 48–51.

Mithen, Steven. *The Singing Neanderthals: The Origins of Music, Language, Mind and Body.* London: Weidenfeld & Nicolson, 2006.

Mittleman, Alan. "From Jewish Street to Public Square." *FT* 125 (September 2002): 29–37.

―――. "Fretful Orthodoxy." *FT* 136 (October 2003): 23–35.

―――. *Religion as a Public Good: Jews and Other Americans on Religion in the Public Square.* Lanham, Md.: Rowman & Littlefield, 2003.

Moevs, Christian. *The Metaphysics of Dante's Comedy.* New York: Oxford University Press, 2005.

Molnar, Thomas. "Tradition, Science and the Centuries." *An* 9 (2003): 171–77.

Monod, Paul Kléber. *The Power of Kings: Monarchy and Religion in Europe, 1589–1715.* New Haven, Conn.: Yale University Press, 1999.

Montag, John. "Revelation: The False Legacy of Suarez." In *Radical Orthodoxy: A New Theology,* edited by John Milbank et al., 38–63. London: Routledge, 1999.

Morgan, Edmund S. "The Whirlwind." *NYRB* 51, 14 (September 23, 2004): 34–39.

―――. "The Other Founders." *NYRB* 52, 14 (September 22, 2005): 41–43.

Motzkin, Gabriel. *Time and Transcendence: Secular History, the Catholic Reaction, and the Rediscovery of the Future.* Dordrecht: Kluwer Academic Publishers, 1992.

Muir, Diana. "The Value of the Nation-State." *HS* 7, 1 (September October 2005): 37–40.

Müller, Gerhard Ludwig. "Can Mankind Understand the Spirit of the Liturgy Anymore?" *Antiphon* 7, 2 (2002): 2–5.

Muller, Jerry Z. *The Mind and the Market: Capitalism in Modern European Thought.* New York: Knopf, 2002.

Munson, Lynne. *Exhibitionism: Art in an Era of Intolerance.* Chicago: Ivan R. Dee, 2000.

Munz, Peter. "Past and Present Cross-Fertilized." *HS* 5, 5 (May/June 2004): 26–28.

Murphy, Francesca Aran. *Art and Intellect in the Philosophy of Étienne Gilson.* Columbia: University of Missouri Press, 2004.

Murphy, Mark, ed. *Alasdair MacIntyre.* Cambridge: Cambridge University Press, 2003.

Murphy Jr., William F. "Henri de Lubac's Mystical Tropology." *Co* 27 (2000): 171–201.

Murray, John Courtney. "The Problem of Pluralism." Reprint of 1954 article. *Thought* 65 (1990): 323–58.

Murray, Penelope, and Peter Wilson, eds. *Music and the Muses: The Culture of Mousike in the Classical Athenian City.* New York: Oxford University Press, 2004.

Napier, A. David, *The Righting of Passage: Perceptions of Change After Modernity.* Philadelphia: University of Pennsylvania Press, 2004.

Ndalianis, Angela. *Neo-Baroque Aesthetics and Contemporary Entertainment.* Cambridge, Mass.: MIT Press, 2004.

Nederman, Cary J. "The Meaning of 'Aristotelianism' in Medieval Moral and Political Thought." *JHI* 57 (1996): 563–85.

―――. *Worlds of Difference: European Discourses of Toleration, c. 1100–c. 1550.* University Park: Pennsylvania State University Press, 2000.

―――, ed. and trans. *Political Thought in Early Fourteenth-Century England: Trea-*

tises by Walter of Milemete, William of Pagula, and William of Ockham. Tempe: Arizona Center for Medieval and Renaissance Studies, 2002.

Nehamas, Alexander. "Foreword." In Alain Renaut, *The Era of the Individual: A Contribution to a History of Subjectivity,* translated by M. B. DeBevoise and Franklin Philip. Princeton, N.J.: Princeton University Press, 1997.

Nelson, Eric. *The Greek Tradition in Republican Thought.* Cambridge: Cambridge University Press, 2004.

Nelson, Robert H. *Economics as Religion: From Samuelson to Chicago and Beyond.* University Park: Pennsylvania State University Press, 2001.

Neocleous, Mark. *Fascism.* Minneapolis: University of Minnesota Press, 1997.

Nesteruk, Alexei V. *Light from the East: Theology, Science, and the Eastern Orthodox Tradition.* Minneapolis: Fortress Press, 2004.

Neubauer, Hanns Peter. "Die Kirchenweihbeschreibungen von Saint-Denis." In *Mittelalterliches Kunsterleben nach Quellen des 11. bis 13. Jahrhunderts,* edited by Andreas Speer and Günther Binding. Stuttgart–Bad Cannstatt: Frommann-Holzboog, 1994.

Neuhaus, Richard John. *The Catholic Moment: The Paradox of the Church in the Post-Modern World.* San Francisco: Harper & Row, 1987.

———. "Religion within the Limits of Morality Alone." *FT* 72 (April 1997): 58–61.

———. "The Liberalism of John Paul II." *FT* 73 (May 1997): 16–21.

———. "The Idea of Moral Progress." *FT* 95 (August/September 1999): 21–27.

———. "Secularization in Theory and Fact." *FT* 104 (June/July 2000): 86–89.

———. "Explaining the Strange Death of American Liberalism." *FT* 120 (February 2002): 83–86.

———. "The Hermeneutics of Love." *FT* 124 (June/July 2002): 85–88.

———. "The Bishops Get Their Report Card." *FT* 141 (March 2004): 57–61.

———. "To Be American." *FT* 145 (August/September 2004): 93–97.

———. "The Public Square." *FT* 163 (May 2006): 59–64.

———. "Le Danse Macabre." *FT* 171 (March 2007): 56–57.

———. "The Much Exaggerated Death of Europe." *FT* 173 (May 2007): 32–38.

———. "Who Will Rid Us of This Turbulent Democracy." *FT* 73 (May 1997): 65.

"News." *SA* 12 (2006): 8.

Newman, Barbara. *Saint Hildegard of Bingen: Symphonia.* Ithaca, N.Y.: Cornell University Press, 1988.

———. "What Did It Mean to Say 'I Saw'? The Clash between Theory and Practice in Medieval Visionary Culture." *Sp* 80 (2005): 1–43.

Newman, John Henry. *Essay on the Development of Christian Doctrine.* New York: D. Appleton, 1845.

———. *Parochial and Plain Sermons.* New ed., 8 vols. London: Longmans, Green, 1894.

Nichols, Aidan. *Looking at the Liturgy: A Critical View of Its Contemporary Form.* San Francisco: Ignatius Press, 1996.

———. *Scattering the Seed: A Guide Through Balthasar's Early Writings on Philosophy and the Arts.* Washington, D.C.: The Catholic University of America Press, 2006.

———. *Redeeming Beauty: Soundings in Sacral Aesthetics.* Burlington, Vt.: Ashgate, 2007.

Nicholson, Kelly. *Body and Soul: The Transcendence of Materialism.* Boulder, Colo.: Westview Press, 1997.

Niebuhr, Reinhold. *The Nature and Destiny of Man; a Christian Interpretation.* New York: Scribner, 1949.

Nietzsche, Friedrich. *On the Genealogy of Morality: A Polemic.* Translated by M. Clark and A. J. Swensen. Indianapolis: Hackett, 1998.

"The 19th Annual Clarke Family Medical Ethics Conference." *EC* (June 2004): 2–3.

Nisbet, Robert. *Twilight of Authority.* New York: Oxford University Press, 1975.

Noble, David W. *Death of a Nation: American Culture and the End of Exceptionalism.* Minneapolis: University of Minnesota Press, 2002.

Noble, Thomas F. X. *Images, Iconoclasm, and the Carolingians.* Philadelphia: University of Pennsylvania Press, 2009.

Noll, Mark. *America's God: From Jonathan Edwards to Abraham Lincoln.* New York: Oxford University Press, 2002.

———. "Founding Fathers?" *FT* 140 (February 2004): 38–41.

———. *The Civil War as a Theological Crisis.* Chapel Hill: University of North Carolina Press, 2006.

Nolte, Ernst. *Three Faces of Fascism: Action Française, Italian Fascism, National Socialism.* Translated by Leila Vennewitz. New York: Holt, Rinehart and Winston, 1966.

Noriega Bastos, José. "The Origin and Destiny of Freedom." *Co* 30 (2003): 282–336.

Norris, Pippa, and Ronald Inglehart. *Sacred and Secular: Religion and Politics Worldwide.* Cambridge: Cambridge University Press, 2004.

Novak, David. *Natural Law in Judaism.* Cambridge: Cambridge University Press, 1998.

———. "What's Best for the Jews?" *FT* 110 (February 2001): 37–42.

Novak, Michael. "Running into a Wall." *FT* 166 (October 206): 44–47.

Novick, Peter. *That Noble Dream: The "Objectivity Question" and the American Historical Profession.* Cambridge: Cambridge University Press, 1988.

Nuechterlein, James. "Lincoln Both Great and Good." *FT* 165 (August/September 2006): 36–41.

Oakeshott, Michael. *The Politics of Faith and the Politics of Scepticism.* Edited by Timothy Fuller. New Haven, Conn.: Yale University Press, 1996.

Oakley, Francis. *Natural Law, Laws of Nature, and Natural Rights: Continuity and Discontinuity in the History of Ideas.* New York: Continuum, 2005.

———. *Kingship: The Politics of Enchantment.* Malden, Mass.: Blackwell, 2006.

O'Boyle, Edward J. "Getting the Hard-Core Concepts of Economics Right." *Lo* 7, 1 (Winter 2004): 147–73.

Obrist, Barbara. *La cosmologie médiévale. Textes et images,* vol. 1, *Les fondements antiques.* Florence: SISMEL/Edizioni del Galluzzo, 2004.

"Observations on the proposed retranslation of the 1975 *Missale Romanum.*" *AB* 8, 4 (June 2002): 4–5.

O'Callaghan, Paul. "Is Christianity a Religion? The Role of Violence, Myth and Witness in Religion." *FCSQ* 29, 4 (Winter 2006): 13–28.

O'Donovan, Oliver. *The Desire of the Nations: Rediscovering the Roots of Political Theology.* New York: Cambridge University Press, 1996.

——— and Joan Lockwood O'Donovan, eds. *From Irenaeus to Grotius; A Sourcebook in Christian Political Thought, 100–1625.* Grand Rapids, Mich.: Eerdmans, 1999.

———. *Bonds of Imperfection: Christian Politics, Past and Present.* Grand Rapids, Mich.: Eerdmans, 2004.

O'Hagan, Andrew. "Back in the US of A." *NYRB* 51, 8 (May 27, 2004): 12–16.

O'Hear, Anthony. *Beyond Evolution.* Oxford: Oxford University Press, 1997.

Ohly, Friedrich. *Sensus Spiritualis: Studies in Medieval Significs and the Philology of Culture.* Edited by Samuel P. Jaffe, translated by Kenneth J. Northcott. Chicago: University of Chicago Press, 2005.

Oliver, Simon. "Motion According to Aquinas and Newton." *MT* 17, 2 (2001): 163–99.

———. *Philosophy, God, and Motion.* New York: Routledge, 2005.

Olsen, Glenn W. "'You Can't Legislate Morality': Reflections on a Bromide." *Co* 2 (1975): 148–62.

———. "Lay Spirituality *ad majorem Dei gloriam.*" *Co* 6 (1979): 405–12.

———. "The Maturity of Christian Culture: Some Reflections on the Views of Christopher Dawson." In *The Dynamic Character of Christian Culture: Essays on Dawsonian Themes,* edited by Peter J. Cataldo, 97–125. Lanham, Md.: University Press of America, 1984.

———. "The Catholic Moment?" *Co* 15 (1988): 474–87.

———. "The Meaning of Christian Culture: A Historical View." In *Catholicism and Secularization in America,* edited David L. Schindler, 98–130. Notre Dame, Ind.: Communio Books, 1990.

———. "One Heart and One Soul (Acts 4:32 and 34) in Dhuoda's *Manual.*" *CH* 61 (1992): 23–33.

———. "John Rawls and the Flight from Authority: The Quest for Equality as an Exercise in Primitivism." *In* 21 (1994): 419–36.

———. "Separating Church and State." *FR* 20 (1994): 403–25.

———. "American Culture and Liberal Ideology in the Thought of Christopher Dawson." *Co* 22 (1995): 702–20.

———. "Cultural Dynamics: Secularization and Sacralization." In *Christianity and Western Civilization,* ed. Wethersfield Institute, 97–122. San Francisco: Ignatius Press, 1995.

———. "Religion, Politics, and America at the Millennium." *FR* 22 (1996): 285–315.

———. "Unity, Plurality, and Subsidiarity in Twentieth Century Context." In *Actas del III Congreso "Cultura Europea,"* edited by Enrique Banús, 311–17. Pamplona: Aranzadi, 1996.

———. "Christian philosophy, Christian history: Parallel Ideas?" In *Eternity in Time: Christopher Dawson and the Catholic Idea of History,* edited by Stratford Caldecott and John Morrill, 131–50. Edinburgh: T & T Clark, 1997.

———. "America as an Enlightenment Culture." In *Actas del IV Congreso "Cultura Europea,"* edited by Enrique Banús and Beatriz Elío, 121–28. Pamplona: Aranzadi, 1998.

———. "John of Salisbury's Humanism." In *Gli Umanesimi Medievali,* edited by Claudio Leonardi, 447–68. Florence: SISMEL/Edizioni del Galluzzo, 1998.

———. "On the Frontiers of Eroticism: The Romanesque Monastery of San Pedro de Cervatos." *MS* 8 (1999): 89–104.

———. "The Changing Understanding of the Making of Europe from Christopher Dawson to Robert Bartlett." In *Actas del V Congreso "Cultura Europea,"* edited by Enrique Banús and Beatriz Elío, 203–10. Pamplona: Aranzadi, 2000. Reprinted in another version in *Quidditas* 20 (1999): 193–201.

———. "The Quest for a Public Philosophy in Twentieth-Century American Political Thought." *Co* 27 (2000): 340–62.

————. "Why and How to Study the Middle Ages." *Lo* 3:3 (Summer 2000): 50–75.

————, ed. *Christian Marriage: A Historical Study.* New York: Herder and Herder, 2001.

————. "Problems with the Contrast between Circular and Linear Views of Time in the Interpretation of Ancient and Early Medieval History." *FQI* 1 (2001): 41–65.

————. "Stubborn Myths." *The University Bookman* 42, 4 (2003): 5–9.

————. *Beginning at Jerusalem: Five Reflections on the History of the Church.* San Francisco: Ignatius Press, 2004.

————. "Humanism: The Struggle to Possess a Word." *Lo* 7 (2004): 97–116.

————. "The *Ecclesia Primitiua* in John Cassian, the Ps. Jerome *Commentary* on Mark, and Bede." In *Biblical Studies in the Early Middle Ages,* edited by Claudio Leonardi and Giovanni Orlandi, 5–27. Florence: SISMEL/Edizioni del Galluzzo, 2005.

————. "The Return of Purpose." *Co* 33 (2006): 666–81.

————. "Setting Boundaries: Early Medieval Reflections on Religious Toleration and their Jewish Roots." *HPS* 2 (2007): 164–92.

————. "The Spiritual Sense(s) Today." In *The Bible and the University,* edited by David Lyle Jeffrey and C. Stephen Evans. Scripture and Hermeneutics Series, vol. 8, 116–38. Grand Rapids, Mich.: Eerdmans, 2007.

————. "The Middle Ages in the History of Toleration: A Prolegomena." *MS* 16 (2008): 1–20.

————. "Why We Need Christopher Dawson." *Co* 35 (2008): 115–44.

————. "The Natural Law: The First Grace." *Co* 35 (2008): 354–73.

————. "The Two Europes." *The European Legacy: Toward New Paradigms. Journal of the International Society for the Study of European Ideas* 14, 1 (2009): 133–48.

————. "Canon Law." In *The Oxford Guide to the Historical Reception of Augustine,* gen. ed. Karla Pollmann. To be published.

O'Malley, John. *Four Cultures of the West.* Cambridge, Mass.: Belknap Press, 2004.

Ong, Walter J. *Orality and Literacy: The Technologizing of the Word.* New York: Methuen, 1982.

Osler, Margaret J., ed. *Rethinking the Scientific Revolution.* New York: Cambridge University Press, 2000.

Østrem, E. "Deus artifex and homo creator: Art between the Human and the Divine." In *Creations, Medieval Rituals, the Arts, and the Concept of Creation,* edited by Sven Rune Havsteen et al. Turnhout: Brepols, 2007.

Ouellet, Marc. "Trinity and Eucharist: A Covenantal Mystery." *Co* 27 (2000): 262–83.

————. "Theological Perspectives on Marriage." *Co* 31 (2004): 419–34.

Owen, J. Judd. *Religion and the Demise of Liberal Rationalism: The Foundational Crisis of the Separation of Church and State.* Chicago: University of Chicago Press, 2001.

Paglia, Camille. "Religion and the Arts in America." *Arion* 15, 1 (2007).

Palmer, G. E. H., Philip Sherrard, and Kallistos Ware, eds. and trans. *Philokalia.* 4 vols. London: Faber and Faber, 1979.

Pamuk, Orhan. "Freedom to Write." *NYRB* 53, 9 (May 25, 2006): 6.

Pantelic, Brataislav. *The Architecture of Decani and the Role of Archbishop Danilo II.* Wiesbaden: Reichert, 2002.

Parish, Helen L. *Monks, Miracles and Magic: Reformation Representations of the Medieval Church.* New York: Routledge, 2005.

Parks, Tim. "The Non-Conformist." *NYRB* 47, 14 (September 21, 2000): 30–35.

———. "Soccer: A Matter of Love and Hate." *NYRB* 49, 12 (July 18, 2002): 38–40.

———. "Tyrol: Retreat to Reality." *NYRB* 51, 9 (May 27, 2004): 50–52.

———. "The Illusionist." *NYRB* 52, 6 (April 7, 2005): 54–58.

———. "The Genius of Bad News." *NYRB* 54, 1 (January 11, 2007): 46–49.

Partner, Peter. *God of Battles: Holy Wars of Christianity and Islam.* Princeton, N.J.: Princeton University Press, 1998.

Passerin d'Entrèves, Maurizio, and Seyla Benhabib, eds. *Habermas and the Unfinished Project of Modernity: Critical Essays on the Philosophical Discourse of Modernity.* Cambridge, Mass.: MIT Press, 1997.

Patterson, Lee. "Chaucer's Pardoner on the Couch: Psyche and Clio in Medieval Literary Studies." *Sp* 76 (2001): 638–80.

Pavlischek, Keith J. "At the Border of Church and State." *FT* 72 (April 1997): 47–50.

Paxton, Robert O. *The Anatomy of Fascism.* New York: Knopf, 2004.

Payne, Stanley. *A History of Fascism: 1914–1945.* Madison: University of Wisconsin Press, 1995.

Pecora, Vincent. *Households of the Soul.* Baltimore: Johns Hopkins University Press, 1997.

Peers, Glenn. *Sacred Shock: Framing Visual Experience in Byzantium.* University Park: Pennsylvania State University Press, 2004.

Péguy, Charles. *Oeuvres en prose,* II. Paris: Gallimard, 1957.

Pelikan, Jaroslav. *Bach among the Theologians.* Philadelphia: Fortress Press, 1986.

Pell, George Cardinal. "The Inconvenient Conscience." *FT* 153 (May 2005): 22–26.

Perl, Jed. *Paris without End: On French Art Since World War I.* San Francisco: North Point Press, 1988.

———. *New Art City.* New York: Knopf, 2005.

Perlman, Jill. *Inventing American Modernism: Joseph Hudnut, Walter Gropius, and the Bauhaus Legacy at Harvard.* Charlottesville: University of Virginia Press, 2007.

Pesmen, Dale. *Russia and Soul: an Exploration.* Ithaca, N.Y.: Cornell University Press, 2000.

Peter Lombard. *The Sentences: Book 1: The Mystery of the Trinity.* Translated by Giulio Silano. Toronto: Pontifical Institute of Medieval Studies, 2007.

Petersen, N. H. "Ritual and Creation: Medieval Liturgy as Foreground and Background for Creation." In *Creations, Medieval Rituals, the Arts, and the Concept of Creation,* edited Sven Rune Havsteen et al. Turnhout: Brepols, 2007.

Pfaff, William. *The Bullet's Song: Romantic Violence and Utopia.* New York: Simon & Schuster, 2004.

———. "France: The Children's Hour." *NYRB* 53, 8 (May 11, 2006): 40–43.

———. "Manifest Destiny: A New Direction for America." *NYRB* 54, 2 (February 15, 2007): 54–59.

Philip, Robert. *Performing Music in the Age of Recording.* New Haven, Conn.: Yale University Press, 2005.

Phillips, Kevin. *Wealth and Democracy: A Political History of the American Rich.* New York: Broadway Books, 2002.

Pickstock, Catherine. *After Writing: On the Liturgical Consummation of Philosophy.* Oxford: Blackwell, 1998.

———. "Music: Soul, City, and Cosmos after Augustine." In *Radical Orthodoxy: A New Theology,* edited by John Milbank et al., 243–77. London: Routledge, 1999.

———. "Medieval Liturgy and Modern Reform." *Antiphon* 6, 1 (2001): 19–25.

Pieper, Josef, *In Tune With the World: A Theory of Festivity*. Translated by Richard and Clara Winston. New York: Harcourt, Brace & World, 1965.

Pike, David L. *Passage through Hell: Modernist Descents, Medieval Underworlds*. Ithaca, N.Y.: Cornell University Press, 1997.

Pinckaers, Servais. *The Sources of Christian Ethics*. Translated by Mary Thomas Noble. Washington, D.C.: The Catholic University of America Press, 1995.

———. *Morality: The Catholic View*. Preface by Alasdair MacIntyre, translated by Michael Sherwin. South Bend, Ind.: St. Augustine's Press, 2001.

———. *The Pinckaers Reader: Renewing Thomistic Moral Theology*. Edited by John Berkman and Craig Steven Titus. Washington, D.C.: The Catholic University of America Press, 2005.

Pippin, Robert B. *Modernism as a Philosophical Problem: On the Dissatisfactions of European High Culture*. 2nd ed. Malden, Mass.: Blackwell, 1999.

Plotinus. *Enneads*. Translated by Stephen MacKenna. 4th ed. London: Faber & Faber, 1969.

Pocock, J. G. A. *Barbarism and Religion*. 4 vols. New York: Cambridge University Press, 1999–2005.

Poewe, Karla. *New Religions and the Nazis*. London: Routledge, 2006.

Polzonetti, Pierpaolo. *Giuseppe Tartini e la musica secondo natura*. Lucca: LIM, 2001.

Poor, Sara S. *Mechthild of Magdeburg and Her Book: Gender and the Making of Textual Authority*. Philadelphia: University of Pennsylvania Press, 2004.

"The Pope at the National Prayer Breakfast." *FT* 104 (June–July 2000): 85–86.

Porter, Glenn. *The Rise of Big Business*. 2nd ed. Wheeling, Ill.: Harlan Davidson, 1992.

Portier, William L. "Americanism and Inculturation: 1899–1999." *Co* 27 (2000): 139–60.

———. "'The Eminent Evangelist from Boston': Father Thomas A. Judge as an Evangelical Catholic." *Co* 30 (2003): 300–19.

———. "Here Come the Evangelical Catholics." *Co* 31 (2004): 35–66.

Posner, Richard A. *Law, Pragmatism, and Democracy*. Cambridge, Mass.: Harvard University Press, 2003.

Post, Gaines. *Studies in Medieval Legal Thought: Public Law and the State, 1100–1322*. Princeton, N.J.: Princeton University Press, 1964.

Postman, Neil. *Building a Bridge to the Eighteenth Century: How the Past Can Improve Our Future*. New York: Knopf, 1999.

Powers, Elizabeth. "The Self in Full." *FT* 97 (November 1999): 21–27.

Powers, Thomas. "An American Tragedy." *NYRB* 52, 14 (September 22, 2005): 73–79.

Prades, Javier. "'From the Economic to the Immanent Trinity': Remarks on a Principle of Renewal in Trinitarian Theology." *Co* 27 (2000): 240–61.

———. "Is God at the Center of Life?" *Co* 30 (2003): 180–208.

Prodi, Paolo. *Una storia della giustizia; Dal pluralismo dei fori al moderno dualismotra coscienza e diritto*. Bologna: Il Mulino, 2000.

Prothero, Stephen. *Religious Literacy: What Every American Needs to Know—And Doesn't*. San Francisco: HarperSanFrancisco, 2007.

Prufer, Thomas. "A Protrepic: What is Philosophy?" *Co* 30 (2003): 337–58.

Putnam, Hilary. *The Threefold Cord: Mind, Body, and World*. New York: Columbia University Press, 1999.

Putnam, Robert D. *Bowling Alone: The Collapse and Revival of American Community*. New York: Simon & Schuster, 2000.

———. *E Pluribus Unum: Diversity and Community in the Twenty-First Century.* Malden, Mass.: Blackwell, 2007.

Quasten, Johannes. *Music and Worship in Pagan and Christian Antiquity.* Translated by Boniface Ramsey. Washington, D.C.: National Association of Pastoral Musicians, 1983.

Quinn, John F. "Why *Is* He a Catholic? Garry Wills' Spiritual Odyssey." *FCSQ* 27, 2 (Summer 2004): 12–23.

Quintavalle, Arturo Carlo. "Il viaggio, l'immagine, l'eresia: la trasformazione del sistema simbolico della Chiesa fra Riforma gregoriana ed eresia catara." In *Arti e storia nel medioevo,* vol. 3: *Del vedere: pubblicii, forme e funzioni,* edited by Enrico Castelnuovo and Giuseppe Sergi, 593–669. Turin: G. Einaudi, 2004.

Rahner, Karl. "Theology and the Arts." *Thought* 65 (1990): 385–99.

Rastall, Richard. *The Heavens Singing: Music in Early English Religious Drama.* Vol. 1. Cambridge: Brewer, 1996.

Reichmann, James B. *Evolution, Animal "Rights," and the Environment.* Washington, D.C.: The Catholic University of America Press, 2000.

Reid, Alcuin. *The Organic Development of the Liturgy: The Principles of Liturgical Reform and their Relation to the Twentieth Century Liturgical Movement Prior to the Second Vatican Council.* San Francisco: Ignatius Press, 2005.

Reid Jr., Charles J. *Power Over the Body, Equality in the Family: Rights and Domestic Relations in Medieval Canon Law.* Grand Rapids, Mich.: Eerdmans, 2004.

Reilly, John J. "Art's Truth." *FT* 141 (March 2004): 49–52.

Reilly, Robert R. "John Nelson: To God Be the Glory." *Crisis* 18, 4 (April 2000): 52–55.

Reiss, Timothy J. *Mirages of the Selfe: Patterns of Personhood in Ancient and Early Modern Europe.* Stanford, Calif.: Stanford University Press, 2003.

Renaut, Alain. *The Era of the Individual: A Contribution to a History of Subjectivity.* Translated by M. B. DeBevoise and Franklin Philip, with a foreword by Alexander Nehamas. Princeton, N.J.: Princeton University Press, 1997.

Reno, R. R. *In the Ruins of the Church: Sustaining Faith in an Age of Diminished Christianity.* Grand Rapids, Mich.: Brazos Press, 2002.

———. "The Great Delayer." *FT* 145 (August/September 2004): 63–69.

———. "The End of Criticism." *IR* 42, 1 (Spring 2007): 42–46.

———. "Theology After the Revolution." *FT* 173 (May 2007): 15–21.

Repp, Kevin. *Reformers, Critics, and the Paths of German Modernity: Anti-Politics and the Search for Alternatives, 1890–1914.* Cambridge, Mass.: Harvard University Press, 2000.

Réville, Albert. *Prolegomena of the History of Religions.* Translated by A. S. Squire. London: Williams and Norgate, 1884.

Rex, Richard. *The Theology of John Fisher.* New York: Cambridge University Press, 1991.

Rey García, Emilio. "Algunos Aspectos de la Vida Musical Hispánica en la Edad Media." In *Vida Cotidiana en la España Medieval,* 85–106. Aguilar de Campóo: Fundación Sta. María la Real, Centro de Estudios del Románico, 1998.

Reynolds, David. *One World Divisible: A Global History since 1945.* New York: W. W. Norton, 2000.

Rhonheimer, Martin. "The Holocaust: What Was Not Said." *FT* 137 (November 2003): 18–27.

Ribuffo, Leo P. "The American Catholic Church and Ordered Liberty." *HS* (September/October 2004): 26–28.

Ricoeur, Paul. *History and Truth.* Translated, with an introduction, by Charles A. Kelbley. Evanston, Ill.: Northwestern University Press, 1965.

Rieff, Philip. *Freud: The Mind of the Moralist.* Chicago: University of Chicago Press, 1979.

———. *My Life Among the Deathworks: Illustrations of the Aesthetics of Authority.* Charlottesville: University of Virginia Press, 2006.

———. *Sacred Order/Social Order,* vol. 2: *The Crisis of the Officer Class, the Decline of the Tragic Sensibility.* Charlottesville: University of Virginia Press, 2007.

Rieger, Matthias. *Helmholtz Musicus: Die Objektivierung der Musik im 19. Jh. durch Helmholtz' Lehre von den Tonempfindungen.* Darmstadt: Wissenschaftliche Buchgesellschaft, 2006.

Ries, Julien. *Il mito e il suo significato.* Milan: Jaca Book, 2005. Translation of French original.

Riklin, Alois. *Machtteilung: Geschichte der Mischverfassung.* Darmstadt: Wissenschaftliche Buchgesellschaft, 2006.

Riquer, Borja de, et al. *Modernismo: Architecture and Design in Catalonia.* New York: Monacelli Press, 2003.

Rist, John M. *Real Ethics: Rethinking the Foundations of Morality.* Cambridge: Cambridge University Press, 2002.

Rivera Rivera, Mayna. "Radical Transcendence? Divine and Human Otherness in Radical Orthodoxy and Liberation Theology." In *Interpreting the Postmodern: Responses to "Radical Orthodoxy,"* edited by Rosemary Radford Ruether and Marion Grau, 119–38. New York: T & T Clark, 2006.

Robb, Graham. *The Discovery of France: A Historical Geography from the Revolution to the First World War.* New York: W. W. Norton, 2007.

Roberts, Jennifer Tolbert. *Athens on Trial: The Antidemocratic Tradition in Western Thought.* Princeton, N.J.: Princeton University Press, 1996.

Roberts, Jon H. "'The Idea that Wouldn't Die': The Warfare between Science and Christianity." *HS* 4, 3 (February 2003): 21–24.

Robichaud, Paul. *Making the Past Present: David Jones, the Middle Ages, and Modernism.* Washington, D.C.: The Catholic University of America Press, 2007.

Robinson, William H., et al. *Barcelona and Modernity: Picasso, Gaudi, Miro, Dali.* New Haven, Conn.: Yale University Press, 2006.

Rodenbeck, Max. "Witch Hunt in Egypt." *NYRB* 47, 19 (November 16, 2000): 39–41.

———. "Islam Confronts Its Demons." *NYRB* 51, 7 (April 29, 2004): 14–18.

Rose, Michael S. *Ugly as Sin: Why They Changed Our Churches from Sacred Places to Meeting Spaces—and How We Can Change Them Back Again.* Manchester, N.H.: Sophia Institute Press, 2001.

———. *In Tiers of Glory: The Organic Development of Church Architecture Through the Ages.* Cincinnati: Mesa Folio Editions, 2004.

———. "The Wisdom of Hindsight." *AB* 10, 8 (November 2004): 6–7.

Rosen, Charles. "The Future of Music." *NYRB* 48, 20 (December 20, 2001): 60–65.

———. "Should We Adore Adorno?" *NYRB* 49, 16 (October 24, 2002): 59–66.

———. "Culture on the Market." *NYRB* 50, 17 (November 6, 2003): 70–73.

———. "Playing Music: The Lost Freedom." *NYRB* 52, 17 (November 3, 2005): 47–50.

———. "From the Troubadours to Frank Sinatra, Parts I and II." *NYRB* 53, 4 and 6 (February 23 and March 9, 2006): 41–45, 44–48.

———. "The Best Book on Mozart." *NYRB* 54, 16 (October 25, 2007): 25–27.

——— and Henri Zerner. "Red-Hot MoMA." *NYRB* 52, 1 (January 13, 2005): 18–21.

Rosenwein, Barbara H. "Worrying about Emotions in History." *AHR* 107 (2002): 821–45.

Rosponi, Cristiano, and Giampaolo Rossi. *Reconquistare lo spazio sacro: riscoprire la tradizione nell'architetura liturgica del XX secolo.* Rome: Editrice Il bosco e la nave, 1999.

———, with Duncan Stroik. *Reconquistare lo spazio sacro: la chiesa nella città del terzo millennio.* Rome: Editrice Il bosco e la nave, 2000.

Ross, Alex. *The Rest Is Noise: Listening to the Twentieth Century.* New York: Farrar, Straus and Giroux, 2007.

Ross, Ronald J. *The Failure of Bismarck's Kulturkampf: Catholicism and State Power in Imperial Germany, 1871–1887.* Washington, D.C.: The Catholic University of America Press, 1998.

Rowland, Ingrid. "Eastern Glory." *NYRB* 51, 9 (May 27, 2004): 23–25.

———. "The Magician." *NYRB* 51, 20 (December 16, 2004): 16–20.

Rowland, Tracey. *Culture and the Thomist Tradition after Vatican II.* London: Routledge, 2003.

Rubenstein, Jay. *Guibert of Nogent: Portrait of a Medieval Mind.* New York: Routledge, 2002.

Ruddy, Christopher. "Heroism, Hospitality, and Holiness: Generational Perspectives on the Church-World Relationship." *Lo* 7, 1 (2004): 45–62.

Rudolph, Conrad. *Artistic Change at St.-Denis: Abbot Suger's Program and the Early Twelfth-Century Controversy over Art.* Princeton, N.J.: Princeton University Press, 1990.

———. *The "Things of Greater Importance": Bernard of Clairvaux's Apologia and the Medieval Attitude toward Art.* Philadelphia: University of Pennsylvania Press, 1990.

———. *"First, I Find the Center Point": Reading the Text of Hugh of Saint Victor's The Mystic Ark.* Philadelphia: American Philosophical Society, 2004.

———. "La resistenza all'arte nell'Occidente." In *Arti e storia nel medioevo,* vol. 3: *Del vedere: pubblici, forme e funzioni,* edited by Enrico Castelnuovo and Giuseppe Sergi, 49–84. Turin: G. Einaudi, 2004.

———. "A Sense of Loss: An Overview of the Historiography of Romanesque and Gothic Art." In *A Companion to Medieval Art,* edited by Conrad Rudolph, 295–313. Oxford: Blackwell, 2006.

Ruiz, Teofilo F. *From Heaven to Earth: The Reordering of Castilian Society, 1150–1350.* Princeton, N.J.: Princeton University Press, 2004.

Russell, Jeffrey Burton. *A History of Heaven: The Singing Silence.* Princeton, N.J.: Princeton University Press, 1997.

Russell, Norman. *The Doctrine of Deification in the Greek Patristic Tradition.* Oxford: Oxford University Press, 2005.

Ruthven, Malise. "The Islamic Optimist." *NYRB* 54, 13 (August 16, 2007): 61–65.

Ryan, Alan. "My Way." *NYRB* 47, 13 (August 10, 2000): 47–50.

———. "Live and Let Live." *NYRB* 48, 8 (May 17, 2001): 54–56.

———. "The Group." *NYRB* 48, 9 (May 31, 2001): 16–20.

———. "The Power of Positive Thinking." *NYRB* 50, 1 (January 16, 2003): 43–46.

————. "The Way to Reason." *NYRB* 50, 19 (December 4, 2003): 43–45.

————. "Time Out?" *NYRB* 51, 16 (October 21, 2004): 51–53.

————. "Faith-Based History." *NYRB* 51, 19 (December 2, 2004): 22–24.

————. "Freedom Fighter." *NYRB* 52, 5 (March 26, 2005): 40–43.

Rybczynski, Witold. *The Look of Architecture.* New York: Oxford University Press, 2001.

————. "The Triumph of a Distinguished Failure." *NYRB* 51, 16 (October 21, 2004): 30–32.

————. "Genius in Concrete." *NYRB* 54, 8 (May 10, 2007): 34–36.

Rychlak, Ronald J. "Goldhagen v. Pius XII." *FT* 124 (June/July 2002): 37–54.

Sagan, Eli. *Citizens and Cannibals: The French Revolution, the Struggle for Modernity, and the Origins of Ideological Terror.* Lanham, Md.: Rowman & Littlefield, 2001.

Samons, Loren J., II. *What's Wrong with Democracy? From Athenian Practice to American Worship.* Berkeley: University of California Press, 2004.

Samuelsson, Kurt. *Religion and Economic Action: The Protestant Ethic, the Rise of Capitalism, and the Abuses of Scholarship.* Translated by E. Geoffrey French, edited by D. C. Coleman. Toronto: University of Toronto Press, 1993.

Sandel, Michael J. *Liberalism and the Limits of Justice.* 2nd ed. New York: Cambridge University Press, 1998.

————. *The Case Against Perfection: Ethics in the Age of Genetic Engineering.* Cambridge, Mass.: Belknap Press, 2007.

Sarna, Jonathan D. "American Judaism in Historical Perspective." *HS* 5, 5 (May/June 2004): 11–15.

Sauerländer, Willibald. "The Great Outsider: Meyer Schapiro." In *Romanesque Art: Problems and Monuments.* 2 vols., II, 833–49. London: Pindar, 2004.

————. "The Artist Historian." *NYRB* 54, 11 (June 28, 2007): 55–62.

Scaperlanda, Michael A., and Teresa Collett, eds. *Recovering Self-Evident Truths: Catholic Perspectives on American Law.* Washington, D.C.: The Catholic University of America Press, 2006.

Scarry, Elaine. *On Beauty and Being Just.* Princeton, N.J.: Princeton University Press, 1999.

Schaefer, Edward E. "The Expressive and Formative Roles of Music: A Search for Balance in Liturgical Reform." *Antiphon* 7, 2 (2002): 21–36.

Schall, James V. "Structures of Evil—Structures of Good: On the Centrality of Personal Sin." *FCSQ* 32, 1 (Winter 2000): 7–14.

Schapiro, Meyer. "On the Aesthetic Attitude in Romanesque Art." In *Romanesque Art,* 1–27. New York: George Braziller, 1977.

————. *Romanesque Architectural Sculpture.* Edited by Linda Seidel. Chicago: University of Chicago Press, 2006.

Schatz, Adam. "In Search of Hezbollah." *NYRB* 51, 7 (April 29, 2004): 41–44.

Scherzberg, Lucia. *Kirchenreform mit Hilfe des Nationalsozialismus: Karl Adam als kontextueller Theologe.* Darmstadt: Wissenschaftliche Buchgesellschaft, 2001.

Schindler, David C. "Toward a Non-Possessive Concept of Knowledge: On the Relation Between Reason and Love in Aquinas and Balthasar." *MT* 22, 4 (October 2006): 577–607.

Schindler, David L. "Sanctity and the Intellectual Life." *Co* 20 (1993): 652–752.

————. "The Meaning of the Human in a Technological Age: *Homo Faber, Homo Sapiens, Homo amans.*" *Co* 26 (1999): 80–104.

———. "Homelessness and the Modern Condition: The Family, Evangelization, and the Global Economy." *Lo* 3, 4 (Fall 2000): 34–56.

———. "Creation and Nuptiality: A Reflection on Feminism in Light of Schmemann's Liturgical Theology." *Co* 28 (2001): 265–95.

———. "Toward a Culture of Life: The Eucharist, the 'Restoration' of Creation, and the 'Worldly' Task of the Laity in Liberal Societies." *Co* 29, 1 (2002): 679–90.

———. "The Significance of World and Culture for Moral Theology." *Co* 31 (2004): 111–42.

Schlesinger Jr., Arthur. *War and the American Presidency.* New York: W. W. Norton, 2004.

———. "The Making of a Mess." *NYRB* 51, 14 (September 23, 2004): 40–43.

———. "History and National Stupidity." *NYRB* 53, 7 (April 27, 2006): 14–16.

———. "The Turning Point." *NYRB* 54, 15 (October 11, 2007): 10–12.

Schmemann, Alexander. *For the Life of the World: Sacraments and Orthodoxy.* Crestwood, N.Y.: St. Vladimir's Seminary Press, 1982.

———. *The Eucharist: Sacrament of the Kingdom.* Crestwood, N.Y.: St. Vladimir's Seminary Press, 1987.

Schmidt, Dennis. *On Germans and Other Greeks: Tragedy and Ethical Life.* Bloomington: Indiana University Press, 2001.

Schmidt, Hans-Joachim, ed. *Tradition, Innovation, Invention. Fortschrittsverweigerung und Fortschrittsbewusstsein im Mittelalter.* Berlin: De Gruyter, 2005.

Schmitt, Carl. *The Challenge of Carl Schmitt.* Edited by Chantal Mouffe. New York: Verso, 1999.

Schmitz, Kenneth. "To Father Norris Clarke in Appreciation." *Co* 31 (2004): 447–56.

Scholes, Robert. *Paradoxy of Modernism.* New Haven, Conn.: Yale University Press, 2006.

Schorske, Carl E. *Thinking with History: Explorations in the Passage to Modernism.* Princeton, N.J.: Princeton University Press, 1998.

Schotte, Jan Cardinal. 1999 Commencement Address at Thomas Aquinas College in California. *Thomas Aquinas College Newsletter,* Summer 1999.

Schrag, Peter, and Stephan Thernstrom. "'Must Schools Fail?' An Exchange." *NYRB* 52, 3 (February 24, 2004).

Schuessler, Jennifer. "The Terrified Copyist." *NYRB* 53, 16 (October 19, 2006): 18.

Schulz, Michael. "'Fallen' Nature: How Sin Affects the Creation." *Co* 29 (2002): 490–505.

Schwartz, Adam. "Swords of Honor: The Revival of Orthodox Christianity in Twentieth-Century Britain." *Lo* 4, 1 (2001): 11–31.

———. *The Third Spring: G. K. Chesterton, Graham Greene, Christopher Dawson, and David Jones.* Washington, D.C.: The Catholic University of America Press, 2005.

Schwartz, Sanford. "The Devil and Giacometti." *NYRB* 49, 1 (January 17, 2002): 22–24.

———. "Ladies in Satin." *NYRB* 52, 2 (February 10, 2005): 8–11.

———. "White Secrets." *NYRB* 53, 2 (February 9, 2006): 8–9.

Scott, Joan Wallach. *The Politics of the Veil.* Princeton, N.J.: Princeton University Press, 2007.

Scruton, Roger. *The West and the Rest: Globalization and Terrorist Threat.* Wilmington, Del.: ISI Books, 2002.

———. "Regaining My Religion." In Roger Scruton, *Gentle Regrets: Thoughts from a Life*. New York: Continuum, 2005.

Seabright, Paul. "The Road Upward." *NYRB* 48, 5 (March 26, 2001): 41–43.

Seasoltz, R. Kevin. *A Sense of the Sacred: Theological Foundations of Christian Architecture and Art*. New York: Continuum, 2005.

Sebastian, Santiago. *Mensaje Simbólico del Arte Medieval. Arquitectura, Liturgia e Iconografía*. Madrid: Encuentro Ediciones, 1994.

Seidel, Linda. "Introduction." In Meyer Schapiro, *Romanesque Architectural Sculpture,* edited by Linda Seidel. Chicago: University of Chicago Press, 2006.

Seixas, Peter. "Collective Memory, History Education, and Historical Consciousness." *HS* 7, 2 (November/December 2005): 17–19.

Seligman, Adam B. *Modernity's Wager: Authority, the Self, and Transcendence*. Princeton, N.J.: Princeton University Press, 2000.

Sen, Amartya. "East and West: The Reach of Reason." *NYRB* 47, 12 (July 20, 2000): 33–38.

Sequeri, Pier Angelo. *L'estro di Dio: saggio e estetica*. Milan: Glossa, 2000.

Servais, Jacques. "Finding God in All Things." *Co* 30 (2003): 260–81.

Severino, Emanuele. *La filosofia antica*. Milan: Rizzoli, 1984.

Shagan, Ethan H. *Popular Politics and the English Reformation*. New York: Cambridge University Press, 2003.

Shain, Barry Alan. *The Myth of American Individualism: The Protestant Origins of American Political Thought*. Princeton, N.J.: Princeton University Press, 1994.

Shannon, Christopher. *Conspicuous Criticism: Tradition, the Individual, and Culture in American Social Thought, from Veblen to Mills*. Baltimore: Johns Hopkins University Press, 1996.

———. "Catholicism as the Other." *FT* 139 (January, 2004): 46–52.

Shattuck, Roger. *Forbidden Knowledge: from Prometheus to Pornography*. New York: St. Martin's Press, 1996.

———. "Decline and Fall?" *NYRB* 47, 11 (June 29, 2000): 55–58.

Shawn, Allen. *Arnold Schoenberg's Journey*. New York: Farrar, Straus and Giroux, 2002.

Sheehan, James J. "The Problem of Sovereignty in European History." *AHR* 111 (2006): 1–15.

Sherrard, Philip. "The Desanctification of Nature." In *Sanctity and Secularity: The Church and the World,* edited by Derek Baker, 1–20. Oxford: Blackwell, 1973.

———. *The Sacred In Life and Art*. Ipswich, England: Golgonooza Press, 1990.

———. *Human Image, World Image: The Death and Resurrection of Sacred Cosmology*. Ipswich, England: Golgonooza Press, 1992.

Shivanandan, Mary. "Body Narratives: Language of Truth?" *Lo* 3, 3 (Summer 2000): 166–93.

Shults, F. LeRon, ed. *The Evolution of Rationality: Interdisciplinary Essays in Honor of J. Wentzel van Huyssteen*. Grand Rapids, Mich.: Eerdmans, 2005.

Simic, Charles. "Paradise Lost." *NYRB* 48, 14 (September 20, 2001): 62–64.

———. "A World Gone Up in Smoke." *NYRB* 48, 20 (December 20, 2001): 14–18.

———. "Difference in Similarity." *NYRB* 51, 4 (March 11, 2004): 21–23.

———. "The Memory Piano." *NYRB* 52, 3 (February 24, 2005): 39–41.

———. "The Powers of Invention." *NYRB* 53, 4 (March 6, 2006): 10–14.

———. "The Power of Ruins." *NYRB* 53, 11 (June 22, 2006): 16–19.

———. "Making It New." *NYRB* 53, 13 (August 10, 2006): 10–13.

Simpson, James. *The Oxford English Literary History,* vol. 2, *1350–1547: Reform and Cultural Revolution.* New York: Oxford University Press, 2002.

———. *Burning to Read: English Fundamentalism and Its Reformation Opposition.* Cambridge, Mass.: Belknap Press, 2007.

Singer, David. "For Torah and Culture." *FT* 153 (May 2005): 27–32.

Slaughter, Anne-Marie. *A New World Order.* Princeton, N.J.: Princeton University Press, 2004.

Smith, Anthony D. *Chosen Peoples: Sacred Sources of National Identity.* New York: Oxford University Press, 2003.

Smith, Christian, ed. *The Secular Revolution: Power, Interests, and Conflict in the Secularization of American Public Life.* Berkeley: University of California Press, 2003.

Smith, Christine, et al. *Before and After the End of Time: Architecture and the Year 1000.* New York: Harvard Design School/George Braziller, 2000.

Smith, Huston. *Essays on World Religion.* New York: Paragon House, 1992.

Smith, Jeffrey Chipps. *Sensuous Worship: Jesuits and the Art of the Early Catholic Reformation in Germany.* Princeton, N.J.: Princeton University Press, 2002.

Smith, Neil. *The Endgame of Globalization.* New York: Routledge, 2005.

Smith, Ryan K. *Gothic Arches, Latin Crosses: Anti-Catholicism and American Church Designs in the Nineteenth Century.* Chapel Hill: University of North Carolina Press, 2006.

Smith, Steven D. *Getting over Equality: A Critical Diagnosis of Religious Freedom in America.* New York: New York University Press, 2001.

Soergel, Philip M. "Ritual and Faith Formation in Early Modern Catholic Europe." In *Educating People of Faith: Exploring the History of Jewish and Christian Communities,* edited by John Van Engen, 314–29. Grand Rapids, Mich.: Eerdmans, 2004.

Sokolowski, Robert. *The God of Faith and Reason: Foundations of Christian Theology.* With a new preface. Washington, D.C.: The Catholic University of America Press, 1995.

———. "The Eucharist and Transubstantiation." *Co* 24 (1997): 867–80.

———. *Christian Faith and Human Understanding: Studies on the Eucharist, Trinity, and the Human Person.* Washington, D.C.: The Catholic University of America Press, 2006.

Soloveitchik, Joseph B.. "Majesty and Humility." *Tradition* 17 (Spring 1978): 25–37.

Sorabji, Richard. *Emotion and Peace of Mind: From Stoic Agitation to Christian Temptation.* New York: Oxford University Press, 2000.

Soros, George. *George Soros on Globalization.* New York: Public Affairs, 2002.

Soufas, C. Christopher. *The Subject in Question: Early Contemporary Spanish Literature and Modernism.* Washington, D.C.: The Catholic University of America Press, 2007.

Spence, Jonathan. "The Whole World in Their Hands." *NYRB* 50, 15 (October 9, 2003): 35.

Spinner-Halev, Jeff. *Surviving Diversity: Religion and Democratic Citizenship.* Baltimore: Johns Hopkins University Press, 2000.

Spitzer, Leo. *Classical and Christian Ideas of World Harmony.* Edited by Anna Hatcher. Baltimore: Johns Hopkins University Press, 1963.

Spurlling, Hilary. "Matisse's Pajamas." *NYRB* 52, 13 (August 11, 2005): 33–36.

Steel, Ronald. "Mr. Fix-It." *NYRB* 47, 15 (October 5, 2000): 19–21.

———. "The Missionary." *NYRB* 50, 18 (November 20, 2003): 26–35.

———. "George Kennan at 100." *NYRB* 51, 7 (April 29, 2004): 8–9.

———. "Where It Began." *NYRB* 51, 14 (September 23, 2004): 58–61.

Steiner, Wendy. *Venus in Exile: The Rejection of Beauty in Twentieth-Century Art.* New York: Free Press, 2001.

Steinmetz, David C. "Luther and Formation in Faith." In *Educating People of Faith: Exploring the History of Jewish and Christian Communities,* edited by John Van Engen, 253–69. Grand Rapids, Mich.: Eerdmans, 2004.

Sternhell, Zeev. *Neither Right nor Left: Fascist Ideology in France.* Berkeley: University of California Press, 1986.

———, with Mario Sznajder and Maia Asheri. *The Birth of Fascist Ideology: From Cultural Rebellion to Political Revolution.* Translated by David Maisel. Princeton, N.J.: Princeton University Press, 1994.

Stiglitz, Joseph E. "A Fair Deal for the World." *NYRB* 49, 9 (May 23, 2002): 24–28.

———. *Globalization and Its Discontents.* New York: W. W. Norton, 2002.

Stille, Alexander. "Apocalypse Soon." *NYRB* 49, 17 (November 7, 2002): 47.

Stimpson, Emily. "Civilization in Crisis: The Loss of Faith in Western Europe." *Franciscan Way* (Autumn 2006): 14–15.

Stock, Brian. *Myth and Science in the Twelfth Century: A Study of Bernard Silvester.* Princeton, N.J.: Princeton University Press, 1972.

———. *Augustine the Reader: Meditation, Self-Knowledge, and the Ethics of Interpretation.* Cambridge, Mass.: Belknap Press, 1996.

Stocken, Frederick. "Music as a Christian Art." *SS* 5 (2004): 55–59.

Stone, Maria Susan. *The Patron State: Culture and Politics in Fascist Italy.* Princeton, N.J.: Princeton University Press, 1998.

Storck, Thomas. *Foundations of a Catholic Political Order.* Beltsville, Md.: Four Faces Press, 1998.

Storr, Robert. *Modern Art Despite Modernism.* New York: Museum of Modern Art, 2000.

Stout, Jeffrey. *Democracy and Tradition.* Princeton, N.J.: Princeton University Press, 2004.

Strauss, Barry. "The Rebirth of Narrative." *HS* 6, 6 (July/August 2005): 2–5.

Strauss, Leo. *Natural Right and History.* Chicago: University of Chicago Press, 2000.

Stroik, Duncan G. "One Step Forward: An Analysis of *Built of Living Stones.*" *SA* 8 (2003): 20–24.

Sturzo, Luigi. *Church and State.* 2 vols. Translated by A. Robert Caponigri. Notre Dame, Ind.: University of Notre Dame Press, 1962.

Suger. *Abbot Suger: On the Abbey Church of St. Denis and Its Art Treasures.* Edited by Erwin Panofsky. Princeton, N.J.: Princeton University Press, 1946.

Sullivan, Jem. "The Beauty of Faith: Sacred Architecture and Catechesis." *SA* 11 (2006): 12–14.

Sullivan, John. "Reading Habits, Scripture and the University." In *The Bible and the University,* edited by David Lyle Jeffrey and C. Stephen Evans, 216–39. Grand Rapids, Mich.: Zondervan, 2007.

Sullivan, Winnifred Fallers. *The Impossibility of Religious Freedom.* Princeton, N.J.: Princeton University Press, 2005.

Sunstein, Cass. *The Partial Constitution.* Cambridge, Mass.: Harvard University Press, 1993.

Sweetman, Brendan, ed. *The Failure of Modernism: The Cartesian Legacy and Contemporary Pluralism.* Mishawaka, Ind.: American Maritain Association, 1999.

Taft, Robert F. *The Liturgy of the Hours in East and West: The Origin of the Divine Office and its Meaning for Today.* Collegeville, Minn.: Liturgical Press, 1993.

———. "'Eastern Presuppositions' and Western Liturgical Renewal." *Antiphon* 5, 1 (2000): 10–22.

———. *Beyond East and West: Problems in Liturgical Understanding.* 2nd ed. Rome: Edizioni Orientalia Christiana, Pontifical Oriental Institute, 2001.

Talmon, Shemaryahu. *The World of Qumran from Within: Collected Studies.* Jerusalem: Magnes Press, 1989.

Tammen, Björn R. *Musik und Bild im Chorraum mittelalterlicher Kirchen, 1100–1500.* Berlin: Reimer, 2000.

Tanner, Marcus. *Ireland's Holy Wars: The Struggle for a Nations' Soul, 1500–2000.* New Haven, Conn.: Yale University Press, 2001.

Tanner, Norman, and Sethina Watson. "Least of the Laity: the Minimum Requirements for a Medieval Christian." *Journal of Medieval History* 32 (2006): 395–423.

Tarragó, Rafael E. "Bloody Bess: The Persecution of Catholics in Elizabethan England." *Lo* 7, 1 (Winter 2004): 117–33.

Tavener, John. *The Music of Silence: A Composer's Testament.* Edited by Brian Keeble. London: Faber and Faber, 1999.

Taylor, Charles. *A Catholic Modernity? Charles Taylor's Marianist Award Lecture.* Edited by James L. Heft. New York: Oxford University Press, 1999.

———. *Varieties of Religion Today: William James Revisited.* Cambridge, Mass.: Harvard University Press, 2002.

———. "A Different Kind of Courage." *NYRB* 54, 7 (April 26, 2007): 4–8.

———. *A Secular Age.* Cambridge, Mass.: Harvard University Press, 2007.

Taylor, Mark C. *Disfiguring: Art, Architecture, Religion.* Chicago: University of Chicago Press, 1992.

Teachout, Terry. *A Terry Teachout Reader.* New Haven, Conn.: Yale University Press, 2004.

Tentler, Leslie Woodcock. *Catholics and Contraception: An American History.* Ithaca, N.Y.: Cornell University Press, 2004.

———, ed. *The Church Confronts Modernity: Catholicism since 1950 in the United States, Ireland, and Quebec.* Washington, D.C.: The Catholic University of America Press, 2007.

Teusch, Ulrich. *Was ist Globalisierung? Ein Überblick.* Darmstadt: Wissenschaftliche Buchgesellschaft, 2004.

Thiemann, Ronald F. *Religion in Public Life: A Dilemma for Democracy.* Washington, D.C.: Georgetown University Press, 1996.

Thompson, Augustine. *Cities of God: The Religion of the Italian Communes, 1125–1325.* University Park: Pennsylvania State University Press, 2005.

Thümmel, Hans Georg. *Die Konzilien zur Bilderfrage im 8. und 9. Jarhhundert: Das 7. Ökumenische Konzil in Nikaia 787.* Paderborn: Ferdinand Schöningh, 2005.

Tierney, Brian. *The Idea of Natural Rights: Studies on Natural Rights, Natural Law, and Church Law, 1150–1625.* Atlanta: Scholars Press, 1997.

———. "Dominion of Self and Natural Rights before Locke and After." In *Transformations in Medieval and Early-Modern Rights Discourse,* edited by Virpi Mäkinen and Petter Korkman, 173–203. Dordrecht: Springer, 2006.

Tinder, Glenn. "The Anti-Gnostic." *FT* 128 (December 2002): 47–51.

Tingley, Edward. "Gadamer & the Light of the Word." *FT* 139 (January, 2004): 38–45.

Todd, Emmanuel. *After the Empire: The Breakdown of the American Order.* New York: Columbia University Press, 2003.

Todorov, Tzvetan. *Hope and Memory: Lessons from the Twentieth Century.* Translated by David Bellos. Princeton, N.J.: Princeton University Press, 2003.

Tóibin, Colm. "Henry James's New York." *NYRB* 53, 2 (February 9, 2006): 33–37.

———. "A Thousand Prayers." *NYRB* 53, 19 (November 30, 2006): 50–53.

Tonsor, Stephen J. *Equality, Decadence, and Modernity: The Collected Essays of Stephen J. Tonsor.* Edited by Gregory L. Schneider. Wilmington, Del.: ISI Books, 2005.

Torevell, David. *Losing the Sacred: Ritual, Modernity, and Liturgical Reform.* Edinburgh: T & T Clark, 2000.

Torgerson, Mark A. *An Architecture of Immanence: Architecture for Worship and Ministry Today.* Grand Rapids, Mich.: Eerdmans, 2007.

Tracy, David. *The Analogical Imagination: Christian Theology and the Culture of Pluralism.* New York: Crossroad, 1981.

Tracy, James D. "Believers, Non-Believers, and the Historian's Unspoken Assumptions." *CHR* 86 (2000): 403–19.

Trapp, Waldemar. *Vorgeschichte und Ursprung der liturgischen Bewegung: vorwiegend in Hinsicht auf das deutsche Sprachgebiet.* Würzburg: R. Mayr, 1939.

Traub, James. "Sierra Leone: The Worst Place on Earth." *NYRB* 47, 11 (June 29, 2000): 61–66.

Treadgold, Warren. "Imaginary Early Christianity." *International History Review* 15 (1993): 535–45.

———. "Taking Sources on their Own Terms and on Ours: Peter Brown's Late Antiquity." *Antiquité Tardive* 2 (1994): 153–59.

Treitel, Corinna. *A Science for the Soul: Occultism and the Genesis of the German Modern.* Baltimore: Johns Hopkins University Press, 2004.

Treitler, Leo. "Written Music and Oral Music: Improvisation in Medieval Performance." In *El Códice Calixtino y la música de su tiempo,* edited by José López-Calo and Carlos Villanueva, 113–34. A Coruña: Fundación Pedro Barrié de la Maza, 2001.

Tribe, Shawn. "'The Genius of the Roman Liturgy' CIEL Colloquium 2006." *Antiphon* 10 (2006): 314–22.

Turner, James. *Without God, Without Creed: The Origins of Unbelief in America.* Baltimore: Johns Hopkins University Press, 1985.

Tyerman, Christopher. *God's War: A New History of the Crusades.* Cambridge, Mass.: Belknap Press, 2006.

Uhalde, Kevin. *Expectations of Justice in the Age of Augustine.* Philadelphia: University of Pennsylvania Press, 2007.

Uhlmann, Michael M. "The Supreme Court Rules." *FT* 136 (October 2003): 26–35.

Updike, John. "A Wistful Master." *NYRB* 47, 6 (April 13, 2000): 18–20.

———. "The Thing Itself." *NYRB* 48, 19 (November 19, 2001): 10–12.

———. "Singular in Everything." *NYRB* 50, 17 (November 6, 2003): 14–18.

———. "Determined Spirit." *NYRB* 52, 19 (December 1, 2005): 13–14.

Urquhart, Brian. "'A Great Day in History.'" *NYRB* 51, 1 (January 15, 2004): 8–10.

Valliere, Paul. *Modern Russian Theology: Bukharev, Soloviev, Bulgakov: Orthodox Theology in a New Key.* Grand Rapids, Mich.: Eerdmans, 2000.

Vanderburg, William H. *Living in the Labyrinth of Technology.* Toronto: University of Toronto Press, 2005.

Van der Laan, Hans. *The Play of Forms: Nature, Culture, and Liturgy.* Leiden: Brill, 2005.

Van der Veer, Peter. *Conversion to Modernities: The Globalization of Christianity.* New York: Routledge, 1995.

Van Dülmen, Richard, ed. *Entdeckung des Ich: Die Geschichte der Individualisierung vom Mittelalter bis zur Gegenwart.* Cologne: Böhlau, 2001.

Van Engen, John. "Introduction: Formative Religious Practices in Premodern European Life." In *Educating People of Faith: Exploring the History of Jewish and Christian Communities,* edited by John Van Engen, 1–26. Grand Rapids, Mich.: Eerdmans, 2004.

Van Hove, Brian. "Reflections on *Toward Ritual Transformation: Remembering Robert Hovda.*" *FCSQ* 27, 1 (Summer 2004): 3–11.

Van Huyssteen, J. Wentzel. *Alone in the World? Human Uniqueness in Science and Theology.* Grand Rapids, Mich.: Eerdmans, 2007.

Varnedoe, Kirk. *Pictures of Nothing: Abstract Art since Pollock.* Princeton, N.J.: Princeton University Press, 2006.

Vasoli, R. H. *What God Has Joined Together: The Annulment Crisis in American Catholicism.* New York: Oxford University Press, 1998.

Vattimo, Gianni. *After Christianity.* Translated by Luca D'Isanto. New York: Columbia University Press, 2002.

Velkely, Richard L. *Being After Rousseau: Philosophy and Culture in Question.* Chicago: University of Chicago Press, 2002.

Vella, John M. "The Jesuits and Political Power." *MA* 48, 2 (Spring 2006): 158–163.

Verbaal, W. "Invocatio musae: Inspired by the Muse, the Inescapable Reality." In *Creations, Medieval Rituals, the Arts, and the Concept of Creation,* edited by Sven Rune Havsteen et al. Turnhout: Brepols, 2007.

Vergo, Peter. *That Divine Order: Music and Visual Arts from Antiquity to the Eighteenth Century.* New York: Phaidon, 2005.

Versfeld, Martin. *The Perennial Order.* London: Society of St. Paul, 1954.

Vico, Giambattista. *The New Science of Giambattista Vico.* Translated from the 3rd ed. (1744) by Thomas Goddard Bergin and Max Harold Fisch. Ithaca, N.Y.: Cornell University Press, 1948.

Vidmar, John. *The Catholic Church Through the Ages: A History.* New York: Paulist Press, 2005.

Vietta, Silvio, and Herbert Uerlings, eds. *Ästhetik und Säkularisierung,* I: *Von der Renaissance zur Romantik.* Munich: Wilhelm Fink, 2008.

Virilio, Paul. *Art and Fear.* Translated by Julie Rose. New York: Continuum, 2003.

———. *The Paul Virilio Reader.* Edited by Steve Redhead. New York: Columbia University Press, 2004.

———. *City of Panic.* Translated by Julie Rose. New York: Oxford University Press, 2005.

Voegelin, Eric. *The Ecumenic Age.* Baton Rouge: Louisiana State University Press, 1974.

———. *Conversations with Eric Voegelin.* Edited by R. Eric O'Connor. Montreal: Thomas More Institute, 1980.

———. *Modernity without Restraint: The Political Religions, The New Science of*

Politics and Science, Politics, and Gnosticism. Edited by Manfred Henningsen. Columbia: University of Missouri Press, 2000.

Von Balthasar, Hans Urs. *Love Alone: The Way of Revelation.* London: Burns & Oates, 1968.

———. *Love Alone.* Translated by Alexander Dru. New York: Herder and Herder, 1969.

———. *The von Balthasar Reader.* Edited by Medard Kehl and Werner Loser. New York: Crossroad, 1982.

———. *The Glory of the Lord: A Theological Aesthetics.* 7 vols. Translated by Erasmo Leiva-Merikakis, edited by Joseph Fessio and John Riches. San Francisco: Ignatius Press, 1983–91.

———. *Epilog.* Einsiedeln: Johannes Verlag, 1987.

———. "Tribute to Mozart." *Co* 28 (2001): 398–99.

———. *Cosmic Liturgy: The Universe According to Maximus the Confessor.* San Francisco: Ignatius Press, 2003.

Von Ivánka, Endre. *Plato Christianus. Übernahme und Umgestaltung des Platonismus durch die Vater.* Einsiedeln: Johannes Verlag, 1964.

Waldron, Jeremy. *God, Locke, and Equality.* New York: Cambridge University Press, 2002.

———. "What Would Hannah Say." *NYRB* 54, 4 (March 15, 2007): 8–12.

Walker, Adrian. "Introduction." *Co* 30 (2003): 177–79.

———. "Introduction." *Co* 31 (2004): 1–3.

———. "On 'Rephilosophizing' Theology." *Co* 31 (2004): 143–67.

———. "Personal Singularity and the *Communio Personarum.*" *Co* 31 (2004): 457–80.

———. "Not Neutral: Technology and the 'Theology of the Body.'" *SS* 7 (2006): 26–32.

———. "'Constitutive Relations': Towards a Spiritual Reading of *Physis.*" To be published in a Festschrift for David L. Schindler.

Walkowitz, Rebecca L. *Cosmopolitan Style: Modernism Beyond the Nation.* New York: Columbia University Press, 2006.

Wallace, Peter. "The Long European Reformation: A Proposal for a New Interpretive Model." *HS* 6, 2 (November/December 2004): 2–4.

Wallace, William A. *Causality and Scientific Explanation.* 2 vols. Ann Arbor: University of Michigan Press, 1972–74.

Walsh, David. *After Ideology: Recovering the Spiritual Foundations of Freedom.* Washington, D.C.: The Catholic University of America Press, 1995.

———. *Guarded by Mystery: Meaning in a Postmodern Age.* Washington, D.C.: The Catholic University of America Press, 1999.

Walsh, Stephen. *Stravinsky: The Second Exile: France and America, 1934–71.* New York: Knopf, 2006.

Walzer, Michael. "Can There be a Decent Left." *Dissent* (Spring 2002): 19–23.

Wandel, Lee Palmer. "Zwingli and Reformed Practice." In *Educating People of Faith: Exploring the History of Jewish and Christian Communities,* edited by John Van Engen, 270–93. Grand Rapids, Mich.: Eerdmans, 2004.

Ward, Keith. *Is Religion Dangerous?* Grand Rapids, Mich.: Eerdmans, 2007.

Washburn, Jennifer. *University Inc.: The Corporate Corruption of American Higher Education.* New York: Basic Books, 2004.

Watson, Richard A. *The Breakdown of Cartesian Metaphysics.* Atlantic Highlands, N.J.: Humanities Press International, 1987.

Weaver, Richard M. *Ideas Have Consequences.* Chicago: University of Chicago Press, 1948.

Weber, Eugen. *Peasants into Frenchmen: The Modernization of Rural France, 1870–1914.* Stanford, Calif.: Stanford University Press, 1976.

Weigel, George. *The Final Revolution: the Resistance Church and the Collapse of Communism.* New York: Oxford University Press, 1992.

———. "Europe's Problem—and Ours." *FT* 140 (February 24, 2004): 18–25.

———. *The Cube and the Cathedral: Europe, America, and Politics Without God.* San Francisco: Basic Books, 2005.

Welton, Donn. *The Other Husserl: The Horizons of Transcendental Phenomenology.* Bloomington: Indiana University Press, 2000.

Wessels, Tom. *The Myth of Progress: Toward a Sustainable Future.* Hanover: University of Vermont Press, 2006.

Weston, Richard. *Modernism.* London: Phaidon, 1996.

———. *The Paradox of Contemporary Architecture.* Edited by Peter Cook et al. Chichester: Wiley, 2001.

Whalen, Robert Weldon. *Sacred Spring: God and the Birth of Modernism in Fin de Siècle Vienna.* Grand Rapids, Mich.: Eerdmans, 2007.

White, Stephen D. *Re-Thinking Kinship and Feudalism in Early Medieval Europe.* Burlington, Vt.: Ashgate, 2006.

Whitford, David M. "*Cura Religionis* or Two Kingdoms: The Late Luther on Religion and the State in the Lectures on Genesis." *CH* 73 (2004): 41–62.

Wilde, Oscar. *The Complete Works of Oscar Wilde.* Edited by J. B. Foreman. London: Book Club, 1966.

Wilken, Robert Louis. "Angels and Archangels: The Worship of Heaven and Earth." *Antiphon* 6, 1 (2001): 10–18.

———. *The Spirit of Early Christian Thought: Seeking the Face of God.* New Haven, Conn.: Yale University Press, 2003.

———. "The Church as Culture." *FT* 142 (April 2004): 31–36.

———. "The Church's Way of Speaking." *FT* 155 (August/September 2005): 27–31.

Williams, Louise Blakeney. *Modernism and the Ideology of History: Literature, Politics, and the Past.* New York: Cambridge University Press, 2002.

Williams, Rowan, ed. *Sergii Bulgakov: Towards a Russian Political Theology.* Edinburgh: T & T Clark, 1999.

———. *Grace and Necessity: Reflections on Art and Love.* Harrisburg, Pa.: Morehouse, 2005.

Wills, Garry. "Lessons of a Master." *NYRB* 51, 11 (June 24, 2004): 12–14.

———. "An American Hero." *NYRB* 54, 12 (July 19, 2007): 43–44.

Wilson, Edward O. *Consilience: The Unity of Knowledge.* New York: Knopf, 1998.

Winch, Donald. *Riches and Poverty: An Intellectual History of Political Economy in Britain, 1750–1834.* Cambridge: Cambridge University Press, 1996.

Winroth, Anders. *The Making of Gratian's "Decretum."* Cambridge: Cambridge University Press, 2000.

Wippermann, Wolfgang. *Faschismustheorien: Die Entwicklung der Diskussion von den Anfängen bis heute.* Darmstadt: Wissenschaftliche Buchgesellschaft, 1997.

Woell, Edward J. *Small Town Martyrs and Murderers: Religious Revolution and Coun-*

terrevolution in Western France, 1774–1914. Milwaukee, Wis.: Marquette University Press, 2006.

Wolf, Martin. *Why Globalization Works.* New Haven, Conn.: Yale University Press, 2004.

Wolfe, Christopher. "American Liberalism: Past, Present, Future." In *Razón práctica y multiculturalismo,* edited by Enrique Banús and Alejandro Llano. Studia Europea Navarrensis, vol. 1, 207–14. Pamplona: Centro de Estudios Europeos, Universidad de Navarra, 1999.

Wolfe, Gregory. *Intruding Upon the Timeless: Meditations on Art, Faith and Mystery.* Baltimore: Johns Hopkins University Press, 2003.

Wolin, Richard. *The Seduction of Unreason: The Intellectual Romance with Fascism: from Nietzsche to Postmodernism.* Princeton, N.J.: Princeton University Press, 2004.

Wolter, Allan B., ed. *Duns Scotus on the Will and Morality.* Translated by William A. Frank. Washington, D.C.: The Catholic University of America, 1997.

Wolterstorff, Nicholas. *Justice: Rights and Wrongs.* Princeton, N.J.: Princeton University Press, 2008.

Womersley, David, ed. *Liberty and American Experience in the Eighteenth Century.* Indianapolis, Ind.: Liberty Fund, 2006.

Wood, Gordon S. "Early American Get-Up-and-Go." *NYRB* 47, 11 (June 29, 2000): 50–53.

———. "All in the Family." *NYRB* 48, 3 (February 22, 2001): 11–12.

———. "The Hidden France." *NYRB* 51, 4 (March 11, 2004): 31–34.

———. "What Slavery Was Really Like." *NYRB* 51, 18 (November 18, 2004): 43–47.

———. "Apologies to the Iroquois." *NYRB* 53, 7 (April 6, 2006): 50–52.

———. "American Religion: The Great Retreat." *NYRB* 53, 10 (June 8, 2006): 60–63.

Wood, Peter. *Diversity: The Invention of a Concept.* San Francisco: Encounter Books, 2003.

Wood, Paul. *Modernism in Dispute: Art since the Forties.* New Haven, Conn.: Yale University Press, 1993.

Wood, Ralph C. "Ivan Karamazov's Mistake." *FT* 128 (December 2002): 29–36.

Woodruff, Paul. *First Democracy: The Challenge of an Ancient Idea.* New York: Oxford University Press, 2005.

Woods, Thomas E., Jr. *The Church Confronts Modernity: Catholic Intellectuals and the Progressive Era.* New York: Columbia University Press, 2004

Wuthnow, Robert. *After the Baby Boomers: How Twenty- and Thirty-Somethings Are Shaping the Future of American Religion.* Princeton, N.J.: Princeton University Press, 2007.

Wyrick, Jed. *The Ascension of Authorship: Attribution and Canon Formation in Jewish, Hellenistic and Christian Traditions.* Cambridge, Mass.: Harvard University Press, 2004.

Yarza Luaces, Joaquin, and Gerado Boto Varela, eds. *Claustros Románicos Hispanos.* León: Edilesa, 2003.

Yeago, David. "Messiah's People: The Culture of the Church in the Midst of the Nations." *Pro Ecclesia* 6 (Spring 1997).

Year Book 2000–2001. The American Philosophical Society. Philadelphia: American Philosophical Society, 2001.

Yeats, W. B. *Autobiographies.* London: Macmillan, 1955.

Yerxa, Donald A. "Cultures of Defeat: An Interview with Wolfgang Schivelbusch." *HS* 5, 2 (November 2003): 16–17.

———. "Einstein's Clocks, Poincaré's Maps: An Interview with Peter Galison, Part I." *HS* 5, 2 (November 2003): 5–9.

Young, Frances M. "Prelude: Jesus Christ, Foundation of Christianity." In *The Cambridge History of Christianity: Origins to Constantine,* edited by Margaret M. Mitchell and Frances M. Young. Cambridge: Cambridge University Press, 2006.

Young, R. V. "The Reformations of the Sixteenth and Seventeenth Centuries." In *Christian Marriage: A Historical Study,* edited by Glenn W. Olsen, 269–301. New York: Herder and Herder, 2001.

Zagajewski, Adam. "On Czeslaw Milosz (1911–2004)." *NYRB* 51, 14 (September 23, 2004): 65–66.

Zahner, Paul. *Die Fülle des Heils in der Endlicheit der Geschichte: Bonaventuras Theologie als Antwort auf die franziskanischen Joachiten.* Werl: D.-Coelde-Verlag, 1999.

Zakal, Avihu. *Jonathan Edward's Philosophy of History: The Re-Enchantment of the World in the Age of Enlightenment.* Princeton, N.J.: Princeton University Press, 2003.

———. "Jonathan Edwards's Vision of History." *HS* (June 2003): 28–30.

Zakaria, Fareed. *The Future of Freedom: Illiberal Democracy at Home and Abroad.* New York: W. W. Norton, 2003.

Zambrano, María. *Hacia un saber sobre el alma.* Madrid: Alianza, 2001.

Zammito, John H. *A Nice Derangement of Epistemes: Post-Positivism in the Study of Science from Quine to Latour.* Chicago: University of Chicago Press, 2004.

Zitser, Ernest A. "Review Essay. Post-Soviet Peter: New Histories of the Late Muscovite and Early Imperial Russian Court." *HS* 7, 2 (November/December 2005): 37–39.

Zizek, Slavoj. *The Fragile Absolute: Or, Why Is the Christian Legacy Worth Fighting For?* London: Verso, 2000.

Zmirak, John. *Wilhelm Röpke: Swiss Localist, Global Economist.* Wilmington, Del.: ISI Books, 2001.

Zwick, Mark and Louise. "New Biography of John Paul II." *HCW* 19, 7 (December 1999): 7–9.

———. *The Catholic Worker Movement: Intellectual and Spiritual.* New York: Paulist Press, 2005.

Zycinski, Józef. *God and Evolution: Fundamental Questions of Christian Evolutionism.* Translated by Kenneth W. Kemp and Zuzanna Maslanka. Washington, D.C.: The Catholic University of America Press, 2006.

INDEX

The Turn to Transcendence: The Role of Religion in the Twenty-First Century was designed and typeset by Kachergis Book Design of Pittsboro, North Carolina. It was printed on 60-pound Natures Book Natural and bound by Thomson-Shore of Dexter, Michigan.